# THE NEVERENDING HUNT

# A BIBLIOGRAPHY OF ROBERT E. HOWARD

## Edited by Paul Herman

# TABLE OF CONTENTS

# INTRODUCTION

When I began collecting the works of Robert E. Howard ("REH") more than twenty years ago, I was faced with the straightforward challenges of finding out (1) what REH had written, and (2) where it had been published. While simple challenges to state, obtaining complete answers were a much more difficult problem. This stemmed from a number of issues surrounding REH that continue to the present day.

First, REH himself made little effort to track what he wrote, what he did with it, or who published it. REH was in the business of selling literary works for money, and made no bones about it. He was NOT especially interested in leaving detailed records. He never created, as far as is known, a comprehensive listing of all the places his works had been published. Occasionally REH would generate a partial list of stories he had sold, likely to track who owed him money, but these lists were hardly comprehensive.

Second, REH left no descendants to look after his works. He never married, and had no children, no siblings. His mother died the day after he did, and his father died just a few years later, without remarrying. The nearest living next of kin were some cousins, and they had no interest in his writings. Out of the mass of jumbled papers that were salvaged from REH's room by his father, the agent acquired a few stories, which he proceeded to sell some of over the next couple decades. The rest of the papers, literally tens of thousands of randomly mixed-up pages, were sent in 1944 to Ed Price in California. He would read through them, and pass them around to his friends, but never did sort them all out.

Third, REH's father left the rights he had in the then unpublished works to a friend. From the 1940s into the 1960s, the copyright owners were only interested in selling the stories for money. So not only did no one track information during REH's lifetime, no one did for more than 25 years after his death.

Fourth, the various folks that had some control or power over the works of REH for the next 45 years felt no need to identify everything extant, though they have certainly been at least partially helpful on occasion.

And last, the only serious attempt at a comprehensive bibliography was THE LAST CELT in 1975, thirty years ago, and just before one of the biggest periods of REH publishing took place.

So for a collector like me, the search for information became the Neverending Hunt.

The first person to seriously dedicate time and effort to figuring out the details of REH's bibliography was Glenn Lord, starting in the late 1950s, more than twenty years after REH died. After several years Glenn was able to locate the cache of papers Ed Price had, and purchase it. Glenn also, in a serendipitous twist of fate, became the agent for the then current owners of REH's copyrights, and served as their agent for more than 25 years. The twin points of having the cache of papers and being the agent in charge enabled Glenn to not only see a lot of background to REH's work, and control to a certain extent what was to come, but also served as an introduction for him to all sorts of people in the field of weird fiction (authors, publishers, collectors), all of whom could help him fill in more blanks, locate more lost REH material. It also gave him sufficient panache to obtain copies of various REH works that were still extant but in the hands of others, including a large number of letters written by REH.

Glenn published his first bibliography in THE HOWARD COLLECTOR, in 1961. The entire set of listings took only a few pages in his small but elegant chapbook. At that point in time, there were still many previously published pulps, amateur journals, newspaper and school publications that Glenn did not know about. This was also just before he purchased the Ed Price cache of papers. That cache would include dozens and dozens of previously unpublished stories and hundreds of poems.

Glenn's next bibliography, and the standard up until this volume, was THE LAST CELT ("TLC") published by Grant in 1975, and included data up through 1973. TLC included references to a lot of material that had come out of the Ed Price cache, as well as works that had been published since 1961. It also included references to some of the unpublished works for the first time, though certainly not all of it. The timing was interesting. The first REH "Boom" was just starting, with several publishers having a strong interest in anything by REH, thanks to the success of REH's character, Conan. So while that volume was a quantum leap larger in size and scope, it came out just before the most extensive period of REH publications since the 1930s.

To track and locate what was published after 1973 required a collector to create his own listings, constantly updated and modified. As the world became interconnected via the Internet, collectors could access chat groups, book search engines, and eBay, to discover again and again previously unknown (to the individual collector) works and publications. And the chat groups led to some people sharing some of their own carefully collected and sorted information, slowly allowing a steady build up to a more and more complete bibliography.

Which brings us to this volume, more than thirty years after THE LAST CELT. You hold in your hand a bibliography based on the editor's personal lists, over 500 pages of nothing but pure data. While TLC was also a bit of a biography as well as a place to reprint all sorts of interesting odds and ends, this volume is virtually nothing but raw facts and figures. It likely contains more than twice as much information as TLC. In addition to what was known at the time of publication of TLC, this volume includes here for the first time in any mainstream publication:

(1) updated publication listings for 1973 through late-2007
(2) older publications discovered since 1973 (a new one was discovered as recently as a few years ago)
(3) the addition of amateur publications
(4) the addition of a letters index
(5) a much more thorough listing of unpublished works of various types, though likely still not complete

Note that this volume is designed to impart information about REH's works and where to find them, the current results of the Hunt, not to provide all the details that one would find in a traditional bibliography. It certainly would not offend me if someone else wants to start with this volume and turn it into a traditional formal bibliography, of no doubt double the size of this volume. But that is simply not the point of this volume.

This volume is split into two main sections: **The Works** and **The Publications**.

**The Works** includes the following listings:

**Prose Index**, including stories, articles, plays, etc. There are separate listings for English and non-English publication citations;
**Verse Index**, with both English and non-English publications included together; and,
**Letters Index**, also with English and non-English publications included together.

**The Publications** are split into six listings:

**Books in English**
**Periodicals**
**Anthologies**
**Chapbooks and other unusual formats**
**A sampling of books in non-English languages**
**A sampling of comics**

Each set of listings includes some introductory information regarding how the index is sorted, conventions used in it, etc. One general convention that will show up throughout this volume concerns people's names. Specifically, certain people's names show up very often, and so to try to hold down the overall length of this work, their names have been shortened to initials in most instances. To wit,

Robert E. Howard – REH
H.P. Lovecraft – HPL
Tevis Clyde Smith – TCS
L. Sprague de Camp – LSDC

As a small bonus, at the end of the listings I have included a few "Top Ten" type lists created by various noted REH scholars, which I hope you'll find of interest.

With regard to deciding what publications go under Books, or Periodicals, or Chapbooks, my general rule is that if it has a flat spine it will be listed under Books (if mostly REH conent) or Anthologies (if not mostly REH content), specifically excepting pulps, which are listed under Periodicals. Facsimile replicas of pulps, a new trend in publishing, are under Chapbooks, listed by the pulp title. Periodicals are generally any publication that came out in a series. Trying to decide which items should be listed under Chapbooks and which should be listed under Periodicals based on the "pro-ness" of the work is an exercise in opinion forming, and I have done just that here. Since I do not know the history of many of the listed items, there is a certain amount of guesswork involved. So please remember to check more than one place for that which you seek, presuming that I may have erroneously placed a publication in the wrong list.

Note that in general I do not state a judgment as to the quality of the text in various different versions of works, though there are some exceptions. While some people regularly express concern about what one editor did or another, actual detailed analysis to back up the concerns is generally lacking, and in my own rather extensive study of the issue in preparing numerous volumes of REH material for publication, I have come to the conclusion that changes of an extra comma every 500 words is hardly ruinous of the text, and that in general, one text is pretty much as good as the next to the average reader in presenting REH accurately, again with a few noted exceptions.

In preparing such a work, one can only report accurately what one actually knows. I do not possess copies of all the works and publications listed herein. Given that so many items here exist as only a single copy, or only a dozen or fewer copies, it is simply impossible for one person to possess one of everything. So I am forced on numerous occasions to accept what others tell me, to count on them for accuracy, IF I can find someone willing to provide any information at all. Thankfully, there are a large number of collectors who are on occasion willing to assist. Unfortunately, experience has shown that on rare occasions incorrect information is provided to me. So please understand that I am presenting what I know, along with what has been represented to me as factual. There are bound to be a few errors in this volume (including my own introduced errors), especially when it comes to obscure, rare, or unpublished items, and you are warned accordingly.

And last, I want to express my heartfelt thanks and appreciation to all those who have helped create this work. Such a volume as this could not be created by one person, and such is not the case here, even in this, the individualist world of REH. First and foremost is Glenn Lord, whose tireless efforts to find everything, and then to disseminate a great amount of the information, is the touchstone for starting any such project. Glenn provided innumerable details for this volume, and can easily take credit for supplying the largest portion of the information in this volume. Thanks also to all the Usual Suspects within REH fandom, who have either quietly or openly worked on parts or pieces of this, and have graciously provided information from their own collections. This would include Rusty Burke, Patrice Louinet, David Gentzel, Joe Marek, Scotty Henderson and Dennis McHaney, along with innumerable others, REHupans and otherwise, from the States and from abroad, who have filled in bits and pieces along the way these last twenty years. Providing copies of rare pulp pages and amateur publications for scholarly review are The Library of Congress, Texas A&M University, the University of Texas Harry Ransom Center, Bowling Green University, and the University of Maryland, Baltimore Campus, among others. Old Texas newspapers can be found at Texas Tech University, a wonderful source.

So enjoy, be amazed, wonder, and realize how woefully pitiful and lacking your collection really is. But next Lotto . . .

Paul Herman

*To Glenn Lord, the first and best paladin of Robert E. Howard, the standard that may never be equaled.*

# PROSE INDEX

## INCLUDES FICTIONAL WORKS, ARTICLES, ESSAYS, FRAGMENTS AND SYNOPSES PUBLISHED IN ENGLISH

This index includes fictional works, articles, essays, fragments and synopses; in short, all of REH's prose writings, except for letters. All works solely by REH unless noted otherwise. There are just under 600 works listed, not counting alternate titles. The editor has attempted to include every known prose work of REH, whether it has been published or not, whether a copy even exists or not.

In general, publications and notes are listed under the first published title. Hence, alternate titles will cross-reference back to the first published title, and have no further data.

If the work is published under an alternate title, reference is noted to this after the publication name. If a pseudonym is used in place of REH's own name in any given instance, it is noted after the publication reference.

If the work is a true co-authored work (i.e., both authors agreed to work with each other), it is noted under author. If a work is derivative of an original REH piece, the person completing or altering the work is listed in the notes.

This list only includes publications in English, with the exception of a few stories that made their First Appearance in French and were published by NeO, as all First Appearances are included in this list. Most of the publications listed here can be found in the BOOKS IN ENGLISH list. Publications with (Anth.) at the end can be found in the ANTHOLOGIES list. Publications with (Chpbk.) at the end can be found in the CHAPBOOKS list. Publications that are periodicals, such as pulps or magazines, will generally include dates or numbers and can be found in the PERIODICALS list. If multiple books have the same title but differing contents, I have listed the publisher as well, to indicate which book is appropriate.

*Format of Entries*
**TITLE**
By [if not by just REH]
Alternate Title: [If it has one]
Featuring: [If a significant REH hero]
First appeared in: [If published]
  All other publications in English of the story
  Notes

**44-40 OR FIGHT**
A story that REH said he wrote, but no copy exists

**THE ABBEY**
First appeared in FANTASY CROSSROADS #4/5
  NAMELESS CULTS (completed by C.J. Henderson)
  This is a fragment only

**AFTER THE GAME**
First appeared in the YELLOW JACKET, October 27, 1926
  CERTIORARI ACCEPTED #1 (Chpbk.)
  THE COMPLETE YELLOW JACKET
  WEST IS WEST AND OTHERS
  This is a play

**AGE LASTING LOVE**
First appeared in LA TOMBE DU DRAGON (French)
  THE NEW HOWARD READER #7 (Chpbk.)
  Unfinished

**AHA! OR THE MYSTERY OF THE QUEEN'S NECKLACE**
First appeared in THE TATTLER, March 1, 1923
  THE HOWARD COLLECTOR #4
  THE NEW HOWARD READER #2 (Chpbk.)
  WEST IS WEST AND OTHERS

**AKRAM THE MYSTERIOUS**
Alternate title: THE TOWER OF TIME

**ALLEYS OF DARKNESS**
Alternate title: ALLEYS OF SINGAPORE
Featuring DENNIS DORGAN
First appeared in MAGIC CARPET MAGAZINE, January 1934 (author listed as "Patrick Ervin")
  THE INCREDIBLE ADVENTURES OF DENNIS DORGAN
  THE MAGIC CARPET MAGAZINE, Odyssey Publications (Anth., author listed as "Patrick Ervin")
  THE IRON MAN, WITH THE ADVENTURES OF DENNIS DORGAN
  WATERFRONT FISTS AND OTHERS
  WINDY CITY PULP STORIES #7 (Chpbk.)

**ALLEYS OF PERIL**
Alternate title: LEATHER LIGHTNING
Featuring STEVE COSTIGAN
First appeared in FIGHT STORIES, January 1931
  FIGHT STORIES, Winter, 1940 (as "Leather Lightning", author listed as "Mark Adam")
  REH'S FIGHT MAGAZINE #2 (Chpbk.)
  WATERFRONT FISTS AND OTHERS

**ALLEYS OF SINGAPORE**
Alternate title: ALLEYS OF DARKNESS

## ALLEYS OF TRECHERY
Alternate title: THE MANDARIN RUBY
Featuring DENNIS DORGAN
First appeared in THE HOWARD COLLECTOR #8 (author listed as "Patrick Ervin")
    THE INCREDIBLE ADVENTURES OF DENNIS DORGAN
    THE IRON MAN, WITH THE ADVENTURES OF DENNIS DORGAN, (as "The Mandarin Ruby")

## ALMURIC
First appeared as a 3-part serial in WEIRD TALES: May 1939; June-July 1939; and August 1939
    ALMURIC, Ace and New English Library
    ALMURIC, Grant, Berkley, and Sphere
    THE WEIRD WRITINGS OF ROBERT E. HOWARD, VOLUME TWO
    ALMURIC, Pulpville Press
    ALMURIC, Paizo Press
    Likely not all REH, as there is a first draft that dwindles to an outline, then a partial second draft that is not
        finished; Glenn Lord thinks that it most likely was finished by Farnsworth Wright; WEIRD TALES
        itself has a different story in its intro, which most scholars do not believe; some have suggested that it
        might have been Otto Binder who did the rewrite

## THE ALTAR AND THE SCORPION
Featuring KULL
    First appeared in KING KULL
    KULL: THE FABULOUS WARRIOR KING
    KULL
    KULL: EXILE OF ATLANTIS

## AMBITION BY MOONLIGHT
Alternate title: AMBITION IN THE MOONLIGHT
First appeared in THE JUNTO, January 1929
    TRUMPET #7 (Chpbk.)
    THE NEW HOWARD READER #1 (Chpbk.)
    THE ROAD TO VELITRIUM #30 (Chpbk.)

## AMBITION IN THE MOONLIGHT
Alternate title: AMBITION BY MOONLIGHT

## THE APACHE MOUNTAIN WAR
Featuring BRECKINRIDGE ELKINS
First appeared in: ACTION STORIES, December 1935
    THE PRIDE OF BEAR CREEK
    THE SUMMIT COUNTY JOURNAL, October 20, 27, November 3, 10, 17, 24, 1972 (series was dropped
        before publication of the series was completed)
    HEROES OF BEAR CREEK
    THE COMPLETE ACTION STORIES
    Grant removed all the italics for THE PRIDE OF BEAR CREEK, which was carried over in later editions; THE
        SUMMIT COUNTY JOURNAL appearance changed the name to "Breckenridge", to be like the town
        it was published in; THE COMPLETE ACTION STORIES returned the text to its original published
        form, including the italics

## APPARITION IN THE PRIZE RING
Alternate title: THE SPIRIT OF TOM MOLYNEAUX
Featuring ACE JESSEL
First appeared in GHOST STORIES, April 1929 (author listed as "John Taverel")

STORIES OF GHOSTS (Anth.)
BOYS OWN FANTASY ANNUAL (Chpbk.)
WATERFRONT FISTS AND OTHERS
BOXING STORIES (as "The Spirit of Tom Molyneaux")
GHOST STORIES version is first person, as it's a "confessional" magazine, earlier drafts of the story are written in third person; REH turned it into first person for the published form

## APPARITION OF JOSIAH WILBARGER
Alternate title: THE STRANGE CASE OF JOSIAH WILBARGER
First appeared in THE WEST, September 1967
THE NEW HOWARD READER #5 (Chpbk.)
THE BLACK STRANGER AND OTHER AMERICAN TALES
THE END OF THE TRAIL: WESTERN STORIES
The published version of this story is just a few pages; a list from the Kline Agency listed two versions of this story, one at 117 pages, one at 134 pages

## THE ATAVIST
First appeared in THE LAST OF THE TRUNK OCH BREV I URVAL BREV I URVAL (Chpbk.)
THE LAST OF THE TRUNK
Unfinished

## AN AUTOBIOGRAPHY
First appeared in THE LAST CELT
THE NEW HOWARD READER #8 (Chpbk.)

## BASTARDS ALL!
First appeared in LEWD TALES (Chpbk.)
THE LAST OF THE TRUNK OCH BREV I URVAL BREV I URVAL (Chpbk.)
THE COLLECTED LETTERS OF ROBERT E. HOWARD, VOLUME 1: 1923-1929
This is a play; from a letter to TCS, ca. March 1929 ("Salaam: / Black Dawn")

## THE BATTLING SAILOR
Featuring STEVE COSTIGAN
First appeared in DENNIS DORGAN (French)
THE LAST OF THE TRUNK OCH BREV I URVAL BREV I URVAL (Chpbk.)
THE LAST OF THE TRUNK

## THE BEAST FROM THE ABYSS
Alternate title: THE FELINE MYSTIQUE
First appeared in THE HOWARD COLLECTOR #15
THE HOWARD REVIEW #3 (Chpbk.)
THE HOWARD COLLECTOR, Ace
THE LAST CAT BOOK
ROD SERLING'S THE TWILIGHT ZONE MAGAZINE, August 1984 (as "The Feline Mystique")

## BEYOND THE BLACK RIVER
Featuring CONAN
First appeared as a 2-part serial in WEIRD TALES: May 1935; and June 1935
KING CONAN
CONAN THE WARRIOR
THE MIGHTY SWORDSMEN (Anth.)
RED NAILS, Berkley & Putnam
BARBARIANS (Anth.)

THE ESSENTIAL CONAN, SFBC Fantasy
THE ULTIMATE TRIUMPH: THE HEROIC FANTASY OF ROBERT E. HOWARD
THE CONAN CHRONICLES, VOLUME 2, Millenium
SAVAGE ADVENTURES (Chpbk.)
THE CONQUERING SWORD OF CONAN
THE COMPLETE CHRONICLES OF CONAN
THE WEIRD WRITINGS OF ROBERT E. HOWARD, VOLUME TWO
CRIMSON SHADOWS: THE BEST OF ROBERT E. HOWARD, VOLUME 1
PEOPLE OF THE BLACK CIRCLE
BEYOND THE BLACK RIVER: THE WEIRD WORKS OF ROBERT E. HOWARD, VOLUME 7

**BILL SMALLEY AND THE POWER OF THE HUMAN EYE**
Alternate title: THE POWER OF THE HUMAN EYE
First appeared in THE DARK MAN #2 (Chpbk.)
   Unfinished

**BLACK ABYSS**
Alternate title: THE BLACK CITY

**THE BLACK BEAR BITES**
Alternate title: BLACK JOHN'S VENGEANCE
First appeared in FROM BEYOND THE DARK GATEWAY #3
   SWORDS OF SHAHRAZAR, Berkley and Ace
   NAMELESS CULTS

**BLACK CANAAN**
First appeared in WEIRD TALES, June 1936
   SKULL-FACE AND OTHERS
   SKULL-FACE OMNIBUS
   SKULL-FACE OMNIBUS, VOLUME 1
   THE SECOND BOOK OF ROBERT E. HOWARD
   BLACK CANAAN
   TRAILS IN DARKNESS
   ROBERT E. HOWARD'S STRANGE TALES
   THE BLACK STRANGER AND OTHER AMERICAN TALES
   THE WEIRD WRITINGS OF ROBERT E. HOWARD, VOLUME TWO
   Was voted best story in its original WEIRD TALES appearance by the fans; an earlier synopsis exists, had the
         lead character as Saul Claver instead of Saul Stark; supposedly based on the factual(?) Kelly the
         Conjure-Man up in Arkansas; REH complained in a letter that he had had to "cut the guts out of it" to
         get it published, Glenn Lord MAY have a carbon of that original draft; there is also a synopsis

**THE BLACK CITY**
Featuring KULL
Alternate title: BLACK ABYSS
   First appeared in KING KULL
   KULL: THE FABULOUS WARRIOR KING
   KULL
   KULL: EXILE OF ATLANTIS
   An unfinished REH work, these listings are for the fragment; Lin Carter finished it for the KING KULL book,
         Lancer, starting with Chapter 3; the original title on the fragment was "The Black City", Carter's
         completion is titled "Black Abyss"

## BLACK COLOSSUS
Featuring CONAN
First appeared in WEIRD TALES, June 1933
> CONAN THE BARBARIAN, Gnome
> CONAN THE FREEBOOTER
> BLACK COLOSSUS
> THE CONAN CHRONICLES 1, Sphere and Orbit
> THE CONAN CHRONICLES I: THE PEOPLE OF THE BLACK CIRCLE
> ROBERT E. HOWARD'S COMPLETE CONAN OF CIMMERIA, VOLUME 1
> THE COMING OF CONAN THE CIMMERIAN
> THE COMPLETE CHRONICLES OF CONAN
> THE WEIRD WRITINGS OF ROBERT E. HOWARD, VOLUME ONE
> THE VALLEY OF THE WORM: THE WEIRD WORKS OF ROBERT E. HOWARD, VOLUME 5
> THE PHOENIX ON THE SWORD (Chpbk.)
> THREE TALES OF CONAN THE BARBARIAN
> Voted best story in its original WEIRD TALES appearance by the fans; WEIRD TALES version includes an E. Hoffmann Price quote at the start, from Price's "The Girl from Samarcand"

## BLACK COUNTRY
First appeared in WEIRDBOOK #6
> GOOSEFLESH! (Anth.)
> THE NEW HOWARD READER #5 (Chpbk.)
> REH: TWO-GUN RACONTEUR #8

## BLACK EONS
Alternate title: Untitled ("Beneath the glare of the sun . . .")

## BLACK HOUND OF DEATH
First appeared in WEIRD TALES, November 1936
> WEIRD TALES, Neville-Spearman, Carroll & Graf and Xanadu (Anth.)
> DARK PHANTASMS #1 (Chpbk.)
> WEIRD TALES, VOLUME 1, Sphere (Anth.)
> TRAILS IN DARKNESS
> THE WEIRD WRITINGS OF ROBERT E. HOWARD, VOLUME TWO

## BLACK JOHN'S VENGEANCE
Alternate title: THE BLACK BEAR BITES

## THE BLACK MOON
Featuring STEVE HARRISON
First appeared in BRAN MAK MORN: A PLAY & OTHERS (Chpbk.)

## THE BLACK STONE
First appeared in WEIRD TALES, November 1931
> GRIM DEATH (Anth.)
> SLEEP NO MORE (Anth.)
> SKULL-FACE AND OTHERS
> WEIRD TALES, November 1953
> WOLFSHEAD, Lancer
> TALES OF THE CTHULHU MYTHOS (Anth.)
> TALES OF THE CTHULHU MYTHOS, VOLUME 1 (Anth.)
> SKULL-FACE OMNIBUS
> CHRISTOPHER LEE'S "X" CERTIFICATE #1 (Anth.)

SKULL-FACE OMNIBUS, VOLUME 1
FROM THE ARCHIVES OF EVIL (Anth.)
WOLFSHEAD, Bantam
CTHULHU THE MYTHOS AND KINDRED HORRORS
TO SLEEP PERCHANCE TO DREAM, NIGHTMARE (Anth.)
NAMELESS CULTS
PEOPLE OF THE DARK: THE WEIRD WORKS OF ROBERT E. HOWARD, VOLUME 3
THE WEIRD WRITINGS OF ROBERT E. HOWARD, VOLUME ONE
THE WEIRD WRITINGS OF ROBERT E. HOWARD, VOLUME TWO
CRIMSON SHADOWS: THE BEST OF ROBERT E. HOWARD, VOLUME 1
The version in WEIRD WRITINGS, VOLUME ONE is a facsimile of the original pages from WEIRD TALES
    from the 1930s; the version in WEIRD WRITINGS, VOLUME TWO is a facsimile of the original
    pages from WEIRD TALES from the 1950s

## THE BLACK STRANGER
Alternate titles: THE TREASURE OF TRANICOS; SWORDS OF THE BROTHERHOOD
Featuring CONAN
First appeared in FANTASY FICTION MAGAZINE, March 1953 (LSDC-edited version, with additional editing by
    Lester Del Rey)
    KING CONAN (LSDC-edited version)
    CONAN THE USURPER (LSDC-edited version)
    ECHOES OF VALOR (Anth., REH1, first appearance)
    THE CONAN CHRONICLES, VOLUME 2, Millenium (REH1)
    THE BLACK STRANGER (Chpbk., REH1)
    THE BLACK STRANGER AND OTHER AMERICAN TALES (REH1)
    THE CONQUERING SWORD OF CONAN (plus two earlier drafts)
    THE COMPLETE CHRONICLES OF CONAN
    Originally written by REH as a Conan story, was not accepted, so REH rewrote it into a Black Vulmea story
        ("Swords of the Red Brotherhood"), also not accepted; LSDC used the original Conan story, but
        heavily rewrote it to make it fit into his "epic", and titled it "The Treasure of Tranicos"; hence, there
        are 3 different versions of this story, REH1, REH2 (listed here under "Swords of the Red
        Brotherhood"), and the LSDC-edited version; the Wandering Star publication is a facsimile
        reproduction of the original loose typescript pages in a folder

## BLACK TALONS
Alternate title: TALONS IN THE DARK
First appeared in STRANGE DETECTIVE STORIES, December 1933
    THE BOOK OF ROBERT E. HOWARD
    PULP REVIEW #13
    GRAVEYARD RATS AND OTHERS
    ROBERT E. HOWARD: WORLD'S GREATEST PULPSTER #1
    THE HOWARD REVIEW #12 (Chpbk.)

## BLACK VULMEA'S VENGEANCE
Featuring TERENCE VULMEA
First appeared in GOLDEN FLEECE, November 1938
    BLACK VULMEA'S VENGEANCE
    ROBERT E. HOWARD OMNIBUS
    TREASURES OF TARTARY AND OTHERS
    THE BLACK STRANGER AND OTHER AMERICAN TALES
    GOLDEN FLEECE, NOVEMBER 1938, Girasol Collectables
    THE GRIM LAND: THE BEST OF ROBERT E. HOWARD, VOLUME 2
    Jack Byrne of ARGOSY liked the story, but was overstocked on such; the GOLDEN FLEECE version is a
        facsimile reproduction of the original pulp

## BLACK WIND BLOWING
First appeared in THRILLING MYSTERY, June 1936
    THE BOOK OF ROBERT E. HOWARD
    PULP REVIEW #5
    GRAVEYARD RATS AND OTHERS

## BLACK-COUNTRY
Different from the published one above, note hyphen, complete story, unpublished

## BLADES FOR FRANCE
Featuring AGNES DE CHASTILLON
First appeared in BLADES FOR FRANCE
    SWORD WOMAN

## BLADES OF THE BROTHERHOOD
Alternate titles: BLUE FLAME OF VENGEANCE; BLUE FLAME OF DEATH

## THE BLOCK
First appeared in PAY DAY (Chpbk.)

## THE BLOND GODDESS OF BAL-SAGOTH
Alternate title: THE GODS OF BAL-SAGOTH

## THE BLOOD OF BELSHAZZAR
Featuring CORMAC FITZGEOFFREY
First appeared in ORIENTAL STORIES, Fall 1931
    HAWKS OF OUTREMER
    GATES OF EMPIRE AND OTHERS
    LORD OF SAMARCAND AND OTHER ADVENTURES OF THE OLD ORIENT
    ORIENTAL STORIES, AUTUMN 1931, Girasol Press (Chpbk.)
    THE COMPLETE ORIENTAL STORIES (Anth.)

## BLOOD OF THE GODS
Featuring EL BORAK
First appeared in TOP-NOTCH, July 1935
    SON OF THE WHITE WOLF
    BLOOD OF THE GODS AND OTHER STORIES
    THE "EL BORAK" STORIES - BLOOD OF THE GODS; THE DAUGHTER OF ERLIK KHAN; HAWK OF
        THE HILLS; SON OF THE WHITE WOLF; THE COUNTRY OF THE KNIFE

## THE BLOODSTAINED GOD
Alternate titles: CURSE OF THE CRIMSON GOD; TRAIL OF THE BLOODSTAINED GOD
Featuring CONAN
First appeared in  TALES OF CONAN
    FANTASTIC UNIVERSE, April 1956
    CONAN OF CIMMERIA
    THE CONAN CHRONICLES 1, Sphere and Orbit
This is an LSDC derivative rewrite of a then-unpublished REH historical adventure story called "Curse of the
    Crimson God", LSDC turning it into a Conan story

## BLOODSTONES AND EBONY
First appeared in ETCHINGS IN IVORY (Chpbk.)
    THE BOOK OF ROBERT E. HOWARD

**BLOW THE CHINKS DOWN!**
Alternate title: THE HOUSE OF PERIL
Featuring STEVE COSTIGAN
First appeared in ACTION STORIES, October 1931
    THE COMPLETE ACTION STORIES
    Was originally a Mike Dorgan and Bill McGlory story, straight adventure, editor turned it into a Costigan story

**THE BLUE FLAME OF DEATH**
Alternate titles: BLADES OF THE BROTHERHOOD; THE BLUE FLAME OF VENGEANCE

**THE BLUE FLAME OF VENGEANCE**
Featuring SOLOMON KANE
Alternate titles: BLADES OF THE BROTHERHOOD; THE BLUE FLAME OF DEATH
First appeared in OVER THE EDGE (REH/JP, Anth.)
    RED SHADOWS (REH, as "Blades of the Brotherhood")
    SOLOMON KANE, Centaur and Haddock (REH)
    SOLOMON KANE: SKULLS IN THE STARS (REH)
    SOLOMON KANE, Baen (REH)
    THE SAVAGE TALES OF SOLOMON KANE (REH, as "The Blue Flame of Vengeance")
    THE RIGHT HAND OF DOOM AND OTHER TALES OF SOLOMON KANE
    THE LEGEND OF SOLOMON KANE
    BLADES OF THE BROTHERHOOD (Chpbk., Malachi Grim version)
  The first publication of this story was extensively rewritten by John Pocsik, adding a weird element, used only a small portion of actual REH text, and took the title "Blue Flame of Vengeance"; when the original REH version was going to be published Glenn Lord switched the title of the original to "Blades of the Brotherhood", that title being used by several publishers; however, THAT title actually goes to a shorter version written by REH that featured Malachi Grim instead of Solomon Kane; the Malachi Grim story is yet another instance of the "By This Axe I Rule" / "Phoenix" syndrome; THE SAVAGE TALES OF SOLOMON KANE was the first publication to restore the title to the original REH story; the Solomon Kane version was written ca. May 1929, and the Malachi Grim version is sometime between June and November 1932, probably October or November; "Blue Flame of Death" was the title on an earlier draft

**BLUE RIVER BLUES**
Featuring STEVE COSTIGAN
First appeared in STEVE COSTIGAN LE CHAMPION (French)
    THE LAST OF THE TRUNK OCH BREV I URVAL BREV I URVAL (Chpbk.)
    THE LAST OF THE TRUNK

**BOOKMEN AND BOOKS**
First appeared in THE RIGHT HOOK, VOLUME 1, #1 (Chpbk.)
    AUSTIN, VOLUME 3, #2 (Chpbk.)
    ROBERT E. HOWARD—THE POWER OF THE WRITING MIND
    This is an article

**BOOT-HILL PAYOFF**
By Robert E. Howard & R.E. Allen
Alternate title: THE LAST RIDE
First appeared in WESTERN ACES, October 1935
    THE LAST RIDE (as "The Last Ride")
    TREASURES OF TARTARY AND OTHERS
    THE END OF THE TRAIL: WESTERN STORIES (as "The Last Ride")
  This story was originally written by Chandler Whipple, whose pen name was Robert Enders Allen; he couldn't figure out how to finish it, and his agent suggested that he have REH finish it; REH did, and it sold,

with REH and CW splitting the profit 50/50; REH's part starts with Chapter 7; the original title was "The Last Ride", WESTERN ACES changed it to "Boot-Hill Payoff"

## THE BORED OF THE COW
First appeared in THE LAST OF THE TRUNK OCH BREV I URVAL BREV I URVAL (Chpbk.)
>THE COLLECTED LETTERS OF ROBERT E. HOWARD, VOLUME 1: 1923-1929
>From a letter to TCS, April 6, 1925 ("Salaam, sahib: / What ho! I have . . .")

## A BOY, A BEEHIVE, AND A CHINAMAN
First appeared in THE DARK BARBARIAN (first page only)
>THE LAST OF THE TRUNK OCH BREV I URVAL BREV I URVAL (first complete appearance) (Chpbk.)
>THE ROBERT E. HOWARD FOUNDATION NEWSLETTER, VOLUME 1, #2
>THE LAST OF THE TRUNK
>Hand-written, and dated December 1, 1920; the REHFNL publication is a facsimile reproduction of the original handwritten pages

## BRACHEN THE KELT
Featuring JAMES ALLISON
First appeared in THE BARBARIAN SWORDSMEN (Anth.)
>THE NEW HOWARD READER #1 (Chpbk., restored version)
>The version published in THE BARBARIAN SWORDSMEN has the majority of the final paragraph deleted and the first sentence (all that remained) grafted on to the preceding paragraph, to make it sound "finished", though in fact it is incomplete; there were also some changes to REH's original spelling to conform to customary British form in THE BARBARIAN SWORDSMEN: civilization->civilisation, clamor->clamour, moulded->molded

## BRAN MAK MORN
Alternate title: Untitled ("The story of a forgotten age . . .")
Featuring BRAN MAK MORN
First appeared in  CROMLECH #3 (Chpbk.)
>UNAUSSPRECHLICHEN KULTEN #1 (Chpbk.)
>THE NEW HOWARD READER #3 (Chpbk.)
>BRAN MAK MORN – THE LAST KING (as "Synopsis")

## BRAN MAK MORN: A PLAY
Alternate title: BRAN MAK MORN
Featuring BRAN MAK MORN
First appeared in BRAN MAK MORN: A PLAY & OTHERS (Chpbk.)
>CROMLECH #3, Cryptic, 1988
>UNAUSSPRECHLICHEN KULTEN #1, October 1990
>BRAN MAK MORN – THE LAST KING (as "Bran Mak Morn")
>The Wandering Star appearance also includes a copy of the original manuscript

## THE BRAND OF SATAN
Alternate title: Untitled ("This is the tale of Shaitan Khan, . . .")
First appeared in THE LAST OF THE TRUNK OCH BREV I URVAL BREV I URVAL (Chpbk.)
>THE LAST OF THE TRUNK
>Unfinished

**THE BRAZEN PEACOCK**
First appeared in REH: LONE STAR FICTIONEER #3
  SWORDS OF SHAHRAZAR, Berkley and Ace

**BREED OF BATTLE**
Alternate titles: THE FIGHTIN'EST PAIR; SAMPSON HAD A SOFT SPOT
Featuring STEVE COSTIGAN
First appeared in ACTION STORIES, November 1931
  FIGHT STORIES, Spring, 1942 (as "Sampson Had a Soft Spot", author listed as "Mark Adam")
  REH'S FIGHT MAGAZINE #2 (Chpbk.)
  THE COMPLETE ACTION STORIES
  BREED OF BATTLE (Chpbk.)
  BOXING STORIES (as "The Fightin'est Pair")
  CRIMSON SHADOWS: THE BEST OF ROBERT E. HOWARD, VOLUME 1

**BROTHERLY ADVICE**
Featuring THE SONORA KID
First appeared in THE SONORA KID (Chpbk.)

**THE BULL DOG BREED**
Alternate title: YOU GOT TO KILL A BULLDOG
Featuring STEVE COSTIGAN
First appeared in FIGHT STORIES, February 1930
  FIGHT STORIES, Winter, 1937-38 (as "You Got to Kill a Bulldog", author listed as "Mark Adam")
  REH'S FIGHT MAGAZINE #1 (Chpbk.)
  WATERFRONT FISTS AND OTHERS
  BOXING STORIES
  THE GRIM LAND: THE BEST OF ROBERT E. HOWARD, VOLUME 2

**BY THE LAW OF THE SHARK**
Featuring STEVE COSTIGAN
First appeared in STEVE COSTIGAN LE CHAMPION (French)
  REH'S FIGHT MAGAZINE #4 (Chpbk.)

**BY THIS AXE I RULE!**
Featuring KULL
First appeared in KING KULL
  KULL: THE FABULOUS WARRIOR KING
  KULL
  KULL: EXILE OF ATLANTIS
  THE GRIM LAND: THE BEST OF ROBERT E. HOWARD, VOLUME 2
  Originally submitted to ADVENTURE and ARGOSY; may not have been submitted to WEIRD TALES, as no
    weird element; after rejections it was rewritten by REH into the first Conan story, "The Phoenix on the
    Sword"

**THE CAIRN ON THE HEADLAND**
First appeared in STRANGE TALES, January 1933
  SKULL-FACE AND OTHERS
  AVON FANTASY READER #7
  THE MACABRE READER (Anth.)
  WOLFSHEAD, Lancer
  SKULL-FACE OMNIBUS
  SKULL-FACE OMNIBUS, VOLUME 1

RIVALS OF WEIRD TALES (Anth.)
BEYOND THE BORDERS
STRANGE TALES, JANUARY 1933, Girasol Collectables (facsimile reprint)
STRANGE TALES, JANUARY 1933, Wildside Press (facsimile reprint)
ROBERT E. HOWARD'S STRANGE TALES
WINGS IN THE NIGHT: THE WEIRD WORKS OF ROBERT E. HOWARD, VOLUME 4

## CANNIBAL FISTS
Alternate title: FIST AND FANG

## THE CASE OF THE COLLEGE TOILET
First appeared in YESTERYEAR #4 (Chpbk.)
THE COLLECTED LETTERS OF ROBERT E. HOWARD, VOLUME 1: 1923-1929
From a letter to TCS, ca. February 1929 ("Salaam: / Last night the Sunday School . . .")

## CASONETTO'S LAST SONG
Alternate title: CASANETTO'S LAST SONG
First appeared in ETCHINGS AND ODYSSEYS #1 (Chpbk.)
THE CHRONICLER OF CROSS PLAINS #1
THE GODS OF BAL-SAGOTH
BEYOND THE BORDERS
Title varies from publication to publication

## THE CASTLE OF THE DEVIL
Featuring SOLOMON KANE and JOHN SILENT
First appeared in RED SHADOWS
SOLOMON KANE, Centaur and Haddock
SOLOMON KANE: SKULLS IN THE STARS (completed by Ramsey Campbell)
SOLOMON KANE, Baen (restored text, completed by Ramsey Campbell)
THE SAVAGE TALES OF SOLOMON KANE
THE LEGEND OF SOLOMON KANE
This is a fragment

## THE CAT AND THE SKULL
Alternate title: DELCARDES' CAT

## THE CELTICA NOTES OF ROBERT E. HOWARD
Alternate title: Untitled (" . . . which has characterized . . .")
First appeared in DEEPER THAN YOU THINK, January 1968 (offset reproduction of an original holographic
     manuscript)
THE NEW HOWARD READER #4 (Chpbk.)
This is an essay

## THE CHALLENGE FROM BEYOND
By Robert E. Howard, C.L. Moore, A. Merritt, HPL, & Frank Belknap Long
First appeared in FANTASY MAGAZINE, September 1935
BEYOND THE WALLS OF SLEEP (Anth.)
THE CHALLENGE FROM BEYOND, Pennsylvania Dutch Cheese Press (FAPA)
HORRORS UNKNOWN (Anth.)
THE CHALLENGE FROM BEYOND, Necronomicon
NAMELESS CULTS
SWORD AND FANTASY #4
THE ROAD TO VELITRIUM #49 (Chpbk.)

THE CROSS PLAINSMAN, December 2005 (Chpbk.)
BEYOND THE BLACK RIVER: THE WEIRD WORKS OF ROBERT E. HOWARD, VOLUME 7
This is an interesting exercise, dreamed up by the editor of Fantasy Magazine; he lined up five SF writers in one team, and five fantasy writers in a second team (REH's team), gave them just the title, then asked each team to write the story sequentially, allowed each author on a team to write a certain number of words, then pass it on to the next author, each being allowed to do whatever they wanted with the story; REH went fourth on his team, and completely turned the story over on its ear; a wonderful example of the differences between REH's themes and style and most other fantasy authors of the day

## CHAMP OF THE FORECASTLE
Alternate titles: CHAMP OF THE SEVEN SEAS; THE CHAMPION OF THE FORECASTLE
Featuring STEVE COSTIGAN
First appeared in FIGHT STORIES, November 1930
    FIGHT STORIES, June-July 1938 (as "Champ of the Seven Seas", author listed as "Mark Adam")
    REH'S FIGHT MAGAZINE #2
    WATERFRONT FISTS AND OTHERS
    BOXING STORIES (as "The Champion of the Forecastle")
    "The Champion" was changed to "Champ" by FIGHT STORIES

## CHAMP OF THE SEVEN SEAS
Alternate title: CHAMP OF THE FORECASTLE

## THE CHILDREN OF ASSHUR
Featuring SOLOMON KANE
First appeared in RED SHADOWS
    THE HAND OF KANE (unfinished fragment)
    SOLOMON KANE: THE HILLS OF THE DEAD (completed by Ramsey Campbell)
    SOLOMON KANE, Baen (restored text, completed by Ramsey Campbell)
    THE SAVAGE TALES OF SOLOMON KANE
    THE LEGEND OF SOLOMON KANE (completed by Ramsey Campbell)
    Unfinished

## THE CHILDREN OF THE NIGHT
First appeared in WEIRD TALES, April-May 1931
    THE DARK MAN AND OTHERS
    THE SPAWN OF CTHULHU (Anth.)
    PIGEONS FROM HELL, Zebra & Ace
    THE DARK MAN OMNIBUS, VOLUME 2
    BEYOND THE BORDERS
    BRAN MAK MORN – THE LAST KING
    NAMELESS CULTS
    PEOPLE OF THE DARK: THE WEIRD WORKS OF ROBERT E. HOWARD, VOLUME 3
    THE WEIRD WRITINGS OF ROBERT E. HOWARD, VOLUME ONE
    This story received a Class II rating in the O. Henry Memorial Prize Annual for 1931

## THE CHIMING OF THE GONG
Alternate title: THE STRIKING OF THE GONG

## THE CHRONICLES OF PATRICKUS
Listed on a Kline Agency list of REH stories, listed as 1 page long, don't know what happened to it

**CIRCUS CHARADE**
First appeared in THE LAST OF THE TRUNK OCH BREV I URVAL BREV I URVAL (Chpbk.)
        THE LAST OF THE TRUNK

**CIRCUS FISTS**
Alternate title: SLUGGER BAIT
Featuring STEVE COSTIGAN
First appeared in FIGHT STORIES, December 1931
        FIGHT STORIES, Summer, 1942 (as "Slugger Bait", author listed as "Mark Adam")
        REH'S FIGHT MAGAZINE #3 (Chpbk.)
        WATERFRONT FISTS AND OTHERS

**CLUTCHERS AT THE FRINGE**
Listed on a Kline Agency list of REH stories, listed as 170(!) pages long, don't know what happened to it

**CLUTHCHES AT THE FRINGES**
Listed on a Kline Agency list of REH stories, listed as 36 pages long, don't know what happened to it

**THE COBRA IN THE DREAM**
First appeared in WEIRDBOOK #1
        FEAST OF FEAR (Anth.)
        BLACK CANAAN
        BEYOND THE BORDERS

**COLLEGE SOCKS**
Alternate title: A STUDENT OF SOCKOLOGY
Featuring KID ALLISON
First appeared in SPORT STORY MAGAZINE, September 25, 1931
        FANTASY CROSSROADS #7

**THE COMING OF EL BORAK**
Featuring EL BORAK
First appeared in EL BORAK L'ETERNEL (French)
        THE COMING OF EL BORAK (Chpbk.)

**CONAN, MAN OF DESTINY**
Alternate titles: THE ROAD OF THE EAGLES; THE WAY OF THE SWORD
Featuring CONAN
First appeared in  FANTASTIC UNIVERSE, December 1955
        TALES OF CONAN
        CONAN THE FREEBOOTER
        THE CONAN CHRONICLES 1, Sphere and Orbit
        A derivative work created by LSDC, starting with a then-unpublished historical adventure, then turning it into a
                Conan story; LSDC later changed the name to match the original "The Road of the Eagles"; the
                original story was finally published as "The Way of the Sword" in THE ROAD OF AZRAEL

**CONAN THE CONQUEROR**
Alternate title: THE HOUR OF THE DRAGON

**THE CONQUERIN' HERO OF THE HUMBOLTS**
Alternate titles: POLITICS AT BLUE LIZARD; POLITICS AT LONESOME LIZARD
Featuring BRECKINRIDGE ELKINS
First appeared in ACTION STORIES, October 1936

THE PRIDE OF BEAR CREEK
HEROES OF BEAR CREEK
THE COMPLETE ACTION STORIES
THE RIOT AT BUCKSNORT AND OTHER WESTERN TALES
Grant removed all the italics for THE PRIDE OF BEAR CREEK, which was carried over in the Ace edition; the original title that REH had was "Politics at Blue Lizard", though Glenn Lord in THE LAST CELT pointed out that surely REH meant "Politics at Lonesome Lizard", as that is the name of the town in the story; both THE COMPLETE ACTION STORIES restores the story to its original published form

## COSTIGAN VS. KID CAMERA
Alternate title: SAILORS' GRUDGE

## THE COUNTRY OF THE KNIFE
Alternate title: SONS OF THE HAWK
Featuring EL BORAK
First appeared in COMPLETE STORIES, August 1936
    SON OF THE WHITE WOLF
    BLOOD OF THE GODS AND OTHER STORIES
    THE "EL BORAK" STORIES - BLOOD OF THE GODS; THE DAUGHTER OF ERLIK KHAN; HAWK OF THE HILLS; SON OF THE WHITE WOLF; THE COUNTRY OF THE KNIFE

## THE CRIMSON LINE
A story that REH said he wrote, but no copy exists

## CROWD-HORROR
First appeared in ARGOSY ALL-STORY WEEKLEY, July 20, 1929
    BOXING STORIES
    ARGOSY shortened the story, per REH; REH to TCS, ca. April 1929: ". . . I got a letter from Argosy, accepting that story that I told you about. They said it was still far too long but they'd cut it down and make the necessary changes themselves."

## CULTURED CAULIFLOWERS
Alternate title: IN HIGH SOCIETY

## CUPID FROM BEAR CREEK
Alternate title: THE PEACEFUL PILGRIM
Featuring BRECKINRIDGE ELKINS
First appeared in ACTION STORIES, August 1935
    THE SUMMIT COUNTY JOURNAL, March 26, April 2, 9, 16, 23, 30, May 7, 14, 21, 28, June 4, 11, 18, 26, 1970 (14-part serial, same as book version)
    THE COMPLETE ACTION STORIES
    Was altered slightly to become Chapter 9 of the "A Gent from Bear Creek" novel; "The Peaceful Pilgrim" is a slightly different story; THE SUMMIT COUNTY JOURNAL appearance changed the name to "Breckenridge", to be like the town it was published in

## CUPID VS. POLLUX
First appeared in THE YELLOW JACKET, February 10, 1927
    THE HOWARD COLLECTOR #7
    THE HOWARD COLLECTOR, Ace
    THE COMPLETE YELLOW JACKET
    WEST IS WEST AND OTHERS

## THE CURLY WOLF OF SAWTOOTH
Alternate titles: A ELSTON TO THE RESCUE; A ELKINS NEVER SURRENDERS
Featuring BEARFIELD ELSTON; BRECKINRIDGE ELKINS
First appeared in STAR WESTERN, September 1936 (as "The Curly Wolf of Sawtooth")
> THE SUMMIT COUNTY JOURNAL, January 12, 19, 26, February 2, 9, 1968 (as "A Elkins Never
>> Surrenders")
> MAYHEM ON BEAR CREEK (as "A Elkins Never Surrenders")
> HEROES OF BEAR CREEK (as "A Elkins Never Surrenders")
> A ELKINS NEVER SURRENDERS ( as "A Elkins Never Surrenders", chpbk.)
> The version titled "The Curly Wolf of Sawtooth" features Bearfield Elston, REH making that change; the
>> version titled "A Elkins Never Surrenders" comes from an earlier draft, and features Breckinridge
>> Elkins; THE SUMMIT COUNTY JOURNAL appearance changed the name to "Breckenridge", to be
>> like the town it was published in; the chapbook version is based on an earlier draft

## THE CURSE OF GREED
First appeared in FANTASY CROSSWINDS #1
> LURID CONFESSIONS #1 (Chpbk.)
> THE NEW HOWARD READER #7 (Chpbk.)

## THE CURSE OF THE CRIMSON GOD
Alternate titles: TRAIL OF THE BLOODSTAINED GOD; THE BLOODSTAINED GOD
Featuring KIRBY O'DONNELL
First appeared in SWORDS OF SHAHRAZAR (all editions)
> This story was used as the basis for an LSDC derivative story, called "The Bloodstained God", his version
>> being a Conan story

## THE CURSE OF THE GOLDEN SKULL
Featuring KULL
First appeared in THE HOWARD COLLECTOR #9
> FANTASY CROSSROADS #2
> FROM THE HELLS BENEATH THE HELLS (Chpbk.)
> THE BOOK OF ROBERT E. HOWARD
> THE GODS OF BAL-SAGOTH
> THE HOWARD COLLECTOR, Ace
> KULL, Baen
> KULL: EXILE OF ATLANTIS
> CRIMSON SHADOWS: THE BEST OF ROBERT E. HOWARD, VOLUME 1

## DAGON MANOR
First appeared in SHUDDER STORIES #4 (Chpbk., completed by C.J. Henderson)
> DIFFERENT WORLDS #42 (Chpbk., completed by C.J. Henderson)
> THE NEW HOWARD READER #3 (Chpbk.)
> Incomplete fragment

## THE DARK MAN
Featuring TURLOGH DUBH O'BRIEN
First appeared in WEIRD TALES, December 1931
> WEIRD TALES, September 1954
> THE DARK MAN AND OTHERS (Accidentally published incomplete)
> BRAN MAK MORN, Dell
> WORMS OF THE EARTH
> THE DARK MAN ONMIBUS, VOLUME 1
> BARN MAK MORN, Baen
> BRAN MAK MORN – THE LAST KING

THE HOWARD REVIEW #13 (Chpbk., facsimile of original pages)
PEOPLE OF THE DARK: THE WEIRD WORKS OF ROBERT E. HOWARD, VOLUME 3
THE WEIRD WRITINGS OF ROBERT E. HOWARD, VOLUME ONE
THE WEIRD WRITINGS OF ROBERT E. HOWARD, VOLUME TWO
CRIMSON SHADOWS: THE BEST OF ROBERT E. HOWARD, VOLUME 1
The version in WEIRD WRITINGS, VOLUME ONE is a facsimile of the original pages from WEIRD TALES
    from the 1930s; the version in WEIRD WRITINGS, VOLUME TWO is a facsimile of the original
    pages from WEIRD TALES from the 1950s

## DARK SHANGHAI
Alternate title: ONE SHANGHAI NIGHT
Featuring STEVE COSTIGAN
First appeared in ACTION STORIES, January 1932
    THE COMPLETE ACTION STORIES
    THE ROBERT E. HOWARD FOUNDATION NEWSLETTER, VOLUME 1, #2 (synopsis only)
    Was originally a Mike Dorgan / Bill McGlory story, straight adventure, ACTION STORIES editors changed it
        to a Sailor Steve Costigan story; there is a surviving synopsis of the original Dorgan/McGlory version

## THE DAUGHTER OF ERLIK KHAN
Featuring EL BORAK
First appeared in TOP-NOTCH, December 1934
    THE LOST VALLEY OF ISKANDER
    ROBERT E. HOWARD'S WORLD OF HEROES
    BLOOD OF THE GODS AND OTHER STORIES
    THE DAUGHTER OF ERLIK KHAN
    THE "EL BORAK" STORIES - BLOOD OF THE GODS; THE DAUGHTER OF ERLIK KHAN; HAWK OF
        THE HILLS; SON OF THE WHITE WOLF; THE COUNTRY OF THE KNIFE

## DAUGHTERS OF FEUD
First appeared in FANTASY CROSSROADS #8
    THE SHE DEVIL

## DEAD MAN'S DOOM
    Alternate title: LORD OF THE DEAD, Grant

## THE DEAD REMEMBER
First appeared in ARGOSY, August 15, 1936
    FANTASTIC, December 1961
    THE DARK MAN AND OTHERS (Accidentally published incomplete)
    HORROR TIMES TEN
    PIGEONS FROM HELL, Zebra & Ace
    THE DARK MAN OMNIBUS, VOLUME 2
    HAUNTED AMERICA (Anth.)
    TRAILS IN DARKNESS
    REHUPA #156 (Chpbk.)
    THE END OF THE TRAIL: WESTERN STORIES

## DEATH'S BLACK RIDERS
Featuring SOLOMON KANE
First appeared in THE HOWARD COLLECTOR #10
    REH: LONE STAR FICTIONEER #1
    THE HOWARD COLLECTOR, Ace
    THE RAVEN #1 (Chpbk.)
    FANTASY BOOK, June 1984 (completed by Fred Blosser)

SOLOMON KANE, Baen
THE SAVAGE TALES OF SOLOMON KANE
THE CRYPT OF CTHULHU #105 (Chpbk., completed by CJ Henderson)
THE RIGHT HAND OF DOOM AND OTHER TALES OF SOLOMON KANE
THE LEGEND OF SOLOMON KANE
Unfinished

## DELCARDES' CAT
Alternate title: THE CAT AND THE SKULL
Featuring KULL
First appeared in KING KULL
    KULL: THE FABULOUS WARRIOR KING
    KULL
    KULL: EXILE OF ATLANTIS (as "The Cat and the Skull", also includes an early draft)
    REH changed the title to "The Cat and The Skull"

## DELENDA EST
First appeared in WORLDS OF FANTASY #1
    FANTASY CROSSROADS #1
    BLACK CANAAN
    MORE TALES OF UNKNOWN HORROR (Anth.)
    THE THIRD BOOK OF UNKNOWN TALES OF HORROR (Anth.)
    EONS OF THE NIGHT

## DERMOD'S BANE
First appeared in MAGAZINE OF HORROR #17
    ROBERT E. HOWARD OMNIBUS
    BLACK CANAAN
    BARBARIAN SCROLL #7 (Chpbk.)
    BEYOND THE BORDERS

## DESERT BLOOD
Alternate title: REVENGE BY PROXY
Featuring WILD BILL CLANTON
First appeared in SPICY-ADVENTURE STORIES, June 1936 (author listed as "Sam Walser")
    SPICY-ADVENTURE STORIES, September 1942 (as "Revenge by Proxy", author listed as "William
        Decatur")
    INCREDIBLE ADVENTURES #1 (Chpbk.)
    THE SHE DEVIL
    THE CHRONICLER OF CROSS PLAINS #2 (Chpbk.)
    SPICY-ADVENTURE STORIES, JUNE 1936 (Chpbk.)

## DESERT RENDEZVOUS
Featuring THE SONORA KID
First appeared in THE SONORA KID (Chpbk.)

## THE DESTINY GORILLA
Alternate titles: SAILOR DORGAN AND THE DESTINY GORILLA; SAILOR COSTIGAN AND THE DESTINY
        GORILLA
Featuring DENNIS DORGAN; STEVE COSTIGAN
First appeared in THE INCREDIBLE ADVENTURES OF DENNIS DORGAN
    THE IRON MAN, WITH THE ADVENTURES OF DENNIS DORGAN
    THE DESTINY GORILLA (Chpbk.)

Original typescript lists author as "Patrick Ervin", a pseudonym REH used in connection with his Dennis
Dorgan stories; a draft exists with the Costigan charcter

## THE DEVIL IN HIS BRAIN
First appeared in LURID CONFESSIONS #1 (Chpbk.)
    THE NEW HOWARD READER #3 (Chpbk.)

## THE DEVIL IN IRON
Featuring CONAN
First appeared in WEIRD TALES, August 1934
    CONAN THE BARBARIAN, Gnome
    CONAN THE WANDERER
    THE DEVIL IN IRON, Grant and Grossett & Dunlap
    THE PEOPLE OF THE BLACK CIRCLE, Berkley & Putnam
    THE CONAN CHRONICLES 2, Orbit
    THE ESSENTIAL CONAN, SFBC Fantasy
    THE CONAN CHRONICLES I: THE PEOPLE OF THE BLACK CIRCLE
    ROBERT E. HOWARD'S COMPLETE CONAN OF CIMMERIA, VOLUME 1
    THE COMING OF CONAN THE CIMMERIAN
    STRANGE WORLDS #12 (Chpbk., facsimile repro of pulp pages)
    SAVAGE ADVENTURES
    THE DEVIL IN IRON, Incarna
    THE COMPLETE CHRONICLES OF CONAN
    THE WEIRD WRITINGS OF ROBERT E. HOWARD, VOLUME TWO
    THE GARDEN OF FEAR: THE WEIRD WORKS OF ROBERT E. HOWARD, VOLUME 6
    WEIRD TALES, AUGUST 1934 (Chpbk.)

## THE DEVIL'S JEST
Alternate titles: THE DEVIL'S JOKER; OUTLAW TRAILS

## THE DEVIL'S JOKER
Alternate titles: THE DEVIL'S JEST; OUTLAW TRAILS
Featuring THE SONORA KID
First appeared in CROSS PLAINS #6
    REH: TWO GUN RACONTEUR #3
    THE LAST RIDE
    THE END OF THE TRAIL: WESTERN STORIES

## THE DEVILS OF DARK LAKE
First appeared in WT 50: A TRIBUTE TO WEIRD TALES
    THE ROAD TO VELITRIUM #25 (Chpbk.)
    THE NEW HOWARD READER #1 (Chpbk.)
    A 5 page synopsis also exists

## THE DEVIL'S WOODCHOPPER
First appeared in THE GRIM LAND AND OTHERS (Chpbk., completed by TCS)
    ROBERT E. HOWARD—THE POWER OF THE WRITING MIND (just REH's portion)
    RAZORED ZEN #82 (Chpbk., completed by Charles Gramlich)
    An incomplete story

## THE DIABLOS TRAIL
Featuring PIKE BEARFIELD
First appeared in BRAN MAK MORN: A PLAY & OTHERS (Chpbk.)
    CROMLECH #3 (Chpbk.)
    THE COLLECTED LETTERS OF ROBERT E. HOWARD, VOLUME 3: 1934-1936 (synopsis only)
    Unfinished; an unfinished synopsis of this story appears in a letter to Jack Byrne, April 21, 1936 ("My agent,
        O.A. Kline, tells me . . .")

## DIG ME NO GRAVE
Alternate title: JOHN GRIMLAN'S DEBT
First appeared in WEIRD TALES, February 1937
    THE DARK MAN AND OTHERS
    EIGHT STRANGE TALES (Anth.)
    THE 2<sup>ND</sup> MAYFLOWER BOOK OF BLACK MAGIC STORIES (Anth.)
    PIGEONS FROM HELL, Zebra & Ace
    THE DARK MAN OMNIBUS, VOLUME 2
    CTHULHU THE MYTHOS AND KINDRED HORRORS
    BEYOND THE BORDERS
    NAMELESS CULTS
    THE WEIRD WRITINGS OF ROBERT E. HOWARD, VOLUME TWO

## DIOGENES OF TODAY
By Robert E. Howard & Tevis Clyde Smith
First appeared in RED BLADES OF BLACK CATHAY

## THE DOMINANT MALE
First appeared in THE LAST OF THE TRUNK OCH BREV I URVAL BREV I URVAL (Chpbk.)
    THE LAST OF THE TRUNK

## THE DOOK OF STORK
First appeared in THE LAST OF THE TRUNK OCH BREV I URVAL BREV I URVAL (Chpbk.)
    THE COLLECTED LETTERS OF ROBERT E. HOWARD, VOLUME 1: 1923-1929
    From a letter to TCS, July 7, 1923 ("To Clyde bahadur-sahib, greeting: / I got . . .")

## THE DOOR TO THE GARDEN
Alternate title: THE DOOR TO THE WORLD
First appeared in FANTASY CROSSWINDS #2
    NAMELESS CULTS (completed by Joseph S. Pulver)
    ROBERT E. HOWARD—THE POWER OF THE WRITING MIND
    This is a fragment

## THE DOOR TO THE WORLD
Alternate title: THE DOOR TO THE GARDEN

## DOUBLE CROSS
Featuring ACE JESSEL
First appeared in BRAN MAK MORN: A PLAY & OTHERS (Chpbk.)
    ROBERT E. HOWARD—THE POWER OF THE WRITING MIND

**THE DRAGON OF KAO TSU**
Featuring WILD BILL CLANTON
First appeared in SPICY-ADVENTURE STORIES, September 1936 (author listed as "Sam Walser")
    THE SHE DEVIL
    SPICY ADVENTURE STORIES, SEPTEMBER 1936, Girasol Collectables (Chpbk.)

**THE DRAWING CARD**
Featuring KID ALLISON
First appeared in THE LAST OF THE TRUNK OCH BREV I URVAL (Chpbk.)
    THE LAST OF THE TRUNK

**A DREAM**
Alternate title: Untitled ("I remember a most curious dream . . .")
First appeared in THE HOWARD COLLECTOR #14
    THE NEW HOWARD READER #2 (Chpbk.)
    Originally this story appeared in a letter to HPL, ca. December 1930 ("As always, your letter proved highly
        enjoyable.") and was untitled

**THE DREAM SNAKE**
First appeared in WEIRD TALES, February 1928
    THE DARK MAN AND OTHERS
    PIGEONS FROM HELL, Zebra & Ace
    THE DARK MAN OMNIBUS, VOLUME 2
    BEYOND THE BORDERS
    SHADOW KINGDOMS: THE WEIRD WORKS OF ROBERT E. HOWARD, VOLUME 1 (Wildside Press,
        Cosmos & AudioRealms)
    THE WEIRD WRITINGS OF ROBERT E. HOWARD, VOLUME ONE

**THE DRIFTER**
First appeared in THE LAST OF THE TRUNK OCH BREV I URVAL (Chpbk.)
    THE LAST OF THE TRUNK
    Incomplete

**DRUMS OF HORROR**
A story that REH said he wrote, but no copy exists

**DRUMS OF THE SUNSET**
Alternate title: RIDERS OF THE SUNSET
First appeared in THE CROSS PLAINS REVIEW, November 2, 9, 16, 23, 30, December 7, 14, 21, 1928; January 4,
    1929 (9-part serial)
    FANTASY CROSSROADS #2
    THE VULTURES OF WHAPETON
    ROBERT E. HOWARD OMNIBUS
    THE END OF THE TRAIL: WESTERN STORIES

**DRUMS OF TOMBULKU**
Featuring CONAN
First appeared in CONAN THE ADVENTURER (completed by LSDC)
    THE FANTASTIC SWORDSMEN (Anth., claims to be the first printing of this story, LSDC version)
    THE POOL OF THE BLACK ONE (fragment only, bowdlerized)
    CROMLECH #3 (Chpbk., first appearance of the original synopsis)
    THE CONAN CHRONICLES 2, Orbit (LSDC version)
    THE CONAN CHRONICLES I: THE PEOPLE OF THE BLACK CIRCLE (fragment)

ROBERT E. HOWARD'S COMPLETE CONAN OF CIMMERIA, VOLUME 2 (fragment and synopsis)
THE BLOODY CROWN OF CONAN (fragment and synopsis)
THE COMPLETE CHRONICLES OF CONAN (fragment only)
Originally just a fragment and a synopsis, the story was completed by LSDC; THE FANTASTIC
        SWORDSMEN claims to be first appearance, even though its publishing date is several months after
        CONAN THE ADVENTURER, perhaps their publishers didn't know about the pending publication of
        the other book

## DULA DUE TO BE CHAMPION
First appeared in THE BROWNWOOD BULLETIN, July 18, 1928
        POST OAKS AND SAND ROUGHS
        WATERFRONT FISTS AND OTHERS
        WEST IS WEST AND OTHERS
        A factual report on the Kid Dula - Duke Tramel bout, Fort Worth, July 13, 1928

## THE DWELLERS UNDER THE TOMB
First appeared in LOST FANTASIES #4
        BLACK CANAAN
        Two drafts known, one 13 pages and one 18 pages, both titled

## EDUCATE OR BUST
Alternate title: SHARP'S GUN SERENADE
First appeared in A GENT FROM BEAR CREEK (as Chapter 11)
        SUMMIT COUNTY JOURNAL, September 25; October 2, 9, 16, 23, 30; November 6, 13, 20, 27, 1970 (10-
                part serial)
        HEROES OF BEAR CREEK
        "Sharp's Gun Serenade" is somewhat different; THE SUMMIT COUNTY JOURNAL appearance changed the
                name to "Breckenridge", to be like the town it was published in

## EIGHTTOES MAKES A PLAY
By Robert E. Howard & Tevis Clyde Smith
First appeared in RED BLADES OF BLACK CATHAY
        THE HOWARD COLLECTOR #15 (first appearance of alternate ending)
        THE NEW HOWARD READER #6 (Chpbk., original ending)
        Based on an outline by REH and TCS, TCS actually wrote the story

## EL BORAK (1, "I emptied my revolver . . .")
Featuring EL BORAK
First appeared in EL BORAK L'ETERNEL (French)
        THE COMING OF EL BORAK (Chpbk.)

## EL BORAK (2, "Were you ever stranded . . .")
Featuring EL BORAK & THE SONORA KID
First appeared in EL BORAK L'ETERNEL (French)
        NORTH OF KHYBER (Chpbk.)

## EL BORAK SYNOPSIS
Unpublished

## A ELKINS NEVER SURRENDERS
Alternate title: THE CURLY WOLF OF SAWTOOTH

**A ELSTON TO THE RESCUE**
Alternate title: THE CURLY WOLF OF SAWTOOTH

**ETCHED IN EBONY**
First appeared in TRUMPET #7 (Chpbk.)
    THE NEW HOWARD READER #3 (Chpbk.)
    THE ROAD TO VELITRIUM #30 (Chpbk.)

**ETCHINGS IN IVORY**
First appeared in ETCHINGS IN IVORY (Chpbk.)
    THE BOOK OF ROBERT E. HOWARD

**EVIL DEEDS AT RED COUGAR**
Featuring BRECKINRIDGE ELKINS
First appeared in ACTION STORIES, June 1936
    THE SUMMIT COUNTY JOURNAL, July 7, 14, 21, 28; August 11, 18, 25; September 1, 1967 (8-part serial,
        8/11 was reprint of 8/4, which had inadvertently had some text missing)
    MAYHEM ON BEAR CREEK
    HEROES OF BEAR CREEK
    THE COMPLETE ACTION STORIES
    THE SUMMIT COUNTY JOURNAL appearance changed the name to "Breckenridge", to be like the town it
        was published in; there is also a synopsis, never published

**EXILE OF ATLANTIS**
Featuring KULL
First appeared in KING KULL
    KULL: THE FABULOUS WARRIOR KING
    KULL
    KULL: EXILE OF ATLANTIS

**THE EXTERMINATION OF YELLOW DONARY**
Alternate title: THE KILLING OF YELLOW DONARY
First appeared in ZANE GREY WESTERN MAGAZINE, June 1970 (heavily edited)
    THE LAST RIDE (better text)
    THE END OF THE TRAIL: WESTERN STORIES

**A FAITHFUL SERVANT**
First appeared in THE LAST OF THE TRUNK OCH BREV I URVAL (Chpbk.)
    THE LAST OF THE TRUNK
    Hand-written, and dated February 9, 1921

**FALL GUY**
Alternate title: THE IRON MAN

**FANGS OF GOLD**
Alternate title: PEOPLE OF THE SERPENT
Featuring STEVE HARRISON
First appeared in STRANGE DETECTIVE STORIES, February 1934
    PHANTASY DIGEST #2
    PULP REVIEW #15
    THE NEW HOWARD READER #5 (Chpbk.)
    GRAVEYARD RATS AND OTHERS

Almost certainly an error by the staff of STRANGE DETECTIVE STORIES in assigning the original title, as it
    has nothing to do with this story, but would be a great title for the OTHER REH story that appeared in
    the same issue

## FANGS OF THE COPPERHEAD
Listed on a Kline Agency list of REH stories, listed as 10 pages long, don't know what happened to it

## THE FANGS OF THE YELLOW COBRA
Alternate title: THE YELLOW COBRA; SAILOR DORGAN AND THE YELLOW COBRA; A NIGHT ASHORE;
    A KOREAN NIGHT
Featuring STEVE COSTIGAN
Unpublished version of "The Yellow Cobra", a Dennis Dorgan story; "A Korean Night" is a slightly different, earlier
    original draft of this Costigan version

## THE FASTIDIOUS FOOEY MANCUCU
First appeared in THE COLLECTED LETTERS OF ROBERT E. HOWARD, VOLUME 1: 1923-1929
    From a letter to TCS, ca. October 1927 ("Salaam: / Seeking cognizance of things . . ."); also contains the poem
        Untitled ("Tell me not in coocoo numbers")

## FATE IS THE KILLER
First appeared in THE LAST OF THE TRUNK OCH BREV I URVAL (Chpbk.)
    THE LAST OF THE TRUNK
    Unfinished

## THE FEAR-MASTER
First appeared in CRYPT OF CTHULHU #22 (Chpbk.)
    THE NEW HOWARD READER #5 (Chpbk.)

## THE FEARSOME TOUCH OF DEATH
Alternate title: THE TOUCH OF DEATH
First appeared in WEIRD TALES, February 1930
    THE HOWARD REVIEW #1 (Chpbk.)
    THE NEW HOWARD READER #2 (Chpbk., as "The Touch of Death")
    ROBERT E. HOWARD'S STRANGE TALES
    MOON OF SKULLS: THE WEIRD WORKS OF ROBERT E. HOWARD, VOLUME 2
    SHADOW KINGDOMS: THE WEIRD WORKS OF ROBERT E. HOWARD, VOLUME 1 (Cosmos)
    THE WEIRD WRITINGS OF ROBERT E. HOWARD, VOLUME ONE

## THE FELINE MYSTIQUE
Alternate title: THE BEAST FROM THE ABYSS

## THE FEMALE OF THE SPECIES
First appeared in THE LAST OF THE TRUNK OCH BREV I URVAL (Chpbk.)
    THE LAST OF THE TRUNK
    Incomplete; incorrectly previously listed at "The Feminine of the Species"

## THE FEROCIOUS APE
First appeared in THE LAST OF THE TRUNK OCH BREV I URVAL (Chpbk.)
    THE LAST OF THE TRUNK

**THE FEUD BUSTER**
Featuring BRECKINRIDGE ELKINS
First appeared in ACTION STORIES, June 1935
> THE SUMMIT COUNTY JOURNAL, April 4, 11, 18, 25; May 2, 9, 16, 23, 30; June 6, 13, 20, 27; July 4, 11, 18, 1969 (16-part serial, similar to book version)
> THE NEW HOWARD READER #5 (Chpbk., original magazine version)
> THE COMPLETE ACTION STORIES
> THE RIOT AT BUCKSNORT AND OTHER WESTERN TALES
> Was altered slightly to become Chapter 6 of the the "A Gent from Bear Creek" novel; THE SUMMIT COUNTY JOURNAL appearance changed the name to "Breckenridge", to be like the town it was published in

**THE FIGHTIN' DUMBBELL**
A story that REH said he wrote, but no copy exists

**THE FIGHTIN'EST PAIR**
Alternate title: BREED OF BATTLE

**THE FIGHTING FURY**
First appeared in THE LAST OF THE TRUNK OCH BREV I URVAL (Chpbk.)
> THE LAST OF THE TRUNK

**FIGHTING NERVES**
Featuring KID ALLISON
First appeared in THE LAST OF THE TRUNK OCH BREV I URVAL (Chpbk.)
> THE LAST OF THE TRUNK

**THE FIRE OF ASSHURBANIPAL**
First appeared in WEIRD TALES, December 1936
> SKULL-FACE AND OTHERS
> WOLFSHEAD, Lancer
> THE HOWARD COLLECTOR #16 (a slightly different, straight adventure version)
> SKULL-FACE OMNIBUS
> SKULL-FACE OMNIBUS, VOLUME 2
> WOLFSHEAD, Bantam
> CTHULHU THE MYTHOS AND KINDRED HORRORS
> TALES OF THE LOVECRAFT MYTHOS (Anth., straight adventure version)
> BEYOND THE BORDERS
> THE NEW HOWARD READER #7 (Chpbk., straight adventure version)
> NAMELESS CULTS
> THE HOWARD REVIEW #13 (Chpbk., facsimile of original WT pages)
> THE WEIRD WRITINGS OF ROBERT E. HOWARD, VOLUME TWO

**THE FISHING TRIP**
First appeared in THE LAST OF THE TRUNK OCH BREV I URVAL (Chpbk.)
> THE LAST OF THE TRUNK
> Hand-written, and dated October 6, 1922

**FIST AND FANG**
Alternate title: CANNIBAL FISTS
Featuring STEVE COSTIGAN
First appeared in FIGHT STORIES, May 1930
> FIGHT STORIES, Winter, 1938-39 (as "Cannibal Fists", author listed as "Mark Adam")

REH'S FIGHT MAGAZINE #1 (Chpbk.)
WATERFRONT FISTS AND OTHERS

## FISTCE MASQUERADE
Listed on a Kline Agency list of REH stories, listed as 17 pages long, don't know what happened to it

## FISTIC PSYCHOLOGY
Featuring KID ALLISON
First appeared in THE LAST OF THE TRUNK OCH BREV I URVAL (Chpbk.)
    THE LAST OF THE TRUNK

## FISTS OF THE DESERT
Alternate title: IRON-JAW

## FISTS OF THE REVOLUTION
First appeared in FANTASY CROSSROADS, SPECIAL EDITION #1

## THE FLAME KNIFE
Alternate title: THREE-BLADED DOOM
Featuring CONAN
First appeared in TALES OF CONAN
    FANTASTIC UNIVERSE, December 1955
    CONAN THE WANDERER
    THE CONAN CHRONICLES 2, Orbit
    An LSDC derivative work, starting with the long version of the then-unpublished "Three-Bladed Doom", and
        turning it into a Conan story

## FLAMING MARBLE
First appeared in ETCHINGS IN IVORY (Chpbk.)
    THE BOOK OF ROBERT E. HOWARD
    There is also a poem with the same title, but is different

## FLYING KNUCKLES
Featuring STEVE COSTIGAN
First appeared in STEVE COSTIGAN LE CHAMPION (French)
    REH'S FIGHT MAGAZINE #4 (Chpbk.)

## THE FOLLY OF CONCEIT
First appeared in THE LAST OF THE TRUNK OCH BREV I URVAL (Chpbk.)
    THE LAST OF THE TRUNK
    Unfinished

## THE FOOTFALLS WITHIN
Featuring SOLOMON KANE
First appeared in WEIRD TALES, September 1931
    RED SHADOWS
    THE MOON OF SKULLS
    THE SECOND BOOK OF ROBERT E. HOWARD
    ROBERT E. HOWARD OMNIBUS
    SOLOMON KANE: THE HILLS OF THE DEAD
    SOLOMON KANE, Baen (Grant text)
    THE SAVAGE TALES OF SOLOMON KANE
    SAVAGE ADVENTURES

PEOPLE OF THE DARK: THE WEIRD WORKS OF ROBERT E. HOWARD, VOLUME 3
THE WEIRD WRITINGS OF ROBERT E. HOWARD, VOLUME ONE
THE RIGHT HAND OF DOOM AND OTHER TALES OF SOLOMON KANE
THE LEGEND OF SOLOMON KANE
THE 'SOLOMAN CRANE' STORIES

## FOOTPRINTS OF FEAR
Listed on a Kline Agency list of REH stories, listed as 9 pages long, don't know what happened to it

## "FOR THE LOVE OF BARBARA ALLEN"
First appeared in MAGAZINE OF FANTASY & SCIENCE FICTION, August 1966
    THE SECOND BOOK OF ROBERT E. HOWARD
    MARCHERS OF VALHALLA, Sphere and Berkley
    TIME WARPS (Anth.)
    THE FANTASTIC CIVIL WAR (Anth.)
    TRAILS IN DARKNESS
    CRIMSON SHADOWS: THE BEST OF ROBERT E. HOWARD, VOLUME 1

## FRIENDS
First appeared in THE LAST OF THE TRUNK OCH BREV I URVAL (Chpbk.)
    THE LAST OF THE TRUNK
    Hand-written, and dated October 19, 1922

## THE FROST-GIANT'S DAUGHTER
Alternate titles: GODS OF THE NORTH; THE FROST-KING'S DAUGHTER
First appeared in THE COMING OF CONAN
    FANTASY FICTION #1
    FANTASTIC UNIVERSE, December 1956
    CONAN OF CIMMERIA
    ROGUES IN THE HOUSE
    ECHOES OF VALOR II (Anth.)
    THE CONAN CHRONICLES 1, Sphere and Orbit
    THE DARK MAN #1 (Chpbk., an early draft)
    THE CONAN CHRONICLES I: THE PEOPLE OF THE BLACK CIRCLE
    ROBERT E. HOWARD'S COMPLETE CONAN OF CIMMERIA, VOLUME 1
    THE COMING OF CONAN THE CIMMERIAN
    THE COMPLETE CHRONICLES OF CONAN
    THE PHOENIX ON THE SWORD (Chpbk.)
    Originally written by REH as a Conan story titled "The Frost-Giant's Daughter", it was not accepted, so he rewrote it with a different hero (Amra), changed the title to "The Frost-King's Daughter", and gave it away to THE FANTASY FAN; when published by THE FANTASY FAN, they changed the title to "Gods of the North"; LSDC found the original manuscript, but extensively rewrote it, and called it "The Frost Giant's Daughter" (LSDC-edited version, note no hyphen); LSDC changed it each time it got republished, up through the Lancer version); starting with Grant Press' ROGUES IN THE HOUSE, the text has been restored to original typescript form; listings for "Gods of the North" are under its own heading; ECHOES OF VALOR II has both REH versions of the story

## THE FROST-KING'S DAUGHTER
Alternate titles: THE FROST GIANT'S DAUGHTER; GODS OF THE NORTH

## THE FUNNIEST BOUT
First appeared in THE LAST OF THE TRUNK OCH BREV I URVAL (Chpbk.)
    THE LAST OF THE TRUNK

## THE FURTHER ADVENTURES OF LAL SINGH
Featuring LAL SINGH
First appeared in THE ADVENTURES OF LAL SINGH (Chpbk.)

## THE GALVESTON AFFAIR
First appeared in THE JUNTO, December 1928
> TRUMPET #7 (Chpbk.)
> THE NEW HOWARD READER #3 (Chpbk.)
> THE ROAD TO VELITRIUM #30 (Chpbk.)

## THE GARDEN OF FEAR
Featuring JAMES ALLISON
First appeared in MARVEL TALES, July-August 1934
> THE GARDEN OF FEAR AND OTHER STORIES OF THE BIZARRE AND FANTASTIC (Anth.)
> FANTASTIC, May 1961
> THE DARK MAN AND OTHERS
> NEW WORLDS FOR OLD (Anth.)
> PIGEONS FROM HELL, Zebra & Ace
> THE DARK MAN OMNIBUS, VOLUME 2
> EONS OF THE NIGHT
> ROBERT E. HOWARD'S STRANGE TALES
> THE GARDEN OF FEAR: THE WEIRD WORKS OF ROBERT E. HOWARD, VOLUME 6

## GATES OF EMPIRE
Alternate title: THE ROAD OF THE MOUNTAIN LION
First appeared in GOLDEN FLEECE, January 1939
> GOLDEN FLEECE, Odyssey Publications (Anth.)
> ROBERT E. HOWARD OMNIBUS
> THE ROAD OF AZRAEL
> WINDY CITY PULP AND PAPERBACK SHOW 2ND ANNUAL, March 2002
> GATES OF EMPIRE AND OTHERS
> LORD OF SAMARCAND AND OTHER ADVENTURES OF THE OLD ORIENT

## GENERAL IRONFIST
Featuring STEVE COSTIGAN
First appeared in JACK DEMPSEY'S FIGHT MAGAZINE, June 1934
> REH'S FIGHT MAGAZINE #3 (Chpbk.)
> WATERFRONT FISTS AND OTHERS
> THE ROBERT E. HOWARD FOUNDATION NEWSLETTER, VOLUME 1, #2 (synopsis only)
> A short synopsis also exists for this story

## GENSERIC'S SON
Alternate titles: GENSERIC'S FIFTH BORN SON; Untitled ("Long, long ago a son was born . . ."); GHOR, KIN-
> SLAYER

## GENSERIC'S FIFTH BORN SON
Alternate titles: Untitled ("Long, long ago a son was born . . ."); GHOR, KIN-SLAYER; GENSERIC'S SON
Featuring JAMES ALLISON
First appeared in FANTASY CROSSROADS #10 (REH portion)
> GHOR, KIN-SLAYER (Anth., complete story)
> THE NEW HOWARD READER #6 (Chpbk., REH portion only)
> This is a round robin, 17-chapter story, derived from a short unfinished work by REH; REH's portion served as
> > Chapter 1, and each following author wrote another chapter; the other authors were Karl Edward

Wagner, Joseph Brennan, Richard L. Tierney, Michael Moorcock, Charles R. Saunders, Andrew J. Offutt, Manly Wade Wellman, Darrell Schwietzer, A.E. Van Vogt, Brian Lumley, Frank Belknap Long, Adrian Cole, Ramsey Campbell, H. Warner Munn, Marion Zimmer Bradley, and finally Richard A. Lupoff; all but the REH portion was written in the 1970's; originally scheduled to be published serially in several episodes in FANTASY CROSSROADS, only 12 of the 17 got published; the Necronomicon Press edition is the first complete publication of the story; Jonathan Bacon took the original untitled fragment, and called it "Genseric's Son"

## A GENT FROM BEAR CREEK (Novel)
Featuring BRECKINRIDGE ELKINS
First appeared in  A GENT FROM BEAR CREEK
    HEROES OF BEAR CREEK
    A GENT FROM BEAR CREEK AND OTHERS
    Title of both an original short story, as well as a novel created by combining several previous short stories with some new material; the previously published short stories were altered a little to create chapters with a continuous story line, and new material was added as additional chapters; the chapters are: "Striped Shirts and Busted Hearts" (new); "Mountain Man"; "Meet Cap'n Kidd" (new); "Guns of the Mountains"; "A Gent from Bear Creek"; "The Feud Buster"; "The Road to Bear Creek"; "The Scalp Hunter"; "Cupid from Bear Creek"; "The Haunted Mountain"; "Educate or Bust" (new); "War on Bear Creek"; "When Bear Creek Came to Chawed Ear" (new); the first Grant edition is photo-offset from the Jenkins, so identical; Grant's second edition is retypeset, introduces a few errors and editorial changes, including removal of all italics; A GENT FROM BEAR CREEK AND OTHERS restores the text back to original published form

## A GENT FROM BEAR CREEK (Short Story)
Featuring BRECKINRIDGE ELKINS
First appeared in ACTION STORIES, October 1934
    THE SUMMIT COUNTY JOURNAL, December 20, 27, 1968; January 3, 10, 17, 24, 31; February 7, 14, 21, 28; march 7, 14, 21, 28, 1969 (15-part serial, similar to book version)
    THE NEW HOWARD READER #4 (Chpbk., original magazine version)
    THE COMPLETE ACTION STORIES
    Title of both an original short story as well as a novel; this short story became Chapter 5 of the novel; THE SUMMIT COUNTY JOURNAL appearance changed the name to "Breckenridge", to be like the town it was published in

## A GENT FROM THE PECOS
Alternate title: SHAVE THAT HAWG!
Featuring PIKE BEARFIELD
First appeared in ARGOSY, October 3, 1936
    MAX BRAND'S WESTERN MAGAZINE, January 1950 (as "Shave That Hawg!")
    MAX BRAND'S WESTERN MAGAZINE #2 (UK), date unknown (as "Shave That Hawg!")
    WRITER OF THE DARK
    THE RIOT AT BUCKSNORT AND OTHER WESTERN TALES

## GENTS IN BUCKSKIN
Alternate title: "NO COWHERDERS WANTED"

## GENTS ON THE LYNCH
Featuring PIKE BEARFIELD
First appeared in ARGOSY, October 17, 1936
    THE BOOK OF ROBERT E. HOWARD
    THE RIOT AT BUCKSNORT AND OTHER WESTERN TALES
    THE GRIM LAND: THE BEST OF ROBERT E. HOWARD, VOLUME 2

## GENTS ON THE RAMPAGE
Alternate title: HIGH HORSE RAMPAGE

## GHOR, KIN-SLAYER
Alternate titles: GENSERIC'S FIFTH BORN SON; Untitled ("Long, long ago a son was born . . ."); GENSERIC'S
     SON

## THE GHOST BEHIND THE GLOVES
First appeared in AQUILA NIDAS, April 2006 (Chpbk.)
     THE LAST OF THE TRUNK OCH BREV I URVAL (Chpbk.)
     THE LAST OF THE TRUNK
     Incomplete

## GHOST IN THE DOORWAY
First appeared in THE HOWARD COLLECTOR #11
     THE NEW HOWARD READER #2 (Chpbk.)
     Original typescript lists author as "Patrick McConaire", one of REH's pseudonyms

## THE GHOST OF BALD ROCK RANCH
Featuring BILL SMALLEY
First appeared in THE LAST OF THE TRUNK OCH BREV I URVAL (Chpbk.)
     THE LAST OF THE TRUNK
     Hand-written, and dated Decemer 13, 1921

## THE GHOST OF CAMP COLORADO
First appeared in TEXACO STAR, April 1931
     COLEMAN DEMOCRAT-VOICE, May 28, 1931
     FRONTIER TIMES, June 1931
     COLEMAN DEMOCRAT-VOICE, September 27, 1934
     COLEMAN DEMOCRAT-VOICE, November 12, 1936
     RUNES OF AHRH-EIH-ECHE (Chpbk.)
     THE SPELL OF CONAN (Anth.)
     THE NEW HOWARD READER #3 (Chpbk., facsimile reproduction of the original publication, including
          photos by REH)
     THE END OF THE TRAIL: WESTERN STORIES
     WEST IS WEST AND OTHERS
     The original publication in the TEXACO STAR included some photographs that REH apparently took, the
          photographs were never reprinted until THE NEW HOWARD READER publication

## GHOST WITH THE SILK HAT
Featuring STEVE BENDER, WEARY McGREW and THE WHALE
First appeared in WRITER OF THE DARK
     THE MAN FROM CROSS PLAINS (Anth.)

## THE GHOSTS OF JACKSONVILLE
First appeared in THE LAST OF THE TRUNK OCH BREV I URVAL (Chpbk.)
     THE LAST OF THE TRUNK
     Hand-written, and dated November 3, 1920

## THE GIRL ON THE HELL SHIP
Alternate title: SHE DEVIL

## A GLASS OF VODKA
First appeared in THE COLLECTED LETTERS OF ROBERT E. HOWARD, VOLUME 2: 1930-1932
    From a letter to TCS, ca. September 1932 ("Fear Finn: / You owe me a letter . . .")


## THE GOD IN THE BOWL
Featuring CONAN
First appeared in SPACE SCIENCE FICTION, September 1952 (significantly edited by LSDC)
    SPACE SCIENCE FICTION (UK), VOLUME 1, #1 (edited by LSDC)
    THE COMING OF CONAN (edited by LSDC)
    CONAN (edited by LSDC)
    THE TOWER OF THE ELEPHANT (original draft)
    THE CONAN CHRONICLES 1, Sphere and Orbit (edited by LSDC)
    THE CONAN CHRONICLES I: THE PEOPLE OF THE BLACK CIRCLE (edited by LSDC)
    ROBERT E. HOWARD'S COMPLETE CONAN OF CIMMERIA, VOLUME 1 (original draft)
    THE COMING OF CONAN THE CIMMERIAN (original draft)
    THE COMPLETE CHRONICLES OF CONAN
    LSDC had altered this story significantly, and rewrote each time it was published, up to the Lancer version;
        REH scholar Scotty Henderson says there are three different drafts by REH


## THE GODS OF BAL-SAGOTH
Alternate title: THE BLONDE GODDESS OF BAL-SAGOTH
Featuring TURLOGH DUBH O'BRIEN
First appeared in WEIRD TALES, October 1931
    AVON FANTASY READER #12 (as "The Blond Goddess of Bal-Sagoth")
    THE DARK MAN AND OTHERS
    THE SECOND AVON FANTASY READER (Anth.)
    PIGEONS FROM HELL, Zebra & Ace
    THE DARK MAN ONMIBUS, VOLUME 1
    THE GODS OF BAL-SAGOTH
    ROBERT E. HOWARD'S WORLD OF HEROES
    BARN MAK MORN, Baen
    NAMELESS CULTS
    THE BLACK STRANGER AND OTHER AMERICAN TALES
    PEOPLE OF THE DARK: THE WEIRD WORKS OF ROBERT E. HOWARD, VOLUME 3
    THE WEIRD WRITINGS OF ROBERT E. HOWARD, VOLUME ONE


## GODS OF THE NORTH
Alternate titles: THE FROST-GIANT'S DAUGHTER (slightly different); THE FROST-KING'S DAUGHTER;
    THE FROST GIANT'S DAUGHTER
Featuring CONAN
First appeared in FANTASY FAN, March 1934
    THE ILLUSTRATED GODS OF THE NORTH (Chpbk.)
    ECHOES OF VALOR II (Anth.)
    ROBERT E. HOWARD'S STRANGE TALES
    THE VALLEY OF THE WORM: THE WEIRD WORKS OF ROBERT E. HOWARD, VOLUME 5
    ROBERT E. HOWARD IN THE FANTASY FAN (Chpbk.)
    PEOPLE OF THE BLACK CIRCLE
    Originally written by REH as a Conan story titled "The Frost-Giant's Daughter", it was not accepted, so he
        rewrote it with a different hero (Amra), changed the title to "The Frost-King's Daughter", and gave it
        away to THE FANTASY FAN; when published by THE FANTASY FAN, they changed the title to
        "Gods of the North"; LSDC found the original manuscript, but extensively rewrote it, and called it
        "The Frost Giant's Daughter" (LSDC-edited version, note no hyphen); LSDC changed it each time it
        got republished, up through the Lancer version); starting with Grant Press' ROGUES IN THE

HOUSE, the text has been restored to original typescript form; listings for "The Frost-Giant's Daughter" are under its own heading; ECHOES OF VALOR II has both REH versions of the story

## THE GODS THAT MEN FORGOT
First appeared in ETCHINGS IN IVORY (Chpbk.)
    THE BOOK OF ROBERT E. HOWARD

## GOLD FROM TARTARY
Alternate title: THE TREASURES OF TARTARY

## "GOLDEN HOPE" CHRISTMAS
First appeared in THE TATTLER, December 22, 1922
    CROSS PLAINS #1
    REH: TWO-GUN RACONTEUR #4
    THE NEW HOWARD READER #4 (Chpbk.)
    "GOLDEN HOPE" CHRISTMAS (Chpbk.)
    THE END OF THE TRAIL: WESTERN STORIES
    WEST IS WEST AND OTHERS

## GOLNAR THE APE
First appeared in CRYPT OF CTHULHU #31 (Chpbk.)
    THE NEW HOWARD READER #2 (Chpbk.)
    Unfinished; Listed as "Golnar" in The Last Celt, appeared as "Golnor" in CoC and TNHR

## THE GONDARIAN MAN
First appeared in FANTASY CROSSROADS #6
    THE NEW HOWARD READER #4 (Chpbk.)

## THE GOOD KNIGHT
Alternate title: KID GALAHAD
Featuring KID ALLISON
First appeared in SPORT STORY MAGAZINE, December 25, 1931
    FANTASY CROSSROADS #3
    THE SECOND BOOK OF ROBERT E. HOWARD
    ROBERT E. HOWARD OMNIBUS
    BOXING STORIES (as "Kid Galahad")

## GRAVEYARD RATS
Featuring STEVE HARRISON
First appeared in THRILLING MYSTERY, February 1936
    PHANTASY DIGEST #1
    WRITER OF THE DARK
    GRAVEYARD RATS AND OTHERS

## THE GREAT MUNNEY RING
First appeared in THE RIGHT HOOK, VOLUME 1, #1 (Chpbk.)
    AUSTIN, VOLUME 3, #2 (Chpbk.)
    ROBERT E. HOWARD—THE POWER OF THE WRITING MIND
    This is an article

## THE GREY GOD PASSES
Alternate titles: THE TWILIGHT OF THE GREY GODS; THE SPEARS OF CLONTARF (a non-fantastic version)
Featuring TURLOGH DUBH O'BRIEN

First appeared in DARK MIND, DARK HEART (Anth.)
>    THE GREY GOD PASSES (Chpbk.)
>    BEYOND MIDNIGHT (Anth.)
>    MARCHERS OF VALHALLA, Grant
>    ROBERT E. HOWARD OMNIBUS
>    MARCHERS OF VALHALLA, Sphere and Berkley
>    EONS OF THE NIGHT
>    CRIMSON SHADOWS: THE BEST OF ROBERT E. HOWARD, VOLUME 1
>    This story has an extended history, per REH scholar Patrice Louinet; "Spears of Clontarf" was written in the second half of May 1931, submitted June 1st to Clayton Publications, and rejected; REH tried it with ADVENTURE (June 19) and ARGOSY (July 1), to no avail; he rewrote it sometime later in 1931 as "The Grey God Passes"; this was rejected by WEIRD TALES on December 28; REH recycled some elements of the story in "The Cairn on the Headland", which he submitted - and sold - to Clayton Publications in January 1932, and was subsequently published in STRANGE TALES, January 1933; typescript sold at auction, along with a rejection letter, for $7877, in Feburary 2006

## THE GRISLY HORROR
Alternate title: MOON OF ZAMBEBWEI
First appeared in WEIRD TALES, February 1935
>    MAGAZINE OF HORROR, April 1971
>    BLACK CANAAN (as "Moon of Zambebwei")
>    TRAILS IN DARKNESS (as "Moon of Zambebwei")
>    THE WEIRD WRITINGS OF ROBERT E. HOWARD, VOLUME TWO
>    BEYOND THE BLACK RIVER: THE WEIRD WORKS OF ROBERT E. HOWARD, VOLUME 7

## THE GROVE OF LOVERS
First appeared in THE LAST OF THE TRUNK OCH BREV I URVAL (Chpbk.)
>    THE LAST OF THE TRUNK
>    Unfinished

## THE GUARDIAN OF THE IDOL
Featuring JAMES ALLISON
First appeared in WEIRD TALES #3, Zebra (Anth., completed by Gerald W. Page)
>    THE NEW HOWARD READER #8 (Chpbk., first appearance of just fragment and synopsis)
>    An unfinished story, with an untitled synopsis ("The story begins with Gorm . . .")

## GUESTS OF THE HOODOO ROOM
First appeared in SHUDDER STORIES #1 (Chpbk.)
>    THE NEW HOWARD READER #4 (Chpbk.)

## GUNMAN'S DEBT
First appeared in THE LAST RIDE
>    THE END OF THE TRAIL: WESTERN STORIES

## GUNS OF KHARTUM
First appeared in REH: LONE STAR FICTIONEER #3
>    THE SECOND BOOK OF ROBERT E. HOWARD
>    THE SHE DEVIL

## GUNS OF THE MOUNTAINS
Featuring BRECKINRIDGE ELKINS
First appeared in ACTION STORIES, May-June 1934

THE SUMMIT COUNTY JOURNAL, October 4, 11, 18, 25; November 1, 8, 15, 22, 29; December 6, 13, 1968
(11-part serial, similar to book version)
THE NEW HOWARD READER #3 (Chpbk., original magazine version)
THE COMPLETE ACTION STORIES
THE RIOT AT BUCKSNORT AND OTHER WESTERN TALES
This short story was altered slightly to become Chapter 4 of the "A Gent from Bear Creek" novel; THE
SUMMIT COUNTY JOURNAL appearance changed the name to "Breckenridge", to be like the town
it was published in

## THE HALL OF THE DEAD
Featuring CONAN
First appeared in MAGAZINE OF FANTASY AND SCIENCE FICTION, February 1967 (completed by LSDC)
CONAN (LSDC version)
FANTASY CROSSROADS #1 (first appearance of synopsis)
THE LAST CELT (synopsis)
THE CONAN CHRONICLES 1, Sphere and Orbit (completed by LSDC)
THE CONAN CHRONICLES I: THE PEOPLE OF THE BLACK CIRCLE (synopsis)
IN LANDS THAT NEVER WERE (Anth.)
THE COMPLETE CHRONICLES OF CONAN (synopsis)
Just a synopsis

## HALT! WHO GOES THERE?
First appeared in THE YELLOW JACKET, September 24, 1924
AQUILA NIDUS #29 (Chpbk.)
THE NEW HOWARD READER #5 (Chpbk.)
THE COMPLETE YELLOW JACKET
WEST IS WEST AND OTHERS

## THE HAND IN THE DARK
Listed on a Kline Agency list of REH stories, listed as 11 pages long, don't know what happened to it

## THE HAND OF NERGAL
Alternate title: Untitled ("The battlefield stretched silent . . .")
Featuring CONAN
First appeared in CONAN (completed by Lin Carter)
BEYOND THE GATES OF DREAM (Anth., Lin Carter version)
THE LAST CELT (first appearance of untitled and unfinished draft)
THE CONAN CHRONICLES 1, Sphere and Orbit (Lin Carter version)
THE CONAN CHRONICLES I: THE PEOPLE OF THE BLACK CIRCLE (draft)
ROBERT E. HOWARD'S COMPLETE CONAN OF CIMMERIA, VOLUME 1 (draft)
THE COMING OF CONAN THE CIMMERIAN (draft)
THE COMING OF CONAN THE CIMMERIAN, SFBC, December 2003 (draft)
THE COMPLETE CHRONICLES OF CONAN (draft)
Originally an unfinished draft

## THE HAND OF OBEAH
First appeared in CRYPT OF CTHULHU #16 (Chpbk.)
THE NEW HOWARD READER #3 (Chpbk.)

## HAND OF THE BLACK GODDESS
Alternate title: SCARLET TEARS
Featuring GORMAN & KIRBY
First appeared in BRAN MAK MORN: A PLAY & OTHERS (Chpbk.)
 WEIRD TALES #1, Zebra (Anth., as "Scarlet Tears", extensively rewritten by Lin Carter)

## HARD-FISTED SENTIMENT
Featuring STEVE COSTIGAN
First appeared in DENNIS DORGAN (French)
 REH'S FIGHT MAGAZINE #4 (Chpbk.)
 BOXING STORIES

## THE HASHISH LAND
First appeared in FANTOME #1 (Chpbk.)
 THE NEW HOWARD READER #3 (Chpbk.)

## THE HAUNTED HUT
First appeared in WEIRDBOOK #2
 ABSINTHE PISSED (Chpbk.)
 THE NEW HOWARD READER #4 (Chpbk.)
 REH: TWO-GUN RACONTEUR #7

## THE HAUNTED MOUNTAIN
Featuring BRECKINRIDGE ELKINS
First appeared in ACTION STORIES, February 1935
 THE SUMMIT COUNTY JOURNAL, July 3, 10, 17, 24, 31; August 7, 14, 21, 28; September 4, 11, 18, 1970
 (12-part serial, similar to book version)
 THE COMPLETE ACTION STORIES
 THE RIOT AT BUCKSNORT AND OTHER WESTERN TALES
Was altered slightly to become Chapter 10 of the "A Gent from Bear Creek" novel; THE SUMMIT COUNTY
 JOURNAL appearance changed the name to "Breckenridge", to be like the town it was published in

## THE HAUNTER OF THE RING
First appeared in WEIRD TALES, June 1934
 STARTLING MYSTERY STORIES, VOLUME 2, #5, Winter 1968/69
 BLACK CANAAN
 THE CIMMERIAN SCROLL (Chpbk.)
 BEYOND THE BORDERS
 THE WEIRD WRITINGS OF ROBERT E. HOWARD, VOLUME ONE
 THE GARDEN OF FEAR: THE WEIRD WORKS OF ROBERT E. HOWARD, VOLUME 6

## THE HAWK OF BASTI
Featuring SOLOMON KANE
First appeared in RED SHADOWS (unfinished fragment)
 THE HAND OF KANE (unfinished fragment)
 SOLOMON KANE: THE HILLS OF THE DEAD (completed by Ramsey Campbell)
 SOLOMON KANE, Baen (completed by Ramsey Campbell)
 THE SAVAGE TALES OF SOLOMON KANE
 THE LEGEND OF SOLOMON KANE (completed by Ramsey Campbell)

## HAWK OF THE HILLS
Featuring EL BORAK
First appeared in TOP-NOTCH, June 1935

THE LOST VALLEY OF ISKANDER
BLOOD OF THE GODS AND OTHER STORIES
CRIMSON SHADOWS: THE BEST OF ROBERT E. HOWARD, VOLUME 1
THE "EL BORAK" STORIES - BLOOD OF THE GODS; THE DAUGHTER OF ERLIK KHAN; HAWK OF
    THE HILLS; SON OF THE WHITE WOLF; THE COUNTRY OF THE KNIFE

## HAWKS OF OUTREMER
Featuring CORMAC FITZGEOFFREY
First appeared in ORIENTAL STORIES, Spring (April-May-June) 1931
    ROBERT E. HOWARD OMNIBUS
    HAWKS OF OUTREMER
    ROBERT E. HOWARD'S WORLD OF HEROES
    GATES OF EMPIRE AND OTHERS
    LORD OF SAMARCAND AND OTHER ADVENTURES OF THE OLD ORIENT
    ORIENTAL STORIES, SPRING 1931 (Chpbk.)
    THE COMPLETE ORIENTAL STORIES (Anth.)

## HAWKS OVER EGYPT
Alternate titles: HAWKS OVER SHEM; THE MAN WHO WOULD BE GOD
    First appeared in THE ROAD OF AZRAEL
    LORD OF SAMARCAND AND OTHER ADVENTURES OF THE OLD ORIENT
    LSDC created a derivative work from this then-unpublished historical adventure story, titled "Hawks over
        Shem", a Conan story

## HAWKS OVER SHEM
Alternate title: HAWKS OVER EGYPT
Featuring CONAN
First appeared in FANTASTIC UNIVERSE, October 1955
    TALES OF CONAN
    CONAN THE FREEBOOTER
    THE CONAN CHRONICLES 1, Sphere and Orbit
    An LSDC derivative work, being a rewrite of a previously unpublished REH historical adventure story called
        "Hawks over Egypt", turning it into a Conan story

## A HEAD IN THE HOLLOW STUMP
Listed on a Kline Agency list of REH stories, listed as 4 pages long, don't know what happened to it

## THE HEATHEN
First appeared in THE HOWARD COLLECTOR #13
    THE HOWARD COLLECTOR, Ace
    THE NEW HOWARD READER #2 (Chpbk.)

## HIGH HORSE RAMPAGE
Alternate title: GENTS ON THE RAMPAGE
Featuring BRECKINRIDGE ELKINS
First appeared in ACTION STORIES, August 1936
    THE PRIDE OF BEAR CREEK
    THE SUMMIT COUNTY JOURNAL, June 16, 23, 30; July 7, 14, 21, 28; August 4, 11, 18, 25; September 1,
        8, 15, 22, 29; October 6, 13, 1972 (18-part serial)
    HEROES OF BEAR CREEK
    THE COMPLETE ACTION STORIES
    Grant removed all the italics, which was carried over in later editions; THE SUMMIT COUNTY JOURNAL
        appearance changed the name to "Breckenridge", to be like the town it was published in; THE
        COMPLETE ACTION STORIES restored the text back to original publication form

**THE HILLS OF THE DEAD**
Featuring SOLOMON KANE
First appeared in WEIRD TALES, August 1930
    SKULL-FACE AND OTHERS
    RED SHADOWS
    THE HAND OF KANE
    WARLOCKS AND WARRIORS (Anth.)
    SKULL-FACE OMNIBUS
    SKULL-FACE OMNIBUS, VOLUME 2
    SOLOMON KANE: THE HILLS OF THE DEAD
    A TASTE FOR BLOOD (Anth.)
    SOLOMON KANE, Baen
    THE SAVAGE TALES OF SOLOMON KANE
    SAVAGE ADVENTURES
    MOON OF SKULLS: THE WEIRD WORKS OF ROBERT E. HOWARD, VOLUME 2
    THE WEIRD WRITINGS OF ROBERT E. HOWARD, VOLUME ONE
    THE RIGHT HAND OF DOOM AND OTHER TALES OF SOLOMON KANE
    THE LEGEND OF SOLOMON KANE
    THE 'SOLOMAN CRANE' STORIES

**HIS BROTHER'S SHOES**
A story title that is listed in Kline's records as being an REH story he had, 6650 words, but either lost or published under a different title; Glenn thought this might have become "The Dwellers Under the Tombs", but those stories were written at the wrong time

**THE HONOR OF THE SHIP**
Featuring STEVE COSTIGAN
    REH'S FIGHT MAGAZINE #4 (Chpbk.)

**THE HOOFED THING**
Alternate title: USURP THE NIGHT

**THE HORROR FROM THE MOUND**
First appeared in WEIRD TALES, May 1932
    SKULL-FACE AND OTHERS
    WOLFSHEAD, Lancer
    THE DARK OF THE SOUL (Anth.)
    SKULL-FACE OMNIBUS
    SKULL-FACE OMNIBUS, VOLUME 1
    WOLFSHEAD, Bantam
    VAMPIRE (Anth.)
    WEIRD VAMPIRE TALES (Anth.)
    TRAILS IN DARKNESS
    THE BLACK STRANGER AND OTHER AMERICAN TALES
    PEOPLE OF THE DARK: THE WEIRD WORKS OF ROBERT E. HOWARD, VOLUME 3
    THE WEIRD WRITINGS OF ROBERT E. HOWARD, VOLUME ONE
    THE MAMMOTH BOOK OF MONSTERS (Anth.)

## A HORROR IN THE NIGHT
First appeared in CROSS PLAINS #3
    PAY DAY (Chpbk.)
    REH: TWO-GUN RACONTEUR #5

## THE HOUR OF THE DRAGON
Alternate title: CONAN THE CONQUEROR
Featuring CONAN
First appeared as a 5-part serial in WEIRD TALES: December 1935; January 1936; February 1936; March 1936; and
    April 1936
    CONAN THE CONQUEROR
    THE HOUR OF THE DRAGON, Berkley & Putnam
    THE HOUR OF THE DRAGON, Grant
    THE ESSENTIAL CONAN, SFBC Fantasy
    THE CONAN CHRONICLES, VOLUME 2, Millenium
    PULP FICTION CLASSICS #1: THE HOUR OF THE DRAGON
    ROBERT E. HOWARD'S COMPLETE CONAN OF CIMMERIA, VOLUME 2 (plus synopsis, first
        appearance)
    THE BLOODY CROWN OF CONAN (plus synopsis)
    THE COMPLETE CHRONICLES OF CONAN
    THE WEIRD WRITINGS OF ROBERT E. HOWARD, VOLUME TWO
    HOURS OF THE DRAGON
    Parts 1 and 5 were voted best story in their respective original WEIRD TALES appearance, Part 5 having the
        highest total votes for its year; all original drafts as well as the original publication don't have a
        chapter 20, likely just a numbering error by REH

## THE HOUSE
Alternate title: THE HOUSE IN THE OAKS

## THE HOUSE IN THE OAKS
By Robert E. Howard & August Derleth
Alternate title: THE HOUSE
First appeared in DARK THINGS (Anth., completed by August Derleth)
    BLACK CANAAN (Completed by August Derleth)
    IN LOVECRAFT'S SHADOW (Anth., completed by August Derleth)
    NAMELESS CULTS(Completed by August Derleth)
    THE NEW HOWARD READER #8 (Chpbk., as "The House", fragment only)
    Originally a fragment, Derleth's portion begins with the second sentence of the paragraph that begins "We had
        passed through the circling . . ."; Derleth added a verse heading, which was from an early draft of "The
        Children of the Night", as well as the poems "Arkham" and "An Open Window"

## THE HOUSE OF ARABU
Alternate title: WITCH FROM HELL'S KITCHEN

## HOUSE OF FEAR
Alternate title: THE HOUSE OF SUSPICION

## THE HOUSE OF OM
First appeared in SHUDDER STORIES #2 (Chpbk., synopsis only)
    THE NEW HOWARD READER #1 (Chpbk., synopsis only)

## THE HOUSE OF PERIL
Alternate title: BLOW THE CHINKS DOWN!

**THE HOUSE OF SUSPICION**
Alternate title: HOUSE OF FEAR
Featuring STEVE HARRISON
First appeared in  THE SECOND BOOK OF ROBERT E. HOWARD

**THE HYBORIAN AGE**
Featuring CONAN
First appeared as a 3-part serial in THE PHANTAGRAPH: February 1936; August 1936; and October-November
    1936 (incomplete, only goes up till the time of Conan)
    THE HYBORIAN AGE, LANY Coop. (Chpbk., first complete publication)
    SKULL-FACE AND OTHERS
    THE COMING OF CONAN (just the first half)
    KING KULL (portions)
    CONAN (first half)
    CONAN THE AVENGER (just the second half)
    SKULL-FACE OMNIBUS
    RED NAILS, Grant
    SKULL-FACE OMNIBUS, VOLUME 3
    RED NAILS, Berkley & Putnam
    KULL: THE FABULOUS WARRIOR KING
    KULL
    THE CONAN CHRONICLES 1, Sphere and Orbit
    THE ESSENTIAL CONAN, SFBC Fantasy
    THE CONAN CHRONICLES I: THE PEOPLE OF THE BLACK CIRCLE
    ROBERT E. HOWARD'S COMPLETE CONAN OF CIMMERIA, VOLUME 1
    THE COMING OF CONAN THE CIMMERIAN
    THE COMPLETE CHRONICLES OF CONAN
    HOURS OF THE DRAGON

**THE HYENA**
First appeared in WEIRD TALES, March 1928
    THE DARK MAN AND OTHERS
    PIGEONS FROM HELL, Zebra & Ace
    THE DARK MAN OMNIBUS, VOLUME 2
    BEYOND THE BORDERS
    SHADOW KINGDOMS: THE WEIRD WORKS OF ROBERT E. HOWARD, VOLUME 1 (Wildside Press,
        Cosmos & AudioRealms)
    THE WEIRD WRITINGS OF ROBERT E. HOWARD, VOLUME ONE

**THE IDEAL GIRL**
First appeared in THE TATTLER, January 6, 1925
    THE NEW HOWARD READER #6 (Chpbk.)
    WEST IS WEST AND OTHERS

**IN HIGH SOCIETY**
Alternate title: CULTURED CAULIFLOWERS
Featuring DENNIS DORGAN
First appeared in THE INCREDIBLE ADVENTURES OF DENNIS DORGAN
    THE IRON MAN, WITH THE ADVENTURES OF DENNIS DORGAN
    BOXING STORIES (as "Cultured Cauliflowers", rewritten back to original Costigan version)
    Original typescript lists author as "Patrick Ervin", a pseudonym REH used in connection with his Dennis
        Dorgan stories

**IN HIS OWN IMAGE**

First appeared in THE LAST OF THE TRUNK OCH BREV I URVAL (Chpbk.)
    THE LAST OF THE TRUNK

## IN THE FOREST OF VILLEFERE
First appeared in WEIRD TALES, August 1925
    THE DARK MAN AND OTHERS
    PIGEONS FROM HELL, Zebra & Ace
    THE DARK MAN ONMIBUS, VOLUME 1
    EONS OF THE NIGHT
    SHADOW KINGDOMS: THE WEIRD WORKS OF ROBERT E. HOWARD, VOLUME 1 (Wildside Press)
    THE WEIRD WRITINGS OF ROBERT E. HOWARD, VOLUME ONE

## "... INCLUDING THE SCANDINAVIAN!"
Alternate title: VIKINGS OF THE GLOVES

## INCONGRUITY
First appeared in THE LAST OF THE TRUNK OCH BREV I URVAL (Chpbk.)
    THE LAST OF THE TRUNK
    Unfinished

## THE INFLUENCE OF THE MOVIES
First appeared in THE LAST OF THE TRUNK OCH BREV I URVAL (Chpbk.)
    THE LAST OF THE TRUNK

## INTRIGUE IN KURDISTAN
Featuring EL BORAK
First appeared in EL BORAK L'ETERNEL (French)
    PULSE-POUNDING ADVENTURE STORIES #1 (Chpbk.)
    THE NEW HOWARD READER #5 (Chpbk.)

## THE IRON MAN
Alternate titles: IRON MEN; FALL GUY
First appeared in FIGHT STORIES, June 1930
    FIGHT STORIES, Fall 1938 (as "Fall Guy", author listed as"John Starr", slightly edited from the first
        appearance)
    THE IRON MAN
    THE IRON MAN, WITH THE ADVENTURES OF DENNIS DORGAN
    WATERFRONT FISTS AND OTHERS
    BOXING STORIES (as "Iron Men")
    The Bison version is the original as written by REH, over 10K words longer

## IRON MEN
Alternate title: THE IRON MAN

## IRON SHADOWS IN THE MOON
Alternate title: SHADOWS IN THE MOONLIGHT

## THE IRON TERROR
Featuring EL BORAK
First appeared in EL BORAK L'ETERNEL (French)
    THE COMING OF EL BORAK (Chpbk.)

**IRON-CLAD FISTS**
Alternate title: A KNIGHT OF THE ROUND TABLE

**IRON-JAW**
Alternate title: FISTS OF THE DESERT
First appeared in DIME SPORTS MAGAZINE, April 1936
    THE IRON MAN (as "Fists of the Desert")
    THE IRON MAN, WITH THE ADVENTURES OF DENNIS DORGAN (as "Fists of the Desert")
    BOXING STORIES (as "Fists of the Desert")

**IRONY**
First appeared in THE COLLECTED LETTERS OF ROBERT E. HOWARD, VOLUME 1: 1923-1929
    From a letter to TCS, ca. July 1929 ("Salaam: / The main reason I'm writing . . .")

**THE ISLE OF PIRATES' DOOM**
First appeared in THE ISLE OF PIRATES' DOOM (Chpbk.)
    BLACK VULMEA'S VENGEANCE

**THE ISLE OF THE EONS**
First appeared in  THE GODS OF BAL-SAGOTH
    THE DARK MAN, VOLUME 3, #1
    First begun in 1925, was unfinished, started again in 1929 or later, again unfinished; the version in the First
        Appearance is the later draft, as far as it goes, followed by more from the first draft; all five known
        drafts are included in the THE DARK MAN

**THE IVORY CAMEL**
First appeared in THE LAST OF THE TRUNK OCH BREV I URVAL (Chpbk.)
    THE LAST OF THE TRUNK
    Unfinished

**THE JADE GOD**
First appeared in UNAUSSPRECHLICHEN KULTEN #2 (Chpbk.)
    THE NEW HOWARD READER #3 (Chpbk.)
    Unfinished

**THE JADE MONKEY**
Alternate titles: SAILOR COSTIGAN AND THE JADE MONKEY; SAILOR DORGAN AND THE JADE
    MONKEY

**JAZZ MUSIC**
First appeared in THE GOLDEN CALIPH (Chpbk.)
    THE LAST CELT

**THE JEWELS OF GWAHLUR**
Alternate titles: TEETH OF GWAHLUR; THE SERVANTS OF BIT-YAKIN
Featuring CONAN
First appeared in WEIRD TALES, March 1935
    KING CONAN
    CONAN THE WARRIOR
    THE PEOPLE OF THE BLACK CIRCLE, Berkley & Putnam (SFBC)
    THE JEWELS OF GWAHLUR
    ROBERT E. HOWARD'S WORLD OF HEROES
    THE ESSENTIAL CONAN, SFBC Fantasy

THE CONAN CHRONICLES, VOLUME 2, Millenium
SAVAGE ADVENTURES
THE CONQUERING SWORD OF CONAN (as "The Servants of Bit-Yakin")
THE COMPLETE CHRONICLES OF CONAN
THE WEIRD WRITINGS OF ROBERT E. HOWARD, VOLUME TWO
PEOPLE OF THE BLACK CIRCLE
BEYOND THE BLACK RIVER: THE WEIRD WORKS OF ROBERT E. HOWARD, VOLUME 7
Possibly based on the city-fortress of Gwalior, capital of the Mahratta state of that name, is situated at the base of a precipitous, isolated rock, about 80 miles S. from the city of Agra, and 772 N.W. of Calcutta, in 26° 18' N. lat., and 78° 30' E. long; the celebrated hill-fortress, from which its chief importance is derived, is built upon the rock mentioned, which is one mile and a-half in length, by about 300 yards wide; the elevation from the plain, at the northern extremity of the plateau, being 343 feet; the sides of the rock are precipitous and rugged, and are impossible of ascent but by ladders, or by a single approach on the north-eastern side, where it gradually dips toward the plain; around the brink of the precipice a stone parapet is erected, within which rises the fort of the Maharajah Sindia, a native prince of India

## THE JINX
Featuring KID ALLISON
First appeared in THE LAST OF THE TRUNK OCH BREV I URVAL (Chpbk.)
    THE LAST OF THE TRUNK

## JOHN GRIMLAN'S DEBT
Alternate title: DIG ME NO GRAVE

## JOHN MORRISSEY, ADVENTURER OF EARLY NEW YORK
Listed on a Kline Agency list of REH stories, listed as 5 pages long, don't know what happened to it

## THE JUDGEMENT OF THE DESERT
Alternate title: SHOWDOWN AT HELL'S CANYON

## KELLY THE CONJURE-MAN
First appeared in THE HOWARD COLLECTOR #5
    THE SECOND BOOK OF ROBERT E. HOWARD
    THE HOWARD COLLECTOR, Ace
    TRAILS IN DARKNESS
    THE BLACK STRANGER AND OTHER AMERICAN TALES
    According to a Kline Agency list, this story came with photos, don't know what happened to those

## KHODA KHAN'S TALE
Featuring EL BORAK
First appeared in EL BORAK L'ETERNEL (French)
    THE COMING OF EL BORAK (Chpbk.)

## KID GALAHAD
Alternate title: THE GOOD KNIGHT

## THE KILLER'S DEBT
Listed on a Kline Agency list of REH stories, listed as 21 pages long, don't know what happened to it

## THE KILLING OF YELLOW DONARY
Alternate title: THE EXTERMINATION OF YELLOW DONARY

## KING BAHTHUR'S COURT
First appeared in THE LAST OF THE TRUNK OCH BREV I URVAL (Chpbk.)
    THE COLLECTED LETTERS OF ROBERT E. HOWARD, VOLUME 3: 1933-1936
    From a letter to TCS, undated ("King Bahthur's Court . . .")

## KING HOOTUS
First appeared in THE COLLECTED LETTERS OF ROBERT E. HOWARD, VOLUME 1: 1923-1929
    From a letter to TCS, ca. January 1928 ("I wasnt [sic] lying . . .")

## KING OF THE FORGOTTEN PEOPLE
Alternate title: THE VALLEY OF THE LOST (1)

## KINGS OF THE NIGHT
Featuring BRAN MAK MORN and KULL
First appeared in WEIRD TALES, November 1930
    SKULL-FACE AND OTHERS
    MAGAZINE OF HORROR #21
    BRAN MAK MORN, Dell
    WORMS OF THE EARTH
    SKULL-FACE OMNIBUS
    SKULL-FACE OMNIBUS, VOLUME 2
    ROBERT E. HOWARD'S WORLD OF HEROES
    THE ETERNAL CITY (Anth.)
    BARN MAK MORN, Baen
    BRAN MAK MORN – THE LAST KING
    PEOPLE OF THE DARK: THE WEIRD WORKS OF ROBERT E. HOWARD, VOLUME 3
    THE WEIRD WRITINGS OF ROBERT E. HOWARD, VOLUME ONE
    KULL: EXILE OF ATLANTIS
    CRIMSON SHADOWS: THE BEST OF ROBERT E. HOWARD, VOLUME 1
    Was voted the best story in its original WEIRD TALES appearance, had the highest total vote for that year, and
        had the 40th highest total ever

## THE KING'S SERVICE
First appeared in THE KING'S SERVICE (Chpbk.)
    SWORD WOMAN

## KNIFE, BULLET AND NOOSE
Alternate title: KNIFE, GUN AND NOOSE
Featuring THE SONORA KID
First appeared in THE HOWARD COLLECTOR #6
    THE BOOK OF ROBERT E. HOWARD
    THE LAST RIDE
    THE HOWARD COLLECTOR, Ace
    THE END OF THE TRAIL: WESTERN STORIES

## KNIFE, GUN AND NOOSE
Alternate title: KNIFE, BULLET AND NOOSE

## KNIFE-RIVER PRODIGAL
Alternate title: A TEXAS PRODIGAL
Featuring BUCKNER J. GRIMES
First appeared in COWBOY STORIES, July 1937
    REH: LONE STAR FICTIONEER #1

THE SECOND BOOK OF ROBERT E. HOWARD
ROBERT E. HOWARD OMNIBUS
THE RIOT AT BUCKSNORT AND OTHER WESTERN TALES

## A KNIGHT OF THE ROUND TABLE
Alternate titles: IRON-CLAD FISTS; possibly SAILOR DORGAN AND THE WIZARD
Featuring DENNIS DORGAN
First appeared in THE INCREDIBLE ADVENTURES OF DENNIS DORGAN
    THE IRON MAN, WITH THE ADVENTURES OF DENNIS DORGAN
    THE ROBERT E. HOWARD FOUNDATION NEWSLETTER, VOLUME 1, #2 (synopsis only)
    A short synopsis also exists for this story

## A KOREAN NIGHT
Alternate titles: SAILOR DORGAN AND THE YELLOW COBRA; THE YELLOW COBRA; A NIGHT
      ASHORE; THE FANGS OF THE YELLOW COBRA

## LAL SINGH, ORIENTAL GENTLEMAN
Featuring LAL SINGH
First appeared in THE ADVENTURES OF LAL SINGH (Chpbk.)

## THE LAME MAN
Alternate title: LORD OF SAMARCAND

## THE LAND OF FORGOTTEN AGES
Alternate title: THE TRAIL OF THE MAMMOTH; THE TRAIL OF THE DINOSAUR
First appeared in THE LAST OF THE TRUNK OCH BREV I URVAL (Chpbk.)
    THE LAST OF THE TRUNK
    Unfinished

## THE LAND OF MYSTERY
Featuring EL BORAK & THE SONORA KID
First appeared in EL BORAK L'ETERNEL (French)
    NORTH OF KHYBER (Chpbk.)

## THE LAST LAUGH
Alternate title: Untitled ("The rising sun was behind the wild figure.")
First appeared in FANTASY CROSSROADS #9
    THE NEW HOWARD READER #1 (Chpbk.)
    An untitled incomplete work

## THE LAST MAN
Alternate title: Untitled ("The flaming sun of the year 2000 . . .")
First appeared in THE LAST OF THE TRUNK OCH BREV I URVAL (Chpbk.)
    THE LAST OF THE TRUNK
    Unfinished; listed erroneously as "The Last White Man" in TLC; likely a first cut, telling a different part of the
        story from "The Last White Man"; likely written in 1925, and mentioned in a letter to TCS, August 4,
        1923 ("Clyde Sahib; / You say I'll be in Kabul.")

## THE LAST RIDE
Alternate title: BOOT-HILL PAYOFF

**THE LAST WHITE MAN**
First appeared in THE HOWARD COLLECTOR #5
    THE NEW HOWARD READER #7 (Chpbk.)

**LAW GUNS OF COWTOWN**
Alternate title: LAW-SHOOTERS OF COWTOWN

**LAW-SHOOTERS OF COWTOWN**
Alternate title: LAW GUNS OF COWTOWN
Featuring GRIZZLY ELKINS
First appeared in CROSS PLAINS #4
    THE LAST RIDE
    THE END OF THE TRAIL: WESTERN STORIES

**LE GENTIL HOMME LE DIABLE**
First appeared in THE TOREADOR, June 1925 (Chpbk.)
    THE RIGHT HOOK, VOLUME 1, #2, 1925 (Not sure which of these two it appeared in first)
    AUSTIN, VOLUME 3, #2 (Chpbk., facsimile of THE RIGHT HOOK)
    AUSTIN, VOLUME 3, #3 (Chpbk., facsimile of THE TOREADOR)
    THE NEW HOWARD READER #6 (Chpbk.)

**LEATHER LIGHTNING**
Alternate title: ALLEYS OF PERIL

**LEGEND**
First appeared in THE LAST OF THE TRUNK OCH BREV I URVAL (Chpbk.)
    THE COLLECTED LETTERS OF ROBERT E. HOWARD, VOLUME 1: 1923-1929
    From a letter to TCS, late August or early September 1927 ("ARE YOU THE YOUNG MAN . . .")

**THE LION GATE**
Alternate title: Untitled ("'No place for a girl,' I growled . . .")
First appeared in THE LAST OF THE TRUNK OCH BREV I URVAL (Chpbk.)
    THE LAST OF THE TRUNK
    Unfinished

**THE LION OF TIBERIAS**
First appeared in THE MAGIC CARPET MAGAZINE, July 1933
    THE SOWERS OF THE THUNDER
    GATES OF EMPIRE AND OTHERS
    LORD OF SAMARCAND AND OTHER ADVENTURES OF THE OLD ORIENT
    MAGIC CARPET MAGAZINE, JULY 1933 (Chpbk.)

**THE LITTLE PEOPLE**
First appeared in COVEN 13, January 1970
    THE FIRST BOOK OF UNKNOWN TALES OF HORROR (Anth.)
    BARBARIAN SCROLL #12 (Chpbk.)
    BRAN MAK MORN – THE LAST KING
    NAMELESS CULTS
    A page was apparently missing from the original manuscript; the editor of COVEN 13, Gerald W. Page, just made up some stuff to fill the gap, never said anything, that became the published version ever since; the Wandering Star book took Page's edits back out, and also includes a copy of the original typescript

## LIVES AND CRIMES OF NOTABLE ARTISTS
First appeared in THE HOWARD REVIEW #11 (Chpbk.)
>THE LAST OF THE TRUNK OCH BREV I URVAL (Chpbk.)
>THE COLLECTED LETTERS OF ROBERT E. HOWARD, VOLUME 2: 1930-1932
>Originally from a letter to TCS, ca. July 1930 ("Salaam, Fear Finn: / Well, me bauld buccaneer . . .")

## LOBO VOLANTE
Unfinished, unpublished

## LORD OF SAMARCAND
Alternate title: THE LAME MAN
First appeared in ORIENTAL STORIES, Spring 1932
>THE SOWERS OF THE THUNDER
>THE ULTIMATE TRIUMPH: THE HEROIC FANTASY OF ROBERT E. HOWARD
>GATES OF EMPIRE AND OTHERS
>LORD OF SAMARCAND AND OTHER ADVENTURES OF THE OLD ORIENT
>ORIENTAL STORIES, SPRING 1932 (Chpbk.)
>THE GRIM LAND: THE BEST OF ROBERT E. HOWARD, VOLUME 2
>THE COMPLETE ORIENTAL STORIES (Anth.)

## LORD OF THE DEAD
Alternate title: DEAD MAN'S DOOM
Featuring STEVE HARRISON
First appeared in SKULL-FACE, Berkley
>THE YEAR'S BEST FANTASY STORIES: 5 (Anth.)
>LORD OF THE DEAD
>CRIMSON SHADOWS: THE BEST OF ROBERT E. HOWARD, VOLUME 1
>"Dead Man's Doom" was the title under which it was announced in the final, February 1934 issue of STRANGE DETECTIVE STORIES

## THE LOSER
First appeared in REH: LONE STAR FICTIONEER #1
>PAY DAY (Chpbk.)

## THE LOST RACE
Featuring BRAN MAK MORN
First appeared in WEIRD TALES, January 1927
>BRAN MAK MORN, Dell
>WORMS OF THE EARTH
>BARN MAK MORN, Baen
>BRAN MAK MORN – THE LAST KING
>SHADOW KINGDOMS: THE WEIRD WORKS OF ROBERT E. HOWARD, VOLUME 1 (Wildside Press, Cosmos & AudioRealms)
>THE WEIRD WRITINGS OF ROBERT E. HOWARD, VOLUME ONE

## THE LOST VALLEY OF ISKANDER
Alternate title: SWORDS OF THE HILLS
Featuring EL BORAK
First appeared in  THE LOST VALLEY OF ISKANDER

## MAN
First appeared in THE LAST OF THE TRUNK OCH BREV I URVAL (Chpbk.)
>THE LAST OF THE TRUNK

**A MAN AND A BROTHER**
First appeared in THE LAST OF THE TRUNK OCH BREV I URVAL (Chpbk.)
    THE LAST OF THE TRUNK

**A MAN OF PEACE**
First appeared in THE LAST OF THE TRUNK OCH BREV I URVAL (Chpbk.)
    THE LAST OF THE TRUNK

**THE MAN ON THE GROUND**
First appeared in WEIRD TALES, July 1933
    THE DARK MAN AND OTHERS
    WEIRD TALES, Fall 1973
    PIGEONS FROM HELL, Zebra & Ace
    THE 14TH FONTANA BOOK OF GREAT GHOST STORIES (Anth.)
    THE DARK MAN ONMIBUS, VOLUME 1
    GETTING EVEN (Anth.)
    THE RAVEN #1, Kovacs (Chpbk.)
    TRAILS IN DARKNESS
    THE END OF THE TRAIL: WESTERN STORIES
    THE WEIRD WRITINGS OF ROBERT E. HOWARD, VOLUME ONE
    THE VALLEY OF THE WORM: THE WEIRD WORKS OF ROBERT E. HOWARD, VOLUME 5
    THE GRIM LAND: THE BEST OF ROBERT E. HOWARD, VOLUME 2

**MAN WITH THE MYSTERY MITTS**
Featuring KID ALLISON
First appeared in SPORT STORY MAGAZINE, October 25, 1931
    FANTASY CROSSROADS #4/5
    IRON LEGIONS, VOLUME 3, #3 (Chpbk.)

**THE MAN WHO WENT BACK**
First appeared in THE LAST OF THE TRUNK OCH BREV I URVAL (Chpbk.)
    THE LAST OF THE TRUNK
    Unfinished

**THE MAN WHO WOULD BE GOD**
Alternate title: HAWKS OVER EGYPT

**THE MAN-EATERS OF ZAMBOULA**
Alternate title: SHADOWS IN ZAMBOULA

**A MAN-EATING JEOPARD**
Featuring BUCKNER J. GRIMES
First appeared in COWBOY STORIES, June 1936
    THE CROSS PLAINS REVIEW, June 19, 1936
    SKULL-FACE AND OTHERS
    SKULL-FACE OMNIBUS
    SKULL-FACE OMNIBUS, VOLUME 2
    REHUPA #124 (Chpbk.)
    A MAN-EATING JEOPARD (Chpbk.)
    THE RIOT AT BUCKSNORT AND OTHER WESTERN TALES

**THE MANDARIN RUBY**
Alternate title: ALLEYS OF TRECHERY

**MANILA MANSLAUGHTER**
Alternate title: THE PIT OF THE SERPENT

**MARCHERS OF VALHALLA**
Featuring JAMES ALLISON
First appeared in MARCHERS OF VALHALLA, Grant
    MARCHERS OF VALHALLA, Sphere and Berkley
    EONS OF THE NIGHT
    THE BLACK STRANGER AND OTHER AMERICAN TALES

**THE MARK OF A BLOODY HAND**
Alternate title: Untitled ("Ring fans will recall . . .")
First appeared in WRITER OF THE DARK
    CRYPT OF CTHULHU #47 (Chpbk.)

**A MATTER OF AGE**
First appeared in LURID CONFESSIONS #1 (Chpbk.)
    THE NEW HOWARD READER #6 (Chpbk.)

**MAYHEM AND TAXES**
Featuring BRECKINRIDGE ELKINS
First appeared in SUMMIT COUNTY JOURNAL, September 8, 15, 22, 29, 1967 (4-part serial)
    MAYHEM ON BEAR CREEK
    HEROES OF BEAR CREEK
    THE SUMMIT COUNTY JOURNAL appearance changed the name to "Breckenridge", to be like the town it
        was published in

**ME, WHALE AND WEARY**
Listed on a Kline Agency list of REH stories, listed as 20 pages long, don't know what happened to it

**MEDALLIONS IN THE MOON**
First appeared in ETCHINGS IN IVORY (Chpbk.)
    THE BOOK OF ROBERT E. HOWARD

**MEET CAP'N KIDD**
Featuring BRECKINRIDGE ELKINS
First appeared in A GENT FROM BEAR CREEK (as Chapter 3)
    THE SUMMIT COUNTY JOURNAL, July 19, 26; August 2, 9, 16, 23, 30; September 6, 13, 20, 27; October
        4, 1968 (12-part serial)
    SWORDSMEN AND SUPERMEN (Anth.)
    HEROES OF BEAR CREEK (book version)
    THE RIOT AT BUCKSNORT AND OTHER WESTERN TALES
    THE SUMMIT COUNTY JOURNAL appearance changed the name to "Breckenridge", to be like the town it
        was published in

**MEN OF IRON**
    First appeared in THE IRON MAN
    THE IRON MAN, WITH THE ADVENTURES OF DENNIS DORGAN
    BOXING STORIES

**MEN OF THE SHADOWS**
Featuring BRAN MAK MORN
First appeared in BRAN MAK MORN, Dell

WORMS OF THE EARTH
BARN MAK MORN, Baen
BRAN MAK MORN – THE LAST KING
Includes the poems "Chant of the White Beard", "Rune", and "Song of the Pict", all as untitled verse within the
  story

## MIDNIGHT
First appeared in THE JUNTO, September 1928
  THE HOWARD COLLECTOR #1
  THE HOWARD COLLECTOR, Ace
  THE NEW HOWARD READER #7 (Chpbk.)
  WEST IS WEST AND OTHERS

## THE MIRRORS OF TUZUN THUNE
Featuring KULL
First appeared in WEIRD TALES, September 1929
  SKULL-FACE AND OTHERS
  AVON FANTASY READER #2
  THE COMING OF CONAN (edited by LSDC)
  KING KULL (edited by Lin Carter)
  THE MAGIC OF ATLANTIS (Anth.)
  SKULL-FACE OMNIBUS
  FROM THE HELLS BENEATH THE HELLS (Chpbk.)
  SKULL-FACE OMNIBUS, VOLUME 3
  DARK IMAGININGS: A COLLECTION OF GOTHIC FANTASY (Anth.)
  KULL: THE FABULOUS WARRIOR KING
  KULL
  YGGDRASIL, VOLUME 1, #1 (Chpbk.)
  SHADOW KINGDOMS: THE WEIRD WORKS OF ROBERT E. HOWARD, VOLUME 1 (Wildside Press,
      Cosmos & AudioRealms)
  THE WEIRD WRITINGS OF ROBERT E. HOWARD, VOLUME ONE
  KULL: EXILE OF ATLANTIS
  THE GRIM LAND: THE BEST OF ROBERT E. HOWARD, VOLUME 2

## MISS HIGH-HAT
First appeared in RISQUE STORIES #4 (Chpbk.)
  THE NEW HOWARD READER #2 (Chpbk.)

## MISTO' DEMPSEY
First appeared in THE LAST OF THE TRUNK OCH BREV I URVAL (Chpbk.)
  THE LAST OF THE TRUNK
  A group of 7 humorous boxing sketches

## MISTRESS OF DEATH
Featuring AGNES DE CHASTILLON
First appeared in WITCHCRAFT AND SORCERY, January-February 1971 (completed by Gerald W. Page)
  SWORD WOMAN (completed by Gerald W. Page)
  Originally an unfinished draft and a synopsis, the original forms have never been published

## THE MOON OF SKULLS
Featuring SOLOMON KANE
First appeared as a 2-part serial in WEIRD TALES: June 1930; and July 1930
  RED SHADOWS
  THE MOON OF SKULLS

SOLOMON KANE: SKULLS IN THE STARS
WHITE WOLF MAGAZINE #9 (part 1 of 3)
SOLOMON KANE, Baen
THE SAVAGE TALES OF SOLOMON KANE
SAVAGE ADVENTURES
THE DEVIL IN IRON, Incarna
MOON OF SKULLS: THE WEIRD WORKS OF ROBERT E. HOWARD, VOLUME 2
THE WEIRD WRITINGS OF ROBERT E. HOWARD, VOLUME ONE
THE RIGHT HAND OF DOOM AND OTHER TALES OF SOLOMON KANE
THE LEGEND OF SOLOMON KANE
THE 'SOLOMAN CRANE' STORIES

## MOON OF ZAMBEBWEI
Alternate title: THE GRISLY HORROR

## MORE EVIDENCES OF THE INNATE DIVINITY OF MAN
First appeared in THE JUNTO, October 1928
     FANTASY CROSSROADS SPECIAL EDITION #1
     THE NEW HOWARD READER #6 (Chpbk.)
     This is an article

## MORE OR LESS DANGEROUS
Listed on a Kline Agency list of REH stories, listed as 4 pages long, don't know what happened to it; the Kline reference states "MORE OR LESS DANGEROUS – No Title"

## MOUNTAIN MAN
Featuring BRECKINRIDGE ELKINS
First appeared in ACTION STORIES, March-April 1934
     THE SUMMIT COUNTY JOURNAL, May 10, 17, 24, 31; June 7, 14, 21, 28; July 5, 12, 19, 1968 (11-part
        serial, same as book)
     THE NEW HOWARD READER #2 (Chpbk., the original magazine version)
     THE COMPLETE ACTION STORIES
     THE RIOT AT BUCKSNORT AND OTHER WESTERN TALES
     TALES FROM THE PULPS, VOLUME 1, #3
     Was altered slightly to become Chapter 2 of the "A Gent from Bear Creek" novel; THE SUMMIT COUNTY
        JOURNAL appearance changed the name to "Breckenridge", to be like the town it was published in

## THE MOUNTAINS OF THIBET
Alternate title: Untitled ("The way it came about that Steve Allison, Timoleon . . .")

## MR. DOWSER BUYS A CAR
First appeared in THE LAST OF THE TRUNK OCH BREV I URVAL (Chpbk.)
     THE LAST OF THE TRUNK
     Hand-written, and dated January 26, 1921

## MURDERER'S GROG
Alternate title: OUTLAW WORKING
Featuring WILD BILL CLANTON
First appeared in SPICY-ADVENTURE STORIES, January 1937 (author listed as "Sam Walser")
     SPICY-ADVENTURE STORIES, November 1942 (as "Outlaw Working", author listed as Max Neilson")
     THE SHE DEVIL
     SPICY-ADVENTURE STORIES, JANUARY 1937, Girasol Collectables (Chpbk.)

## MUSINGS
First appeared in THE JUNTO, September 1928
TRUMPET #7 (Chpbk.)
THE SECOND BOOK OF ROBERT E. HOWARD
THE NEW HOWARD READER #2 (Chpbk.)
THE ROAD TO VELITRIUM #30 (Chpbk.)

## MUSINGS OF A MORON
First appeared in THE HOWARD COLLECTOR #10
THE HOWARD COLLECTOR, Ace
THE NEW HOWARD READER #6 (Chpbk.)

## THE MUTINY OF THE HELLROARER
First appeared in THE LAST OF THE TRUNK OCH BREV I URVAL (Chpbk.)
THE COLLECTED LETTERS OF ROBERT E. HOWARD, VOLUME 2: 1930-1932
From a letter to TCS, ca. April 1930 ("Salaam: / Well, Fear Finn, I believe . . .")

## THE MYSTERY OF SUMMERTON CASTLE
Listed on a Kline Agency list of REH stories, listed as 9 pages long, don't know what happened to it

## THE MYSTERY OF TANNERNOE LODGE
Featuring STEVE HARRISON
First appeared in LORD OF THE DEAD (completed by Fred Blosser)
THE NEW HOWARD READER #8 (Chpbk., just fragment)
A fragment

## NAMES IN THE BLACK BOOK
Featuring STEVE HARRISON
First appeared in SUPER-DETECTIVE STORIES, May 1934
SKULL-FACE, Berkley
LORD OF THE DEAD, Grant
TOUGH GUYS AND DANGEROUS DAMES (Anth.)
GRAVEYARD RATS AND OTHERS

## NEKHT SEMERKEHT
First appeared in SWORDS AGAINST DARKNESS (Anth., completed by Andrew J. Offutt)
YEAR'S BEST FANTASY STORIES: 4 (Anth., completed by Andrew J. Offutt)
THE GODS OF BAL-SAGOTH (Anth., completed by Andrew J. Offutt)
THE BLACK STRANGER AND OTHER AMERICAN TALES (first draft only)
THE ROBERT E. HOWARD FOUNDATION NEWSLETTER, VOLUME 1, #2 (page 15 of first draft)
Originally there was a complete first draft, though the later portions of it were in synopsis form, and a second draft which was started but didn't go very far; Glenn Lord gave Offutt the second draft beginning with the remaining portion of the first draft, Offutt worked from that; supposedly the last story REH ever worked on; certainly one of the very last stories REH wrote, as the original is on a yellow paper that REH acquired in 1936 and used for his last stories; the REHFNL publication is in color, to show that yellow paper

## NERVE
First appeared in PAY DAY (Chpbk.)

## A NEW GAME FOR COSTIGAN
Alternate titles: PLAYING JOURNALIST; A NEW GAME FOR DORGAN

**A NEW GAME FOR DORGAN**
Alternate titles: PLAYING JOURNALIST; A NEW GAME FOR COSTIGAN

**A NIGHT ASHORE**
Alternate titles: SAILOR COSTIGAN AND THE YELLOW COBRA; THE YELLOW COBRA; A KOREAN
        NIGHT; THE FANGS OF THE YELLOW COBRA

**NIGHT ENCOUNTER**
First appeared in THE LAST OF THE TRUNK OCH BREV I URVAL (Chpbk.)
        THE LAST OF THE TRUNK
        Incomplete

**NIGHT OF BATTLE**
Alternate title: SHORE LEAVE FOR A SLUGGER
Featuring STEVE COSTIGAN
First appeared in FIGHT STORIES, March 1932
        FIGHT STORIES, Fall, 1942 ("Shore Leave for a Slugger", author listed as "Mark Adam")
        REH'S FIGHT MAGAZINE #3 (Chpbk.)
        WATERFRONT FISTS AND OTHERS
        There is also a surviving synopsis for this story

**THE NIGHT OF THE WOLF**
Featuring CORMAC MAC ART
First appeared in BRAN MAK MORN, Dell
        TIGERS OF THE SEA
        CORMAC MAC ART, Baen
        THE ULTIMATE TRIUMPH: THE HEROIC FANTASY OF ROBERT E. HOWARD

**"NO COWHERDERS WANTED"**
Alternate title: GENTS IN BUCKSKIN
Featuring BRECKINRIDGE ELKINS
First appeared in ACTION STORIES, September 1936
        THE SUMMIT COUNTY JOURNAL, November 24; December 1, 8, 15, 22, 29, 1967; January 5, 1968 (7-part
                serial, the first installment was mistitled as "While Smoke Rolled")
        MAYHEM ON BEAR CREEK
        HEROES OF BEAR CREEK
        THE COMPLETE ACTION STORIES
        THE RIOT AT BUCKSNORT AND OTHER WESTERN TALES
        THE SUMMIT COUNTRY JOURNAL appearance changed the name to "Breckenridge", to be like the town it
                was published in

**NO MAN NEEDS 3 HANDS**
Listed on a Kline Agency list of REH stories, listed as 9 pages long, don't know what happened to it

**NORTH OF KHYBER**
Featuring EL BORAK & THE SONORA KID
First appeared in EL BORAK L'ETERNEL (French)
        NORTH OF KHYBER (Chpbk.)

## THE NOSELESS HORROR
First appeared in THE MAGAZINE OF HORROR #31
　　THE HOWARD REVIEW #5 (Chpbk.)
　　BLACK CANAAN

## NOTES FOR A GENT FROM BEAR CREEK
First appeared in COSTIGAN #19 (Chpbk.)

## NOTES ON VARIOUS PEOPLES OF THE HYBORIAN AGE
First appeared in A GAZETTER OF THE HYBORIAN WORLD OF CONAN AND AN
　　ETHNOGEOGRAPHICAL DICTIONARY OF PRINCIPLE PEOPLES OF THE ERA (Chpbk.)
　　THE CONAN CHRONICLES, VOLUME 2, Millenium
　　ROBERT E. HOWARD'S COMPLETE CONAN OF CIMMERIA, VOLUME 1
　　THE COMING OF CONAN THE CIMMERIAN
　　THE COMPLETE CHRONICLES OF CONAN
　　This is an essay, REH scholars Rusty Burke and Patrice Louinet believe that the first page, dealing mainly with
　　　　Aquilonians, Gundermen, and Cimmerians, may have been composed very early in the Conan series,
　　　　perhaps around the same time as "The Hyborian Age," while the page covering the Westermarck was
　　　　clearly composed as background material for "Wolves Beyond the Border"

## NOTHING TO LOSE
Alternate title: THE PURPLE HEART OF ERLIK

## THE NUT'S SHELL
First appeared in PAY DAY (Chpbk.)

## OLD FRIENDS – OLD FOES
Listed on a Kline Agency list of REH stories, listed as 13 pages long, don't know what happened to it

## OLD GARFIELD'S HEART
First appeared in WEIRD TALES, December 1933
　　THE DARK MAN AND OTHERS
　　PIGEONS FROM HELL, Zebra & Ace
　　THE DARK MAN OMNIBUS, VOLUME 2
　　CTHULHU THE MYTHOS AND KINDRED HORRORS
　　THE BLACK STRANGER AND OTHER AMERICAN TALES
　　THE DARK HORSE BOOK OF THE DEAD
　　THE WEIRD WRITINGS OF ROBERT E. HOWARD, VOLUME ONE
　　THE VALLEY OF THE WORM: THE WEIRD WORKS OF ROBERT E. HOWARD, VOLUME 5
　　AMERICAN SUPERNATURAL TALES (Anth.)
　　THE GRIM LAND: THE BEST OF ROBERT E. HOWARD, VOLUME 2

## ON READING – AND WRITING
First appeared in THE LAST CELT
　　MEDIASCENE #20
　　This is a collection of portions of various REH letters, all dealing with REH's choices in reading and writing
　　　　techniques

## ONE OF A VANISHING RACE
Listed on a Kline Agency list of REH stories, listed as 20 pages long, don't know what happened to it

## ONE SHANGAI NIGHT
Alternate title: DARK SHANGHAI

## OUT OF THE DEEP
First appeared in MAGAZINE OF HORROR #18
    FAR BELOW AND OTHER HORRORS (Anth.)
    MARCHERS OF VALHALLA, Sphere and Berkley
    THE BARBARIAN SCROLL #6 (Chpbk.)
    EONS OF THE NIGHT

## OUTLAW TRAILS
Alternate titles: THE DEVIL'S JOKER; THE DEVIL'S JEST

## OUTLAW WORKING
Alternate title: MURDERER'S GROG

## OVER THE ROCKIES IN A FORD
First appeared in THE NEVERENDING HUNT

## THE PARADOX
First appeared in THE LAST OF THE TRUNK OCH BREV I URVAL (Chpbk.)
    THE LAST OF THE TRUNK
    Unfinished

## PAY DAY
First appeared in PAY DAY (Chpbk.)

## THE PEACEFUL PILGRIM
Alternate title: CUPID FROM BEAR CREEK
Featuring BRECKINRIDGE ELKINS
First appeared in SUMMIT COUNTY JOURNAL, February 16, 23; March 1, 8, 15, 22, 29, 1968 (7-part serial)
    MAYHEM ON BEAR CREEK
    HEROES OF BEAR CREEK
    THE RIOT AT BUCKSNORT AND OTHER WESTERN TALES
    "Cupid from Bear Creek" first appeared in ACTION STORIES, this version is slightly different; THE
        SUMMIT COUNTY JOURNAL appearance changed the name to "Breckenridge", to be like the town
        it was published in

## THE PEOPLE OF THE BLACK CIRCLE
Featuring CONAN
First appeared as a 3-part serial in WEIRD TALES: September 1934; October 1934; and November 1934
    THE SWORD OF CONAN
    CONAN THE ADVENTURER
    FANTASTIC, January 1967
    THE PEOPLE OF THE BLACK CIRCLE, Grant
    THE PEOPLE OF THE BLACK CIRCLE, Berkley & Putnam
    THE CONAN CHRONICLES 2, Orbit
    ISAAC ASIMOV'S MAGICAL WORLD OF FANTASY #1: WIZARDS (Anth.)
    ISAAC ASIMOV'S MAGICAL WORLDS OF FANTASY: WITCHES & WIZARDS (Anth.)
    THE ESSENTIAL CONAN, SFBC Fantasy
    THE CONAN CHRONICLES I: THE PEOPLE OF THE BLACK CIRCLE
    ROBERT E. HOWARD'S COMPLETE CONAN OF CIMMERIA, VOLUME 2 (plus synopsis, first
        appearance; both story and synopsis from original typescripts)
    THE BLOODY CROWN OF CONAN (plus synopsis, both story and synopsis from original typescripts)
    THE COMPLETE CHRONICLES OF CONAN
    THE WEIRD WRITINGS OF ROBERT E. HOWARD, VOLUME TWO

THE GARDEN OF FEAR: THE WEIRD WORKS OF ROBERT E. HOWARD, VOLUME 6
CRIMSON SHADOWS: THE BEST OF ROBERT E. HOWARD, VOLUME 1
PEOPLE OF THE BLACK CIRCLE
THREE TALES OF CONAN THE BARBARIAN

## PEOPLE OF THE BLACK COAST
First appeared in SPACEWAY SCIENCE FICTION, September-October 1969
   NIGHT CHILLS (Anth.)
   BLACK CANAAN
   TALES OF DUNGEONS & DRAGONS (Anth.)
   BEYOND THE BORDERS

## PEOPLE OF THE DARK
First appeared in STRANGE TALES, June 1932
   THE DARK MAN AND OTHERS
   STRANGE TALES OF MYSTERY & TERROR (Anth.)
   PIGEONS FROM HELL, Zebra & Ace
   THE DARK MAN OMNIBUS, VOLUME 2
   CTHULHU THE MYTHOS AND KINDRED HORRORS
   NAMELESS CULTS
   ROBERT E. HOWARD AND WEIRD TALES #4 (Chpbk.)
   STRANGE TALES, JUNE 1932, Girosal Collectables
   ROBERT E. HOWARD'S STRANGE TALES
   PEOPLE OF THE DARK: THE WEIRD WORKS OF ROBERT E. HOWARD, VOLUME 3
   This story was written three months prior to the first Conan the Cimmerian story, and was likely the prototype
      for the later Conan; the hero in this story is also named Conan, but a different character of more recent
      times, also swears by Crom

## PEOPLE OF THE SERPENT
Alternate title: FANGS OF GOLD

## PEOPLE OF THE WINGED SKULLS
First appeared in THE LAST OF THE TRUNK OCH BREV I URVAL (Chpbk.)
   THE COLLECTED LETTERS OF ROBERT E. HOWARD, VOLUME 1: 1923-1929
   From a letter to TCS, ca. November 1928 ("Salaam: / I'll swear . . ."); this work also contains the following
      poems: Untitled ("Oh, we are the children . . ."); Untitled ("The tall man answered: . . ."); Untitled
      ("The tall man rose and said: . . ."); Untitled ("The tall man said: . . .")

## THE PHANTOM OF OLD EGYPT
 Listed on a Kline Agency list of REH stories, listed as 9 pages long, don't know what happened to it

## THE PHANTOM TARANTULA
Listed on a Kline Agency list of REH stories, listed as 9 pages long, don't know what happened to it

## THE PHOENIX ON THE SWORD
Featuring CONAN
First appeared in WEIRD TALES, December 1932
   SKULL-FACE AND OTHERS
   KING CONAN
   CONAN THE USURPER
   SKULL-FACE OMNIBUS
   SKULL-FACE OMNIBUS, VOLUME 3
   THE CONAN CHRONICLES, VOLUME 2, Millenium

ROBERT E. HOWARD'S COMPLETE CONAN OF CIMMERIA, VOLUME 1
THE COMING OF CONAN THE CIMMERIAN
WINGS IN THE NIGHT: THE WEIRD WORKS OF ROBERT E. HOWARD, VOLUME 4
THE COMPLETE CHRONICLES OF CONAN
THE WEIRD WRITINGS OF ROBERT E. HOWARD, VOLUME ONE
THE PHOENIX ON THE SWORD (Chpbk.)
FIVE TALES OF CONAN THE BARBARIAN

## PICTURES IN THE FIRE
First appeared in THE LAST CELT, 1973 (original holograph form, first page only)
LA MANOIR DE LA TERREUR (French, first complete publication)
THE NEW HOWARD READER #7 (Chpbk.)
This was a paper REH wrote for English class in high school

## PIGEONS FROM HELL
First appeared in WEIRD TALES, May 1938
WEIRD TALES, November 1951
THRILLER, episode #14140 (Chpbk.)
THE DARK MAN AND OTHERS
WEIRD TALES, Pyramid
THE BOOK OF ROBERT E. HOWARD
PIGEONS FROM HELL, Zebra & Ace
THE DARK MAN ONMIBUS, VOLUME 1
PIGEONS FROM HELL, Script from Darkroom (Chpbk.)
CTHULHU THE MYTHOS AND KINDRED HORRORS
THE HORROR HALL OF FAME (Anth.)
YOUNG BLOOD (Anth.)
SAVAGE ADVENTURES
THE BLACK STRANGER AND OTHER AMERICAN TALES
THE WEIRD WRITINGS OF ROBERT E. HOWARD, VOLUME TWO
THE GRIM LAND: THE BEST OF ROBERT E. HOWARD, VOLUME 2
Was voted best story in its original WEIRD TALES appearance by the fans; the producer of THRILLER, Doug
Benton, said that "Pigeons from Hell" was his favorite episode; the Weird Writings volume contains
the story twice, the original 1930s pages as well as the pages from a WT reprint in the 1950s

## PIGSKIN SCHOLAR
First appeared in THE LAST OF THE TRUNK OCH BREV I URVAL (Chpbk.)
THE LAST OF THE TRUNK
Fragment

## PILGRIMS TO THE PECOS
Alternate title: WEARY PILGRIMS ON THE ROAD
Featuring BRECKINRIDGE ELKINS
First appeared in ACTION STORIES, February 1936
THE PRIDE OF BEAR CREEK
THE SUMMIT COUNTY JOURNAL, January 28; February 4, 11, 18, 25; March 3, 10, 17, 24, 31; April 7, 14,
21, 28; May 5, 12, 19, 26; June 2, 9, 1972 (20-part serial)
HEROES OF BEAR CREEK
THE COMPLETE ACTION STORIES
Grant removed all the italics, which was carried over in later editions; THE SUMMIT COUNTY JOURNAL
appearance changed the name to "Breckenridge", to be like the town it was published in; THE
COMPLETE ACTION STORIES restored the text to original publication form

## A PIRUT STORY

First appeared in THE RIGHT HOOK, VOLUME 1, #2 (Chpbk.)
　　AUSTIN, VOLUME 3, #2 (Chpbk.)

## PISTOL POLITICS
Featuring BRECKINRIDGE ELKINS
First appeared in ACTION STORIES, April 1936
　　THE PRIDE OF BEAR CREEK
　　HEROES OF BEAR CREEK
　　THE COMPLETE ACTION STORIES
　　THE RIOT AT BUCKSNORT AND OTHER WESTERN TALES
　　Grant removed all the italics, which was carried over in HEROES OF BEAR CREEK; THE COMPLETE
　　　　ACTION STORIES and THE RIOT AT BUCKSNORT both restored the text to original publication
　　　　form

## THE PIT OF THE SERPENT
Alternate title: MANILA MANSLAUGHTER
Featuring STEVE COSTIGAN
First appeared in FIGHT STORIES, July 1929
　　FIGHT STORIES, Fall, 1937 (as "Manila Manslaughter", author listed as "Mark Adam")
　　THE BOOK OF ROBERT E. HOWARD
　　REH'S FIGHT MAGAZINE #1 (Chpbk.)
　　WATERFRONT FISTS AND OTHERS
　　BOXING STORIES

## PLAYING JOURNALIST
Alternate titles: A NEW GAME FOR DORGAN; A NEW GAME FOR COSTIGAN
Featuring DENNIS DORGAN
First appeared in THE INCREDIBLE ADVENTURES OF DENNIS DORGAN
　　THE IRON MAN, WITH THE ADVENTURES OF DENNIS DORGAN
　　BOXING STORIES (as "A New Game for Costigan", Costigan version)
　　Original typescript lists author as "Patrick Ervin", a pseudonym REH used in connection with his Dennis
　　　　Dorgan stories

## PLAYING SANTA CLAUS
Alternate title: A TWO-FISTED SANTA CLAUS
Featuring DENNIS DORGAN
First appeared in THE INCREDIBLE ADVENTURES OF DENNIS DORGAN
　　THE IRON MAN, WITH THE ADVENTURES OF DENNIS DORGAN
　　Original typescript lists author as "Patrick Ervin", a pseudonym REH used in connection with his Dennis
　　　　Dorgan stories

## POLITICS AT BLUE LIZARD
Alternate titles: THE CONQUERIN' HERO OF THE HUMBOLTS; POLITICS AT LONESOME LIZARD

## POLITICS AT LONESOME LIZARD
Alternate titles: THE CONQUERIN' HERO OF THE HUMBOLTS; POLITICS AT BLUE LIZARD

## THE POOL OF THE BLACK ONE
Featuring CONAN
First appeared in WEIRD TALES, October 1933
　　THE SWORD OF CONAN
　　CONAN THE ADVERTURER
　　ROBERT E. HOWARD OMNIBUS

THE POOL OF THE BLACK ONE
THE CONAN CHRONICLES 2, Orbit
THE CONAN CHRONICLES I: THE PEOPLE OF THE BLACK CIRCLE
ROBERT E. HOWARD'S COMPLETE CONAN OF CIMMERIA, VOLUME 1
THE COMING OF CONAN THE CIMMERIAN
WEIRD TALES, OCTOBER 1933, Girasol Collectables (Chpbk.)
THE COMPLETE CHRONICLES OF CONAN
THE WEIRD WRITINGS OF ROBERT E. HOWARD, VOLUME ONE
THE VALLEY OF THE WORM: THE WEIRD WORKS OF ROBERT E. HOWARD, VOLUME 5

## POST OAKS AND SAND ROUGHS
First appeared in LE REBELLE (French)
POST OAKS AND SAND ROUGHS
There are two complete drafts for the novel, and both are carbons (which probably explains why the novel isn't titled as REH would usually give titles after he had completed his stories); Glenn Lord stated that the drafts are in horrible shape and that it had taken him a very loooong time to type a copy for Don Grant to use

## THE POST OF THE SAPPY SKIPPER
First appeared in THE LAST OF THE TRUNK OCH BREV I URVAL (Chpbk.)
THE COLLECTED LETTERS OF ROBERT E. HOWARD, VOLUME 1: 1923-1929
From a letter to TCS, April 6, 1925 ("Salaam, sahib: / What ho! I have never . . .")

## A POWER AMONG THE ISLANDS
Featuring EL BORAK & THE SONORA KID
First appeared in EL BORAK L'ETERNEL (French)
NORTH OF KHYBER (Chpbk.)

## PROEM
First appeared in ETCHINGS IN IVORY (Chpbk.)

## THE PUNCH
First appeared in THE LAST OF THE TRUNK OCH BREV I URVAL (Chpbk.)
THE LAST OF THE TRUNK

## PURITANS
First appeared in THE RIGHT HOOK, VOLUME 1, #1 (Chpbk.)
AUSTIN, VOLUME 3, #2 (Chpbk.)
ROBERT E. HOWARD—THE POWER OF THE WRITING MIND
This is an article

## THE PURPLE HEART OF ERLIK
Alternate title: NOTHING TO LOSE
Featuring WILD BILL CLANTON
First appeared in SPICY-ADVENTURE STORIES, November 1936 (author listed as "Sam Walser")
SPICY-ADVENTURE STORIES, October 1942 ( as "Nothing to Lose", author listed as "R.T. Maynard")
THE PULPS: FIFTY YEARS OF AMERICAN POP CULTURE (Anth.)
THE SHE DEVIL
SPICY-ADVENTURE STORIES, NOVEMBER 1936, Girasol Collectables (Chpbk.)

## QUEEN OF THE BLACK COAST
Featuring CONAN
First appeared in WEIRD TALES, May 1934
> AVON FANTASY READER #8
> THE COMING OF CONAN
> CONAN OF CIMMERIA
> SWORD AND SORCERY ANNUAL, 1975
> QUEEN OF THE BLACK COAST, Grant
> THE CONAN CHRONICLES 1, Sphere and Orbit
> THE CONAN CHRONICLES I: THE PEOPLE OF THE BLACK CIRCLE
> ROBERT E. HOWARD'S COMPLETE CONAN OF CIMMERIA, VOLUME 1
> THE COMING OF CONAN THE CIMMERIAN
> THE COMPLETE CHRONICLES OF CONAN
> THE WEIRD WRITINGS OF ROBERT E. HOWARD, VOLUME ONE
> THE GARDEN OF FEAR: THE WEIRD WORKS OF ROBERT E. HOWARD, VOLUME 6
> FIVE TALES OF CONAN THE BARBARIAN
> QUEEN OF THE BLACK COAST (Chpbk., early "Taramis" draft)
> The heroine of the story was originally named Taramis, though REH later changed it to Belit.

## THE QUESTION OF THE EAST
First appeared in THE LAST OF THE TRUNK OCH BREV I URVAL (Chpbk.)
> THE LAST OF THE TRUNK

## RATTLE OF BONES
Featuring SOLOMON KANE
First appeared in WEIRD TALES, June 1929
> SKULL-FACE AND OTHERS
> MAGAZINE OF HORROR, November 1965
> RED SHADOWS
> SOLOMON KANE, Centaur and Haddock
> SKULL-FACE OMNIBUS
> SKULL-FACE OMNIBUS, VOLUME 2
> SOLOMON KANE: SKULLS IN THE STARS
> SOLOMON KANE, Baen
> THE SAVAGE TALES OF SOLOMON KANE
> SHADOW KINGDOMS: THE WEIRD WORKS OF ROBERT E. HOWARD, VOLUME 1 (Wildside Press,
> Cosmos & AudioRealms)
> THE WEIRD WRITINGS OF ROBERT E. HOWARD, VOLUME ONE
> THE ROBERT E. HOWARD NEWSLETTER, VOLUME 1, #1 (early draft)
> THE RIGHT HAND OF DOOM AND OTHER TALES OF SOLOMON KANE
> THE LEGEND OF SOLOMON KANE
> THE 'SOLOMAN CRANE' STORIES
> An earlier draft of the story gives the villain a different reason for his killings

## THE RECALCITRANT
First appeared in THE LAST OF THE TRUNK OCH BREV I URVAL (Chpbk.)
> THE LAST OF THE TRUNK

## RECAP OF HAROLD LAMB'S THE WOLF CHASER
First appeared in LORD OF SAMARCAND AND OTHER ADVENTURE TALES OF THE OLD ORIENT
> REH rewrote this into his own synopsis, though he never turned it into a story, his version is Untitled ("The
> Persians had all fled . . .")

## RED BLADES OF BLACK CATHAY

By Robert E. Howard & Tevis Clyde Smith
First appeared in ORIENTAL STORIES, February-March 1931
     RED BLADES OF BLACK CATHAY, Grant
     THE BOOK OF ROBERT E. HOWARD
     REHUPA #167 (Chpbk.)
     GATES OF EMPIRE AND OTHERS
     ORIENTAL STORIES, FEBRUARY-MARCH 1931, Girasol Collectables (Chpbk.)
     LORD OF SAMARCAND AND OTHER ADVENTURES OF THE OLD ORIENT
     THE COMPLETE ORIENTAL STORIES (Anth.)

## RED CURLS AND BOBBED HAIR
Featuring THE SONORA KID
First appeared in THE SONORA KID (Chpbk.)

## RED NAILS
Featuring CONAN
First appeared as a 3-part serial in WEIRD TALES: July 1936; August-September 1936; and October 1936
     THE SWORD OF CONAN
     CONAN THE WARRIOR
     RED NAILS, Grant
     RED NAILS, Berkley & Putnam
     BAKER'S DOZEN: 13 SHORT FANTASY NOVELS (Anth.)
     THE MAMMOTH BOOK OF SHORT FANTASY NOVELS (Anth.)
     THE ESSENTIAL CONAN, SFBC Fantasy
     THE CONAN CHRONICLES, VOLUME 2, Millenium
     STRANGE WORLDS #12
     STRANGE WORLDS
     RED NAILS, Incarna Publishing
     THE CONQUERING SWORD OF CONAN (plus an earlier draft)
     THE COMPLETE CHRONICLES OF CONAN
     THE WEIRD WRITINGS OF ROBERT E. HOWARD, VOLUME TWO
     THE GRIM LAND: THE BEST OF ROBERT E. HOWARD, VOLUME 2
     Parts 2 and 3 were voted best story in their respective original WEIRD TALES appearance by the fans; story may have been based on REH's visit to the Bonito Valley, home of the Lincoln County War; in his letters on the subject, very similar feel there, and this story was written just after that visit, per analysis by REH Scholar Rusty Burke

## RED SHADOWS
Alternate title: SOLOMON KANE
Featuring SOLOMON KANE
First appeared in WEIRD TALES, August 1928
     RED SHADOWS
     SOLOMON KANE, Centaur and Haddock
     SOLOMON KANE: SKULLS IN THE STARS
     SOLOMON KANE, Baen
     THE SAVAGE TALES OF SOLOMON KANE
     SHADOW KINGDOMS: THE WEIRD WORKS OF ROBERT E. HOWARD, VOLUME 1 (Wildside Press, Cosmos & AudioRealms)
     THE WEIRD WRITINGS OF ROBERT E. HOWARD, VOLUME ONE
     CRIMSON SHADOWS: THE BEST OF ROBERT E. HOWARD, VOLUME 1
     THE RIGHT HAND OF DOOM AND OTHER TALES OF SOLOMON KANE
     THE LEGEND OF SOLOMON KANE
     THE 'SOLOMAN CRANE' STORIES

## THE RED STONE
First appeared in THE LAST OF THE TRUNK OCH BREV I URVAL (Chpbk.)
> THE LAST OF THE TRUNK
> Unfinished

## REDFLAME
Featuring JOHN SILENT
First appeared in REDFLAME #3 (Chpbk.)
> THE NEW HOWARD READER #5 (Chpbk.)
> This is a fragment

## THE REFORMATION: A DREAM
First appeared in THE YELLOW JACKET, April 21, 1927
> THE HOWARD REVIEW #3 (Chpbk., as "The Reformation of a Dream")
> THE COMPLETE YELLOW JACKET
> WEST IS WEST AND OTHERS

## RESTLESS WATERS
First appeared in WITCHCRAFT AND SORCERY #10
> THE GODS OF BAL-SAGOTH

## THE RETURN OF SKULL-FACE
Alternate titles: Untitled ("Sir Haldred Taverel . . ."); TAVEREL MANOR
Featuring GORDON & COSTIGAN
First appeared in THE RETURN OF SKULLFACE (completed by Richard Lupoff)
> SKULL-FACE, Berkley (fragment only, as "Taverel Manor")
> THE NEW HOWARD READER #8 (Chpbk., fragment only, as "Taveral Manor")
> Originally an untitled and unfinished story, was finished by Lupoff and retitled as "The Return of Skull-Face";
>> the original untitled fragment was later published as "Taverel Manor"

## THE RETURN OF THE SORCERER
First appeared in BICENTENNIAL SALUTE TO REH (Chpbk.)
> THE NEW HOWARD READER #3 (Chpbk.)

## REVENGE
Alternate title: VENGEANCE
First appeared in UNAUSSPRECHLICHEN KULTEN #1 (Chpbk.)
> THE LAST OF THE TRUNK OCH BREV I URVAL (Chpbk.)
> THE COLLECTED LETTERS OF ROBERT E. HOWARD, VOLUME 1: 1923-1929
> Contained in a letter to TCS, late August or early September 1927 ("ARE YOU THE YOUNG MAN . . .")

## REVENGE BY PROXY
Alternate title: DESERT BLOOD

## RIDERS BEYOND THE SUNRISE
By Robert E. Howard & Lin Carter
Alternate title: Untitled ("'Thus,' said Tu . . .")
Featuring KULL
First appeared in KING KULL
> LOST WORLDS (Anth.)
> Originally an unfinished REH draft, Carter added 2 main sections for the KING KULL book; the original
>> fragment is published in KULL, Grant, Bantam, and Baen; see untitled stories for details

**RIDERS OF THE SUNSET**
Alternate title: DRUMS OF THE SUNSET

**THE RIGHT HAND OF DOOM**
Featuring SOLOMON KANE
First appeared in RED SHADOWS
    SOLOMON KANE, Centaur and Haddock
    SOLOMON KANE: SKULLS IN THE STARS
    SOLOMON KANE, Baen
    THE SAVAGE TALES OF SOLOMON KANE
    THE RIGHT HAND OF DOOM AND OTHER TALES OF SOLOMON KANE
    THE LEGEND OF SOLOMON KANE

**RIGHT HOOK**
First appeared in POING D'ACIER (French)
    THE LAST OF THE TRUNK OCH BREV I URVAL (Chpbk.)
    THE LAST OF THE TRUNK

**RINGSIDE TALES**
First appeared in THE RIGHT HOOK, VOLUME 1, #3 (Chpbk.)
    AUSTIN, VOLUME 3, #2 (Chpbk.)

**A RINGTAILED TORNADO**
Alternate title: TEXAS JOHN ALDEN

**THE RIOT AT BUCKSNORT**
Featuring PIKE BEARFIELD
First appeared in ARGOSY, October 31, 1936
    THE HOWARD REVIEW #2 (Chpbk.)
    THE RIOT AT BUCKSNORT AND OTHER WESTERN TALES

**THE RIOT AT COUGAR PAW**
Featuring BRECKINRIDGE ELKINS
First appeared in ACTION STORIES, October 1935
    THE PRIDE OF BEAR CREEK
    THE SUMMIT COUNTY JOURNAL, September 24; October 1, 8, 15, 22, 29; November 5, 12, 19, 26;
        December 3, 10, 17, 24, 31, 1971; January 7, 14, 21, 1972 (18-part serial)
    HEROES OF BEAR CREEK
    THE COMPLETE ACTION STORIES
    THE RIOT AT BUCKSNORT AND OTHER WESTERN TALES
    Grant removed all the italics, which was carried over in later editions; THE SUMMIT COUNTY JOURNAL
        appearance changed the name to "Breckenridge", to be like the town it was published in; THE
        COMPLETE ACTION STORIES and THE RIOT AT BUCKSNORT both restored the text to original
        publication form

**THE RIVALS**
Unpublished

**THE ROAD OF AZRAEL**
First appeared in CHACAL #1, Winter 1976
    THE ROAD OF AZRAEL
    LORD OF SAMARCAND AND OTHER ADVENTURES OF THE OLD ORIENT
    There are both a long and short version of this story, the short version has never been published

## THE ROAD OF THE EAGLES
Alternate titles: CONAN, MAN OF DESTINY; THE WAY OF THE SWORD

## THE ROAD OF THE MOUNTAIN LION
Alternate title: GATES OF EMPIRE

## THE ROAD TO BEAR CREEK
Featuring BRECKINRIDGE ELKINS
First appeared in ACTION STORIES, December 1934
> THE SUMMIT COUNTY JOURNAL, July 18, 24; August 7, 14, 21, 28; September 4, 11, 18, 25; October 2,
>> 9, 16, 23, 30; November 6, 1969 (16-part serial, book version)
> THE NEW HOWARD READER #6 (Chpbk., original magazine version)
> THE COMPLETE ACTION STORIES
> Was altered slightly to become Chapter 7 of the "A Gent from Bear Creek" novel; THE SUMMIT COUNTY
>> JOURNAL appearance changed the name to "Breckenridge", to be like the town it was published in

## ROGUES IN THE HOUSE
Featuring CONAN
First appeared in WEIRD TALES, January 1934
> TERROR BY NIGHT (Anth.)
> SKULL-FACE AND OTHERS
> THE COMING OF CONAN
> MORE NOT AT NIGHT (Anth.)
> CONAN
> NEVER AT NIGHT (Anth.)
> SKULL-FACE OMNIBUS
> SKULL-FACE OMNIBUS, VOLUME 3
> ROGUES IN THE HOUSE
> THE CONAN CHRONICLES 1, Sphere and Orbit
> THE CONAN CHRONICLES I: THE PEOPLE OF THE BLACK CIRCLE
> ROBERT E. HOWARD'S COMPLETE CONAN OF CIMMERIA, VOLUME 1
> THE COMING OF CONAN THE CIMMERIAN
> SAVAGE ADVENTURES
> SAVAGE PULP #1, Incarna Publishing
> THE COMPLETE CHRONICLES OF CONAN
> THE WEIRD WRITINGS OF ROBERT E. HOWARD, VOLUME ONE
> THE VALLEY OF THE WORM: THE WEIRD WORKS OF ROBERT E. HOWARD, VOLUME 5
> FIVE TALES OF CONAN THE BARBARIAN

## A ROOM IN LONDON
First appeared in THE LAST OF THE TRUNK OCH BREV I URVAL (Chpbk.)
> THE LAST OF THE TRUNK
> This is only an outline

## THE ROVING BOYS ON A SANDBURG
First appeared in THE LAST OF THE TRUNK OCH BREV I URVAL (Chpbk.)
> THE LAST OF THE TRUNK

## THE RUMP OF SWIFT
First appeared in THE LAST OF THE TRUNK OCH BREV I URVAL (Chpbk.)
> THE COLLECTED LETTERS OF ROBERT E. HOWARD, VOLUME 1: 1923-1929
> From a letter to TCS, ca. June 1928 ("Salaam; / Ho, ho, the long lights lift . . .")

## SAILOR COSTIGAN AND THE DESTINY GORILLA
Alternate titles: SAILOR DORGAN AND THE DESTINY GORILLA; THE DESTINY GORILLA

## SAILOR COSTIGAN AND THE JADE MONKEY
Alternate title: SAILOR DORGAN AND THE JADE MONKEY

## SAILOR COSTIGAN AND THE SWAMI
Featuring STEVE COSTIGAN
First appeared in THE HOWARD REVIEW #7 (Chpbk.)
    REH'S FIGHT MAGAZINE #4 (Chpbk.)

## SAILOR DORGAN AND THE DESTINY GORILLA
Alternate titles: THE DESTINY GORILLA; SAILOR COSTIGAN AND THE DESTINY GORILLA

## SAILOR DORGAN AND THE JADE MONKEY
Alternate titles: SAILOR COSTIGAN AND THE JADE MONKEY; THE JADE MONKEY
Featuring DENNIS DORGAN
First appeared in THE HOWARD COLLECTOR #14
    THE INCREDIBLE ADVENTURES OF DENNIS DORGAN
    THE IRON MAN, WITH THE ADVENTURES OF DENNIS DORGAN
    Announced in the final January 1934 edition of THE MAGIC CARPET MAGAZINE; the original typescript
        sold on eBay in 2000 for around $1500; in the original publication, Glenn Lord listed the author as
        "Patrick Ervin" in its first publication, the pseudonym that REH used with some of his Dennis Dorgan
        stories

## SAILOR DORGAN AND THE TURKISH MENACE
Alternate title: THE TURKISH MENACE

## SAILOR DORGAN AND THE WIZARD
Alternate title: A KNIGHT OF THE ROUND TABLE
This may be a possible alternate title

## SAILOR DORGAN AND THE YELLOW COBRA
Alternate titles: THE YELLOW COBRA; A NIGHT ASHORE; THE FANGS OF THE YELLOW COBRA; A
KOREAN NIGHT

## SAILOR STEVE O'BRIEN
Alternate title: ALLEYS OF PERIL
Unpublished
    This is a titled synopsis that became the story "Alleys of Peril", but this synopsis features Sailor Steve O'Brien,
        teamed with Bill McGlory; in the published story it's Sailor Steve Costigan, ship and dog name
        changed accordingly, no McGlory; perhaps he meant it to be sold to ACTION STORIES, which had
        published a couple other Dorgan/McGlory stories, then for some reason changed it to Costigan for
        FIGHT STORIES, or perhaps the editors made the changes, as the magazines were commonly owned
        and had the same editors

## SAILORS' GRUDGE
Alternate title: COSTIGAN VS. KID CAMERA
Featuring STEVE COSTIGAN
First appeared in FIGHT STORIES, March 1930
   FIGHT STORIES, Spring, 1938 (as "Costigan vs. Kid Camera", author listed as "Mark Adam")
   REH'S FIGHT MAGAZINE #1 (Chpbk.)
   WATERFRONT FISTS AND OTHERS

## SAMPSON HAD A SOFT SPOT
Alternate titles: BREED OF BATTLE; THE FIGHTIN'EST PAIR

## SANCTUARY OF THE SUN
A story that REH said he wrote, but no copy exists

## THE SAPPIOUS FEW MENCHEW
First appeared in THE LAST OF THE TRUNK OCH BREV I URVAL (Chpbk.)
   THE COLLECTED LETTERS OF ROBERT E. HOWARD, VOLUME 1: 1923-1929
   From a letter to TCS, March 17, 1925 ("The top o' the marnin', O'Clydo . . .")

## THE SCALP HUNTER
Alternate title: A STRANGER IN GRIZZLY CLAW
Featuring BRECKINRIDGE ELKINS
First appeared in ACTION STORIES, August 1934
   THE SUMMIT COUNTY JOURNAL, November 13, 20, 27; December 4, 11, 18, 25, 1969; January 1, 8, 15,
        22, 29; February 5, 12, 26; March 5, 12, 19, 1970 (18-part serial, same as book version)
   THE NEW HOWARD READER #7 (Chpbk.)
   THE COMPLETE ACTION STORIES
   Was altered slightly to become Chapter 8 of the "A Gent from Bear Creek" novel; THE SUMMIT COUNTY
        JOURNAL appearance changed the name to "Breckenridge", to be like the town it was published in

## THE SCARLET CITADEL
Featuring CONAN
First appeared in WEIRD TALES, January 1933
   SKULL-FACE AND OTHERS
   KING CONAN
   CONAN THE USURPER
   SKULL-FACE OMNIBUS
   SKULL-FACE OMNIBUS, VOLUME 3
   THE CONAN CHRONICLES, VOLUME 2, Millenium
   ROBERT E. HOWARD'S COMPLETE CONAN OF CIMMERIA, VOLUME 1
   THE COMING OF CONAN THE CIMMERIAN
   WINGS IN THE NIGHT: THE WEIRD WORKS OF ROBERT E. HOWARD, VOLUME 4
   THE COMPLETE CHRONICLES OF CONAN
   THE WEIRD WRITINGS OF ROBERT E. HOWARD, VOLUME ONE
   THE PHOENIX ON THE SWORD (Chpbk.)
   FIVE TALES OF CONAN THE BARBARIAN
   Voted best story in its original WEIRD TALES appearance, third highest total for that year; after the story was
        published in WEIRD TALES, REH included it in a collection he sent to Archer in the UK for possible
        publication; for that collection, REH actually retyped the story from scratch, and cleaned up a few
        typos, errors, inconsistencies, etc., from the WEIRD TALES appearance; this "later" draft is the one
        that is used and first published in the Wandering Star book

**SCARLET TEARS**
Alternate title: HAND OF THE BLACK GODDESS

**THE SCREAMING SKULL OF SILENCE**
Alternate title: THE SKULL OF SILENCE

**SEA CURSE**
First appeared in WEIRD TALES, May 1928
    THE HOWARD COLLECTOR #4
    WEIRD TALES, Winter 1973
    WAVES OF TERROR (Chpbk.)
    MARCHERS OF VALHALLA, Sphere and Berkley
    THE DIVERSIFIER #20 (Chpbk.)
    THE HOWARD COLLECTOR, Ace
    SEA-CURSED (Anth.)
    EONS OF THE NIGHT
    WEIRD TALES: SEVEN DECADES OF TERROR (Chpbk.)
    SHADOW KINGDOMS: THE WEIRD WORKS OF ROBERT E. HOWARD, VOLUME 1 (Wildside Press)
    THE WEIRD WRITINGS OF ROBERT E. HOWARD, VOLUME ONE
    FANTASTIC ADVENTURE STORIES, VOLUME 1, #2

**SECRET OF LOST VALLEY**
Alternate title: THE VALLEY OF THE LOST (2)
    First appeared in STARTLING MYSTERY STORIES #4
    THE VALLEY OF THE LOST
    ROBERT E. HOWARD OMNIBUS
    MARCHERS OF VALHALLA, Sphere and Berkley
    TRAILS IN DARKNESS (as "The Valley of the Lost")
    ARKHAM'S MASTERS OF HORROR: A 60TH ANNIVERSARY ANTHOLOGY RESTROSPECTIVE OF
        THE FIRST 30 YEARS OF ARKHAM HOUSE (Chpbk.)
    THE BLACK STRANGER AND OTHER AMERICAN TALES (as "The Valley of the Lost")
    Begins "As a wolf spies . . ." Glenn Lord had erroneously titled another story "The Valley of the Lost", as he
        thought it was the story that had been announced for the last issue of STRANGE TALES that never
        got published; in fact, that first story was "King of the Forgotten People"; and when this, the correct
        story, showed up, Glenn Lord titled it "The Secret of Lost Valley"; since this initial screwup, everyone
        has gone back to the proper titles

**SENTIMENT**
First appeared in THE JUNTO, September 1928
    THE HOWARD COLLECTOR #9
    THE HOWARD COLLECTOR, Ace
    THE NEW HOWARD READER #7 (Chpbk.)

**SERPENT VINES**
First appeared in WT 50: A TRIBUTE TO WEIRD TALES
    THE NEW HOWARD READER #3 (Chpbk.)

**THE SERVANTS OF BIT-YAKIN**
Alternate titles: THE JEWELS OF GWAHLUR; THE TEETH OF GWAHLUR

**SHACKLED MITTS**
Alternate title: Untitled ("I am a man of few words . . .")
First appeared in LA TOMBE DU DRAGON (French)

THE LAST OF THE TRUNK OCH BREV I URVAL (Chpbk.)
THE LAST OF THE TRUNK
Title was erroneously applied to this story, as Glenn Lord thought it was a story of that title mentioned in
REH's papers, which REH said he had offered to Fiction House in April, 1931; but as this story was
not written until after early 1932, this cannot be that story

## THE SHADOW IN THE WELL
First appeared in CROMLECH #2 (Chpbk., synopsis only)
THE NEW HOWARD READER #1 (Chpbk., synopsis only)
THE LAST OF THE TRUNK OCH BREV I URVAL (Chpbk.)
THE LAST OF THE TRUNK (first appearance of draft)

## THE SHADOW KINGDOM
Featuring KULL
First appeared in WEIRD TALES, August 1929
SKULL-FACE AND OTHERS
THE COMING OF CONAN
KING KULL
SKULL-FACE OMNIBUS
SKULL-FACE OMNIBUS, VOLUME 3
KULL: THE FABULOUS WARRIOR KING
KULL
ISAAC ASIMOV'S MAGICAL WORLDS OF FANTASY #9: ATLANTIS (Anth.)
WEIRD TALES: 32 UNEARTHED TALES (Anth.)
ROBERT E. HOWARD'S WORLD OF HEROES
NAMELESS CULTS
SHADOW KINGDOMS: THE WEIRD WORKS OF ROBERT E. HOWARD, VOLUME 1 (Wildside Press &
Cosmos)
THE WEIRD WRITINGS OF ROBERT E. HOWARD, VOLUME ONE
KULL: EXILE OF ATLANTIS (also included an ealy draft)
CRIMSON SHADOWS: THE BEST OF ROBERT E. HOWARD, VOLUME 1
Voted best story by the fans in original WEIRD TALES appearance, with one of the 50 highest totals ever

## THE SHADOW OF DOOM
First appeared in THE HOWARD COLLECTOR #8 (author listed as "John Taverel")
THE NEW HOWARD READER #1 (Chpbk.)
REH: TWO-GUN RACONTEUR #9
TCS said regarding this story: "(It) is based on an actual incident which occurred about fifty years ago. Bob
was in San Antonio at the time, and the beheading received special treatment from the press, and wide
discussion among the people. It made a real impression on Bob, and he referred to the grisly murder
several times during the course of our acquaintance." From THE HOWARD COLLECTOR #9

## THE SHADOW OF THE BEAST
First appeared in THE SHADOW OF THE BEAST (Chpbk.)
THE GODS OF BAL-SAGOTH
CTHULHU THE MYTHOS AND KINDRED HORRORS

## THE SHADOW OF THE HUN
Featuring TURLOGH DUBH O'BRIEN
First appeared in SHADOW OF THE HUN (Chpbk.)
SWORD WOMAN
LORD OF SAMARCAND AND OTHER ADVENTURES OF THE OLD ORIENT

## THE SHADOW OF THE VULTURE

First appeared in THE MAGIC CARPET MAGAZINE, January 1934
>    THE SOWERS OF THE THUNDER
>    ECHOES OF VALOR III (Anth.)
>    GATES OF EMPIRE AND OTHERS
>    LORD OF SAMARCAND AND OTHER ADVENTURES OF THE OLD ORIENT
>    THE GRIM LAND: THE BEST OF ROBERT E. HOWARD, VOLUME 2

## SHADOWS IN THE MOONLIGHT
Alternate title: IRON SHADOWS IN THE MOON
Featuring CONAN
First appeared in WEIRD TALES, April 1934
>    CONAN THE BARBARIAN
>    SWORDS AND SORCERY (Anth.)
>    CONAN THE FREEBOOTER
>    BLACK COLOSSUS
>    THE CONAN CHRONICLES 1, Sphere and Orbit
>    THE CONAN CHRONICLES I: THE PEOPLE OF THE BLACK CIRCLE
>    ROBERT E. HOWARD'S COMPLETE CONAN OF CIMMERIA, VOLUME 1
>    THE COMING OF CONAN THE CIMMERIAN
>    THE COMPLETE CHRONICLES OF CONAN
>    THE WEIRD WRITINGS OF ROBERT E. HOWARD, VOLUME ONE
>    THE VALLEY OF THE WORM: THE WEIRD WORKS OF ROBERT E. HOWARD, VOLUME 5
>    Original title was "Iron Shadows in the Moon"; REH to Clark Ashton Smith, ca. October 1933 ("Thanks very much for the kind things . . ."), "Wright has three more Conan yarns yet unpublished: 'Iron Shadows in the Moon,' 'The Queen of the Black Coast,' and 'Rogues in the House.'" More, REH to HPL, ca. July 1934: "Thanks for the kind things you said about my 'Shadows in the Moonlight.' (My original title was 'Iron Shadows in the Moon.')"

## SHADOWS IN ZAMBOULA
Alternate title: THE MAN-EATERS OF ZAMBOULA
Featuring CONAN
First appeared in WEIRD TALES, November 1935
>    SKULL-FACE AND OTHERS
>    CONAN THE BARBARIAN
>    THE SPELL OF SEVEN (Anth.)
>    CONAN THE WANDERER
>    SKULL-FACE OMNIBUS
>    SKULL-FACE OMNIBUS, VOLUME 3
>    THE DEVIL IN IRON
>    RED NAILS, Berkley and Putnam
>    THE CONAN CHRONICLES 2, Orbit
>    THE ESSENTIAL CONAN, SFBC Fantasy
>    THE CONAN CHRONICLES I: THE PEOPLE OF THE BLACK CIRCLE
>    SAVAGE ADVENTURES
>    THE CONQUERING SWORD OF CONAN (as "The Man-Eaters of Zamboula", plus an earlier draft)
>    THE COMPLETE CHRONICLES OF CONAN
>    THE WEIRD WRITINGS OF ROBERT E. HOWARD, VOLUME TWO
>    BEYOND THE BLACK RIVER: THE WEIRD WORKS OF ROBERT E. HOWARD, VOLUME 7

## SHANGHIED MITTS
Alternate title: TEXAS FISTS

## SHARP'S GUN SERENADE
Alternate title: EDUCATE OR BUST

Featuring BRECKINRIDGE ELKINS
First appeared in ACTION STORIES, January 1937 (slightly different from the book version "Educate or Bust")
    THE SUMMIT COUNTY JOURNAL, September 25; October 2, 9, 16, 23, 30; November 6, 13, 20, 27, 1970
    MAYHEM ON BEAR CREEK
    HEROES OF BEAR CREEK
    THE COMPLETE ACTION STORIES
    CRIMSON SHADOWS: THE BEST OF ROBERT E. HOWARD, VOLUME 1
    THE SUMMIT COUNTY JOURNAL appearance changed the name to "Breckenridge", to be like the town it
        was published in

## SHAVE THAT HAWG!
Alternate title: A GENT FROM THE PECOS

## SHE DEVIL
Alternate title: THE GIRL ON THE HELL SHIP
Featuring WILD BILL CLANTON
First appeared in SPICY-ADVENTURE STORIES, April 1936 (author listed as "Sam Walser")
    THE BOOK OF ROBERT E. HOWARD
    THE SHE DEVIL
    SPICY-ADVENTURE STORIES, APRIL 1936, Girasol Collectables (Chpbk.)

## SHE-CATS OF SAMARCAND
Alternate title: Untitled ("John Gorman found himself in Samarkand, . . .")

## THE SHEIK
First appeared in THE TATTLER, March 15, 1923
    THE NEW HOWARD READER #7 (Chpbk.)
    WEST IS WEST AND OTHERS

## SHIP IN MUTINY
Featuring WILD BILL CLANTON
First appeared in THE SHE DEVIL
    BRAN MAK MORN: A PLAY & OTHERS (Chpbk.)

## SHORE LEAVE FOR A SLUGGER
Alternate title: NIGHT OF BATTLE

## SHOWDOWN AT HELL'S CANYON
Alternate title: THE JUDGEMENT OF THE DESERT
First appeared in THE VULTURES
    THE VULTURES OF WHAPETON
    THE END OF THE TRAIL: WESTERN STORIES (as "The Judgment of the Desert")

## THE SHUNNED CASTLE
Featuring EL BORAK & THE SONORA KID
First appeared in EL BORAK L'ETERNEL (French)
    NORTH OF KHYBER (Chpbk.)

## THE SIGN OF THE SNAKE
Featuring STEVE COSTIGAN
First appeared in ACTION STORIES, June 1931
    CROSS PLAINS #2
    THE CHRONICLER OF CROSS PLAINS #1

THE COMPLETE ACTION STORIES
Was originally a Mike Dorgan / Bill McGlory story, straight adventure, ACTION STORIES editors turned it
        into a Sailor Steve Costigan story, didn't get the dog and ship names consistently correct

## THE SILVER HEEL
Featuring STEVE HARRISON
First appeared in TWO-FISTED DETECTIVE STORIES (Chpbk.)
        THE ROBERT E. HOWARD FOUNDATION NEWSLETTER, VOLUME 1, #2 (synopsis only)
        Only one page, page 5, remaining of the synopsis

## SISTERS
First appeared in THE RIGHT HOOK, VOLUME 1, #1 (Chpbk.)
        AUSTIN, VOLUME 3, #2 (Chpbk.)
        ROBERT E. HOWARD—THE POWER OF THE WRITING MIND
        This is an article

## SIX-GUN INTERVIEW
Unfinished, unpublished

## THE SKULL OF SILENCE
Alternate title: THE SCREAMING SKULL OF SILENCE
Featuring KULL
First appeared in KING KULL
        KULL: THE FABULOUS WARRIOR KING
        KULL, Grant
        KULL, Baen (restored text, including verse heading)
        KULL: EXILE OF ATLANTIS

## SKULL-FACE
First appeared as a serial in WEIRD TALES: Part 1, October 1929; Part 2, November 1929; Part 3, December 1929
        SKULL-FACE AND OTHERS
        FAMOUS FANTASTIC MYSTERIES, December 1952
        SKULL-FACE OMNIBUS
        SKULL-FACE OMNIBUS, VOLUME 1
        SKULL-FACE, Berkley
        NAMELESS CULTS
        MOON OF SKULLS: THE WEIRD WORKS OF ROBERT E. HOWARD, VOLUME 2
        SHADOW KINGDOMS: THE WEIRD WORKS OF ROBERT E. HOWARD, VOLUME 1 (Cosmos)
        THE WEIRD WRITINGS OF ROBERT E. HOWARD, VOLUME ONE
        SKULL-FACE, Medusa Expressions
        Parts 1 and 3 were voted best story in their respective WEIRD TALES issues by the fans

## SKULLS AGAINST THE DAWN
Unpublished, from a letter to TCS, undated ("Salaam: / Skulls Against the Dawn . . .")

## SKULLS AND ORCHIDS
First appeared in ETCHINGS IN IVORY (Chpbk.)
        THE BOOK OF ROBERT E. HOWARD

## SKULLS IN THE STARS
Featuring SOLOMON KANE
First appeared in WEIRD TALES, January 1929
>SKULL-FACE AND OTHERS
>MAGAZINE OF HORROR #9
>RED SHADOWS
>THE MOON OF SKULLS
>SKULL-FACE OMNIBUS
>SKULL-FACE OMNIBUS, VOLUME 2
>WEIRD LEGACIES (Anth.)
>SOLOMON KANE: SKULLS IN THE STARS
>WEIRD TALES: THE MAGAZINE THAT NEVER DIES (Anth.)
>SOLOMON KANE, Baen
>THE SAVAGE TALES OF SOLOMON KANE
>SAVAGE ADVENTURES
>SHADOW KINGDOMS: THE WEIRD WORKS OF ROBERT E. HOWARD, VOLUME 1 (Wildside Press, Cosmos & AudioRealms)
>THE WEIRD WRITINGS OF ROBERT E. HOWARD, VOLUME ONE
>THE RIGHT HAND OF DOOM AND OTHER TALES OF SOLOMON KANE
>THE LEGEND OF SOLOMON KANE
>THE 'SOLOMAN CRANE' STORIES

## THE SLAVE-PRINCESS
Featuring CORMAC FITZGEOFFREY
First appeared in HAWKS OF OUTREMER (completed by Richard Tierney)
>THE NEW HOWARD READER #8 (Chpbk., unfinished draft with synopsis for the last portion added)
>LORD OF SAMARCAND AND OTHER ADVENTURES OF THE OLD ORIENT (unfinished portion and synopsis)
>An unfinished story, REH wrote the first six chapters, Tierney wrote the last two; a complete synopsis also exists

## THE SLAYER
First appeared in THE LAST OF THE TRUNK OCH BREV I URVAL (Chpbk.)
>THE LAST OF THE TRUNK
>Unfinished

## SLEEPING BEAUTY
First appeared in THE YELLOW JACKET, October 27, 1926
>THE COMPLETE YELLOW JACKET
>WEST IS WEST AND OTHERS
>This is a play

## THE SLITHERING SHADOW
Alternate title: XUTHAL OF THE DUSK
Featuring CONAN
First appeared in WEIRD TALES, September 1933
>THE SWORD OF CONAN
>CONAN THE ADVENTURER
>THE CONAN CHRONICLES 2, Orbit
>THE SLITHERING SHADOW (Chpbk.)
>THE CONAN CHRONICLES I: THE PEOPLE OF THE BLACK CIRCLE, Millennium Fantasy Masterworks
>ROBERT E. HOWARD'S COMPLETE CONAN OF CIMMERIA, VOLUME 1

THE COMING OF CONAN THE CIMMERIAN
THE COMPLETE CHRONICLES OF CONAN
THE WEIRD WRITINGS OF ROBERT E. HOWARD, VOLUME ONE
THE VALLEY OF THE WORM: THE WEIRD WORKS OF ROBERT E. HOWARD, VOLUME 5

## SLUGGER BAIT
Alternate title: CIRCUS FISTS

## THE SLUGGER'S GAME
Featuring STEVE COSTIGAN
    First appeared in JACK DEMPSEY'S FIGHT MAGAZINE, May 1934
    REH'S FIGHT MAGAZINE #3 (Chpbk.)
    WATERFRONT FISTS AND OTHERS
    JACK DEMPSEY'S FIGHT MAGAZINE, MAY 1934 (Chpbk.)
    THE ROBERT E. HOWARD FOUNDATION NEWSLETTER, VOLUME 1, #2 (synopsis only)
    A short synopsis also exists for this story

## SLUGGERS OF THE BEACH
Featuring STEVE COSTIGAN
First appeared in JACK DEMPSEY'S FIGHT MAGAZINE, August 1934
    REH'S FIGHT MAGAZINE #3 (Chpbk.)
    WATERFRONT FISTS AND OTHERS
    THE ROBERT E. HOWARD FOUNDATION NEWSLETTER, VOLUME 1, #2 (synopsis only)
    A short synopsis also exists for this story

## THE SNOUT IN THE DARK
Featuring CONAN
First appeared in CONAN OF CIMMERIA (completed by LSDC and Lin Carter)
    JEWELS OF GWAHLUR (first appearance of fragment only)
    CROMLECH #3 (Chpbk., first appearance of the original synopsis)
    THE CONAN CHRONICLES 1, Sphere and Orbit (completed by LSDC and Lin Carter)
    THE CONAN CHRONICLES I: THE PEOPLE OF THE BLACK CIRCLE, Millennium Fantasy Masterworks
    THE COMPLETE CHRONICLES OF CONAN (draft)
    LSDC and Lin Carter finished this then-unpublished, unfinished story, which came with a synopsis for the
        remainder of the story

## SOLOMON KANE
Alternate title: RED SHADOWS

## SOME PEOPLE WHO HAVE HAD INFLUENCE OVER ME
First appeared in THE GHOST, May 1945
    ROBERT E. HOWARD—THE POWER OF THE WRITING MIND
    WEST IS WEST AND OTHERS
    Originally a high school theme

## SOMETHING ABOUT EVE
First appeared in AMRA, VOLUME 2, #47
    THE CONAN GRIMOIRE (Anth.)
    THE SPELL OF CONAN (Anth.)
    HORROR! 100 BEST BOOKS (Anth.)
    THE NEW HOWARD READER #1 (Chpbk.)
    THE BURKBURNETT PAPERS, February 2004 (Chpbk.)
    A review of the James Branch Cabell book

**SON OF THE WHITE WOLF**
Featuring EL BORAK
First appeared in THRILLING ADVENTURES, December 1936
  SON OF THE WHITE WOLF
  TREASURES OF TARTARY AND OTHERS
  ADVENTURE TALES #4
  THE "EL BORAK" STORIES - BLOOD OF THE GODS; THE DAUGHTER OF ERLIK KHAN; HAWK OF
    THE HILLS; SON OF THE WHITE WOLF; THE COUNTRY OF THE KNIFE
  THE GRIM LAND: THE BEST OF ROBERT E. HOWARD, VOLUME 2

**SONGS OF BASTARDS**
First appeared in LEWD TALES (Chpbk.)
  THE LAST OF THE TRUNK OCH BREV I URVAL (Chpbk.)
  THE COLLECTED LETTERS OF ROBERT E. HOWARD, VOLUME 1: 1923-1929
  This is a play; from a letter to TCS, ca. March 1929 ("Salaam: / Black Dawn"); also contains the following
    poems: Untitled ("I knocked upon her lattice – soft!"); Untitled ("Let us up in the hills . . ."); Untitled
    ("Life is a lot of hooey"); Untitled ("Men are toys . . .")

**THE SONORA KID—COWHAND**
Featuring THE SONORA KID
First appeared in THE SONORA KID (Chpbk.)

**THE SONORA KID'S WINNING HAND**
Featuring THE SONORA KID
First appeared in THE SONORA KID (Chpbk.)

**SONS OF HATE**
Featuring GORMAN & KIRBY
First appeared in TWO-FISTED DETECTIVE STORIES (Chpbk.)

**SONS OF THE HAWK**
Alternate title: THE COUNTRY OF THE KNIFE

**THE SOPHISTICATE**
First appeared in PAY DAY (Chpbk.)

**A SOUTH SEA STORM**
First appeared in THE LAST OF THE TRUNK OCH BREV I URVAL (Chpbk.)
  THE LAST OF THE TRUNK
  Unfinished; hand-written, and dated March 2, 1921

**THE SOWERS OF THE THUNDER**
First appeared in ORIENTAL STORIES, Winter 1932
  THE SOWERS OF THE THUNDER
  GATES OF EMPIRE AND OTHERS
  LORD OF SAMARCAND AND OTHER ADVENTURES OF THE OLD ORIENT
  ORIENTAL STORIES, WINTER 1932, Girasol Collectables (Chpbk.)
  THE COMPLETE ORIENTAL STORIES (Anth.)
  The story does not feature Cormac Fitzgeoffrey, but does mention him

## SPANISH GOLD ON DEVIL HORSE
First appeared in THE HOWARD COLLECTOR #17 (part 1 of 2)
>    THE HOWARD COLLECTOR #18 (part 2 of 2)
>    THE HOWARD COLLECTOR, Ace
>    THE NEW HOWARD READER #7 (Chpbk.)

## SPEAR AND FANG
First appeared in WEIRD TALES, July 1925
>    THE HOWARD COLLECTOR #7
>    WEIRD TALES, Summer 1973
>    EONS OF THE NIGHT
>    THE ULTIMATE TRIUMPH: THE HEROIC FANTASY OF ROBERT E. HOWARD
>    SHADOW KINGDOMS: THE WEIRD WORKS OF ROBERT E. HOWARD, VOLUME 1 (Wildside Press)
>    WEIRD TALES, JULY 1925, Girasol Collectables (Chpbk.)
>    THE WEIRD WRITINGS OF ROBERT E. HOWARD, VOLUME ONE

## SPEARS OF CLONTARF
Alternate titless: THE GREY GOD PASSES; THE TWILIGHT OF THE GREY GODS (both fantastic versions of
>    the same story)

Featuring TURLOGH DUBH O'BRIEN
First appeared in SPEARS OF CLONTARF, Hamilton (Chpbk.)
>    SPEARS OF CLONTARF, Dark Carneval (Chpbk.)
>    WRITER OF THE DARK
>    THE ULTIMATE TRIUMPH: THE HEROIC FANTASY OF ROBERT E. HOWARD
>    "Spears of Clontarf" was written in the second half of May 1931, submitted June 1st to Clayton Publications,
>    and rejected; REH tried it with ADVENTURE (June 19) and ARGOSY (July 1), to no avail; he
>    rewrote it sometime later in 1931 as "The Grey God Passes";.this was rejected it by WEIRD TALES
>    on December 28; REH recycled some elements of the story in "The Cairn on the Headland", which he
>    submitted - and sold - to Clayton Publications in January 1932, and which was subsequently published
>    in STRANGE TALES, January 1933

## SPEARS OF THE EAST
First appeared in THE GOLDEN CALIPH (Chpbk.)
>    THE LAST CELT

## SPECTRES IN THE DARK
First appeared in CROMLECH #1 (Chpbk.)
>    THE NEW HOWARD READER #2 (Chpbk.)

## THE SPELL OF DAMBALLAH
First appeared in REVELATIONS FROM YUGGOTH #1 (Chpbk.)
>    THE NEW HOWARD READER #4 (Chpbk.)

## THE SPIRIT OF BRIAN BORU
First appeared in LA TOMBE DU DRAGON (French)
>    THE NEW HOWARD READER #6 (Chpbk., in English)

## THE SPIRIT OF TOM MOLYNEAUX
Alternate title: APPARITION IN THE PRIZE RING

## THE SPLENDID BRUTE
First appeared in THE LAST OF THE TRUNK OCH BREV I URVAL (Chpbk.)
    THE LAST OF THE TRUNK
    Incomplete

## STAND UP AND SLUG!
Alternate title: WATERFRONT FISTS

## THE STONES OF DESTINY
First appeared in PULP MAGAZINE #1 (Chpbk.)
    THE NEW HOWARD READER #4 (Chpbk.)

## THE STRANGE CASE OF JOSIAH WILBARGER
Alternate title: APPARITION OF JOSIAH WILBARGER

## A STRANGER IN GRIZZLY CLAW
Alternate title: THE SCALP HUNTER

## THE STREET OF GREY BEARDS
Listed on a Kline Agency list of REH stories, listed as 6 pages long, don't know what happened to it

## THE STRIKING OF THE GONG
Alternate title: THE CHIMING OF THE GONG
Featuring KULL
First appeared in KING KULL
    THE SECOND BOOK OF ROBERT E. HOWARD (original text)
    KULL: THE FABULOUS WARRIOR KING
    KULL
    KULL: EXILE OF ATLANTIS
    The KING KULL edition versions are heavily edited by Lin Carter; originally submitted to ARGOSY, rejected;
        mentioned by REH as "The Chiming of the Gong" in a letter to TCS, ca. February 1929 ("Salaam: /
        Ancient English Balladel")

## STRIPED SHIRTS AND BUSTED HEARTS
Featuring BRECKINRIDGE ELKINS
First appeared in A GENT FROM BEAR CREEK (as Chapter 1)
    THE SUMMIT COUNTY JOURNAL, June 9, 16, 23, 30, 1967 (4-part serial)
    THE SUMMIT COUNTY JOURNAL, April 5, 12, 19, 26; May 3, 10, 1968 (6-part serial)
    HEROES OF BEAR CREEK
    THE SUMMIT COUNTY JOURNAL appearance changed the name to "Breckenridge", to be like the town it
        was published in

## A STUDENT OF SOCKOLOGY
Alternate title: COLLEGE SOCKS

## SUCKER!
Alternate title: WINNER TAKE ALL

## SUNDAY IN A SMALL TOWN
First appeared in THE HOWARD COLLECTOR #11
    THE HOWARD COLLECTOR, Ace
    THE NEW HOWARD READER #7 (Chpbk.)

## THE SUPREME MOMENT
First appeared in CRYPT OF CTHULHU #25 (Chpbk.)
  THE NEW HOWARD READER #1 (Chpbk.)

## SURRENDER—YOUR MONEY OR YOUR VICE
First appeared in THE JUNTO, September 1928
  TRUMPET #7 (Chpbk.)
  THE ROAD TO VELITRIUM #30 (Chpbk.)
  THE NEW HOWARD READER #7 (Chpbk.)
  Some movie reviews

## THE SWORD
First appeared in THE GOLDEN CALIPH (Chpbk.)
  THE LAST CELT

## SWORD WOMAN
Featuring AGNES DE CHASTILLON
First appeared in REH: LONE STAR FICTIONEER #2
  THE SECOND BOOK OF ROBERT E. HOWARD
  SWORD WOMAN
  Also contains the poems "Drums in My Ears" and "The Ballad of Dark Agnes", as verse headings for Chapters
    3 & 4, respectively.

## SWORDS OF SHAHRAZAR
Alternate title: THE TREASURE OF SHAIBAR KHAN
Featuring KIRBY O'DONNELL
First appeared in TOP-NOTCH, October 1934
  SWORDS OF SHAHRAZAR (FAX edition is titled THE SWORDS OF SHAHRAZAR)
  ROBERT E. HOWARD'S WORLD OF HEROES (as "The Treasure of Shaibar Khan")
  BLOOD OF THE GODS AND OTHER STORIES

## SWORDS OF THE HILLS
Alternate title: THE LOST VALLEY OF ISKANDER

## SWORDS OF THE NORTHERN SEA
Featuring CORMAC MAC ART
First appeared in TIGERS OF THE SEA
  CORMAC MAC ART, Baen

## SWORDS OF THE PURPLE KINGDOM
Featuring KULL
  First appeared in KING KULL
  REALMS OF WIZARDRY (Anth.)
  KULL: THE FABULOUS WARRIOR KING
  A TREASURY OF FANTASY (Anth.)
  KULL
  KULL: EXILE OF ATLANTIS

## SWORDS OF THE RED BROTHERHOOD
Featuring TERENCE VULMEA
First appeared in BLACK VULMEA'S VENGEANCE
  REH's rewrite of "The Black Stranger", a Conan story, trying to sell it to an adventure-type pulp as a Black
    Vulmea pirate story

**THE TALE OF AM-RA**
First appeared in THE NEW HOWARD READER #2 (Chpbk.)
    KULL: EXILE OF ATLANTIS
    Unfinished

**THE TALE OF THE RAJAH'S RING**
Featuring LAL SINGH
First appeared in THE ADVENTURES OF LAL SINGH (Chpbk.)

**TALLYHO!**
First appeared in THE DARK MAN, VOLUME 3, #1

**TALONS IN THE DARK**
Alternate title: BLACK TALONS

**TAVEREL MANOR**
Alternate title: THE RETURN OF SKULL-FACE

**TEETH OF DOOM**
Alternate title: THE TOMB'S SECRET

**THE TEETH OF GWAHLUR**
Alternate title: JEWELS OF GWAHLUR

**THE TEMPLE OF ABOMINATION**
Featuring CORMAC MAC ART
First appeared in TIGERS OF THE SEA (completed by Richard Tierney)
    SAVAGE HEROES, TALES OF SORCERY & BLACK MAGIC (Anth., completed by Richard Tierney)
    THE YEAR'S BEST FANTASY STORIES (Anth., completed by Richard Tierney)
    SAVAGE HEROES, TALES OF MAGICAL FANTASY (Anth., completed by Richard Tierney)
    CORMAC MAC ART, Baen (first appearance of original version, both the "long version" as well as the
        outline)

**TEMPTRESS OF THE TOWER OF TORTURE AND SIN**
Alternate title: THE VOICE OF EL-LIL

**TEN MINUTES ON A STREET CORNER**
First appeared in THE LAST OF THE TRUNK OCH BREV I URVAL (Chpbk.)
    THE LAST OF THE TRUNK
    Hand-written, undated

**TEXAS FISTS**
Alternate title: SHANGHIED MITTS
Featuring STEVE COSTIGAN
First appeared in FIGHT STORIES, May 1931
    FIGHT STORIES, Summer, 1939 (as "Shanghied Mitts", author listed as "Mark Adam")
    REH'S FIGHT MAGAZINE #2
    WATERFRONT FISTS AND OTHERS
    BOXING STORIES

**TEXAS JOHN ALDEN**
Alternate title: A RINGTAILED TORNADO
Featuring BRECKINRIDGE ELKINS (PIKE BEARFIELD)

First appeared in MASKED RIDER WESTERN, May 1944
    HOPALONG CASSIDY'S WESTERN MAGAZINE, Fall 1950
    TOP WESTERN FICTION ANNUAL, 1952
    THE PRIDE OF BEAR CREEK (as "A Ringtailed Tornado")
    HEROES OF BEAR CREEK (as "A Ringtailed Tornado")
    A GENT FROM BEAR CREEK AND OTHERS
    This was originally a Pike Bearfield story, the Klein agency, likely OAK himself, significantly rewrote it to turn it into a Breckinridge Elkins story, altering town and character names, added some material, lots of inconsistencies; original REH title was "A Ring-Tailed Tornado"; Grant removed all the italics, which was carried over in HEROES OF BEAR CREEK; italics restored in A GENT FROM BEAR CREEK AND OTHERS

## A TEXAS PRODIGAL
Alternate title: KNIFE-RIVER PRODIGAL

## THE TEXAS WILDCAT
Alternate title: THE WILDCAT AND THE STAR

## THEM
First appeared in TRUMPET #7 (Chpbk.)
    THE NEW HOWARD READER #1 (Chpbk.)
    THE ROAD TO VELITRIUM #30 (Chpbk.)

## THE THESSALIANS
First appeared in THE YELLOW JACKET, January 13, 1927
    THE HOWARD COLLECTOR #6
    THE HOWARD COLLECTOR, Ace
    THE NEW HOWARD READER #4 (Chpbk.)
    THE COMPLETE YELLOW JACKET
    WEST IS WEST AND OTHERS

## THEY ALWAYS COME BACK
First appeared in THE IRON MAN
    THE IRON MAN, WITH THE ADVENTURES OF DENNIS DORGAN
    BOXING STORIES

## THE THING ON THE ROOF
First appeared in WEIRD TALES, February 1932
    THE DARK MAN AND OTHERS
    HORROR HUNTERS (Anth.)
    THE SIXTH MAYFLOWER BOOK OF BLACK MAGIC STORIES (Anth.)
    THE DARK MAN OMNIBUS, VOLUME 2
    CTHULHU THE MYTHOS AND KINDRED HORRORS
    NAMELESS CULTS
    TALES OF THE LOVECRAFT MYTHOS (Anth.)
    PEOPLE OF THE DARK: THE WEIRD WORKS OF ROBERT E. HOWARD, VOLUME 3
    THE WEIRD WRITINGS OF ROBERT E. HOWARD, VOLUME ONE

## THOROUGHBREDS
First appeared in LA TOMBE DU DRAGON (French)
    THE HOWARD REVIEW #11 (Chpbk.)

## THREE PERILS OF SAILOR COSTIGAN
Featuring STEVE COSTIGAN
First appeared in THE HOWARD REVIEW #2 (Chpbk.)
> This is three unfinished stories, all previously unpublished, they are: untitled story ("I had just hung by sparring partner, Battling O'Toole . . ."); untitled story ("It was the end of the fourth round."); untitled story ("The night Sailor Steve Costigan fought Battling O'Rourke . . .")

## THREE-BLADED DOOM
Alternate title: THE FLAME KNIFE
Featuring EL BORAK
First appeared in REH: LONE STAR FICTIONEER #4 (short version)
> THREE-BLADED DOOM (long version)
> THE NEW HOWARD READER #7 (Chpbk., short version)
> There is both a long (42,000 words) and a short (24,000 words) version of this story; LSDC created a derivative Conan work based on the long version, "The Flame Knife"; records from the Kline Agency also say there is a 12 page version of this story, much shorter than the known two versions

## THROUGH THE AGES
First appeared in THE LAST OF THE TRUNK OCH BREV I URVAL (Chpbk.)
> THE LAST OF THE TRUNK
> Unfinished

## A THUNDER OF TRUMPETS
By Robert E. Howard & Frank Thurston Torbett
First appeared in WEIRD TALES, September 1938
> THE HOWARD REVIEW #1 (Chpbk.)
> MARCHERS OF VALHALLA, Sphere and Berkley
> ROBERT E. HOWARD'S STRANGE TALES
> THE WEIRD WRITINGS OF ROBERT E. HOWARD, VOLUME TWO
> Torbett was the son of Dr. Frank Torbett, who worked in John Walter Torbett Sr's Sanatorium in Marlin, TX; REH sent letters from there in 1923 and 1932, and even mentioned Thurston in that latter letter; Torbett originated the plot and wrote a rough draft for the story; REH polished this up, introducing some changes in the trend of the story; the hero of this story, Ranjit Bhatarka, appears to be similar to Khemsa, the young magician in "The People of the Black Circle"; Torbett died in 1982

## THE THUNDER-RIDER
First appeared in MARCHERS OF VALHALLA, Grant
> MARCHERS OF VALHALLA, Sphere and Berkley
> THE BLACK STRANGER AND OTHER AMERICAN TALES
> One of the very last stories REH wrote, as the original is on a yellow paper that REH acquired in 1936 and used for his last stories

## TIGERS OF THE SEA
Featuring CORMAC MAC ART
First appeared in TIGERS OF THE SEA (completed to Richard Tierney)
> CORMAC MAC ART, Baen (completed by David Drake)
> This is a fragment

## THE TNT PUNCH
Alternate titles: WATERFRONT LAW; THE WATERFRONT WALLOP
Featuring STEVE COSTIGAN
First appeared in ACTION STORIES, January 1931
> FIGHT STORIES, Fall, 1941 (as "The Waterfront Wallop", author listed as "Mark Adam")

THE HOWARD REVIEW #4 (Chpbk.)
ROBERT E. HOWARD FIGHT MAGAZINE #2 (Chpbk.)
THE COMPLETE ACTION STORIES
BOXING STORIES (as "Waterfront Law")

## TO A MAN WHOSE NAME I NEVER KNEW
First appeared in TRUMPET #7 (Chpbk.)
     THE NEW HOWARD READER #2 (Chpbk.)
     THE ROAD TO VELITRIUM #30 (Chpbk.)

## THE TOM THUMB MOIDER MYSTERY
First appeared in THE COLLECTED LETTERS OF ROBERT E. HOWARD, VOLUME 2: 1930-1932
     From a letter to TCS, ca. May 1932 ("Fear Finn: / Lo, friend, I approach . . .")

## TOM SHARKEY—MANKILLER
A story that REH said he wrote, but no copy exists

## THE TOMB OF THE DRAGON
First appeared in THE SHADOW OF THE BEAST (Chpbk.)
     A Mike Dorgan / Bill McGlory story

## THE TOMB'S SECRET
Alternate title: TEETH OF DOOM
Featuring BROCK ROLLINS
First appeared in STRANGE DETECTIVE STORIES, February 1934 (author listed as "Patrick Ervin")
     WRITER OF THE DARK (as "The Teeth of Doom", hero changed back to Steve Harrison)
     PULP REVIEW #17 (photocopy of original)
     GRAVEYARD RATS AND OTHERS
     ROBERT E. HOWARD: WORLD'S GREATEST PULPSTER #1
     THE HOWARD REVIEW #12 (Chpbk.)
     Originally was written as a Steve Harrison story, STRANGE DETECTIVE wanted to run it in the same issue
          with another Steve Harrison, so they change the author to "Patrick Ervin", and the hero to Brock
          Rollins

## A TOUCH OF COLOR
First appeared in PAY DAY (Chpbk.)
     REH: TWO-GUN RACONTEUR #11

## THE TOUCH OF DEATH
Alternate title: THE FEARSOME TOUCH OF DEATH

## A TOUCH OF TRIVIA
First appeared in THE LAST CELT
     THE NEW HOWARD READER #8 (Chpbk.)

## A TOUGH NUT TO CRACK
Featuring KID ALLISON
First appeared in THE LAST OF THE TRUNK OCH BREV I URVAL (Chpbk.)
     THE LAST OF THE TRUNK

**THE TOWER OF THE ELEPHANT**
Featuring CONAN
First appeared in WEIRD TALES, March 1933
>     SKULL-FACE AND OTHERS
>     THE COMING OF CONAN
>     CONAN
>     SKULL-FACE OMNIBUS
>     TOWER OF THE ELEPHANT, Grant and Grossett & Dunlap
>     SKULL-FACE OMNIBUS, VOLUME 3
>     THE TOWER OF THE ELEPHANT, Moondance Records (Chpbk.)
>     THIRTEEN TALES OF TERROR (Anth.)
>     THE BARBARIAN SWORDSMEN (Anth.)
>     THE CONAN CHRONICLES 1, Sphere and Orbit
>     THE OXFORD BOOK OF FANTASY STORIES (Anth.)
>     THE PRENTICE HALL ANTHOLOGY OF SCIENCE FICTION AND FANTASY (Anth.)
>     THE CONAN CHRONICLES I: THE PEOPLE OF THE BLACK CIRCLE, Millennium Fantasy Masterworks
>     ROBERT E. HOWARD'S COMPLETE CONAN OF CIMMERIA, VOLUME 1
>     THE COMING OF CONAN THE CIMMERIAN
>     WINGS IN THE NIGHT: THE WEIRD WORKS OF ROBERT E. HOWARD, VOLUME 4
>     THE COMPLETE CHRONICLES OF CONAN
>     THE WEIRD WRITINGS OF ROBERT E. HOWARD, VOLUME ONE
>     THE PHOENIX ON THE SWORD (Chpbk.)
>     FIVE TALES OF CONAN THE BARBARIAN
>     THE GRIM LAND: THE BEST OF ROBERT E. HOWARD, VOLUME 2

**THE TOWER OF TIME**
Alternate title: AKRAM THE MYSTERIOUS
Featuring JAMES ALLISON
First appeared in FANTASTIC STORIES, June 1975 (completed by Lin Carter)
>     THE NEW HOWARD READER #2 (Chpbk., original fragment)

**THE TOY RATTLE MURDER CASE**
First appeared in THE COLLECTED LETTERS OF ROBERT E. HOWARD, VOLUME 2: 1930-1932
>     From a letter to TCS, May 1932 ("Fear Finn: / Thank you very much . . .")

**THE TRACK OF BOHEMUND**
>     First appeared in THE ROAD OF AZRAEL
>     LORD OF SAMARCAND AND OTHER ADVENTURES OF THE OLD ORIENT

**TRAIL OF THE BLOODSTAINED GOD**
Alternate titles: THE CURSE OF THE CRIMSON GOD; THE BLOODSTAINED GOD

**THE TRAIL OF THE DINOSAUR**
Alternate title: THE LAND OF FORGOTTEN AGES; THE TRAIL OF THE MAMMOTH

**THE TRAIL OF THE MAMMOTH**
Alternate title: THE LAND OF FORGOTTEN AGES; THE TRAIL OF THE DINOSAUR

**THE TRAIL OF THE SINGLE FOOT**
A story that REH said he wrote, but no copy exists

**TRAIL OF THE SNAKE**
First appeared in THE LAST OF THE TRUNK OCH BREV I URVAL (Chpbk.)
    THE LAST OF THE TRUNK

**THE TREASURE OF HENRY MORGAN**
First appeared in THE LAST OF THE TRUNK OCH BREV I URVAL (Chpbk.)
    THE LAST OF THE TRUNK
    Unfinished

**THE TREASURE OF SHAIBAR KHAN**
Alternate title: SWORDS OF SHAHRAZAR

**THE TREASURE OF TRANICOS**
Alternate title: THE BLACK STRANGER

**THE TREASURES OF TARTARY**
Alternate title: GOLD FROM TARTARY
Featuring KIRBY O'DONNELL
First appeared in THRILLING ADVENTURES, January 1935
    SWORDS OF SHAHRAZAR (all editions)
    TREASURES OF TARTARY AND OTHERS

**THE TURKISH MENACE**
Alternate title: SAILOR DORGAN AND THE TURKISH MENACE
Featuring DENNIS DORGAN
First appeared in THE INCREDIBLE ADVENTURES OF DENNIS DORGAN (completed by Darrell C.
    Richardson)
    THE IRON MAN, WITH THE ADVENTURES OF DENNIS DORGAN (completed by Darrell C. Richardson)
    THE NEW HOWARD READER #8 (Chpbk.)
    Original typescript lists author as "Patrick Ervin", a pseudonym REH used in connection with his Dennis
        Dorgan stories; story also includes Mike Dorgan (here called "Leary") and Bill McGlory; story was
        accepted by MAGIC CARPET MAGAZINE, but never got published; when the typescript
        was found, several pages were missing, including pages3, 21, and ten out of the middle of the story;
        this incomplete story was completed by Darrell C. Richardson

**TWENTIETH CENTURY SLAVE TRADE**
First appeared in THE RIGHT HOOK, VOLUME 1, #1 (Chpbk.)
    AUSTIN, VOLUME 3, #2 (Chpbk.)
    ROBERT E. HOWARD—THE POWER OF THE WRITING MIND

**A TWENTIETH-CENTURY RIP VAN WINKLE**
First appeared in THE LAST OF THE TRUNK OCH BREV I URVAL (Chpbk.)
    THE LAST OF THE TRUNK
    Hand-written, and dated October 13, 1920

**THE TWILIGHT OF THE GREY GODS**
Alternate title: THE GREY GOD PASSES

**TWO AGAINST TYRE**
First appeared in THE HOWARD COLLECTOR #12
      TWO AGAINST TYRE (Chpbk.)
      THE SECOND BOOK OF ROBERT E. HOWARD
      THE HOWARD COLLECTOR, Ace
      LORD OF SAMARCAND AND OTHER ADVENTURES OF THE OLD ORIENT


**TWO WRONGS MAKE A WRIGHT**
A story that REH said he wrote, but no copy exists


**A TWO-FISTED SANTA CLAUS**
Alternate title: PLAYING SANTA CLAUS


**UNDER THE BAOBAB TREE**
First appeared in CROSS PLAINS #5
      THE NEW HOWARD READER #4 (Chpbk.)
      REH: TWO GUN RACONTEUR #6


**UNDER THE GREAT TIGER**
By Robert E. Howard & Tevis Clyde Smith
First appeared as a 2-part serial in THE ALL-AROUND MAGAZINE: #3-4, May-June 1923; and #5, July 1923
      REPORT ON A WRITING MAN (Chpbk., facsimile of original publication)
      Unfinished


**UNHAND ME, VILLIAN**
First appeared in THE TATTLER, February 15, 1923
      THE NEW HOWARD READER #6 (Chpbk.)
      WEST IS WEST AND OTHERS


**A UNIQUE HAT**
First appeared in THE LAST OF THE TRUNK OCH BREV I URVAL (Chpbk.)
      THE LAST OF THE TRUNK


**UNTITLED ("'Arrange, Madam, arrange!'")**
First appeared in THE LAST OF THE TRUNK OCH BREV I URVAL (Chpbk.)
      THE LAST OF THE TRUNK
      Unfinished


**UNTITLED ("As he approached the two, he swept off his feathered hat . . .")**
First appeared in THE LAST OF THE TRUNK OCH BREV I URVAL (Chpbk.)
      THE LAST OF THE TRUNK
      Incomplete; two untitled poems embodied in this story HAVE been published, titled "Trail's End" and
            "Shadow Thing"


**UNTITLED ("As my dear public remembers . . .")**
First appeared in THE COLLECTED LETTERS OF ROBERT E. HOWARD, VOLUME 3: 1933-1936
      From a letter to TCS, undated ("Salaam: / As my dear public remembers . . .")


**UNTITLED ("The battlefield stretched silent . . .")**
Alternate title: THE HAND OF NERGAL

**UNTITLED ("Beneath the glare of the sun . . .")**
Alternate title: BLACK EONS
First appeared in THE HOWARD COLLECTOR #9 (as an untitled fragment)
    THE HOWARD COLLECTOR, Ace
    FANTASY BOOK #16, June 1985 (completed by Robert M. Price, and titled "Black Eons")
    THE NEW HOWARD READER #6 (Chpbk.)
    NAMELESS CULTS (Price-completed version)
    This is a fragment; featured a character named James Allison, but not the same as the past lives character

**UNTITLED ("Better a man should remain in kindly ignorance, than . . .")**
Unfinished, unpublished

**UNTITLED ("Between berserk battle-rages, the black despair of melancholy . . .")**
Unfinished, unpublished

**UNTITLED ("A blazing sun in a blazing sky, reflected from . . .")**
Featuring THE SONORA KID
First appeared in THE SONORA KID (Chpbk.)
    Unfinished

**UNTITLED ("A Cossack and a Turk . . .")**
First appeared in THE GOLDEN CALIPH (Chpbk.)
    THE LAST CELT

**UNTITLED ("The Dane came in with a rush, hurtling his huge body forward . . .")**
Featuring TURLOGH DUBH O'BRIEN
First appeared in SHADOW OF THE HUN (Chpbk.)
    REH: TWO-GUN RACONTEUR #4
    UNAUSSPRECHLICHEN KULTEN #2 (Chpbk.)
    THE NEW HOWARD READER #3 (Chpbk.)

**UNTITLED (" . . . determined. So I set out up the hill-trail as if on a hunt and . . .")**
First appeared in KULL: EXILE OF ATLANTIS
    Incomplete

**UNTITLED ("First Draft: James Norris.")**
First appeared in THE LAST OF THE TRUNK OCH BREV I URVAL (Chpbk.)
    THE LAST OF THE TRUNK
    Incomplete; THE LAST CELT had listed a portion of this as Untitled ("Joe Rogers had been working the stock
        market.")

**UNTITLED ("The flaming sun of the year 2000 . . .")**
Alternate title: THE LAST MAN

**UNTITLED ("Franey was a fool.")**
First appeared in THE LAST OF THE TRUNK OCH BREV I URVAL (Chpbk.)
    THE LAST OF THE TRUNK
    Incomplete

**UNTITLED ("From the black, bandit-haunted mountains of Kang . . .")**
Unfinished, unpublished

**UNTITLED ("Gordon, the American whom the Arabs call El Borak, . . .")**

Featuring EL BORAK
First appeared in EL BORAK L'ETERNEL (French)
 THE COMING OF EL BORAK (Chpbk.)
 Unfinished

## UNTITLED ("A gray sky arched . . .")
Featuring BRAN MAK MORN
First appeared in BRAN MAK MORN, Dell
 WORMS OF THE EARTH
 BARN MAK MORN, Baen
 BRAN MAK MORN – THE LAST KING

## UNTITLED ("The Hades Saloon and gambling hall, Buffalotown, . . .")
Featuring THE SONORA KID
First appeared in THE SONORA KID (Chpbk.)
 Incomplete

## UNTITLED ("'Hatrack!'")
First appeared in THE LAST OF THE TRUNK OCH BREV I URVAL (Chpbk.)
 THE COLLECTED LETTERS OF ROBERT E. HOWARD, VOLUME 1: 1923-1929
 From a letter to TCS, ca. March 1929 ("Salaam: / Black Dawn")

## UNTITLED ("He knew De Bracy, they having fought against the Saracens . . .")
First appeared in LORD OF SAMARCAND AND OTHER ADVENTURES OF THE OLD ORIENT
 Unfinished

## UNTITLED ("'Help! Help! They're murderin' me!'")
Unfinished, unpublished

## UNTITLED ("Hernando de Guzman: . . .")
First appeared in THE ROBERT E. HOWARD FOUNDATION NEWSLETTER, VOLUME 1, #2 (synopsis only)
 A short biographical piece, setting up how this character will be used in "Nekht Semerkeht"

## UNTITLED ("The hot Arizona sun had not risen high enough to heat . . .")
Featuring THE SONORA KID
First appeared in THE SONORA KID (Chpbk.)
 Unfinished

## UNTITLED ("'Huh?' I was so dumbfounded I was clean off . . .")
Featuring KID ALLISON
First appeared in THE LAST OF THE TRUNK OCH BREV I URVAL (Chpbk.)
 THE LAST OF THE TRUNK
 Incomplete, consisted of pages 10-14 of 14 page manuscript

## UNTITLED ("Hunwulf, an American . . .")
First appeared in THE LAST OF THE TRUNK OCH BREV I URVAL (Chpbk.)
 THE LAST OF THE TRUNK
 Incomplete; this is a synopsis

## UNTITLED ("I am a man of few words . . .")
Alternate title: SHACKLED MITTS

**UNTITLED ("I had just hung by sparring partner, Battling O'Toole . . .")**
First appeared in THE HOWARD REVIEW #2 (Chpbk.)
   Fragment, appeared under the title "Three Perils of Sailor Costigan", which was this unfinished story and two
      others, untitled story ("It was the end of the fourth round."), and untitled story ("The night Sailor Steve
      Costigan fought Battling O'Rourke . . .")

**UNTITLED ("I have been . . .")**
Alternate title: WEEKLY SHORT STORY

**UNTITLED ("I met him first in the Paradise saloon.")**
First appeared in THE LAST OF THE TRUNK OCH BREV I URVAL (Chpbk.)
   THE LAST OF THE TRUNK
   Unfinished

**UNTITLED ("I remember a most curious dream . . .")**
Alternate title: A DREAM

**UNTITLED ("'I', said Cuchulain, 'was a man, at least.'")**
Unfinished, unpublished

**UNTITLED ("I'm writing this with a piece of pencil on the backs of old . . .")**
Unfinished, unpublished

**UNTITLED ("It was a strange experience, and I don't expect anyone . . .")**
Unfinished, unpublished

**UNTITLED ("It was the end of the fourth round.")**
Featuring STEVE COSTIGAN
First appeared in THE HOWARD REVIEW #2 (Chpbk.)
   REH'S FIGHT MAGAZINE #4 (Chpbk.)
   Unfinished; appeared in THE HOWARD REVIEW #2 under the title "Three Perils of Sailor Costigan", which
      was this unfinished story and two others, untitled story ("I had just hung by sparring partner, Battlin'
      O'Toole, . . ."), and untitled story ("The night Sailor Steve Costigan fought Battling O'Rourke . . .")

**UNTITLED ("John Gorman found himself in Samarkand, . . .")**
Alternate title: SHE-CATS OF SAMARKAND
First appeared in RISQUE STORIES #1 (Chpbk.)
   THE NEW HOWARD REVIEW #4 (Chpbk.)
   This is a synopsis; RISQUE STORIES includes both the original synopsis as well as a short story with the
      author listed as "Sam Walser", but actually written by Charles Hoffman and Marc A. Cerasini based
      on the original synopsis; the SHE-CATS name was also applied to the synopsis in THE NEW
      HOWARD REVIEW #4

**UNTITLED ("John L. Sullivan knocked out Ryan . . .")**
Unpublished; a ficticious fight between John Jeffries and Jack Dempsey; Jeffries wins

**UNTITLED ("Knute Hansen")**
Unpublished; notes for a ficticious boxing tournament, in which Steve Brennon, at 7 feet and 310 lbs, wins; mostly
      just notes on various fictional fighters and how they compare

**UNTITLED ("A land of wild, fantastic beauty; of mighty trees . . .")**
First appeared in KULL: EXILE OF ATLANTIS
    Unfinished

**UNTITLED ("The lazy quiet of the mid-summer day was shattered . . .")**
First appeared in THE LAST OF THE TRUNK OCH BREV I URVAL (Chpbk.)
    THE LAST OF THE TRUNK
    Unfinished

**UNTITLED ("Long, long ago a son was born . . .")**
Alternate titles: GENSERIC'S FIFTH BORN SON; GHOR, KIN-SLAYER; GENSERIC'S SON

**UNTITLED ("Madge Meraldson set her traveling-bag on the station . . .")**
Featuring THE SONORA KID
First appeared in THE SONORA KID (Chpbk.)
    Fragment

**UNTITLED ("'A man', said my friend Larry Aloysius O'Leary . . .")**
First appeared in THE LAST OF THE TRUNK OCH BREV I URVAL (Chpbk.)
    THE LAST OF THE TRUNK
    Unfinished

**UNTITLED ("The matter seemed so obvious that my only answer . . .")**
Incomplete, unpublished

**UNTITLED ("Maybe it don't seem like anything interesting and . . .")**
First appeared in THE LAST OF THE TRUNK OCH BREV I URVAL (Chpbk.)
    THE LAST OF THE TRUNK
    Unfinished

**UNTITLED ("Men have had vision ere now.")**
Alternate title: THE WHEEL TURNS
First appeared in BRAN MAK MORN – THE LAST KING, Del Rey ONLY
    Unfinished

**UNTITLED ("Mike Costigan, writer and self-avowed futilist, gazed . . .")**
First appeared in THE LAST OF THE TRUNK OCH BREV I URVAL (Chpbk.)
    THE LAST OF THE TRUNK
    Unfinished

**UNTITLED ("MUNN! MUNN! . . .")**
First Appeared in THE RIGHT HOOK, VOLUME1, #2 (Chpbk.)
    AUSTIN, VOLUME 3, #2 (Chpbk.)
    This is an article

**UNTITLED ("My name is Sam Culotte.")**
First appeared in THE RIGHT HOOK, VOLUME 1, #3 (Chpbk.)
    AUSTIN, VOLUME 3, #2 (Chpbk.)

**UNTITLED ("The next day I was sluggish and inefficient in my work.")**
Incomplete, unpublished

**UNTITLED ("The night Sailor Steve Costigan fought Battling O'Rourke . . .")**
Featuring STEVE COSTIGAN
First appeared in THE HOWARD REVIEW #2 (Chpbk.)
    REH'S FIGHT MAGAZINE #4 (Chpbk.)
    Fragment; appeared in THE HOWARD REVIEW #2 under the title "Three Perils of Sailor Costigan", which
        was this unfinished story and two others, untitled story ("It was the end of the fourth round."), and
        untitled story ("I had just hung my sparring partner, Battlin' O'Toole . . .")

**UNTITLED ("The night was damp, misty, the air possessing a certain . . .")**
First appeared in FANTASY CROSSROADS #7
    THE NEW HOWARD READER #1 (Chpbk.)
    Incomplete

**UNTITLED ("'No place for a girl,' I growled . . .")**
Alternate title: THE LION GATE

**UNTITLED ("Old Man Jacobsen crunched his powerful teeth through . . .")**
Unfinished, unpublished

**UNTITLED ("The Persians had all fled . . .")**
First appeared in LORD OF SAMARCAND AND OTHER ADVENTURE TALES OF THE OLD ORIENT
    Unfinished

**UNTITLED ("Ring fans will recall . . .")**
Alternate title: THE MARK OF A BLOODY HAND

**UNTITLED ("The rising sun was behind the wild figure.")**
Alternate title: THE LAST LAUGH

**UNTITLED ("The Seeker thrust . . .")**
First appeared in THE LAST OF THE TRUNK OCH BREV I URVAL (Chpbk.)
    THE ROBERT E. HOWARD FOUNDATION NEWSLETTER, VOLUME 1, #2
    THE COLLECTED LETTERS OF ROBERT E. HOWARD, VOLUME 3: 1933-1936
    From a letter to TCS, undated ("The Seeker Thrust . . .")

**UNTITLED ("Sir Haldred Taverel . . .")**
Alternate titles: THE RETURN OF SKULL-FACE; TAVEREL MANOR

**UNTITLED ("So there I was.")**
First appeared in THE LAST OF THE TRUNK OCH BREV I URVAL (Chpbk.)
    THE LAST OF THE TRUNK
    Incomplete

**UNTITLED ("Spike Morissey was as tough a kid as ever came . . .")**
Fragment, unpublished

**UNTITLED ("Steve Allison settled himself down comfortably in . . .")**
Featuring THE SONORA KID
First appeared in THE SONORA KID (Chpbk.)
    Unfinished

**UNTITLED ("Steve Harrison received a wire from Joan Wiltshaw.")**
Featuring STEVE HARRISON
First appeared in TWO-FISTED DETECTIVE STORIES (Chpbk.)
      This is a synopsis

**UNTITLED ("The story begins with Gorm . . .")**
Alternate title: THE GUARDIAN OF THE IDOL

**UNTITLED ("The story of a forgotten age . . .")**
Alternate title: BRAN MAK MORN

**UNTITLED ("The tale has always been doubted and scoffed at, . . .")**
Fragment, unpublished

**UNTITLED (". . . that is, the artistry is but a symbol for the thought!")**
First appeared in THE LAST OF THE TRUNK OCH BREV I URVAL (Chpbk.)
      THE LAST OF THE TRUNK
      Incomplete, unfinished

**UNTITLED ("This is the tale of Shaitan Khan, . . .")**
Alternate title: THE BRAND OF SATAN

**UNTITLED ("Three men sat at a . . .")**
Alternate title WIZARD AND WARRIOR
Featuring KULL
First appeared in KULL: THE FABULOUS WARRIOR KING
      KULL
      KULL: EXILE OF ATLANTIS
      This fragment was completed by Lin Carter, and titled "Wizard and Warrior", which first appeared in KING
            KULL; Carter's portion begins with "It was the Sungara . . ."; the Bantam edition was the first
            appearance of just the fragment

**UNTITLED ("Thure Khan gazed out across the shifting vastness . . .")**
First appeared in THE LAST OF THE TRUNK OCH BREV I URVAL (Chpbk.)
      THE LAST OF THE TRUNK
      Unfinished

**UNTITLED ("'Thus', said Tu, . . .")**
Alternate title: RIDERS BEYOND THE SUNRISE
Featuring KULL
First appeared in KULL: THE FABULOUS WARRIOR KING
      KULL
      KULL: EXILE OF ATLANTIS
      This fragment was completed by Lin Carter as "Riders Beyond the Sunrise", first appearing in KING KULL;
            Carter's portion begins with the paragraph "'Safety!', Kull grunted.", and ends with the paragraph "A
            feral light", and begins again with "'Then come, king.'"; the Bantam edition was the first publication
            of just the fragment; REH left no notes as to how the story should end

**UNTITLED ("Trail led through dense jungle.")**
First appeared in THE LAST OF THE TRUNK OCH BREV I URVAL (Chpbk.)
      THE LAST OF THE TRUNK
      Fragment

**UNTITLED ("Tumba Hooey.")**
First appeared in THE LAST OF THE TRUNK OCH BREV I URVAL (Chpbk.)
    THE COLLECTED LETTERS OF ROBERT E. HOWARD, VOLUME 1: 1923-1929
    From a letter to TCS, November 1928 ("Salaam: / I got such a laugh . . .")

**UNTITLED ("Two men were standing in the bazaar at Delhi.")**
First appeared in THE LAST OF THE TRUNK OCH BREV I URVAL (Chpbk.)
    THE LAST OF THE TRUNK
    Unfinished

**UNTITLED ("A typical small town drugstore . . .")**
First appeared in THE LAST OF THE TRUNK OCH BREV I URVAL (Chpbk.)
    THE COLLECTED LETTERS OF ROBERT E. HOWARD, VOLUME 1: 1923-1929
    A play; from a letter to TCS, ca. February 1928 ("The fellow who wrote The Kasidah . . .")

**UNTITLED ("The way it came about that Steve Allison, Timoleon . . .")**
Featuring THE SONORA KID
Alternate title: THE MOUNTAINS OF THIBET
First appeared in THE SONORA KID (Chpbk.)
    Unfinished

**UNTITLED ("When Yar Ali Khan crept into the camp of Zumal Khan, . . .")**
First appeared in THE LAST OF THE TRUNK OCH BREV I URVAL (Chpbk.)
    THE LAST OF THE TRUNK
    Unfinished

**UNTITLED (". . . which has characterized . . .")**
Alternate title: THE CELTICA NOTES OF ROBERT E. HOWARD

**UNTITLED ("Who I am it matters little.")**
First appeared in THE LAST OF THE TRUNK OCH BREV I URVAL (Chpbk.)
    THE LAST OF THE TRUNK
    Unfinished

**UNTITLED ("William Aloysius McGraw's father was red-headed and . . .")**
Featuring STEVE BENDER, WEARY McGREW and THE WHALE
First appeared in THE LAST OF THE TRUNK OCH BREV I URVAL (Chpbk.)
    THE LAST OF THE TRUNK
    Unfinished

**UNTITLED ("The wind from the Mediterranean wafted. . .")**
First appeared in AMRA, VOLUME 2, #7
    THE CONAN GRIMOIRE (Anth.)
    THE SPELL OF CONAN (Anth.)
    THE NEW HOWARD READER #1 (Chpbk.)
    LORD OF SAMARCAND AND OTHER ADVENTURES OF THE OLD ORIENT
    WEST IS WEST AND OTHERS
    Unfinished

**UNTITLED ("'Yessah,' said Mrs. , . . .")**
First appeared in THE LAST OF THE TRUNK OCH BREV I URVAL (Chpbk.)
    THE LAST OF THE TRUNK
    Unfinished

**UNTITLED ("'You,' said Shifty Griddle, pointing his finger at me . . .")**
Unfinished, unpublished

**USURP THE NIGHT**
Alternate title: THE HOOFED THING
First appeared in WEIRDBOOK #3
     THE HAUNT OF HORROR, June 1973
     THE GODS OF BAL-SAGOTH
     TRAILS IN DARKNESS (as "The Hoofed Thing")
     NAMELESS CULTS

**THE VALE OF LOST WOMEN**
Featuring CONAN
First appeared in MAGAZINE OF HORROR #15 (edited by R.A.W. Lowndes)
     CONAN OF CIMMERIA (LSDC-edited version)
     QUEEN OF THE BLACK COAST, Grant (Donald Grant-edited version)
     THE CONAN CHRONICLES 1, Sphere and Orbit (LSDC-edited version)
     THE CONAN CHRONICLES I: THE PEOPLE OF THE BLACK CIRCLE, Millennium Fantasy Masterworks
     ROBERT E. HOWARD'S COMPLETE CONAN OF CIMMERIA, VOLUME 1 (edited by Patrice Louinet)
     THE COMING OF CONAN THE CIMMERIAN
     THE COMPLETE CHRONICLES OF CONAN
     Each of the edited versions (RAWL, LSDC, DMG, PL) are all different, and differ from the original typescript; the original story has never been published, and indeed may now be lost

**VALLEY OF THE GOLDEN WEB**
Listed on a Kline Agency list of REH stories, listed as 18 pages long, don't know what happened to it

**THE VALLEY OF THE LOST (1, "Jim Brill licked his parched lips . . .")**
Alternate title: KING OF THE FORGOTTEN PEOPLE
First appeared in MAGAZINE OF HORROR #13
     THE GODS OF BAL-SAGOTH
     BEYOND THE BORDERS
     Glenn Lord had erroneously titled this story "The Valley of the Lost", as he thought it was the story that had been announced for the last issue of STRANGE TALES that never got published; as it turns out, he was wrong, and when the proper story showed up, Glenn Lord titled it "The Secret of Lost Valley"; Since this initial screwup, everyone has gone back to the proper titles

**THE VALLEY OF THE LOST (2)**
Alternate title: SECRET OF LOST VALLEY

**THE VALLEY OF THE WORM**
Featuring JAMES ALLISON
First appeared in WEIRD TALES, February 1934
     SKULL-FACE AND OTHERS
     WORLDS OF WEIRD (Anth.)
     WOLFSHEAD, Lancer
     THE YOUNG MAGICIANS (Anth.)
     THE PULPS: FIFTY YEARS OF AMERICAN POP CULTURE (Anth.)
     SKULL-FACE OMNIBUS
     SKULL-FACE OMNIBUS, VOLUME 2
     BLOODSTAR
     WOLFSHEAD, Bantam
     LURKING SHADOWS (Anth.)

THE FANTASY HALL OF FAME (Anth.)
CTHULHU THE MYTHOS AND KINDRED HORRORS
BARBARIANS II (Anth.)
ROBERT E. HOWARD'S WORLD OF HEROES
THE ULTIMATE TRIUMPH: THE HEROIC FANTASY OF ROBERT E. HOWARD
THE MAMMOTH BOOK OF FANTASY (Anth.)
SAVAGE ADVENTURES
THE DEVIL IN IRON, Incarna
THE WEIRD WRITINGS OF ROBERT E. HOWARD, VOLUME ONE
THE VALLEY OF THE WORM: THE WEIRD WORKS OF ROBERT E. HOWARD, VOLUME 5
CRIMSON SHADOWS: THE BEST OF ROBERT E. HOWARD, VOLUME 1

## VENGEANCE
Alternate title: REVENGE

## VENGEANCE OF A WOMAN
First appeared in THE RIGHT HOOK, VOLUME 1, #1 (Chpbk.)
    AUSTIN, VOLUME 3, #2 (Chpbk.)
    ROBERT E. HOWARD—THE POWER OF THE WRITING MIND

## THE VICAR OF WAKEFIELD
First appeared in REHUPA #118 (Chpbk., facsimile reproduction of original school paper)
    THE NEW HOWARD READER #5 (Chpbk.)
    A review of this book, he didn't like it; the document is published along with a letter from Glenn Lord in
        REHUPA #118

## VIKINGS OF THE GLOVES
Alternate title: ". . . INCLUDING THE SCANDINAVIAN!"
Featuring STEVE COSTIGAN
First appeared in FIGHT STORIES, February 1932
    FIGHT STORIES, Fall, 1940 (as "Including the Scandinavian!", author listed as "Mark Adam")
    THE HOWARD REVIEW #2 (Chpbk.)
    REH'S FIGHT MAGAZINE #3 (Chpbk.)
    WATERFRONT FISTS AND OTHERS
    BOXING STORIES

## THE VOICE OF DEATH
Featuring STEVE HARRISON
First appeared in TWO-FISTED DETECTIVE STORIES (Chpbk.)
    REH: TWO-GUN RACONTEUR #10

## THE VOICE OF DOOM
First appeared in CRYPT OF CTHULHU #39 (Chpbk.)

## THE VOICE OF EL-LIL
Alternate title: TEMPTRESS OF THE TOWER OF TORTURE AND SIN
First appeared in ORIENTAL STORIES, October-November 1930
    AVON FANTASY READER #14 (as "Temptress of the Tower of Torture and Sin")
    THE DARK MAN AND OTHERS
    ORIENTAL STORIES, Odyssey Publications
    THE BOOK OF ROBERT E. HOWARD
    PIGEONS FROM HELL, Zebra & Ace
    THE DARK MAN ONMIBUS, VOLUME 1

BEYOND THE BORDERS
ORIENTAL STORIES, OCTOBER-NOVEMBER 1930, Girasol Collectables (Chpbk.)
THE HOWARD REVIEW #13 (Chpbk., facsimile of original pages)
ROBERT E. HOWARD'S STRANGE TALES
MOON OF SKULLS: THE WEIRD WORKS OF ROBERT E. HOWARD, VOLUME 2
SHADOW KINGDOMS: THE WEIRD WORKS OF ROBERT E. HOWARD, VOLUME 1 (Cosmos & AudioRealms)
ORIENTAL STORIES, THE MAGIC CARPET MAGAZINE & THE SOUK
THE COMPLETE ORIENTAL STORIES (Anth.)

## THE VOICE OF THE MOB
First appeared in LURID CONFESSIONS #1 (Chpbk.)
THE NEW HOWARD READER #4 (Chpbk.)

## VOYAGES WITH VILLAINS
First appeared in THE COLLECTED LETTERS OF ROBERT E. HOWARD, VOLUME 2: 1930-1932
From a letter to TCS, ca. July or August 1930 ("Well, Fear Finn, / I haven't heard . . .")

## THE VULTURES
Alternate title: THE VULTURES OF WHAPETON

## THE VULTURES OF TETON GULCH
Alternate title: THE VULTURES OF WHAPETON

## THE VULTURES OF WHAPETON
Alternate titles: THE VULTURES OF TETON GULCH; THE VULTURES
First appeared in SMASHING NOVELS MAGAZINE, December 1936 (printed with 2 endings)
THE VULTURES (printed with just one ending)
CROSS PLAINS #5 (alternate ending)
THE VULTURES OF WHAPETON
CROMLECH #3 (Chpbk., alternate ending)
THE NEW HOWARD READER #6 (Chpbk., both endings, as "The Vultures of Wahpeton")
TREASURES OF TARTARY AND OTHERS (both endings)
THE END OF THE TRAIL: WESTERN STORIES (as "The Vultures of Wahpeton", with both endings)
THE GRIM LAND: THE BEST OF ROBERT E. HOWARD, VOLUME 2
In other stories, used the town name of Wahpeton, so likely that was the correct spelling

## THE VULTURE'S ROOST
Listed on a Kline Agency list of REH stories, listed as 12 pages long, don't know what happened to it

## VULTURES' SANCTUARY
First appeared in ARGOSY, November 28, 1936
MAX BRAND'S WESTERN MAGAZINE, June 1950
THE LAST RIDE
THE END OF THE TRAIL: WESTERN STORIES

## THE WANDERING YEARS
First appeared in THE GHOST, May 1945
THE LAST CELT
WEST IS WEST AND OTHERS

## WAR ON BEAR CREEK
Featuring BRECKINRIDGE ELKINS
First appeared in ACTION STORIES, April 1935
>    THE SUMMIT COUNTY JOURNAL, December 4, 11, 18, 25, 1970; January 1, 8, 15, 22, 29; February 5, 12,
>        19, 26; March 5, 12, 1971 (15-part serial)
>    THE COMPLETE ACTION STORIES
>    THE RIOT AT BUCKSNORT AND OTHER WESTERN TALES
>    Was altered slightly to become Chapter 12 of the "A Gent from Bear Creek" novel; THE SUMMIT COUNTY
>        JOURNAL appearance changed the name to "Breckenridge", to be like the town it was published in

## WATERFRONT FISTS
Alternate title: STAND UP AND SLUG!
Featuring STEVE COSTIGAN
First appeared in FIGHT STORIES, September 1930
>    FIGHT STORIES, Summer, 1940 (as "Stand Up and Slug!", author listed as "Mark Adam")
>    REH'S FIGHT MAGAZINE #1 (Chpbk.)
>    WATERFRONT FISTS AND OTHERS
>    BOXING STORIES

## WATERFRONT LAW
Alternate title: THE TNT PUNCH

## THE WATERFRONT WALLOP
Alternate title: THE TNT PUNCH

## THE WAY OF THE SWORDS
Alternate title: THE ROAD OF THE EAGLES; CONAN, MAN OF DESTINY
>    First appeared in THE ROAD OF AZRAEL
>    LORD OF SAMARCAND AND OTHER ADVENTURES OF THE OLD ORIENT (as "The Road of the
>        Eagles")
>    Story was originally titled "The Road of the Eagles"; it was rewritten by LSDC into a Conan story back in the
>        1950s, first called "Conan, Man of Destiny", then later changed to "The Road of the Eagles"; the
>        original story was printed here; note that there are two versions of this story, an earlier draft owned by
>        Glenn Lord, and a later draft owned by Cross Plains Public Library; THE ROAD OF AZRAEL uses
>        the later draft, the LORD OF SAMARCAND book uses the earlier draft

## THE WEAKER SEX
First appeared in LA TOMBE DU DRAGON (French)
>    THE NEW HOWARD READER #6 (Chpbk.)

## WEARY PILGRIMS ON THE ROAD
Alternate title: PILGRIMS TO THE PECOS

## WEEKLY SHORT STORY
Alternate title: Untitled ("I have been . . .")
First appeared in THE YELLOW JACKET, November 3, 1926
>    THE COMPLETE YELLOW JACKET
>    WEST IS WEST AND OTHERS

## THE WEEPING WILLOW
First appeared in POING D'ACIER (French)
>    THE LAST OF THE TRUNK OCH BREV I URVAL (Chpbk.)
>    THE LAST OF THE TRUNK

**THE WEREWOLF MURDER CASE**
First appeared in THE LAST OF THE TRUNK OCH BREV I URVAL (Chpbk.)
        THE COLLECTED LETTERS OF ROBERT E. HOWARD, VOLUME 3: 1933-1936
From a letter to TCS, undated ("Ahatou noyon, Fear Finn. . .")

**WEST IS WEST**
First appeared in THE TATTLER, December 22, 1922
        THE HOWARD COLLECTOR #3
        THE HOWARD COLLECTOR, Ace
        THE NEW HOWARD READER #7 (Chpbk.)
        WEST IS WEST AND OTHERS

**THE WEST TOWER**
Featuring THE SONORA KID
First appeared in THE SONORA KID (Chpbk.)
        Fragment

**WESTWARD HO!**
Featuring STEVE BENDER, WEARY McGREW and THE WHALE
First appeared in THE LAST OF THE TRUNK OCH BREV I URVAL (Chpbk.)
        THE LAST OF THE TRUNK
        Incomplete

**WHAT THE DEUCE?**
First appeared in THE LAST OF THE TRUNK OCH BREV I URVAL (Chpbk.)
        THE LAST OF THE TRUNK
        Unfinished

**WHAT THE NATION OWES THE SOUTH**
First appeared in THE BROWNWOOD BULLETIN, May 26, 1923 (A high school theme)
        THE CROSS PLAINS REVIEW, August 14, 1936
        THE DARK MAN #3 (Chpbk.)
        WEST IS WEST AND OTHERS

**THE WHEEL TURNS**
Alternate title: Untitled ("Men have had visions ere now.")

**WHEN BEAR CREEK CAME TO CHAWED EAR**
Featuring BRECKINRIDGE ELKINS
First appeared in A GENT FROM BEAR CREEK (as Chapter 13)
        THE SUMMIT COUNTY JOURNAL, March 19, 26; April 2, 9, 16, 23, 30; May 7, 14, 21, 28; June 4, 11, 18,
                25; July 2, 9, 16, 23, 30; August 6, 13, 20, 27; September 3, 10, 17, 1971 (27-part serial)
        HEROES OF BEAR CREEK (book version)
        THE SUMMIT COUNTY JOURNAL appearance changed the name to "Breckenridge", to be like the town it
                was published in

**WHEN HELL BROKE LOOSE**
Listed on a Kline Agency list of REH stories, listed as 16 "long" pages long, don't know what happened to it

**WHEN TOMORROW BECOMES YESTERDAY**
Listed on a Kline Agency list of REH stories, listed as 5 pages long, don't know what happened to it

**WHEN TWO WRONGS MAKE A WRIGHT**
Listed on a Kline Agency list of REH stories, listed as 9 pages long, don't know what happened to it

**WHERE STRANGE GODS SQUALL**
First appeared in THE LAST OF THE TRUNK OCH BREV I URVAL (Chpbk.)
     THE COLLECTED LETTERS OF ROBERT E. HOWARD, VOLUME 1: 1923-1929
        From two letter to TCS, ca. August/September 1927 ("Salaam, Singing Dan: / Having satisfactorily disposed . .
          .") and ca. Fall 1927 ("Salaam: / Then the little boy said . . .")

**WHILE SMOKE ROLLED**
Featuring BRECKINRIDGE ELKINS or PIKE BEARFIELD
Alternate title: WHILE THE SMOKE ROLLED
First appeared in DOUBLE-ACTION WESTERN, December 1956
     THE SUMMIT COUNTY JOURNAL, October 5, 13, 20, 27; November 3, 10, 17, 1967 (7-part serial)
     MAYHEM ON BEAR CREEK
     HEROES OF BEAR CREEK
     A GENT FROM BEAR CREEK AND OTHERS
     Was originally a Pike Bearfield story titled "While the Smoke Rolled", the agent, maybe Otis A. Kline,
        switched it to a Breckinridge Elkins story and shortened the title; THE SUMMIT COUNTY
        JOURNAL appearance changed the name to "Breckenridge", to be like the town it was published in

**THE WHITE JADE RING**
First appeared in THE LAST OF THE TRUNK OCH BREV I URVAL (Chpbk.)
     THE LAST OF THE TRUNK
     Unfinished

**THE WILD MAN**
Featuring STEVE BENDER, WEARY McGREW and THE WHALE
First appeared in THE LAST OF THE TRUNK OCH BREV I URVAL (Chpbk.)
     THE LAST OF THE TRUNK

**WILD WATER**
First appeared in  CROSS PLAINS #7
     THE VULTURES OF WHAPETON
     THE GRIM LAND: THE BEST OF ROBERT E. HOWARD, VOLUME 2
     WILD WATER (Chpbk.)

**THE WILDCAT AND THE STAR**
Featuring KID ALLISON
Alternate title: THE TEXAS WILDCAT
First appeared in THE LAST OF THE TRUNK OCH BREV I URVAL (Chpbk.)
     THE LAST OF THE TRUNK

**WINDIGO! WINDIGO!**
A story that REH said he wrote, but no copy exists

**WINGS IN THE NIGHT**
Featuring SOLOMON KANE
First appeared in WEIRD TALES, July 1932
     SKULL-FACE AND OTHERS
     RED SHADOWS
     THE HAND OF KANE
     SKULL-FACE OMNIBUS

SKULL-FACE OMNIBUS, VOLUME 2
SOLOMON KANE: THE HILLS OF THE DEAD
ROBERT E. HOWARD'S WORLD OF HEROES
SOLOMON KANE, Baen
THE SAVAGE TALES OF SOLOMON KANE
SAVAGE ADVENTURES
WINGS IN THE NIGHT: THE WEIRD WORKS OF ROBERT E. HOWARD, VOLUME 4
THE WEIRD WRITINGS OF ROBERT E. HOWARD, VOLUME ONE
THE RIGHT HAND OF DOOM AND OTHER TALES OF SOLOMON KANE
THE LEGEND OF SOLOMON KANE
THE 'SOLOMAN CRANE' STORIES
THE GRIM LAND: THE BEST OF ROBERT E. HOWARD, VOLUME 2

## THE WINGS OF THE BAT
First appeared in THE LAST OF THE TRUNK OCH BREV I URVAL (Chpbk.)
THE LAST OF THE TRUNK
Incomplete; hand-written

## WINNER TAKE ALL
Alternate title: SUCKER!
Featuring STEVE COSTIGAN
First appeared in FIGHT STORIES, July 1930
FIGHT STORIES, Winter, 1939-40 (as "Sucker!", author listed as "Mark Adam")
REH'S FIGHT MAGAZINE #1 (Chpbk.)
WATERFRONT FISTS AND OTHERS

## WITCH FROM HELL'S KITCHEN
Alternate title: THE HOUSE OF ARABU
First appeared in AVON FANTASY READER #18
WOLFSHEAD, Lancer (as "The House of Arabu")
THE AVON FANTASY READER (Anth.)
ROBERT E. HOWARD OMNIBUS
WOLFSHEAD, Bantam
EONS OF THE NIGHT (as "The House of Arabu")
THE ULTIMATE TRIUMPH: THE HEROIC FANTASY OF ROBERT E. HOWARD
Original title was "The House of Arabu", the guys at Avon came up with the strange title; there apparently were
two drafts, Oscar Friend worked over and sold the second draft to Avon, and charged a "rewrite" fee;
there are only a few pages from the second draft extant; THE ULTIMATE TRIUMPH uses the first
draft and bits and pieces from the second draft to create their version

## A WITCH SHALL BE BORN
Featuring CONAN
First appeared in WEIRD TALES, December 1934
AVON FANTASY READER #10
CONAN THE BARBARIAN, Gnome
CONAN THE FREEBOOTER
THE MIGHTY BARBARIANS (Anth.)
A WITCH SHALL BE BORN
THE PEOPLE OF THE BLACK CIRCLE, Berkley & Putnam (SFBC)
THE CONAN CHRONICLES 1, Sphere and Orbit
THE ESSENTIAL CONAN, SFBC Fantasy
THE CONAN CHRONICLES I: THE PEOPLE OF THE BLACK CIRCLE, Millennium Fantasy Masterworks
ROBERT E. HOWARD'S COMPLETE CONAN OF CIMMERIA, VOLUME 2 (plus synopsis, first
appearance; both story and synopsis from original typescripts)

THE BLOODY CROWN OF CONAN (plus synopsis, both story and synopsis from original typescripts)
THE COMPLETE CHRONICLES OF CONAN
THE WEIRD WRITINGS OF ROBERT E. HOWARD, VOLUME TWO
THE GARDEN OF FEAR: THE WEIRD WORKS OF ROBERT E. HOWARD, VOLUME 6
PEOPLE OF THE BLACK CIRCLE
THREE TALES OF CONAN THE BARBARIAN
Voted best story in its original WEIRD TALES appearance by the fans

## WITH A SET OF RATTLESNAKE RATTLES
First appeared in LEAVES #1, Summer, 1937
    THE HOWARD COLLECTOR #1
    THE HOWARD COLLECTOR, Ace
    THE NEW HOWARD READER #4 (Chpbk.)
    DEAR HPL: LETTERS, ROBERT E. HOWARD TO H.P. LOVECRAFT, 1930-1936 (Chpbk.)
    WEST IS WEST AND OTHERS
    Apparently from an unidentified letter to HPL in which REH included some rattlesnake rattles; REH later
        commented about this in another letter to HPL, November 11, 1933 ("Glad you liked the rattles.")

## WIZARD AND WARRIOR
By Robert E. Howard & Lin Carter
Alternate title: Untitled ("Three men sat at a . . .")
Featuring KULL
First appeared in KING KULL
    Originally an untitled and unfinished draft, Carter finished it for this book; the original fragment was published
        in KULL, Grant, Bantam and Baen editions

## WOLFSDUNG
First appeared in CROMLECH #3 (Chpbk.)
    WOLFSDUNG (Chpbk.)
    THE NEW HOWARD READER #5 (Chpbk.)
    THE COLLECTED LETTERS OF ROBERT E. HOWARD, VOLUME 1: 1923-1929
    From a letter to TCS, ca. January 1928 ("Salaam: / Listen, you crumb . . .")

## WOLFSHEAD
First appeared in WEIRD TALES, April 1926
    SKULL-FACE AND OTHERS
    WOLFSHEAD, Lancer
    SKULL-FACE OMNIBUS
    SKULL-FACE OMNIBUS, VOLUME 1
    WOLFSHEAD, Bantam
    WEREWOLF: HORROR STORIES OF THE MAN-BEAST (Anth.)
    EONS OF THE NIGHT
    SHADOW KINGDOMS: THE WEIRD WORKS OF ROBERT E. HOWARD, VOLUME 1 (Wildside Press)
    WEIRD TALES, APRIL 1926 (Chpbk.)
    THE WEIRD WRITINGS OF ROBERT E. HOWARD, VOLUME ONE
    Won fans' vote for 2nd best story in its original WEIRD TALES appearance

## WOLVES—AND A SWORD
First appeared in THE LAST OF THE TRUNK OCH BREV I URVAL (Chpbk.)
    THE LAST OF THE TRUNK
    Incomplete

## WOLVES BEYOND THE BORDER
Featuring CONAN
First appeared in CONAN THE USURPER (completed by LSDC)
THE CONAN CHRONICLES, VOLUME 2, Millenium (completed by LSDC)
THE CONQUERING SWORD OF CONAN (two original drafts)
THE COMPLETE CHRONICLES OF CONAN (draft)
Originally a complete first draft, though the later portions of it were just in synopsis form, then REH wrote a new second draft, which he didn't finish; LSDC took this second draft, and using the rest of the story from the first draft, created a new work; the complete first draft has never been published

## WORMS OF THE EARTH
Featuring BRAN MAK MORN
First appeared in WEIRD TALES, November 1932
KEEP ON THE LIGHT (Anth.)
WEIRD TALES, October 1939
SKULL-FACE AND OTHERS
FAMOUS FANTASTIC MYSTERIES, June 1953
MAGAZINE OF HORROR #22
BRAN MAK MORN, Dell
WORMS OF THE EARTH
SKULL-FACE OMNIBUS
SKULL-FACE OMNIBUS, VOLUME 2
CTHULHU THE MYTHOS AND KINDRED HORRORS
ROBERT E. HOWARD'S WORLD OF HEROES
FAMOUS FANTASTIC MYSTERIES (Anth.)
BARN MAK MORN, Baen
BRAN MAK MORN – THE LAST KING
WORMS OF THE EARTH (Chpbk., this is a compact disk)
NAMELESS CULTS
WINGS IN THE NIGHT: THE WEIRD WORKS OF ROBERT E. HOWARD, VOLUME 4
THE WEIRD WRITINGS OF ROBERT E. HOWARD, VOLUME ONE
CRIMSON SHADOWS: THE BEST OF ROBERT E. HOWARD, VOLUME 1
Was voted best story in its original appearance in WEIRD TALES; the BRAN MAK MORN – THE LAST KING printing also includes an early draft version

## XUTHAL OF THE DUSK
Alternate title: THE SLITHERING SHADOW

## YE COLLEGE DAYS
First appeared in THE YELLOW JACKET, January 20, 1927
THE HOWARD COLLECTOR #11
THE HOWARD COLLECTOR, Ace
THE COMPLETE YELLOW JACKET
WEST IS WEST AND OTHERS

## THE YELLOW COBRA
Alternate title: SAILOR DORGAN AND THE YELLOW COBRA; A NIGHT ASHORE; A KOREAN NIGHT; THE FANGS OF THE YELLOW COBRA
Featuring DENNIS DORGAN
First appeared in THE INCREDIBLE ADVENTURES OF DENNIS DORGAN
THE IRON MAN, WITH THE ADVENTURES OF DENNIS DORGAN
Original typescript lists author as "Patrick Ervin", a pseudonym REH used in connection with his Dennis Dorgan stories; there is also an original Costigan typescript, titled "The Fangs of the Yellow Cobra"; "A Korean Night" is a slightly different, earlier original draft of the Costigan version

**YELLOW LAUGHTER**
Incomplete, unpublished, rejected by WEIRD TALES
      Also contains the poem UNTITLED ("I'm more than a man . . .")

**YOU GOT TO KILL A BULLDOG**
Alternate title: THE BULL DOG BREED

# NON-ENGLISH PROSE INDEX

## INCLUDES FICTIONAL WORKS, ARTICLES, ESSAYS, FRAGMENTS AND SYNOPSES

All works solely by REH unless noted otherwise. Notes, alternate titles, character references, and first appearances for the various works are under the ENGLISH PROSE INDEX, unless some information specifically applies to a non-English edition. Stories are sorted by first published title. The ENGLISH PROSE INDEX provides the cross-referencing of titles. The books listed herein can be found in the NON-ENGLISH BOOKS list, the periodicals in the PERIODICALS list, and chapbooks (indicated with (Chpbk.)) in the CHAPBOOKS list. Any anthologies will be in the NON-ENGLISH BOOKS list.

**AGE LASTING LOVE**
First appeared in LA TOMBE DU DRAGON (French)

**ALLEYS OF DARKNESS**
　　DENNIS DORGAN (French)

**ALLEYS OF PERIL**
　　STEVE COSTIGAN ET LE SIGNE DU SERPENT (French)

**ALLEYS OF TRECHERY**
　　DENNIS DORGAN (French)

**ALMURIC**
　　MAKYO-WAKUSEI ALMURIC (Japanese)
　　ALMURIC (Greek)
　　ALMOURIK (Greek)
　　ALMURIC (French)
　　ALMURIC (Dutch)
　　ALMURIA (Hungarian)
　　ALMURIC (Italian)
　　ALMURIC (Polish)
　　ALMURIK I INNE OPOWIADANIA (Polish)
　　ALMURIC (Spanish)
　　ALMURIC (German)

**THE ALTAR AND THE SCORPION**
　　KULL (Greek)
　　KULL VON ATLANTIS (German)
　　KULL DI VALUSIA (Italian)
　　KULL LE ROI BARBARE (French)
　　TZAR KULL (Russian)
　　HOSOK KORA (Hungarian)
　　REY KULL (Spanish)

**APPARITION IN THE PRIZE RING**
　　LA FLAMME DE LA VENGEANCE (French)

**BASTARDS ALL!**
IL SEGNO DEL SERPENTE (Italian)

**THE BATTLING SAILOR**
First appeared in DENNIS DORGAN (French)

**THE BEAST FROM THE ABYSS**
MONOLITH 002 (Croatian)
CIEN BESTII (Polish)

**BEYOND THE BLACK RIVER**
S-F MAGAZINE, October 1969 (Japanese)
FUSISHO CONAN (Japanese)
CONAN TO HONO'O NO TAMKEN (Japanese)
CONAN EL GUERRERO (Spanish)
CONAN TO KODAI-OHKOKU NO HIHOU (Japanese)
CONAN DE KRIJGER (Dutch)
REH: CONAN JA DEMONIT (Finnish)
CONAN PERA APO TON MAVRO POTAMO (Greek)
KONAN UNISHTOZHITELYA (Bulgarian)
O PIRGOS TOU ERPETOU – PERA APO TON MAVRO POTAMO (Greek)
CONAN IZ CIMERII (Russian)
CONAN DE CIMMERIA III (Spanish)
IL REGNO DI CONAN (Italian)
IL REGNO DI CONAN IL GRANDE (Italian)
L'URLO DI CONAN (Italian)
TUTTI I CICLI FANTASTICI, VOLUME 2: IL CICLO DI CONAN, VOLUME 2 (Italian)
KONAN I POVELITELY PESHTER (Russian)
CONAN WOJOWNIK (Polish)
CONAN: ZA CZARNA RZEKA (Polish)
A SZOLDAS BARBAR (Hungarian)
CONAN A KIMMERIAI (Hungarian)
CONAN PERA APO TON MAVRO POTAMO (Greek)
CONAN JA PUNANE KANTS (Estonian)
CONAN DOBYVATEL (Czech)
CONAN (Czech)
CONAN KRIGEREN (Norwegian)
CONAN KRIGAREN (Swedish)
CONAN: DROGA DO TRONU (Polish)
CONAN LA NAISSANCE DU MONDE (French)
CONAN LE GUERRIER (French)

**THE BLACK BEAR BITES**
KIRBY O'DONNELL (French)

**BLACK ABYSS**
KULL VON ATLANTIS (German)
REY KULL (Spanish)

**THE BLACK BEAR BITES**
DER SCHATZ DER TATAREN (German)
KOGHOT DRAKONA (Russian)

## BLACK CANAAN

KEN TO MAHOU NO MONGATARI (Japanese)
LE PACTE NOIR (French, NeO)
FUREUR NOIRS (French)
ROSTRO DE CALAVERA (Spanish)
OUTOJA TARINOITA #4 (Finnish)
PIMEDUSE RAHVAS (Estonian)
CHERNYE KANAAN (Russian)
WILCZA GLOWA (Polish)
EL TEMPLO DE YUN-SHATU (Spanish)
ROSTRO DE CALAVERA (Spanish, Ediciones Martinez Roca, S.A.)

## THE BLACK CITY

KULL (Greek)
KULL DI VALUSIA (Italian)
KULL LE ROI BARBARE (French)
KULL VON ATLANTIS (German, later edition only)
TZAR KULL (Russian)

## BLACK COLOSSUS

KYOSENSHI CONAN (Japanese)
CONAN TO ARAWASHI NO MICHI (Japanese)
SAVAGE TALES OF CONAN #2 (Conan)
L'ERA DI CONAN (Italian)
CONAN DER VRIJBUITER (Dutch)
REH: CONAN TAISTELIJA (Finnish)
CONAN - ESPADA & MAGIA #2 (Brazil, in Portugese)
SKIES STO FAGGAROFOTO (Greek)
CHERNYAT KOLOS (Bulgarian)
CONAN IZ CIMERII (Russian)
CONAN (Russian, original publication plus synopsis)
OSSZES CONAN, TORTENETE 1 (Hungarian)
LA LEGGENDA DI CONAN IL CIMMERO (Italian)
BARBARZYNCA (Polish)
CONAN ZDOBYWCA (Polish)
CONAN (French, a later, much larger edition)
CONAN A KIMMERIAI (Hungarian)
KONAN: PROKLETSTVO MONOLITA (Yugoslavian, part 1)
KONAN: CRNI KOLOS (Yugoslavian, part 2)
CONAN JA MUSTA RANNIKU KUNINGANNA (Estonian)
CONAN BARBAR (Czech)
CONAN (Czech)
CONAN A BARBAR (Hungarian)
CONAN TAISTELIJA (Finnish)
CONAN FRIBYTTEREN (Norwegian)
CONAN, WHVG, 2003 (German)
CONAN DER FREIBEUTER (German)
CONAN IL CIMMERO (Italian)
CONAN IL PIRATA (Italian)
CONAN PIRATEN (Swedish)
CONAN PIRAT (Polish)
CONAN LE FLIBUSTIER (French)
CONAN EL PIRATA (Spanish)

**BLACK COUNTRY**
LE SIGNEUR DE SAMARCANDE (French)

**BLACK HOUND OF DEATH**
LE CHIEN DE LA MORT (French)
WILCZA GLOWA (Polish)

**THE BLACK MOON**
STEVE HARRISON ET LE TALON D'ARGENT (French)

**THE BLACK STONE**
DE ZWARTE STEEN (Dutch)
S-F MAGAZINE, September 1972 (Japanese)
LEGENDES DU MYTHE DE CTHULHU (French)
ISTORIES FRIKIS (Greek)
KUTHURU #5 (Japanese)
LE TERTRE MAUDIT (French)
KURO NO ISHIBUMI (Japanese)
ROSTRO DE CALAVERA (Spanish)
DAS HAUS DES GRAUENS (German)
MUSTA KIVI (Finnish)
LOS GUSANOS DE LA TIERRA Y OTROS RELATES DE HORROR SOBRENATURAL (Spanish)
CHERNYE KANAAN (Russian)
CIEN BESTII (Polish)
ZMIERZCH NAD STONEHENGE (Polish)
CHERNUY KAMEN (Russian)
CULTI INNOMINABILI (Italian)
ROSTRO DE CALAVERA (Spanish, Ediciones Martinez Roca, S.A.)

**THE BLACK STRANGER**
MUSTAN JUMALAN SUUDELMA (Finnish)
ALMURIA (Hungarian)
CONAN ETERNAL (Russian, LSDC version)
OSSZES CONAN, TORTENETE 1 (Hungarian)
CONAN DE CIMMERIA III (Spanish)

**BLACK TALONS**
LE CHIEN DE LA MORT (French)

**BLACK VULMEA'S VENGEANCE**
VULMEA LE PIRATE NOIR (French)

**BLACK WIND BLOWING**
LES HABITANTS DES TOMBES (French)
KOGHOT DRAKONA (Russian)
WILCZA GLOWA (Polish)

**BLADES FOR FRANCE**
HORDE AUS DEM MORGENLAND (German)
AGNES DE CHASTILLON (French)

## BLADES OF THE BROTHERHOOD
SOLOMON KANE (French, REH1)
DEGEN DER GERECHTIGKEIT (German, REH1)
LA LUNA DEI TESCHI (Italian)
SOLOMON KEIN (Russian)
CZERWONE CIENIE (Polish)
LAS AVENTURAS DE SOLOMON KANE (Spanish)
A KIPONYAK HOLDJA (Hungarian)
I LOFI TON NEKRON KAI ALLA DIEGEMATA (Greek)

## THE BLOCK
LA TOMBE DU DRAGON (French)

## THE BLOOD OF BELSHAZZAR
CORMAC FITZGEOFFREY (French)
JASTZEBIE OUTREMERU (Polish)

## BLOOD OF THE GODS
EL BORAK LE REDOUTABLE (French)
KROV BOGOV (Russian)
IM LAND DER MESSER (German)

## THE BLOODSTAINED GOD (LSDC version)
CONAN VAN CIMMERIE (Dutch)
ARAJISHI CONAN (Japanese)
CONAN TO SEKIHI NO NORI (Japanese)
JEGMAGIA (Hungarian)
LA LEGGENDA DI CONAN IL CIMMERO (Italian)
CONAN (Polish)
CONAN: STRAZNICY LARSHA / OKRWAWIONY BOG (Polish)
CONAN Z CYNERII (Polish)
CONAN (French, a later, much larger edition)
KONAN: GRAD LOBANJA (Yugoslavian)
CONAN EN DE KONINGIN VAN DE ZWARTE KUST (Dutch)
CONAN VON CIMMERIA (German)
CONAN DI CIMMERIA (Italian)
CONAN IL CIMMERO (Italian)
CONAN CIMMERIERN (Swedish)
CONAN LE CIMMERIEN (French)
CONAN DE CIMMERIA (Spanish)

## BLOODSTONES AND EBONY
WYSLANCY WALHALLI (Polish)

## BLUE FLAME OF VENGEANCE (John Pocsik supernatural version)
SOLOMON KANE (Italian)
SOLOMON KANE IL GIUSTIZIERE (Italian)

## BLUE RIVER BLUES
First appeared in STEVE COSTIGAN LE CHAMPION (French)

## BRACHEN THE KELT
L'ILE DES EPOUVANTES (French)
WYSLANCY WALHALLI (Polish)

## THE BRAZEN PEACOCK
KIRBY O'DONNELL (French)
DER SCHATZ DER TATAREN (German)
KOGHOT DRAKONA (Russian)

## BREED OF BATTLE
STEVE COSTIGAN ET LE SIGNE DU SERPENT (French)

## THE BULL DOG BREED
STEVE COSTIGAN (French)

## BY THE LAW OF THE SHARK
First appeared in STEVE COSTIGAN LE CHAMPION (French)

## BY THIS AXE I RULE!
KULL (Greek)
KULL DI VALUSIA (Italian)
KULL LE ROI BARBARE (French)
HERR VON VALUSIEN (German)
REH: YÖN KUNINKAAT (Finnish)
KULL VON ATLANTIS (German, later edition only)
TZAR KULL (Russian)
HOSOK KORA (Hungarian)
CONAN BARBAR A JINE POVIDKY (Czech)
REY KULL (Spanish)

## THE CAIRN ON THE HEADLAND
HAYAKAWA MYSTERY MAGAZINE, November 1969 (Japanese)
LE PACTE NOIR (French, NeO)
LE PACTE NOIR (French, Marabout)
KEN TO MAHOU NO MONGATARI (Japanese)
DAS HAUS DES GRAUENS (German)
ROSTRO DE CALAVERA (Spanish)
LE PACTE NOIR, VOLUME 1 or 2 (French)
PIMEDUSE RAHVAS (Estonian)
WYSLANCY WALHALLI (Polish)

## CASONETTO'S LAST SONG
LE CHIEN DE LA MORT (French)

## THE CASTLE OF THE DEVIL
SOLOMON KANE (French)
I FIGLI DI ASSHUR (Italian)
SOLOMON KANE (Italian)
SOLOMON KANE IL GIUSTIZIERE (Italian)
DIE KRIEGER VON ASSUR (German)
CZERWONE CIENIE (Polish)
LAS AVENTURAS DE SOLOMON KANE (Spanish)

**THE CHALLENGE FROM BEYOND**
>LAS MEJORES HISTORIAS DE HORROR (Spanish)
>UNIVERS 01 (French)
>DAS GROSSE LESEBUCH DER FANTASY (German)
>DER LOVECRAFT-ZIRKEL (German)

**CHAMP OF THE FORECASTLE**
>STEVE COSTIGAN (French)

**THE CHILDREN OF ASSHUR**
>LE RETOUR DE KANE (French)
>I FIGLI DI ASSHUR (Italian)
>SOLOMON KANE (Italian)
>SOLOMON KANE IL GIUSTIZIERE (Italian)
>DIE KRIEGER VON ASSUR (German)
>SOLOMON KEIN (Russian)
>CZERWONE CIENIE (Polish)
>LAS AVENTURAS DE SOLOMON KANE (Spanish)

**THE CHILDREN OF THE NIGHT**
>HAYAKAWA MYSTERY MAGAZINE, November 1971 (Japanese)
>L'HOMME NOIR (French)
>WAIDO #3 (Japanese)
>LA MASCHERA DI CTHULHU (Italian)
>LOS GUSANOS DE LA TIERRA Y OTROS RELATES DE HORROR SOBRENATURAL (Spanish)
>NIE KOPCIE MI GROBU (Polish)

**CIRCUS FISTS**
>STEVE COSTIGAN ET LE SIGNE DU SERPENT (French)
>LIK SMERCHA (Russian)

**THE COBRA IN THE DREAM**
>LES HABITANTS DES TOMBES (French)

**THE COMING OF EL BORAK**
First appeared in EL BORAK L'ETERNEL (French)
>KROV BOGOV (Russian)

**THE COUNTRY OF THE KNIFE**
>EL BORAK LE REDOUTABLE (French)
>KROV BOGOV (Russian)
>IM LAND DER MESSER (German)

**CROWD-HORROR**
>POING D'ACIER (French)

**THE CURSE OF GREED**
>LA TOMBE DU DRAGON (French)

**THE CURSE OF THE CRIMSON GOD**
  KIRBY O'DONNELL (French)
  DER SCHATZ DER TATAREN (German)
  SZABLE SZAHRAZARU (Polish)

**THE CURSE OF THE GOLDEN SKULL**
  HERR VON VALUSIEN (German)
  EL BORAK LE MAGNIFIQUE (French)
  PRZEKLENSTWO ZLOTEJ CZASZKI (Polish)

**DAGON MANOR**
  LA FLAMME DE LA VENGEANCE (French)

**THE DARK MAN**
  L'HOMME NOIR (French)
  RACHER DER VERDAMMTEN (German)
  HERRSCHER DER NACHT (German)
  REH: YÖN KUNINKAAT (Finnish)
  LOS GUSANOS DE LA TIERRA Y OTROS RELATES DE HORROR SOBRENATURAL (Spanish)
  BRAN MAK MORN (Czech)
  I SIGNORI DELLA SPADA (Italian)
  BOGOWIE BAL-SAGOTH (Polish)
  ROBAKI ZIEMI (Polish)
  ARNYKIRALYOK (Hungarian)
  TYGRI MORE (Czech)
  CONAN BARBAR A JINE POVIDKY (Czech)
  GUSANOS DE LA TIERRE (Spanish)

**DARK SHANGHAI**
  STEVE COSTIGAN ET LE SIGNE DU SERPENT (French)

**THE DAUGHTER OF ERLIK KHAN**
  EL BORAK L'INVINCIBLE (French)
  ZNAK OGNYA (Russian)
  ZAGINIONA DOLINA ISKANDERA (Polish)

**DAUGHTERS OF THE FEUD**
  WILD BILL CLANTON (French)

**THE DEAD REMEMBER**
  HAYAKAWA MYSTERY MAGAZINE, August 1967 (Japanese)
  CORMAC FITZGEOFFREY (French)
  LOS GUSANOS DE LA TIERRA Y OTROS RELATES DE HORROR SOBRENATURAL (Spanish)
  CIEN BESTII (Polish)
  NIE KOPCIE MI GROBU (Polish)

**DEATH'S BLACK RIDERS**
  LA FLAMME DE LA VENGEANCE (French)
  THE RAVEN #1 (Chpbk., German)
  LE ALI NOTTURNE (Italian)
  SOLOMON KANE (Italian)
  LAS AVENTURAS DE SOLOMON KANE (Spanish)

**DELCARDES' CAT**
>    KULL (Greek)
>    KULL VON ATLANTIS (German)
>    KULL DI VALUSIA (Italian)
>    KULL LE ROI BARBARE (French)
>    TZAR KULL (Russian)
>    HOSOK KORA (Hungarian)
>    REY KULL (Spanish)

**DELENDA EST**
>    LES HABITANTS DES TOMBES (French)

**DERMOD'S BANE**
>    LES HABITANTS DES TOMBES (French)
>    CIEN BESTII (Polish)

**DESERT BLOOD**
>    WILD BILL CLANTON (French)

**THE DESTINY GORILLA**
>    DENNIS DORGAN (French)

**THE DEVIL IN HIS BRAIN**
>    LA TOMBE DU DRAGON (French)

**THE DEVIL IN IRON**
>    KYOSENSHI CONAN (Japanese)
>    CONAN DER ZWERVER (Dutch)
>    TÄHTIVAELTAJA, April 1991 (Finnish)
>    OI MAVROI PROPHITES (Greek)
>    CONAN IZ CIMERII (Russian)
>    CONAN (Russian)
>    OSSZES CONAN, TORTENETE 1 (Hungarian)
>    SFERA (Polish)
>    KONAN SKITNIKA (Bulgarian)
>    L'IRA DI CONAN (Italian)
>    KONAN I POVELITELY PESHTER (Russian)
>    CONAN (Polish)
>    CONAN NAJEMNIK (Polish)
>    CONAN OBIEZYSWIAT (Polish)
>    CONAN (French, a later, much larger edition)
>    CONAN A KIMMERIAI (Hungarian)
>    KONAN: DRVO SMRTI (Yugoslavian, first part)
>    KONAN: DEMONSKO OSTROVO (Yugoslavian, second part)
>    CONAN JA MUSTA RANNIKU KUNINGANNA (Estonian)
>    CONAN BARBAR (Czech)
>    CONAN (Czech)
>    CONAN A BARBAR (Hungarian)
>    CONAN SNIKMORDERNES BY (Norwegian)
>    CONAN, WHVG, 2003 (German)
>    CONAN DER WANDERER (German)
>    CONAN LO ZINGARO (Italian)
>    CONAN FORGORAREN (Swedish)

CONAN: REKA NERGALA / STALOWY DEMON (Polish)
CONAN LE VAGABOND (French)
CONAN EL VAGABUNDO (Spanish)

**THE DEVILS OF DARK LAKE**
LE SIGNEUR DE SAMARCANDE (French)

**THE DEVIL'S WOODCHOPPER**
LA TOMBE DU DRAGON (French)

**DIG ME NO GRAVE**
DE BEWONER VAN HET MEER (Dutch)
L'HOMME NOIR (French)
KUTHURU #4 (Japanese)
ANTHOLOGIA EPISTIMONIKIS FANTASIAS - ISTORIES TIS MITHOLOGIAS CHTULHU, VOLUME
        17 (Greek)
KURO NO ISHIBUMI (Japanese)
KAUHUPOKKARI #1 (Finnish)
LOS GUSANOS DE LA TIERRA Y OTROS RELATES DE HORROR SOBRENATURAL (Spanish)
NIE KOPCIE MI GROBU (Polish)
ZMIERZCH NAD STONEHENGE (Polish)
CULTI INNOMINABILI (Italian)

**THE DOOR TO THE GARDEN**
LA TOMBE DU DRAGON (French)

**DOUBLE CROSS**
LA FLAMME DE LA VENGEANCE (French)

**THE DRAGON OF KAO TSU**
WILD BILL CLANTON (French)

**A DREAM**
LE MANOIR DE LA TERREUR (French)

**THE DREAM SNAKE**
NOUVELLES HISTOIRES D'OUTRE-MONDE (French)
HISTOIRES DE CAUCHEMARS (French)
HORA ANDO FANTAZI KESSOKUSEN #1 (Japanese)
LE TERTRE MAUDIT (French)
LA GRANDE ANTHOLOGIE DU FANTASTIQUE (Anth., French)
LOS GUSANOS DE LA TIERRA Y OTROS RELATES DE HORROR SOBRENATURAL (Spanish)
CIEN BESTII (Polish)
NIE KOPCIE MI GROBU (Polish)

**DRUMS OF THE SUNSET**
NIE KOPCIE MI GROBU (Polish)

## DRUMS OF TOMBULKU

CONAN EL AVENTURERO (Spanish)
CONAN DE AVONTURIER (Dutch, LSDC version)
CONAN TO KUROI YOGENSHA (Japanese, LSDC version)
CONAN ETERNAL (Russian, LSDC version)
OSSZES CONAN, TORTENETE 1 (Hungarian)
KONAN AVANTURISTA (Bulgarian)
LA LEGGENDA DI CONAN IL CIMMERO (Italian)
CONAN I IZTOCHNIK SUDEB (Russian)
KONAN HO TYKHODIOKTES (Greek)
KONAN: CRNI LAVIRINT (Yugoslavian, part 1)
KONAN: TAJANSTVENI GAZAL (Yugoslavian, part 2)
CONAN EVENTYREREN (Norwegian)
CONAN, WHVG, 2003 (German)
CONAN DER ABENTEURER (German)
CONAN AVENTYRAREN (Swedish)
CONAN RYZYKANT (Polish)
CONAN LA FIN DE L'ATLANTIDE (French)
CONAN L'AVENTURIER (French)

## DWELLERS UNDER THE TOMB

LES HABITANTS DES TOMBES (French)
ZHIVUSCHIE POD USPYA INITSAMI (Chpbk., Russian)
CHERNYE KANAAN (Russian)

## EL BORAK (1)

First appeared in EL BORAK L'ETERNEL (French)

## EL BORAK (2)

First appeared in EL BORAK L'ETERNEL (French)

## ETCHINGS IN IVORY

WYSLANCY WALHALLI (Polish)

## EXILE OF ATLANTIS

KULL (Greek)
KULL VON ATLANTIS (German)
KULL DI VALUSIA (Italian)
KULL LE ROI BARBARE (French)
REH: KADOTUKSEN KUILU (Finnish)
TZAR KULL (Russian)
ZMIERZCH NAD STONEHENGE (Polish)
HOSOK KORA (Hungarian)
KADOTUSSEN KUILU (Finnish)
REY KULL (Spanish)

## THE EXTERMINATION OF YELLOW DONARY

KOGHOT DRAKONA (Russian)

## FANGS OF GOLD

STEVE HARRISON ET LE MAITRE DES MORTS (French)

**THE FEAR-MASTER**
> LA TOMBE DU DRAGON (French)

**THE FEARSOME TOUCH OF DEATH**
> LE SIGNEUR DE SAMARCANDE (French)

**THE FIRE OF ASSHURBANIPAL**
> DE ZWARTE STEEN (Dutch)
> SUKARU FEISU (Japanese)
> LE PACTE NOIR (French, NeO)
> FUREUR NOIRS (French)
> KEN TO MAHOU NO MONGATARI (Japanese)
> ROSTRO DE CALAVERA (Spanish)
> ANTHOLOGIA EPISTIMONIKIS FANTASIAS - ISTORIES MAGIAS KE TROMOU, VOLUME 7 (Greek)
> KURO NO ISHIBUMI (Japanese)
> KUTHURU #7 (Japanese)
> LE PACTE NOIR, VOLUME 1 or 2 (French)
> BURY NAD ORIENTA (Bulgarian)
> PLOMIEN ASSURBANIPALA (Polish)
> ZMIERZCH NAD STONEHENGE (Polish)
> LA CUIDAD MUERTA (Spanish)
> TYGRI MORE (Czech)
> CHERNUY KAMEN (Russian)
> CHAS DRAKONA (Russian, printed in Belarus)
> CULTI INNOMINABILI (Italian)

**FIST AND FANG**
> STEVE COSTIGAN (French)

**THE FLAME KNIFE**
> CONAN DER ZWERVER (Dutch)
> CONAN TO HONO'O NO TAMKEN (Japanese)
> ARAJISHI CONAN (Japanese)
> CONAN – ESPADA & MAGIA #5 (Brazil, in Portugese)
> CONAN ETERNAL (Russian, LSDC version)
> KONAN SKITNIKA (Bulgarian)
> CONAN – CORSAR (Russian)
> CONAN OBIEZYSWIAT (Polish)
> CONAN (French, a later, much larger edition)
> KONAN: DEMONSKO OSTROVO (Yugoslavian, first part)
> KONAN: OPKOLJENI VUKOVI (Yugoslavian, second part)
> CONAN SNIKMORDERNES BY (Norwegian)
> CONAN DER WANDERER (German)
> CONAN UND DER FALMMENDOLCH (German)
> CONAN LO ZINGARO (Italian)
> CONAN FORGORAREN (Swedish)
> CONAN LE VAGABOND (French)
> CONAN EL VAGABUNDO (Spanish)

**FLAMING MARBLE**
> WYSLANCY WALHALLI (Polish)

**FLYING KNUCKLES**
First appeared in STEVE COSTIGAN LE CHAMPION (French)

**THE FOOTFALLS WITHIN**
LE RETOUR DE KANE (French)
DEGEN DER GERECHTIGKEIT (German)
REH: KADOTUKSEN KUILU (Finnish)
I FIGLI DI ASSHUR (Italian)
SOLOMON KANE (Italian)
SOLOMON KANE IL GIUSTIZIERE (Italian)
KSIEZYC CZASZEK (Polish)
LAS AVENTURAS DE SOLOMON KANE (Spanish)
KADOTUSSEN KUILU (Finnish)

**"FOR THE LOVE OF BARBARA ALLEN"**
LE TERTRE MAUDIT (French)
FICTION #223, May 1973 (French)
WILCZA GLOWA (Polish)

**THE FROST-GIANT'S DAUGHTER**
HAYAKAWA MYSTERY MAGAZINE, October 1969 (Japanese)
BOKENSHA CONAN (Japanese)
CONAN TO SEKIHI NO NORI (Japanese)
LA TOMBE DU DRAGON (French)
CONAN VAN CIMMERIE (Dutch)
CONAN - ESPADA & MAGIA #1 (Brazil, in Portugese)
REH: CONAN CIMMERIALAINEN (Finnish)
ANTHOLOGIA EPISTIMONIKIS FANTASIAS - ISTORIES ME THEOUS KE DEMONES /2, VOLUME 60
        (Greek, LSDC version)
I VASILIA TIS MAVRIS AKTIS (Greek)
CONAN IZ CIMERII (Russian)
FIL KULESI (Turkish)
CONAN (Russian)
OSSZES CONAN, TORTENETE 1 (Hungarian)
KONAN VARVARYNA (Bulgarian)
LA LEGGENDA DI CONAN IL CIMMERO (Italian)
L'URLO DI CONAN (Italian)
CONAN Z CYNERII (Polish)
CONAN Z CIMMERII (Polish)
CONAN (French, a later, much larger edition)
CONAN A KIMMERIAI (Hungarian)
KONAN: GRAD LOBANJA (Yugoslavian)
CONAN EN DE KONINGIN VAN DE ZWARTE KUST (Dutch)
KONAN I GOROD PLENENIYCH DOUSH (Russian)
CONAN BARBAR (Czech)
CONAN: MEC S FENIXEM (Czech)
CONAN (Czech)
CONAN, WHVG, 2003 (German)
CONAN VON CIMMERIA (German)
CONAN DI CIMMERIA (Italian)
CONAN IL CIMMERO (Italian)
CONAN CIMMERIERN (Swedish)
CONAN LE CIMMERIEN (French)
CONAN DE CIMMERIA (Spanish)

## THE GARDEN OF FEAR
GENSOU TO KAIKI #12 (Japanese)
SUKARU FEISU (Japanese)
O KIPOS TOU FOVOU (Greek)
L'HOMME NOIR (French)
GEISTER DER NACHT (German)
PORTTI, April 1993 (Finnish)
LOS GUSANOS DE LA TIERRA Y OTROS RELATES DE HORROR SOBRENATURAL (Spanish)
WYSLANCY WALHALLI (Polish)
EL REINE DE LAS SOMBRAS (Spanish)

## GATES OF EMPIRE
LA ROUTE D'AZRAEL (French)
BRAMY IMPERIUM (Polish)

## GENERAL IRONFIST
STEVE COSTIGAN LE CHAMPION (French)
LIK SMERCHA (Russian)

## GENSERIC'S FIFTH BORN SON
L'ILE DES EPOUVANTES (French)

## A GENT FROM BEAR CREEK (novel)
GENTELMEN S MEDVEZHEY RECHKI (Russian)

## GHOST IN THE DOORWAY
LA MANOIR DE LA TERREUR (French)

## GHOST WITH THE SILK HAT
LA FLAMME DE LA VENGEANCE (French)

## THE GOD IN THE BOWL
BOKENSHA CONAN (Japanese)
CONAN TO DOKURO NO MIYAKO (Japanese, LSDC version)
CONAN (Dutch, LSDC version)
CONAN (French, LSDC version)
CONAN - ESPADA & MAGIA #1 (Brazil, in Portugese)
I VASILIA TIS MAVRIS AKTIS (Greek)
CONAN ETERNAL (Russian, LSDC version)
FIL KULESI (Turkish)
CONAN (Russian)
OSSZES CONAN, TORTENETE 1 (Hungarian)
LA LEGGENDA DI CONAN IL CIMMERO (Italian)
L'URLO DI CONAN (Italian)
CONAN (Polish)
CONAN ZDOBYWCA (Polish)
CONAN (French, a later, much larger edition)
BARBAROK ES VARAZSLOK (Hungarian)
CONAN A KIMMERIAI (Hungarian)
CONAN (Croatian)
KONAN (Yugoslavian)
CONAN (Romanian)
KONANAS (Lithuanian)

CONAN BARBAR (Czech)
CONAN (Czech)
CONAN (Norwegian)
CONAN, WHVG (German)
CONAN, WHVG, 2003 (German)
CONAN! (Italian)
CONAN IL CIMMERO (Italian)
CONAN (Swedish)
CONAN (Polish, 1991 edition)
CONAN (Spanish)

**THE GODS OF BAL-SAGOTH**
O KIPOS TOU FOVOU (Greek)
L'HOMME NOIR (French)
DIE BESTIE VON BAL-SAGOTH (German)
PIMEYDEN LINNAKE (Finnish)
BRAN MAK MORN (Czech)
LOS GUSANOS DE LA TIERRA Y OTROS RELATES DE HORROR SOBRENATURAL (Spanish)
BOGOWIE BAL-SAGOTH (Polish)
PRZEKLENSTWO ZLOTEJ CZASZKI (Polish)
ARNYKIRALYOK (Hungarian)
TYGRI MORE (Czech)
VOZVRASHTENYE CONANA (Russian, print in Belerus)

**THE GODS THAT MEN FORGOT**
WYSLANCY WALHALLI (Polish)

**THE GOOD KNIGHT**
KOGHOT DRAKONA (Russian)

**GRAVEYARD RATS**
STEVE HARRISON ET LE TALON D'ARGENT (French)

**THE GREY GOD PASSES**
DE STEM VAN EL-LIL (Dutch)
BRAN MAK MORN (French)
GEISTER DER NACHT (German)
REH: KADOTUKSEN KUILU (Finnish)
TO LIKOFOS TON GKRIZON THEON (Greek)
I SIGNORI DELLA SPADA (Italian)
WEDROWCY Z VALHALLI (Polish)
ZMIERZCH NAD STONEHENGE (Polish)
KADOTUSSEN KUILU (Finnish)

**THE GRISLY HORROR**
LES HABITANTS DES TOMBES (French)
CHERNYE KANAAN (Russian)

**THE GUARDIAN OF THE IDOL**
L'ILE DES EPOUVANTES (French)

**GUESTS OF THE HOODOO ROOM**
LA MAIN DE LA DEESSE NOIRE (French)

## GUNS OF KHARTUM
WILD BILL CLANTON (French)
KOGHOT DRAKONA (Russian)

## THE HALL OF THE DEAD
CONAN (Dutch, LSDC version)
CONAN TO DOKURO NO MIYAKO (Japanese, LSDC version)
CONAN (French, LSDC version)
CONAN – ESPADA & MAGIA #3 (Brazil, in Portugese, LSDC version)
AZ ALKONY KIRALYAI (Hungarian)
CONAN ETERNAL (Russian, LSDC version)
FIL KULESI (Turkish, synopsis)
CONAN (Russian)
OSSZES CONAN, TORTENETE 1 (Hungarian)
LA LEGGENDA DI CONAN IL CIMMERO (Italian)
CONAN (Polish)
CONAN: STRAZNICY LARSHA / OKRWAWIONY BOG (Polish)
CONAN (French, a later, much larger edition)
CONAN (Croatian)
KONAN (Yugoslavian)
CONAN (Romanian)
KONANAS (Lithuanian)
CONAN (Norwegian)
CONAN, WHVG (German)
CONAN, WHVG, 2003 (German)
CONAN! (Italian)
CONAN IL CIMMERO (Italian)
CONAN (Swedish)
CONAN (Polish, 1991 edition)
CONAN (Spanish)

## THE HAND OF NERGAL
CONAN (Dutch, Lin Carter version)
CONAN TO DOKURO NO MIYAKO (Japanese, LSDC version)
CONAN (French, Lin Carter version)
CONAN – ESPADA & MAGIA #2 (Brazil, in Portugese, LSDC version)
AZ ALKONY KIRALYAI (Hungarian)
CONAN ETERNAL (Russian, Lin Carter version)
FIL KULESI (Turkish, fragment only)
CONAN (Russian)
OSSZES CONAN, TORTENETE 1 (Hungarian)
SFERA (Polish)
LA LEGGENDA DI CONAN IL CIMMERO (Italian)
CONAN (Polish)
CONAN (French, a later, much larger edition)
CONAN (Croatian)
KONAN: GRAD LOBANJA (Yugoslavian)
CONAN (Romanian)
KONANAS (Lithuanian)
CONAN (Norwegian)
CONAN, WHVG (German)
CONAN, WHVG, 2003 (German)
CONAN! (Italian)
CONAN IL CIMMERO (Italian)

CONAN (Swedish)
CONAN (Polish, 1991 edition)
CONAN: REKA NERGALA / STALOWY DEMON (Polish)
CONAN (Spanish)

**THE HAND OF OBEAH**
LA TOMBE DU DRAGON (French)

**HAND OF THE BLACK GODDESS**
LA MAIN DE LA DEESSE NOIRE (French)

**HARD-FISTED SENTIMENT**
First appeared in DENNIS DORGAN (French)

**THE HAUNTED HUT**
LE SIGNEUR DE SAMARCANDE (French)

**THE HAUNTER OF THE RING**
LES HABITANTS DES TOMBES (French)
CHERNYE KANAAN (Russian)
CIEN BESTII (Polish)

**THE HAWK OF BASTI**
LE RETOUR DE KANE (French)
LE ALI NOTTURNE (Italian)
SOLOMON KANE (Italian)
SOLOMON KANE IL GIUSTIZIERE (Italian)
DIE KRIEGER VON ASSUR (German)
SOLOMON KEIN (Russian)
KSIEZYC CZASZEK (Polish)
LAS AVENTURAS DE SOLOMON KANE (Spanish)

**HAWK OF THE HILLS**
EL BORAK L'INVINCIBLE (French)
MOICHANIE IDOLA (Russian)
ZAGINIONA DOLINA ISKANDERA (Polish)

**HAWKS OF OUTREMER**
CORMAC FITZGEOFFREY (French)
JASTZEBIE OUTREMERU (Polish)
HOSOK KORA (Hungarian)

**HAWKS OVER EGYPT**
O KIPOS TOU FOVOU (Greek)
LA ROUTE D'AZRAEL (French)
BRAMY IMPERIUM (Polish)

**HAWKS OVER SHEM**
CONAN DER VRIJBUITER (Dutch)
CONAN TO ARAWASHI NO MICHI (Japanese)
ARAJISHI CONAN (Japanese)
LA LEGGENDA DI CONAN IL CIMMERO (Italian)
CONAN (French, a later, much larger edition)

KONAN: PROKLETSTVO MONOLITA (Yugoslavian)
CONAN FRIBYTTEREN (Norwegian)
CONAN DER FREIBEUTER (German)
CONAN IL CIMMERO (Italian)
CONAN IL PIRATA (Italian)
CONAN PIRATEN (Swedish)
CONAN PIRAT (Polish)
CONAN LE FLIBUSTIER (French)
CONAN EL PIRATA (Spanish)

## THE HILLS OF THE DEAD
DE STEM VAN EL-LIL (Dutch)
LE RETOUR DE KANE (French)
HORA ANDO FANTAZI KESSOKUSEN #2 (Japanese)
ROSTRO DE CALAVERA (Spanish)
I LOFI TON NECRON KAI ALLA DIEGEMATA (Greek)
DEGEN DER GERECHTIGKEIT (German)
REH: YÖN KUNINKAAT (Finnish)
I FIGLI DI ASSHUR (Italian)
SOLOMON KANE (Italian)
SOLOMON KANE IL GIUSTIZIERE (Italian)
SOLOMON KEIN (Russian)
KSIEZYC CZASZEK (Polish)
LAS AVENTURAS DE SOLOMON KANE (Spanish)
A KIPONYAK HOLDJA (Hungarian)
LAS EXTRANAS AVENTURAS DE SOLOMON KANE (Spanish)

## THE HONOR OF THE SHIP
First appeared in DENNIS DORGAN (French)

## THE HORROR FROM THE MOUND
DE STEM VAN EL-LIL (Dutch)
CHI DI VAMPIRO FERISCE: H.P. LOVECRAFT & OTHERS (Italian)
HISTOIRES ANGLO-SAXONNES DE VAMPIRES (French)
LE TERTRE MAUDIT (French)
KEN TO MAHOU NO MONGATARI (Japanese)
ROSTRO DE CALAVERA (Spanish)
OUTOJA TARINOITA #5 (Finnish)
CIEN BESTII (Polish)
LA CUIDAD MUERTA (Spanish)
ROSTRO DE CALAVERA (Spanish, Ediciones Martinez Roca, S.A.)

## A HORROR IN THE NIGHT
LA MANOIR DE LA TERREUR (French)

## THE HOUR OF THE DRAGON
SEIFUKU-O CONAN (Japanese)
BOKENO CONAN (Japanese, toned-down by translator for juvenile market)
CONAN EL CONQUISTADOR (Spanish)
CONAN DE BARBAAR: HET UUR VAN DE DRAAK (Dutch)
CONAN LE CONQUERANT (French)
REH: CONAN VOITTAJA (Finnish)
FATIH CONAN (Turkish)
CONAN IZ CIMERII (Russian)

DRAAKONI TUND (Estonian)
CONAN ZAVOEVATELYA (Bulgarian)
KONAN: CHASUT NA DRAKONA (Bulgarian)
IL REGNO DI CONAN (Italian)
IL REGNO DI CONAN IL GRANDE (Italian)
L'ORA DEL DRAGONE (Italian)
L'ORA DI CONAN (Italian)
TUTTI I CICLI FANTASTICI, VOLUME 2: IL CICLO DI CONAN, VOLUME 2 (Italian)
CONAN: GODZINA SMOKA (Polish)
CONAN ZDOBYWCA (Polish)
CONAN A BOSSZUALLO (Hungarian)
KONAN HO KATAKTETES (Greek)
CONAN JA PUNANE KANTS (Estonian)
CHAS DRAKONA (Russian, printed in Belarus)
CONAN DOBYVATEL (Czech)
CONAN – HODINA DRAKA (Czech)
CONAN DER EROBERER (German)
CONAN HARSKAREN (Swedish)

## THE HOUSE IN THE OAKS
SHIN KU RITORU SIHWA TAIKEI #9 (Japanese)
LES HABITANTS DES TOMBES (French)
CHERNYE KANAAN (Russian)
CULTI INNOMINABILI (Italian)

## THE HOUSE OF SUSPICION
STEVE HARRISON ET LE TALON D'ARGENT (French)
KOGHOT DRAKONA (Russian)

## THE HYBORIAN AGE
DE STEM VAN EL-LIL (Dutch)
CONAN TO DOKURO NO MIYAKO (Japanese, part 1)
DAI-TEIO CONAN (Japanese, part 2)
KULL (German, part 1)
KULL VON ATLANTIS (German, part 1)
KULL DI VALUSIA (Italian)
KULL DI VALUSIA (Greek, portions)
CONAN (Dutch, part 1)
CONAN (French, part 1)
HERR VON VALUSIEN (German, part 2)
ROSTRO DE CALAVERA (Spanish)
KONAN UNISHTOZHITELYA (Bulgarian)
CONAN IZ CIMERII (Russian)
FIL KULESI (Turkish)
CONAN (Russian)
OSSZES CONAN, TORTENETE 1 (Hungarian)
LA LEGGENDA DI CONAN IL CIMMERO (Italian)
L'ERA HYBORIANA DI CONAN (Italian)
L'ERA HYBORIANA DI CONAN IL CIMMERO (Italian)
CONAN (Polish, later printing only)
CONAN Z CIMMERII (Polish)
CONAN (French, a later, much larger edition)
CONAN (Croatian)
CONAN (Romanian)

CONAN BARBAR (Czech)
CONAN DOBYVATEL (Czech)
CONAN BARBAR A JINE POVIDKY (Czech)
CONAN (Czech)
CONAN (Norwegian)
CONAN, WHVG (German, later edition only)
CONAN, WHVG, 2003 (German)
CONAN IL CIMMERO (Italian)
CONAN (Swedish)
CONAN CIMMERIERN (Swedish)
CONAN: DROGA DO TRONU (Polish)
CONAN (Spanish)
REY KULL (Spanish)

## THE HYENA
KIRBY O'DONNELL (French)
PIMEDUSE RAHVAS (Estonian)
CIEN BESTII (Polish)
NIE KOPCIE MI GROBU (Polish)

## IN HIGH SOCIETY
DENNIS DORGAN (French)

## IN THE FOREST OF VILLEFERE
WOLFSHEAD (Chpbk., German)
L'HOMME NOIR (French)
DAS HAUS DES GRAUENS (German)
DER LOVECRAFT-ZIRKEL (German)
LOS GUSANOS DE LA TIERRA Y OTROS RELATES DE HORROR SOBRENATURAL (Spanish)
PIMEDUSE RAHVAS (Estonian)
CHERNYE KANAAN (Russian)
NIE KOPCIE MI GROBU (Polish)
EL REINE DE LAS SOMBRAS (Spanish)

## INTRIGUE IN KURDISTAN
First appeared in EL BORAK L'ETERNEL (French)

## THE IRON MAN
POING D'ACIER (French)

## THE IRON TERROR
First appeared in EL BORAK L'ETERNEL (French)
KROV BOGOV (Russian)

## IRON-JAW
POING D'ACIER (French)

## THE ISLE OF PIRATES' DOOM
VULMEA LE PIRATE NOIR (French)
PRZEKLENSTWO ZLOTEJ CZASZKI (Polish)

## THE ISLE OF THE EONS
L'ILE DES EPOUVANTES (French)

**THE JEWELS OF GWAHLUR**
    FUSISHO CONAN (Japanese)
    CONAN EL GUERRERO (Spanish)
    CONAN TO KODAI-OHKOKU NO HIHOU (Japanese)
    CONAN DE KRIJGER (Dutch)
    REH: CONAN CIMMERIALAINEN (Finnish)
    CONAN IZ CIMERII (Russian)
    CONAN DE CIMMERIA III (Spanish)
    IL REGNO DI CONAN (Italian)
    IL REGNO DI CONAN IL GRANDE (Italian)
    L'IRA DI CONAN (Italian)
    TUTTI I CICLI FANTASTICI, VOLUME 2: IL CICLO DI CONAN, VOLUME 2 (Italian)
    KONAN I POVELITELY PESHTER (Russian)
    CONAN (Polish)
    CONAN NAJEMNIK (Polish)
    CONAN WOJOWNIK (Polish)
    A SZOLDAS BARBAR (Hungarian)
    CONAN A KIMMERIAI (Hungarian)
    KONAN: DRAGULJI GVAHLURA (Yugoslavian)
    CONAN JA VARELEV VARI (Estonian)
    CONAN DOBYVATEL (Czech)
    CONAN (Czech)
    CONAN KRIGEREN (Norwegian)
    CONAN KRIGAREN (Swedish)
    CONAN LA NAISSANCE DU MONDE (French)
    CONAN LE GUERRIER (French)

**KHODA KHAN'S TALE**
First appeared in EL BORAK L'ETERNEL (French)
    KROV BOGOV (Russian)

**KING OF THE FORGOTTEN PEOPLE**
    ALMURIK I INNE OPOWIADANIA (Polish)

**KINGS OF THE NIGHT**
    DE STEM VAN EL-LIL (Dutch)
    HERRSCHER DER NACHT (German)
    BRAN MAK MORN (French)
    GENSOU BUNGAKU #19, July 1987 (Japanese)
    REH: YÖN KUNINKAAT (Finnish)
    BRAN MAK MORN (Czech)
    I SIGNORI DELLA SPADA (Italian)
    KROLOWIE NOCY (Polish)
    ROBAKI ZIEMI (Polish)
    ARNYKIRALYOK (Hungarian)
    GUSANOS DE LA TIERRE (Spanish)

**THE KING'S SERVICE**
    AGNES DE CHASTILLON (French)

**KNIFE, BULLET & NOOSE**
    KROV BOGOV (Russian)

**KNIFE-RIVER PRODIGAL**
  LA TOMBE DU DRAGON (French)
  KOGHOT DRAKONA (Russian)

**A KNIGHT OF THE ROUND TABLE**
  DENNIS DORGAN (French)

**LAL SINGH, ORIENTAL GENTLEMAN**
  KROV BOGOV (Russian)

**THE LAND OF MYSTERY**
First appeared in EL BORAK L'ETERNEL (French)

**THE LAST WHITE MAN**
  L'ULTIMO UOMO BIANCO (Italian)

**THE LION OF TIBERIAS**
  DIE BESTIE VON BAL-SAGOTH (German)
  SONYA LA ROUGE (French)
  BURY NAD ORIENTA (Bulgarian)
  ZNAK OGNYA (Russian)

**THE LITTLE PEOPLE**
  LE SIGNEUR DE SAMARCANDE (French)

**LORD OF SAMARCAND**
  LE SIGNEUR DE SAMARCANDE (French)
  GEISTER DER NACHT (German)
  BURY NAD ORIENTA (Bulgarian)

**LORD OF THE DEAD**
  STEVE HARRISON ET LE MAITRE DES MORTS (French)
  O ARCHONTAS TON NECRON (Greek)
  MOICHANIE IDOLA (Russian)

**THE LOSER**
  LA TOMBE DU DRAGON (French)

**THE LOST RACE**
  HAYAKAWA MYSTERY MAGAZINE, July 1970 (Japanese)
  HERRSCHER DER NACHT (German)
  BRAN MAK MORN (French)
  BRAN MAK MORN (Czech)
  ROBAKI ZIEMI (Polish)
  HOSOK KORA (Hungarian)
  TYGRI MORE (Czech)
  GUSANOS DE LA TIERRE (Spanish)

**THE LOST VALLEY OF ISKANDER**
 EL BORAK L'INVINCIBLE (French)
 ZNAK OGNYA (Russian)
 ZAGINIONA DOLINA ISKANDERA (Polish)

**THE MAN ON THE GROUND**
 HISTOIRES D'OUTRE-MONDE (French)
 DE STEM VAN EL-LIL (Dutch)
 LE TERTRE MAUDIT (French)
 THE RAVEN #1 (Chpbk., German)
 LOS GUSANOS DE LA TIERRA Y OTROS RELATES DE HORROR SOBRENATURAL (Spanish)
 CIEN BESTII (Polish)
 NIE KOPCIE MI GROBU (Polish)

**A MAN-EATING JEOPARD**
 ROSTRO DE CALAVERA (Spanish)
 LA TOMBE DU DRAGON (French)

**MARCHERS OF VALHALLA**
 LE PACTE NOIR (French, NeO)
 FUREUR NOIRS (French)
 LE PACTE NOIR, VOLUME 1 or 2 (French)
 GESPENSTER DER VERGANGENHEIT (German)
 WEDROWCY Z VALHALLI (Polish)
 WYSLANCY WALHALLI (Polish)

**THE MARK OF THE BLOODY HAND**
 LA MANOIR DE LA TERREUR (French)

**A MATTER OF AGE**
 LA TOMBE DU DRAGON (French)

**MEDALLIONS IN THE MOON**
 WYSLANCY WALHALLI (Polish)

**MEN OF IRON**
 POING D'ACIER (French)

**MEN OF THE SHADOWS**
 HERRSCHER DER NACHT (German)
 BRAN MAK MORN (French)
 BRAN MAK MORN (Czech)
 ROBAKI ZIEMI (Polish)
 HOSOK KORA (Hungarian)
 TYGRI MORE (Czech)
 GUSANOS DE LA TIERRE (Spanish)

**THE MIRRORS OF TUZUN THUNE**
 LOS CUENTOS FANTASTICOS, October 1948 (Spanish)
 KULL (Greek)
 S-F MAGAZINE, October 1971 (Japanese)
 KULL DI VALUSIA (Italian)
 LES MEILLEURS RECITS DE WEIRD TALES, VOLUME 1 (French)

KULL LE ROI BARBARE (French)
HERR VON VALUSIEN (German)
REH: YÖN KUNINKAAT (Finnish)
KULL VON ATLANTIS (German, later edition only)
TZAR KULL (Russian)
HOSOK KORA (Hungarian)
EL REINE DE LAS SOMBRAS (Spanish)
REY KULL (Spanish)

**MISS HIGH-HAT**
LA TOMBE DU DRAGON (French)

**MISTRESS OF DEATH**
HORDE AUS DEM MORGENLAND (German)
AGNES DE CHASTILLON (French)

**THE MOON OF SKULLS**
SOLOMON KANE (French)
RACHER DER VERDAMMTEN (German)
ATLANTIDES (French)
REH: KADOTUKSEN KUILU (Finnish)
LA LUNA DEI TESCHI (Italian)
SOLOMON KANE (Italian)
SOLOMON KANE IL GIUSTIZIERE (Italian)
SOLOMON KEIN (Russian)
KSIEZYC CZASZEK (Polish)
LAS AVENTURAS DE SOLOMON KANE (Spanish)
A KIPONYAK HOLDJA (Hungarian)
KADOTUSSEN KUILU (Finnish)
LAS EXTRANAS AVENTURAS DE SOLOMON KANE (Spanish)

**MURDERER'S GROG**
WILD BILL CLANTON (French)

**MUSINGS OF A MORON**
THE RAVEN #1 (Chpbk., German)

**THE MYSTERY OF TANNERNOE LODGE**
STEVE HARRISON ET LE MAITRE DES MORTS (French)

**NAMES IN THE BLACK BOOK**
STEVE HARRISON ET LE MAITRE DES MORTS (French)
O ARCHONTAS TON NECRON (Greek)
MOICHANIE IDOLA (Russian)

**NEKHT SEMERKEHT**
LE CHIEN DE LA MORT (French)
ANTHOLOGIA EPISTIMONIKIS FANTASIAS - ISTORIES APO PARAXENOUS TOPOUS, VOLUME 18
    (Greek)
DIE BESTEN FANTASY-STORES 4 (German)

**NERVE**
LA TOMBE DU DRAGON (French)

**NIGHT OF BATTLE**
 STEVE COSTIGAN LE CHAMPION (French)
 LIK SMERCHA (Russian)

**THE NIGHT OF THE WOLF**
 KRIEGER DES NORDENS (German)
 CORMAC MAC ART (French)
 TYGRI MORE (Czech)
 VOZVRASHTENYE CONANA (Russian, print in Belerus)

**NORTH OF KHYBER**
First appeared in EL BORAK L'ETERNEL (French)

**THE NOSELESS HORROR**
 EL BORAK LE MAGNIFIQUE (French)
 CHERNYE KANAAN (Russian)
 CIEN BESTII (Polish)

**NOTES ON THE VARIOUS PEOPLES OF THE HYBORIAN AGE**
 CONAN (Russian)
 CONAN, WHVG, 2003 (German)

**THE NUT'S SHELL**
 LA TOMBE DU DRAGON (French)

**OLD GARFIELD'S HEART**
 VINGT PAS DANS L'AU-DELA (French)
 LE TERTRE MAUDIT (French)
 KURO NO ISHIBUMI (Japanese)
 LOS GUSANOS DE LA TIERRA Y OTROS RELATES DE HORROR SOBRENATURAL (Spanish)
 PIMEDUSE RAHVAS (Estonian)
 CHERNYE KANAAN (Russian)
 CIEN BESTII (Polish)
 NIE KOPCIE MI GROBU (Polish)
 ZMIERZCH NAD STONEHENGE (Polish)

**OUT OF THE DEEP**
 LE TERTRE MAUDIT (French)

**PAY DAY**
 LA TOMBE DU DRAGON (French)

**THE PEOPLE OF THE BLACK CIRCLE**
 FU'UNJI CONAN (Japanese)
 CONAN TO KUROI YOGENSHA (Japanese)
 CONAN EL AVENTURERO (Spanish)
 REH: CONAN JA DEMONIT (Finnish)
 CONAN DE AVONTURIER (Dutch)
 MAGOS (Brazil, in Portugese)
 OI MAVROI PROPHITES (Greek)
 CONAN IZ CIMERII (Russian)
 OSSZES CONAN, TORTENETE 1 (Hungarian)
 KONAN AVANTURISTA (Bulgarian)

KONAN VARVARYNA (Bulgarian)
I VEGGENTI NERI (Italian)
LA LEGGENDA DI CONAN IL CIMMERO (Italian)
L'IRA DI CONAN (Italian)
LUDZIE CZARNEGO KREGU (Polish)
CONAN A KIMMERIAI (Hungarian)
KONAN HO TYKHODIOKTES (Greek)
KONAN: OPKOLJENI VUKOVI (Yugoslavian, first part)
KONAN: PRINC CAROBNJAKA (Yugoslavian, second part)
CONAN JA VARELEV VARI (Estonian)
CHAS DRAKONA (Russian, printed in Belarus)
CONAN BARBAR (Czech)
CONAN (Czech)
CONAN EVENTYREREN (Norwegian)
CONAN DER ABENTEURER (German)
CONAN AVENTYRAREN (Swedish)
CONAN RYZYKANT (Polish)
CONAN LA FIN DE L'ATLANTIDE (French)
CONAN L'AVENTURIER (French)

## PEOPLE OF THE BLACK COAST
LES HABITANTS DES TOMBES (French)
ALMURIK I INNE OPOWIADANIA (Polish)
CHERNUY KAMEN (Russian)

## PEOPLE OF THE DARK
HAYAKAWA MYSTERY MAGAZINE, November 1973 (Japanese)
LE PACTE NOIR (French, NeO)
LE PACTE NOIR (French, Marabout)
GESPENSTER DER VERGANGENHEIT (German)
ANTHOLOGIA EPISTIMONIKIS FANTASIAS – ISTORIES IROIKIS FANTASIAS, VOLUME 12 (Greek)
LE PACTE NOIR, VOLUME 1 or 2 (French)
REH: KADOTUKSEN KUILU (Finnish)
KURO NO ISHIBUMI (Japanese)
LOS GUSANOS DE LA TIERRA Y OTROS RELATES DE HORROR SOBRENATURAL (Spanish)
PIMEDUSE RAHVAS (Estonian)
WYSLANCY WALHALLI (Polish)
KADOTUSSEN KUILU (Finnish)

## THE PHOENIX ON THE SWORD
PLANÈTE #24, September-October 1965 (French)
DAI-TEIO CONAN (Japanese)
ROSTRO DE CALAVERA (Spanish)
L'ERA DI CONAN (Italian)
CONAN L' USURPATORE (Italian)
CONAN DE OVERWELDIGER (Dutch)
REH: CONAN TAISTELIJA (Finnish)
CONAN - ESPADA & MAGIA #1 (Brazil, in Portugese)
CHERNYAT KOLOS (Bulgarian)
CONAN IZ CIMERII (Russian)
CONAN (Russian, first published plus first draft versions)
IL REGNO DI CONAN (Italian)
IL REGNO DI CONAN IL GRANDE (Italian)
TUTTI I CICLI FANTASTICI, VOLUME 2: IL CICLO DI CONAN, VOLUME 2 (Italian)

BARBARZYNCA (Polish)
CONAN (Polish)
CONAN UZURPATOR (Polish)
CONAN ZDOBYWCA (Polish)
BARBAROK ES VARAZSLOK (Hungarian)
CONAN A KIMMERIAI (Hungarian)
CONAN JA PUNANE KANTS (Estonian)
CONAN EN DE SCHARLAKEN CITADEL (Dutch)
CONAN DOBYVATEL (Czech)
CONAN (Czech)
CONAN TAISTELIJA (Finnish)
CONAN TRONRANEREN (Norwegian)
CONAN, WHVG, 2003 (German)
CONAN DER THRONRAUBER (German)
CONAN DER USURPATOR (German)
CONAN SEGRAREN (Swedish)
CONAN L'USURPATEUR (French)
CONAN EL USURPADOR (Spanish)

## PICTURES IN THE FIRE
LA MANOIR DE LA TERREUR (French, first complete publication)

## PIGEONS FROM HELL
ANKOKU NO SAIKI (Japanese)
L'HOMME NOIR (French)
OUTOJA TARINOITA #1 (Finnish)
DAS HAUS DES GRAUENS (German)
KURO NO ISHIBUMI (Japanese)
KARANLIKTA 33 YAZAR (Turkish)
LOS GUSANOS DE LA TIERRA Y OTROS RELATES DE HORROR SOBRENATURAL (Spanish)
CHERNYAT KOLOS (Bulgarian)
CHERNYE KANAAN (Russian)
KRWAWY MONOLIT (Polish)
WILCZA GLOWA (Polish)
CHAS DRAKONA (Russian, printed in Belarus)

## THE PISTOL POLITICS
ZAKAZANE MIASTO GOTHAN (Polish)

## THE PIT OF THE SERPENT
STEVE COSTIGAN (French)

## PLAYING JOURNALIST
DENNIS DORGAN (French)

## PLAYING SANTA CLAUS
DENNIS DORGAN (French)

## THE POOL OF THE BLACK ONE
FU'UNJI CONAN (Japanese)
CONAN TO KUROI YOGENSHA (Japanese)
CONAN EL AVENTURERO (Spanish)
CONAN - ESPADA & MAGIA #5 (Brazil, in Portugese)

CONAN DE AVONTURIER (Dutch)
REH: CONAN CIMMERIALAINEN (Finnish)
CONAN IZ CIMERII (Russian)
CONAN (Russian)
KONAN AVANTURISTA (Bulgarian)
LA LEGGENDA DI CONAN IL CIMMERO (Italian)
L'IRA DI CONAN (Italian)
CONAN (Polish)
CONAN NAJEMNIK (Polish)
CONAN ZDOBYWCA (Polish)
KONAN HO TYKHODIOKTES (Greek)
KONAN: TAJANSTVENI GAZAL (Yugoslavian)
CONAN JA VARELEV VARI (Estonian)
CONAN BARBAR (Czech)
CONAN (Czech)
CONAN EVENTYREREN (Norwegian)
CONAN, WHVG, 2003 (German)
CONAN DER ABENTEURER (German)
CONAN AVENTYRAREN (Swedish)
CONAN RYZYKANT (Polish)
CONAN LA FIN DE L'ATLANTIDE (French)
CONAN L'AVENTURIER (French)

## POST OAKS AND SAND ROUGHS
First appeared in LE REBELLE (French)
RAUHER SAND UND WILDE EICHEN (German)

## A POWER AMONG THE ISLANDS
First appeared in EL BORAK L'ETERNEL (French)

## THE PURPLE HEART OF ERLIK
HAYAKAWA MYSTERY MAGAZINE, December 1974 (Japanese)
WILD BILL CLANTON (French)

## QUEEN OF THE BLACK COAST
CUENTOS DE ABUELITO – LA REINA DE LA COSTA NEGRA, ca. 1952 (Spanish, comic series)
LA REINA DE LA COSTA NEGRA, 1958-1966 (Spanish, comic)
CONAN VAN CIMMERIE (Dutch)
HAYAKAWA MYSTERY MAGAZINE, October 1969 (Japanese)
HAYAKAWA MYSTERY MAGAZINE, November 1969 (Japanese)
CONAN TO SEKIHI NO NORI (Japanese)
BOKENSHA CONAN (Japanese)
REH: CONAN JA DEMONIT (Finnish)
CONAN - ESPADA & MAGIA #4 (Brazil, in Portugese)
ANTHOLOGIA EPISTIMONIKIS FANTASIAS - ISTORIES EMATOS KE PATHOUS, VOLUME 49
        (Greek)
I VASILIA TIS MAVRIS AKTIS (Greek)
KONAN UNISHTOZHITELYA (Bulgarian)
CONAN IZ CIMERII (Russian)
FIL KULESI (Turkish)
CONAN (Russian)
OSSZES CONAN, TORTENETE 1 (Hungarian)
LA LEGGENDA DI CONAN IL CIMMERO (Italian)
L'IRA DI CONAN (Italian)

CONAN Z CYNERII (Polish)
CONAN Z CIMMERII (Polish)
CONAN (French, a later, much larger edition)
CONAN A KIMMERIAI (Hungarian)
KONAN: GRAD LOBANJA (Yugoslavian, part 1)
KONAN: PROKLETSTVO MONOLITA (Yugoslavian, part 2)
CONAN JA MUSTA RANNIKU KUNINGANNA (Estonian)
CONAN EN DE KONINGIN VAN DE ZWARTE KUST (Dutch)
KONAN I GOROD PLENENIYCH DOUSH (Russian)
CONAN BARBAR (Czech)
CONAN (Czech)
CONAN, WHVG, 2003 (German)
CONAN VON CIMMERIA (German)
CONAN DI CIMMERIA (Italian)
CONAN IL CIMMERO (Italian)
CONAN CIMMERIERN (Swedish)
CONAN LE CIMMERIEN (French)
CONAN DE CIMMERIA (Spanish)

## RATTLE OF BONES

SOLOMON KANE (French)
ROSTRO DE CALAVERA (Spanish)
DEGEN DER GERECHTIGKEIT (German)
I LOFI TON NECRON KAI ALLA DIEGEMATA (Greek)
LE ALI NOTTURNE (Italian)
SOLOMON KANE (Italian)
SOLOMON KANE IL GIUSTIZIERE (Italian)
SOLOMON KEIN (Russian)
CZERWONE CIENIE (Polish)
LAS AVENTURAS DE SOLOMON KANE (Spanish)
A KIPONYAK HOLDJA (Hungarian)
LAS EXTRANAS AVENTURAS DE SOLOMON KANE (Spanish)

## RED BLADES OF BLACK CATHAY

CORMAC FITZGEOFFREY (French)

## RED NAILS

FUSISHO CONAN (Japanese)
CONAN TO KODAI-OHKOKU NO HIHOU (Japanese)
DE STEM VAN EL-LIL (Dutch)
CONAN EL GUERRERO (Spanish)
REH: CONAN TAISTELIJA (Finnish)
CONAN DE KRIJGER (Dutch)
CONAN O PIRGOS TOU ERPETOU (Greek)
PREGOS VERMELHOS (Brazil, in Portugese)
KONAN UNISHTOZHITELYA (Bulgarian)
O PIRGOS TOU ERPETOU – PERA APO TON MAVRO POTAMO (Greek)
CONAN IZ CIMERII (Russian)
CONAN DE CIMMERIA III (Spanish)
IL REGNO DI CONAN (Italian)
IL REGNO DI CONAN IL GRANDE (Italian)
L'URLO DI CONAN (Italian)
TUTTI I CICLI FANTASTICI, VOLUME 2: IL CICLO DI CONAN, VOLUME 2 (Italian)
KONAN I POVELITELY PESHTER (Russian)

CONAN WOJOWNIK (Polish)
CLAVOS ROJOS (Spanish)
A SZOLDAS BARBAR (Hungarian)
CONAN A KIMMERIAI (Hungarian)
KONAN: TAJANSTVENI GAZAL (Yugoslavian, part 1)
KONAN: DRAGULJI GVAHLURA (Yugoslavian, part 2)
CONAN JA VARELEV VARI (Estonian)
CONAN DOBYVATEL (Czech)
CONAN (Czech)
CONAN TAISTELIJA (Finnish)
CONAN KRIGEREN (Norwegian)
CHIODI ROSSI (Italian)
CONAN KRIGAREN (Swedish)
CONAN: CZERWONE CWIEKI (Polish)
CONAN: DROGA DO TRONU (Polish)
CONAN LA NAISSANCE DU MONDE (French)
CONAN LE GUERRIER (French)

## RED SHADOWS
SOLOMON KANE (French)
DEGEN DER GERECHTIGKEIT (German)
REH: YÖN KUNINKAAT (Finnish)
LE ALI NOTTURNE (Italian)
SOLOMON KANE (Italian)
SOLOMON KANE IL GIUSTIZIERE (Italian)
SOLOMON KEIN (Russian)
CZERWONE CIENIE (Polish)
LAS AVENTURAS DE SOLOMON KANE (Spanish)
A KIPONYAK HOLDJA (Hungarian)
VOZVRASHTENYE CONANA (Russian, print in Belerus)
LAS EXTRANAS AVENTURAS DE SOLOMON KANE (Spanish)

## RESTLESS WATERS
LE CHIEN DE LA MORT (French)

## THE RETURN OF SKULL-FACE
LA MANOIR DE LA TERREUR (French, as "Taverel Manor")
BRAT BOURY (Bulgarian, as "Taverel Manor")

## THE RETURN OF THE SORCERER
LA TOMBE DU DRAGON (French)

## RIDERS BEYOND THE SUNRISE
KULL (Greek)
KULL DI VALUSIA (Italian)
KULL LE ROI BARBARE (French)
HERR VON VALUSIEN (German)
REY KULL (Spanish)

## THE RIGHT HAND OF DOOM
SOLOMON KANE (French)
RACHER DER VERDAMMTEN (German)
LE ALI NOTTURNE (Italian)
SOLOMON KANE (Italian)

SOLOMON KANE IL GIUSTIZIERE (Italian)
SOLOMON KEIN (Russian)
CZERWONE CIENIE (Polish)
LAS AVENTURAS DE SOLOMON KANE (Spanish)
HOSOK KORA (Hungarian)
LAS EXTRANAS AVENTURAS DE SOLOMON KANE (Spanish)

**RIGHT HOOK**
First appeared in POING D'ACIER (French)

**THE ROAD OF AZRAEL**
LA ROUTE D'AZRAEL (French)
DIE KRIEGER VON ASSUR (German)
BRAMY IMPERIUM (Polish)

**THE ROAD OF EAGLES (LSDC version)**
CONAN DER VRIJBUITER (Dutch)
CONAN TO ARAWASHI NO MICHI (Japanese)
ARAJISHI CONAN (Japanese)
LA LEGGENDA DI CONAN IL CIMMERO (Italian)
CONAN (French, a later, much larger edition)
KONAN: CRNI KOLOS (Yugoslavian)
CONAN FRIBYTTEREN (Norwegian)
CONAN DER FREIBEUTER (German)
CONAN IL CIMMERO (Italian)
CONAN IL PIRATA (Italian)
CONAN PIRATEN (Swedish)
CONAN PIRAT (Polish)
CONAN LE FLIBUSTIER (French)
CONAN EL PIRATA (Spanish)

**ROGUES IN THE HOUSE**
BOKENSHA CONAN (Japanese)
CONAN TO DOKURO NO MIYAKO (Japanese)
ROSTRO DE CALAVERA (Spanish)
CONAN (Dutch)
CONAN (French)
REH: CONAN JA DEMONIT (Finnish)
I VASILIA TIS MAVRIS AKTIS (Greek)
CONAN IZ CIMERII (Russian)
FIL KULESI (Turkish)
CONAN (Russian)
OSSZES CONAN, TORTENETE 1 (Hungarian)
LA LEGGENDA DI CONAN IL CIMMERO (Italian)
L'IRA DI CONAN (Italian)
CONAN Z CIMMERII (Polish)
CONAN (French, a later, much larger edition)
LA CUIDAD MUERTA (Spanish)
BARBAROK ES VARAZSLOK (Hungarian)
CONAN A KIMMERIAI (Hungarian)
CONAN (Croatian)
KONAN (Yugoslavian)
CONAN JA MUSTA RANNIKU KUNINGANNA (Estonian)
CONAN (Romanian)

KONANAS (Lithuanian)
CONAN BARBAR (Czech)
CONAN (Czech)
CONAN (Norwegian)
CONAN, WHVG (German)
CONAN, WHVG, 2003 (German)
CONAN! (Italian)
CONAN IL CIMMERO (Italian)
CONAN (Swedish)
CONAN (Polish, 1991 edition)
CONAN (Spanish)

## SAILOR COSTIGAN AND THE SWAMI
STEVE COSTIGAN LE CHAMPION (French)

## SAILOR DORGAN AND THE JADE MONKEY
DENNIS DORGAN (French)

## SAILORS' GRUDGE
STEVE COSTIGAN (French)

## THE SCARLET CITADEL
LA CITADELLE ECARLATE (French)
DAI-TEIO CONAN (Japanese)
ROSTRO DE CALAVERA (Spanish)
CONAN DE OVERWELDIGER (Dutch)
CONAN L' USURPATORE (Italian)
L'ERA DI CONAN (Italian)
REH: CONAN TAISTELIJA (Finnish)
LES MEILLEURS RECITS DE WEIRD TALES, VOLUME 2 (French)
SARLATOVA CITADELA (Czech)
CONAN IZ CIMERII (Russian)
CONAN (Russian, original version plus synopsis)
IL REGNO DI CONAN (Italian)
IL REGNO DI CONAN IL GRANDE (Italian)
TUTTI I CICLI FANTASTICI, VOLUME 2: IL CICLO DI CONAN, VOLUME 2 (Italian)
CONAN UZURPATOR (Polish)
LA CUIDAD MUERTA (Spanish)
BARBAROK ES VARAZSLOK (Hungarian)
CONAN A KIMMERIAI (Hungarian)
CONAN JA PUNANE KANTS (Estonian)
CONAN EN DE SCHARLAKEN CITADEL (Dutch)
CONAN DOBYVATEL (Czech)
CONAN (Czech)
CONAN TAISTELIJA (Finnish)
CONAN TRONRANEREN (Norwegian)
CONAN, WHVG, 2003 (German)
CONAN DER THRONRAUBER (German)
CONAN DER USURPATOR (German)
CONAN SEGRAREN (Swedish)
CONAN: DROGA DO TRONU (Polish)
CONAN L'USURPATEUR (French)
CONAN EL USURPADOR (Spanish)

## SEA CURSE
LE TERTRE MAUDIT (French)
CHERNYAT KOLOS (Bulgarian)

## SECRET OF LOST VALLEY
LE TERTRE MAUDIT (French)
REH: KADOTUKSEN KUILU (Finnish)
CHERNYE KANAAN (Russian)
NIE KOPCIE MI GROBU (Polish)
PRZEKLENSTWO ZLOTEJ CZASZKI (Polish)
KADOTUSSEN KUILU (Finnish)

## SERPENT VINES
LA MANOIR DE LA TERREUR (French)

## SHACKLED MITTS
First appeared in LA TOMBE DU DRAGON (French)

## THE SHADOW KINGDOM
DE ZWARTE STEEN (Dutch)
KULL (Greek)
KULL (German)
KULL VON ATLANTIS (German)
KULL DI VALUSIA (Italian)
ANTHOLOGIA EPISTIMONIKIS FANTASIAS - ISTORIES APO FANTASTIKOUS COSMOUS,
  VOLUME 1 (Greek)
KULL LE ROI BARBARE (French)
WEIRD TALES #2 (Japanese)
ATLANTIDES (French)
REH: YÖN KUNINKAAT (Finnish)
TZAR KULL (Russian)
ARNYKIRALYOK (Hungarian)
EL REINE DE LAS SOMBRAS (Spanish)
REY KULL (Spanish)

## THE SHADOW OF DOOM
LA MANOIR DE LA TERREUR (French)
YORICK #32/33 (Italian)

## THE SHADOW OF THE BEAST
LE CHIEN DE LA MORT (French)
KURO NO ISHIBUMI (Japanese)
LOS GUSANOS DE LA TIERRA Y OTROS RELATES DE HORROR SOBRENATURAL (Spanish)
CIEN BESTII (Polish)
ZMIERZCH NAD STONEHENGE (Polish)

## THE SHADOW OF THE HUN
AGNES DE CHASTILLON (French)

## THE SHADOW OF THE VULTURE
HORDE AUS DEM MORGENLAND (German)
SONYA LA ROUGE (French)
REH: KADOTUKSEN KUILU (Finnish)

BURY NAD ORIENTA (Bulgarian)
KADOTUSSEN KUILU (Finnish)
EL REINE DE LAS SOMBRAS (Spanish)
LAS EXTRANAS AVENTURAS DE SOLOMON KANE (Spanish)

## SHADOWS IN THE MOONLIGHT

S-F MAGAZINE, April 1969 (Japanese)
CONAN TO ARAWASHI NO MICHI (Japanese)
KYOSENSHI CONAN (Japanese)
REH: CONAN CIMMERIALAINEN (Finnish)
CONAN DER VRIJBUITER (Dutch)
ANTHOLOGIA EPISTIMONIKIS FANTASIAS - ISTORIES APO PARAXENES THALASES / 2,
        VOLUME 55 (Greek)
SKIES STO FAGGAROFOTO (Greek)
CONAN IZ CIMERII (Russian)
CONAN (Russian)
OSSZES CONAN, TORTENETE 1 (Hungarian)
LA LEGGENDA DI CONAN IL CIMMERO (Italian)
L'IRA DI CONAN (Italian)
CONAN (Polish)
CONAN NAJEMNIK (Polish)
CONAN ZDOBYWCA (Polish)
CONAN (French, a later, much larger edition)
CONAN A KIMMERIAI (Hungarian)
KONAN: CRNI KOLOS (Yugoslavian)
CONAN JA MUSTA RANNIKU KUNINGANNA (Estonian)
KONAN I GOROD PLENENIYCH DOUSH (Russian)
CONAN BARBAR (Czech)
CONAN (Czech)
CONAN A BARBAR (Hungarian)
CONAN FRIBYTTEREN (Norwegian)
CONAN, WHVG, 2003 (German)
CONAN DER FREIBEUTER (German)
CONAN IL CIMMERO (Italian)
CONAN IL PIRATA (Italian)
CONAN PIRATEN (Swedish)
CONAN PIRAT (Polish)
CONAN LE FLIBUSTIER (French)
CONAN EL PIRATA (Spanish)

## SHADOWS IN ZAMBOULA

DE ZWARTE STEEN (Dutch)
CONAN DER ZWERVER (Dutch)
CONAN TO HONO'O NO TAMKEN (Japanese)
KYOSENSHI CONAN (Japanese)
ROSTRO DE CALAVERA (Spanish)
VELHOJEN VALTAKUNTA (Finnish)
PRIZRAKI ZAMBUL (Chpbk., Russian)
KONAN UNISHTOZHITELYA (Bulgarian)
OI MAVROI PROPHITES (Greek)
CONAN IZ CIMERII (Russian)
OSSZES CONAN, TORTENETE 1 (Hungarian)
CONAN DE CIMMERIA III (Spanish)
KONAN SKITNIKA (Bulgarian)

KONAN VARVARYNA (Bulgarian)
L'URLO DI CONAN (Italian)
PRIZRAKI ZAMBULI (Russian)
CONAN (Polish)
CONAN OBIEZYSWIAT (Polish)
CONAN ZDOBYWCA (Polish)
CONAN (French, a later, much larger edition)
CONAN A KIMMERIAI (Hungarian)
KONAN: DRVO SMRTI (Yugoslavian)
CONAN JA MUSTA RANNIKU KUNINGANNA (Estonian)
CONAN BARBAR (Czech)
CONAN: MEC S FENIXEM (Czech)
CONAN (Czech)
CONAN A BARBAR (Hungarian)
CONAN LO ZINGARO (Italian)
CONAN SNIKMORDERNES BY (Norwegian)
CONAN DER WANDERER (German)
CONAN FORGORAREN (Swedish)
CONAN LE VAGABOND (French)
CONAN EL VAGABUNDO (Spanish)

**SHE DEVIL**
WILD BILL CLANTON (French)

**SHIP IN MUTINY**
WILD BILL CLANTON (French)

**THE SHUNNED CASTLE**
First appeared in EL BORAK L'ETERNEL (French)

**THE SIGN OF THE SNAKE**
STEVE COSTIGAN ET LE SIGNE DU SERPENT (French)
IL SEGNO DEL SERPENTE (Italian)

**THE SILVER HEEL**
STEVE HARRISON ET LE TALON D'ARGENT (French)

**THE SKULL OF SILENCE**
KULL (Greek)
KULL VON ATLANTIS (German)
KULL DI VALUSIA (Italian)
LA CITADELLE ECARLATE (French)
KULL LE ROI BARBARE (French)
REH: KADOTUKSEN KUILU (Finnish)
TZAR KULL (Russian)
HOSOK KORA (Hungarian)
KADOTUSSEN KUILU (Finnish)
REY KULL (Spanish)

**SKULL-FACE**
SUKARU FEISU (Japanese)
LE PACTE NOIR (French, NeO)
LE PACTE NOIR (French, Marabout)

ROSTRO DE CALAVERA (Spanish)
LE PACTE NOIR, VOLUME 1 or 2 (French)
O MAGOS APO TIN ATLANTIDA (Greek)
MOICHANIE IDOLA (Russian)
TRUPIOGLOWY (Polish)
EL TEMPLO DE YUN-SHATU (Spanish)
ROSTRO DE CALAVERA (Spanish, Ediciones Martinez Roca, S.A.)

## SKULLS AND ORCHIDS
WYSLANCY WALHALLI (Polish)

## SKULLS IN THE STARS
SOLOMON KANE (French)
ROSTRO DE CALAVERA (Spanish)
I LOFI TON NECRON KAI ALLA DIEGEMATA (Greek)
DEGEN DER GERECHTIGKEIT (German)
LE ALI NOTTURNE (Italian)
SOLOMON KANE (Italian)
SOLOMON KANE IL GIUSTIZIERE (Italian)
SOLOMON KEIN (Russian)
KSIEZYC CZASZEK (Polish)
LAS AVENTURAS DE SOLOMON KANE (Spanish)
A KIPONYAK HOLDJA (Hungarian)
LAS EXTRANAS AVENTURAS DE SOLOMON KANE (Spanish)

## THE SLAVE-PRINCESS
CORMAC FITZGEOFFREY (French)
JASTZEBIE OUTREMERU (Polish)

## THE SLITHERING SHADOW
HAYAKAWA MYSTERY MAGAZINE, April 1969 (Japanese)
FU'UNJI CONAN (Japanese)
CONAN EL AVENTURERO (Spanish)
CONAN TO KUROI YOGENSHA (Japanese)
CONAN DE AVONTURIER (Dutch)
L'ERA DI CONAN (Italian)
REH: CONAN CIMMERIALAINEN (Finnish)
CHERNYAT KOLOS (Bulgarian)
CONAN IZ CIMERII (Russian)
CONAN (Russian)
OSSZES CONAN, TORTENETE 1 (Hungarian)
KONAN AVANTURISTA (Bulgarian)
LA LEGGENDA DI CONAN IL CIMMERO (Italian)
CONAN Z CIMMERII (Polish)
CONAN A KIMMERIAI (Hungarian)
KONAN HO TYKHODIOKTES (Greek)
KONAN: CRNI LAVIRINT (Yugoslavian)
CONAN JA VARELEV VARI (Estonian)
CONAN BARBAR (Czech)
CONAN BARBAR A JINE POVIDKY (Czech)
CONAN (Czech)
CONAN EVENTYREREN (Norwegian)
CONAN, WHVG, 2003 (German)
CONAN DER ABENTEURER (German)

CONAN AVENTYRAREN (Swedish)
CONAN RYZYKANT (Polish)
CONAN LA FIN DE L'ATLANTIDE (French)
CONAN L'AVENTURIER (French)

**THE SLUGGER'S GAME**
STEVE COSTIGAN LE CHAMPION (French)
LIK SMERCHA (Russian)

**SLUGGERS OF THE BEACH**
STEVE COSTIGAN LE CHAMPION (French)
LIK SMERCHA (Russian)

**THE SNOUT IN THE DARK**
CONAN VAN CIMMERIE (Dutch, LSDC version)
CONAN TO SEKIHI NO NORI (Japanese, LSDC version)
CONAN – ESPADA & MAGIA #3 (Brazil, in Portugese, LSDC version)
CONAN ETERNAL (Russian, LSDC version)
BARBAR POKOL (Hungarian)
FIL KULESI (Turkish, fragment only)
OSSZES CONAN, TORTENETE 1 (Hungarian)
LA LEGGENDA DI CONAN IL CIMMERO (Italian)
CONAN Z CYNERII (Polish)
CONAN (French, a later, much larger edition)
KONAN: PROKLETSTVO MONOLITA (Yugoslavian)
CONAN EN DE KONINGIN VAN DE ZWARTE KUST (Dutch)
CONAN VON CIMMERIA (German)
CONAN DI CIMMERIA (Italian)
CONAN IL CIMMERO (Italian)
CONAN CIMMERIERN (Swedish)
CONAN LE CIMMERIEN (French)
CONAN DE CIMMERIA (Spanish)

**SON OF THE WHITE WOLF**
EL BORAK LE REDOUTABLE (French)
KROV BOGOV (Russian)
IM LAND DER MESSER (German)

**SONS OF HATE**
LA MAIN DE LA DEESSE NOIRE (French)

**THE SOPHISTICATE**
LA TOMBE DU DRAGON (French)

**THE SOWERS OF THE THUNDER**
DIE BESTIE VON BAL-SAGOTH (German)
SONYA LA ROUGE (French)
BURY NAD ORIENTA (Bulgarian)

**SPANISH GOLD ON DEVIL HORSE**
LA MANOIR DE LA TERREUR (French)
KROV BOGOV (Russian)
NIE KOPCIE MI GROBU (Polish)

**SPEAR AND FANG**
> ORBITES #4 (French)
> LE TERTRE MAUDIT (French)
> RAUHER SAND UND WILDE EICHEN (German)
> KOGHOT DRAKONA (Russian)

**SPEARS OF CLONTARF**
> L'ILE DES EPOUVANTES (French)

**SPECTRES IN THE DARK**
> DES SPECTRES DANS LA TENEBRES (French)

**THE SPELL OF DAMBALLAH**
> LA TOMBE DU DRAGON (French)

**THE SPIRIT OF BRIAN BORU**
First appeared in LA TOMBE DU DRAGON (French)

**THE STONES OF DESTINY**
> LA TOMBE DU DRAGON (French)

**THE STRIKING OF THE GONG**
> KULL (Greek)
> KULL VON ATLANTIS (German)
> KULL DI VALUSIA (Italian)
> KULL LE ROI BARBARE (French)
> TZAR KULL (Russian)
> HOSOK KORA (Hungarian)
> REY KULL (Spanish)

**THE SUPREME MOMENT**
> LA FLAMME DE LA VENGEANCE (French)

**SWORD WOMAN**
> HORDE AUS DEM MORGENLAND (German)
> AGNES DE CHASTILLON (French)

**SWORDS OF SHAHRAZAR**
> KIRBY O'DONNELL (French)
> DER SCHATZ DER TATAREN (German)
> SZABLE SZAHRAZARU (Polish)

**SWORDS OF THE NORTHERN SEA**
> KRIEGER DES NORDENS (German)
> CORMAC MAC ART (French)
> TYGRI MORE (Czech)
> VOZVRASHTENYE CONANA (Russian, print in Belerus)

**SWORDS OF THE PURPLE KINGDOM**
> KULL (Greek)
> KULL DI VALUSIA (Italian)
> KULL LE ROI BARBARE (French)
> HERR VON VALUSIEN (German)

REH: KADOTUKSEN KUILU (Finnish)
KULL VON ATLANTIS (German, later edition only)
TZAR KULL (Russian)
HOSOK KORA (Hungarian)
KADOTUSSEN KUILU (Finnish)
REY KULL (Spanish)

## SWORDS OF THE RED BROTHERHOOD
VULMEA LE PIRATE NOIR (French)

## THE TALE OF THE RAJAH'S RING
KROV BOGOV (Russian)

## THE TEMPLE OF ABOMINATION
KRIEGER DES NORDENS (German)
CORMAC MAC ART (French)
I SIGNORI DELLA SPADA (Italian)
TYGRI MORE (Czech)
VOZVRASHTENYE CONANA (Russian, print in Belerus)

## TEXAS FISTS
STEVE COSTIGAN ET LE SIGNE DU SERPENT (French)

## THEY ALWAYS COME BACK
POING D'ACIER (French)

## THE THING ON THE ROOF
KYOUFU TSUSHIN #2 (Japanese)
KU RITORU RITORU SHINWASHU (Japanese)
L'HOMME NOIR (French)
ANTHOLOGIA EPISTIMONIKIS FANTASIAS - ISTORIES APO EFIALTIKOUS COSMOUS, VOLUME
    10 (Greek)
KURO NO ISHIBUMI (Japanese)
DAS HAUS DES GRAUENS (German)
KUTHURU #8 (Japanese)
LOS GUSANOS DE LA TIERRA Y OTROS RELATES DE HORROR SOBRENATURAL (Spanish)
CHERNYAT KOLOS (Bulgarian)
PLOMIEN ASSURBANIPALA (Polish)
ZMIERZCH NAD STONEHENGE (Polish)
CHAS DRAKONA (Russian, printed in Belarus)
CULTI INNOMINABILI (Italian)

## THOROUGHBREDS
First appeared in LA TOMBE DU DRAGON (French)

## THREE-BLADED DOOM
EL BORAK LE MAGNIFIQUE (French, long version)
ZNAK OGNYA (Russian)

**A THUNDER OF TRUMPETS**
  LE TERTRE MAUDIT (French)
  CHERNYE KANAAN (Russian)
  ALMURIK I INNE OPOWIADANIA (Polish)
  CHERNUY KAMEN (Russian)

**THE THUNDER-RIDER**
  GESPENSTER DER VERGANGENHEIT (German)
  LE TERTRE MAUDIT (French)
  KOGHOT DRAKONA (Russian)
  WEDROWCY Z VALHALLI (Polish)
  WYSLANCY WALHALLI (Polish)

**TIGERS OF THE SEA**
  KRIEGER DES NORDENS (German)
  CORMAC MAC ART (French)
  TYGRI MORE (Czech)
  VOZVRASHTENYE CONANA (Russian, print in Belerus)

**THE TNT PUNCH**
  STEVE COSTIGAN (French)

**THE TOMB OF THE DRAGON**
  LA TOMBE DU DRAGON (French)

**THE TOMB'S SECRET**
  STEVE HARRISON ET LE MAITRE DES MORTS (French)

**A TOUCH OF COLOR**
  LA TOMBE DU DRAGON (French)

**THE TOWER OF THE ELEPHANT**
  S-F MAGAZINE, November 1970 (Japanese)
  BOKENSHA CONAN (Japanese)
  CONAN TO DOKURO NO MIYAKO (Japanese)
  DE STEM VAN EL-LIL (Dutch)
  ROSTRO DE CALAVERA (Spanish)
  L'ERA DI CONAN (Italian)
  REH: CONAN JA DEMONIT (Finnish)
  CONAN (Dutch)
  CONAN (French)
  CONAN - ESPADA & MAGIA #1 (Brazil, in Portugese)
  ANTHOLOGIA EPISTIMONIKIS FANTASIAS - ISTORIES ME MAGOUS KE MAGISES, VOLUME 28
      (Greek)
  I VASILIA TIS MAVRIS AKTIS (Greek)
  CONAN IZ CIMERII (Russian)
  FIL KULESI (Turkish)
  CONAN (Russian)
  OSSZES CONAN, TORTENETE 1 (Hungarian)
  LA LEGGENDA DI CONAN IL CIMMERO (Italian)
  CONAN (French, a later, much larger edition)
  BARBAROK ES VARAZSLOK (Hungarian)
  CONAN A KIMMERIAI (Hungarian)

CONAN (Croatian)
KONAN (Yugoslavian)
CONAN JA MUSTA RANNIKU KUNINGANNA (Estonian)
CONAN (Romanian)
KONANAS (Lithuanian)
CONAN BARBAR (Czech)
CONAN: MEC S FENIXEM (Czech)
CONAN (Czech)
CONAN (Norwegian)
CONAN, WHVG (German)
CONAN, WHVG, 2003 (German)
CONAN! (Italian)
CONAN IL CIMMERO (Italian)
CONAN (Swedish)
CONAN (Polish, 1991 edition)
CONAN (Spanish)

**THE TOWER OF TIME**
L'ILE DES EPOUVANTES (French)

**THE TRACK OF BOHEMUND**
LA ROUTE D'AZRAEL (French)
BRAMY IMPERIUM (Polish)

**THE TRAIL OF THE BLOOD-STAINED GOD**
MOICHANIE IDOLA (Russian)

**THE TREASURES OF TARTARY**
KIRBY O'DONNELL (French)
DER SCHATZ DER TATAREN (German)
MOICHANIE IDOLA (Russian)
SZABLE SZAHRAZARU (Polish)

**THE TREASURE OF TRANICOS**
CONAN DE OVERWELDIGER (Dutch)
CONAN L' USURPATORE (Italian)
DAI-TEIO CONAN (Japanese)
IL REGNO DI CONAN (Italian)
IL REGNO DI CONAN IL GRANDE (Italian)
L'URLO DI CONAN (Italian)
TUTTI I CICLI FANTASTICI, VOLUME 2: IL CICLO DI CONAN, VOLUME 2 (Italian)
CONAN UZURPATOR (Polish)
CONAN EN DE SCHARLAKEN CITADEL (Dutch)
KONAN I GOROD PLENENIYCH DOUSH (Russian)
VOZVRASHTENYE CONANA (Russian, print in Belerus)
CONAN TRONRANEREN (Norwegian)
CONAN DER THRONRAUBER (German)
CONAN DER USURPATOR (German)
CONAN UND DER SCHATZ DES TRANICOS (German)
CONAN SEGRAREN (Swedish)
CONAN L'USURPATEUR (French)
CONAN EL USURPADOR (Spanish)
EL TESORO DE TRANICOS (Spanish)

**THE TURKISH MENACE**
DENNIS DORGAN (French)

**TWO AGAINST TYRE**
GESPENSTER DER VERGANGENHEIT (German)
L'ILE DES EPOUVANTES (French)

**UNDER THE BAOBAB TREE**
LA TOMBE DU DRAGON (French)

**UNTITLED ("Gordon, the American whom the Arabs call El Borak, . . .")**
First appeared in EL BORAK L'ETERNEL (French)

**UNTITLED ("A gray sky arched . . .")**
HERRSCHER DER NACHT (German)
BRAN MAK MORN (Czech)
GUSANOS DE LA TIERRE (Spanish)

**UNTITLED ("It was the end of the fourth round.")**
DENNIS DORGAN (French)

**UNTITLED ("The night Sailor Steve Costigan fought Battling O'Rourke . . .")**
DENNIS DORGAN (French)

**UNTITLED ("Steve Harrison received a wire from Joan Wiltshaw.")**
STEVE HARRISON ET LE TALON D'ARGENT (French)

**UNTITLED ("Three men sat at a table . . .")**
KULL VON ATLANTIS (German, later edition only)
TZAR KULL (Russian)

**UNTITLED ("'Thus,' said Tu, . . .")**
KULL VON ATLANTIS (German, later edition only)
TZAR KULL (Russian)

**USURP THE NIGHT**
SHIN KU RITORU SIHWA TAIKEI #3 (Japanese)
LE CHIEN DE LA MORT (French)

**THE VALE OF LOST WOMEN**
CONAN - ESPADA & MAGIA #4 (Brazil, in Portugese)
CONAN VAN CIMMERIE (Dutch) (LSDC version)
REH: KADOTUKSEN KUILU (Finnish)
I VASILIA TIS MAVRIS AKTIS (Greek)
CONAN ETERNAL (Russian, LSDC version)
FIL KULESI (Turkish)
CONAN (Russian)
OSSZES CONAN, TORTENETE 1 (Hungarian)
LA LEGGENDA DI CONAN IL CIMMERO (Italian)
L'URLO DI CONAN (Italian)
BARBARZYNCA (Polish)
CONAN (Polish)
CONAN Z CYNERII (Polish)

CONAN ZDOBYWCA (Polish)
CONAN (French, a later, much larger edition)
CONAN A KIMMERIAI (Hungarian)
KONAN: PROKLETSTVO MONOLITA (Yugoslavian)
CONAN EN DE KONINGIN VAN DE ZWARTE KUST (Dutch)
CONAN BARBAR (Czech)
CONAN BARBAR A JINE POVIDKY (Czech)
KADOTUSSEN KUILU (Finnish)
CONAN, WHVG, 2003 (German)
CONAN VON CIMMERIA (German)
CONAN DI CIMMERIA (Italian)
CONAN IL CIMMERO (Italian)
CONAN CIMMERIERN (Swedish)
CONAN LE CIMMERIEN (French)
CONAN DE CIMMERIA (Spanish)

## THE VALLEY OF THE LOST (1)
LE CHIEN DE LA MORT (French)

## THE VALLEY OF THE WORM
HAYAKAWA MYSTERY MAGAZINE, November 1969 (Japanese)
KAIKI TO GENSOU #1 (Japanese)
CONAN TO SEKIHI NO NORI (Japanese)
LE PACTE NOIR (French, NeO)
FUREUR NOIRS (French)
GESPENSTER DER VERGANGENHEIT (German)
ROSTRO DE CALAVERA (Spanish)
PORTTI, January 1990 (Finnish)
LE PACTE NOIR, VOLUME 1 or 2 (French)
KURO NO ISHIBUMI (Japanese)
ANTHOLOGIA EPISTIMONIKIS FANTASIAS - ISTORIES APO VELOUDO KE ATSALI, VOLUME 20
      (Greek)
LOS GUSANOS DE LA TIERRA Y OTROS RELATES DE HORROR SOBRENATURAL (Spanish)
DOLINA GROZY (Polish)
ZMIERZCH NAD STONEHENGE (Polish)
LA CUIDAD MUERTA (Spanish)

## VIKINGS OF THE GLOVES
STEVE COSTIGAN LE CHAMPION (French)
LIK SMERCHA (Russian)

## THE VOICE OF DOOM
LA MANOIR DE LA TERREUR (French)

## THE VOICE OF EL-LIL
DE STEM VAN EL-LIL (Dutch)
LE PACTE NOIR (French, NeO)
FUREUR NOIRS (French)
LE PACTE NOIR, VOLUME 1 or 2 (French)
LOS GUSANOS DE LA TIERRA Y OTROS RELATES DE HORROR SOBRENATURAL (Spanish)
PRZEKLENSTWO ZLOTEJ CZASZKI (Polish)

## THE VOICE OF THE MOB
LA TOMBE DU DRAGON (French)

**VULTURES OF WHAPETON**
    IM SCHATTEN DER GEIER (German)

**WATERFRONT FISTS**
    STEVE COSTIGAN (French)

**THE WAY OF THE SWORDS**
    LE SIGNEUR DE SAMARCANDE (French)
    BRAMY IMPERIUM (Polish)

**THE WEAKER SEX**
First appeared in LA TOMBE DU DRAGON (French)

**THE WEEPING WILLOW**
First appeared in POING D'ACIER (French)

**THE WEST TOWER**
    KOGHOT DRAKONA (Russian)

**WILD WATER**
    IL SEGNO DEL SERPENTE (Italian)

**WINGS IN THE NIGHT**
    DE ZWARTE STEEN (Dutch)
    LE RETOUR DE KANE (French)
    RACHER DER VERDAMMTEN (German)
    WEIRD TALES #3 (Japanese)
    ROSTRO DE CALAVERA (Spanish)
    I LOFI TON NECRON KAI ALLA DIEGEMATA (Greek)
    REH: YÖN KUNINKAAT (Finnish)
    LE ALI NOTTURNE (Italian)
    SOLOMON KANE (Italian)
    SOLOMON KANE IL GIUSTIZIERE (Italian)
    CZERWONE CIENIE (Polish)
    PLOMIEN ASSURBANIPALA (Polish)
    LAS AVENTURAS DE SOLOMON KANE (Spanish)
    HOSOK KORA (Hungarian)
    CHAS DRAKONA (Russian, printed in Belarus)
    LAS EXTRANAS AVENTURAS DE SOLOMON KANE (Spanish)

**WINNER TAKE ALL**
    STEVE COSTIGAN (French)

**WITCH FROM HELL'S KITCHEN**
    O KIPOS TOU FOVOU (Greek)
    CORMAC MAC ART (French)
    KEN TO MAHOU NO MONGATARI (Japanese)
    GEISTER DER NACHT (German)
    CHERNYE KANAAN (Russian)
    PRZEKLENSTWO ZLOTEJ CZASZKI (Polish)
    CHERNUY KAMEN (Russian)

**A WITCH SHALL BE BORN**
MAJO NO TANJO (Japanese)
CONAN TO ARAWASHI NO MICHI (Japanese)
KYOSENSHI CONAN (Japanese)
CONAN DER VRIJBUITER (Dutch)
REH: CONAN TAISTELIJA (Finnish)
CONAN - ESPADA & MAGIA #3 (Brazil, in Portugese)
SKIES STO FAGGAROFOTO (Greek)
CONAN IZ CIMERII (Russian)
OSSZES CONAN, TORTENETE 1 (Hungarian)
ISE RODI VESHICA (Bulgarian)
LA LEGGENDA DI CONAN IL CIMMERO (Italian)
L'IRA DI CONAN (Italian)
CONAN Z CIMMERII (Polish)
CONAN (French, a later, much larger edition)
CONAN A KIMMERIAI (Hungarian)
KONAN: CRNI KOLOS (Yugoslavian, first part)
KONAN: DRVO SMRTI (Yugoslavian, second part)
CONAN JA MUSTA RANNIKU KUNINGANNA (Estonian)
KONANAS (Lithuanian)
CONAN BARBAR (Czech)
CONAN: MEC S FENIXEM (Czech)
CONAN (Czech)
CONAN A BARBAR (Hungarian)
CONAN TAISTELIJA (Finnish)
CONAN FRIBYTTEREN (Norwegian)
CONAN DER FREIBEUTER (German)
CONAN IL CIMMERO (Italian)
CONAN IL PIRATA (Italian)
CONAN PIRATEN (Swedish)
CONAN PIRAT (Polish)
CONAN LE FLIBUSTIER (French)
CONAN EL PIRATA (Spanish)

**WITH A SET OF RATTLESNAKE RATTLES**
MYSTERO #22, March 2002 (Italian)

**WIZARD AND WARRIOR**
KULL (Greek)
KULL VON ATLANTIS (German)
KULL DI VALUSIA (Italian)
KULL LE ROI BARBARE (French)
REY KULL (Spanish)

**WOLFSHEAD**
SUKARU FEISU (Japanese)
LE PACTE NOIR (French, NeO)
LE PACTE NOIR (French, Marabout)
KEN TO MAHOU NO MONGATARI (Japanese)
ROSTRO DE CALAVERA (Spanish)
ANTHOLOGIA EPISTIMONIKIS FANTASIAS - ISTORIES MAGIAS KE TROMOU, VOLUME 7 (Greek)
DAS HAUS DES GRAUENS (German)
LE PACTE NOIR, VOLUME 1 or 2 (French)
PIMEDUSE RAHVAS (Estonian)

CHERNYE KANAAN (Russian)
WILCZA GLOWA (Polish)
ROSTRO DE CALAVERA (Spanish, Ediciones Martinez Roca, S.A.)

## WOLVES BEYOND THE BORDER
CONAN L' USURPATORE (Italian, LSDC version)
CONAN DE OVERWELDIGER (Dutch, LSDC version)
CONAN ETERNAL (Russian, LSDC version)
CONAN DE CIMMERIA III (Spanish)
IL REGNO DI CONAN (Italian)
IL REGNO DI CONAN IL GRANDE (Italian)
CONAN UZURPATOR (Polish)
CONAN EN DE SCHARLAKEN CITADEL (Dutch)
KONAN I GOROD PLENENIYCH DOUSH (Russian)
VOZVRASHTENYE CONANA (Russian, print in Belerus)
CONAN TRONRANEREN (Norwegian)
CONAN DER THRONRAUBER (German)
CONAN DER USURPATOR (German)
CONAN SEGRAREN (Swedish)
CONAN L'USURPATEUR (French)
CONAN EL USURPADOR (Spanish)

## WORMS OF THE EARTH
DE ZWARTE STEEN (Dutch)
SUKARU FEISU (Japanese)
HERRSCHER DER NACHT (German)
AKUMA NO YUME, TENSHI NO TAMEIKI (Japanese)
BRAN MAK MORN (French)
ROSTRO DE CALAVERA (Spanish)
REH: YÖN KUNINKAAT (Finnish)
KURO NO ISHIBUMI (Japanese)
LOS GUSANOS DE LA TIERRA Y OTROS RELATES DE HORROR SOBRENATURAL (Spanish)
BRAN MAK MORN (Czech)
I SIGNORI DELLA SPADA (Italian)
DOLINA GROZY (Polish)
ROBAKI ZIEMI (Polish)
ARNYKIRALYOK (Hungarian)
GUSANOS DE LA TIERRE (Spanish)

## THE YELLOW COBRA
DENNIS DORGAN (French)

# VERSE INDEX

All works solely by REH. Approximately 680 works listed, not counting alternate titles.

I have attempted to include every known poetic work of REH, whether it has been published or not, whether a copy even exists or not. There are likely some snippets of verse contained within some stories that have not been captured here, and quite possibly others I am not aware of.

This list includes publications in English as well as non-English, as there are relatively few of the latter. Most of the publications listed here can be found in the BOOKS IN ENGLISH list. Publications with (Anth.) at the end can be found in the ANTHOLOGIES list. Publications with (Chpbk.) at the end can be found in the CHAPBOOKS list. Publications that are periodicals, such as pulps or magazines, can be found in the PERIODICALS list. Non-English publications can be found in either the NON-ENGLISH BOOK list, CHAPBOOK list, or PERIODICALS list, as appropriate.

If multiple books have the same title but differing contents, I have listed the publisher as well, to indicate which book is appropriate.

*Format of Entries*
**TITLE**
Alternate Title: [If it has one]
Featuring: [If a significant REH hero]
First appeared in: [If published]
    All other publications of the story
    Notes

**ABE LINCOLN**
First appeared in SHADOWS OF DREAMS
    THE COLLECTED LETTERS OF ROBERT E. HOWARD, VOLUME 2: 1930-1932
    From a letter to TCS, ca. May 1932 ("Fear Finn: / Lo, friend, . . .")

**ACE HIGH**
First appeared in A RHYME OF SALEM TOWN AND OTHER POEMS (Chpbk. & HB)

**THE ACTOR**
Alternate title: Untitled ("I am an actor . . .")
First appeared in A RHYME OF SALEM TOWN AND OTHER POEMS (Chpbk. & HB)

**ADVENTURE (1, "Adventure, I have followed your beck")**
Alternate title: Untitled ("Adventure, I have followed your beck")
First appeared in OMNIUMGATHUM (Chpbk.)
    NIGHT IMAGES
    DARK VALLEY DESTINY (Anth., lines 1-5 and 13-14, page 239)

**ADVENTURE (2, "I am the spur . . .")**
First appeared in THE CROSS PLAINSMAN, August 2004 (Chpbk.)
    THE LAST OF THE TRUNK OCH BREV I URVAL (Chpbk.)
    THE COLLECTED LETTERS OF ROBERT E. HOWARD, VOLUME 1: 1923-1929
    From a letter to TCS, June 23, 1926 ("Salaam: / I'm trying to write again . . .")

**ADVENTURER**
First appeared in THE LAST OF THE TRUNK OCH BREV I URVAL (Chpbk.)
    THE COLLECTED LETTERS OF ROBERT E. HOWARD, VOLUME 1: 1923-1929
    From a letter to TCS, June 23, 1926 ("Salaam: / I'm trying to write again . . .")

**THE ADVENTURER**
First appeared in THE GRIM LAND AND OTHERS (Chpbk.)
    THE HOWARD READER #8 (Chpbk.)
    THE CROSS PLAINSMAN, October 2003 (Chpbk.)
    THE CROSS PLAINSMAN, August 2004 (Chpbk.)

**THE ADVENTURER'S MISTRESS (1, "The scarlet standards of the sun")**
Alternate title: Untitled ("The scarlet standards of the sun")
First appeared in THE GHOST OCEAN AND OTHER POEMS OF THE SUPERNATURAL (Chpbk.)

**THE ADVENTURER'S MISTRESS (2, "The fogs of night")**
Alternate title: THE DANCE WITH DEATH

**THE AFFAIR AT THE TAVERN**
First appeared in A RHYME OF SALEM TOWN AND OTHER POEMS (Chpbk. & HB)

**AFTER A FLAMING NIGHT**
Alternate title: MARK OF THE BEAST

**AGE**
Alternate title: TO THE OLD MEN
First appeared in THE JUNTO, September 1928
    THE HOWARD COLLECTOR #14
    NIGHT IMAGES
    There are two slightly variant versions of this

**AGE COMES TO RABELAIS**
First appeared in THE HOWARD COLLECTOR #8
    ECHOES FROM AN IRON HARP
    THE DARK BARBARIAN (Anth., lines 7, 8, 11, 12, p. 47)

**THE AGES STRIDE ON GOLDEN FEET**
Alternate title: Untitled ("The ages stride on golden feet")
First appeared in A RHYME OF SALEM TOWN AND OTHER POEMS (Chpbk. & HB)

**THE ALAMO**
First appeared in THE LAST OF THE TRUNK OCH BREV I URVAL (Chpbk.)
    THE COLLECTED LETTERS OF ROBERT E. HOWARD, VOLUME 1: 1923-1929
    RHYMES OF TEXAS AND THE OLD WEST
    From a letter to TCS, June 23, 1926 ("Salaam: / I'm trying to write again . . .")

**ALIEN**

First appeared in VERSES IN EBONY (Chpbk.)
    THE HOWARD READER #8 (Chpbk.)

## ALL HALLOWS EVE
Alternate title: Untitled ("Now anthropoid and leprous shadows lope")
First appeared in AMAZING STORIES, March 1986
    THE NEW HOWARD READER #1 (Chpbk.)

## ALTARS AND JESTERS
Alternate title: AN OPIUM DREAM
First appeared in ALTARS AND JESTERS (Chpbk.)
    FROM THE HELLS BENEATH THE HELLS (Chpbk.)
    NIGHT IMAGES

## ALWAYS COMES EVENING
First appeared in THE PHANTAGRAPH, August 1936
    STIRRING SCIENCE STORIES, February 1941
    UNCANNY TALES, September-October 1943
    DARK OF THE MOON (Anth.)
    ALWAYS COMES EVENING
    FANTASY CROSSROADS #2
    NIGHT IMAGES (lines 1-14 only)
    VOICES OF THE NIGHT AND OTHER POEMS (Chpbk.)
    STARMONT READER'S GUIDE #35: ROBERT E. HOWARD (Anth., lines 5-12)
    EIN TRAUMER AUS TEXAS (Chpbk.)
    CHANTS DE GUERRE ET DE MORT
    HARDWIRED HINTERLAND, VOLUME 2, #7 (Chpbk.)
    PFADE INS FANTASTIQUE, BOOK 1 (Chpbk.)
    THE NEW HOWARD READER #7 (Chpbk.)
    SPECTRUM SUPER SPECIAL #2
    ODES AT THE BLACK DOG (Chpbk.)
    WINDS OF TIME

## AMBITION
First appeared in THE COLLECTED LETTERS OF ROBERT E. HOWARD, VOLUME 2: 1930-1932
    Unpublished, from a letter to TCS, ca. April 1930 ("Well, Fear Finn, you mention . . .")

## AN AMERICAN
First appeared in THE LAST OF THE TRUNK OCH BREV I URVAL (Chpbk.)
    THE COLLECTED LETTERS OF ROBERT E. HOWARD, VOLUME 1: 1923-1929
    From a letter to TCS, ca. December 1928 ("Salaam: / Out in front of Goldstein's . . .")

## AN AMERICAN EPIC
First appeard in THE COLLECTED LETTERS OF ROBERT E. HOWARD, VOLUME 1: 1923-1929
    From a letter to TCS, ca. April 1929 ("Salaam: / The iron harp that Adam christened life . . .")

## AM-RA THE TA-AN
First appeared in A RHYME OF SALEM TOWN AND OTHER POEMS (Chpbk. & HB)
    KULL: EXILE OF ATLANTIS
    Unfinished

## ANCIENT ENGLISH BALLADEL
First appeared in LEWD TALES (Chpbk.)
>THE LAST OF THE TRUNK OCH BREV I URVAL (Chpbk.)
>THE COLLECTED LETTERS OF ROBERT E. HOWARD, VOLUME 1: 1923-1929
>From a letter to TCS, ca. February 1929 ("Salaam: / Ancient English Balladel")

## AND BEOWULF RIDES AGAIN
First appeared in SPOOR ANTHOLOGY #1 (Chpbk.)
>NIGHT IMAGES

## AND MAN WAS GIVEN THE EARTH TO RULE
Alternative Title: FOR MAN WAS GIVEN THE EARTH TO RULE; THE OLD GODS BROOD

## AND SO I SANG
First appeared in A RHYME OF SALEM TOWN AND OTHER POEMS (Chpbk. & HB)

## ANOTHER HYMN OF HATE
First appeared in A RHYME OF SALEM TOWN AND OTHER POEMS (Chpbk. & HB)

## ARCADIAN DAYS
First appeared in THE LAST OF THE TRUNK OCH BREV I URVAL (Chpbk.)
>THE COLLECTED LETTERS OF ROBERT E. HOWARD, VOLUME 1: 1923-1929
>From a letter to TCS, August 6, 1926 ("Salaam, sahib; / In the first place . . .")

## ARKHAM
First appeared in WEIRD TALES, August 1932
>DARK OF THE MOON (Anth.)
>GARGOYLE #1 (Chpbk.)
>ALWAYS COMES EVENING
>DARK THINGS (Anth., slightly different version)
>RHYMES OF DEATH (Chpbk.)
>BLACK CANAAN (DARK THINGS version)
>CTHULHU THE MYTHOS AND KINDRED HORRORS
>KURO NO ISHIBUMI (Japanese)
>SHIN KU RITORU RITORU SIHWA TAIKEI 9 (Japanese)
>FANTASY COMMENTATOR #45/46 (lines 1-4)
>DEAR HPL: LETTERS, ROBERT E. HOWARD TO H.P. LOVECRAFT, 1930-1936 (Chpbk.)
>LOS GUSANOS DE LA TIERRA Y OTROS RELATES DE HORROR SOBRENATURAL (Spanish)
>WINGS IN THE NIGHT: THE WEIRD WORKS OF ROBERT E. HOWARD, VOLUME 4
>THE WEIRD WRITINGS OF ROBERT E. HOWARD, VOLUME ONE
>THE COLLECTED LETTERS OF ROBERT E. HOWARD, VOLUME 2: 1930-1932
>First appeared in a letter to HPL, December 9, 1931 ("I would have answered . . .")

## ARTIFICE
Alternate title: Untitled ("All is pose and artifice")
First appeared in A RHYME OF SALEM TOWN AND OTHER POEMS (Chpbk. & HB)

## AS I RODE DOWN TO LINCOLN TOWN
Alternate title: Untitled ("As I rode down to Lincoln Town")
First appeared in A RHYME OF SALEM TOWN AND OTHER POEMS (Chpbk. & HB)

## ASTARTE'S IDOL STANDS ALONE
First appeared in A RHYME OF SALEM TOWN AND OTHER POEMS (Chpbk. & HB)

**AT THE BAZAAR**
First appeared in THE LAST OF THE TRUNK OCH BREV I URVAL (Chpbk.)
    THE COLLECTED LETTERS OF ROBERT E. HOWARD, VOLUME 1: 1923-1929
    From a letter to TCS, ca. March 1929 ("Salaam: / Black Dawn")

**ATTILA RIDES NO MORE**
First appeared in SINGERS IN THE SHADOWS

**AUTHORIAL VERSION OF DUNA**
First appeared in ROBERT E. HOWARD: SELECTED LETTERS: 1931-1936 (Chpbk.)
    THE COLLECTED LETTERS OF ROBERT E. HOWARD, VOLUME 2: 1930-1932
    From a letter to TCS, ca. May 1932 ("Fear Finn: / Lo, friend, . . .")

**AUTUMN**
Alternate title: A DREAM OF AUTUMN; THE AUTUMN OF THE WORLD
First appeared in WEIRD TALES, April 1933
    ALWAYS COMES EVENING
    CHANTS DE GUERRE ET DE MORT
    SWORD #4 (Chpbk., Spanish)
    PALE HORSE, unknown number (Chpbk.)
    WINGS IN THE NIGHT: THE WEIRD WORKS OF ROBERT E. HOWARD, VOLUME 4
    ODES AT THE BLACK DOG (Chpbk.)
    THE WEIRD WRITINGS OF ROBERT E. HOWARD, VOLUME ONE
    THE COLLECTED LETTERS OF ROBERT E. HOWARD, VOLUME 2: 1930-1932
    Originally titled "The Autumn of the World", from a letter to TCS, ca. March 1930 ("Well, Fear Finn, tell
        Cuchullain the Dutchess . . .")

**THE AUTUMN OF THE WORLD**
Alternate title: AUTUMN; THE DREAM OF AUTUMN

**"AW COME ON AND FIGHT!"**
First appeared in THE COLLECTED LETTERS OF ROBERT E. HOWARD, VOLUME 2: 1930-1932
    From a letter to TCS, ca. March 1930 ("Well, Fear Finn, tell Cuchullain the Dutchess . . .")

**BAAL**
Alternate title: Untitled ("My name is Baal . . .")
First appeared in A RHYME OF SALEM TOWN AND OTHER POEMS (Chpbk. & HB)

**BAAL-PTEOR**
Alternate title: Untitled ("High on his throne Baal-Pteor sat")
First appeared in A RHYME OF SALEM TOWN AND OTHER POEMS (Chpbk. & HB)

**BABEL**
First appeared in FANTASY FAN, January 1935
    THE NEW HIEROGLYPH, March 1944
    ALWAYS COMES EVENING
    ETCHINGS AND ODYSSEYS #1 (Chpbk.)
    VOICES OF THE NIGHT AND OTHER POEMS (Chpbk.)
    CHANTS DE GUERRE ET DE MORT
    THE HOWARD REVIEW #13, (Chpbk.)

WEST IS WEST AND OTHERS
ROBERT E. HOWARD IN THE FANTASY FAN (Chpbk.)
WINDS OF TIME
From a letter to TCS, undated ("The Seeker thrust . . ."); part 2 of 5 of "The Voices of the Night" cycle

## BABYLON
Alternate title: Untitled ("For I have seen the lizards crawl")
First appeared in ALWAYS COMES EVENING
        LANDS OF WONDER #3 (Chpbk.)
        GREAT CITIES OF THE ANCIENT WORLD (Anth., lines 1-8)
        CHANTS DE GUERRE ET DE MORT

## THE BALLAD OF ABE SLICKEMMORE
First appeared in THE CROSS PLAINSMAN, August 2004 (Chpbk.)
        THE LAST OF THE TRUNK OCH BREV I URVAL (Chpbk.)
        THE COLLECTED LETTERS OF ROBERT E. HOWARD, VOLUME 1: 1923-1929
        From a letter to TCS, ca. November 1928 ("Salaam: / Listen you . . .")

## THE BALLAD OF BAIBARS
Alternate title: THE SOWERS OF THE THUNDER (Verse heading)

## A BALLAD OF BEER
Alternate title: Untitled ("I was once, I declare, a grog-shop man")
First appeared in SHADOWS OF DREAMS
        THE LAST OF THE TRUNK OCH BREV I URVAL (Chpbk.)
        THE COLLECTED LETTERS OF ROBERT E. HOWARD, VOLUME 2: 1930-1932
        Originally untitled, from a letter to TCS, ca. July 1930 ("Salaam, Fear Finn: / Then Stein the peddler . . .")

## THE BALLAD OF BUCKSHOT ROBERTS
Alternate title: THE BALLAD OF BUCKSNORT ROBERTS
First appeared in RHYMES OF DEATH (Chpbk.)
        THE END OF THE TRAIL: WESTERN STORIES
        RHYMES OF TEXAS AND THE OLD WEST
        Incorrectly titled as "Ballad of Bucksnort Roberts" by McHaney; Buckshot Roberts was a historical figure,
                involved in the Lincoln County War, famous for holding up in a cabin and shooting it out with an
                entire posse, getting killed, naturally

## THE BALLAD OF BUCKSNORT ROBERTS
Alternate title: THE BALLAD OF BUCKSHOT ROBERTS

## A BALLAD OF INSANITY
First appeared in THE COLLECTED LETTERS OF ROBERT E. HOWARD, VOLUME 1: 1923-1929
        From a letter to TCS, ca. November 1928 ("Salaam: / I'll swear . . .")

## THE BALLAD OF DARK AGNES (appearances apart from the story "Sword Woman")
Alternate title: verse heading for Chapter 4 of "Sword Woman"
Never published separately

## THE BALLAD OF KING GERAINT
Alternate title: Untitled ("This is the tale of a nameless fight")
First appeared in THE BALLAD OF KING GERAINT (Chpbk.)
    THE NEW HOWARD READER #6 (Chpbk.)
        Titled provided by Lenore Preece; portions of this were included in a letter to Harold Preece, January 4, 1930
            ("Yes, we fade from youth swiftly.")

## THE BALLAD OF MONK KICKAWHORE
First appeared in THE COLLECTED LETTERS OF ROBERT E. HOWARD, VOLUME 1: 1923-1929
    From a letter to TCS, ca. November 1928 ("Salaam: / I'll swear . . .")

## THE BALLAD OF NAUGHTY NELL
Alternate title: THE BALLAD OF SINGAPORE NELL; THE BALLAD OF NELL OF SINGAPORE

## THE BALLAD OF NELL OF SINGAPORE
Alternate title: THE BALLAD OF SINGAPORE NELL; THE BALLAD OF NAUGHTY NELL

## THE BALLAD OF SINGAPORE NELL
Alternate title: Untitled draft ("There are grim things did"); THE BALLAD OF NELL OF SINGAPORE; THE
        BALLAD OF NAUGHTY NELL
First appeared in CHACAL #1
    DESIRE AND OTHER EROTIC POEMS (Chpbk.)
    The draft is from a letter to TCS, undated (Salaam: / There once was a wicked old elf . . .")

## BALLADE
First appeared in SHADOWS OF DREAMS
    THE LAST OF THE TRUNK OCH BREV I URVAL (Chpbk.)
    THE COLLECTED LETTERS OF ROBERT E. HOWARD, VOLUME 3: 1933-1936
    From a letter to TCS, undated ("Salaam: / I have forgotten . . .")

## THE BANDIT
Alternate title: Untitled ("Out of the Texas desert . . .")
First appeared in A RHYME OF SALEM TOWN AND OTHER POEMS (Chpbk. & HB)
    RHYMES OF TEXAS AND THE OLD WEST

## THE BAR BY THE SIDE OF THE ROAD
First appeared in THE HOWARD COLLECTOR #17
    THE BOOK OF ROBERT E. HOWARD
    THE HOWARD COLLECTOR, Ace

## THE BARON AND THE WENCH
Alternate title: Untitled ("The baron quaffed a draught of wine . . .")
First appeared in A RHYME OF SALEM TOWN AND OTHER POEMS (Chpbk. & HB)
    Unfinished

## THE BELL OF MORNI
Alternate title: Untitled ("There's a bell that hangs in a hidden cave")
First appeared in BRAN MAK MORN – THE LAST KING
    COLD STEEL #121 (Chpbk.)

**BELSHAZZAR**
Alternate title: BELSHAZZER
First appeared in THE HOWARD COLLECTOR #5
    ECHOES FROM AN IRON HARP
    THE COLLECTED LETTERS OF ROBERT E. HOWARD, VOLUME 2: 1930-1932
    From a letter to Harold Preece, ca. October or early November 1930 ("Well, Harold, I'm sorry to hear your nose . . ."); titled "Belshazzer" in the original letter

**BELSHAZZER**
Alternate title: BELSHAZZAR

**BLACK CHANT IMPERIAL**
Alternate title: EMPIRE
First appeared in WEIRD TALES, September 1930
    ALWAYS COMES EVENING
    WEIRD TALES IN THE THIRTIES (Chpbk.)
    REHUPA #84/85 (Chpbk.)
    CHANTS DE GUERRE ET DE MORT
    THE BOOK OF MADNESS (Chpbk., lines 1-4)
    PFADE INS FANTASTIQUE, BOOK 1 (Chpbk.)
    MOON OF SKULLS: THE WEIRD WORKS OF ROBERT E. HOWARD, VOLUME 2
    ROBERT E. HOWARD'S POEMS ON THE EDGE
    THE WEIRD WRITINGS OF ROBERT E. HOWARD, VOLUME ONE
    WINDS OF TIME
    Identical to lines 1-4, 9-12, 21-32, 37-40 of "Empire"

**BLACK DAWN**
First appeared in BLACK DAWN, Roy Squires, 1972
    VERSES IN EBONY (Chpbk., dummy prototype)
    NIGHT IMAGES
    THE NEW HOWARD READER #5 (facsimile reproduction of VERSES IN EBONY by Glenn Lord)
    THE LAST OF THE TRUNK OCH BREV I URVAL (Chpbk.)
    THE COLLECTED LETTERS OF ROBERT E. HOWARD, VOLUME 1: 1923-1929
    A cycle of 5 numbered, untitled poems of, respectively, 20, 13, 26, 32, 14 lines, none published separately; in 1985 another manuscript was found in which each poem was titled respectively, "Shadows", "Clouds", "Shrines", "The Iron Harp", and "Invocation"; originally from a letter to TCS, ca. March 1929 ("Salaam: / Black Dawn")

**BLACK HARPS IN THE HILLS**
Alternate title: Untitled ("Thomas Fitzgerald, Shane O'Neill")
First appeared in OMNIUMGATHUM (Chpbk.)
    NIGHT IMAGES
    THE GRIM LAND: THE BEST OF ROBERT E. HOWARD, VOLUME 2
    A shorter and slightly different untitled version of this poem appeared in a letter to Harold Preece, April 1930 ("Thanks for the St. Padraic's card.")

**BLACK MASS**
Alternate title: A VISION

**BLACK MICHAEL'S STORY**
Alternate title: RETRIBUTION; THE SONG OF MURTAGH O'BRIEN; Untitled ("The moon above the Kerry hills . . .")

**BLACK SEAS**
First appeared in FANTASY BOOK #23
  SHADOWS OF DREAMS
  THE COLLECTED LETTERS OF ROBERT E. HOWARD, VOLUME 1: 1923-1929
  ZMIERZCH NAD STONEHENGE (Polish)
  From a letter to TCS, ca. June 1929 ("Salaam: / I received an announcement . . .")

**THE BLACK STONE (Verse heading, appearances apart from story)**
First appeared in INSIDE & SCIENCE FICTION ADVERTISER, September 1956
  THE SHUTTERED ROOM (Anth.)
  DARK THINGS (Anth., added by Derleth to the story "The House")
  THE CALLER OF THE BLACK, (Anth.)
  ECHOES FROM AN IRON HARP
  LOVECRAFT: A LOOK BEHIND THE CTHULHU MYTHOS (Anth.)
  BLACK CANAAN
  THE RAVEN #1 (Chpbk.)
  CRYPT OF CTHULHU #3 (Chpbk.)
  SHIN KU RITORU RITORU SIHWA TAIKEI 9 (Japanese)
  A ROBERT E. HOWARD MEMORIAL: JUNE 13-15, 1986 (Chpbk.)

**THE BLOOD OF BELSHAZZAR (Verse heading, appearances apart from story)**
Alternate title: THE SONG OF THE RED STONE
First appeared in ECHOES FROM AN IRON HARP

**THE BOMBING OF GON FANFEW**
First appeard in THE LAST OF THE TRUNK OCH BREV I URVAL (Chpbk.)
  THE COLLECTED LETTERS OF ROBERT E. HOWARD, VOLUME 1: 1923-1929
  From a letter to TCS, February 25, 1925 ("Salaam, sahib: / Chapter XIX")

**THE BRIDE OF CUCHULAIN**
First appeared in SINGERS IN THE SHADOWS
  DARK VALLEY DESTINY (Anth., lines 18-24)
  EIN TRAUMER AUS TEXAS (Chpbk.)
  PFADE INS FANTASTIQUE, BOOK 1 (Chpbk.)
  ROBERT E. HOWARD'S POEMS ON THE EDGE
  WINDS OF TIME

**THE BROKEN WALLS OF BABEL**
Alternate title: Untitled ("The broken walls of Babel")
First appeared in A RHYME OF SALEM TOWN AND OTHER POEMS (Chpbk. & HB)

**A BUCCANEER SPEAKS**
First appeared in NIGHT IMAGES

**BUCCANEER TREASURE**
First appeared in AMAZING SCIENCE FICTION STORIES, January 1985
  THE NEW HOWARD READER #2 (Chpbk.)

**THE BUILDERS (1, "We reared up Babel's towers")**
First appeared in A RHYME OF SALEM TOWN AND OTHER POEMS (Chpbk. & HB)

**THE BUILDERS (2, "We reared Bab-ilu's towers")**
First appeared in THE COLLECTED LETTERS OF ROBERT E. HOWARD, VOLUME 1: 1923-1929
    From a letter to TCS, ca. October 1927 ("Salaam: / Seeking cognizance of things . . ."); a slightly different
        version

**THE BUILDERS (3, "The towers stand recorders")**
First appeared in THE ROBERT E. HOWARD FOUNDATION NEWSLETTER, VOLUME 1, #2

**BUT THE HILLS WERE ANCIENT THEN**
Alternate title: Untitled ("Now is a summer come out of the sea")
First appeared in AMRA, VOLUME 2, #8
    ECHOES FROM AN IRON HARP
    LA CITADELLE ECARLATE (French)
    WEST IS WEST AND OTHERS
    RHYMES OF TEXAS AND THE OLD WEST
    George Scithers came up with the title

**THE CALL OF PAN**
Alternate title: Untitled ("My heart is a silver drum tonight")
First appeared in SHADOWS OF DREAMS
        THE COLLECTED LETTERS OF ROBERT E. HOWARD, VOLUME 1: 1923-1929
        From a letter to TCS, ca. November 1928 ("Heh heh! At last I've sold . . .")

**THE CALL OF THE SEA**
First appeared in DARK VALLEY DESTINY (Anth., lines 1-6)
        A RHYME OF SALEM TOWN AND OTHER POEMS (Chpbk., first complete publication)

**A CALLING TO ROME**
Alternate title: Untitled ("There's a calling, and a calling . . .")
First appeared in A RHYME OF SALEM TOWN AND OTHER POEMS (Chpbk. & HB)

**THE CAMPUS AT NIGHT**
First appeared in OMNIUMGATHUM (Chpbk.)
    NIGHT IMAGES
    THE LAST OF THE TRUNK OCH BREV I URVAL (Chpbk.)
    THE COLLECTED LETTERS OF ROBERT E. HOWARD, VOLUME 1: 1923-1929
    From a letter to Edna Mann, October 30, 1926 ("Dear Friend: As usual I have to start . . .")

**CANDLES**
First appeared in CANDLES (Chpbk.)
    ONE MORE BARBARIAN #13 (Chpbk.)
    HYBORIAN CHUNTERINGS #6 (Chpbk.)
    THE GHOST OCEAN AND OTHER POEMS OF THE SUPERNATURAL (Chpbk.)
    EIN TRAUMER AUS TEXAS (Chpbk.)
    PFADE INS FANTASTIQUE, BOOK 1 (Chpbk.)
    THE NEW HOWARD READER #1 (Chpbk.)
    WINDS OF TIME
    Glenn Lord questions whether this is really an REH poem; poem was apparently discovered in a book, or some
        such, by Horvat

**CASTAWAY**
First appeared in SHADOWS OF DREAMS

**THE CATS OF ANUBIS**
First appeared in WHISPERS #1
    NIGHT IMAGES

**THE CELLS OF THE COLISEUM**
First appeared in A RHYME OF SALEM TOWN AND OTHER POEMS (Chpbk. & HB)

**A CHALLENGE TO BAST**
Alternate title: Untitled (draft, "She came in the grey of . . .")
First appeared in FANTASY BOOK, September 1986
    SHADOWS OF DREAMS
    DESIRE AND OTHER EROTIC POEMS (Chpbk.)
    THE LAST OF THE TRUNK OCH BREV I URVAL (Chpbk.)
    THE COLLECTED LETTERS OF ROBERT E. HOWARD, VOLUME 3: 1933-1936
    From a letter to TCS, undated ("Well, Fear Finn, I read . . .")

**THE CHAMP**
Alternate title: Untitled ("The champion sneered . . .")
First appeared in REH FIGHT MAGAZINE #2 (Chpbk.)

**THE CHANT DEMONIAC**
First appeared in WEIRD TALES #295, Winter 1989-90
    THE NEW HOWARD READER #3 (Chpbk.)
    THE COLLECTED LETTERS OF ROBERT E. HOWARD, VOLUME 1: 1923-1929
    From a letter to TCS, ca. January 1928 ("I wasn't lying . . .")

**CHANT OF THE WHITE BEARD**
Alternate title: Untitled ("O'er lakes agleam . . .")
First appeared in ALWAYS COMES EVENING
    LANDS OF WONDER #1 (Chpbk.)
    BRAN MAK MORN, Dell
    WORMS OF THE EARTH
    HERRSCHER DER NACHT (German)
    MAGIRA #33 (Chpbk.)
    BARN MAK MORN, Baen
    BRAN MAK MORN – THE LAST KING
    BRAN MAK MORN (Czech)
    An untitled poem embodied in the story "Men of the Shadows" in BRAN MAK MORN, WORMS OF THE
        EARTH, and BRAN MAK MORN – THE LAST KING

**THE CHIEF OF THE MATABELES**
Alternate title: Untitled ("The warm veldt spread . . .")
First appeared in A RHYME OF SALEM TOWN AND OTHER POEMS (Chpbk. & HB)
    Unfinished

**THE CHILDREN OF THE NIGHT (Verse heading, appearances apart from story)**
Alternate title: THE HOUSE IN THE OAKS (Verse heading)

**THE CHINESE GONG**
First appeared in THE COLLECTED LETTERS OF ROBERT E. HOWARD, VOLUME 1: 1923-1929
    From a letter to TCS, ca. March 1928 ("Salaam: / Glad you're writing . . .")

## THE CHOIR GIRL
First appeared in THE LAST OF THE TRUNK OCH BREV I URVAL (Chpbk.)
> THE COLLECTED LETTERS OF ROBERT E. HOWARD, VOLUME 1: 1923-1929
> From a letter to TCS, ca. March 1928 ("Salaam: / Not having much . . .")

## CIMMERIA
First appeared in THE HOWARD COLLECTOR #7
> ECHOES FROM AN IRON HARP
> THE BOOK OF ROBERT E. HOWARD
> 4$^{TH}$ WORLD FANTASY CONVENTION PROGRAM (Chpbk.)
> LA CITADELLE ECARLATE (French)
> THE RAVEN #1 (Chpbk.)
> DARK VALLEY DESTINY (Anth.)
> HARDWIRED HINTERLAND #8 (Chpbk.)
> CONAN DE BARBAAR: HET UUR VAN DE DRAAK (lines 2-5, 18, Dutch)
> EIN TRAUMER AUS TEXAS (Chpbk.)
> REH: CONAN CIMMERIALAINEN (Finnish)
> CONAN, VARVAR IZ CIMMERIA (Russian)
> THE NEW HOWARD READER #1 (Chpbk., "pure text")
> THE CONAN CHRONICLES, VOLUME 2, Millenium
> ROBERT E. HOWARD'S COMPLETE CONAN OF CIMMERIA, VOLUME 1
> THE COMING OF CONAN THE CIMMERIAN
> CONAN, WHVG (German)
> OSSZES CONAN, TORTENETE 1 (Hungarian)
> ROBERT E. HOWARD'S POEMS ON THE EDGE
> THE COMPLETE CHRONICLES OF CONAN
> HOWARD'S HAUNTS (Anth.)
> CONAN, WHVG, 2003 (German)
> RHYMES OF TEXAS AND THE OLD WEST
> WINDS OF TIME
> THE COLLECTED LETTERS OF ROBERT E. HOWARD, VOLUME 3: 1933-1936
> THE GRIM LAND: THE BEST OF ROBERT E. HOWARD, VOLUME 2
> From a letter to Emil Petaja, December 17, 1934 ("Thank you very much . . ."); many of these publications, especially the earlier ones, do not include the last six lines of the longer version; it is unknown which version was sent to Petaja, as it was an attachment that has been lost

## CLOUDS
Alternate title: Part 2 of the BLACK DAWN cycle

## CODE
Alternate title: Untitled ("We're a jolly good bunch of buns")
First appeared in A RHYME OF SALEM TOWN AND OTHER POEMS (Chpbk. & HB)

## THE COMING OF BAST
First appeared in LONE STAR UNIVERSE (Anth.)
> THE NEW HOWARD READER #4 (Chpbk.)
> THE LAST OF THE TRUNK OCH BREV I URVAL (Chpbk.)
> THE COLLECTED LETTERS OF ROBERT E. HOWARD, VOLUME 3: 1933-1936
> A slightly different draft version of this poem appeared in a letter to TCS, undated ("Ha, Ha! Your [sic] not going . . .")

**CONN'S SAGA (appearances apart from "The Grey God Passes")**
Alternate title: verse heading for Chapter 5 of "The Grey God Passes"
Never published separately

**THE COOLING OF SPIKE MCRUE**
First appeared in WRITER OF THE DARK
    A parody of Robert W. Service

**CORNISH JACK**
Alternate title: Untitled ("Away in the dusky barracoon")
First appeared in A RHYME OF SALEM TOWN AND OTHER POEMS (Chpbk. & HB)

**COUNTERSPELLS**
Alternate title: Untitled ("The doine sidhe sang to our swords . . .")
First appeared in UNAUSSPRECHLICHEN KULTEN #1 (Chpbk.)
    THE NEW HOWARD READER #5 (Chpbk.)

**COWBOY**
First appeared in THE LAST OF THE TRUNK OCH BREV I URVAL (Chpbk.)
    THE COLLECTED LETTERS OF ROBERT E. HOWARD, VOLUME 1: 1923-1929
    RHYMES OF TEXAS AND THE OLD WEST
    From a letter to TCS, June 23, 1926 ("Salaam: / I'm trying to write again . . .")

**CRETE**
First appeared in WEIRD TALES, February 1929
    ALWAYS COMES EVENING
    DARK VALLEY DESTINY (Anth., lines 1-4)
    THE DARK BARBARIAN (Anth., lines 13-16)
    EIN TRAUMER AUS TEXAS (Chpbk., lines 1-4)
    CHANTS DE GUERRE ET DE MORT
    SHADOW KINGDOMS: THE WEIRD WORKS OF ROBERT E. HOWARD, VOLUME 1 (Wildside Press & Cosmos)
    THE WEIRD WRITINGS OF ROBERT E. HOWARD, VOLUME ONE

**A CROWN FOR A KING**
Alternate title: Part 5 of 5 of the VOICES OF THE NIGHT cycle
First appeared in ARIEL #1
    ALWAYS COMES EVENING, Underwood-Miller only
    CHANTS DE GUERRE ET DE MORT
    SWORD #4 (Chpbk., Spanish)
    From a letter to TCS, undated ("The Seeker thrust . . .")

**CRUSADE**
First appeared in THE LAST OF THE TRUNK OCH BREV I URVAL (Chpbk.)
    THE COLLECTED LETTERS OF ROBERT E. HOWARD, VOLUME 3: 1933-1936
    From an undated, enclosed separate document sent with a letter to TCS

**THE CRY EVERLASTING**
First appeared in A RHYME OF SALEM TOWN AND OTHER POEMS (Chpbk. & HB)

## THE CUCKOO'S REVENGE
First appeared in RISQUE STORIES #5 (Chpbk.)
    THE NEW HOWARD READER #1 (Chpbk.)
    THE LAST OF THE TRUNK OCH BREV I URVAL (Chpbk.)
    THE COLLECTED LETTERS OF ROBERT E. HOWARD, VOLUME 3: 1933-1936
    From a letter to TCS, undated ("Well, Fear Finn, I read . . .")

## CUSTOM
First appeared in UNAUSSPRECHLICHEN KULTEN #1 (Chpbk.)
    THE NEW HOWARD READER #2 (Chpbk.)

## DANCE MACABRE
Alternate title: Untitled ("I saw the grass on the hillside bend")
First appeared in WEIRDBOOK #12
    THE NEW HOWARD READER #3 (Chpbk.)

## THE DANCE WITH DEATH
Alternate title: THE ADVENTURER'S MISTRESS (2, "The fogs of night")
First appeared in MAGIRA #38 (Chpbk., German)
    PFADE INS FANTASTIQUE, BOOK 2 (Chpbk.)
    THE NEW HOWARD READER #5 (Chpbk.)
    THE LAST OF THE TRUNK OCH BREV I URVAL (Chpbk.)
    WINDS OF TIME
    THE COLLECTED LETTERS OF ROBERT E. HOWARD, VOLUME 3: 1933-1936
    From an undated, enclosed separate document sent with a letter to TCS, titled "The Adventurer's Mistress" in
        the original typescript

## DANCER
First appeared in THE LAST OF THE TRUNK OCH BREV I URVAL (Chpbk.)
    THE COLLECTED LETTERS OF ROBERT E. HOWARD, VOLUME 1: 1923-1929
    From a letter to TCS, June 23, 1926 ("Salaam: / I'm trying to write again . . .")

## THE DANCER
First appeared in THE LAST OF THE TRUNK OCH BREV I URVAL (Chpbk.)
    THE COLLECTED LETTERS OF ROBERT E. HOWARD, VOLUME 1: 1923-1929
    From a letter to TCS, April 14, 1926 ("Salaam; / Being in an (un)poetical mood . . .")

## DAUGHTER OF EVIL
Alternate title: Untitled ("They cast her out of the . . .")
First appeared in CHACAL #2
    DESIRE AND OTHER EROTIC POEMS (Chpbk.)
    ROBERT E. HOWARD: SELECTED LETTERS: 1923-1930 (Chpbk.)
    THE COLLECTED LETTERS OF ROBERT E. HOWARD, VOLUME 2: 1930-1932
    From a letter to TCS, ca. September 1930 ("Well, Fear Finn: / I hope you'll . . .")

## A DAWN IN FLANDERS
Alternate title: Untitled ("I can recall a quiet sky . . .")
First appeared in THE HOWARD COLLECTOR #5
    ECHOES FROM AN IRON HARP
    THE DARK BARBARIAN (Anth.)

**THE DAY BREAKS OVER SIMLA**
First appeared in FANTASY CROSSROADS #4/5
    NIGHT IMAGES

**THE DAY THAT I DIE**
First appeared in THE HOWARD COLLECTOR #9
    ECHOES FROM AN IRON HARP
    THE BOOK OF ROBERT E. HOWARD

**DAYS OF GLORY**
Alternate title: Untitled ("Ah, those were glittering, jeweled days")
First appeared in NIGHT IMAGES

**DE OLE RIVER OX**
First appeared in THE GRIM LAND AND OTHERS (Chpbk.)
    THE HOWARD READER #8 (Chpbk.)

**DEAD MAN'S HATE**
First appeared in WEIRD TALES, January 1930
    ALWAYS COMES EVENING
    THE HOWARD REVIEW #1 (Chpbk., 2$^{nd}$ edition only)
    CHANTS DE GUERRE ET DE MORT
    ROBERT E. HOWARD: WORLD'S GREATEST PULPSTER #1
    MOON OF SKULLS: THE WEIRD WORKS OF ROBERT E. HOWARD, VOLUME 2
    SHADOW KINGDOMS: THE WEIRD WORKS OF ROBERT E. HOWARD, VOLUME 1 (Cosmos)
    THE WEIRD WRITINGS OF ROBERT E. HOWARD, VOLUME ONE

**THE DEAD SLAVER'S TALE**
First appeared in WEIRDBOOK #8
    NIGHT IMAGES

**DEATH'S BLACK RIDERS (Verse heading, appearances apart from story)**
First appeared in ECHOES FROM AN IRON HARP

**THE DEED BEYOND THE DEED**
First appeared in THE LAST OF THE TRUNK OCH BREV I URVAL (Chpbk.)
    THE COLLECTED LETTERS OF ROBERT E. HOWARD, VOLUME 1: 1923-1929
    From a letter to TCS, ca. December 1928 ("Salaam: / Out in front of Goldstein's . . .")

**DEEPS**
First appeared in THE LAST OF THE TRUNK OCH BREV I URVAL (Chpbk.)
    THE COLLECTED LETTERS OF ROBERT E. HOWARD, VOLUME 1: 1923-1929
    From a letter to TCS, June 23, 1926 ("Salaam; / I'm trying to write again . . .")

**THE DESERT**
Alternate title: Untitled ("Wide and free ranging . . .")
First appeared in A RHYME OF SALEM TOWN AND OTHER POEMS (Chpbk. & HB)

**DESERT DAWN**
First appeared in WEIRD TALES, March 1939
        WEIRD TALES, January 1945 (Canadian)
        ALWAYS COMES EVENING
        CHANTS DE GUERRE ET DE MORT
        THE WEIRD WRITINGS OF ROBERT E. HOWARD, VOLUME TWO

**THE DESERT HAWK**
First appeared in A RHYME OF SALEM TOWN AND OTHER POEMS (Chpbk. & HB)

**DESIRE**
Alternate title: Untitled ("'Turn out the light.' I raised a willing hand")
First appeared in DESIRE AND OTHER EROTIC POEMS (Chpbk.)
        RISQUE STORIES #1 (Chpbk.)

**DESTINATION**
First appeared in THE MAGAZINE OF HORROR #12
        SINGERS IN THE SHADOWS
        REVELATIONS FROM YUGGOTH #3 (Chpbk.)

**DESTINY (1, "I think I was born . . .")**
First appeared in SAVAGE SWORD OF CONAN #193 (Comics)
        THE NEW HOWARD READER #7 (Chpbk.)

**DESTINY (2, "What is there . . .")**
First appeared in SHADOWS OF DREAMS
        THE CROSS PLAINSMAN, August 2004 (Chpbk.)
        THE LAST OF THE TRUNK OCH BREV I URVAL (Chpbk.)
        THE COLLECTED LETTERS OF ROBERT E. HOWARD, VOLUME 1: 1923-1929
        From a letter to TCS, April 14, 1926 ("Salaam; / Being in an (un)poetical mood . . .")

**DESTINY (3, "I am a white trail . . .")**
First appeared in THE LAST OF THE TRUNK OCH BREV I URVAL (Chpbk.)
        THE COLLECTED LETTERS OF ROBERT E. HOWARD, VOLUME 1: 1923-1929
        From a letter to TCS, June 23, 1926 ("Salaam; / I'm trying to write again . . .")

**DEVON OAK**
Alternate title: Untitled ("I am a Devon oak")
First appeared in A RHYME OF SALEM TOWN AND OTHER POEMS (Chpbk. & HB)

**DOOM**
Alternate title: THE WHEEL OF DESTINY

**THE DOOM CHANT OF THAN-KUL**
First appeared in WEIRD TALES #4 (Anth.)
        THE NEW HOWARD READER #5 (Chpbk.)

**DOWN THE AGES**
Alternate title: Untitled ("Forever down the ages")
First appeared in A RHYME OF SALEM TOWN AND OTHER POEMS (Chpbk. & HB)
        Unfinished

**DRAKE SINGS OF YESTERDAY**

First appeared in WEIRDBOOK #15
    THE NEW HOWARD READER #1 (Chpbk.)

## THE DREAM AND THE SHADOW
First appeared in WEIRD TALES, September 1937
    ALWAYS COMES EVENING
    L'HERNE #12 (Chpbk.)
    CHANTS DE GUERRE ET DE MORT
    THE WEIRD WRITINGS OF ROBERT E. HOWARD, VOLUME TWO
    THE CROSS PLAINSMAN, April 2006 (Chpbk.)
    One of the "Sonnets Out of Bedlam"

## A DREAM OF AUTUMN
Alternate title: AUTUMN; THE AUTUMN OF THE WORLD

## DREAMER
First appeared in THE LAST OF THE TRUNK OCH BREV I URVAL (Chpbk.)
    THE COLLECTED LETTERS OF ROBERT E. HOWARD, VOLUME 1: 1923-1929
    From a letter to TCS, June 23, 1926 ("Salaam; / I'm trying to write again . . .")

## DREAMING
First appeared in THE LAST OF THE TRUNK OCH BREV I URVAL (Chpbk.)
    THE COLLECTED LETTERS OF ROBERT E. HOWARD, VOLUME 3: 1933-1936
    From a letter to TCS, undated ("Salaam / Again glancing . . .")

## DREAMING IN ISRAEL
First appeared in SHADOWS OF DREAMS
    THE LAST OF THE TRUNK OCH BREV I URVAL (Chpbk.)
    THE COLLECTED LETTERS OF ROBERT E. HOWARD, VOLUME 2: 1930-1932
    From a letter to TCS, ca. August 1932 ("Fear Finn; / I don't know when . . .")

## DREAMING ON DOWNS
Alternate title: KING ALFRED RIDES AGAIN
First appeared in POET'S SCROLL, April 1929 (author listed as "Patrick Howard")
    THE NEW HOWARD READER #2 (Chpbk.)
    WEST IS WEST AND OTHERS

## DREAMS
First appeared in UP JOHN KANE! AND OTHER POEMS (Chpbk.)
    THE NEW HOWARD READER #5 (Chpbk.)

## THE DREAMS OF MEN
First appeared in SHADOWS OF DREAMS
    THE COLLECTED LETTERS OF ROBERT E. HOWARD, VOLUME 1: 1923-1929
    BRAMY IMPERIUM (Polish)
    From a letter to TCS, ca. October 1927 ("Salaam: / Seeking cognizance of things . . .")

**DREAMS OF NINEVEH**
First appeared in GOLDEN ATOM, 20^TH Anniversary Issue, 1959-1960
    ECHOES FROM AN IRON HARP
    LA CITADELLE ECARLATE (French)
    THE DARK BARBARIAN (Anth., lines 1-8)
    ODES AT THE BLACK DOG (Chpbk.)
    WEST IS WEST AND OTHERS

**DROWNED**
First appeared in TOADSTOOL WINE (Chpbk.)
    THE NEW HOWARD READER #3 (Chpbk.)

**THE DRUM**
Alternate title: Untitled ("I heard the drum as I went . . .")
First appeared in A RHYME OF SALEM TOWN AND OTHER POEMS (Chpbk. & HB)

**A DRUM BEGINS TO THROB**
Alternate title: OUT OF THE DEEP; THE VOICES WAKEN MEMORY

**DRUM GODS**
First appeared in ETCHINGS AND ODYSSEYS #9 (Chpbk.)
    THE NEW HOWARD READER #4 (Chpbk.)

**DRUMMINGS ON AN EMPTY SKULL**
First appeared in THE LAST OF THE TRUNK OCH BREV I URVAL (Chpbk.)
    THE COLLECTED LETTERS OF ROBERT E. HOWARD, VOLUME 3: 1933-1936
    From an undated letter to TCS ("Salaam:/ Skulls Against the Dawn")

**DRUMS IN MY EARS**
Alternate title: verse heading for Chapter 3 of "Sword Woman"
Never published separately

**THE DRUMS OF PICTDOM**
Alternate title: Untitled ("How can I wear the harness of toil")
First appeared in BRAN MAK MORN, Dell
    WORMS OF THE EARTH
    HERRSCHER DER NACHT (German)
    BRAN MAK MORN, Baen
    BRAN MAK MORN – THE LAST KING
    BRAN MAK MORN (Czech)
    ROBAKI ZIEMI (Polish)
    Appeared in the Foreword of all these copies, except for the Wandering Star edition

**A DULL SOUND AS OF KNOCKING**
First appeared in A RHYME OF SALEM TOWN AND OTHER POEMS (Chpbk. & HB)

**A DUNGEON OPENS**
First appeared in EIN TRAUMER AUS TEXAS (Chpbk.)
    THE NEW HOWARD READER #2 (Chpbk.)

**THE DUST DANCE (1, "Ah, its little they knew . . .")**
First appeared in THE HOWARD COLLECTOR #10
    ECHOES FROM AN IRON HARP (lines 1-80)
    DARK VALLEY DESTINY (Anth.)
    THE DARK BARBARIAN (Anth., lines 1-4)
    SHADOWS OF DREAMS (lines 81-96)
    THE COLLECTED LETTERS OF ROBERT E. HOWARD, VOLUME 1: 1923-1929 (various portions)
    Very similar to the other poem of the same title; Lines 9-12, 29-32, 45-48, 49-52, and 85-88 identical to 1-4, 5-
        8, 13-16, 9-12, and 21-24, respectively, of the other version; portions from a letter to TCS, March
        1928 ("Salaam: / Glad you're writing . . .")

**THE DUST DANCE (2, "For I, with the . . .")**
Alternate title: Untitled ("For I, with the . . .")
First appeared in THE HOWARD COLLECTOR #7
    THE RIVERSIDE QUARTERLY, June 1966 (lines 5-20)
    ECHOES FROM AN IRON HARP
    THE BOOK OF ROBERT E. HOWARD
    THE DARK BARBARIAN (Anth., lines 9-12)
    DESIRE AND OTHER EROTIC POEMS (Chpbk.)
    THE BOOK OF MADNESS (Chpbk., lines 69-72)
    THE COLLECTED LETTERS OF ROBERT E. HOWARD, VOLUME 1: 1923-1929 (various portions)
    CRIMSON SHADOWS: THE BEST OF ROBERT E. HOWARD, VOLUME 1
    Consists of four parts, of 24, 12, 16, and 20 lines; Lines 33-36 virtually identical to lines 1-4 of "The Song of
        Horsa's Galley"; lines 69-72 virtually identical to lines 1-4 of "The Road to Hell"; originally untitled,
        portions were included in a letter to TCS, ca. March 1928 ("Salaam: / Glad you're writing . . .")

**THE DWELLER IN DARK VALLEY**
First appeared in MAGAZINE OF HORROR #11
    ECHOES FROM AN IRON HARP
    A STRANGE GLORY (Anth.)
    DARK VALLEY DESTINY (Anth., lines 9-12, 17-20)
    ROBERT E. HOWARD'S POEMS ON THE EDGE
    RHYMES OF TEXAS AND THE OLD WEST
    WINDS OF TIME

**A DYING PIRATE SPEAKS OF TREASURE**
First appeared in UP JOHN KANE! AND OTHER POEMS (Chpbk.)
    THE NEW HOWARD READER #4 (Chpbk.)

**EARTH-BORN**
First appeared in FIRE AND SLEET AND CANDLELIGHT (Anth.)
    ECHOES FROM AN IRON HARP
    PFADE INS FANTASTIQUE, BOOK 2 (Chpbk.)
    THE WINDS OF TIME

**EASTER ISLAND**
First appeared in WEIRD TALES, December 1928
    ALWAYS COMES EVENING
    ANCIENT RUINS AND ARCHEOLOGY (Anth., lines 1-4, 9-14)
    CITADELS OF MYSTERY (Anth., lines 1-4, 9-14)
    ECHOES FROM THE BLACK STONE #12 (Chpbk., lines 9-14)
    CHANTS DE GUERRE ET DE MORT
    REHUPA #127 (Chpbk., in an LSDC letter, don't know which zine, lines 1-4)
    ROBERT E. HOWARD: WORLD'S GREATEST PULPSTER #1

BLUFFTOWN BARBARIAN #8 (Chpbk.)
SHADOW KINGDOMS: THE WEIRD WORKS OF ROBERT E. HOWARD, VOLUME 1 (Wildside Press &
    Cosmos)
THE WEIRD WRITINGS OF ROBERT E. HOWARD, VOLUME ONE

## ECHOES FROM AN ANVIL
First appeared in NIGHT IMAGES
    A RHYME OF SALEM TOWN AND OTHER POEMS (Chpbk. & HB)
    THE GRIM LAND: THE BEST OF ROBERT E. HOWARD, VOLUME 2

## ECHOES FROM AN IRON ANVIL
First appeared in VERSES IN EBONY (Chpbk.)
    HEAVY METAL #3
    THE DARK BARBARIAN (Anth., lines 13-16, 19, 22)

## AN ECHO FROM THE IRON HARP
Alternate title: THE GOLD AND THE GREY

## ECHOING SHADOWS
Alternate title: THE IRON HARP (2); VOICES OF THE NIGHT

## ECSTASY
Alternate title: Untitled ("There is a strangeness in my soul")
First appeared in RHYMES OF DEATH (Chpbk.)
    THE HOWARD READER #8 (Chpbk.)

## THE ECSTASY OF DESOLATION
Alternate title: Untitled ("Long were the years . . .")
First appeared in SHADOWS OF DREAMS
    THE COLLECTED LETTERS OF ROBERT E. HOWARD, VOLUME 1: 1923-1929
    BRAMY IMPERIUM (Polish)
    From a letter to TCS, ca. October 1928 ("Salaam: / I could have gone . . .")

## EDGAR GUEST
Alternate title: Untitled ("How long have you written, Eddie Guest?")
First appeared in A RHYME OF SALEM TOWN AND OTHER POEMS (Chpbk. & HB)
    Unfinished

## EGYPT
First appeared in WHISPERS #2
    NIGHT IMAGES

## EMANCIPATION
First appeared in ALWAYS COMES EVENING
    RHYMES OF DEATH (Chpbk.)
    DARK VALLEY DESTINY (Anth., lines 18-20)
    CHANTS DE GUERRE ET DE MORT
    PALE HORSE, unknown number (Chpbk.)

## EMPIRE

Alternate title: BLACK CHANT IMPERIAL
First appeared in VERSES IN EBONY (Chpbk.)
    THE BOOK OF ROBERT E. HOWARD
    NIGHT IMAGES
    "Black Chant Imperial" is a shortened version of this poem, using lines 1-4, 9-12, 21-32, and 37-40

## EMPIRE'S DESTINY

Alternate title: OH BABYLON, LOST BABYLON
First appeared in POET'S SCROLL, June 1929 (author listed as "Patrick Howard")
    THE NEW HOWARD READER #3 (Chpbk.)
    WEST IS WEST AND OTHERS
    "Oh Babylon, Lost Babylon" is a slightly different version, one line shorter

## THE END OF THE GLORY TRAIL

First appeared in RHYMES OF DEATH (Chpbk.)
    RHYMES OF TEXAS AND THE OLD WEST

## ENVOY

First appeared in THE LAST OF THE TRUNK OCH BREV I URVAL (Chpbk.)
    THE COLLECTED LETTERS OF ROBERT E. HOWARD, VOLUME 2: 1930-1932
    From a letter to TCS, ca. November 1932 ("Fear Finn: / Well, I finally get around . . .")

## ERIC OF NORWAY

First appeared in A RHYME OF SALEM TOWN AND OTHER POEMS (Chpbk. & HB)

## ESCAPE

First appeared in A RHYME OF SALEM TOWN AND OTHER POEMS (Chpbk. & HB)

## ETERNITY

First appeared in THE LAST OF THE TRUNK OCH BREV I URVAL (Chpbk.)
    THE COLLECTED LETTERS OF ROBERT E. HOWARD, VOLUME 1: 1923-1929
    From a letter to TCS, June 23, 1926 ("Salaam; / I'm trying to write again . . .")

## EXHORTATION

Alternate title: Untitled ("Oh, ye who tread the narrow way")
First appeared in A RHYME OF SALEM TOWN AND OTHER POEMS (Chpbk. & HB)

## A FABLE FOR CRITICS

Alternate title: Untitled ("Now come the days of high . . .")
First appeared in SHADOWS OF DREAMS
    THE LAST OF THE TRUNK OCH BREV I URVAL (Chpbk.)
    THE COLLECTED LETTERS OF ROBERT E. HOWARD, VOLUME 1: 1923-1929
    From a letter to TCS, ca. November-December 1928 ("Salaam: / Heh heh!")

## FABLES FOR LITTLE FOLKS

First appeared in DANIEL BAKER COLLEGIAN, March 15, 1926
    ECHOES FROM AN IRON HARP
    ONION TOPS #3 (Chpbk.)
    ODES AT THE BLACK DOG (Chpbk.)
    WEST IS WEST AND OTHERS

## A FAR COUNTRY

First appeared in SHADOWS OF DREAMS
  THE COLLECTED LETTERS OF ROBERT E. HOWARD, VOLUME 1: 1923-1929
  From a letter to TCS, ca. November 1928 ("Salaam: / I'll swear . . .")

## FAR IN THE GLOOMY NORTHLAND
Alternate title: Untitled ("Far in the gloomy northland")
First appeared in A RHYME OF SALEM TOWN AND OTHER POEMS (Chpbk. & HB)

## FAREWELL, PROUD MUNSTER
Alternate title: Untitled ("Night in the county of Donegal")
First appeared in A RHYME OF SALEM TOWN AND OTHER POEMS (Chpbk. & HB)

## "FEACH AIR MUIR LIONADHI GEALACH BUIDHE MAR OR"
First appeared in THE JUNTO, August 1929
  COVEN 13, March 1970
  ECHOES FROM AN IRON HARP
  THE WINDS OF TIME

## THE FEAR THAT FOLLOWS
First appeared in SINGERS IN THE SHADOWS

## THE FEARSOME TOUCH OF DEATH (Verse heading, appearances apart from story)
First appeared in ECHOES FROM AN IRON HARP
  THE DEAD MAN'S KISS (Anth.)

## FEBRUARY
Alternate title: PARODY

## THE FEUD
Alternate title: Untitled ("He did not glance above the trail . . .")
First appeared in FANTASY CROSSROADS #13
  THE NEW HOWARD READER #5 (Chpbk.)
  RHYMES OF TEXAS AND THE OLD WEST

## FLAMING MARBLE
Alternate title: Untitled ("I carved a woman out of marble when")
First appeared in POET'S SCROLL, January 1929 (author listed as "Patrick Howard")
  SHADOWS OF DREAMS
  WEST IS WEST AND OTHERS
  THE LAST OF THE TRUNK OCH BREV I URVAL (Chpbk.)
  THE COLLECTED LETTERS OF ROBERT E. HOWARD, VOLUME 1: 1923-1929
  Also in a letter to TCS, ca. November-December 1928 ("Salaam: / Heh heh!"); there is also a short prose piece
      with the same title, but is different

## FLIGHT
Alternate title: Untitled ("A jackal laughed from a thicket still, . . .")
First appeared in WITCHCRAFT & SORCERY #6
  NIGHT IMAGES
  SHAYOL #1 (Chpbk., lines 17-24)
  AMERICAN AND EUROPEAN MANUSCRIPTS AND PRINTED BOOKS, December 19, 1986 (early
      incomplete version)
  COLD STEEL #10 (Chpbk., early incomplete version)
  MANUSCRIPTS FROM GOWER-PENN, VOLUME 2, #3 (Chpbk., early incomplete version)

FLIGHT
MIDNIGHT SUN (Anth., lines 17-24)
THE COLLECTED LETTERS OF ROBERT E. HOWARD, VOLUME 1: 1923-1929 (early incomplete
    version)
The early incomplete version is slightly different, using lines 1-2, 5-8, 15-20, 23-24; that slightly shorter
    version is from an earlier untitled draft of the poem that appeared in a letter to TCS, ca. September 1927
    ("Salaam: / Having just got your letter . . ."); those appearances are facsimile reproductions of the page of
    the letter containing that poem, other than in THE COLLECTED LETTERS, which is transcribed

**FLINT'S PASSING**
First appeared in FANTASY CROSSROADS #3
    FLIGHT
    THE NEW HOWARD READER #1 (Chpbk.)
    THE GRIM LAND: THE BEST OF ROBERT E. HOWARD, VOLUME 2

**THE FLOOD**
Alternate title: TO ALL EVANGELISTS
First appeared in THE GHOST OCEAN AND OTHER POEMS OF THE SUPERNATURAL (Chpbk.)
    THE HOWARD READER #8 (Chpbk.)

**THE FOLLOWER**
First appeared in THE GOLDEN CALIPH, 1922 or 1923
    THE LAST CELT

**FOR MAN WAS GIVEN THE EARTH TO RULE**
Alternate title: AND MAN WAS GIVEN THE EARTH TO RULE; THE OLD GODS BROOD
First appeared in FANTASY BOOK, September 1986
    THE NEW HOWARD READER #2 (Chpbk.)
    Mistakenly listed as "And . . ." in the Table of Contents of FANTASY BOOK

**FORBIDDEN MAGIC**
First appeared in WEIRD TALES, July 1929
    ALWAYS COMES EVENING
    CHANTS DE GUERRE ET DE MORT
    SHADOW KINGDOMS: THE WEIRD WORKS OF ROBERT E. HOWARD, VOLUME 1 (Wildside Press &
        Cosmos)
    THE WEIRD WRITINGS OF ROBERT E. HOWARD, VOLUME ONE

**FRAGMENT**
First appeared in WEIRD TALES, December 1937
    ALWAYS COMES EVENING
    RHYMES OF DEATH (Chpbk.)
    DARK VALLEY DESTINY (Anth., lines 1-4, 19-28)
    EIN TRAUMER AUS TEXAS (Chpbk., German, HB & PB, lines 1-28)
    CHANTS DE GUERRE ET DE MORT
    THE WEIRD WRITINGS OF ROBERT E. HOWARD, VOLUME TWO

**FREEDOM**
Alternate title: Untitled ("The world is rife, say I")
First appeared in A RHYME OF SALEM TOWN AND OTHER POEMS (Chpbk. & HB)

**FUTILITY (1, "Golden goats . . .")**
Alternate title: MOONLIGHT ON A SKULL
First appeared in WEIRD TALES, November 1937
>      DARK OF THE MOON (Anth.)
>      ALWAYS COMES EVENING
>      RHYMES OF DEATH (Chpbk.)
>      MAGIRA #27 (Chpbk., German)
>      CHANTS DE GUERRE ET DE MORT
>      IN MEMORIUM: CONAN THE BARBARIAN, 1970-1993 (Chpbk., lines 28-30)
>      THE MIDTOWN DOWNTOWN SPECIAL TRESTLER: THE ILLUSTRATORS OF R.E.H.: TOM FOSTER
>      THE WEIRD WRITINGS OF ROBERT E. HOWARD, VOLUME TWO
>      Virtually identical to "Moonlight on a Skull"

**FUTILITY (2, "Time races on . . .")**
First appeared in DANIEL BAKER COLLEGIAN, May 25, 1926
>      THE HOWARD COLLECTOR #4
>      ECHOES FROM AN IRON HARP
>      CHACAL #1 (as heading for a David C. Smith story)
>      WEST IS WEST AND OTHERS

**THE GATES OF BABYLON**
First appeared in THE GHOST OCEAN AND OTHER POEMS OF THE SUPERNATURAL (Chpbk.)

**THE GATES OF NINEVEH**
First appeared in WEIRD TALES, July 1928
>      ALWAYS COMES EVENING
>      CHANTS DE GUERRE ET DE MORT
>      ROBERT E. HOWARD: WORLD'S GREATEST PULPSTER #1
>      BLUFFTOWN BARBARIAN #8 (Chpbk.)
>      SHADOW KINGDOMS: THE WEIRD WORKS OF ROBERT E. HOWARD, VOLUME 1 (Wildside Press &
>           Cosmos)
>      THE HOWARD REVIEW #12 (Chpbk.)
>      THE WEIRD WRITINGS OF ROBERT E. HOWARD, VOLUME ONE

**GHOST DANCERS**
First appeared in WRITER OF THE DARK
>      ROBERT E. HOWARD'S POEMS ON THE EDGE
>      RHYMES OF TEXAS AND THE OLD WEST
>      WINDS OF TIME

**THE GHOST KINGS**
First appeared in WEIRD TALES, December 1938
>      WEIRD TALES, September 1944 (Canadian)
>      DARK OF THE MOON (Anth.)
>      ALWAYS COMES EVENING
>      FANTASY CROSSROADS #3
>      NIGHT IMAGES
>      LITERARY SWORDSMEN AND SORCERERS (Anth., lines 7-9)
>      HEAVY METAL #3
>      DARK FANTASY #16 (Chpbk., Canadian)
>      MIRROR OF FANTASY #4 (Chpbk., German)
>      DARK VALLEY DESTINY (Anth., lines 1-3)
>      CHANTS DE GUERRE ET DE MORT
>      ODES AT THE BLACK DOG (Chpbk.)

THE WEIRD WRITINGS OF ROBERT E. HOWARD, VOLUME TWO
CRIMSON SHADOWS: THE BEST OF ROBERT E. HOWARD, VOLUME 1
THE CROSS PLAINSMAN, December 2006 (Chpbk.)

## THE GHOST OCEAN
Alternate title: Untitled ("There is a sea and a silent moon")
First appeared in THE GHOST OCEAN AND OTHER POEMS OF THE SUPERNATURAL (Chpbk.)
EIN TRAUMER AUS TEXAS (Chpbk.)
THE HOWARD READER #8 (Chpbk.)
THE WINDS OF TIME

## GIRL
First appeared in THE LAST OF THE TRUNK OCH BREV I URVAL (Chpbk.)
THE COLLECTED LETTERS OF ROBERT E. HOWARD, VOLUME 1: 1923-1929
From a letter to TCS, June 23, 1926 ("Salaam; / I'm trying to write again . . .")

## GIRLS
First appeared in THE TOREADOR, July 5, 1925
REHUPA #117 (Chpbk.)
THE NEW HOWARD READER #3 (Chpbk.)

## THE GLADIATOR AND THE LADY
First appeared in SHADOWS OF DREAMS
THE COLLECTED LETTERS OF ROBERT E. HOWARD, VOLUME 2: 1930-1932
From a letter to TCS, ca. April 1930 ("Well, Fear Finn, you mention . . .")

## THE GODS I WORSHIPPED
First appeared in A RHYME OF SALEM TOWN AND OTHER POEMS (Chpbk. & HB)

## THE GODS OF EASTER ISLAND
Alternate title: Untitled ("Long ere Priapus . . .")
First appeared in ALWAYS COMES EVENING
CHANTS DE GUERRE ET DE MORT

## THE GODS OF THE JUNGLE DRUMS
First appeared in THE GRIM LAND AND OTHERS (Chpbk.)
THE HOWARD READER #8 (Chpbk.)

## THE GODS REMEMBER (1, "Lost wonders of the ages")
First appeared in THE COLLECTED LETTERS OF ROBERT E. HOWARD, VOLUME 1: 1923-1929
From a letter to TCS, ca. October 1927 ("Salaam: / Seeking cognizance of things . . ."); an early draft, somewhat different from (2)

## THE GODS REMEMBER (2, "The glories of the ages")
First appeared in ETCHINGS AND ODYSSEYS #9 (Chpbk.)
THE NEW HOWARD READER #4 (Chpbk.)

## THE GOLD AND THE GREY
Alternate title: AN ECHO FROM THE IRON HARP
First appeared in THE GOLD AND THE GREY (Chpbk.)
VERSES IN EBONY (Chpbk., dummy prototype)
THE BOOK OF ROBERT E. HOWARD
NIGHT IMAGES

SERVANT OF THE WARSMAN #8 (Chpbk., lines 29-32)
RED RUINS #1 (Chpbk.)
THE NEW HOWARD READER #5 (Chpbk., facsimile reproduction of VERSES IN EBONY by Glenn Lord)
THE ULTIMATE TRIUMPH (as "An Echo from the Iron Harp", a previously unpublished version)
CRIMSON SHADOWS: THE BEST OF ROBERT E. HOWARD, VOLUME 1
THE CROSS PLAINSMAN, December 2006 (Chpbk.)

## GOOD MISTRESS BROWN
Alternate title: Untitled ("A sturdy housewife was . . .")
First appeared in DESIRE AND OTHER EROTIC POEMS (Chpbk.)

## A GREAT MAN SPEAKS
First appeared in THE COLLECTED LETTERS OF ROBERT E. HOWARD, VOLUME 1: 1923-1929
    From a letter to TCS, ca. November 1928 ("Salaam: / I'll swear . . .")

## THE GREY GOD PASSES (Verse heading, appearances apart from story)
Alternate title: CONN'S SAGA
First appeared in ECHOES FROM AN IRON HARP (Chapters 2 and 5)
    Only the heading for Chapter 5 is titled "Conn's Saga"

## THE GREY LOVER
First appeared in THE COLLECTED LETTERS OF ROBERT E. HOWARD, VOLUME 1: 1923-1929
    From a letter to TCS, ca. January 1928 ("I wasn't lying . . .")

## THE GRIM LAND
Alternate title: SONORA TO DEL RIO
First appeared in THE GRIM LAND AND OTHERS (Chpbk.)
    DARK VALLEY DESTINY (Anth., lines 1-8)
    DEAR HPL: LETTERS, ROBERT E. HOWARD TO H.P. LOVECRAFT, 1930-1936, REHP, 2002
    THE HOWARD READER #8 (Chpbk.)
    THE BLACK STRANGER AND OTHER AMERICAN TALES
    RHYMES OF TEXAS AND THE OLD WEST
    THE GRIM LAND: THE BEST OF ROBERT E. HOWARD, VOLUME 2
    Lines 1-8 and 17-24 are virtually identical to lines 1-16 of "Sonora to Del Rio"; originally from a letter to HPL,
        June 1931 ("I didn't take much of a trip . . .")

## THE GUISE OF YOUTH
Alternate title: Untitled ("Men say my years . . .")
First appeared in SCIENCE-FANTASY CORRESPONDENT #1 (Chpbk.)
    THE SECOND BOOK OF ROBERT E. HOWARD
    SPECTRUM SUPER SPECIAL #2 (lines 13-20)

## HADRIAN'S WALL
First appeared in SINGERS IN THE SHADOWS

## A HAIRY CHESTED IDEALIST SINGS
Alternate title: A HAIRY-CHESTED IDEALIST SINGS
First appeared in THE JUNTO, October 1928
    RHYMES OF DEATH (Chpbk.)
    EIN TRAUMER AUS TEXAS (Chpbk.)
    THE HOWARD READER #8 (Chpbk.)

## THE HARLOT

First appeared in RISQUE STORIES #3 (Chpbk.)
>   DESIRE AND OTHER EROTIC POEMS (Chpbk.)

## THE HARP OF ALFRED
First appeared in WEIRD TALES, September 1928
>   DARK OF THE MOON (Anth.)
>   ALWAYS COMES EVENING
>   CHANTS DE GUERRE ET DE MORT
>   ROBERT E. HOWARD: WORLD'S GREATEST PULPSTER #1
>   BLUFFTOWN BARBARIAN #8 (Chpbk.)
>   THE CROSS PLAINSMAN, VOLUME 2003, #1 (Chpbk.)
>   SHADOW KINGDOMS: THE WEIRD WORKS OF ROBERT E. HOWARD, VOLUME 1 (Wildside Press & Cosmos)
>   THE HOWARD REVIEW #12 (Chpbk.)
>   ODES AT THE BLACK DOG (Chpbk.)
>   THE WEIRD WRITINGS OF ROBERT E. HOWARD, VOLUME ONE

## HARVEST
Alternate title: Untitled ("We reap and bind the bitter yield")
First appeared in THE HOWARD COLLECTOR #17
>   THE HOWARD COLLECTOR, Ace
>   THE NEW HOWARD READER #6 (Chpbk.)

## HATE'S DAWN
First appeared in THE JUNTO, July 1929
>   THE DARK MAN #6 (Chpbk.)

## HAUNTING COLUMNS
First appeared in WEIRD TALES, February 1938
>   ALWAYS COMES EVENING
>   NIGHT IMAGES
>   WEIRD TALES, Neville-Spearman and Carroll & Graf (Anth.)
>   WEIRD TALES, VOLUME 1, Sphere (Anth.)
>   CHANTS DE GUERRE ET DE MORT
>   THE WEIRD WRITINGS OF ROBERT E. HOWARD, VOLUME TWO
>   THE CROSS PLAINSMAN, April 2006 (Chpbk.)
>   One of the "Sonnets Out of Bedlam"

## THE HEART OF THE SEA'S DESIRE
Alternate title: MATE OF THE SEA; Untitled ("The stars beat up . . .")
First appeared in ALWAYS COMES EVENING
>   NIGHT IMAGES
>   HEAVY METAL #3
>   DARK VALLEY DESTINY (Anth., lines 1-8)
>   EIN TRAUMER AUS TEXAS (Chpbk., lines 1-12, 17-24, embodied in article titled "Ein Traumer Aus Texas")
>   CHANTS DE GUERRE ET DE MORT
>   HARDWIRED HINTERLAND #7 (Chpbk.)
>   Originally was discovered as an untitled poem, title created by Dale Hart; a later final version was found, titled "Mate of the Sea"

**HERITAGE (1, "My people came . . .")**
First appeared in THE JUNTO, August 1929
    THE HOWARD COLLECTOR #10
    ECHOES FROM AN IRON HARP
    FANTASY CROSSROADS #2

**HERITAGE (2, "Saxon blood . . .")**
First appeared in FANTASY CROSSROADS #2
    THE NEW HOWARD READER #5 (Chpbk.)

**HIGH BLUE HALLS**
First appeared in THE COLLECTED LETTERS OF ROBERT E. HOWARD, VOLUME 1: 1923-1929
    From a letter to TCS, ca. April 1929 ("Salaam: / The iron harp that . . .")

**THE HILLS OF KANDAHAR**
First appeared in WEIRD TALES, June-July 1939
    ALWAYS COMES EVENING
    CHANTS DE GUERRE ET DE MORT
    THE WEIRD WRITINGS OF ROBERT E. HOWARD, VOLUME TWO

**HOPE EMPTY OF MEANING**
First appeared in THE HOWARD COLLECTOR #15
    FANTASY CROSSROADS #6
    NIGHT IMAGES
    THE HOWARD COLLECTOR, Ace
    THE RAVEN #1 (Chpbk.)
    THE DARK BARBARIAN (Anth., lines 1, 7-8)
    EIN TRAUMER AUS TEXAS (Chpbk.)
    CIEN BESTII (Polish)

**HOPES OF DREAMS**
First appeared in WITCHCRAFT & SORCERY #7
    NIGHT IMAGES

**THE HOUR OF THE DRAGON (Verse heading, appearances apart from story)**
First appeared in THE HOWARD COLLECTOR #11
    ECHOES FROM AN IRON HARP
    MIRROR OF FANTASY #3 (Chpbk., German)
    WINDS OF TIME
    Did not appear in the original publication, instead was first used with the story in the Berkeley editions

**THE HOUSE IN THE OAKS (Verse heading, appearances apart from story)**
Alternate title: CHILDREN OF THE NIGHT (Verse heading)
First appeared in DARK THINGS (Anth.)
    BLACK CANAAN
    LES HABITANTS DES TOMBES (French)
    IN LOVECRAFT'S SHADOW (Anth.)
    Originally this was an unused verse heading for "Children of the Night", Derleth used this as the verse heading
        for this story; attributed to Justin Geoffrey

**THE HOUSE OF GAEL**
Alternate title: Untitled ("The ancient boast, the ancient song")
First appeared in A RHYME OF SALEM TOWN AND OTHER POEMS (Chpbk. & HB)

## HOW TO SELECT A SUCCESSFUL EVANGELIST
First appeared in THE LAST OF THE TRUNK OCH BREV I URVAL (Chpbk.)
    THE COLLECTED LETTERS OF ROBERT E. HOWARD, VOLUME 1: 1923-1929
    From a letter to TCS, ca. March 1928 ("Salaam: / Not having much . . .")

## HY-BRASIL
Alternate title: THE ISLE OF HY-BRASIL

## HYMN OF HATRED
Alternate title: A RATTLESNAKE SINGS IN THE GRASS
First appeared in ALWAYS COMES EVENING
    DARK VALLEY DESTINY (Anth.)
    CHANTS DE GUERRE ET DE MORT
    Lines 1-8 and 9-12 same as 1-8 and 17-20 of "A Rattlesnake Sings in the Grass"

## I PRAISE MY NATIVITY
First appeared in FANTASY BOOK #23, March 1987
    SHADOWS OF DREAMS
    THE LAST OF THE TRUNK OCH BREV I URVAL (Chpbk.)
    THE COLLECTED LETTERS OF ROBERT E. HOWARD, VOLUME 3: 1933-1936
    From a letter to TCS, undated ("Salaam: / Again glancing . . .")

## ILLUSION
First appeared in DANIEL BAKER COLLEGIAN, March 15, 1926
    ECHOES FROM AN IRON HARP
    WEST IS WEST AND OTHERS

## IN THE RING
Alternate title: Untitled ("Over the place the lights go out")
First appeared in REH FIGHT MAGAZINE #4 (Chpbk.)
    BOXING STORIES

## AN INCIDENT OF THE MUSCOVY-TURKISH WAR
First appeared in A RHYME OF SALEM TOWN AND OTHER POEMS (Chpbk. & HB)

## INVECTIVE
Alternate title: Untitled ("There burns in me . . .")
First appeared in ALWAYS COMES EVENING
    DARK VALLEY DESTINY (Anth.)
    EIN TRAUMER AUS TEXAS (Chpbk.)
    CHANTS DE GUERRE ET DE MORT

## INVOCATION
Last poem in the BLACK DAWN cycle

## THE IRON HARP (1, a cycle of five poems)
Alternate title: VOICES OF THE NIGHT; ECHOING SHADOWS
First appeared in THE LAST OF THE TRUNK OCH BREV I URVAL (as "The Iron Harp")
    THE COLLECTED LETTERS OF ROBERT E. HOWARD, VOLUME 3: 1933-1936
A cycle of five poems, including "Out of the Deep"; "Babel"; "Laughter in the Gulf"; "Moon Shame"; "A Crown for
    a King"; from a letter to TCS, undated ("The Seeker thrust . . .")

## THE IRON HARP (2, a separate poem)

Alternate title: Fourth poem in the BLACK DAWN cycle

## THE ISLE OF HY-BRASIL
Alternate title: SHIPS
First appeared in THE GHOST OCEAN AND OTHER POEMS OF THE SUPERNATURAL (Chpbk.)
    Lines 1-4 and 20-38 identical to lines 1-4 and 5-22 of "Ships"

## IVORY IN THE NIGHT
First appeared in THE LAST OF THE TRUNK OCH BREV I URVAL (Chpbk.)
    THE COLLECTED LETTERS OF ROBERT E. HOWARD, VOLUME 1: 1923-1929
    From a letter to TCS, undated ("Salaam: / Life is a yellow mist . . .")

## JACK DEMPSEY
First appeared in THE RIGHT HOOK, VOLUME 1, #2 (Chpbk.)
    AUSTIN, VOLUME 3, #2 (Chpbk.)

## THE JACKAL
First appeared in OMNIUMGATHUM (Chpbk.)
    NIGHT IMAGES

## JOHN BROWN
First appeared in SHADOWS OF DREAMS
    THE COLLECTED LETTERS OF ROBERT E. HOWARD, VOLUME 2: 1930-1932
    From a letter to TCS, ca. May 1932 ("Fear Finn: / Lo, friend, . . .")

## JOHN KELLEY
First appeared in THE COLLECTED LETTERS OF ROBERT E. HOWARD, VOLUME 2: 1930-1932
    From a letter to TCS, ca. May 1932 ("Fear Finn: / Lo, friend, . . .")

## JOHN L. SULLIVAN
First appeared in THE RIGHT HOOK, VOLUME 1, #2 (Chpbk.)
    AUSTIN, VOLUME 3, #2 (Chpbk.)
    THE NEW HOWARD READER #1 (Chpbk.)

## JOHN RINGOLD
First appeared in THE HOWARD COLLECTOR #5
    ECHOES FROM AN IRON HARP
    THE END OF THE TRAIL: WESTERN STORIES
    RHYMES OF TEXAS AND THE OLD WEST

## JU-JU DOOM
Alternate title: Untitled ("As a great spider grows to monstrous girth")
First appeared in A RHYME OF SALEM TOWN AND OTHER POEMS (Chpbk. & HB)

## KELLY THE CONJURE-MAN (Verse heading, appearances apart from story)
First appeared in ECHOES FROM AN IRON HARP

## KERESA, KERESITA
Alternate title: Untitled ("Keresa, Keresita")
First appeared in SHADOWS OF DREAMS
    THE COLLECTED LETTERS OF ROBERT E. HOWARD, VOLUME 1: 1923-1929
    From a letter to TCS, ca. March 1928 ("The only reason . . .")

## KID LAVIGNE IS DEAD
First appeared in THE RING, June 1928
    ECHOES FROM AN IRON HARP
    WATERFRONT FISTS AND OTHERS
    WATERFRONT FISTS AND OTHERS PROMO POSTCARD
    BOXING STORIES
    ODES AT THE BLACK DOG (Chpbk.)

## KING ALFRED RIDES AGAIN
Alternate title: DREAMING ON DOWNS

## THE KING AND THE MALLET
First appeared in THE JUNTO, July 1929
    NIGHT IMAGES

## THE KING AND THE OAK
First appeared in WEIRD TALES, February 1939
    WEIRD TALES, March 1945 (Canadian)
    DARK OF THE MOON (Anth.)
    THE COMING OF CONAN
    ALWAYS COMES EVENING
    KING KULL
    KULL (Greek)
    KULL DI VALUSIA (Italian)
    NIGHT IMAGES
    HERR VON VALUSIEN (German)
    THE DARK BARBARIAN (Anth., lines 1-3)
    KULL
    LHORK EXTRA #3 (Chpbk., Spanish)
    EXPECTING THE BARBARIANS #8 (Chpbk., lines 4-24)
    THE NEW HOWARD READER #1 (Chpbk., "pure text")
    BUSTED RIBS AND BROKEN ENGLISH, VOLUME 6, #2 (Chpbk.)
    ODES AT THE BLACK DOG (Chpbk.)
    THE WEIRD WRITINGS OF ROBERT E. HOWARD, VOLUME TWO
    KULL: EXILE OF ATLANTIS (also an early draft)
    TZAR KULL (Russian)
    REY KULL (Spanish)
    THE GRIM LAND: THE BEST OF ROBERT E. HOWARD, VOLUME 2
    There are two versions of this poem, both of which come from separate typescripts; the first was published in WEIRD TALES, the second include a few extra lines at the start, and some other minor changes, REH scholar Patrice Louinent says it was only a draft, the WEIRD TALES published version is the one REH meant to publish

## KING BAHTHUR'S COURT (verse contained therein)
Only published with the story; from a letter to TCS, undated ("King Bahthur's Court . . .")

**THE KING OF THE AGES COMES**
Alternate title: Untitled ("I stand in the streets of the city")
First appeared in NIGHT IMAGES

**KING OF THE SEA**
First appeared in A RHYME OF SALEM TOWN AND OTHER POEMS (Chpbk. & HB)

**THE KING OF TRADE**
First appeared in A RHYME OF SALEM TOWN AND OTHER POEMS (Chpbk. & HB)
    Incomplete

**KINGS OF THE NIGHT (Verse heading, appearances apart from story)**
Alternate title: THE SONG OF BRAN
First appeared in ALWAYS COMES EVENING
    NIGHT IMAGES

**THE KIOWA'S TALE**
First appeared in FANTASY CROSSWINDS #1
    NIGHT IMAGES
    RHYMES OF TEXAS AND THE OLD WEST

**THE KISSING OF SAL SNOOBOO**
First appeared in THE TATTLER, January 6, 1925
    ECHOES FROM AN IRON HARP
    ODES AT THE BLACK DOG (Chpbk.)
    WEST IS WEST AND OTHERS
    ONION TOPS #9 (Chpbk.)
    A parody of Robert W. Service's "The Shooting of Dan McGrew"

**KRAKORUM**
Alternate title: Untitled ("A thousand years ago great Genghis reigned")
First appeared in A RHYME OF SALEM TOWN AND OTHER POEMS (Chpbk. & HB)
An introduction to this poem, written by REH and copied over by Glenn Lord, says: "The following is a poem
    written by me in the early part of my seventeenth year. Even at that puerile age it reflects the cheery
    optimism that characterizes all my writings."

**KUBLAI KHAN**
First appeared in THE GOLDEN CALIPH, 1922 or 1923
    THE LAST CELT
    THE RAVEN #1 (Chpbk.)

**THE LADDER OF LIFE**
Alternate title: Untitled ("Life is a ladder . . .")
First appeared in A RHYME OF SALEM TOWN AND OTHER POEMS (Chpbk. & HB)

**A LADY'S CHAMBER**
First appeared in AMERICAN POET, April 1929 (author listed as "Patrick Howard")
    LE MANOIR DES ROSES (French)
    ECHOES FROM AN IRON HARP
    LE MANOIR DES ROSES (French)
    THE DARK BARBARIAN (Anth., lines 3, 4, 10, 11)
    WEST IS WEST AND OTHERS

**THE LAND OF MYSTERY (Verse heading, appearances apart from story)**
Never published separately

**LAND OF THE PIONEER**
Alternate title: Untitled ("The wild bees hum . . .")
First appeared in A RHYME OF SALEM TOWN AND OTHER POEMS (Chpbk. & HB)

**THE LAST DAY**
Alternate title: THE LAST HOUR
First appeared in WEIRD TALES, March 1932
    ECHOES FROM AN IRON HARP
    MANUSCRIPTS FROM GOWER-PENN, VOLUME 2, #3 (Chpbk.)
    PEOPLE OF THE DARK: THE WEIRD WORKS OF ROBERT E. HOWARD, VOLUME 3
    THE WEIRD WRITINGS OF ROBERT E. HOWARD, VOLUME ONE
    THE LAST OF THE TRUNK OCH BREV I URVAL (Chpbk.)
    THE COLLECTED LETTERS OF ROBERT E. HOWARD, VOLUME 2: 1930-1932
    A slightly different version of "The Last Hour"; included in a letter to TCS, ca. November 1931 ("Fear Finn: / Here are the blasted . . .")

**THE LAST HOUR**
Alternate title: THE LAST DAY
First appeared in WEIRD TALES, June 1938
    DARK OF THE MOON (Anth.)
    ALWAYS COMES EVENING
    CHANTS DE GUERRE ET DE MORT
    THE WEIRD WRITINGS OF ROBERT E. HOWARD, VOLUME TWO
    THE CROSS PLAINSMAN, April 2006 (Chpbk.)
    One of the "Sonnets Out of Bedlam"; almost identical to "The Last Day"

**THE LAST WORDS HE HEARD**
Alternate title: Untitled ("The chariots were chanting . . .")
First appeared in SHADOWS OF DREAMS
    THE LAST OF THE TRUNK OCH BREV I URVAL (Chpbk.)
    THE COLLECTED LETTERS OF ROBERT E. HOWARD, VOLUME 1: 1923-1929
    ZMIERZCH NAD STONEHENGE (Polish)
    Originally untitled from a letter to TCS, ca. December 1928 ("Salaam: / Out in front of Goldstein's . . .")

**LAUGHTER**
First appeared in THE LAST OF THE TRUNK OCH BREV I URVAL (Chpbk.)
    THE COLLECTED LETTERS OF ROBERT E. HOWARD, VOLUME 1: 1923-1929
    From a letter to TCS, April 14, 1926 ("Salaam; / Being in an (un)poetical mood . . .")

**LAUGHTER IN THE GULFS**
Alternate title: AN ECHO OF LAUGHTER IN THE GULFS; VOICES OF THE NIGHT
First appeared in ALWAYS COMES EVENING
    LANDS OF WONDER #3 (Chpbk., German)
    CHANTS DE GUERRE ET DE MORT
    Verse 3 of 5 of "Voices of the Night"; from a letter to TCS, undated ("The Seeker thrust . . .")

**THE LEGACY OF TUBAL-CAIN**
Alternate title: Untitled ("'No more!' they swear . . .")
First appeared in THE HOWARD COLLECTOR #18
    NIGHT IMAGES
    THE HOWARD COLLECTOR, Ace
    BELTRIC WRITES #56 (Chpbk.)


**A LEGEND**
First appeared in WRITER OF THE DARK


**A LEGEND OF FARING TOWN**
First appeared in VERSES IN EBONY (Chpbk.)


**L'ENVOI (1, "Live like a wolf then")**
First appeared in THE RIGHT HOOK, VOLUME 1, #1 (Chpbk.)
    AUSTIN, VOLUME 3, #2 (Chpbk.)
    THE NEW HOWARD READER #3 (Chpbk.)
    ROBERT E. HOWARD—THE POWER OF THE WRITING MIND


**L'ENVOI (2, "Harlots and choir girls")**
First appeared in THE RIGHT HOOK, VOLUME 1, #2 (Chpbk.)
    AUSTIN, VOLUME 3, #2 (Chpbk.)
    THE NEW HOWARD READER #2 (Chpbk.)


**L'ENVOI (3, "Twilight striding o'er the mountain")**
First appeared in THE RIGHT HOOK, VOLUME 1, #3 (Chpbk.)
    AUSTIN, VOLUME 3, #2 (Chpbk.)
    THE NEW HOWARD READER #4 (Chpbk.)


**LESBIA (1, "From whence this grim desire")**
First appeared in THE LAST OF THE TRUNK OCH BREV I URVAL (Chpbk.)
    THE COLLECTED LETTERS OF ROBERT E. HOWARD, VOLUME 1: 1923-1929
    From a letter to TCS, ca. June 1928 ("Salaam; / Ho, ho, the long lights . . ."); a slightly different earlier version
        from (2)


**LESBIA (2, "From whence this grim desire")**
First appeared in DESIRE AND OTHER EROTIC POEMS (Chpbk.)
    RISQUE STORIES #1 (Chpbk.)


**LET THE GODS DIE**
First appeared in WEIRDBOOK #10
    WRITER OF THE DARK


**LIBERTINE**
First appeared in THE LAST OF THE TRUNK OCH BREV I URVAL (Chpbk.)
    THE COLLECTED LETTERS OF ROBERT E. HOWARD, VOLUME 1: 1923-1929
    From a letter to TCS, June 23, 1926 ("Salaam; / I'm trying to write again . . .")


**THE LIES**
First appeared in A RHYME OF SALEM TOWN AND OTHER POEMS (Chpbk. & HB)

**LIFE (1, "About me rise the primal mists")**
First appeared in THE COLLECTED LETTERS OF ROBERT E. HOWARD, VOLUME 1: 1923-1929
　　From a letter to TCS, ca. January 1928 ("I wasn't lying . . .")

**LIFE (2, "They bruised my soul . . .")**
First appeared in THE HOWARD COLLECTOR #18
　　THE SECOND BOOK OF ROBERT E. HOWARD
　　THE HOWARD COLLECTOR, Ace
　　From a letter to R.H. Barlow, June 14, 1934 ("If I ever decide . . .")

**LILITH**
First appeared in THE GHOST OCEAN AND OTHER POEMS OF THE SUPERNATURAL (Chpbk.)
　　DESIRE AND OTHER EROTIC POEMS (Chpbk.)
　　THE COLLECTED LETTERS OF ROBERT E. HOWARD, VOLUME 1: 1923-1929
　　From a letter to TCS, ca. October 1927 ("Salaam: / Seeking cognizance of things . . .")

**LIMERICKS TO SPANK BY**
Alternate title: Untitled ("There was a young girl from Siberia")
First appeared in DESIRE AND OTHER EROTIC POEMS (Chpbk.)
　　A collection of three five-line limericks

**LINES TO G. B. SHAW**
First appeared in THE LAST OF THE TRUNK OCH BREV I URVAL (Chpbk.)
　　THE COLLECTED LETTERS OF ROBERT E. HOWARD, VOLUME 2: 1930-1932
　　From a letter to TCS, ca. November 1932 ("Fear Finn: / Well, I finally get around . . ."), don't think he liked
　　　him

**LINES WRITTEN IN THE REALIZATION THAT I MUST DIE**
First appeared in WEIRD TALES, August 1938
　　SKULL-FACE AND OTHERS
　　DARK OF THE MOON (Anth.)
　　ALWAYS COMES EVENING
　　SKULL-FACE OMNIBUS
　　THE SECOND BOOK OF ROBERT E. HOWARD
　　SKULL-FACE OMNIBUS, VOLUME 3 (THE SHADOW KINGDOM AND OTHERS)
　　THE RAVEN #1 (Chpbk.)
　　DARK VALLEY DESTINY (Anth., lines 5-10)
　　THE DARK BARBARIAN (Anth., lines 5, 23, 24)
　　ROSTRO DE CALAVERA (Chpbk., Spanish)
　　EIN TRAUMER AUS TEXAS (Chpbk., German, lines 5-8, 13-16, 21-24)
　　CHANTS DE GUERRE ET DE MORT
　　MUSINGS #2 (Chpbk.)
　　PALE HORSE, unknown number (Chpbk.)
　　SERVANT OF THE WARSMAN #2 (Chpbk.)
　　ODES AT THE BLACK DOG (Chpbk.)
　　THE WEIRD WRITINGS OF ROBERT E. HOWARD, VOLUME TWO
　　WINDS OF TIME
　　CRIMSON SHADOWS: THE BEST OF ROBERT E. HOWARD, VOLUME 1

**THE LION OF TIBERIAS (Verse heading, appearances apart from story)**
First appeared in ECHOES FROM AN IRON HARP (Chapter 3)

**LITTLE BELL OF BRASS**
Alternate title: Untitled ("Tingle, jingle, dingle, tingle . . .")
First appeared in A RHYME OF SALEM TOWN AND OTHER POEMS (Chpbk. & HB)

**LITTLE BROWN MAN OF NIPPON**
Alternate title: Untitled ("Little brown man from Nippon . . .")
First appeared in A RHYME OF SALEM TOWN AND OTHER POEMS (Chpbk. & HB)
        THE COLLECTED LETTERS OF ROBERT E. HOWARD, VOLUME 2: 1930-1932
        From a letter to TCS, ca. April 1932 ("Fear Finn: / I heard from that bone-crushing . . .")

**LONG AGO**
First appeared in WRITER OF THE DARK

**LONGFELLOW REVISED**
First appeared in A RHYME OF SALEM TOWN AND OTHER POEMS (Chpbk. & HB)

**LOST ALTARS**
First appeared in WAYFARER #4
        ECHOES FROM AN IRON HARP

**THE LOST GALLEY**
First appeared in SINGERS IN THE SHADOWS

**THE LOST MINE**
Alternate title: THE LOST SAN SABA MINE

**THE LOST SAN SABA MINE**
Alternate title: THE LOST MINE; Untitled ("Under the grim San Saba hills")
First appeared in A RHYME OF SALEM TOWN AND OTHER POEMS (Chpbk. & HB)
        RHYMES OF TEXAS AND THE OLD WEST
        THE COLLECTED LETTERS OF ROBERT E. HOWARD, VOLUME 3: 1933-1936
        Originally an untitled poem in a letter to HPL, April 23, 1933 ("I'm enclosing some of the latest . . .")

**LOVE**
First appeared in SHADOWS OF DREAMS
        BIMBOS AND BARBARIANETTES (Chpbk.)
        THE COLLECTED LETTERS OF ROBERT E. HOWARD, VOLUME 1: 1923-1929
        From a letter to TCS, ca. January 1928 ("I wasn't lying . . .")

**LOVE'S YOUNG DREAM**
First appeared in SHADOWS OF DREAMS
        SEANCHAI #74 (Chpbk.)
        SPECTRUM SUPER SPECIAL #2 (lines 21-28)

**LUNACY CHANT**
First appeared in A RHYME OF SALEM TOWN AND OTHER POEMS (Chpbk. & HB)

**LUST**
First appeared in THE LAST OF THE TRUNK OCH BREV I URVAL (Chpbk.)
        THE COLLECTED LETTERS OF ROBERT E. HOWARD, VOLUME 1: 1923-1929
        From a letter to TCS, June 23, 1926 ("Salaam; / I'm trying to write again . . .")

**MAD MEG GILL**
First appeared in UP JOHN KANE! AND OTHER POEMS (Chpbk.)
    THE NEW HOWARD READER #4 (Chpbk.)

**MADAM GOOSE'S RHYMES**
Alternate title: Untitled ("Hark, hark, the jackals bark")
First appeared in FANTASY CROSSROADS #7
    THE NEW HOWARD READER #5 (Chpbk.)

**THE MADNESS OF CORMAC**
First appeared in THE LAST OF THE TRUNK OCH BREV I URVAL (Chpbk.)
    THE COLLECTED LETTERS OF ROBERT E. HOWARD, VOLUME 3: 1933-1936
    From a letter to TCS, undated ("Well, Fear Finn, I read . . .")

**MAHOMET**
Alternate title: Untitled ("Mahomet! Man of Mecca!")
First appeared in A RHYME OF SALEM TOWN AND OTHER POEMS (Chpbk. & HB)

**THE MAIDEN OF KERCHEEZER**
First appeared in THE PROGRESS, VOLUME 1, #2
    ODDS AND ENDS #1 (Chpbk.)
    THE NEW HOWARD READER #1 (Chpbk.)
    WEST IS WEST AND OTHERS

**A MAN**
First appeared in RAUHER SAND UND WILDE EICHEN (English & German)
    THE NEW HOWARD READER #2 (Chpbk.)
    THE COLLECTED LETTERS OF ROBERT E. HOWARD, VOLUME 1: 1923-1929
    From a letter to TCS, ca. January 1928 ("I wasn't lying . . .")

**MAN AM I**
First appeared in THE GHOST OCEAN AND OTHER POEMS OF THE SUPERNATURAL (Chpbk.)
    THE HOWARD READER #8 (Chpbk.)

**MAN, THE MASTER**
Alternate title: SONG AT MIDNIGHT

**MANKIND**
Alternate title: Untitled ("The world has changed")
First appeared in A RHYME OF SALEM TOWN AND OTHER POEMS (Chpbk. & HB)

**MARCHING SONG OF CONNACHT**
First appeared in THE HOWARD COLLECTOR #16
    NIGHT IMAGES
    THE HOWARD COLLECTOR, Ace
    THE COLLECTED LETTERS OF ROBERT E. HOWARD, VOLUME 2: 1930-1932
    CRIMSON SHADOWS: THE BEST OF ROBERT E. HOWARD, VOLUME 1
    THE CROSS PLAINSMAN, December 2006 (Chpbk.)
    THE WINDS OF TIME
    From a letter to TCS, ca. May 1930 ("Well, Fear Finn, I was in . . .")

## MARK OF THE BEAST
Alternate title: AFTER A FLAMING NIGHT
First appeared in WEIRDBOOK #9
    NIGHT IMAGES

## THE MASTER-DRUM
Alternate title: Untitled ("The Master beat on his master-drum")
First appeared in NIGHT IMAGES

## MATE OF THE SEA
Alternate title: THE HEART OF THE SEA'S DESIRE; Untitled ("The stars beat up . . .")

## MEMORIES (1, "I rose . . .")
Alternate title:
First appeared in SHANGRI L'AFFAIRES #72, April 1, 1968
    ECHOES FROM AN IRON HARP

## MEMORIES (2, "Shall we remember, friend of the morning")
First appeared in FANTASY TALES, Autumn 1988 (UK)
    WEIRD TALES #297, Summer 1990
    THE GIANT BOOK OF FANTASY TALES (Anth., Australia)
    THE NEW HOWARD READER #2 (Chpbk.)
    THE COLLECTED LETTERS OF ROBERT E. HOWARD, VOLUME 1: 1923-1929
    From a letter to TCS, ca. October 1927 ("Salaam: / Seeking cognizance of things . . .")

## MEMORIES OF ALFRED
First appeared in THE GHOST OCEAN AND OTHER POEMS OF THE SUPERNATURAL (Chpbk.)

## MEN BUILD THEM HOUSES
First appeared in VERSES IN EBONY (Chpbk.)
    THE HOWARD READER #8 (Chpbk.)

## MEN OF THE SHADOWS (Verse heading, appearances apart from the story)
Alternate title: Untitled ("From the dim red dawn of Creation")
First appeared in ALWAYS COMES EVENING
    MAGIRA #25 (Chpbk.)
    EIN TRAUMER AUS TEXAS (Chpbk.)
    HARDWIRED HINTERLAND #7 (Chpbk.)
    ROBERT E. HOWARD'S BRAN MAK MORN: A SKETCHBOOK (Chpbk.)
    The Underwood-Miller ALWAYS COMES EVENING version is significantly edited; the original appearance
        in the Arkham House edition is missing two lines

## THE MEN THAT WALK WITH SATAN
First appeared in SINGERS IN THE SHADOWS
    FANTASIA #11, (Chpbk., German)
    EIN TRAUMER AUS TEXAS (Chpbk.)
    WINDS OF TIME

## A MICK IN ISRAEL
First appeared in THE LAST OF THE TRUNK OCH BREV I URVAL (Chpbk.)
    THE COLLECTED LETTERS OF ROBERT E. HOWARD, VOLUME 2: 1930-1932
    From a letter to TCS, ca. November 1932 ("Fear Finn: / Well, I finally get around . . ."), discussing King Saul
        as a drunk Scotsman

**MIHIRAGULA**
First appeared in A RHYME OF SALEM TOWN AND OTHER POEMS (Chpbk. & HB)
>From a letter to Harold Preece, ca. October or early November 1930 ("Well, Harold, I'm sorry to hear your nose . . .")

**MINE BUT TO SERVE**
Alternate title: Untitled ("The moonlight glimmered white . . .")
First appeared in A RHYME OF SALEM TOWN AND OTHER POEMS (Chpbk. & HB)

**MISER'S GOLD**
First appeared in FANTASY CROSSROADS #8
>THE NEW HOWARD READER #3 (Chpbk.)

**A MISTY SEA**
Alternate title: Untitled ("There is a misty sea . . .")
First appeared in A RHYME OF SALEM TOWN AND OTHER POEMS (Chpbk. & HB)

**MODEST BILL**
First appeared in A RHYME OF SALEM TOWN AND OTHER POEMS (Chpbk. & HB)
>RHYMES OF TEXAS AND THE OLD WEST

**A MOMENT**
First appeared in THE HOWARD COLLECTOR #13
>ECHOES FROM AN IRON HARP
>DARK VALLEY DESTINY (Anth., lines 13-16)
>PFADE INS FANTASTIQUE, BOOK 2 (Chpbk.)
>WINDS OF TIME

**MONARCHS**
First appeared in THE CROSS PLAINSMAN, August 2004 (Chpbk.)
>THE LAST OF THE TRUNK OCH BREV I URVAL (Chpbk.)
>THE COLLECTED LETTERS OF ROBERT E. HOWARD, VOLUME 1: 1923-1929
>From a letter to TCS, June 23, 1926 ("Salaam; / I'm trying to write again . . .")

**MOON MOCKERY**
First appeared in WEIRD TALES, April 1929
>DARK OF THE MOON (Anth.)
>ALWAYS COMES EVENING
>THE HOWARD REVIEW #1 (Chpbk., 2nd edition only)
>EIN TRAUMER AUS TEXAS (Chpbk.)
>CHANTS DE GUERRE ET DE MORT
>SHADOW KINGDOMS: THE WEIRD WORKS OF ROBERT E. HOWARD, VOLUME 1 (Wildside Press & Cosmos)
>THE WEIRD WRITINGS OF ROBERT E. HOWARD, VOLUME ONE

**MOON SHAME**
Alternate title: THE MOON WOMAN; VOICES OF THE NIGHT
First appeared in ALWAYS COMES EVENING
>CHANTS DE GUERRE ET DE MORT
>PALE HORSE, unknown number (Chpbk.)
>This poem is Verse 4 of "Voices of the Night"; from a letter to TCS, undated ("The Seeker thrust . . ."); there are at least two drafts of this poem

**THE MOON WOMAN**
Alternate title: MOON SHAME

**MOONLIGHT ON A SKULL**
Alternate title: FUTILITY ("Golden goats . . .")
First appeared in WEIRD TALES, May 1933
    ECHOES FROM AN IRON HARP
    MAGIRA #21 (Chpbk., German)
    LA CITADELLE SCARLATE (French)
    EIN TRAUMER AUS TEXAS (Chpbk.)
    MANUSCRIPTS FROM GOWER-PENN, VOLUME 2, #3 (Chpbk.)
    WINGS IN THE NIGHT: THE WEIRD WORKS OF ROBERT E. HOWARD, VOLUME 4
    THE WEIRD WRITINGS OF ROBERT E. HOWARD, VOLUME ONE
    THE LAST OF THE TRUNK OCH BREV I URVAL (Chpbk.)
    THE COLLECTED LETTERS OF ROBERT E. HOWARD, VOLUME 2: 1930-1932
    Virtually identical to "Futility ('Golden goats . . .')"; included in a letter to TCS, ca. November 1931 ("Fear
        Finn: / Here are the blasted . . .")

**THE MOOR GHOST**
First appeared in WEIRD TALES, September 1929
    ALWAYS COMES EVENING
    CHANTS DE GUERRE ET DE MORT
    SHADOW KINGDOMS: THE WEIRD WORKS OF ROBERT E. HOWARD, VOLUME 1 (Wildside Press &
        Cosmos)
    THE WEIRD WRITINGS OF ROBERT E. HOWARD, VOLUME ONE

**THE MOTTOES OF THE BOY SCOUTS**
First appeared in THE LAST OF THE TRUNK OCH BREV I URVAL (Chpbk.)
    THE COLLECTED LETTERS OF ROBERT E. HOWARD, VOLUME 1: 1923-1929
    From a letter to TCS, ca. August/September 1927 ("ARE YOU THE YOUNG MAN . . .")

**THE MOUNTAINS OF CALIFORNIA**
First appeared in THE LAST OF THE TRUNK OCH BREV I URVAL (Chpbk.)
    THE COLLECTED LETTERS OF ROBERT E. HOWARD, VOLUME 1: 1923-1929
    From a letter to TCS, June 23, 1926 ("Salaam; / I'm trying to write again . . .")

**MUSINGS (1, "The little poets . . .")**
First appeared in WITCHCRAFT & SORCERY #5
    THE MISKATONIC (Chpbk.)
    THE SECOND BOOK OF ROBERT E. HOWARD
    NIGHT IMAGES
    ARIEL #3
    WOLFSHEAD #0 (Chpbk.)
    WHISPERS AT NIGHT (Chpbk.)
    EIN TRAUMER AUS TEXAS (Chpbk.)
    THE GRIM LAND: THE BEST OF ROBERT E. HOWARD, VOLUME 2

**MUSINGS (2, "To every man his trade")**
First appeared in SHADOWS OF DREAMS
    THE LAST OF THE TRUNK OCH BREV I URVAL (Chpbk.)
    THE COLLECTED LETTERS OF ROBERT E. HOWARD, VOLUME 2: 1930-1932
    From a letter to TCS, ca. November 1932 ("Fear Finn: / Well, I finally get around . . .")

## MY CHILDREN

First appeared in THE LAST OF THE TRUNK OCH BREV I URVAL (Chpbk.)
    THE COLLECTED LETTERS OF ROBERT E. HOWARD, VOLUME 1: 1923-1929
    From a letter to TCS, ca. December 1928 ("Salaam: / Out in front of Goldstein's . . .")

## MY SENTIMENTS SET TO JAZZ

First appeared in THE RIGHT HOOK, VOLUME 1, #3 (Chpbk.)
    AUSTIN, VOLUME 3, #2 (Chpbk.)
    THE NEW HOWARD READER #4 (Chpbk.)

## THE MYSTERIES

First appeared in YESTERYEAR #4 (Chpbk.)
    THE COLLECTED LETTERS OF ROBERT E. HOWARD, VOLUME 1: 1923-1929
    From a letter to TCS, ca. February 1929 ("Salaam: / Last night the Sunday School . . .")

## MYSTIC

First appeared in THE LAST OF THE TRUNK OCH BREV I URVAL (Chpbk.)
    THE COLLECTED LETTERS OF ROBERT E. HOWARD, VOLUME 1: 1923-1929
    From a letter to TCS, June 23, 1926 ("Salaam; / I'm trying to write again . . .")

## MYSTIC LORE

Alternate title: Untitled ("A wizard who dwelt in Drumnakill")
First appeared in A RHYME OF SALEM TOWN AND OTHER POEMS (Chpbk. & HB)

## THE MYTH

First appeared in DESIRE AND OTHER EROTIC POEMS (Chpbk.)

## NANCY HAWK - A LEGEND OF VIRGINITY

First appeared in THE LAST OF THE TRUNK OCH BREV I URVAL (Chpbk.)
    THE COLLECTED LETTERS OF ROBERT E. HOWARD, VOLUME 1: 1923-1929
    From a letter to TCS, ca. November 1928 ("Salaam: / I got such a laugh . . .")

## NATIVE HELL

First appeared in A RHYME OF SALEM TOWN AND OTHER POEMS (Chpbk. & HB)

## NECTAR

First appeared in THE JUNTO, September 1929
    THE GRIM LAND AND OTHERS (Chpbk.)
    THE HOWARD READER #8 (Chpbk.)

## A NEGRO GIRL

First appeared in DESIRE AND OTHER EROTIC POEMS (Chpbk.)

## NEOLITHIC LOVE SONG

First appeared in NEOLITHIC LOVE SONG (Chpbk.)
    BARNSWOGGLE #1 (Chpbk.)
    AUSTIN, VOLUME 3, #1 (Chpbk.)
    THE NEW HOWARD READER #4 (Chpbk.)
    THE LAST OF THE TRUNK OCH BREV I URVAL (Chpbk.)
    THE COLLECTED LETTERS OF ROBERT E. HOWARD, VOLUME 1: 1923-1929
    From a letter to TCS, June 8, 1923 ("Hello Clyde, / May the blessings . . .")

## NEVER BEYOND THE BEAST

Alternate title: Untitled ("Rise to the peak of the ladder")
First appeared in THE GHOST OCEAN AND OTHER POEMS OF THE SUPERNATURAL (Chpbk.)
    SEANCHAI #46 (Chpbk.)
    SEANCHAI #74 (Chpbk.)
    THE GRIM LAND: THE BEST OF ROBERT E. HOWARD, VOLUME 2

## NIFLHEIM
First appeared in ALWAYS COMES EVENING
    RHYMES OF DEATH (Chpbk.)
    EIN TRAUMER AUS TEXAS (Chpbk.)
    CHANTS DE GUERRE ET DE MORT
    SWORD #4 (Chpbk., Spanish)
    ROBERT E. HOWARD'S POEMS ON THE EDGE
    THE WINDS OF TIME

## NIGHT MOOD
First appeared in SINGERS IN THE SHADOWS

## THE NIGHT WINDS
Alternate title: Untitled ("The night winds whisper . . .")
First appeared in VERSES IN EBONY (Chpbk.)

## NIGHTS TO BOTH OF US KNOWN
First appeared in SHADOWS OF DREAMS
    THE LAST OF THE TRUNK OCH BREV I URVAL (Chpbk.)
    THE COLLECTED LETTERS OF ROBERT E. HOWARD, VOLUME 1: 1923-1929
    From a letter to TCS, ca. June 1928 ("Salaam; / Ho, ho, the long lights . . .")

## NISAPUR
Alternate title: Untitled ("The day that towers, ...")
First appeared in ALWAYS COMES EVENING
    MAGIRA #11 (Chpbk., German)
    CHANTS DE GUERRE ET DE MORT

## NO MAN'S LAND
Alternate title: Untitled ("Across the wastes of No Man's Land . . .")
First appeared in A RHYME OF SALEM TOWN AND OTHER POEMS (Chpbk. & HB)

## NO MORE THE SERPENT PROW
Alternate title: Untitled ("The House of Asgaard passes . . .")
First appeared in THE HOWARD COLLECTOR #14
    NIGHT IMAGES

## NOCTURNE
Alternate title: Untitled ("Night falls")
First appeared in WEIRDBOOK #11
    THE NEW HOWARD READER #5 (Chpbk.)

## NOT ONLY IN DEATH THEY DIE
First appeared in MAGAZINE OF HORROR #28
    ECHOES FROM AN IRON HARP

## NOW AND THEN

Alternate title: Untitled ("'Twas twice a hundred centuries ago")
First appeared in A RHYME OF SALEM TOWN AND OTHER POEMS (Chpbk. & HB)

## NUN
First appeared in THE CROSS PLAINSMAN, August 2004 (Chpbk.)
    THE LAST OF THE TRUNK OCH BREV I URVAL (Chpbk.)
    THE COLLECTED LETTERS OF ROBERT E. HOWARD, VOLUME 1: 1923-1929
    From a letter to TCS, June 23, 1926 ("Salaam; / I'm trying to write again . . .")

## O THE BRAVE SEA-ROVER
Alternate title: Untitled ("Ah, the rover hides . . .")
First appeared in A RHYME OF SALEM TOWN AND OTHER POEMS (Chpbk. & HB)

## THE OAKS
Alternate title: Untitled ("The great gray oaks . . .")
First appeared in A RHYME OF SALEM TOWN AND OTHER POEMS (Chpbk. & HB)

## OCEAN-THOUGHTS
First appeared in THE CROSS PLAINSMAN (Chpbk., August 2006)
    THE LAST OF THE TRUNK OCH BREV I URVAL (Chpbk.)
    THE COLLECTED LETTERS OF ROBERT E. HOWARD, VOLUME 1: 1923-1929
    From a letter to TCS, August 21, 1926 ("Bohut salaam, sahib: / I think you owe me . . .")

## THE ODYSSEY OF ISRAEL
Alternate title: Untitled ("Moses was our leader . . .")
First appeared in SHADOWS OF DREAMS
    ROBERT E. HOWARD: SELECTED LETTERS: 1923-1930 (Chpbk.)
    THE COLLECTED LETTERS OF ROBERT E. HOWARD, VOLUME 1: 1923-1929
    Selections from a projected longer work, originally untitled from a letter to TCS, ca. March 1928 ("Salaam: / Glad you're writing . . ."), in multiple parts

## OH BABYLON, LOST BABYLON
Alternate title: EMPIRE'S DESTINY
First appeared in GREAT CITIES OF THE ANCIENT WORLD, by LSDC, Doubleday, 1972 (lines 19-24 only)
    NIGHT IMAGES (First complete appearance)
    FANTASY CROSSROADS #14
    "Empire's Destiny" is slightly different, one line longer; the appearance in NIGHT IMAGES is the first complete appearance

## OLD BALLAD
Alternate title: THE SCARLET CITADEL (Verse heading for Chapters 1 and 3)

## THE OLD GODS BROOD
Alternative Titles: FOR MAN WAS GIVEN THE EARTH TO RULE; AND MAN WAS GIVEN THE EARTH TO RULE

## THE OLD ONES
Alternate title: THE THING ON THE ROOF (Verse heading); OUT OF THE OLD LAND

**ON WITH THE PLAY**
Alternate title: Untitled ("Up with the curtain, lo, . . .")
First appeared in THE HOWARD COLLECTOR #17
      THE HOWARD COLLECTOR, Ace
      THE NEW HOWARD READER #6 (Chpbk.)
      A RHYME OF SALEM TOWN AND OTHER POEMS (Chpbk. & HB)
      THE WINDS OF TIME

**THE ONE BLACK STAIN**
First appeared in THE HOWARD COLLECTOR #2
      RED SHADOWS
      SOLOMON KANE: SKULLS IN THE STARS
      SOLOMON KANE (French)
      WOLFSHEAD #0 (Chpbk.)
      LAS ADVENTURAS DE SOLOMON KANE (Spanish)
      THE GHOST OCEAN AND OTHER POEMS OF THE SUPERNATURAL (Chpbk.)
      A ROBERT E. HOWARD MEMORIAL: JUNE 13-15, 1986 (Chpbk.)
      EIN TRAUMER AUS TEXAS (Chpbk.)
      SOLOMON KANE, Baen
      THE SAVAGE TALES OF SOLOMON KANE
      THE SAVAGE TALES OF SOLOMON KANE CD (Chpbk.)
      WEST IS WEST AND OTHERS
      LA LUNA DEI TESCHI (Italian)
      SOLOMON KANE (Italian)
      SOLOMON KANE IL GIUSTIZIERE (Italian)
      THE CROSS PLAINSMAN, December 2006 (Chpbk.)
      WINDS OF TIME
      CRIMSON SHADOWS: THE BEST OF ROBERT E. HOWARD, VOLUME 1
      THE RIGHT HAND OF DOOM AND OTHER TALES OF SOLOMON KANE
      THE LEGEND OF SOLOMON KANE

**ONE BLOOD STRAIN**
First appeared in THE COLLECTED LETTERS OF ROBERT E. HOWARD, VOLUME 2: 1930-1932
      From a letter to TCS, ca. September 1932 ("Fear Finn: / You owe me a letter . . .")

**ONE WHO COMES AT EVENTIDE**
First appeared in MODERN AMERICAN POETRY (Anth.)
      ALWAYS COMES EVENING
      ONE WHO WALKS ALONE (Anth.)
      CHANTS DE GUERRE ET DE MORT
      PALE HORSE, unknown number (Chpbk.)
      WEST IS WEST AND OTHERS
      THE VALLEY OF THE WORM: THE WEIRD WORKS OF ROBERT E. HOWARD, VOLUME 5

**ONLY A SHADOW ON THE GRASS**
Alternate title: Untitled ("The tribes of men rise up and pass")
First appeared in WEIRDBOOK #13
      THE NEW HOWARD READER #1 (Chpbk.)
      A RHYME OF SALEM TOWN AND OTHER POEMS (Chpbk. & HB)

**AN OPEN WINDOW**
First appeared in WEIRD TALES, September 1932
    ALWAYS COMES EVENING
    DARK THINGS (Anth.)
    RHYMES OF DEATH (Chpbk.)
    THE AUBURN CIRCLE, Spring 1976
    THE MISKATONIC (Chpbk.)
    BLACK CANAAN
    SHIN KU RITORU RITORU SIHWA TAIKEI 9 (Japanese)
    CTHULHU THE MYTHOS AND KINDRED HORRORS
    FANTASY COMMENTATOR #45/46 (lines 1-4)
    KURO NO ISHIBUMI (Japanese)
    THE BOOK OF MADNESS (Chpbk.)
    ADVENTURE TALES #1 (Chpbk.)
    LOS GUSANOS DE LA TIERRA Y OTROS RELATES DE HORROR SOBRENATURAL (Spanish)
    WINGS IN THE NIGHT: THE WEIRD WORKS OF ROBERT E. HOWARD, VOLUME 4
    THE WEIRD WRITINGS OF ROBERT E. HOWARD, VOLUME ONE
    ZMIERZCH NAD STONEHENGE (Polish)
    THE WINDS OF TIME

**THE OPEN WINDOW**
First appeared in A RHYME OF SALEM TOWN AND OTHER POEMS (Chpbk. & HB)

**AN OPIUM DREAM**
Alternate title: ALTARS AND JESTERS

**ORIENTIA**
First appeared in THE LAST OF THE TRUNK OCH BREV I URVAL (Chpbk.)
    THE COLLECTED LETTERS OF ROBERT E. HOWARD, VOLUME 1: 1923-1929
    From a letter to TCS, June 23, 1926 ("Salaam; / I'm trying to write again . . .")

**OUT OF THE DEEP (Part 1 of 5 of VOICES OF THE NIGHT cycle)**
Alternate title: THE VOICES WAKEN MEMORY; A DRUM BEGINS TO THROB

**OUT OF THE OLD LAND**
Alternate title: THE THING ON THE ROOF (Verse heading); THE OLD ONES

**THE OUTCAST**
Alternate title: Untitled ("Forth from the purple . . .")
First appeared in THE GRIM LAND AND OTHERS (Chpbk.)
    FANTASY CROSSWINDS #1

**THE OUTGOING OF SIGURD THE JERUSALEM-FARER**
First appeared in VERSES IN EBONY (Chpbk.)
    THE DARK BARBARIAN (Anth., lines 6, 7, 9, 10)
    THE HOWARD READER #8 (Chpbk.)

**AN OUTWORN STORY**
Alternate title: Untitled ("There come long days . . .")
First appeared in FANTASY TALES, Summer 1987
    THE NEW HOWARD READER #2 (Chpbk.)

## OVER THE OLD RIO GRANDEY
Alternate title: Untitled ("Over the old Rio Grandey")
First appeared in A RHYME OF SALEM TOWN AND OTHER POEMS (Chpbk. & HB)
        RHYMES OF TEXAS AND THE OLD WEST

## THE PALACE OF BAST
Alternate title: PALACE OF BAST
First appeared in CHACAL #2
        DESIRE AND OTHER EROTIC POEMS (Chpbk.)
        Both publications leave out the "The" in the title

## PARODY
Alternate title: PARODY
First appeared in ALWAYS COMES EVENING, Underwood-Miller only

## PASSING OF THE ELDER GODS
Alternate title: Untitled ("The elder gods have fled")
First appeared in A RHYME OF SALEM TOWN AND OTHER POEMS (Chpbk. & HB)

## THE PASSIONATE TYPIST
First appeared in THE HOWARD REVIEW #5 (Chpbk.)

## THE PATH OF THE STRANGE WANDERERS
First appeared in SHADOWS OF DREAMS
        THE LAST OF THE TRUNK OCH BREV I URVAL (Chpbk.)
        THE COLLECTED LETTERS OF ROBERT E. HOWARD, VOLUME 1: 1923-1929
        From a letter to TCS, ca. March 1929 ("Salaam: Black Dawn")

## THE PEASANT ON THE EUPHRATES
First appeared in A RHYME OF SALEM TOWN AND OTHER POEMS (Chpbk. & HB)

## PERSPECTIVE
Alternate title: Untitled ("All men look at life . . .")
First appeared in A RHYME OF SALEM TOWN AND OTHER POEMS (Chpbk. & HB)

## THE PHANTOMS GATHER
Alternate title: Untitled ("Up over the cromlech . . .")
First appeared in A RHYME OF SALEM TOWN AND OTHER POEMS (Chpbk. & HB)

## THE PHASES OF LIFE
Alternate title: Untitled ("Life is the same . . .")
First appeared in UNAUSSPRECHLICHEN KULTEN #2 (Chpbk., French)
        THE NEW HOWARD READER #4 (Chpbk.)
        A RHYME OF SALEM TOWN AND OTHER POEMS (Chpbk. & HB)

## THE PHOENIX ON THE SWORD (Verse heading, appearances apart from story)
Alternate title: THE ROAD OF KINGS
First appeared in CRIT-Q #1 (Chapter 5 only)
        ALWAYS COMES EVENING (all 4 chapters, 2-5)
        ADMIRATIONS (French, Chapter 4 only)
        THE SOWERS OF THE THUNDER
        DIE BESTIE VON BAL-SAGOTH (German, Chapter 2 only)
        NIGHT IMAGES

THE EASTERN KINGDOM SONGBOOK (Chpbk., Chapters 2 & 5 only)
DARK VALLEY DESTINY (Anth., chapter 5 only)
THE FLAMING CIRCLE OF TROGLIS #14 (Chpbk.)
Chapters 2 and 5 are subtitled "The Road of Kings"

## THE PIRATE
First appeared in A RHYME OF SALEM TOWN AND OTHER POEMS (Chpbk. & HB)

## A PIRATE REMEMBERS
First appeared in THE GRIM LAND AND OTHERS (Chpbk.)

## THE PLAINS OF GILBAN
Alternate title: Untitled ("Red swirls of dust")
First appeared in A RHYME OF SALEM TOWN AND OTHER POEMS (Chpbk. & HB)

## A PLEDGE
First appeared in THE HOWARD COLLECTOR #14
    THE NEW HOWARD READER #4 (Chpbk.)

## POET
First appeared in THE CROSS PLAINSMAN, August 2004 (Chpbk.)
    THE LAST OF THE TRUNK OCH BREV I URVAL (Chpbk.)
    THE COLLECTED LETTERS OF ROBERT E. HOWARD, VOLUME 1: 1923-1929
    From a letter to TCS, June 23, 1926 ("Salaam; / I'm trying to write again . . .")

## THE POETS
First appeared in WEIRD TALES, March 1938
    ALWAYS COMES EVENING
    FANTASY CROSSROADS #2
    CHANTS DE GUERRE ET DE MORT
    PALE HORSE, unknown number (Chpbk.)
    ODES AT THE BLACK DOG (Chpbk.)
    THE WEIRD WRITINGS OF ROBERT E. HOWARD, VOLUME TWO

## A POET'S SKULL
Alternate title: Untitled, ("My empty skull is full of dust")
First appeared in SHADOWS OF DREAMS
    THE LAST OF THE TRUNK OCH BREV I URVAL (Chpbk.)
    THE COLLECTED LETTERS OF ROBERT E. HOWARD, VOLUME 3: 1933-1936
    From a letter to TCS, undated ("Fear Finn, / I'm damned if I can . . .")

## THE POOL OF THE BLACK ONE (Verse heading, appearances apart from story)
First appeared in LOST CONTINENTS (Anth.)
    ALWAYS COMES EVENING
    CONAN AND THE BIG ISLE (Chpbk.)

## PRELUDE
Alternate title: Untitled ("I caught Joan alone upon her bed")
First appeared in A RHYME OF SALEM TOWN AND OTHER POEMS (Chpbk. & HB)

**THE PRIMAL URGE**
First appeared in DESIRE AND OTHER EROTIC POEMS (Chpbk.)
    A RHYME OF SALEM TOWN AND OTHER POEMS (Chpbk. & HB)

**PRINCE AND BEGGAR**
Alternate title: Untitled ("I was a prince of China, . . .")
First appeared in ALWAYS COMES EVENING
    CHANTS DE GUERRE ET DE MORT

**PRIVATE MAGRATH OF THE A.E.F.**
First appeared in THE YELLOW JACKET, January 13, 1927
    THE YELLOW JACKET, November 8, 1934
    ECHOES FROM AN IRON HARP
    THE COMPLETE YELLOW JACKET
    WEST IS WEST AND OTHERS

**PRUDE**
First appeared in THE LAST OF THE TRUNK OCH BREV I URVAL (Chpbk.)
    THE COLLECTED LETTERS OF ROBERT E. HOWARD, VOLUME 1: 1923-1929
    From a letter to TCS, June 23, 1926 ("Salaam; / I'm trying to write again . . .")

**A QUATRAIN OF BEAUTY**
First appeared in A RHYME OF SALEM TOWN AND OTHER POEMS (Chpbk. & HB)
    Originally titled "A Quattrain of Beauty", and listed as such in the table of contents for A RHYME OF SALEM
        TOWN AND OTHER POEMS

**QUEEN OF THE BLACK COAST (Verse heading, appearances apart from story)**
Alternate title: THE SONG OF BELIT
First appeared in ALWAYS COMES EVENING
    CONAN: QUEEN OF THE BLACK COAST (Chpbk., as "The Song of Belit")
    DARK VALLEY DESTINY (Anth., Chapter 5 only)
    EIN TRAUMER AUS TEXAS (Chpbk.)
    BELTRIC WRITES #39 (Chpbk.)
    THE FANTASTIC WORLDS OF ROBERT E. HOWARD
    THE WINDS OF TIME

**RATTLE OF DRUMS**
Alternate title: Untitled ("Rattle of drums")
First appeared in A RHYME OF SALEM TOWN AND OTHER POEMS (Chpbk. & HB)

**A RATTLESNAKE SINGS IN THE GRASS**
Alternate title: HYMN OF HATRED
Unpublished; lines 1-8 and 17-20 same as 1-8 and 9-12 of "Hymn of Hatred"

**REBEL**
First appeared in SINGERS IN THE SHADOWS

**REBELLION**
First appeared in POET'S SCROLL, February 1929 (author listed as "Patrick Howard")
    THE NEW HOWARD READER #1 (Chpbk.)
    WEST IS WEST AND OTHERS
    THE COLLECTED LETTERS OF ROBERT E. HOWARD, VOLUME 1: 1923-1929
    From a letter to TCS, ca. November 1928 ("Salaam: / I'll swear . . .")

## RECOMPENSE
First appeared in WEIRD TALES, November 1938
> FANCYCLOPEDIA (Anth.)
> WEIRD TALES, November 1944 (Canadian)
> WEIRD TALES, September 1947 (Canadian)
> DARK OF THE MOON (Anth.)
> CRIT-Q #1
> ALWAYS COMES EVENING
> GEISTER DER NACHT (German)
> FANTASY CROSSROADS #1
> THE BOOK OF ROBERT E. HOWARD
> DARK VALLEY DESTINY (Anth., lines 1-4, 17-24)
> HARDWIRED HINTERLAND #8 (Chpbk.)
> EIN TRAUMER AUS TEXAS (Chpbk.)
> CHANTS DE GUERRE ET DE MORT
> PFADE INS FANTASTIQUE, BOOK 1 (Chpbk.)
> CONAN, VARVAR IZ CIMMERIA (Russian)
> THE KELTIC JOURNAL, VOLUME 21 (Chpbk.)
> ODES AT THE BLACK DOG (Chpbk.)
> ROBERT E. HOWARD AT THE BLACK DOG (Chpbk.)
> THE WEIRD WRITINGS OF ROBERT E. HOWARD, VOLUME TWO
> CRIMSON SHADOWS: THE BEST OF ROBERT E. HOWARD, VOLUME 1
> RAZORED ZEN #82 (Chpbk.)
> COLD STEEL #119 (Chpbk.)
> WINDS OF TIME

## RED BLADES OF BLACK CATHAY (Verse heading, appearances apart from story)
First appeared in ALWAYS COMES EVENING
> LANDS OF WONDER #2 (Chpbk., German)
> MAGIRA #23/24 (Chpbk., German)
> MAGIRA #32 (Chpbk., German)
> HARDWIRED HINTERLAND #7 (Chpbk.)

## RED THUNDER
First appeared in JAPM: THE POETRY WEEKLY, September 16, 1929
> WEIRD TALES #1, Zebra (Anth., a slightly different, 24-line version)
> SEANCHAI #71 (Chpbk., a slightly different, 24-line version)
> THE NEW HOWARD READER #2 (both versions, 24 line in early printings, 25 line in later printings)
> SHADOW KINGDOMS: THE WEIRD WORKS OF ROBERT E. HOWARD, VOLUME 1 (Wildside Press, Cosmos & AudioRealms)
> WEST IS WEST AND OTHERS

## REMEMBRANCE
First appeared in WEIRD TALES, April 1928
> ALWAYS COMES EVENING
> CHANTS DE GUERRE ET DE MORT
> SHADOW KINGDOMS: THE WEIRD WORKS OF ROBERT E. HOWARD, VOLUME 1 (Wildside Press)
> ODES AT THE BLACK DOG (Chpbk.)
> THE WEIRD WRITINGS OF ROBERT E. HOWARD, VOLUME ONE

## RENUNCIATION
First appeared in THE LAST OF THE TRUNK OCH BREV I URVAL (Chpbk.)
> THE COLLECTED LETTERS OF ROBERT E. HOWARD, VOLUME 3: 1933-1936
> From an undated, enclosed separate document sent with a letter to TCS

## REPENTANCE
First appeared in THE LAST OF THE TRUNK OCH BREV I URVAL (Chpbk.)
>THE COLLECTED LETTERS OF ROBERT E. HOWARD, VOLUME 1: 1923-1929
>>From a letter to TCS, ca. March 1928 ("Salaam: / Not having much . . .")

## RETRIBUTION
Alternate title: BLACK MICHAEL'S STORY; THE SONG OF MURTAGH O'BRIEN; Untitled ("The moon above
>the Kerry hills . . .")

First appeared in ALWAYS COMES EVENING
>CHANTS DE GUERRE ET DE MORT
>>First version found was untitled, and titled "Retribution" by Glenn Lord; a later finished version was found,
>>>with the title "The Song of Murtagh O'Brien"

## THE RETURN OF SIR RICHARD GRENVILLE
Alternate title: Untitled ("One slept beneath the branches dim")
First appeared in RED SHADOWS
>SOLOMON KANE, Centaur
>LAS ADVENTURAS DE SOLOMON KANE (Spanish)
>SOLOMON KANE (Italian)
>SOLOMON KANE: THE HILLS OF THE DEAD
>LE RETOUR DE KANE (French)
>MAGIRA #33 (Chpbk., German)
>EIN TRAUMER AUS TEXAS (Chpbk.)
>SOLOMON KANE, Baen
>THE SAVAGE TALES OF SOLOMON KANE
>THE SAVAGE TALES OF SOLOMON KANE CD (Chpbk.)
>ROBERT E. HOWARD'S POEMS ON THE EDGE
>LE ALI NOTTURNE (Italian)
>SOLOMON KANE (Italian)
>SOLOMON KANE IL GIUSTIZIERE (Italian)
>DIE KRIEGER VON ASSUR (German)
>SOLOMON KEIN (Russian)
>KSIEZYC CZASZEK (Polish)
>WINDS OF TIME
>THE RIGHT HAND OF DOOM AND OTHER TALES OF SOLOMON KANE
>THE LEGEND OF SOLOMON KANE

## THE RETURN OF THE SEA-FARER
Alternate title: ("Thorfinn, Thorfinn, where have you been?")
First appeared in WEIRDBOOK #13
>THE RETURN OF THE SEA-FARER (Chpbk.)
>WURG #77 (Chpbk.)
>THE NEW HOWARD READER #4 (Chpbk.)
>THE LAST OF THE TRUNK OCH BREV I URVAL (Chpbk.)
>THE COLLECTED LETTERS OF ROBERT E. HOWARD, VOLUME 2: 1930-1932
>Originally untitled (draft) from a letter to TCS, ca. April 1930 ("Salaam: / Well, Fear Finn, I believe . . .")

## REUBEN'S BIRTHRIGHT
Alternate title: THE SKULL IN THE CLOUDS

**REUBEN'S BRETHREN**
First appeared in THE HOWARD COLLECTOR #11
 ECHOES FROM AN IRON HARP
 THE SECOND BOOK OF ROBERT E. HOWARD
 THE DARK BARBARIAN (Anth., lines 1, 2, 13, 14)
 ROBERT E. HOWARD: SELECTED LETTERS: 1923-1930 (Chpbk.)
 WHICH WILL SCARCELY BE UNDERSTOOD #3 (Chpbk.)
 DEAR HPL: LETTERS, ROBERT E. HOWARD TO H.P. LOVECRAFT, 1930-1936 (Chpbk.)
 THE COLLECTED LETTERS OF ROBERT E. HOWARD, VOLUME 2: 1930-1932
 First appeared in a letter to HPL, October 1930 ("It is with greatest delight that I learn . . .")

**REVOLT PAGAN**
First appeared in VERSES IN EBONY (Chpbk.)

**A RHYME OF SALEM TOWN**
Alternate title: Untitled ("As I went down to Salem town . . .")
First appeared in A RHYME OF SALEM TOWN AND OTHER POEMS (Chpbk. & HB)

**THE RHYME OF THE THREE SLAVERS**
First appeared in THE RHYME OF THE THREE SLAVERS (Chpbk.)
 SPEARS OF CLONTARF (Kovacs, Chpbk., 20 copies only)
 EIN TRAUMER AUS TEXAS (Chpbk.)
 THE NEW HOWARD READER #3 (Chpbk.)

**THE RHYME OF THE VIKING PATH**
Alternate title: THOR'S SON

**THE RIDE OF FALUME**
First appeared in WEIRD TALES, October 1927
 ALWAYS COMES EVENING
 EIN TRAUMER AUS TEXAS (Chpbk.)
 CHANTS DE GUERRE ET DE MORT
 SWORD #4 (Chpbk., Spanish)
 SHADOW KINGDOMS: THE WEIRD WORKS OF ROBERT E. HOWARD, VOLUME 1 (Wildside Press & Cosmos)
 THE WEIRD WRITINGS OF ROBERT E. HOWARD, VOLUME ONE

**THE RIDERS OF BABYLON**
First appeared in WEIRD TALES, January 1928
 ALWAYS COMES EVENING
 LANDS OF WONDER #2 (Chpbk., German)
 THE DARK BARBARIAN (Anth., lines 15-17)
 CHANTS DE GUERRE ET DE MORT
 ROBERT E. HOWARD: WORLD'S GREATEST PULPSTER #1
 SHADOW KINGDOMS: THE WEIRD WORKS OF ROBERT E. HOWARD, VOLUME 1 (Wildside Press & Cosmos)
 THE HOWARD REVIEW #12 (Chpbk.)
 THE WEIRD WRITINGS OF ROBERT E. HOWARD, VOLUME ONE

**RIDING SONG**
First appeared in THE HOWARD REVIEW #2 (Chpbk.)
 Not to be confused with "A Riding Song"

## A RIDING SONG
First appeared in SHADOWS OF DREAMS
>Not to be confused with "Riding Song"

## THE ROAD OF AZRAEL (Verse heading, appearances apart from story)
First appeared in ALWAYS COMES EVENING
>THE DARK BARBARIAN (Anth., lines 1-4)
>THE WINDS OF TIME

## THE ROAD OF KINGS
Alternate title: THE PHOENIX ON THE SWORD (Verse heading); THE SCARLET CITADEL (Verse heading)

## THE ROAD TO BABEL
First appeared in SHADOWS OF DREAMS
>THE COLLECTED LETTERS OF ROBERT E. HOWARD, VOLUME 1: 1923-1929
>From a letter to TCS, ca. October 1927 ("Salaam: / Seeking cognizance of things . . .")

## THE ROAD TO BLISS
First appeared in A RHYME OF SALEM TOWN AND OTHER POEMS (Chpbk. & HB)

## THE ROAD TO FREEDOM
First appeared in CROSS PLAINS #7
>THE NEW HOWARD READER #4 (Chpbk.)
>A RHYME OF SALEM TOWN AND OTHER POEMS (Chpbk. & HB)

## THE ROAD TO HELL
Alternate title: Untitled ("The road to hell . . .")
First appeared in SINGERS IN THE SHADOWS
>AMERICAN AND EUROPEAN MANUSCRIPTS AND PRINTED BOOKS, December 19, 1986 (facsimile reproduction of the second page only of a letter to TCS, ca. September 1927 ("Salaam:/ Then the little boy said . . .") (lines 1-4 and 24-28 only)
>COLD STEEL #10 (Chpbk., facsimile reproduction of the second page only of letter) (lines 1-4 and 24-28 only)
>MANUSCRIPTS FROM GOWER-PENN, VOLUME 2, #3 (Chpbk., facsimile reproduction of the second page only of letter) (lines 1-4 and 24-28 only)
>THE COLLECTED LETTERS OF ROBERT E. HOWARD, VOLUME 1: 1923-1929 (short version)
>The version printed in AMERICAN AND EUROPEAN MANUSCRIPTS AND PRINTED BOOKS, COLD STEEL #10 and MANUSCRIPTS FROM GOWER-PENN, VOLUME 2, #3 is slightly different, using lines 1-4 and 24-28 only; that shorter version is from an earlier untitled draft of the poem that appeared in a letter to TCS, ca. September 1927 ("Salaam: / Having just got your letter . . ."); these two appearances are facsimile reproductions of the page of the letter containing that poem; the full version, with 28 lines, is used in SINGERS IN THE SHADOWS

## THE ROAD TO REST
Alternate title: SURRENDER ("I will rise . . .")

## THE ROAD TO ROME
First appeared in THE ROAD TO ROME (Chpbk.)
>VERSES IN EBONY (Chpbk., dummy prototype)
>NIGHT IMAGES
>THE NEW HOWARD READER #5 (facsimile reproduction of VERSES IN EBONY by Glenn Lord)

**THE ROAD TO YESTERDAY**
First appeared in THE GRIM LAND AND OTHERS (Chpbk.)
 DARK FANTASY #9 (Chpbk., Canadian)
 SEANCHAI #47 (Chpbk.)
 SEANCHAI #51 (Chpbk.)
 THE HOWARD READER #8 (Chpbk.)
 A RHYME OF SALEM TOWN AND OTHER POEMS (Chpbk. & HB)
 Suggested by the Cecil B. DeMille film of the same name

**ROADS**
Alternate title: Untitled ("I too have strode those white-paved roads")
First appeared in THE HOWARD COLLECTOR #17
 THE HOWARD COLLECTOR, Ace
 THE DARK BARBARIAN (Anth.)
 THE NEW HOWARD READER #7 (Chpbk.)
 A RHYME OF SALEM TOWN AND OTHER POEMS (Chpbk. & HB)
 THE CROSS PLAINSMAN, October 2003 (Chpbk.)
 THE WINDS OF TIME

**ROAR, SILVER TRUMPETS**
Alternate title: Untitled ("Roar, silver trumpets")
First appeared in NIGHT IMAGES
 FANTASY CROSSWINDS #3
 A RHYME OF SALEM TOWN AND OTHER POEMS (Chpbk. & HB)

**THE ROBES OF THE RIGHTEOUS**
First appeared in THE LAST OF THE TRUNK OCH BREV I URVAL (Chpbk.)
 THE COLLECTED LETTERS OF ROBERT E. HOWARD, VOLUME 1: 1923-1929
 From a letter to TCS, ca. September 1927 ("Salaam: / Then the little boy said . . .")

**A ROMAN LADY**
First appeared in THE LAST OF THE TRUNK OCH BREV I URVAL (Chpbk.)
 THE COLLECTED LETTERS OF ROBERT E. HOWARD, VOLUME 1: 1923-1929
 From a letter to TCS, ca. June 1928 ("Salaam; / Ho, ho, the long lights . . .")

**ROMANCE (1, "I am king of all the Ages")**
First appeared in A RHYME OF SALEM TOWN AND OTHER POEMS (Chpbk. & HB)

**ROMANCE (2, "Shouting I come, flouting I come")**
First appeared in THE LAST OF THE TRUNK OCH BREV I URVAL (Chpbk.)
 THE COLLECTED LETTERS OF ROBERT E. HOWARD, VOLUME 1: 1923-1929
 From a letter to TCS, June 23, 1926 ("Salaam; / I'm trying to write again . . .")

**ROMANY ROAD**
First appeared in SHADOWS OF DREAMS
 THE COLLECTED LETTERS OF ROBERT E. HOWARD, VOLUME 1: 1923-1929
 From a letter to TCS, ca. January 1928 ("I wasn't lying . . .")

## ROUNDELAY OF THE ROUGHNECK
First appeared in DANIEL BAKER COLLEGIAN, April 12, 1926
    THE HOWARD COLLECTOR #8
    ECHOES FROM AN IRON HARP
    WEST IS WEST AND OTHERS
    RHYMES OF TEXAS AND THE OLD WEST
    THE WINDS OF TIME

## THE ROVER
First appeared in A RHYME OF SALEM TOWN AND OTHER POEMS (Chpbk. & HB)

## THE RULERS
First appeared in A RHYME OF SALEM TOWN AND OTHER POEMS (Chpbk. & HB)

## RULES OF ETIQUETTE
First appeared in THE PROGRESS, VOLUME 1, #2 (Chpbk.)
    ODDS AND ENDS #1 (Chpbk.)
    THE NEW HOWARD READER #5 (Chpbk.)
    WEST IS WEST AND OTHERS

## RUNE
Alternate title: RUNE OF THE ANCIENT ONE
First appeared in ALWAYS COMES EVENING
    BRAN MAK MORN, Dell
    ETCHINGS AND ODYSSEYS #1 (Chpbk.)
    WORMS OF THE EARTH
    HERRSCHER DER NACHT (German)
    WARRIORS OF THE GLENN (Chpbk.)
    EIN TRAUMER AUS TEXAS (Chpbk.)
    PFADE INS FANTASTIQUE, BOOK 1 (Chpbk.)
    BARN MAK MORN, Baen
    BRAN MAK MORN – THE LAST KING
    BRAN MAK MORN (Czech)
    THE WINDS OF TIME
    An untitled poem embodied in the story "Men of the Shadows" in BRAN MAK MORN, WORMS OF THE
        EARTH, and BRAN MAK MORN – THE LAST KING; a copy of the poem exists separately, and
        was titled "Rune of the Ancient One", Glenn Lord retitled it for publication

## RUNE OF THE ANCIENT ONE
Alternate title: RUNE

## SACRIFICE
First appeared in SINGERS IN THE SHADOWS

## SAILOR
First appeared in THE LAST OF THE TRUNK OCH BREV I URVAL (Chpbk.)
    THE COLLECTED LETTERS OF ROBERT E. HOWARD, VOLUME 1: 1923-1929
    From a letter to TCS, June 23, 1926 ("Salaam; / I'm trying to write again . . .")

**SAMSON'S BROODINGS**
First appeared in SHADOWS OF DREAMS
THE LAST OF THE TRUNK OCH BREV I URVAL (Chpbk.)
THE COLLECTED LETTERS OF ROBERT E. HOWARD, VOLUME 2: 1930-1932
From a letter to TCS, ca. August 1932 ("Fear Finn: / I don't know when . . .")

**SAN JACINTO (1, "Flowers bloom on San Jacinto")**
First appeared in THE LAST OF THE TRUNK OCH BREV I URVAL (Chpbk.)
THE COLLECTED LETTERS OF ROBERT E. HOWARD, VOLUME 1: 1923-1929
RHYMES OF TEXAS AND THE OLD WEST
From a letter to TCS, June 23, 1926 ("Salaam; / I'm trying to write again . . .")

**SAN JACINTO (2, "Red fields of glory")**
First appeared in A RHYME OF SALEM TOWN AND OTHER POEMS (Chpbk. & HB)
RHYMES OF TEXAS AND THE OLD WEST

**THE SAND-HILLS' CREST**
Alternate title: Untitled ("Here where the post-oaks . . .")
First appeared in A ROBERT E. HOWARD MEMORIAL: JUNE 13-15, 1986 (Chpbk.)
THE NEW HOWARD READER #1 (Chpbk.)
THE END OF THE TRAIL: WESTERN STORIES
RHYMES OF TEXAS AND THE OLD WEST

**THE SANDS OF THE DESERT**
Alternate title: Untitled ("A sea of molten silver")
First appeared in DRAGONFIELDS #3 (Chpbk.)
THE NEW HOWARD READER #2 (Chpbk.)
THE END OF THE TRAIL: WESTERN STORIES

**THE SANDS OF TIME**
Alternate title: Untitled ("Slow shifts the sands of time . . .")
First appeared in THE HOWARD COLLECTOR #1
FIRE AND SLEET AND CANDLELIGHT (Anth.)
ECHOES FROM AN IRON HARP
THE DARK BARBARIAN (Anth., lines 5, 6, 11, 12)
ROBERT E. HOWARD: SELECTED LETTERS; 1923-1930 (Chpbk., as part of letter to Harold Preece)
SPECTRUM SUPER SPECIAL #2
WEST IS WEST AND OTHERS
THE WINDS OF TIME
THE COLLECTED LETTERS OF ROBERT E. HOWARD, VOLUME 2: 1930-1932
From a letter to Harold Preece, November 24, 1930 ("I hope you'll pardon my negligence . . .")

**SANG THE KING OF MIDIAN**
Alternate title: A SONG OUT OF MIDIAN

**THE SCARLET CITADEL (Verse heading, appearances apart from story)**
Alternate title: THE ROAD OF KINGS; SONG OF THE BOSSONIAN ARCHERS; OLD BALLAD
First appeared in ALWAYS COMES EVENING (Chapters 1, 2, 3, & 5)
ADMIRATIONS (French, Chapters 2 & 5 only)
THE EASTERN KINGDOM SONGBOOK (Chpbk., Chapter 2 only)
The verse heading for Chapter 1 is titled "Old Ballad"; Chapter 2 is "The Road of Kings"; Chapter 3 is the
second part of "Old Ballad"; Chapter 4 has a short proverb; and Chapter 5 is "Song of the Bossonian
Archers"

**THE SEA**
First appeared in THE BAYLOR UNITED STATEMENT, Spring 1923
    CROSS PLAINS REVIEW, June 29, 1923
    ECHOES FROM AN IRON HARP
    DARK VALLEY DESTINY (Anth., lines 1-6)
    CROSS PLAINS REVIEW, June 8, 2000
    WEST IS WEST AND OTHERS
    ONION TOPS #13 (Chpbk.)

**THE SEA AND THE SUNRISE**
First appeared in A RHYME OF SALEM TOWN AND OTHER POEMS (Chpbk. & HB)

**THE SEA GIRL**
First appeared in WHISPERS #4
    NIGHT IMAGES

**SEA-CHANT**
Alternate title: Untitled ("Topaz seas and laughing skies")
First appeared in A RHYME OF SALEM TOWN AND OTHER POEMS (Chpbk. & HB)

**THE SEA-WOMAN**
First appeared in SINGERS IN THE SHADOWS

**SECRETS**
First appeared in THE COLLECTED LETTERS OF ROBERT E. HOWARD, VOLUME 1: 1923-1929
    From a letter to TCS, ca. March 1928 ("Salaam: / Glad you're writing . . .")

**SENOR ZORRO**
First appeared in A RHYME OF SALEM TOWN AND OTHER POEMS (Chpbk. & HB)

**SERPENT**
First appeared in THE LAST OF THE TRUNK OCH BREV I URVAL (Chpbk.)
    THE COLLECTED LETTERS OF ROBERT E. HOWARD, VOLUME 1: 1923-1929
    From a letter to TCS, June 23, 1926 ("Salaam; / I'm trying to write again . . .")

**SEVEN KINGS**
Alternate title: Untitled ("Seven kings of the grey old cities")
First appeared in FANTASY TALES #11, Winter 1982
    THE NEW HOWARD READER #3 (Chpbk.)

**THE SEVEN-UP BALLAD**
First appeared in COSTIGAN SPECIAL #1 (Chpbk.)
    POST OAKS AND SAND ROUGHS

**SHADOW OF DREAMS**
Alternate title: Untitled ("Stay not from me, that veil . . ."); STAY NOT FROM ME
First appeared in POET'S SCROLL, August 1929 (author listed as "Patrick Howard")
    SHADOWS OF DREAMS (as "Stay Not from Me")
    WEST IS WEST AND OTHERS
    THE LAST OF THE TRUNK OCH BREV I URVAL (Chpbk.)
    THE COLLECTED LETTERS OF ROBERT E. HOWARD, VOLUME 1: 1923-1929
    As an untitled poem in a letter to TCS, ca. December 1928 ("Salaam: / Out in front of Goldstein's . . .")

## SHADOW THING
Alternate title: Untitled ("There was a thing of the shadow world")
First appeared in THE GHOST OCEAN AND OTHER POEMS OF THE SUPERNATURAL (Chpbk.)
     Originally embodied as an untitled verse in an untitled story ("As he approached the two . . .")

## SHADOWS (1, "A black moon . . .")
Alternate title: First Part of the BLACK DAWN cycle

## SHADOWS (2, "Grey ghost, . . .")
First appeared in SINGERS IN THE SHADOWS
     EIN TRAUMER AUS TEXAS (Chpbk.)

## SHADOWS (3, "I am that which was . . .")
First appeared in THE LAST OF THE TRUNK OCH BREV I URVAL (Chpbk.)
     THE COLLECTED LETTERS OF ROBERT E. HOWARD, VOLUME 1: 1923-1929
     From a letter to TCS, June 23, 1926 ("Salaam; / I'm trying to write again . . .")

## SHADOWS FROM YESTERDAY
First appeared in THE GHOST OCEAN AND OTHER POEMS OF THE SUPERNATURAL (Chpbk.)
     THE HOWARD READER #8 (Chpbk.)

## SHADOWS OF DREAMS
First appeared in SHADOWS OF DREAMS
     THE LAST OF THE TRUNK OCH BREV I URVAL (Chpbk.)
     THE COLLECTED LETTERS OF ROBERT E. HOWARD, VOLUME 3: 1933-1936
     From a letter to TCS, undated ("Salaam: Shadows of Dreams . . .")

## SHADOWS ON THE ROAD
First appeared in WEIRD TALES, May 1930
     ALWAYS COMES EVENING
     CHANTS DE GUERRE ET DE MORT
     SWORD #4 (Chpbk., Spanish)
     MOON OF SKULLS: THE WEIRD WORKS OF ROBERT E. HOWARD, VOLUME 2
     THE WEIRD WRITINGS OF ROBERT E. HOWARD, VOLUME ONE

## SHIPS
First appeared in WEIRD TALES, July 1938
     ALWAYS COMES EVENING
     CHANTS DE GUERRE ET DE MORT
     ODES AT THE BLACK DOG (Chpbk.)
     THE WEIRD WRITINGS OF ROBERT E. HOWARD, VOLUME TWO
     Lines 1-4 identical to lines 1-4 of "The Isle of Hy-Brasil"; lines 5-22 identical to lines 20-38 of the same

## SHRINES
Alternate title: Third poem of the BLACK DAWN cycle

## SIGHS IN THE YELLOW LEAVES
First appeared in THE LAST OF THE TRUNK OCH BREV I URVAL (Chpbk.)
     THE COLLECTED LETTERS OF ROBERT E. HOWARD, VOLUME 3: 1933-1936
     From a letter to TCS, undated ("Salaam: / I have forgotten . . .")

## THE SIGN OF THE SICKLE
First appeared in A RHYME OF SALEM TOWN AND OTHER POEMS (Chpbk. & HB)

## SILENCE FALLS ON MECCA'S WALLS
Alternate title: Untitled ("Silence falls on Mecca's walls")
First appeared in CTHULHU THE MYTHOS AND KINDRED HORRORS
    SHADOWS OF DREAMS
    KURO NO ISHIBUMI (Japanese)
    THE NYARLATHOTEP CYCLE: STORIES ABOUT THE GOD OF A THOUSAND FORMS (Anth.)
    THE LAST OF THE TRUNK OCH BREV I URVAL (Chpbk.)
    THE COLLECTED LETTERS OF ROBERT E. HOWARD, VOLUME 1: 1923-1929
    ZMIERZCH NAD STONEHENGE (Polish)
    Originally untitled, from a letter to TCS, ca. December 1928 ("Salaam: / Out in front of Goldstein's . . .")

## THE SINGER IN THE MIST
First appeared in WEIRD TALES, April 1938
    DARK OF THE MOON (Anth.)
    ALWAYS COMES EVENING
    IMAGINARY WORLDS (Anth., lines 9-14)
    FANTASY CROSSROADS #1
    LITERARY SWORDSMEN AND SORCERERS (Anth., lines 1-8)
    DARK VALLEY DESTINY (Anth., lines 1-8)
    CHANTS DE GUERRE ET DE MORT
    ADVENTURE TALES #1
    ODES AT THE BLACK DOG (Chpbk.)
    THE WEIRD WRITINGS OF ROBERT E. HOWARD, VOLUME TWO
    THE CROSS PLAINSMAN, April 2006 (Chpbk.)
    One of the "Sonnets Out of Bedlam"

## SINGING HEMP
First appeared in VERSES IN EBONY (Chpbk.)
    NIGHT IMAGES

## SINGING IN THE WIND
First appeared in THE JUNTO, July 1929
    THE HOWARD COLLECTOR #14
    THE HOWARD REVIEW #4 (Chpbk.)

## THE SKULL IN THE CLOUDS
Alternate title: REUBEN'S BIRTHRIGHT
First appeared in THE JUNTO, August 1929
    THE HOWARD COLLECTOR #2
    ECHOES FROM AN IRON HARP
    FANTASIA #11/12 (Chpbk., German)
    EIN TRAUMER AUS TEXAS (Chpbk.)
    ADVENTURE TALES #1
    WEST IS WEST AND OTHERS
    THE WINDS OF TIME

## THE SKULL OF SILENCE (Verse heading, appearances apart from the story)
First appeared in SEANCHAI #82 (Chpbk.)
    Was not published with original story; first used with story in the Baen edition of KULL

**SKULLS**
First appeared in FANTASY BOOK, September 1984
    WRITER OF THE DARK

**SKULLS AGAINST THE DAWN**
Alternate title: SKULLS OVER JUDAH

**SKULLS AND DUST**
First appeared in AMERICAN POET, May 1929 (author listed as "Patrick Howard")
    THE HOWARD COLLECTOR #4
    ECHOES FROM AN IRON HARP
    WEST IS WEST AND OTHERS
    AMERICAN POET awarded a $3 prize with each issue for the best poem, "Skulls and Dust" won in its original
        appearance

**SKULLS OVER JUDAH**
Alternate title: SKULLS AGAINST THE DAWN (original title)
First appeared in THE HOWARD COLLECTOR #9
    ECHOES FROM AN IRON HARP
    THE LAST OF THE TRUNK OCH BREV I URVAL (Chpbk.)
    THE COLLECTED LETTERS OF ROBERT E. HOWARD, VOLUME 3: 1933-1936
    From a letter to TCS, undated ("Salaam: / Skulls Against the Dawn . . .")

**THE SLAYER**
Alternate title: Untitled ("The women come and the women go")
First appeared in A RHYME OF SALEM TOWN AND OTHER POEMS (Chpbk. & HB)
    THE LAST OF THE TRUNK OCH BREV I URVAL (Chpbk.)
    THE COLLECTED LETTERS OF ROBERT E. HOWARD, VOLUME 1: 1923-1929
    From a letter to TCS, ca. December 1928 ("Salaam: / Out in front of Goldstein's . . .")

**SLUGGER'S VOW**
Alternate title: Untitled ("How your right thudded on my jaw")
First appeared in REH FIGHT MAGAZINE #4 (Chpbk.)
    THE LAST OF THE TRUNK OCH BREV I URVAL (Chpbk.)
    THE COLLECTED LETTERS OF ROBERT E. HOWARD, VOLUME 1: 1923-1929
    From a letter to TCS, January 30, 1925 ("Salaam, sahib; / I'm sending you . . .")

**SLUMBER**
First appeared in MAGAZINE OF HORROR #30
    ECHOES FROM AN IRON HARP
    DARK VALLEY DESTINY (Anth.)
    EIN TRAUMER AUS TEXAS (Chpbk.)
    REVELATIONS FROM YUGGOTH #2 (Chpbk.)
    PFADE INS FANTASTIQUE, BOOK 1 (Chpbk.)
    ROBERT E. HOWARD'S POEMS ON THE EDGE
    THE WINDS OF TIME

**SOLOMON KANE'S HOMECOMING (1, original)**
First appeared in FANCIFUL TALES, Fall 1936
    DARK OF THE MOON (Anth.)
    ALWAYS COMES EVENING
    RED SHADOWS
    SOLOMON KANE, Centaur

DE STEM VAN EL-LIL (Dutch)
NIGHT IMAGES
MAGIRA #31 (Chpbk., German)
SOLOMON KANE: THE HILLS OF THE DEAD
FANCIFUL TALES, VOLUME 1, #1 (Chpbk.)
SOLOMON KANE (Italian)
LE RETOUR DE KANE (French)
LAS ADVENTURAS DE SOLOMON KANE (Spanish)
GESPENSTER DER VERGANGENHEIT (German)
THE DARK BARBARIAN (Anth., lines 13, 16, 31)
LE FULMER #25 (Chpbk., French, lines 1-4, 29-36)
EIN TRAUMER AUS TEXAS (Chpbk.)
HARDWIRED HINTERLAND #7 (Chpbk., REHupa # 127, lines 21-32)
A SOLOMON KANE CHRONOLOGY (Chpbk., lines 11-14)
SOLOMON KANE, Baen
THE SOLOMON KANE SKETCHBOOK (Chpbk.)
THE SAVAGE TALES OF SOLOMON KANE
THE SAVAGE TALES OF SOLOMON KANE CD (Chpbk.)
ODES AT THE BLACK DOG (Chpbk.)
LA LUNA DEI TESCHI (Italian)
SOLOMON KANE (Italian)
SOLOMON KANE IL GIUSTIZIERE (Italian)
SOLOMON KEIN (Russian)
CZERWONE CIENIE (Polish)
WINDS OF TIME
THE RIGHT HAND OF DOOM AND OTHER TALES OF SOLOMON KANE
THE LEGEND OF SOLOMON KANE
THE GRIM LAND: THE BEST OF ROBERT E. HOWARD, VOLUME 2
SOLOMON KANE'S HOMECOMING (Chpbk., Pinnacle)

**SOLOMON KANE'S HOMECOMING (2, variant version)**
First appeared in THE HOWARD COLLECTOR #15
THE HOWARD COLLECTOR, Ace
LAS ADVENTURAS DE SOLOMON KANE (Spanish)
A SOLOMON KANE CHRONOLOGY (Chpbk., lines 15-17)
THE SAVAGE TALES OF SOLOMON KANE

**SOMETHING ABOUT EVE (Verse heading, appearances apart from story)**
First appeared in ECHOES FROM AN IRON HARP

**A SON OF SPARTACUS**
First appeared in THE DARK MAN #6 (Chpbk.)

**SONG AT MIDNIGHT**
Alternate title: MAN, THE MASTER
First appeared in THE PHANTAGRAPH, August 1940
THE NEW HIEROGLYPH, March 1944
ORB, VOLUME 3, #1 (Whole number 10, Chpbk.)
ALWAYS COMES EVENING
OPERATION: PHANTASY
VOICES OF THE NIGHT AND OTHER POEMS (Chpbk.)
CHANTS DE GUERRE ET DE MORT
A RHYME OF SALEM TOWN AND OTHER POEMS (Chpbk., as "Man, the Master")
THE ROAD TO VELITRIUM #50 (Chpbk.)

**SONG BEFORE CLONTARF**
First appeared in THE HOWARD REVIEW #2 (Chpbk.)
    NIGHT IMAGES
    WRITER OF THE DARK
    AQUILA NIDUS #6 (Chpbk.)
    From a letter to Harold Preece, pm, March 24, 1930 "(Thanks for the picture.")

**A SONG FOR ALL WOMEN**
First appeared in NIGHT IMAGES (deluxe edition only)
    FEAR DUNN #1 (Chpbk.)
    DESIRE AND OTHER EROTIC POEMS (Chpbk.)

**A SONG FOR MEN THAT LAUGH**
First appeared in THE JUNTO, December 1928
    MAGAZINE OF HORROR #16
    ECHOES FROM AN IRON HARP

**A SONG FROM AN EBONY HEART**
Alternate title: Untitled ("The wine in my cup is . . .")
First appeared in SHADOWS OF DREAMS
    SPECTRUM SUPER SPECIAL #2 (lines 5-8)
    THE COLLECTED LETTERS OF ROBERT E. HOWARD, VOLUME 1: 1923-1929
    Originally untitled from a letter to TCS, ca. November 1928 ("Salaam: / I'll swear . . .")

**SONG OF A FUGITIVE BARD**
Alternate title: Untitled ("They gave me a dollar . . .")
First appeared in SHADOWS OF DREAMS
    THE LAST OF THE TRUNK OCH BREV I URVAL (Chpbk.)
    THE COLLECTED LETTERS OF ROBERT E. HOWARD, VOLUME 1: 1923-1929
    Originally untitled, from a letter to TCS, ca. June 1928 ("Salaam; / Ho, ho, the long lights . . .")

**THE SONG OF A MAD MINSTREL**
First appeared in WEIRD TALES, February-March 1931
    ALWAYS COMES EVENING
    FANTASY CROSSROADS #1
    FROM THE HELLS BENEATH THE HELLS (Chpbk.)
    THE SECOND BOOK OF ROBERT E. HOWARD, Zebra
    THE IRON HARP (Chpbk.)
    CHANTS DE GUERRE ET DE MORT
    PALE HORSE, unknown number (Chpbk.)
    THE BOOK OF MADNESS (Chpbk., lines 1-10, 29-32)
    HARDWIRED HINTERLAND, VOLUME 2, #7 (Chpbk.)
    THE OSSUARY OF ACHERON (Chpbk., lines 1-10)
    PFADE INS FANTASTIQUE, BOOK 2 (Chpbk.)
    PEOPLE OF THE DARK: THE WEIRD WORKS OF ROBERT E. HOWARD, VOLUME 3
    ODES AT THE BLACK DOG (Chpbk.)
    THE WEIRD WRITINGS OF ROBERT E. HOWARD, VOLUME ONE
    THE CROSS PLAINSMAN, December 2006 (Chpbk.)
    WINDS OF TIME
    CRIMSON SHADOWS: THE BEST OF ROBERT E. HOWARD, VOLUME 1

**A SONG OF BARDS**
Alternate title: Untitled ("Chesterton twanged on his lyre")
First appeared in A RHYME OF SALEM TOWN AND OTHER POEMS (Chpbk. & HB)

**THE SONG OF BELIT**
Alternate title: QUEEN OF THE BLACK COAST (Verse Heading)

**THE SONG OF BRAN**
Alternate title: KINGS OF THE NIGHT (Verse heading)

**A SONG OF CHEER**
First appeared in THE LAST OF THE TRUNK OCH BREV I URVAL (Chpbk.)
        THE COLLECTED LETTERS OF ROBERT E. HOWARD, VOLUME 1: 1923-1929
        From a letter to TCS, ca. March 1928 ("Salaam: / Not having much . . .")

**A SONG OF COLLEGE**
First appeared in THE LAST OF THE TRUNK OCH BREV I URVAL (Chpbk.)
        THE COLLECTED LETTERS OF ROBERT E. HOWARD, VOLUME 3: 1933-1936
        From a letter to TCS, undated ("Salaam: / I have forgotten . . .")

**A SONG OF DEFEAT**
Alternate title: Untitled ("We are they")
First appeared in MAGAZINE OF HORROR #34
        ECHOES FROM AN IRON HARP
        THE DARK BARBARIAN (Anth., lines 7, 8, 27, 28)

**A SONG OF GREENWICH**
First appeared in THE LAST OF THE TRUNK OCH BREV I URVAL (Chpbk.)
        THE COLLECTED LETTERS OF ROBERT E. HOWARD, VOLUME 3: 1933-1936
        From a letter to TCS, undated ("Salaam: / I have forgotten . . .")

**THE SONG OF HORSA'S GALLEY**
First appeared in THE HOWARD COLLECTOR #13
        ECHOES FROM AN IRON HARP
        THE SECOND BOOK OF ROBERT E. HOWARD
        THE DARK BARBARIAN (Anth., lines 7, 11, 15, 16)
        HARDWIRED HINTERLAND #6 (Chpbk.)

**THE SONG OF MURTAGH O'BRIEN**
Alternate title: RETRIBUTION; BLACK MICHAEL'S STORY; Untitled ("The moon above the Kerry hills . . .")

**A SONG OF THE ANCHOR CHAIN**
First appeared in SHADOWS OF DREAMS
        THE LAST OF THE TRUNK OCH BREV I URVAL (Chpbk.)
        THE COLLECTED LETTERS OF ROBERT E. HOWARD, VOLUME 1: 1923-1929
        From a letter to TCS, ca. November 1928 ("Salaam: / Listen you . . .")

**THE SONG OF THE BATS**
First appeared in WEIRD TALES, May 1927
        ALWAYS COMES EVENING
        FANTASIA #11/12 (Chpbk., German)
        EIN TRAUMER AUS TEXAS (Chpbk.)
        CHANTS DE GUERRE ET DE MORT

ROBERT E. HOWARD: WORLD'S GREATEST PULPSTER #1
BLUFFTOWN BARBARIAN #6 (Chpbk.)
ROBERT E. HOWARD IN THE PUBLIC DOMAIN (Chpbk.)
SHADOW KINGDOMS: THE WEIRD WORKS OF ROBERT E. HOWARD, VOLUME 1 (Wildside Press & Cosmos)
THE HOWARD REVIEW #12 (Chpbk.)
THE WEIRD WRITINGS OF ROBERT E. HOWARD, VOLUME ONE

## SONG OF THE BOSSONIAN ARCHERS
Alternate title: THE SCARLET CITADEL (Verse heading for Chapter 5)

## A SONG OF THE DON COSSACKS
First appeared in ALWAYS COMES EVENING
    CHANTS DE GUERRE ET DE MORT
    SWORD #4 (Chpbk., Spanish)

## THE SONG OF THE GALLOWS TREE
First appeared in WEIRD TALES #2, Zebra
    WRITER OF THE DARK

## THE SONG OF THE JACKAL
First appeared in NIGHT IMAGES

## THE SONG OF THE LAST BRITON
First appeared in THE GHOST OCEAN AND OTHER POEMS OF THE SUPERNATURAL (Chpbk.)
    THE ULTIMATE TRIUMPH
    CRIMSON SHADOWS: THE BEST OF ROBERT E. HOWARD, VOLUME 1
    THE CROSS PLAINSMAN, December 2006 (Chpbk.)

## A SONG OF THE LEGIONS
First appeared in THE HOWARD COLLECTOR #12
    ECHOES FROM AN IRON HARP

## A SONG OF THE NAKED LANDS
Alternate title: Untitled ("You lolled in gardens where breezes fanned")
First appeared in A SONG OF THE NAKED LANDS (Chpbk.)
    VERSES IN EBONY (Chpbk., dummy prototype)
    THE DARK BARBARIAN (Anth., lines 25-28, 51-52)
    THE NEW HOWARD READER #2 (Chpbk.)
    THE NEW HOWARD READER #5 (facsimile reproduction of VERSES IN EBONY)
    THE ULTIMATE TRIUMPH
    THE GRIM LAND: THE BEST OF ROBERT E. HOWARD, VOLUME 2

## SONG OF THE PICT
Alternate title: Untitled ("Wolf on the height")
First appeared in ALWAYS COMES EVENING
    BRAN MAK MORN, Dell
    WORMS OF THE EARTH
    HERRSCHER DER NACHT (German)
    THE GHOST OCEAN AND OTHER POEMS OF THE SUPERNATURAL (Chpbk.)
    BARN MAK MORN, Baen
    BRAN MAK MORN – THE LAST KING
    BRAN MAK MORN (Czech)

An untitled poem embodied in the story "Men of the Shadows" in BRAN MAK MORN, WORMS OF THE
EARTH, and BRAN MAK MORN – THE LAST KING

## A SONG OF THE RACE
Alternate title: Untitled ("High on his throne sat Bran Mak Morn")
First appeared in BRAN MAK MORN, Dell
    WORMS OF THE EARTH
    MAGIRA #23/24 (Chpbk., German)
    DELIRIUM TREMENS #1 (Chpbk., Spanish)
    HERRSCHER DER NACHT (German)
    EIN TRAUMER AUS TEXAS (Chpbk.)
    BRAN MAK MORN, Baen
    BRAN MAK MORN – THE LAST KING
    BRAN MAK MORN (Czech)
    IL SEGNO DEL SERPENTE (Italian)
    ROBAKI ZIEMI (Polish)
    GUSANOS DE LA TIERRE (Spanish)

## THE SONG OF THE RED STONE
Alternate title: BLOOD OF BELSHAZZAR (verse heading)

## THE SONG OF THE SAGE
First appeared in THE COLLECTED LETTERS OF ROBERT E. HOWARD, VOLUME 2: 1930-1932
    From a letter to TCS, ca. March 1930 ("Well, Fear Finn, tell Cuchullain . . .")

## A SONG OF THE WEREWOLF FOLK
First appeared in ETCHINGS AND ODYSSEYS #10 (Chpbk.)
    THE NEW HOWARD READER #5 (Chpbk.)

## THE SONG OF YAR ALI KHAN
First appeared in ALWAYS COMES EVENING, Underwood-Miller (a loose holographic copy, in deluxe only, and
    a few standard issues)
    ALL FLED, ALL DONE (Chpbk.)
    THE NEW HOWARD READER #4 (Chpbk.)

## A SONG OUT OF MIDIAN
Alternate title: SANG THE KING OF MIDIAN (original title)
First appeared in WEIRD TALES, April 1930
    ALWAYS COMES EVENING
    THE BOOK OF ROBERT E. HOWARD
    DARK VALLEY DESTINY (Anth., lines 1-3, 7-9)
    EIN TRAUMER AUS TEXAS (Chpbk.)
    CHANTS DE GUERRE ET DE MORT
    MOON OF SKULLS: THE WEIRD WORKS OF ROBERT E. HOWARD, VOLUME 2
    THE WEIRD WRITINGS OF ROBERT E. HOWARD, VOLUME ONE
    THE COLLECTED LETTERS OF ROBERT E. HOWARD, VOLUME 3: 1933-1936
    From an undated, enclosed separate document sent with a letter to TCS

## A SONG OUT OF THE EAST
First appeared in NIGHT IMAGES

**A SONNET OF GOOD CHEER**
First appeared in THE HOWARD COLLECTOR #9
    ECHOES FROM AN IRON HARP
    THE BOOK OF ROBERT E. HOWARD

**SONNETS OUT OF BEDLAM**
Alternate title: A cycle of five poems: "The Singer in the Mist", "The Dream and the Shadow", "The Soul-Eater",
    "Haunting Columns", and "The Last Hour"

**SONORA TO DEL RIO**
First appeared in THE HOWARD COLLECTOR #1
    ECHOES FROM AN IRON HARP
    WEST IS WEST AND OTHERS
    RHYMES OF TEXAS AND THE OLD WEST
    Lines 1-16 virtually identical to lines 1-8 and 17-24 of "The Grim Land"

**THE SOUL-EATER**
First appeared in WEIRD TALES, August 1937
    ALWAYS COMES EVENING
    THE HOWARD REVIEW #3 (Chpbk.)
    CHANTS DE GUERRE ET DE MORT
    THE WEIRD WRITINGS OF ROBERT E. HOWARD, VOLUME TWO
    THE CROSS PLAINSMAN, April 2006 (Chpbk.)
    One of the "Sonnets Out of Bedlam"

**THE SOWERS OF THE THUNDER (Verse heading, appearances apart from story)**
Alternate title: THE BALLAD OF BAIBARS
First appeared in ECHOES FROM AN IRON HARP

**STAY NOT FROM ME**
Alternate title: Untitled ("Stay not from me, that veil . . ."); SHADOW OF DREAMS

**A STIRRING OF GREEN LEAVES**
First appeared in SHADOWS OF DREAMS
    THE COLLECTED LETTERS OF ROBERT E. HOWARD, VOLUME 2: 1930-1932
    From a letter to TCS, ca. May 1930 ("Well, Fear Finn, I was in . . .")

**THE STRALSUND**
Alternate title: Untitled ("He has rigged her and tricked her")
First appeared in A RHYME OF SALEM TOWN AND OTHER POEMS (Chpbk. & HB)

**STRANGE PASSION**
Alternate title: Untitled ("Ah, I know black queens . . .")
First appeared in RISQUE STORIES #1 (Chpbk.)
    DESIRE AND OTHER EROTIC POEMS (Chpbk.)

**THE STRANGER**
First appeared in SINGERS IN THE SHADOWS
    EIN TRAUMER AUS TEXAS (Chpbk.)

**SUMMER MORN**
Alternate title: Untitled ("Am-ra stood on a mountain height")
First appeared in KULL: EXILE OF ATLANTIS

**SURRENDER (1, "I will rise . . .")**
Alternate title: THE ROAD TO REST
First appeared in THE JUNTO, August 1929
    THE HOWARD COLLECTOR #3
    ECHOES FROM AN IRON HARP
    THE SECOND BOOK OF ROBERT E. HOWARD
    THE DARK BARBARIAN (Anth., lines 7, 8, 35, 36)
    WEST IS WEST AND OTHERS

**SURRENDER (2, "Open the window and let me go")**
First appeared in SHADOWS OF DREAMS
    SPECTRUM SUPER SPECIAL #2
    THE LAST OF THE TRUNK OCH BREV I URVAL (Chpbk.)
    THE COLLECTED LETTERS OF ROBERT E. HOWARD, VOLUME 3: 1933-1936
    From a letter to TCS, undated ("Salaam: / Again glancing . . .")

**SWAMP MURDER**
First appeared in VERSES IN EBONY (Chpbk.)
    NIGHT IMAGES
    WRITER OF THE DARK

**SWINGS AND SWINGS**
First appeared in THE JUNTO, date unknown
    A RHYME OF SALEM TOWN AND OTHER POEMS (Chpbk. & HB)
    A copy is in the LSDC papers at the Harry Ransom Center at the University of Texas, Austin

**THE SWORD OF LAL SINGH**
Alternate title: Untitled ("Men I have slain with naked steel")
First appeared in A RHYME OF SALEM TOWN AND OTHER POEMS (Chpbk. & HB)

**THE SWORD OF MOHAMMED**
First appeared in THE TOREADOR, July 5, 1925 (Chpbk.)
    REHUPA #117 (Chpbk.)
    THE NEW HOWARD READER #1 (Chpbk.)

**THE SYMBOL**
Alternate title: Untitled ("Eons before the Atlantean days . . .")
First appeared in ARIEL #1
    THE NEW HOWARD READER #2 (Chpbk.)

**SYMBOLS**
First appeared in SHADOWS OF DREAMS
    ROBERT E. HOWARD: SELECTED LETTERS; 1923-1930 (Chpbk.)
    WHICH WILL SCARCELY BE UNDERSTOOD (Chpbk.)
    THE COLLECTED LETTERS OF ROBERT E. HOWARD, VOLUME 1: 1923-1929
    From a letter to TCS, ca. January 1928 ("I wasn't lying . . .")

**THE TALE THE DEAD SLAVER TOLD**
Alternate title: THE DEAD SLAVER'S TALE

**TARANTELLA**
First appeared in DANIEL BAKER COLLEGIAN, May 25, 1926
    ECHOES FROM AN IRON HARP
    DELIRIUM TREMENS #3 (Chpbk., Spanish, lines 32-37)
    WEST IS WEST AND OTHERS

**THE TARTAR RAID**
Alternate title: Untitled ("The snow-capped peaks of Ural . . .")
First appeared in A RHYME OF SALEM TOWN AND OTHER POEMS (Chpbk. & HB)

**THE TAVERN**
First appeared in SINGERS IN THE SHADOWS
    FANTASY COMMENTATOR #43

**THE TEMPTER**
First appeared in CROSS PLAINS REVIEW, June 18, 1937
    ALWAYS COMES EVENING
    RHYMES OF DEATH (Chpbk.)
    LOVECRAFT: A BIOGRAPHY (Anth., lines 17-20)
    LITERARY SWORDSMEN AND SORCERERS (Anth., lines 1-8)
    DALLAS MORNING NEWS, February 24, 1980 (lines 31-40)
    ZARFHANNA #20 (Chpbk., lines 31-40)
    COSTIGAN #24 (Chpbk., lines 31-40)
    SOUTHWEST AIRLINES MAGAZINE, November 1980 (lines 31-40)
    FANTASIA #11/12 (Chpbk., German)
    DARK VALLEY DESTINY (Anth.)
    THE FLAMING CIRCLE OF TROGLIS #8 (Chpbk., lines 17-20)
    THE DARK BARBARIAN (Anth., lines 35, 36, 40)
    EIN TRAUMER AUS TEXAS (Chpbk.)
    CHANTS DE GUERRE ET DE MORT
    CROSS PLAINS REVIEW, July 6, 1990
    REHUPA #104 (Chpbk.)
    MUSINGS #2 (Chpbk.)
    HARDWIRED HINTERLAND #7 (Chpbk., lines 27-40)
    SERVANT OF THE WARSMAN #8 (Chpbk., lines 37-40)
    PFADE INS FANTASTIQUE, BOOK 1 (Chpbk.)
    ODES AT THE BLACK DOG (Chpbk.)
    WEST IS WEST AND OTHERS
    WINDS OF TIME

**THAT WOMEN MAY SING OF US**
First appeared in THE LAST OF THE TRUNK OCH BREV I URVAL (Chpbk.)
    THE COLLECTED LETTERS OF ROBERT E. HOWARD, VOLUME 3: 1933-1936
    From a letter to TCS, undated ("Salaam: / I have forgotten . . .")

**THESE THINGS ARE GODS**
First appeared in UNAUSSPRECHLICHEN KULTEN #2 (Chpbk., French)
    THE NEW HOWARD READER #3 (Chpbk.)

**THE THING ON THE ROOF (Verse heading, appearances apart from story)**
Alternate title: OUT OF THE OLD LAND; THE OLD ONES
First appeared in ECHOES FROM AN IRON HARP
    THE RAVEN #1 (Chpbk.)

A ROBERT E. HOWARD MEMORIAL: JUNE 13-15, 1986 (Chpbk.)
ROBERT E. HOWARD'S POEMS ON THE EDGE
WINDS OF TIME
Attributed to Justin Geoffrey, an REH fictional character; in the published version, the title of the poem is "Out of the Old Land"; in an early draft, it is titled "The Old Ones"; the earlier version has just a couple words different

## THOR
First appeared in THE LAST OF THE TRUNK OCH BREV I URVAL (Chpbk.)
 THE COLLECTED LETTERS OF ROBERT E. HOWARD, VOLUME 1: 1923-1929
 From a letter to TCS, June 23, 1926 ("Salaam; / I'm trying to write again . . .")

## THOR'S SON
Alternate title: THE RHYME OF THE VIKING PATH
First appeared in THE HOWARD COLLECTOR #11
 ECHOES FROM AN IRON HARP
 THE BOOK OF ROBERT E. HOWARD
 CONAN, VARVAR IZ CIMMERIA (Russian)
 THE COLLECTED LETTERS OF ROBERT E. HOWARD, VOLUME 2: 1930-1932
 Original title was "The Rhyme of the Viking Path", from a letter to TCS, ca. May 1930 ("Well, Fear Finn, I
   was in Brownwood . . .")

## A THOUSAND YEARS AGO
Alternate title: Untitled ("I was a chief of the Chatagai")
First appeared in NIGHT IMAGES

## THUS SPAKE SVEN THE FOOL
First appeared in SINGERS IN THE SHADOWS

## THE TIDE
Alternate title: TO A WOMAN (3); Untitled ("Thus in my mood I love you")
First appeared in OMNIUMGATHUM (Chpbk.)
 NIGHT IMAGES
 CRIMSON SHADOWS: THE BEST OF ROBERT E. HOWARD, VOLUME 1

## TIDES
First appeared in CONTEMPORARY VERSE, September 1929
 THE NEW HOWARD READER #5 (Chpbk.)
 WEST IS WEST AND OTHERS

## TIGER GIRL
First appeared in OMNIUMGATHUM (Chpbk.)
 NIGHT IMAGES
 WRITER OF THE DARK

## TIME, THE VICTOR
Alternate title: Untitled ("Swift with your mitts")
First appeared in A RHYME OF SALEM TOWN AND OTHER POEMS (Chpbk. & HB)

## TIMUR-IL-LANG
Alternate title: TIMUR-LANG

**TIMUR-LANG**
Alternate title: TIMUR-IL-LANG
First appeared in THE HOWARD COLLECTOR #5
    ECHOES FROM AN IRON HARP
    THE DARK BARBARIAN (Anth.)
    LORD OF SAMARCAND AND OTHER ADVENTURES OF THE OLD ORIENT
    THE COLLECTED LETTERS OF ROBERT E. HOWARD, VOLUME 2: 1930-1932
    THE GRIM LAND: THE BEST OF ROBERT E. HOWARD, VOLUME 2
    Lines 3, 4, and 6 identical to lines 3, 4, and 10 of "The Sign of the Sickle"; originally from a letter to Harold
        Preece, date unknown ("Salaam: Say, listen, tramp . . .")

**TO A CERTAIN CULTURED WOMAN**
First appeared in THE LAST OF THE TRUNK OCH BREV I URVAL (Chpbk.)
    THE COLLECTED LETTERS OF ROBERT E. HOWARD, VOLUME 3: 1933-1936
    From a letter to TCS, undated ("The Seeker thrust . . .")

**TO A FRIEND**
First appeared in VERSES IN EBONY (Chpbk.)
    NIGHT IMAGES

**TO A KIND MISSIONARY WOIKER**
First appeared in A RHYME OF SALEM TOWN AND OTHER POEMS (Chpbk. & HB)

**TO A MODERN YOUNG LADY**
Alternate title: TO A WOMAN ("Ages ago . . .")

**TO A NAMELESS WOMAN**
First appeared in SHADOWS OF DREAMS
    THE LAST OF THE TRUNK OCH BREV I URVAL (Chpbk.)
    THE COLLECTED LETTERS OF ROBERT E. HOWARD, VOLUME 1: 1923-1929
    From a letter to TCS, ca. November 1928 ("Salaam: / I got such a laugh . . .")

**TO A ROMAN WOMAN**
First appeared in THE LAST OF THE TRUNK OCH BREV I URVAL (Chpbk.)
    THE COLLECTED LETTERS OF ROBERT E. HOWARD, VOLUME 1: 1923-1929
    From a letter to TCS, undated ("Salaam: / Life is a yellow mist . . .")

**TO A WOMAN (1, "Ages ago I came to woo")**
Alternate title: TO A MODERN YOUNG LADY
First appeared in THE GHOST OCEAN AND OTHER POEMS OF THE SUPERNATURAL (Chpbk.)
    THE HOWARD READER #8 (Chpbk.)

**TO A WOMAN (2, "Though fathoms deep . . .")**
First appeared in MODERN AMERICAN POETRY, edited by Gerta Aison, Galleon Press, 1933
    ALWAYS COMES EVENING
    ONE WHO WALKS ALONE (Anth.)
    CHANTS DE GUERRE ET DE MORT
    ODES AT THE BLACK DOG (Chpbk.)
    WEST IS WEST AND OTHERS
    THE VALLEY OF THE WORM: THE WEIRD WORKS OF ROBERT E. HOWARD, VOLUME 5
    ONION TOPS #9 (Chpbk.)
    THE WINDS OF TIME

**TO A WOMAN (3, "Thus in my mood I love you")**
Alternate title: THE TIDE; Untitled ("Thus in my mood I love you")

**TO ALL LORDS OF COMMERCE**
Alternate title: TO ALL THE LORDS OF COMMERCE
First appeared in VERSES IN EBONY (Chpbk.)

**TO ALL SOPHISTICATES**
First appeared in THE GHOST OCEAN AND OTHER POEMS OF THE SUPERNATURAL (Chpbk.)
        SERVANT OF THE WARSMAN #8 (Chpbk., lines 4-7)

**TO AN EARTH-BOUND SOUL**
First appeared in THE GRIM LAND AND OTHERS (Chpbk.)

**TO CERTAIN ORTHODOX BRETHREN**
First appeared in THE HOWARD COLLECTOR #12
        ECHOES FROM AN IRON HARP

**TO HARRY THE OLIAD MAN**
Alternate title: Untitled ("When the first winds of summer . . .")
First appeared in OMNIUMGATHUM (Chpbk.)
        NIGHT IMAGES
        SIMBA #2 (Chpbk.)

**TO LYLE SAXON**
First appeared in SHADOWS OF DREAMS
        THE LAST OF THE TRUNK OCH BREV I URVAL (Chpbk.)
        THE COLLECTED LETTERS OF ROBERT E. HOWARD, VOLUME 3: 1933-1936
        From a letter to TCS, undated ("Salaam: / There once was a wicked . . .")

**TO MODERNS**
First appeared in A RHYME OF SALEM TOWN AND OTHER POEMS (Chpbk. & HB)

**TO THE CONTENTED**
First appeared in THE COLLECTED LETTERS OF ROBERT E. HOWARD, VOLUME 1: 1923-1929
        From a letter to TCS, ca. April 1929 ("Salaam: / The iron harp that . . .")

**TO THE EVANGELISTS**
Alternate title: THE FLOOD
First appeared in THE JUNTO, December 1928
        THE HOWARD READER #8 (Chpbk.)

**TO THE OLD MEN**
Alternate title: AGE

**TO THE STYLISTS**
First appeared in A RHYME OF SALEM TOWN AND OTHER POEMS (Chpbk. & HB)

**TODAY**
First appeared in THE GRIM LAND AND OTHERS (Chpbk.)
        THE DARK BARBARIAN (Anth., lines 10, 18-20)

**THE TOM THUMB MOIDER MYSTERY (Verse heading, appearances apart from story)**
Unpublished, from a letter to TCS, ca. May 1932 ("Lo, friend, . . .")

**TOPER**
First appeared in THE LAST OF THE TRUNK OCH BREV I URVAL (Chpbk.)
    THE COLLECTED LETTERS OF ROBERT E. HOWARD, VOLUME 1: 1923-1929
    From a letter to TCS, June 23, 1926 ("Salaam; / I'm trying to write again . . .")

**THE TOWER OF ZUKALA**
First appeared in A RHYME OF SALEM TOWN AND OTHER POEMS (Chpbk. & HB)
    ONION TOPS #15 (Chpbk.)

**THE TRAIL OF GOLD**
Alternate title: Untitled ("Come with me to the Land of Sunrise")
First appeared in A RHYME OF SALEM TOWN AND OTHER POEMS (Chpbk. & HB)

**TRAIL'S END**
Alternate title: Untitled ("Ho, for a trail that is bloody and long!")
First appeared in A RHYME OF SALEM TOWN AND OTHER POEMS (Chpbk. & HB)
    Originally embodied as an untitled verse in an untitled story ("As he approached the two . . .")

**A TRIBUTE TO THE SPORTSMANSHIP OF THE FANS**
First appeared in THE COLLECTED LETTERS OF ROBERT E. HOWARD, VOLUME 2: 1930-1932
    From a letter to TCS, ca. March 1930 ("Well, Fear Finn, tell Cuchullain . . .")

**TWILIGHT ON STONEHENGE**
First appeared in SHADOWS OF DREAMS
    THE LAST OF THE TRUNK OCH BREV I URVAL (Chpbk.)
    THE COLLECTED LETTERS OF ROBERT E. HOWARD, VOLUME 1: 1923-1929
    ZMIERZCH NAD STONEHENGE (Polish)
    From a letter to TCS, August 21, 1926 ("Bohut salaam, sahib: / I think you owe me . . .")

**THE TWIN GATES**
First appeared in SINGERS IN THE SHADOWS

**TWO MEN**
First appeared in THE GHOST OCEAN AND OTHER POEMS OF THE SUPERNATURAL (Chpbk.)

**UNIVERSE**
First appeared in WEIRD TALES #294, Fall 1989
    THE NEW HOWARD READER #5 (Chpbk.)

**UNTAMED AVATARS**
Alternate title: Untitled ("They break from the pack . . .")
First appeared in A RHYME OF SALEM TOWN AND OTHER POEMS (Chpbk. & HB)

**UNTITLED ("Across the wastes of No Man's Land . . .")**
Alternate title: NO MAN'S LAND

**UNTITLED ("Adam's loins were mountains")**
First appeared in THE COLLECTED LETTERS OF ROBERT E. HOWARD, VOLUME 1: 1923-1929
    From a letter to TCS, ca. November 1928 ("Salaam: / I'll swear . . .")

**UNTITLED ("Adventure, I have followed your beck")**
Alternate title: ADVENTURE (1)

**UNTITLED ("After the trumps are sounded")**
First appeared in THE LAST OF THE TRUNK OCH BREV I URVAL (Chpbk.)
    THE COLLECTED LETTERS OF ROBERT E. HOWARD, VOLUME 1: 1923-1929
    From a letter to TCS, ca. September 1927 ("Salaam: / Then the little boy said . . .")

**UNTITLED ("Against the blood red moon a tower stands")**
First appeared in THE LAST OF THE TRUNK OCH BREV I URVAL (Chpbk.)
    THE COLLECTED LETTERS OF ROBERT E. HOWARD, VOLUME 1: 1923-1929
    From a letter to TCS, ca. August/September 1927 ("ARE YOU THE YOUNG MAN . . .")

**UNTITLED ("The ages stride on golden feet")**
Alternate title: THE AGES STRIDE ON GOLDEN FEET

**UNTITLED ("Ah, I know black queens . . .")**
Alternate title: STRANGE PASSION

**UNTITLED ("Ah, the rover hides . . .")**
Alternate title: O THE BRAVE SEA-ROVER

**UNTITLED ("Ah, those were glittering, jeweled days")**
Alternate title: DAYS OF GLORY

**UNTITLED ("All is pose and artifice")**
Alternate title: ARTIFICE

**UNTITLED ("All men look at life . . .")**
Alternate title: PERSPECTIVE

**UNTITLED ("All the crowd")**
First appeared in THE LAST OF THE TRUNK OCH BREV I URVAL (Chpbk.)
    THE COLLECTED LETTERS OF ROBERT E. HOWARD, VOLUME 1: 1923-1929
    From a letter to TCS, October 9, 1925 ("Salaam, sahib; / Say, boy, you're . . .")

**UNTITLED ("Am-ra stood on a mountain height")**
Alternate title: SUMMER MORN

**UNTITLED ("The ancient boast, the ancient song")**
Alternate title: THE HOUSE OF GAEL

**UNTITLED ("And Bill, he looked at me . . .")**
First appeared in THE RIGHT HOOK, VOLUME 1, #2 (Chpbk.)
    AUSTIN, VOLUME 3, #2 (Chpbk.)
    THE NEW HOWARD READER #2 (Chpbk.)

**UNTITLED ("And Dempsey climbed into the ring and the crowd . . .")**
First appeared in THE COLLECTED LETTERS OF ROBERT E. HOWARD, VOLUME 1: 1923-1929
    From a letter to TCS, July 16, 1925 ("Salaam, sahib: / What ho, milord!")

**UNTITLED ("And there were lethal women, flaming ice and fire")**

First appeared in YESTERYEAR #4 (Chpbk.)
    THE COLLECTED LETTERS OF ROBERT E. HOWARD, VOLUME 1: 1923-1929
    From a letter to TCS, ca. February 1929 ("Salaam: / Last night the Sunday School . . .")

**UNTITLED ("As a great spider grows to monstrous girth")**
Alternate title: JU-JU DOOM

**UNTITLED ("As I rode down to Lincoln town")**
Alternate title: AS I RODE DOWN TO LINCOLN TOWN

**UNTITLED ("As I went down to Salem town . . .")**
Alternate title: A RHYME OF SALEM TOWN

**UNTITLED ("As you dance upon the air")**
First appeared in A RHYME OF SALEM TOWN AND OTHER POEMS (Chpbk. & HB)
    Incomplete

**UNTITLED ("At the Inn of the Gory Dagger, with nothing to . . .")**
First appeared in THE LAST OF THE TRUNK OCH BREV I URVAL (Chpbk.)
    THE COLLECTED LETTERS OF ROBERT E. HOWARD, VOLUME 1: 1923-1929
    From a letter to TCS, ca. February 1929 ("Salaam: / Ancient English Balladel")

**UNTITLED ("Away in the dusky barracoon")**
Alternate title: CORNISH JACK

**UNTITLED ("The Baron of Fenland . . .")**
First appeared in AMERICAN AND EUROPEAN MANUSCRIPTS AND PRINTED BOOKS, December 19, 1986
    COLD STEEL #10 (Chpbk.)
    THE NEW HOWARD READER #4 (Chpbk.)
    MANUSCRIPTS FROM GOWER-PENN, VOLUME 2, #3 (Chpbk.)
    THE COLLECTED LETTERS OF ROBERT E. HOWARD, VOLUME 1: 1923-1929
    Written on the endpapers of PC Wren's BEAU GESTE; also included in a letter to TCS, ca. September 1927
        ("Salaam: / Having just got your letter . . ."); all these publications except THE NEW HOWARD
        READER and COLLECTED LETTERS are facsimile reproductions of the second page of that letter,
        which contains the verse

**UNTITLED ("The baron quaffed a draught of wine . . .")**
Alternate title: THE BARON AND THE WENCH

**UNTITLED ("A beggar, singing without")**
First appeared in THE LAST OF THE TRUNK OCH BREV I URVAL (Chpbk.)
    THE COLLECTED LETTERS OF ROBERT E. HOWARD, VOLUME 1: 1923-1929
    From a letter to TCS, ca. March 1929 ("Salaam: Black Dawn")

**UNTITLED ("Bill Boozy was a pirate bold")**
First appeared in THE LAST OF THE TRUNK OCH BREV I URVAL (Chpbk.)
    THE COLLECTED LETTERS OF ROBERT E. HOWARD, VOLUME 1: 1923-1929
    From a letter to TCS, July 30, 1923 ("Clyde sahib, bohut salaam, bahadur")

**UNTITLED ("Brazen thewed giant of a grimmer Age")**
First appeared in THE ROBERT E. HOWARD FOUNDATION NEWSLETTER, VOLUME 1, #2
    Unfinished

**UNTITLED ("The broken walls of Babel")**
Alternate title: THE BROKEN WALLS OF BABEL

**UNTITLED ("By old Abie Goldstein's pawn shop where the . . .")**
First appeared in THE LAST OF THE TRUNK OCH BREV I URVAL (Chpbk.)
    THE COLLECTED LETTERS OF ROBERT E. HOWARD, VOLUME 1: 1923-1929
    From a letter to TCS, ca. March 1929 ("Salaam: Black Dawn")

**UNTITLED ("The champion sneered . . .")**
Alternate title: THE CHAMP

**UNTITLED ("The chariots were chanting . . .")**
Alternate title: THE LAST WORDS HE HEARD

**UNTITLED ("Chesterton twanged on his lyre")**
Alternate title: A SONG OF BARDS

**UNTITLED ("A Chinese washer, . . .")**
First appeared in THE TOREADOR, July 5, 1925 (Chpbk.)
    REHUPA #117 (Chpbk.)
    THE NEW HOWARD READER #1 (Chpbk.)

**UNTITLED ("Cities brooding beneath the sea")**
Alternate title: WHO IS GRANDPA THEOBOLD?

**UNTITLED ("A clash of steel, a thud of hoofs")**
First appeared in THE LAST OF THE TRUNK OCH BREV I URVAL (Chpbk.)
    THE COLLECTED LETTERS OF ROBERT E. HOWARD, VOLUME 1: 1923-1929
    From a letter to TCS, August 4, 1923 ("Clyde Sahib; / You say I'll be in Kabul.")

**UNTITLED ("Come with me to the Land of Sunrise")**
Alternate title: THE TRAIL OF GOLD

**UNTITLED ("A cringing woman's lot is hard")**
First appeared in THE LAST OF THE TRUNK OCH BREV I URVAL (Chpbk.)
    THE COLLECTED LETTERS OF ROBERT E. HOWARD, VOLUME 1: 1923-1929
    From a letter to TCS, ca. June 1928 ("Salaam; / Ho, ho, the long lights . . .")

**UNTITLED ("Dark are your eyes")**
First appeared in THE LAST OF THE TRUNK OCH BREV I URVAL (Chpbk.)
    THE COLLECTED LETTERS OF ROBERT E. HOWARD, VOLUME 1: 1923-1929
    From a letter to TCS, January 30, 1925 ("Salaam, sahib; / I'm sending you . . .")

**UNTITLED ("The day that towers, ...")**
Alternate title: NISAPUR

**UNTITLED ("The doine sidhe sang to our swords . . .")**
Alternate title: COUNTERSPELLS

**UNTITLED ("Drawers that a girl strips down her thighs")**
First appeared in THE LAST OF THE TRUNK OCH BREV I URVAL (Chpbk.)
    THE COLLECTED LETTERS OF ROBERT E. HOWARD, VOLUME 1: 1923-1929
    From a letter to TCS, ca. November 1928 ("Salaam: / I got such a laugh . . .")

**UNTITLED ("Early in the morning I gazed at the eastern skies")**
First appeared in THE LAST OF THE TRUNK OCH BREV I URVAL (Chpbk.)
    THE COLLECTED LETTERS OF ROBERT E. HOWARD, VOLUME 1: 1923-1929
    From a letter to TCS, June 23, 1926 ("Salaam; / I'm trying to write again . . .")

**UNTITLED ("The east is red and I am dead")**
First appeared in THE COLLECTED LETTERS OF ROBERT E. HOWARD, VOLUME 1: 1923-1929
    THE COLLECTED LETTERS OF ROBERT E. HOWARD, VOLUME 1: 1923-1929
    From a letter to TCS, ca. January 1928 ("Salaam: / Listen, you crumb . . .")

**UNTITLED ("The elder gods have fled")**
Alternate title: PASSING OF THE ELDER GODS

**UNTITLED ("Eons before the Atlantean days . . .")**
Alternate title: THE SYMBOL

**UNTITLED ("Far in the gloomy northland")**
Alternate title: FAR IN THE GLOOMY NORTHLAND

**UNTITLED ("Fill up my goblet")**
First appeared in THE ROBERT E. HOWARD FOUNDATION NEWSLETTER, VOLUME 1, #2

**UNTITLED ("Flappers flicker and flap and flirt")**
First appeared in THE LAST OF THE TRUNK OCH BREV I URVAL (Chpbk.)
    THE COLLECTED LETTERS OF ROBERT E. HOWARD, VOLUME 1: 1923-1929
    From a letter to TCS, ca. December 1928 ("Salaam: / Out in front of Goldstein's . . .")

**UNTITLED ("For I have seen the lizards crawl")**
Alternate title: BABYLON

**UNTITLED ("For I, with the . . .")**
Alternate title: THE DUST DANCE (I)

**UNTITLED ("For what is a maid to the shout of kings")**
First appeared in A RHYME OF SALEM TOWN AND OTHER POEMS (Chpbk. & HB)
    Incomplete

**UNTITLED ("Forever down the ages")**
Alternate title: DOWN THE AGES

**UNTITLED ("Forth from the purple . . .")**
Alternate title: THE OUTCAST

**UNTITLED ("From the dim red dawn of Creation")**
Alternate title: MEN OF THE SHADOWS (Verse heading)

**UNTITLED ("Give ye of my best though the dole be meger")**
First appeared in THE LAST OF THE TRUNK OCH BREV I URVAL (Chpbk.)
    THE COLLECTED LETTERS OF ROBERT E. HOWARD, VOLUME 1: 1923-1929
      From a letter to TCS, June 23, 1926 ("Salaam; / I'm trying to write again . . .")

**UNTITLED ("The great gray oaks . . .")**
Alternate title: THE OAKS

**UNTITLED ("Hark, hark, the jackals bark")**
Alternate title: MADAM GOOSE'S RHYMES

**UNTITLED ("A haunting cadence fills the night with fierce . . .")**
First appeared in YESTERYEAR #4 (Chpbk.)
    THE COLLECTED LETTERS OF ROBERT E. HOWARD, VOLUME 1: 1923-1929
      From a letter to TCS, ca. February 1929 ("Salaam: / Last night the Sunday School . . .")

**UNTITLED ("He clutched his . . .")**
First appeared in THE COLLECTED LETTERS OF ROBERT E. HOWARD, VOLUME 1: 1923-1929
    From a letter to TCS, ca. November 1928 ("Salaam: / I'll swear . . .")

**UNTITLED ("He did not glance above the trail . . .")**
Alternate title: THE FEUD

**UNTITLED ("He has rigged her and tricked her")**
Alternate title: THE STRALSUND

**UNTITLED ("The helmsman gaily, rode down the rickerboo")**
First appeared in THE LAST OF THE TRUNK OCH BREV I URVAL (Chpbk.)
    THE COLLECTED LETTERS OF ROBERT E. HOWARD, VOLUME 1: 1923-1929
      From a letter to TCS, June 22 1923 ("Clyde sahib greeting: / I found your . . .")

**UNTITLED ("Here where the post-oaks . . .")**
Alternate title: THE SAND-HILLS' CREST

**UNTITLED ("High on his throne Baal-Pteor sat")**
Alternate title: BAAL-PTEOR

**UNTITLED ("High on his throne sat Bran Mak Morn")**
Alternate title: A SONG OF THE RACE

**UNTITLED ("High the towers and mighty . . .")**
Alternate title: WHO SHALL SING OF BABYLON?

**UNTITLED ("Hills of the North! Lavender hills")**
First appeared in THE LAST OF THE TRUNK OCH BREV I URVAL (Chpbk.)
    THE COLLECTED LETTERS OF ROBERT E. HOWARD, VOLUME 1: 1923-1929
      From a letter to TCS, January 30, 1925 ("Salaam, sahib; / I'm sending you . . .")

**UNTITLED ("Ho, for a trail that is bloody and long!")**
Alternate title: TRAIL'S END

**UNTITLED ("Ho, ho, the long lights lift amain")**
First appeared in THE LAST OF THE TRUNK OCH BREV I URVAL (Chpbk.)
    THE COLLECTED LETTERS OF ROBERT E. HOWARD, VOLUME 1: 1923-1929
    From a letter to TCS, ca. June 1928 ("Ho, ho, the long lights . . .")

**UNTITLED ("Ho merry bark, . . .")**
First appeared in THE RIGHT HOOK, VOLUME 1, #2 (Chpbk.)
    AUSTIN, VOLUME 3, #2 (Chpbk.)
    THE NEW HOWARD READER #3 (Chpbk.)

**UNTITLED ("The House of Asgaard passes . . .")**
Alternate title: NO MORE THE SERPENT PROW

**UNTITLED ("How can I wear the harness of toil")**
Alternate title: THE DRUMS OF PICTDOM

**UNTITLED ("How long have you written, Eddie Guest?")**
Alternate title: EDGAR GUEST

**UNTITLED ("A hundred years the great war raged")**
First appeared in THE LAST OF THE TRUNK OCH BREV I URVAL (Chpbk.)
    THE COLLECTED LETTERS OF ROBERT E. HOWARD, VOLUME 1: 1923-1929
    From a letter to TCS, August 4, 1923 ("Clyde Sahib; / You say I'll be in Kabul.")

**UNTITLED ("I am a Devon oak")**
Alternate title: DEVON OAK

**UNTITLED ("I am an actor . . .")**
Alternate title: THE ACTOR

**UNTITLED ("I am MAN from the primal, I")**
First appeared in THE LAST OF THE TRUNK OCH BREV I URVAL (Chpbk.)
    THE COLLECTED LETTERS OF ROBERT E. HOWARD, VOLUME 1: 1923-1929
    From a letter to TCS, ca. March 1928 ("Salaam: / Not having much . . .")

**UNTITLED ("I am the Spirit of War!")**
First appeared in THE LAST OF THE TRUNK OCH BREV I URVAL (Chpbk.)
    THE COLLECTED LETTERS OF ROBERT E. HOWARD, VOLUME 1: 1923-1929
    From a letter to TCS, January 30, 1925 ("Salaam, sahib; / I'm sending you . . .")

**UNTITLED ("I can recall a quiet sky . . .")**
Alternate title: A DAWN IN FLANDERS

**UNTITLED ("I carved a woman out of marble when")**
Alternate title: FLAMING MARBLE

**UNTITLED ("I caught Joan alone upon her bed")**
Alternate title: PRELUDE

**UNTITLED ("I cut my teeth on toil and pain")**
Alternate title: WHEN THE GLACIERS RUMBLED SOUTH

**UNTITLED ("I do not sing of a paradise")**
First appeared in THE COLLECTED LETTERS OF ROBERT E. HOWARD, VOLUME 1: 1923-1929
    From a letter to TCS, ca. January 1928 ("Salaam: / Listen, you crumb . . .")

**UNTITLED ("I hate the man who tells me that I lied")**
First appeared in THE COLLECTED LETTERS OF ROBERT E. HOWARD, VOLUME 1: 1923-1929
    From a letter to TCS, ca. November 1928 ("Salaam: / I'll swear . . .")

**UNTITLED ("I heard the drum as I went . . .")**
Alternate title: THE DRUM

**UNTITLED ("I hold all women are a gang of tramps")**
First appeared in THE LAST OF THE TRUNK OCH BREV I URVAL (Chpbk.)
    THE COLLECTED LETTERS OF ROBERT E. HOWARD, VOLUME 1: 1923-1929
    From a letter to TCS, ca. December 1928 ("Salaam: / Out in front of Goldstein's . . .")

**UNTITLED ("I knocked upon her lattice – soft!")**
First appeared in LEWD TALES (Chpbk.)
    THE LAST OF THE TRUNK OCH BREV I URVAL (Chpbk.)
    THE COLLECTED LETTERS OF ROBERT E. HOWARD, VOLUME 1: 1923-1929
    This poem is at the end of Act I, Scene I of "Songs of Bastards"; from a letter to TCS, ca. March 1929
        ("Salaam: / Black Dawn")

**UNTITLED ("I lay in Yen's opium joint")**
First appeared in THE LAST OF THE TRUNK OCH BREV I URVAL (Chpbk.)
    THE COLLECTED LETTERS OF ROBERT E. HOWARD, VOLUME 1: 1923-1929
    From a letter to TCS, January 30, 1925 ("Salaam, sahib; / I'm sending you . . .")

**UNTITLED ("I saw the grass on the hillside bend")**
Alternate title: DANCE MACABRE

**UNTITLED ("I stand in the streets of the city")**
Alternate title: THE KING OF THE AGES COMES

**UNTITLED ("I tell you this my friend . . .")**
First appeared in THE LAST OF THE TRUNK OCH BREV I URVAL (Chpbk.)
    THE COLLECTED LETTERS OF ROBERT E. HOWARD, VOLUME 1: 1923-1929
    From a letter to TCS, August 6, 1925 ("Salaam: / I'm glad you passed . . .")

**UNTITLED ("I too have strode those white-paved roads")**
Alternate title: ROADS

**UNTITLED ("I was a chief of the Chatagai")**
Alternate title: A THOUSAND YEARS AGO

**UNTITLED ("I was a prince of China, . . .")**
Alternate title: PRINCE AND BEGGAR

**UNTITLED ("I, was I there")**
Alternate title: WAS I THERE?

**UNTITLED ("I was once, I declare, a grog-shop man")**
Alternate title: A BALLAD OF BEER

**UNTITLED ("I'm more than a man . . .")**
Unpublished, from the single page of draft of the story "Yellow Laughter"

**UNTITLED ("The iron harp that Adam christened Life")**
First appeared in THE COLLECTED LETTERS OF ROBERT E. HOWARD, VOLUME 1: 1923-1929
    From a letter to TCS, ca. April 1929 ("Salaam: / The iron harp that . . .")

**UNTITLED ("A jackal laughed from a thicket still, . . .")**
Alternate title: FLIGHT

**UNTITLED ("Keep women, thrones and kingly lands")**
First appeared in THE COLLECTED LETTERS OF ROBERT E. HOWARD, VOLUME 1: 1923-1929
    From a letter to TCS, ca. January 1928 ("Salaam: / Listen, you crumb . . .")

**UNTITLED ("Keresa, Keresita")**
Alternate title: KERESA, KERESITA

**UNTITLED ("Let me live as I was born to live")**
First appeared in THE COLLECTED LETTERS OF ROBERT E. HOWARD, VOLUME 1: 1923-1929
    From a letter to TCS, ca. November 1928 ("Salaam: / I'll swear . . .")

**UNTITLED ("Let it rest with the ages mysteries")**
First appeared in THE COLLECTED LETTERS OF ROBERT E. HOWARD, VOLUME 2: 1930-1932
    From a letter to TCS, ca. November 1931 ("Fear Finn:/ I wrote Bradford . . ."); may or may not actually be by
        REH, he may in fact be quoting someone else, possible a variation of a Robert Louis Stevenson verse

**UNTITLED ("Let us up in the hills . . .")**
First appeared in LEWD TALES (Chpbk.)
    THE LAST OF THE TRUNK OCH BREV I URVAL (Chpbk.)
    THE COLLECTED LETTERS OF ROBERT E. HOWARD, VOLUME 1: 1923-1929
    This poem is at the end of Act I, Scene II of "Songs of Bastards"; from a letter to TCS, ca. March 1929
        ("Salaam: / Black Dawn")

**UNTITLED ("Life is a cynical, romantic pig")**
First appeared in THE COLLECTED LETTERS OF ROBERT E. HOWARD, VOLUME 2: 1930-1932
    From a letter to TCS, ca. February 1930 ("Salaam, Fear Ohghruagach . . .")

**UNTITLED ("Life is a lot of hooey")**
First appeared in LEWD TALES (Chpbk.)
    THE LAST OF THE TRUNK OCH BREV I URVAL (Chpbk.)
    THE COLLECTED LETTERS OF ROBERT E. HOWARD, VOLUME 1: 1923-1929
    This poem is contained in Act II, Scene I of "Songs of Bastards"; from a letter to TCS, ca. March 1929
        ("Salaam: / Black Dawn")

**UNTITLED ("Life is a ladder . . .")**
Alternate title: THE LADDER OF LIFE

**UNTITLED ("Life is the same . . .")**
Alternate title: THE PHASES OF LIFE

**UNTITLED ("Little brown man of Nippon . . .")**
Alternate title: LITTLE BROWN MAN OF NIPPON

**UNTITLED ("Lizzen my children and you shall be told")**
First appeared in ROBERT E. HOWARD: SELECTED LETTERS: 1923-1930 (Chpbk.)
    THE LAST OF THE TRUNK OCH BREV I URVAL (Chpbk.)
    THE COLLECTED LETTERS OF ROBERT E. HOWARD, VOLUME 2: 1930-1932
    From a letter to TCS, ca. September 1931 ("Fear Finn: / Lizzen my children . . .")

**UNTITLED ("Long ere Priapus . . .")**
Alternate title: THE GODS OF EASTER ISLAND

**UNTITLED ("Long were the years . . .")**
Alternate title: THE ECSTASY OF DESOLATION

**UNTITLED ("Love is singing soft and low")**
First appeared in THE LAST OF THE TRUNK OCH BREV I URVAL (Chpbk.)
    THE COLLECTED LETTERS OF ROBERT E. HOWARD, VOLUME 1: 1923-1929
    From a letter to TCS, ca. December 1928 ("Salaam: / Out in front of Goldstein's . . .")

**UNTITLED ("Mahomet! Man of Mecca!")**
Alternate title: MAHOMET

**UNTITLED ("Many fell at the grog-shop wall")**
First appeared in ROBERT E. HOWARD: SELECTED LETTERS: 1923-1930 (Chpbk.)
    THE COLLECTED LETTERS OF ROBERT E. HOWARD, VOLUME 2: 1930-1932
    From a letter to TCS, ca. November 1931 ("Fear Finn: / Have you heard anything . . .")

**UNTITLED ("The Master beat on his master-drum")**
Alternate title: THE MASTER-DRUM

**UNTITLED ("Match a toad with a far-winged hawk")**
First appeared in THE LAST OF THE TRUNK OCH BREV I URVAL (Chpbk.)
    THE COLLECTED LETTERS OF ROBERT E. HOWARD, VOLUME 3: 1933-1936
    From an undated, enclosed separate document sent with a letter to TCS ("Poem penned by Akbar Ali . . .")

**UNTITLED ("Men are toys . . .")**
First appeared in LEWD TALES (Chpbk.)
    SEANCHAI #46 (Chpbk.)
    THE LAST OF THE TRUNK OCH BREV I URVAL (Chpbk.)
    THE COLLECTED LETTERS OF ROBERT E. HOWARD, VOLUME 1: 1923-1929
    This poem is contained in "Songs of Bastards"; from a letter to TCS, ca. March 1929 ("Salaam: / Black Dawn")

**UNTITLED ("Men I have slain with naked steel")**
Alternate title: THE SWORD OF LAL SINGH

**UNTITLED ("Men say my years . . .")**
Alternate title: THE GUISE OF YOUTH

**UNTITLED ("Mingle my dust with the burning brand")**
First appeared in THE COLLECTED LETTERS OF ROBERT E. HOWARD, VOLUME 1: 1923-1929
    From a letter to TCS, August 28, 1925 ("Salaam; / I've been thinking.")

**UNTITLED ("The moon above the Kerry hills . . .")**
Alternate title: BLACK MICHAEL'S STORY; THE SONG OF MURTAGH O'BRIEN; RETRIBUTION

**UNTITLED ("Moonlight and shadows barred the land")**
First appeared in THE LAST OF THE TRUNK OCH BREV I URVAL (Chpbk.)
 THE COLLECTED LETTERS OF ROBERT E. HOWARD, VOLUME 3: 1933-1936
 From a letter to TCS, ca. late 1928 ("Salaam: / I swear, if I'd laughed . . .")

**UNTITLED ("The moonlight glimmered white . . .")**
Alternate title: MINE BUT TO SERVE

**UNTITLED ("Moses was our leader . . .")**
Alternate title: THE ODYSSEY OF ISRAEL

**UNTITLED ("Mother Eve, Mother Eve, I name you a fool")**
First appeared in THE COLLECTED LETTERS OF ROBERT E. HOWARD, VOLUME 1: 1923-1929
 From a letter to TCS, ca. January 1928 ("Salaam: / Listen, you crumb . . .")

**UNTITLED ("Murky the night")**
First appeared in A RHYME OF SALEM TOWN AND OTHER POEMS (Chpbk. & HB)
 Unfinished; actually titled "Untitled"

**UNTITLED ("My brother he was a auctioneer")**
First appeared in THE LAST OF THE TRUNK OCH BREV I URVAL (Chpbk.)
 THE COLLECTED LETTERS OF ROBERT E. HOWARD, VOLUME 1: 1923-1929
 From a letter to TCS, ca. November-December 1928 ("Salaam: / Heh heh!")

**UNTITLED ("My heart is a silver drum tonight")**
Alternate title: THE CALL OF PAN

**UNTITLED ("My name is Baal . . .")**
Alternate title: BAAL

**UNTITLED ("Night falls")**
Alternate title: NOCTURNE

**UNTITLED ("Night in the county of Donegal")**
Alternate title: FAREWELL, PROUD MUNSTER

**UNTITLED ("The night winds whisper . . .")**
Alternate title: THE NIGHT WINDS

**UNTITLED ("'No more!' they swear . . .")**
Alternate title: THE LEGACY OF TUBAL-CAIN

**UNTITLED ("Noah was my applesauce")**
First appeared in THE COLLECTED LETTERS OF ROBERT E. HOWARD, VOLUME 1: 1923-1929
 From a letter to TCS, ca. November 1928 ("Salaam: / I'll swear . . .")

**UNTITLED ("Now anthropoid and leprous shadows lope")**
Alternate title: ALL HALLOWS EVE

**UNTITLED ("Now bright, now red, the sabers sped among the . . .")**
First appeared in THE LAST OF THE TRUNK OCH BREV I URVAL (Chpbk.)
    THE COLLECTED LETTERS OF ROBERT E. HOWARD, VOLUME 1: 1923-1929
    From a letter to TCS, June 22 1923 ("Clyde sahib greeting: / I found your . . .")

**UNTITLED ("Now come the days of high . . .")**
Alternate title: A FABLE FOR CRITICS

**UNTITLED ("Now hark to this tale of long ago")**
Alternate title: WHEN MEN WERE BOLD

**UNTITLED ("Now is a summer come out of the sea")**
Alternate title: BUT THE HILLS WERE ANCIENT THEN

**UNTITLED ("Now that the kings have fallen")**
Alternate title: WHERE ARE YOUR KNIGHTS, DONN OTHNA?

**UNTITLED ("O'er lakes agleam . . .")**
Alternate title: CHANT OF THE WHITE BEARD

**UNTITLED ("Oh, the road to glory lay")**
A poem that is contained in "The Pit of the Serpent", attributed to Steve Costigan's fictional shipmate Hansen;
    appears to be a short takeoff from "The Battle of Manila Bay", 1904, an epic poem about a American sea
    victory; poem has appeared with the story in all publications, and has not been published separately

**UNTITLED ("Oh, we are little children, . . .")**
First appeared in THE LAST OF THE TRUNK OCH BREV I URVAL (Chpbk.)
    THE COLLECTED LETTERS OF ROBERT E. HOWARD, VOLUME 1: 1923-1929
    From a letter to TCS, ca. November 1928 ("Salaam: / I'll swear . . ."); this poem is contained in the story
        "People of the Winged Skulls"

**UNTITLED ("Oh, ye who tread the narrow way")**
Alternate title: EXHORTATION

**UNTITLED ("Old Faro Bill was a man of might")**
First appeared in THE COLLECTED LETTERS OF ROBERT E. HOWARD, VOLUME 1: 1923-1929
    RHYMES OF TEXAS AND THE OLD WEST
    From a letter to TCS, ca. November 1928 ("Heh heh! At last I've sold . . .")

**UNTITLED ("One slept beneath the branches dim")**
Alternate title: THE RETURN OF SIR RICHARD GRENVILLE

**UNTITLED ("Out in front of Goldestein's . . .")**
First appeared in THE LAST OF THE TRUNK OCH BREV I URVAL (Chpbk.)
    THE COLLECTED LETTERS OF ROBERT E. HOWARD, VOLUME 1: 1923-1929
    From a letter to TCS, ca. December 1928 ("Salaam: / Out in front of Goldstein's . . .")

**UNTITLED ("Out of Asia the tribesmen came")**
First appeared in THE CROSS PLAINSMAN, August 2004 (Chpbk.)
  THE LAST OF THE TRUNK OCH BREV I URVAL (Chpbk.)
  THE COLLECTED LETTERS OF ROBERT E. HOWARD, VOLUME 1: 1923-1929
  From a letter to TCS, July 30, 1923 ("Clyde sahib, bohut salaam, bahadur")

**UNTITLED ("Out of the Texas desert . . .")**
Alternate title: THE BANDIT

**UNTITLED ("Over the hills the winds . . .")**
Alternate title: THE WINDS OF THE SEA (1)

**UNTITLED ("Over the old Rio Grandey")**
Alternate title: OVER THE OLD RIO GRANDEY

**UNTITLED ("Over the place the lights go out")**
Alternate title: IN THE RING

**UNTITLED ("Palm-trees are waving in the Gulf breeze")**
First appeared in AUSTIN, Vol 3, no. 1 (Chpbk.)
  THE NEW HOWARD READER #5 (Chpbk.)
  THE LAST OF THE TRUNK OCH BREV I URVAL (Chpbk.)
  THE COLLECTED LETTERS OF ROBERT E. HOWARD, VOLUME 1: 1923-1929
  From a letter to TCS, September 7, 1924 ("Salaam, Clyde, / You ought to be here.")

**UNTITLED ("Ramona! Ramona!")**
First appeared in THE LAST OF THE TRUNK OCH BREV I URVAL (Chpbk.)
  THE COLLECTED LETTERS OF ROBERT E. HOWARD, VOLUME 1: 1923-1929
  From a letter to TCS, ca. November-December 1928 ("Salaam: / Heh heh!")

**UNTITLED ("Rattle of drums")**
Alternate title: RATTLE OF DRUMS

**UNTITLED ("Rebel souls from the falling dark")**
First appeared in THE COLLECTED LETTERS OF ROBERT E. HOWARD, VOLUME 1: 1923-1929
  From a letter to TCS, ca. November 1928 ("Heh heh! At last I've sold . . .")

**UNTITLED ("Red swirls of dust")**
Alternate title: THE PLAINS OF GILBAN

**UNTITLED ("Rise to the peak of the ladder")**
Alternate title: NEVER BEYOND THE BEAST

**UNTITLED ("The road to Hell")**
Alternate title: THE ROAD TO HELL

**UNTITLED ("Roar, silver trumpets")**
Alternate title: ROAR, SILVER TRUMPETS

**UNTITLED ("Roses laughed in her pretty hair")**
First appeared in THE COLLECTED LETTERS OF ROBERT E. HOWARD, VOLUME 1: 1923-1929
  From a letter to TCS, August 28, 1925 ("Salaam; / I've been thinking.")

**UNTITLED ("A sappe ther wos and that a crumbe manne")**
First appeared in THE COLLECTED LETTERS OF ROBERT E. HOWARD, VOLUME 1: 1923-1929
    From a letter to TCS, ca. November 1928 ("Heh heh! At last I've sold . . .")

**UNTITLED ("Sappho, the Grecian hills are gold")**
First appeared in THE LAST OF THE TRUNK OCH BREV I URVAL (Chpbk.)
    THE COLLECTED LETTERS OF ROBERT E. HOWARD, VOLUME 1: 1923-1929
    From a letter to TCS, ca. November-December 1928 ("Salaam: / Heh heh!")

**UNTITLED ("Scarlet and gold are the stars tonight")**
First appeared in THE CROSS PLAINSMAN, August 2004 (Chpbk., last four lines only)
    THE COLLECTED LETTERS OF ROBERT E. HOWARD, VOLUME 1: 1923-1929 (first full appearance)
    From a letter to TCS, ca. November 1928 ("Heh heh! At last I've sold . . .")

**UNTITLED ("The scarlet standards of the sun")**
Alternate title: THE ADVENTURER'S MISTRESS

**UNTITLED ("A sea of molten silver")**
Alternate title: THE SANDS OF THE DESERT

**UNTITLED ("Seven kings of the grey old cities")**
Alternate title: SEVEN KINGS

**UNTITLED ("The shades of night were falling faster")**
First appeared in THE LAST OF THE TRUNK OCH BREV I URVAL (Chpbk.)
    THE COLLECTED LETTERS OF ROBERT E. HOWARD, VOLUME 1: 1923-1929
    From a letter to TCS, April 14, 1926 ("Salaam; / Being in an (un)poetical mood . . .")

**UNTITLED (draft, "She came in the grey of . . .")**
Alternate title: A CHALLENGE TO BAST

**UNTITLED ("Silence falls on Mecca's walls")**
Alternate title: SILENCE FALLS ON MECCA'S WALLS

**UNTITLED ("Slow shifts the sands of time . . .")**
Alternate title: THE SANDS OF TIME

**UNTITLED ("The snow-capped peaks of Ural . . .")**
Alternate title: THE TARTAR RAID

**UNTITLED ("The spiders of weariness come on me")**
First appeared in THE COLLECTED LETTERS OF ROBERT E. HOWARD, VOLUME 1: 1923-1929
    From a letter to TCS, ca. March 1928 ("Salaam: / Glad you're writing . . .")

**UNTITLED ("The stars beat up . . .")**
Alternate title: THE HEART OF THE SEA'S DESIRE; MATE OF THE SEA

**UNTITLED ("Stay not from me, that veil . . .")**
Alternate titles: STAY NOT FROM ME; SHADOW OF DREAMS

**UNTITLED ("A sturdy housewife was . . .")**
Alternate title: GOOD MISTRESS BROWN

**UNTITLED ("Swift with your mitts")**
Alternate title: TIME, THE VICTOR

**UNTITLED ("Swords glimmered up the pass")**
First appeared in THE COLLECTED LETTERS OF ROBERT E. HOWARD, VOLUME 1: 1923-1929
    From a letter to TCS, ca. November 1928 ("Salaam: / I'll swear . . .")

**UNTITLED ("Take some honey from a cat")**
First appeared in THE LAST OF THE TRUNK OCH BREV I URVAL (Chpbk.)
    THE COLLECTED LETTERS OF ROBERT E. HOWARD, VOLUME 1: 1923-1929
    From a letter to TCS, ca. August/September 1927 ("ARE YOU THE YOUNG MAN . . .")

**UNTITLED ("The tall man answered: . . .")**
First appeared in THE LAST OF THE TRUNK OCH BREV I URVAL (Chpbk.)
    THE COLLECTED LETTERS OF ROBERT E. HOWARD, VOLUME 1: 1923-1929
    From a letter to TCS, ca. November 1928 ("Salaam: / I'll swear . . ."); this poem is contained in the story
        "People of the Winged Skulls"

**UNTITLED ("The tall man rose and said: . . .")**
First appeared in THE LAST OF THE TRUNK OCH BREV I URVAL (Chpbk.)
    THE COLLECTED LETTERS OF ROBERT E. HOWARD, VOLUME 1: 1923-1929
    From a letter to TCS, ca. November 1928 ("Salaam: / I'll swear . . ."); this poem is contained in the story
        "People of the Winged Skulls"

**UNTITLED ("The tall man said: . . .")**
First appeared in THE LAST OF THE TRUNK OCH BREV I URVAL (Chpbk.)
    THE COLLECTED LETTERS OF ROBERT E. HOWARD, VOLUME 1: 1923-1929
    From a letter to TCS, ca. November 1928 ("Salaam: / I'll swear . . ."); this poem is contained in the story
        "People of the Winged Skulls"

**UNTITLED ("Tell me not in coocoo numbers")**
First appeared in THE COLLECTED LETTERS OF ROBERT E. HOWARD, VOLUME 1: 1923-1929
    From a letter to TCS, ca. October 1927 ("Salaam: / Seeking cognizance . . ."); contained in the story "The
        Fastidious Fooey Mancucu"

**UNTITLED ("Then Stein the peddler with rising joy")**
First appeared in THE LAST OF THE TRUNK OCH BREV I URVAL (Chpbk.)
    THE COLLECTED LETTERS OF ROBERT E. HOWARD, VOLUME 2: 1930-1932
    From a letter to TCS, ca. July 1930 ("Salaam, Fear Finn: / Then Stein the peddler . . .")

**UNTITLED ("There are grim things did")**
First appeared in THE LAST OF THE TRUNK OCH BREV I URVAL (Chpbk.)
    THE COLLECTED LETTERS OF ROBERT E. HOWARD, VOLUME 3: 1933-1936
    From a letter to TCS, undated ("Salaam: / There once was a wicked . . ."); this is a draft form of "The Ballad of
        Singapore Nell"

**UNTITLED ("There burns in me . . .")**
Alternate title: INVECTIVE

**UNTITLED ("There come long days . . .")**
Alternate title: AN OUTWORN STORY

**UNTITLED ("There is a misty sea . . .")**
Alternate title: A MISTY SEA

**UNTITLED ("There is a sea and a silent moon")**
Alternate title: THE GHOST OCEAN

**UNTITLED ("There is a strangeness in my soul")**
Alternate title: ECSTASY

**UNTITLED ("There once was a wicked old elf")**
First appeared in THE LAST OF THE TRUNK OCH BREV I URVAL (Chpbk.)
THE COLLECTED LETTERS OF ROBERT E. HOWARD, VOLUME 3: 1933-1936
From a letter to TCS, undated ("Salaam: / There once was a wicked . . .")

**UNTITLED ("There was a thing of the shadow world")**
Alternate title: SHADOW THING

**UNTITLED ("There was a young girl from Siberia")**
Alternate title: LIMERICKS TO SPANK BY

**UNTITLED ("There were three lads who went their destined ways")**
First appeared in THE LAST OF THE TRUNK OCH BREV I URVAL (Chpbk.)
THE COLLECTED LETTERS OF ROBERT E. HOWARD, VOLUME 3: 1933-1936
From an undated, enclosed separate document sent with a letter to TCS

**UNTITLED ("There's a bell that hangs in a hidden cave")**
Alternate title: THE BELL OF MORNI

**UNTITLED ("There's a calling, and a calling . . .")**
Alternate title: A CALLING TO ROME

**UNTITLED ("There's an isle far away on the breast of the sea")**
First appeared in THE LAST OF THE TRUNK OCH BREV I URVAL (Chpbk.)
THE COLLECTED LETTERS OF ROBERT E. HOWARD, VOLUME 1: 1923-1929
From a letter to TCS, ca. December 1928 ("Salaam: / Out in front of Goldstein's . . .")

**UNTITLED ("They break from the pack . . .")**
Alternate title: UNTAMED AVATARS

**UNTITLED ("They cast her out of the . . .")**
Alternate title: DAUGHTER OF EVIL

**UNTITLED ("They gave me a dollar . . .")**
Alternate title: SONG OF A FUGITIVE BARD

**UNTITLED ("They matched me up that night . . .")**
First appeared in THE LAST OF THE TRUNK OCH BREV I URVAL (Chpbk.)
    THE COLLECTED LETTERS OF ROBERT E. HOWARD, VOLUME 1: 1923-1929
      From a letter to TCS, ca. June 1928 ("Salaam; / Ho, ho, the long lights . . .")

**UNTITLED ("They were there, in the distance dreaming")**
First appeared in DEAR HPL: LETTERS, ROBERT E. HOWARD TO H.P. LOVECRAFT, 1930-1936 (Chpbk.)
    THE COLLECTED LETTERS OF ROBERT E. HOWARD, VOLUME 3: 1933-1936
      From a letter to HPL, April 23, 1933 ("I'm enclosing some of the latest views . . .")

**UNTITLED ("This is the tale of a nameless fight")**
Alternate title: THE BALLAD OF KING GERAINT

**UNTITLED ("This is a young world")**
First appeared in THE RIGHT HOOK, VOLUME 1, #3 (Chpbk.)
    AUSTIN, VOLUME 3, #2 (Chpbk.)
    THE NEW HOWARD READER #1 (Chpbk.)

**UNTITLED ("This is no land for weaklings, . . .")**
Alternate title: ZULULAND

**UNTITLED ("This is the tale the Kaffirs tell . . .")**
Alternate title: THE ZULU LORD

**UNTITLED ("Thorfinn, Thorfinn, where have you been?")**
Alternate title: THE RETURN OF THE SEA-FARER

**UNTITLED ("A thousand years ago great Genghis reigned")**
Alternate title: KRAKORUM

**UNTITLED ("A thousand years, perhaps, have come and gone")**
Alternate title: WHEN DEATH DROPS HER VEIL

**UNTITLED ("Through the mists of silence there came a sound")**
First appeared in YESTERYEAR #4 (Chpbk.)
    THE COLLECTED LETTERS OF ROBERT E. HOWARD, VOLUME 1: 1923-1929
      From a letter to TCS, ca. February 1929 ("Salaam: / Last night the Sunday School . . .")

**UNTITLED ("Thus in my mood I love you")**
Alternate title: THE TIDE; TO A WOMAN (3)

**UNTITLED ("The times, the times . . .")**
First appeared in THE NEW HOWARD READER #5 (Chpbk.)
    This poem was originally handwritten on the endpapers of REH's copy of P.C. Wren's BEAU GESTE

**UNTITLED ("Tingle, jingle, dingle, tingle . . .")**
Alternate title: LITTLE BELL OF BRASS

**UNTITLED ("Toast to the British! Damn their souls to Hell.")**
First appeared in THE LAST OF THE TRUNK OCH BREV I URVAL (Chpbk.)
    THE COLLECTED LETTERS OF ROBERT E. HOWARD, VOLUME 1: 1923-1929
      From a letter to TCS, ca. August/September 1927 ("ARE YOU THE YOUNG MAN . . .")

**UNTITLED ("Topaz seas and laughing skies")**
Alternate title: SEA-CHANT

**UNTITLED ("The towers stand recorders")**
Alternate title: THE BUILDERS (3)

**UNTITLED ("The tribes of men rise up and pass")**
Alternate title: ONLY A SHADOW ON THE GRASS

**UNTITLED ("'Turn out the light.' I raised a willing hand")**
Alternate title: DESIRE

**UNTITLED ("'Twas twice a hundred centuries ago")**
Alternate title: NOW AND THEN

**UNTITLED ("Under the grim San Saba hills")**
Alternate titles: THE LOST SAN SABA MINE; THE LOST MINE

**UNTITLED ("Up over the cromlech . . .")**
Alternate title: THE PHANTOMS GATHER

**UNTITLED ("Up with the curtain, lo, . . .")**
Alternate title: ON WITH THE PLAY

**UNTITLED ("The warm veldt spread . . .")**
Alternate title: THE CHIEF OF THE MATABELES

**UNTITLED ("We are the duckers of crosses")**
First appeared in THE LAST OF THE TRUNK OCH BREV I URVAL (Chpbk.)
    THE COLLECTED LETTERS OF ROBERT E. HOWARD, VOLUME 1: 1923-1929
    From a letter to TCS, April 14, 1926 ("Salaam; / Being in an (un)poetical mood . . .")

**UNTITLED ("We are they")**
Alternate title: A SONG OF DEFEAT

**UNTITLED ("We reap and bind the bitter yield")**
Alternate title: HARVEST

**UNTITLED ("We, the winds that walk the world")**
Alternate title: THE WINDS THAT WALK THE WORLD

**UNTITLED ("We're a jolly good bunch of buns")**
Alternate title: CODE

**UNTITLED ("What's become of Waring")**
First appeared in THE LAST OF THE TRUNK OCH BREV I URVAL (Chpbk.)
    THE COLLECTED LETTERS OF ROBERT E. HOWARD, VOLUME 1: 1923-1929
    From a letter to TCS, ca. Fall 1927 ("Salaam: / Then the little boy said . . .")

**UNTITLED ("When I was a youth")**
Alternate title: WHEN I WAS A YOUTH

**UNTITLED ("When Napoleon down in Africa")**
First appeared in AUSTIN, VOLUME 3, #1 (Chpbk., facsimile reproduction of original letter)
    THE NEW HOWARD READER #4 (Chpbk.)
    THE LAST OF THE TRUNK OCH BREV I URVAL (Chpbk.)
    THE COLLECTED LETTERS OF ROBERT E. HOWARD, VOLUME 1: 1923-1929
    From a letter to TCS, June 8, 1923 ("Hello Clyde, / May the blessings . . .")

**UNTITLED ("When the first winds of summer . . .")**
Alternate title: TO HARRY THE OLIAD MAN

**UNTITLED ("When wolf meets wolf")**
Alternate title: WHEN WOLF MEETS WOLF

**UNTITLED ("When you were a set-up and I was a ham")**
Alternate title: WHEN YOU WERE A SET-UP AND I WAS A HAM

**UNTITLED ("Where the jungles lay dank, exuding")**
Alternate title: WHEN THE GODS WERE KINGS

**UNTITLED ("Who is Grandpa Theobold?")**
Alternate title: WHO IS GRANDPA THEOBOLD?

**UNTITLED ("Wide and free ranging . . .")**
Alternate title: THE DESERT

**UNTITLED ("The wild bees hum . . .")**
Alternate title: LAND OF THE PIONEER

**UNTITLED ("The wine in my cup is . . .")**
Alternate title: A SONG FROM AN EBONY HEART

**UNTITLED ("A wizard who dwelt in Drumnakill")**
Alternate title: MYSTIC LORE

**UNTITLED ("Wolf on the height")**
Alternate title: SONG OF THE PICT

**UNTITLED ("The women come and the women go")**
Alternate title: THE SLAYER

**UNTITLED ("The world goes back to the primitive, yea")**
First appeared in THE COLLECTED LETTERS OF ROBERT E. HOWARD, VOLUME 1: 1923-1929
    From a letter to TCS, ca. January 1928 ("Salaam: / Listen, you crumb . . .")

**UNTITLED ("The world has changed")**
Alternate title: MANKIND

**UNTITLED ("The world is rife, say I")**
Alternate title: FREEDOM

**UNTITLED ("The years are as a knife . . .")**
Alternate title: THE YEARS ARE AS A KNIFE

**UNTITLED ("You have built a world of paper and wood")**
Alternate title: A WARNING (partial version)

**UNTITLED ("You lolled in gardens where breezes fanned")**
Alternate title: A SONG OF THE NAKED LANDS

**UP JOHN KANE!**
First appeared in UP JOHN KANE! AND OTHER POEMS (Chpbk.)
    THE NEW HOWARD READER #3 (Chpbk.)

**VICTORY**
First appeared in NIGHT IMAGES

**THE VIKING OF THE SKY**
First appeared in AUSTIN, VOLUME 3, #3 (Chpbk., facsimile reproduction of original letter)
    THE NEW HOWARD READER #2 (Chpbk.)
    THE LAST OF THE TRUNK OCH BREV I URVAL (Chpbk.)
    THE COLLECTED LETTERS OF ROBERT E. HOWARD, VOLUME 3: 1933-1936
    From a letter to TCS, undated ("If you dont publish this . . .")

**VIKING'S TRAIL**
First appeared in VERSES IN EBONY (Chpbk.)
    NIGHT IMAGES
    THE ULTIMATE TRIUMPH

**VIKING'S VISION**
First appeared in THE GHOST OCEAN AND OTHER POEMS OF THE SUPERNATURAL (Chpbk.)

**A VISION**
Alternate title: BLACK MASS
First appeared in STARTLING MYSTERY STORIES, Fall 1967
    ECHOES FROM AN IRON HARP

**VISIONS**
First appeared in THE HOWARD COLLECTOR #16
    NIGHT IMAGES
    FANTASY CROSSROADS, SPECIAL EDITION #1
    DARK FANTASY #11 (Chpbk., Canadian)
    THE HOWARD COLLECTOR, Ace
    THE RAVEN #1 (Chpbk.)
    ABSINTHE PIE #14 (Chpbk.)
    THE WINDS OF TIME

**VOICES OF THE NIGHT**
Alternate title: ECHOING SHADOWS; THE IRON HARP (2)
A group of five poems: "The Voices Waken Memory"; "Babel"; "Laughter in the Gulfs"; "Moon Shame"; and "A
    Crown for a King"

## THE VOICES WAKEN MEMORY
Alternate title: A DRUM BEGINS TO THROB; OUT OF THE DEEP (original title)
First appeared in FANTASY FAN, September 1934
THE NEW HIEROGLYPH, March 1944
ALWAYS COMES EVENING
VOICES OF THE NIGHT AND OTHER POEMS (Chpbk.)
CHANTS DE GUERRE ET DE MORT
TO YITH AND BEYOND (Chpbk., lines 1-18)
THE HOWARD REVIEW #13 (Chpbk.)
WEST IS WEST AND OTHERS
ROBERT E. HOWARD IN THE FANTASY FAN (Chpbk.)
THE GARDEN OF FEAR: THE WEIRD WORKS OF ROBERT E. HOWARD, VOLUME 6
Part 1 of 5 of the "Voices of the Night" cycle

## THE WANDERER
First appeared in A RHYME OF SALEM TOWN AND OTHER POEMS (Chpbk. & HB)
Incomplete

## WAR TO THE BLIND
First appeared in FANTASY CROSSROADS #4/5
THE NEW HOWARD READER #3 (Chpbk.)

## A WARNING (complete verse)
First appeared in ECHOES FROM AN IRON HARP
The complete version is somewhat different from the partial; the partial is only 16 lines, with lines 1-2, 5-8, and
13-16 being identical to lines 9-10 and 17-24 of the 24 lines "complete" poem

## A WARNING (partial verse, "You have built a world of paper and wood")
Alternate title: Untitled ("You have builded a world of paper and wood")
First appeared in THE HOWARD COLLECTOR #5
IS #6
RUNES OF AHRH EIH ECHE (Chpbk.)
THE HOWARD COLLECTOR, Ace
DARK VALLEY DESTINY (Anth., lines 9-12)
EIN TRAUMER AUS TEXAS (Chpbk., German, lines 1-4)
ROBERT E. HOWARD: SELECTED LETTERS: 1923-1930 (Chpbk.)
DEAR AUGUST: LETTERS, ROBERT E. HOWARD TO AUGUST DERLETH, 1932-1936 (Chpbk.)
THE LAST OF THE TRUNK OCH BREV I URVAL (Chpbk.)
CRIMSON SHADOWS: THE BEST OF ROBERT E. HOWARD, VOLUME 1
THE COLLECTED LETTERS OF ROBERT E. HOWARD, VOLUME 3: 1933-1936
From a letter to August Derleth, May 9, 1936, ("I am indeed sorry to learn of the deaths . . ."); the complete
version is somewhat different from the partial; the partial is only 16 lines, with lines 1-2, 5-8, and 13-
16 being identical to lines 9-10 and 17-24 of the 24 lines "complete" poem

## A WARNING TO ORTHODOXY
First appeared in SHADOWS OF DREAMS
THE LAST OF THE TRUNK OCH BREV I URVAL (Chpbk.)
THE COLLECTED LETTERS OF ROBERT E. HOWARD, VOLUME 1: 1923-1929
From a letter to TCS, ca. July 1928 ("Salaam: / A Warning to Orthodoxy")

## WAS I THERE?
Alternate title: Untitled ("I, was I there")
First appeared in A RHYME OF SALEM TOWN AND OTHER POEMS (Chpbk. & HB)

## THE WEAKLING
First appeared in A ROBERT E. HOWARD MEMORIAL: JUNE 13-15, 1986 (Chpbk.)
   THE NEW HOWARD READER #4 (Chpbk.)

## A WEIRD BALLAD ("The werewolf came across the hill")
First appeared in SHADOWS OF DREAMS
   THE COLLECTED LETTERS OF ROBERT E. HOWARD, VOLUME 2: 1930-1932
   From a letter to TCS, ca. April 1932 ("Fear Finn: / I heard from that bone-crushing . . .")

## WEST
First appeared in A RHYME OF SALEM TOWN AND OTHER POEMS (Chpbk. & HB)

## WHAT IS LOVE?
First appeared in THE RIGHT HOOK, VOLUME 1, #2 (Chpbk.)
   AUSTIN, VOLUME 3, #2 (Chpbk.)
   THE NEW HOWARD READER #5 (Chpbk.)

## THE WHEEL OF DESTINY
Alternate title: DOOM
First appeared in A RHYME OF SALEM TOWN AND OTHER POEMS (Chpbk. & HB)

## WHEN DEATH DROPS HER VEIL
Alternate title: Untitled ("A thousand years, perhaps, have come and gone")
First appeared in UP JOHN KANE! AND OTHER POEMS (Chpbk.)
   THE NEW HOWARD READER #5 (Chpbk.)

## WHEN I WAS A YOUTH
Alternate title: Untitled ("When I was a youth")
First appeared in A RHYME OF SALEM TOWN AND OTHER POEMS (Chpbk. & HB)

## WHEN I WAS IN AFRICA
First appeared in A RHYME OF SALEM TOWN AND OTHER POEMS (Chpbk. & HB)

## WHEN MEN WERE BOLD
Alternate title: Untitled ("Now hark to this tale of long ago")
First appeared in A RHYME OF SALEM TOWN AND OTHER POEMS (Chpbk. & HB)
   Unfinished

## WHEN THE GLACIERS RUMBLED SOUTH
Alternate title: Untitled ("I cut my teeth on toil and pain")
First appeared in THE GHOST OCEAN AND OTHER POEMS OF THE SUPERNATURAL (Chpbk.)
   THE HOWARD READER #8 (Chpbk.)

## WHEN THE GODS WERE KINGS
Alternate title: Untitled ("Where the jungles lay dank, exuding")
First appeared in SPOOR ANTHOLOGY #1 (Chpbk.)
   NIGHT IMAGES

**WHEN WOLF MEETS WOLF**
Alternate title: Untitled ("When wolf meets wolf")
First appeared in THE GOLDEN CALIPH (Chpbk.)
    THE LAST CELT

**WHEN YOU WERE A SET-UP AND I WAS A HAM**
Alternate title: Untitled ("When you were a set-up and I was a ham")
First appeared in REH FIGHT MAGAZINE #2 (Chpbk.)
    BOXING STORIES
    THE LAST OF THE TRUNK OCH BREV I URVAL (Chpbk.)
    THE COLLECTED LETTERS OF ROBERT E. HOWARD, VOLUME 1: 1923-1929
    From a letter to TCS, May 24, 1925 ("Salaam; / Hot zowie, old topper . . .")

**WHERE ARE YOUR KNIGHTS, DONN OTHNA?**
Alternate title: Untitled ("Now that the kings have fallen")
First appeared in THE HOWARD COLLECTOR #11
    ECHOES FROM AN IRON HARP
    EIN TRAUMER AUS TEXAS (Chpbk.)
    PFADE INS FANTASTIQUE, BOOK 1 (Chpbk.)
    WINDS OF TIME

**WHICH WILL SCARCELY BE UNDERSTOOD**
First appeared in WEIRD TALES, October 1937
    SKULL-FACE AND OTHERS
    DARK OF THE MOON (Anth.)
    ALWAYS COMES EVENING
    SKULL-FACE OMNIBUS
    RHYMES OF DEATH (Chpbk.)
    THE SECOND BOOK OF ROBERT E. HOWARD
    SKULL-FACE OMNIBUS, VOLUME 1 (SKULL-FACE AND OTHERS)
    THE DARK BARBARIAN (Anth., lines 1, 7-9, 13, 19-26)
    ROSTRO DE CALAVERA (Spanish)
    EIN TRAUMER AUS TEXAS (Chpbk.)
    CHANTS DE GUERRE ET DE MORT
    SWORD #4 (Chpbk., Spanish)
    PALE HORSE, unknown number (Chpbk.)
    THE COUNT OF THIRTY: A TRIBUTE TO RAMSEY CAMPBELL (Chpbk., lines 42-45)
    THE OSSUARY OF ACHERON (Chpbk., lines 42-45)
    THE WEIRD WRITINGS OF ROBERT E. HOWARD, VOLUME TWO
    THE GRIM LAND: THE BEST OF ROBERT E. HOWARD, VOLUME 2

**WHISPERS**
First appeared in SHADOWS OF DREAMS
    THE COLLECTED LETTERS OF ROBERT E. HOWARD, VOLUME 2: 1930-1932
    From a letter to TCS, ca. March 1930 ("Well Fear Finn: / I trust you are . . .")

**WHISPERS ON THE NIGHTWINDS**
First appeared in SHADOWS OF DREAMS
    THE COLLECTED LETTERS OF ROBERT E. HOWARD, VOLUME 2: 1930-1932
    ZMIERZCH NAD STONEHENGE (Polish)
    From a letter to TCS, ca. April 1930 ("Well, Fear Finn, you mention . . .")

**WHITE THUNDER**
First appeared in SINGERS IN THE SHADOWS
    EIN TRAUMER AUS TEXAS (Chpbk.)

**WHO IS GRANDPA THEOBOLD?**
Alternate title: Untitled ("Cities brooding beneath the seas")
First appeared in THE HOWARD COLLECTOR #6
    HPL (Chpbk.)
    ECHOES FROM AN IRON HARP
    ROBERT E. HOWARD: SELECTED LETTERS: 1931-1936 (Chpbk.)
    THE COLLECTED LETTERS OF ROBERT E. HOWARD, VOLUME 2: 1930-1932
    Originally untitled, from a letter to TCS, ca. November 1931 ("Fear Finn: / I wrote Bradford . . .")

**WHO SHALL SING OF BABYLON?**
Alternate title: Untitled ("High the towers and mighty . . .")
First appeared in A RHYME OF SALEM TOWN AND OTHER POEMS (Chpbk. & HB)

**THE WHOOPANSAT OF HUMOROUS KOOKOOYAM**
First appeared in RISQUE STORIES #2 (Chpbk.)
    THE NEW HOWARD READER #1 (Chpbk.)

**THE WINDS OF THE SEA (1, "Over the hills the winds . . .")**
Alternate title: Untitled ("Over the hills the winds . . .")
First appeared in A RHYME OF SALEM TOWN AND OTHER POEMS (Chpbk. & HB)

**THE WINDS OF THE SEA (2, "Over the hills the winds . . .")**
First appeared in THE LAST OF THE TRUNK OCH BREV I URVAL (Chpbk.)
    THE COLLECTED LETTERS OF ROBERT E. HOWARD, VOLUME 3: 1933-1936
    From a letter to TCS, undated ("The Seeker thrust . . ."); a 16-line version

**THE WINDS THAT WALK THE WORLD**
Alternate title: Untitled ("We, the winds that walk the world")
First appeared in A RHYME OF SALEM TOWN AND OTHER POEMS (Chpbk. & HB)

**THE WITCH**
First appeared in SINGERS IN THE SHADOWS

**A WORD FROM THE OUTER DARK**
First appeared in KADATH #1 (Chpbk.)
    THE SECOND BOOK OF ROBERT E. HOWARD
    NIGHT IMAGES
    HEAVY METAL #3
    MIRROR OF FANTASY #5 (Chpbk., German)
    HARDWIRED HINTERLAND #6 (Chpbk.)
    THE ULTIMATE TRIUMPH
    CRIMSON SHADOWS: THE BEST OF ROBERT E. HOWARD, VOLUME 1

**THE WORSHIPPERS**
First appeared in A RHYME OF SALEM TOWN AND OTHER POEMS (Chpbk. & HB)

## THE YEARS ARE AS A KNIFE
Alternate title: Untitled ("The years are as a knife . . .")
First appeared in MAGAZINE OF HORROR #19
    ECHOES FROM AN IRON HARP

## YESTERDAYS
First appeared in A RHYME OF SALEM TOWN AND OTHER POEMS (Chpbk. & HB)

## YODELS OF GOOD SNEER TO THE PIPPLE, DAMN THEM
First appeared in THE COLLECTED LETTERS OF ROBERT E. HOWARD, VOLUME 1: 1923-1929
    From a letter to TCS, ca. November 1928 ("Salaam: / I'll swear . . .")

## YOUNG LOCKANBARS
First appeared in THE GOLDEN CALIPH, 1922 or 1923 (Chpbk.)
    THE LAST CELT

## A YOUNG WIFE'S TALE
First appeared in RISQUE STORIES #5 (Chpbk.)
    THE NEW HOWARD READER #2 (Chpbk.)
    THE LAST OF THE TRUNK OCH BREV I URVAL (Chpbk.)
    THE COLLECTED LETTERS OF ROBERT E. HOWARD, VOLUME 1: 1923-1929
    From a letter to TCS, ca. June 1928 ("Salaam; / Ho, ho, the long lights . . .")

## YOUTH SPOKE – NOT IN ANGER
Alternate title: LIFE

## ZUKALA'S HOUR
First appeared in SINGERS IN THE SHADOWS
    FANTASIA #11/12 (Chpbk., German, lines 37-40)
    THE DARK BARBARIAN (Anth., lines 37-44)
    EIN TRAUMER AUS TEXAS (Chpbk., lines 37-40)
    ONION TOPS #15 (Chpbk.)

## ZUKALA'S JEST
First appeared in WHISPERS #5
    THE NEW HOWARD READER #3 (Chpbk.)
    ONION TOPS #15 (Chpbk.)

## ZUKALA'S LOVE SONG
Alternate title: ZUKALA'S MATING SONG
First appeared in THE DARK BARBARIAN (Anth., lines 42, 54, 55, 80)
    WEIRD TALES #302, Fall 1991 (HB, Limited HB and PB, first complete appearance)
    THE NEW HOWARD READER #2 (Chpbk.)
    ONION TOPS #15 (Chpbk.)

## ZUKALA'S MATING SONG
Alternate title: ZUKALA'S LOVE SONG
    This is a slightly variant version of the last portion of "Zukala's Love Song"

**THE ZULU LORD**
Alternate title: Untitled ("This is the tale the Kaffirs tell . . .")
First appeared in FANTASY TALES, Winter 1983
        WEIRD TALES #303, Winter 1991-1992
        THE NEW HOWARD READER #4 (Chpbk.)

**ZULULAND**
Alternate title: Untitled ("This is no land for weaklings, . . .")
First appeared in A RHYME OF SALEM TOWN AND OTHER POEMS (Chpbk. & HB)

# LETTERS INDEX

REH enjoyed corresponding with many of his friends, as well as agents, magazines, and other authors or admirers. This index contains a listing of all the known letters that REH wrote. It is likely that he wrote numerous other letters, perhaps multiples of the amount listed here, but they have been lost over the course of time. It is certainly possible that more may be discovered someday.

Most REH letters are typewritten, as his handwriting was atrocious. If I know of one being handwritten, I have noted it as such.

Generally, salutions are not included here in referencing a letter. However, with regard to those letters to TCS, I have included the saluations, as they can be quite varied and interesting. The line break between the saluation and the body of the letter is indicated by a "/".

This index is sorted as follows. The letters are sorted by correspondent's last name, or company or magazine name. Under each correspondent, letters are sorted by date written, as best as can be determined. The date of some letters are estimated, based on scholarly analysis of the contents. Letters of indeterminate date are added at the end of each correspondent's listing. Beneath each letter listing are all known publications of the particular letter.

There are approximately 349 letters in this list.

Some letters, especially those to TCS, may also include short stories or poetry. Note is made here whether the extra work is published with the letter or not in each publication, and whether or not the extra work has been published separately. Any poetry will also be listed in the Verse Index, any prose will also be in the Prose Index. Poetry or Prose in **BOLD** are **First Appearance** in the referenced letter.

This list includes publications in English as well as non-English, as there are relatively few of the latter. Some of the publications listed here can be found in the BOOKS IN ENGLISH list. Publications with (Anth.) at the end can be found in the ANTHOLOGIES list. Publications with (Chpbk.) at the end can be found in the CHAPBOOKS list. Publications that are periodicals, such as pulps or magazines, can be found in the PERIODICALS list. Non-English publications can be found in either the NON-ENGLISH BOOK list, CHAPBOOK list, or PERIODICALS list, as appropriate.

If multiple books have the same title but differing contents, I have listed the publisher as well, to indicate which book is appropriate. Poetry is indicated by (v).

### *Format of Entries*
### To Whom, date, first few words
      Other prose or poetry contents
First appeared in: [If published]
      All other publications of the letter
      Notes

## *TO ADVENTURE MAGAZINE (2)*

**To Adventure, ca. early 1924, Question? I am writing . . .**
First appeared in ADVENTURE, March 20, 1924
    THE NEW HOWARD READER #6 (Chpbk.)
    WEST IS WEST AND OTHERS
    THE COLLECTED LETTERS OF ROBERT E. HOWARD, VOLUME 1: 1923-1929
    **This is the first appearance of REH's name in a pulp magazine, at the age of 18**

**To Adventure, 1924, At what period did the feudal system flourish most. . .**
First appeared in ADVENTURE, August 20, 1924
    THE NEW HOWARD READER #7 (Chpbk.)
    WEST IS WEST AND OTHERS
    THE COLLECTED LETTERS OF ROBERT E. HOWARD, VOLUME 1: 1923-1929

## *TO ARGOSY ALL-STORY WEEKLY MAGAZINE (1)*

**To Argosy All-Story Weekly Magazine, ca. Spring 1929, I was born in Texas about twenty-three . . .**
First appeared in ARGOSY ALL-STORY WEEKLY MAGAZINE, July 20, 1929
    IN THE TOMBS OF KHEMI (Chpbk.)
    THE NEW HOWARD READER #2 (Chpbk.)
    ROBERT E. HOWARD: THE POWER OF THE WRITING MIND
    THE COLLECTED LETTERS OF ROBERT E. HOWARD, VOLUME 1: 1923-1929

## *TO BARLOW, ROBERT H. (8)*

**To Robert H. Barlow, ca. December 1932, Price tells me you are interested . . .**
First appeared in ZARFHAANA #42 (Chpbk.)
    THE NEW HOWARD READER #2 (Chpbk.)
    THE COLLECTED LETTERS OF ROBERT E. HOWARD, VOLUME 2: 1930-1932

**To Robert H. Barlow, ca. December 1932, I'll be glad to sign the title . . .**
First appeared in ZARFHAANA #42 (Chpbk.)
    THE NEW HOWARD READER #1 (Chpbk.)
    THE COLLECTED LETTERS OF ROBERT E. HOWARD, VOLUME 2: 1930-1932

**To Robert H. Barlow, ca. April 2, 1933, Here are some notes . . .**
First appeared in ZARFHAANA #42 (Chpbk.)
    THE NEW HOWARD READER #4 (Chpbk.)
    THE COLLECTED LETTERS OF ROBERT E. HOWARD, VOLUME 3: 1933-1936

**To Robert H. Barlow, June 1, 1934, Concerning the illustrations you . . .**
First appeared in THE HOWARD COLLECTOR #18
    RUNES OF AHRH EIH ECHE (Chpbk.)
    THE HOWARD COLLECTOR, Ace
    ZARFHAANA #42 (Chpbk.)
    THE COLLECTED LETTERS OF ROBERT E. HOWARD, VOLUME 3: 1933-1936

**To Robert H. Barlow, June 14, 1934, If I ever decide to dispose . . .**
First appeared in THE HOWARD COLLECTOR #18
    RUNES OF AHRH EIH ECHE (Chpbk.)
    THE HOWARD COLLECTOR, Ace

ZARFHAANA #42 (Chpbk.)
THE COLLECTED LETTERS OF ROBERT E. HOWARD, VOLUME 3: 1933-1936

**To Robert H. Barlow, July 5, 1934, Here, at last, is the last . . .**
First appeared in ZARFHAANA #42
THE NEW HOWARD READER #5 (Chpbk.)
THE COLLECTED LETTERS OF ROBERT E. HOWARD, VOLUME 3: 1933-1936

**To Robert H. Barlow, Dec 17, 1935, Thank you very much for the copy . . .**
First appeared in THE LAST OF THE TRUNK OCH BREV I URVAL (Chpbk.)
THE COLLECTED LETTERS OF ROBERT E. HOWARD, VOLUME 3: 1933-1936

**To Robert H. Barlow, February 14, 1936, This is to express, somewhat belatedly . . .**
First appeared in ZARFHAANA #42 (Chpbk.)
THE NEW HOWARD READER #3 (Chpbk.)
THE COLLECTED LETTERS OF ROBERT E. HOWARD, VOLUME 3: 1933-1936

## *TO BATES, HARRY (1)*

**To Harry Bates, June 1, 1931, You may, or you may not . . .**
First appeared in SPEARS OF CLONTARF (Chpbk.)
MORGAN VISITS PULP-CON (Chpbk.)
THE COLLECTED LETTERS OF ROBERT E. HOWARD, VOLUME 2: 1930-1932

## *TO BYRNE, JACK (1)*

**To Jack Byrne, April 21, 1936, My agent, O.A. Kline, tells me . . .**
Also contains *The Diablos Trail (synopsis)*
First appeared in THE COLLECTED LETTERS OF ROBERT E. HOWARD, VOLUME 3: 1933-1936
This letter is unfinished, and apparently was never sent; it includes an incomplete outline for the very first proposed Pike Bearfield story, "The Diablos Trail"

## *TO THE CALIFORNIAN MAGAZINE (1)*

**To The Californian Magazine, 1936, Thank you very much . . .**
First appeared in THE CALIFORNIAN, Summer 1936
WEST IS WEST AND OTHERS
THE LAST OF THE TRUNK OCH BREV I URVAL (Chpbk.)
THE COLLECTED LETTERS OF ROBERT E. HOWARD, VOLUME 3: 1933-1936

## *TO CLAYTONS MAGAZINES (1)*

**To The Claytons Magazines, June 13, 1933, A few weeks ago . . .**
First appeared in THE LAST OF THE TRUNK OCH BREV I URVAL (Chpbk.)
THE COLLECTED LETTERS OF ROBERT E. HOWARD, VOLUME 3: 1933-1936

## *TO DENIS ARCHER, PUBLISHER (2)*

**To Denis Archer, May 20, 1934, As you doubtless remember . . .**
First appeared in XENOPHILE #18
ULTIMA THULE #1 (Chpbk.)
THE LAST CELT, Grant, a reproduction of the original letter

DREAMS FROM YOHANETH-LAHAI #38 (Chpbk.)
THE COLLECTED LETTERS OF ROBERT E. HOWARD, VOLUME 3: 1933-1936

**To Denis Archer, May 22, 1934, As you doubtless remember . . .**
First appeared in THE LAST OF THE TRUNK OCH BREV I URVAL (Chpbk.)
THE COLLECTED LETTERS OF ROBERT E. HOWARD, VOLUME 3: 1933-1936
The difference between this letter and the one listed immediately before is that the first letter says Hour of the
Dragon is coming under separate cover, the second letter says enclosed herewith; so either the first is a
draft, or, it was sent first and the second letter included with the actual story, which may have taken
longer to arrive, as a bulkier package

## *TO DERLETH, AUGUST (31) (All available via State Historical Society of Wisconsin)*

**To August Derleth, ca. December (15?) 1932, I had intended answering . . .**
First appeared in DEAR AUGUST: LETTERS, ROBERT E. HOWARD TO AUGUST DERLETH, 1932-1936
(Chpbk.)
THE COLLECTED LETTERS OF ROBERT E. HOWARD, VOLUME 2: 1930-1932

**To August Derleth, ca. December (29?) 1932, I read your recent letter with the greatest interest . . .**
First appeared in IS #6 (Chpbk.)
ROBERT E. HOWARD: SELECTED LETTERS: 1931-1936 (Chpbk.)
DEAR AUGUST: LETTERS, ROBERT E. HOWARD TO AUGUST DERLETH, 1932-1936 (Chpbk.)
THE COLLECTED LETTERS OF ROBERT E. HOWARD, VOLUME 2: 1930-1932

**To August Derleth, ca. January 1933, I was much interested in your accounts . . .**
First appeared in AMRA, VOLUME 2, #30 (excerpt only)
THE CONAN SWORDBOOK (Anth.)
THE NEW HOWARD READER #3 (Chpbk.)
DEAR AUGUST: LETTERS, ROBERT E. HOWARD TO AUGUST DERLETH, 1932-1936 (Chpbk., first
full publication)
THE BLACK STRANGER AND OTHER AMERICAN TALES (excerpt only)
WEST IS WEST AND OTHERS
THE COLLECTED LETTERS OF ROBERT E. HOWARD, VOLUME 3: 1933-1936

**To August Derleth, ca. February 1933, After so long a time, I'm getting around to answering . . .**
First appeared in IS #6 (Chpbk.)
THE NEW HOWARD READER #4 (Chpbk.)
DEAR AUGUST: LETTERS, ROBERT E. HOWARD TO AUGUST DERLETH, 1932-1936 (Chpbk.)
THE COLLECTED LETTERS OF ROBERT E. HOWARD, VOLUME 3: 1933-1936

**To August Derleth, ca. March 1933, I should have told you that I meant to keep . . .**
First appeared in IS #6 (Chpbk.)
THE NEW HOWARD READER #2 (Chpbk.)
DEAR AUGUST: LETTERS, ROBERT E. HOWARD TO AUGUST DERLETH, 1932-1936 (Chpbk.)
THE COLLECTED LETTERS OF ROBERT E. HOWARD, VOLUME 3: 1933-1936

**To August Derleth, ca. March 13, 1933, Many thanks for FRONTIER GENERATIONS . . .**
First appeared in DEAR AUGUST: LETTERS, ROBERT E. HOWARD TO AUGUST DERLETH, 1932-1936
(Chpbk.)
THE COLLECTED LETTERS OF ROBERT E. HOWARD, VOLUME 3: 1933-1936

**To August Derleth, ca. December 1933, I think Scribner's was nuts to turn down "Hawk on . . .**
First appeared in IS #6 (Chpbk.)
    ROBERT E. HOWARD: SELECTED LETTERS: 1931-1936 (Chpbk.)
    DEAR AUGUST: LETTERS, ROBERT E. HOWARD TO AUGUST DERLETH, 1932-1936 (Chpbk.)
    WEST IS WEST AND OTHERS
    THE COLLECTED LETTERS OF ROBERT E. HOWARD, VOLUME 3: 1933-1936

**To August Derleth, ca. December 1933, Hope you had a good Christmas . . .**
First appeared in DEAR AUGUST: LETTERS, ROBERT E. HOWARD TO AUGUST DERLETH, 1932-1936
    (Chpbk.)
    THE COLLECTED LETTERS OF ROBERT E. HOWARD, VOLUME 3: 1933-1936

**To August Derleth, ca. January 1934, I note with sympathy your remarks . . .**
First appeared in DEAR AUGUST: LETTERS, ROBERT E. HOWARD TO AUGUST DERLETH, 1932-1936
    (Chpbk.)
    THE COLLECTED LETTERS OF ROBERT E. HOWARD, VOLUME 3: 1933-1936

**To August Derleth, ca. late March 1934, Pardon this belated letter . . .**
First appeared in DEAR AUGUST: LETTERS, ROBERT E. HOWARD TO AUGUST DERLETH, 1932-1936
    (Chpbk.)
    THE COLLECTED LETTERS OF ROBERT E. HOWARD, VOLUME 3: 1933-1936

**To August Derleth, May 30 1934, I have a feeling that I've been owing . . .**
First appeared in DEAR AUGUST: LETTERS, ROBERT E. HOWARD TO AUGUST DERLETH, 1932-1936
    (Chpbk.)
    THE COLLECTED LETTERS OF ROBERT E. HOWARD, VOLUME 3: 1933-1936

**To August Derleth, ca. June 1934, Having completed several weeks of . . .**
First appeared in DEAR AUGUST: LETTERS, ROBERT E. HOWARD TO AUGUST DERLETH, 1932-1936
    (Chpbk.)
    THE COLLECTED LETTERS OF ROBERT E. HOWARD, VOLUME 3: 1933-1936

**To August Derleth, ca. mid-October 1934, I haven't yet gotten a copy . . .**
First appeared in DEAR AUGUST: LETTERS, ROBERT E. HOWARD TO AUGUST DERLETH, 1932-1936
    (Chpbk.)
    THE COLLECTED LETTERS OF ROBERT E. HOWARD, VOLUME 3: 1933-1936

**To August Derleth, December 11, 1934, I recently found your letter of October 18 in my file . . .**
First appeared in IS #6 (Chpbk.)
    THE NEW HOWARD READER #1 (Chpbk.)
    DEAR AUGUST: LETTERS, ROBERT E. HOWARD TO AUGUST DERLETH, 1932-1936 (Chpbk.)
    THE COLLECTED LETTERS OF ROBERT E. HOWARD, VOLUME 3: 1933-1936

**To August Derleth, ca. February 1935, I would have written you long ago . . .**
First appeared in DEAR AUGUST: LETTERS, ROBERT E. HOWARD TO AUGUST DERLETH, 1932-1936
    (Chpbk.)
    THE COLLECTED LETTERS OF ROBERT E. HOWARD, VOLUME 3: 1933-1936

**To August Derleth, ca. June 1935, I reckon you've wondered at times . . .**
First appeared in DEAR AUGUST: LETTERS, ROBERT E. HOWARD TO AUGUST DERLETH, 1932-1936
    (Chpbk.)
    THE COLLECTED LETTERS OF ROBERT E. HOWARD, VOLUME 3: 1933-1936

**To August Derleth, June 20, 1935, This card was purchased in Lincoln . . .**
First appeared in THE LAST OF THE TRUNK OCH BREV I URVAL (Chpbk.)
    THE COLLECTED LETTERS OF ROBERT E. HOWARD, VOLUME 3: 1933-1936
    This is a post card

**To August Derleth, July 4, 1935, Thanks very much for the article, "Afternoon in June." . . .**
First appeared in IS #6 (Chpbk.)
    ROBERT E. HOWARD: SELECTED LETTERS: 1931-1936 (Chpbk.)
    DEAR AUGUST: LETTERS, ROBERT E. HOWARD TO AUGUST DERLETH, 1932-1936 (Chpbk.)
    THE COLLECTED LETTERS OF ROBERT E. HOWARD, VOLUME 3: 1933-1936

**To August Derleth, November 1, 1935, I should have written you months ago . . .**
First appeared in DEAR AUGUST: LETTERS, ROBERT E. HOWARD TO AUGUST DERLETH, 1932-1936
    (Chpbk.)
    THE COLLECTED LETTERS OF ROBERT E. HOWARD, VOLUME 3: 1933-1936

**To August Derleth, November 28, 1935, Thanks for the opportunity of reading . . .**
First appeared in DEAR AUGUST: LETTERS, ROBERT E. HOWARD TO AUGUST DERLETH, 1932-1936
    (Chpbk.)
    THE COLLECTED LETTERS OF ROBERT E. HOWARD, VOLUME 3: 1933-1936

**To August Derleth, April 15, 1936, Just a hurried line to let you know . . .**
First appeared in DEAR AUGUST: LETTERS, ROBERT E. HOWARD TO AUGUST DERLETH, 1932-1936
    (Chpbk.)
    THE COLLECTED LETTERS OF ROBERT E. HOWARD, VOLUME 3: 1933-1936

**To August Derleth, May 9, 1936, I am indeed sorry to learn of the deaths . . .**
    Also contains *Untitled ("You have built a world of paper and wood") (v)*
First appeared in THE HOWARD COLLECTOR #5
    IS #6 (Chpbk.)
    RUNES OF AHRH EIH ECHE (Chpbk.)
    THE HOWARD COLLECTOR, Ace
    ROBERT E. HOWARD: SELECTED LETTERS: 1931-1936 (Chpbk.)
    DEAR AUGUST: LETTERS, ROBERT E. HOWARD TO AUGUST DERLETH, 1932-1936 (Chpbk.)
    THE LAST OF THE TRUNK OCH BREV I URVAL (Chpbk.)
    THE COLLECTED LETTERS OF ROBERT E. HOWARD, VOLUME 3: 1933-1936
    The poem has been published separately

## *TO THE FANTASY FAN (3)*

**To The Fantasy Fan, ca. 1933, I find the Fantasy Fan . . .**
First appeared in FANTASY FAN, December 1933
    WEST IS WEST AND OTHERS
    ROBERT E. HOWARD IN THE FANTASY FAN (Chpbk.)
    THE COLLECTED LETTERS OF ROBERT E. HOWARD, VOLUME 3: 1933-1936

**To The Fantasy Fan, ca. late 1933, I liked the November issue . . .**
First appeared in FANTASY FAN, January 1934
    WEST IS WEST AND OTHERS
    ROBERT E. HOWARD IN THE FANTASY FAN (Chpbk.)
    THE COLLECTED LETTERS OF ROBERT E. HOWARD, VOLUME 3: 1933-1936

**To The Fantasy Fan, ca. 1934, Smith's poem in the March issue . . .**

First appeared in FANTASY FAN, May 1934
    WEST IS WEST AND OTHERS
    ROBERT E. HOWARD IN THE FANTASY FAN (Chpbk.)
    THE COLLECTED LETTERS OF ROBERT E. HOWARD, VOLUME 3: 1933-1936

## *TO THE FORT WORTH RECORD (1)*

**To The Ft. Worth Record, ca. July 1928, Tunney can't win . . .**
First appeared in FT. WORTH RECORD, July 20, 1928
    THE NEW HOWARD READER #3 (Chpbk.)
    WEST IS WEST AND OTHERS
    THE COLLECTED LETTERS OF ROBERT E. HOWARD, VOLUME 1: 1923-1929

## *TO GAFFORD, R. FOWLER (1)*

**To R. Fowler Gafford, May 20, 1934, This answer to your last letter . . .**
First appeared in THE LAST OF THE TRUNK OCH BREV I URVAL (Chpbk.)
    THE COLLECTED LETTERS OF ROBERT E. HOWARD, VOLUME 3: 1933-1936
    Letter was partly destroyed

## *TO GORDON, ROBERT W. (6)*

**To Robert W. Gordon, February 4, 1925, I am sending you a few songs . . .**
First appeared in SEANCHAI #60 (Chpbk.)
    THE NEW HOWARD READER #5 (Chpbk.)
    THE COLLECTED LETTERS OF ROBERT E. HOWARD, VOLUME 1: 1923-1929

**To Robert W. Gordon, February 15, 1926, I was delighted to receive your letter . . .**
First appeared in SEANCHAI #60 (Chpbk.)
    THE NEW HOWARD READER #2 (Chpbk.)
    THE COLLECTED LETTERS OF ROBERT E. HOWARD, VOLUME 1: 1923-1929

**To Robert W. Gordon, April 9, 1926, I must really ask your pardon, having . . .**
First appeared in SEANCHAI #64 (Chpbk.)
    THE NEW HOWARD READER #1 (Chpbk.)
    THE COLLECTED LETTERS OF ROBERT E. HOWARD, VOLUME 1: 1923-1929

**To Robert W. Gordon, January 2, 1927, Upon seeing a request of yours in a late . . .**
First appeared in SEANCHAI #60 (Chpbk.)
    THE NEW HOWARD READER #5 (Chpbk.)
    THE COLLECTED LETTERS OF ROBERT E. HOWARD, VOLUME 1: 1923-1929

**To Robert W. Gordon, March 17, 1927, This time I have an excuse for not having . . .**
First appeared in SEANCHAI #64 (Chpbk.)
    THE NEW HOWARD READER #4 (Chpbk.)
    THE COLLECTED LETTERS OF ROBERT E. HOWARD, VOLUME 1: 1923-1929

**To Robert W. Gordon, May 14, 1928, Many thanks for the letter, also the paper.**
First appeared in SEANCHAI #64 (Chpbk.)
    THE NEW HOWARD READER #3 (Chpbk.)
    THE COLLECTED LETTERS OF ROBERT E. HOWARD, VOLUME 1: 1923-1929

# *TO HORNIG, CHARLES D. (4)*

**To Charles D. Hornig, November 1, 1933, Thanks for the copy . . .**
First appeared in ROBERT E. HOWARD IN THE FANTASY FAN (Chpbk.)
  THE LAST OF THE TRUNK OCH BREV I URVAL (Chpbk.)
  THE COLLECTED LETTERS OF ROBERT E. HOWARD, VOLUME 3: 1933-1936

**To Charles D. Hornig, November 10, 1933, Here is a short story, "The Frost-King's Daughter" . . .**
First appeared in ECHOES OF VALOR II (Anth.)
  THE NEW HOWARD READER #7 (Chpbk.)
  ROBERT E. HOWARD IN THE FANTASY FAN (Chpbk.)
  THE COLLECTED LETTERS OF ROBERT E. HOWARD, VOLUME 3: 1933-1936

**To Charles D. Hornig, August 10, 1934, Glad you liked the verses . . .**
First appeared in THE LAST CELT (excerpt only, begins "Yes, I received a copy of 'The Battle That . . .'")
  ROBERT E. HOWARD IN THE FANTASY FAN (Chpbk.)
  THE COLLECTED LETTERS OF ROBERT E. HOWARD, VOLUME 3: 1933-1936

**To Charles D. Hornig, May 3, 1935, I'm very sorry . . .**
First appeared in ROBERT E. HOWARD IN THE FANTASY FAN (Chpbk.)
  THE LAST OF THE TRUNK OCH BREV I URVAL (Chpbk.)
  THE COLLECTED LETTERS OF ROBERT E. HOWARD, VOLUME 3: 1933-1936

# *TO JACOBI, CARL (3)*

**To Carl Jacobi, pm, March 22, 1932, I found your recent letter very interesting . . .**
First appeared in LOST IN THE RENTHARPIAN HILLS (Chpbk.)
  THE NEW HOWARD READER #2 (Chpbk.)
  THE COLLECTED LETTERS OF ROBERT E. HOWARD, VOLUME 2: 1930-1932

**To Carl Jacobi, March 17, 1933, I am glad to write to Wright, commenting . . .**
First appeared in LOST IN THE RENTHARPIAN HILLS (Chpbk.)
  THE NEW HOWARD READER #1 (Chpbk.)
  THE COLLECTED LETTERS OF ROBERT E. HOWARD, VOLUME 3: 1933-1936

**To Carl Jacobi, ca. Summer 1934, Thank you for the kind comments . . .**
First appeared in THE HOWARD COLLECTOR #12
  RUNES OF AHRH EIH ECHE (Chpbk.)
  THE NEW HOWARD READER #5 (Chpbk.)
  THE COLLECTED LETTERS OF ROBERT E. HOWARD, VOLUME 3: 1933-1936

# *TO KLINE, OTIS ADELBERT (4)*

**To Otis Adelbert Kline, May 13, 1935, I'm writing this to ask . . .**
First appeared in THE LAST OF THE TRUNK OCH BREV I URVAL (Chpbk.)
  THE COLLECTED LETTERS OF ROBERT E. HOWARD, VOLUME 3: 1933-1936

**To Otis Adelbert Kline, January 8, 1936, A belated acknowledgment . . .**
First appeared in THE LAST OF THE TRUNK OCH BREV I URVAL (Chpbk.)
  THE COLLECTED LETTERS OF ROBERT E. HOWARD, VOLUME 3: 1933-1936

**To Otis Adelbert Kline, January 13, 1936, Just read yours of the 11th.**
First appeared in THE LAST OF THE TRUNK OCH BREV I URVAL (Chpbk.)
    THE COLLECTED LETTERS OF ROBERT E. HOWARD, VOLUME 3: 1933-1936

**To Otis Adelbert Kline, January 18, 1936, Just read your letter of the 15th.**
First appeared in THE LAST OF THE TRUNK OCH BREV I URVAL (Chpbk.)
    THE COLLECTED LETTERS OF ROBERT E. HOWARD, VOLUME 3: 1933-1936

## *TO KOFOED, WILLIAM (1)*

**To William Kofoed, Jan 8, 1935, Glad that Bloomfield can use "Fists of the Desert."**
First appeared in THE LAST OF THE TRUNK OCH BREV I URVAL (Chpbk.)
    THE COLLECTED LETTERS OF ROBERT E. HOWARD, VOLUME 3: 1933-1936

## *TO LENNIGER, AUGUST (3)*

**To August Lenniger, February 20, 1933, Here are the copies of "The Shadow Kingdom"** . . .
First appeared in ZARFHAANA #7 (Chpbk.)
    THE NEW HOWARD READER #3 (Chpbk.)
    THE COLLECTED LETTERS OF ROBERT E. HOWARD, VOLUME 3: 1933-1936

**To August Lenniger, March 8, 1933, This is to inform you that I have** . . .
First appeared in ZARFHAANA #7 (Chpbk.)
    THE NEW HOWARD READER #4 (Chpbk.)
    THE COLLECTED LETTERS OF ROBERT E. HOWARD, VOLUME 3: 1933-1936

**To August Lenniger, Dec 27, 1935, I have received your letter of the 17th.**
First appeared in THE LAST OF THE TRUNK OCH BREV I URVAL (Chpbk.)
    THE COLLECTED LETTERS OF ROBERT E. HOWARD, VOLUME 3: 1933-1936

## *TO LOVECRAFT, H.P. (53) (Those in SELECTED LETTERS may have been edited for racial content)*

**To H.P. Lovecraft, ca. July 1, 1930, I am indeed highly honored to have received** . . .
First appeared in ROBERT E. HOWARD: SELECTED LETTERS: 1923-1930 (Chpbk.)
    DEAR HPL: LETTERS, ROBERT E. HOWARD TO H.P. LOVECRAFT, 1930-1936 (Chpbk.)
    THE COLLECTED LETTERS OF ROBERT E. HOWARD, VOLUME 2: 1930-1932
    On the face of the letter someone has written in pencil "August 9, 1930"

**To H.P. Lovecraft, ca. August 1930, Let me first thank you for the opportunity** . . .
First appeared in ROBERT E. HOWARD: SELECTED LETTERS: 1923-1930 (Chpbk.)
    MOICHANIE IDOLA (Russian)
    DEAR HPL: LETTERS, ROBERT E. HOWARD TO H.P. LOVECRAFT, 1930-1936 (Chpbk.)
    THE COLLECTED LETTERS OF ROBERT E. HOWARD, VOLUME 2: 1930-1932

**To H.P. Lovecraft, ca. September 1930, I envy you your sojourn to Quebec.**
First appeared in ROBERT E. HOWARD: SELECTED LETTERS: 1923-1930 (Chpbk.)
    DEAR HPL: LETTERS, ROBERT E. HOWARD TO H.P. LOVECRAFT, 1930-1936 (Chpbk.)
    THE COLLECTED LETTERS OF ROBERT E. HOWARD, VOLUME 2: 1930-1932

**To H.P. Lovecraft, ca. September 1930, I am very glad that you enjoyed your visit . . .**
First appeared in ROBERT E. HOWARD: SELECTED LETTERS: 1923-1930 (Chpbk.)
 DEAR HPL: LETTERS, ROBERT E. HOWARD TO H.P. LOVECRAFT, 1930-1936 (Chpbk.)
 THE COLLECTED LETTERS OF ROBERT E. HOWARD, VOLUME 2: 1930-1932

**To H.P. Lovecraft, ca. October 1930, It is with greatest delight that I learn . . .**
 Also contains *Reuben's Brethren (v)*
First appeared in ROBERT E. HOWARD: SELECTED LETTERS: 1923-1930 (Chpbk.)
 DEAR HPL: LETTERS, ROBERT E. HOWARD TO H.P. LOVECRAFT, 1930-1936 (Chpbk.)
 THE COLLECTED LETTERS OF ROBERT E. HOWARD, VOLUME 2: 1930-1932
 The poem has been published separately

**To H.P. Lovecraft, ca. December 1930, As always, your letter proved highly . . .**
First appeared in ROBERT E. HOWARD: SELECTED LETTERS: 1923-1930 (Chpbk.)
 NO REFUGE (Chpbk.)
 DEAR HPL: LETTERS, ROBERT E. HOWARD TO H.P. LOVECRAFT, 1930-1936 (Chpbk.)
 THE COLLECTED LETTERS OF ROBERT E. HOWARD, VOLUME 2: 1930-1932

**To H.P. Lovecraft, ca. January 1931, As always I found your recent letter . . .**
First appeared in DEAR HPL: LETTERS, ROBERT E. HOWARD TO H.P. LOVECRAFT, 1930-1936 (Chpbk.)
 THE END OF THE TRAIL: WESTERN STORIES (excerpt only, contained in the article "Billy the Kid and
  the Lincoln County War")
 THE COLLECTED LETTERS OF ROBERT E. HOWARD, VOLUME 2: 1930-1932

**To H.P. Lovecraft, ca. January 1931, This is rather a belated letter thanking . . .**
First appeared in ZARFHAANA #33 (Chpbk.)
 DEAR HPL: LETTERS, ROBERT E. HOWARD TO H.P. LOVECRAFT, 1930-1936 (Chpbk.)
 THE COLLECTED LETTERS OF ROBERT E. HOWARD, VOLUME 2: 1930-1932

**To H.P. Lovecraft, ca. February 1931, I highly appreciate . . .**
First appeared in DEAR HPL: LETTERS, ROBERT E. HOWARD TO H.P. LOVECRAFT, 1930-1936 (Chpbk.)
 THE END OF THE TRAIL: WESTERN STORIES (excerpt only, contained in the article "Billy the Kid and
  the Lincoln County War")
 THE COLLECTED LETTERS OF ROBERT E. HOWARD, VOLUME 2: 1930-1932

**To H.P. Lovecraft, ca. February 1931, I'm writing this letter . . .**
First appeared in DEAR HPL: LETTERS, ROBERT E. HOWARD TO H.P. LOVECRAFT, 1930-1936 (Chpbk.)
 THE COLLECTED LETTERS OF ROBERT E. HOWARD, VOLUME 2: 1930-1932

**To H.P. Lovecraft, ca. June 1931, I didn't take much of a trip after all.**
 Also contains *The Grim Land (v)*
First appeared in ROBERT E. HOWARD: SELECTED LETTERS: 1931-1936 (Chpbk., verse not included)
 DEAR HPL: LETTERS, ROBERT E. HOWARD TO H.P. LOVECRAFT, 1930-1936 (Chpbk.)
 THE COLLECTED LETTERS OF ROBERT E. HOWARD, VOLUME 2: 1930-1932
 The poem has been published separately

**To H.P. Lovecraft, July 14, 1931, Just a line . . .**
First appeared in DEAR HPL: LETTERS, ROBERT E. HOWARD TO H.P. LOVECRAFT, 1930-1936 (Chpbk.)
 THE COLLECTED LETTERS OF ROBERT E. HOWARD, VOLUME 2: 1930-1932

**To H.P. Lovecraft, ca. August 1931, You must indeed . . .**
First appeared in DEAR HPL: LETTERS, ROBERT E. HOWARD TO H.P. LOVECRAFT, 1930-1936 (Chpbk.)
 THE END OF THE TRAIL: WESTERN STORIES (excerpt only, contained in the article "Beyond the Brazos
  River")
 THE COLLECTED LETTERS OF ROBERT E. HOWARD, VOLUME 2: 1930-1932

**To H.P. Lovecraft, ca. October 1931, Thanks for the post-card views.**
First appeared in ZARFHAANA #34
 DEAR HPL: LETTERS, ROBERT E. HOWARD TO H.P. LOVECRAFT, 1930-1936 (Chpbk.)
 THE COLLECTED LETTERS OF ROBERT E. HOWARD, VOLUME 2: 1930-1932

**To H.P. Lovecraft, ca. October 1931, I intended to answer . . .**
First appeared in DEAR HPL: LETTERS, ROBERT E. HOWARD TO H.P. LOVECRAFT, 1930-1936 (Chpbk.)
 THE END OF THE TRAIL: WESTERN STORIES (excerpt only, contained in the article "Beyond the Brazos
  River")
 THE COLLECTED LETTERS OF ROBERT E. HOWARD, VOLUME 2: 1930-1932

**To H.P. Lovecraft, ca. October 1931, Many thanks for the opportunity . . .**
First appeared in THE LAST OF THE TRUNK OCH BREV I URVAL (Chpbk.)
 THE COLLECTED LETTERS OF ROBERT E. HOWARD, VOLUME 2: 1930-1932

**To H.P. Lovecraft, December 9, 1931, I would have answered . . .**
 Also contains *Arkham (v)*
First appeared in DEAR HPL: LETTERS, ROBERT E. HOWARD TO H.P. LOVECRAFT, 1930-1936 (Chpbk.)
 THE COLLECTED LETTERS OF ROBERT E. HOWARD, VOLUME 2: 1930-1932
 The poem has been published separately

**To H.P. Lovecraft, ca. January 1932, Yes, I enjoyed the postcards . . .**
First appeared in WORMS OF THE EARTH (excerpt only)
 HERRSCHER DER NACHT (German, excerpt only)
 DEAR HPL: LETTERS, ROBERT E. HOWARD TO H.P. LOVECRAFT, 1930-1936 (Chpbk., first complete
  appearance)
 THE COLLECTED LETTERS OF ROBERT E. HOWARD, VOLUME 2: 1930-1932

**To H.P. Lovecraft, ca. February 1932, This isn't to flaunt my homely countenance, . . .**
First appeared in THE LAST OF THE TRUNK OCH BREV I URVAL (Chpbk.)
 THE COLLECTED LETTERS OF ROBERT E. HOWARD, VOLUME 2: 1930-1932
 This is a postcard, showing REH standing under a palm tree; the photo has been published many times

**To H.P. Lovecraft, March 2, 1932, I'm finally getting around . . .**
First appeared in DEAR HPL: LETTERS, ROBERT E. HOWARD TO H.P. LOVECRAFT, 1930-1936 (Chpbk.,
  Glenn Lord's transcription, does not include opening line, instead starts with "I was extremely interested in
  your comment . . ."; don't know what else was removed)
 THE COLLECTED LETTERS OF ROBERT E. HOWARD, VOLUME 2: 1930-1932 (first complete
  publication)

**To H.P. Lovecraft, ca. April 1932, At last I've gotten around . . .**
First appeared in DEAR HPL: LETTERS, ROBERT E. HOWARD TO H.P. LOVECRAFT, 1930-1936 (Chpbk.)
 THE COLLECTED LETTERS OF ROBERT E. HOWARD, VOLUME 2: 1930-1932

**To H.P. Lovecraft, May 24, 1932, Glad you liked the Oriental story . . .**
First appeared in DEAR HPL: LETTERS, ROBERT E. HOWARD TO H.P. LOVECRAFT, 1930-1936 (Chpbk.)
 THE COLLECTED LETTERS OF ROBERT E. HOWARD, VOLUME 2: 1930-1932

**To H.P. Lovecraft, ca. August 1933, I am sending on to you the enclosed manuscript . . .**
First appeared in THE HOWARD COLLECTOR #15
    RUNES OF AHRH EIH ECHE (Chpbk.)
    THE HOWARD COLLECTOR, Ace
    THE COLLECTED LETTERS OF ROBERT E. HOWARD, VOLUME 3: 1933-1936
    Includes an enclosed photo postcard of REH standing in the ruins of Fort McKavett; he also sent the same
        picture to August Derleth in a letter; on this particular photo sent to HPL he wrote "Ruins of Fort
        McKavett, July 9, 1933; I like this snap; it makes me feel kind of like a Vandal or Goth standing
        amidst the ruins of a Roman fortress or palace."

**To H.P. Lovecraft, ca. September or October 1933, I was very sorry to hear . . .**
First appeared in DEAR HPL: LETTERS, ROBERT E. HOWARD TO H.P. LOVECRAFT, 1930-1936 (Chpbk.)
    THE COLLECTED LETTERS OF ROBERT E. HOWARD, VOLUME 3: 1933-1936

**To H.P. Lovecraft, November 3, 1933, Glad you liked the rattles.**
First appeared in ROBERT E. HOWARD: SELECTED LETTERS: 1931-1936 (Chpbk.)
    DEAR HPL: LETTERS, ROBERT E. HOWARD TO H.P. LOVECRAFT, 1930-1936 (Chpbk.)
    THE COLLECTED LETTERS OF ROBERT E. HOWARD, VOLUME 3: 1933-1936
    This letter references an earlier and apparently now lost letter, in which REH included sent HPL a set of
        rattlesnake rattles, along with the prose piece "With a Set of Rattlesnake Rattles"

**To H.P. Lovecraft, ca. November 1933, I am so submerged in work . . .**
First appeared in DEAR HPL: LETTERS, ROBERT E. HOWARD TO H.P. LOVECRAFT, 1930-1936 (Chpbk.)
    THE COLLECTED LETTERS OF ROBERT E. HOWARD, VOLUME 3: 1933-1936

**To H.P. Lovecraft, ca. January 1934, I enjoyed very much . . .**
First appeared in DEAR HPL: LETTERS, ROBERT E. HOWARD TO H.P. LOVECRAFT, 1930-1936 (Chpbk.)
    THE COLLECTED LETTERS OF ROBERT E. HOWARD, VOLUME 3: 1933-1936

**To H.P. Lovecraft, ca. January 1934, I deeply appreciate . . .**
First appeared in DEAR HPL: LETTERS, ROBERT E. HOWARD TO H.P. LOVECRAFT, 1930-1936 (Chpbk.)
    THE COLLECTED LETTERS OF ROBERT E. HOWARD, VOLUME 3: 1933-1936

**To H.P. Lovecraft, March 24, 1934, Here's a little item . . .**
First appeared in DEAR HPL: LETTERS, ROBERT E. HOWARD TO H.P. LOVECRAFT, 1930-1936 (Chpbk.)
    THE COLLECTED LETTERS OF ROBERT E. HOWARD, VOLUME 3: 1933-1936

**To H.P. Lovecraft, ca. May 1934, Glad you're having a good time in Florida.**
First appeared in ZARFHAANA #22 (Chpbk.)
    DEAR HPL: LETTERS, ROBERT E. HOWARD TO H.P. LOVECRAFT, 1930-1936 (Chpbk.)
    THE COLLECTED LETTERS OF ROBERT E. HOWARD, VOLUME 3: 1933-1936

**To H.P. Lovecraft, ca. June 1934, Glad you're finding . . .**
First appeared in DEAR HPL: LETTERS, ROBERT E. HOWARD TO H.P. LOVECRAFT, 1930-1936 (Chpbk.)
    THE COLLECTED LETTERS OF ROBERT E. HOWARD, VOLUME 3: 1933-1936

**To H.P. Lovecraft, ca. July 1934, I started writing this months ago . . .**
First appeared in THE BARBARIAN SWORDSMEN (Anth., excerpt only, starting with "Thank you for the kind
    things you said . . .")
    DEAR HPL: LETTERS, ROBERT E. HOWARD TO H.P. LOVECRAFT, 1930-1936 (Chpbk., first complete
        publication)
    ISAACSON'S LEGACY, VOLUME 1, #20 (Chpbk.)
    THE COLLECTED LETTERS OF ROBERT E. HOWARD, VOLUME 3: 1933-1936

**To H.P. Lovecraft, ca. September 1934, Thanks very much for the postcards . . .**
First appeared in DEAR HPL: LETTERS, ROBERT E. HOWARD TO H.P. LOVECRAFT, 1930-1936 (Chpbk.)
    THE COLLECTED LETTERS OF ROBERT E. HOWARD, VOLUME 3: 1933-1936

**To H.P. Lovecraft, ca. December 1934, I read your account . . .**
First appeared in DEAR HPL: LETTERS, ROBERT E. HOWARD TO H.P. LOVECRAFT, 1930-1936 (Chpbk.)
    THE COLLECTED LETTERS OF ROBERT E. HOWARD, VOLUME 3: 1933-1936

**To H.P. Lovecraft, December 3, 1934, Glad you found the cat article of some . . .**
First appeared in ZARFHAANA #22 (Chpbk.)
    DEAR HPL: LETTERS, ROBERT E. HOWARD TO H.P. LOVECRAFT, 1930-1936 (Chpbk.)
    THE COLLECTED LETTERS OF ROBERT E. HOWARD, VOLUME 3: 1933-1936

**To H.P. Lovecraft, ca. January 1935, I have finally found time . . .**
First appeared in THE LAST OF THE TRUNK OCH BREV I URVAL (Chpbk.)
    THE COLLECTED LETTERS OF ROBERT E. HOWARD, VOLUME 3: 1933-1936

**To H.P. Lovecraft, ca. May 1935, The reason I haven't answered . . .**
First appeared in THE LAST OF THE TRUNK OCH BREV I URVAL (Chpbk.)
    THE COLLECTED LETTERS OF ROBERT E. HOWARD, VOLUME 3: 1933-1936

**To H.P. Lovecraft, ca. July 1935, Thanks very much for the fine post-cards . . .**
First appeared in THE END OF THE TRAIL: WESTERN STORIES (excerpt only, contained in the article "Billy
    the Kid and the Lincoln County War")
    THE LAST OF THE TRUNK OCH BREV I URVAL (first complete appearance)
    THE COLLECTED LETTERS OF ROBERT E. HOWARD, VOLUME 3: 1933-1936

**To H.P. Lovecraft, October 3, 1935, Here are some clippings . . .**
First appeared in DEAR HPL: LETTERS, ROBERT E. HOWARD TO H.P. LOVECRAFT, 1930-1936 (Chpbk.)
    THE COLLECTED LETTERS OF ROBERT E. HOWARD, VOLUME 3: 1933-1936

**To H.P. Lovecraft, December 5, 1935, A rather belated reply to your interesting . . .**
First appeared in ROBERT E. HOWARD: SELECTED LETTERS: 1931-1936 (Chpbk.)
    THE BLACK STRANGER AND OTHER AMERICAN TALES
    THE COLLECTED LETTERS OF ROBERT E. HOWARD, VOLUME 3: 1933-1936

**To H.P. Lovecraft, February 11, 1936, Glad you enjoyed the dream write-up I sent you.**
First appeared in ROBERT E. HOWARD: SELECTED LETTERS: 1931-1936 (Chpbk.)
    DEAR HPL: LETTERS, ROBERT E. HOWARD TO H.P. LOVECRAFT, 1930-1936 (Chpbk.)
    THE COLLECTED LETTERS OF ROBERT E. HOWARD, VOLUME 3: 1933-1936

**To H.P. Lovecraft, May 11, 1936, (partial draft of May 13)**
First appeared in THE LAST OF THE TRUNK OCH BREV I URVAL (Chpbk.)
    THE COLLECTED LETTERS OF ROBERT E. HOWARD, VOLUME 3: 1933-1936

**To H.P. Lovecraft, May 13, 1936, I am indeed sorry to hear . . .**
First appeared in DEAR HPL: LETTERS, ROBERT E. HOWARD TO H.P. LOVECRAFT, 1930-1936 (Chpbk.)
    THE COLLECTED LETTERS OF ROBERT E. HOWARD, VOLUME 3: 1933-1936

## TO MAGIC CARPET MAGAZINE (2)

**To Magic Carpet Magazine, January 1933, Thanks very much for the remarks . . .**
First appeared in MAGIC CARPET MAGAZINE, January 1933
    THE EXOTIC WRITINGS OF ROBERT E. HOWARD
    THE COLLECTED LETTERS OF ROBERT E. HOWARD, VOLUME 3: 1933-1936

**To Magic Carpet Magazine, April 1933, Congratulations on the quality . . .**
First appeared in MAGIC CARPET MAGAZINE, January 1933
    THE EXOTIC WRITINGS OF ROBERT E. HOWARD
    THE COLLECTED LETTERS OF ROBERT E. HOWARD, VOLUME 3: 1933-1936

## TO MANN, EDNA (1)

**To Edna Mann, October 30, 1926, As usual I have to start . . .**
    Also contains *The Campus at Midnight (v)*
First appeared in SEANCHAI #112 (Chpbk.)
    THE LAST OF THE TRUNK OCH BREV I URVAL (Chpbk.)
    THE COLLECTED LETTERS OF ROBERT E. HOWARD, VOLUME 1: 1923-1929
    This poem has been published separately

## TO MASHBURN, KIRK (2)

**To Kirk Mashburn, ca. March 1932, I am writing to express my appreciation for . . .**
First appeared in THE HOWARD COLLECTOR #7
    THE NEW HOWARD READER #5 (Chpbk.)
    THE COLLECTED LETTERS OF ROBERT E. HOWARD, VOLUME 2: 1930-1932

**To Kirk Mashburn, ca. Sept 1932, Just a line to congratulate . . .**
First appeared in THE LAST OF THE TRUNK OCH BREV I URVAL (Chpbk.)
    THE COLLECTED LETTERS OF ROBERT E. HOWARD, VOLUME 2: 1930-1932

## TO MILLER, P. SCHUYLER (1)

**To P. Schuyler Miller, SM, March 10, 1936, I feel indeed honored that you and Dr. Clark . . .**
First appeared in THE COMING OF CONAN
    CONAN
    CONAN IZ CIMERII (Russian)
    THE CONQUERING SWORD OF CONAN
    CONAN DE CIMMERIA III (Spanish)
    KONAN VARVARYNA (Bulgarian)
    LA LEGGENDA DI CONAN IL CIMMERO (Italian)
    L'ERA HYBORIANA DI CONAN IL CIMMERO (Italian)
    BARBARZYNCA (Polish)
    CONAN (Polish, later printing only)
    CONAN (French, a later, much larger edition)
    CONAN (Norwegian)
    CONAN, WHVG (German, later edition only)

CONAN! (Italian)
CONAN IL CIMMERO (Italian)
CONAN (Swedish)
CONAN CIMMERIERN (Swedish)
CONAN (Spanish)
THE COLLECTED LETTERS OF ROBERT E. HOWARD, VOLUME 3: 1933-1936

## *TO ORIENTAL STORIES (1)*

**To Oriental Stories, Summer 1932, Brundage did a fine job . . .**
First appeared in ORIENTAL STORIES, Summer 1932
    THE EXOTIC WRITINGS OF ROBERT E. HOWARD
    THE COLLECTED LETTERS OF ROBERT E. HOWARD, VOLUME 2: 1930-1932

## *TO PERRY, ALVIN EARL (1)*

**To Alvin Earl Perry, ca. early 1935, The first character I ever created . . .**
First appeared in FANTASY MAGAZINE, July 1935
    THE HOUR OF THE DRAGON, Berkley and Putnam (small excerpt only)
    THE COLLECTED LETTERS OF ROBERT E. HOWARD, VOLUME 3: 1933-1936
    Originally appeared in a short biographical article by Alvin Earl Perry, it appears that Mr. Perry had received a
        letter from REH talking about all sorts of things, including where most of his characters first started;
        location of original letter unknown, now likely lost; also appears that Mr. Perry paraphrased most of
        the letter, the quoted section is mostly about REH's characters

## *TO PETAJA, EMIL (4)*

**To Emil Petaja, December 17, 1934, Thank you very much for the splendid sonnet.**
    Also contains the *Cimmeria (v)*
First appeared in THE HOWARD COLLECTOR #7
    THE HOWARD COLLECTOR, Ace
    THE HOWARD READER #8 (Chpbk.)
    THE COLLECTED LETTERS OF ROBERT E. HOWARD, VOLUME 3: 1933-1936

**To Emil Petaja, March 6, 1935, Glad the ms. proved satisfactory.**
First appeared in BUNYIPS IN THE MULGA #19 (Chpbk., facsimile reproduction of original letter)
    THE NEW HOWARD READER #1 (Chpbk.)
    THE COLLECTED LETTERS OF ROBERT E. HOWARD, VOLUME 3: 1933-1936

**To Emil Petaja, July 23, 1935, Please believe my delay in answering . . .**
First appeared in REHUPA #23 (Chpbk.)
    THE HYPERBOREAN LEAGUE #5 (Chpbk.)
    THE NEW HOWARD READER #2 (Chpbk.)
    THE COLLECTED LETTERS OF ROBERT E. HOWARD, VOLUME 3: 1933-1936
    Both above appearances consisted of a photo-reproduction of the original letter, as a contribution by R. Alain
        Everts, untitled

**To Emil Petaja, September 6, 1935, Yes, I did like . . .**
First appeared in THE HYBORIAN AGE, distributed through The Hyperborean League (Chpbk.)
    XUTHOL (Chpbk.)
    THE NEW HOWARD READER #3 (Chpbk.)
    THE COLLECTED LETTERS OF ROBERT E. HOWARD, VOLUME 3: 1933-1936

## *TO PREECE, HAROLD (18)*

**To Harold Preece, ca. early 1928, Salaam: You'll have to pardon me . . .**
First appeared in THE LAST OF THE TRUNK OCH BREV I URVAL (Chpbk.)
    THE COLLECTED LETTERS OF ROBERT E. HOWARD, VOLUME 1: 1923-1929

**To Harold Preece, ca. June 1928, Salaam: No, I was not trying to catch flies . . .**
First appeared in THE LAST OF THE TRUNK OCH BREV I URVAL (Chpbk.)
    THE COLLECTED LETTERS OF ROBERT E. HOWARD, VOLUME 1: 1923-1929

**To Harold Preece, June 4, 1928, (No words)**
First appeared in THE HOWARD COLLECTOR #14
    THE COLLECTED LETTERS OF ROBERT E. HOWARD, VOLUME 1: 1923-1929
    Has just an REH drawing of a sailor waving

**To Harold Preece, ca. August 1928, Glad you enjoyed our reunion at Fort Worth.**
First appeared in FANTASY CROSSROADS #7
    RUNES OF AHRH EIH ECHE (Chpbk.)
    THE COLLECTED LETTERS OF ROBERT E. HOWARD, VOLUME 1: 1923-1929

**To Harold Preece, pm, September 5, 1928, Yes, I like the idea of Eldorado . . .**
First appeared in THE HOWARD COLLECTOR #9
    THE NEW HOWARD READER #2 (Chpbk.)
    THE COLLECTED LETTERS OF ROBERT E. HOWARD, VOLUME 1: 1923-1929

**To Harold Preece, pm, September 23, 1928, The tang of winter is in the air . . .**
First appeared in THE HOWARD COLLECTOR #8
    ROBERT E. HOWARD: SELECTED LETTERS: 1923-1930 (Chpbk.)
    THE COLLECTED LETTERS OF ROBERT E. HOWARD, VOLUME 1: 1923-1929

**To Harold Preece, received October 20, 1928 Your stationery is alright.**
First appeared in THE HOWARD COLLECTOR #3
    FANTASY CROSSROADS #2
    RUNES OF AHRH EIH ECHE (Chpbk.)
    ROBERT E. HOWARD: SELECTED LETTERS: 1923-1930 (Chpbk.)
    WEST IS WEST AND OTHERS
    THE COLLECTED LETTERS OF ROBERT E. HOWARD, VOLUME 1: 1923-1929

**To Harold Preece, ca. December 1928, You're right; women are great actors.**
First appeared in THE HOWARD COLLECTOR #13
    FANTASY CROSSROADS #3
    RUNES OF AHRH EIH ECHE (Chpbk.)
    ROBERT E. HOWARD: SELECTED LETTERS: 1923-1930 (Chpbk.)
    THE COLLECTED LETTERS OF ROBERT E. HOWARD, VOLUME 1: 1923-1929
    The publications prior to 1985 were incomplete due to unavailability of complete letter at the time; complete
        letter discovered in 1985

**To Harold Preece, ca. March 1929, I've been very neglectful of my correspondence . . .**
First appeared in THE HOWARD COLLECTOR #7
    ROBERT E. HOWARD: SELECTED LETTERS: 1923-1930 (Chpbk.)
    THE COLLECTED LETTERS OF ROBERT E. HOWARD, VOLUME 1: 1923-1929

**To Harold Preece, ca. September 1929, I've been reading DESTINY BAY and in . . .**
First appeared in THE HOWARD COLLECTOR #12
    RUNES OF AHRH EIH ECHE (Chpbk.)
    ROBERT E. HOWARD: SELECTED LETTERS: 1923-1930 (Chpbk.)
    THE COLLECTED LETTERS OF ROBERT E. HOWARD, VOLUME 1: 1923-1929
    This is dated ca. August 1929 in THE LAST CELT

**To Harold Preece, pm, September 18, 1929, I don't remember saying anything against . . .**
First appeared in RUNES OF AHRH EIH ECHE (Chpbk.)
    THE COLLECTED LETTERS OF ROBERT E. HOWARD, VOLUME 1: 1923-1929

**To Harold Preece, pm, January 4, 1930, Yes, we fade from youth swiftly.**
Also contains *portions of The Ballad of King Geraint (v)*
First appeared in CROSS PLAINS #6
    THE NEW HOWARD READER #3 (Chpbk.)
    THE COLLECTED LETTERS OF ROBERT E. HOWARD, VOLUME 2: 1930-1932
    Need to check earlier appearances, was the poetry included??

**To Harold Preece, ca. February 1930, Go manee jeea git. You're in Kansas now, eh?**
First appeared in THE HOWARD COLLECTOR #10
    FANTASY CROSSROADS #6
    RUNES OF AHRH EIH ECHE (Chpbk.)
    ROBERT E. HOWARD: SELECTED LETTERS: 1923-1930 (Chpbk.)
    THE COLLECTED LETTERS OF ROBERT E. HOWARD, VOLUME 2: 1930-1932

**To Harold Preece, pm, March 24, 1930, Thanks for the picture.**
Also contains *Song Before Clontarf (v)*
First appeared in THE HOWARD COLLECTOR #7
    THE NEW HOWARD READER #4 (Chpbk.)
    THE COLLECTED LETTERS OF ROBERT E. HOWARD, VOLUME 2: 1930-1932
    The poem has been published separately

**To Harold Preece, ca. early Apr 1930 Thanks for the Saint Padraic's card.**
    Also contains *Untitled ("Thomas Fitzgerald, Shane O'Neill") (v)*
First appeared in THE HOWARD COLLECTOR #16
    RUNES OF AHRH EIH ECHE (Chpbk.)
    THE COLLECTED LETTERS OF ROBERT E. HOWARD, VOLUME 2: 1930-1932
    Don't know if the poem made it into the earlier publications, CLv2 may have been the first

**To Harold Preece, ca. October 1930, Well, Harold, how did you like my story . . .**
First appeared in THE HOWARD COLLECTOR #2
    FANTASY CROSSROADS #2
    RUNES OF AHRH EIH ECHE (Chpbk.)
    THE CONAN SWORDBOOK (Anth.)
    ROBERT E. HOWARD: SELECTED LETTERS: 1923-1930 (Chpbk.)
    WEST IS WEST AND OTHERS
    THE COLLECTED LETTERS OF ROBERT E. HOWARD, VOLUME 2: 1930-1932

**To Harold Preece, ca. October or early November 1930 Well, Harold, I'm sorry to hear your nose . .**

  .

Also contains *Mihiragula (v); Belshazzar (v); Timur-Lang (v); A Peasant on the Euphrates (v)*
First appeared in AMRA, VOLUME 2, #29
    THE NEW HOWARD READER #1 (Chpbk.)
    THE COLLECTED LETTERS OF ROBERT E. HOWARD, VOLUME 2: 1930-1932
    The poem has been published separately

**To Harold Preece, pm, November 24, 1930, I hope you'll pardon my negligence . . .**
    Also contains *Untitled ("Slow shifts the sands of time . . .") (v)*
First appeared in THE HOWARD COLLECTOR #13 (verse not included, only the last paragraph of this five-
        paragraph letter)
    RUNES OF AHRH EIH ECHE (Chpbk., verse not included)
    ROBERT E. HOWARD: SELECTED LETTERS: 1923-1930 (Chpbk., verse included)
    THE COLLECTED LETTERS OF ROBERT E. HOWARD, VOLUME 2: 1930-1932
    The verse has been published separately

**To Harold Preece, date unknown, Salaam: Say, listen, tramp . . .**
First appeared in THE COLLECTED LETTERS OF ROBERT E. HOWARD, VOLUME 3: 1933-1936

## *TO PRICE, E. HOFFMANN (3)*

**To E. Hoffmann Price, February 15, 1936, I have eventually found time to answer your cards.**
First appeared in THE GHOST, May 1945
    CROSS PLAINS #6
    THE NEW HOWARD READER #5 (Chpbk.)
    WEST IS WEST AND OTHERS
    THE COLLECTED LETTERS OF ROBERT E. HOWARD, VOLUME 3: 1933-1936

**To E. Hoffmann Price, April 21, 1936, Glad you-all liked "She-Devil."**
First appeared in THE GHOST, May 1945
    THE NEW HOWARD READER #4 (Chpbk.)
    WEST IS WEST AND OTHERS
    THE COLLECTED LETTERS OF ROBERT E. HOWARD, VOLUME 3: 1933-1936

**To E. Hoffmann Price, June 3, 1936, Sorry to hear Pawang Ali has been banished.**
First appeared in THE GHOST, May 1945
    THE NEW HOWARD READER #1 (Chpbk.)
    WEST IS WEST AND OTHERS
    THE COLLECTED LETTERS OF ROBERT E. HOWARD, VOLUME 3: 1933-1936
    This is a postcard

## *TO PRICE, NOVALYNE (10)*

**To Novalyne Price, September 27, 1934, How about going to the show . . .**
First appeared in ONE WHO WALKED ALONE (Anth.)
    THE NEW HOWARD READER #1 (Chpbk.)
    THE COLLECTED LETTERS OF ROBERT E. HOWARD, VOLUME 3: 1933-1936

## TO THE RING MAGAZINE (1)

**To The Ring, ca. 1926, Here is my opinion on the greatest heavyweights. . .**
First appeared in THE RING, April 1926
      THE NEW HOWARD READER #5 (Chpbk.)
      WATERFRONT FISTS AND OTHERS
      WEST IS WEST AND OTHERS
      IRON LEGIONS, VOLUME 5, #2 (Chpbk.)
      THE COLLECTED LETTERS OF ROBERT E. HOWARD, VOLUME 1: 1923-1929

## TO SCHONFIELD, HUGH G. (1)

**To Hugh G. Schonfield, June 15, 1933, As I promised, in answer to your letter . . .**
First appeared in XENOPHILE #18
      ULTIMA THULE #1 (Chpbk.)
      THE NEW HOWARD READER #2 (Chpbk.)
      GLEN LORD'S ULTIMA THULE (Chpbk.)
      THE COLLECTED LETTERS OF ROBERT E. HOWARD, VOLUME 3: 1933-1936

## TO SMITH, CLARK ASHTON (10)

**To Clark Ashton Smith, pm, March 15, 1933, I hardly know how to thank you for the copy . . .**
First appeared in THE HOWARD COLLECTOR #11
      RUNES OF AHRH EIH ECHE (Chpbk.)
      REH: TWO-GUN RACONTEUR #2
      THE HOWARD COLLECTOR, Ace
      THE COLLECTED LETTERS OF ROBERT E. HOWARD, VOLUME 3: 1933-1936

**To Clark Ashton Smith, ca. July 1933, I really must apologize for not having . . .**
First appeared in THE HOWARD COLLECTOR #11
      RUNES OF AHRH EIH ECHE (Chpbk.)
      THE COLLECTED LETTERS OF ROBERT E. HOWARD, VOLUME 3: 1933-1936

**To Clark Ashton Smith, pm, July 22, 1933, I can hardly find words to express . . .**
First appeared in AMRA, VOLUME 2, #39
      THE CONAN GRIMOIRE (Anth.)
      CAS - NYCTALOPS #7 (Chpbk.)
      THE NEW HOWARD READER #3 (Chpbk.)
      THE COLLECTED LETTERS OF ROBERT E. HOWARD, VOLUME 3: 1933-1936

**To Clark Ashton Smith, ca. October 1933, Thanks very much for the kind things . . .**
First appeared in AMRA, VOLUME 2, #39
      THE CONAN GRIMOIRE (Anth.)
      ROBERT E. HOWARD: SELECTED LETTERS: 1931-1936 (Chpbk.)
      THE COLLECTED LETTERS OF ROBERT E. HOWARD, VOLUME 3: 1933-1936

**To Clark Ashton Smith, pm, December 14, 1933, Only the fact that I have been sick . . .**
First appeared in AMRA, VOLUME 2, #39
      THE CONAN GRIMOIRE (Anth.)
      ROBERT E. HOWARD: SELECTED LETTERS: 1931-1936 (Chpbk.)
      THE COLLECTED LETTERS OF ROBERT E. HOWARD, VOLUME 3: 1933-1936

**To Clark Ashton Smith, December 20, 1933 [no text]**
First appeared in THE LAST OF THE TRUNK OCH BREV I URVAL (Chpbk.)
    THE COLLECTED LETTERS OF ROBERT E. HOWARD, VOLUME 3: 1933-1936
    This is a signed Christmas card REH sent to CAS

**To Clark Ashton Smith, ca. January 1934, Thanks again for the drawing of the wizard.**
First appeared in AMRA, VOLUME 2, #39
    THE CONAN GRIMOIRE (Anth.)
    ROBERT E. HOWARD: SELECTED LETTERS: 1931-1936 (Chpbk.)
    THE COLLECTED LETTERS OF ROBERT E. HOWARD, VOLUME 3: 1933-1936

**To Clark Ashton Smith, ca. March 1934, I am sorry to hear you have been indisposed . . .**
First appeared in AMRA, VOLUME 2, #36
    THE CONAN GRIMOIRE (Anth.)
    ROBERT E. HOWARD: SELECTED LETTERS: 1931-1936 (Chpbk.)
    THE COLLECTED LETTERS OF ROBERT E. HOWARD, VOLUME 3: 1933-1936

**To Clark Ashton Smith, pm, May 21 1934, My delay in answering your last letter . . .**
First appeared in ROBERT E. HOWARD: SELECTED LETTERS: 1931-1936 (Chpbk.)
    THE COLLECTED LETTERS OF ROBERT E. HOWARD, VOLUME 3: 1933-1936

**To Clark Ashton Smith, July 23, 1935, I'm ashamed of my long delay in answering . . .**
First appeared in THE HOWARD COLLECTOR #5
    AMRA, VOLUME 2, #39
    THE CONAN GRIMOIRE (Anth.)
    RUNES OF AHRH EIH ECHE (Chpbk.)
    THE HOWARD COLLECTOR, Ace
    THE COLLECTED LETTERS OF ROBERT E. HOWARD, VOLUME 3: 1933-1936

## *TO SMITH, TEVIS CLYDE (136)*

**To Tevis Clyde Smith, June 8, 1923, Hello Clyde, / May the blessing of Allah rest upon you . . .**
    Also contains *Untitled ("When Napoleon down in Africa . . .") (v); Neolithic Love Song (v)*
First appeared in AUSTIN, VOLUME 3, #1 (Chpbk., facsimile reproduction of original letter)
    THE NEW HOWARD READER #4 (Chpbk.)
    THE LAST OF THE TRUNK OCH BREV I URVAL (Chpbk.)
    THE COLLECTED LETTERS OF ROBERT E. HOWARD, VOLUME 1: 1923-1929
    Handwritten, from Marlin, Texas; includes a simple multi-panel cartoon to go with "Neolithic Love Song";
        "Neolithic Love Song" has also been published separately

**To Tevis Clyde Smith, June 22, 1923, Clyde sahib, greeting: / I found your first letter waiting . . .**
    Also contains *Untitled ("The helmsman gaily, rode down the rickerboo . . .") (v); Untitled ("Now bright, now*
        *red, the sabers sped among the racing horde . . .") (v)*
First appeared in THE LAST OF THE TRUNK OCH BREV I URVAL (Chpbk.)
    THE COLLECTED LETTERS OF ROBERT E. HOWARD, VOLUME 1: 1923-1929

**To Tevis Clyde Smith, July 7, 1923, To Clyde bahadur-sahib, greeting: / I got your letter . . .**
    Also contains *The Dook of Stork*
First appeared in THE LAST OF THE TRUNK OCH BREV I URVAL (Chpbk.)
    THE COLLECTED LETTERS OF ROBERT E. HOWARD, VOLUME 1: 1923-1929

**To Tevis Clyde Smith, July 30, 1923, Clyde Sahib, Bohut Salaam, Bahadur: / The picnic has . . .**
> Also contains *Untitled ("Bill Boozy was a pirate bold") (v); Untitled ("Out of Asia the tribesmen came") (v)*
First appeared in THE LAST OF THE TRUNK OCH BREV I URVAL (Chpbk.)
> THE COLLECTED LETTERS OF ROBERT E. HOWARD, VOLUME 1: 1923-1929

**To Tevis Clyde Smith, August 4, 1923, Clyde sahib: / You say I'll be in Kabul.**
> Also contains *Untitled ("A clash of steel, a thud of hoofs") (v); Untitled ("A hundred years the great war raged") (v)*
First appeared in THE LAST OF THE TRUNK OCH BREV I URVAL (Chpbk.)
> THE COLLECTED LETTERS OF ROBERT E. HOWARD, VOLUME 1: 1923-1929

**To Tevis Clyde Smith, August 24, 1923, Bohut Salaam, Clyde sahib: / I was all ready to come over to Brownwood . . .**
First appeared in ROBERT E. HOWARD: SELECTED LETTERS: 1923-1930 (Chpbk.)
> THE COLLECTED LETTERS OF ROBERT E. HOWARD, VOLUME 1: 1923-1929

**To Tevis Clyde Smith, September 9, 1923, Clyde sahib: / First off I must apologize for not having . . .**
First appeared in ROBERT E. HOWARD: SELECTED LETTERS: 1923-1930 (Chpbk.)
> THE COLLECTED LETTERS OF ROBERT E. HOWARD, VOLUME 1: 1923-1929

**To Tevis Clyde Smith, October 5, 1923, Salaam, Clyde: / Maybe you think I've moved away . . .**
First appeared in THE LAST OF THE TRUNK OCH BREV I URVAL (Chpbk.)
> THE COLLECTED LETTERS OF ROBERT E. HOWARD, VOLUME 1: 1923-1929

**To Tevis Clyde Smith, November 4, 1923, Bohut salaam, Clyde bahadur: / It's been quite a while . . .**
First appeared in THE LAST OF THE TRUNK OCH BREV I URVAL (Chpbk.)
> THE COLLECTED LETTERS OF ROBERT E. HOWARD, VOLUME 1: 1923-1929

**To Tevis Clyde Smith, April 21, 1924, Salaam, Clyde sahib: / I should have written you sooner . . .**
First appeared in THE LAST OF THE TRUNK OCH BREV I URVAL (Chpbk.)
> THE COLLECTED LETTERS OF ROBERT E. HOWARD, VOLUME 1: 1923-1929

**To Tevis Clyde Smith, June 19, 1924, Salaam, Clyde sahib: / I suppose you think I'm rather slow . . .**
First appeared in THE LAST OF THE TRUNK OCH BREV I URVAL (Chpbk.)
> THE COLLECTED LETTERS OF ROBERT E. HOWARD, VOLUME 1: 1923-1929

**To Tevis Clyde Smith, September 7, 1924, Salaam, Clyde, / You ought to be here.**
> Also contains *Untitled ("Palm-trees are waving in the Gulf breeze") (v)*
First appeared in AUSTIN, Vol 3, # 1 (Chpbk.)
> THE NEW HOWARD READER #5 (Chpbk.)
> THE LAST OF THE TRUNK OCH BREV I URVAL (Chpbk.)
> THE COLLECTED LETTERS OF ROBERT E. HOWARD, VOLUME 1: 1923-1929
> Handwritten, likely on some hotel notepad; from Weslaco, TX, a small town near Brownsville; likely from a family vacation; includes three hand-drawn cartoons by REH

**To Tevis Clyde Smith, January 7, 1925, Salaam, Clyde sahib: / I was in Brownwood the other day . .**
 **.**
First appeared in THE LAST OF THE TRUNK OCH BREV I URVAL (Chpbk.)
> THE COLLECTED LETTERS OF ROBERT E. HOWARD, VOLUME 1: 1923-1929

**To Tevis Clyde Smith, January 30, 1925, Salaam, sahib: / I'm sending you a lot of junk . . .**

Also contains *Untitled ("Hills of the North! Lavender hills") (v); Untitled ("Dark are your eyes") (v); Slugger's Vow (v); Untitled ("I am the spirit of War!") (v); Untitled ("I lay in Yen's opium joint") (v)*
First appeared in THE LAST OF THE TRUNK OCH BREV I URVAL (Chpbk.)
    THE COLLECTED LETTERS OF ROBERT E. HOWARD, VOLUME 1: 1923-1929
    "Slugger's Vow" has been published separately

**To Tevis Clyde Smith, February 25, 1925, Salaam, sahib: / Chapter XIX / Writers of the Bunkorian Age . . .**
Also contains the poem *The Bombing of Gon Fanfew (v)*
First appeared in THE LAST OF THE TRUNK OCH BREV I URVAL (Chpbk.)
    THE COLLECTED LETTERS OF ROBERT E. HOWARD, VOLUME 1: 1923-1929

**To Tevis Clyde Smith, March 17, 1925, The top o' the marnin', O'Clydo: / Faith and bejabbers!**
Also contains *The Sappious Few Menchew*
First appeared in THE LAST OF THE TRUNK OCH BREV I URVAL (Chpbk.)
    THE COLLECTED LETTERS OF ROBERT E. HOWARD, VOLUME 1: 1923-1929

**To Tevis Clyde Smith, April 6, 1925, Salaam, sahib: / What ho! I have never read the original . . .**
Also contains *The Post of the Sappy Skipper; The Bored of the Cow*
First appeared in THE LAST OF THE TRUNK OCH BREV I URVAL (Chpbk.)
    THE COLLECTED LETTERS OF ROBERT E. HOWARD, VOLUME 1: 1923-1929

**To Tevis Clyde Smith, May 24, 1925, Salaam: / Hot zowie, old topper, we've got the makings . . .**
Also contains *When You Were a Set-Up and I Was a Ham (v)*
First appeared in THE LAST OF THE TRUNK OCH BREV I URVAL (Chpbk.)
    THE COLLECTED LETTERS OF ROBERT E. HOWARD, VOLUME 1: 1923-1929
    The poem has been published separately

**To Tevis Clyde Smith, July 7, 1925, Salaam, sahib: / I believe you owe me a letter.**
First appeared in THE LAST OF THE TRUNK OCH BREV I URVAL (Chpbk.)
    THE COLLECTED LETTERS OF ROBERT E. HOWARD, VOLUME 1: 1923-1929

**To Tevis Clyde Smith, July 16, 1925, Salaam, sahib: / What ho, milord! / Boy, I hope you're . . .**
Also contains *Untitled ("And Dempsey climbed into the ring . . .") (v)*
First appeared in ROBERT E. HOWARD: SELECTED LETTERS: 1923-1930 (Chpbk., doesn't include verse)
    THE COLLECTED LETTERS OF ROBERT E. HOWARD, VOLUME 1: 1923-1929

**To Tevis Clyde Smith, ca. July 1925, Salaam, Clyde: / Old boy, I got your letter. I can't say that it . . .**
First appeared in RAUHER SAND UND WILDE EICHEN (German)
    THE LAST OF THE TRUNK OCH BREV I URVAL (Chpbk.)
    THE COLLECTED LETTERS OF ROBERT E. HOWARD, VOLUME 1: 1923-1929

**To Tevis Clyde Smith, ca. July 1925, Salaam, Clyde sahib, / I haven't got any answer . . .**
First appeared in THE LAST OF THE TRUNK OCH BREV I URVAL (Chpbk.)
    THE COLLECTED LETTERS OF ROBERT E. HOWARD, VOLUME 1: 1923-1929
    This is a postcard

**To Tevis Clyde Smith, August 6, 1925, Salaam: / I'm glad you passed the exams . . .**
 Also contains *Untitled ("I tell you this my friend") (v)*
First appeared in THE LAST OF THE TRUNK OCH BREV I URVAL (Chpbk.)
 THE COLLECTED LETTERS OF ROBERT E. HOWARD, VOLUME 1: 1923-1929

**To Tevis Clyde Smith, August 26, 1925, Salaam: / I've been thinking. What is reality and what is . . .**
First appeared in ROBERT E. HOWARD: SELECTED LETTERS: 1923-1930 (Chpbk.)
 THE COLLECTED LETTERS OF ROBERT E. HOWARD, VOLUME 1: 1923-1929

**To Tevis Clyde Smith, August 28, 1925, Salaam: / I've been thinking. Did you ever stop . . .**
 Also contains *Untitled ("Mingle my dust with the burning brand") (v); Untitled ("Roses laughed in her pretty hair") (v)*
First appeared in ROBERT E. HOWARD: SELECTED LETTERS: 1923-1930 (Chpbk., doesn't include verse)
 THE COLLECTED LETTERS OF ROBERT E. HOWARD, VOLUME 1: 1923-1929

**To Tevis Clyde Smith, October 9, 1925, Salaam, sahib: / Say, bo, you're developing into a real poet.**
 Also contains *Untitled ("All the crowd") (v)*
First appeared in THE LAST OF THE TRUNK OCH BREV I URVAL (Chpbk.)
 THE COLLECTED LETTERS OF ROBERT E. HOWARD, VOLUME 1: 1923-1929

**To Tevis Clyde Smith, January 14, 1926, Salaam, bahadur, bohut salaam: / By Baal I am joyed that . . .**
First appeared in THE LAST OF THE TRUNK OCH BREV I URVAL (Chpbk.)
 THE COLLECTED LETTERS OF ROBERT E. HOWARD, VOLUME 1: 1923-1929

**To Tevis Clyde Smith, January 14, 1926, Salaam: / This is a habit of mine, always was . . .**
First appeared in THE LAST OF THE TRUNK OCH BREV I URVAL (Chpbk.)
 THE COLLECTED LETTERS OF ROBERT E. HOWARD, VOLUME 1: 1923-1929

**To Tevis Clyde Smith, April 14, 1926, Salaam: / Being in an (un)poetical mood . . .**
 Also contains *The Dancer (v); Destiny (2) (v); Laughter (v); Untitled ("We are the duckers of crosses") (v); Untitled ("The shades of night were falling faster") (v)*
First appeared in THE LAST OF THE TRUNK OCH BREV I URVAL (Chpbk.)
 THE COLLECTED LETTERS OF ROBERT E. HOWARD, VOLUME 1: 1923-1929
 "Destiny" (2) has been published separately

**To Tevis Clyde Smith, May 7, 1926, Salaam: / I'm sending you a flock of poetry . . .**
First appeared in THE LAST OF THE TRUNK OCH BREV I URVAL (Chpbk.)
 THE COLLECTED LETTERS OF ROBERT E. HOWARD, VOLUME 1: 1923-1929

**To Tevis Clyde Smith, June 23, 1926, Salaam: / I'm trying to write again, with the usual result . . .**
 Also contains *Untitled ("Give ye of my best . . .") (v); Untitled ("Early in the morning I gazed . . .") (v); Eternity (v); Serpent (v); Shadows (3) (v); Destiny (3) (v); Adventure (2) (v); Libertine (v); Nun (v); Prude (v); Adventurer (v); Poet (v); Dancer (v); Dreamer (v); Sailor (v); Cowboy (v); Toper (v); Girl (v); Deeps (v); Thor (v); Mystic (v); Orientia (v); The Mountains of California (v); Monarchs (v); Lust (v); The Alamo (v); San Jacinto (1) (v); Romance (2) (v)*
First appeared in THE LAST OF THE TRUNK OCH BREV I URVAL (Chpbk.)
 THE COLLECTED LETTERS OF ROBERT E. HOWARD, VOLUME 1: 1923-1929
 "Adventure" (2), and "Adventurer" have both been published separately

**To Tevis Clyde Smith, August 6, 1926, Salaam, sahib: / In the first place, pardon for not having . . .**
> Also contains *Arcadian Days (v)*

First appeared in THE LAST OF THE TRUNK OCH BREV I URVAL (Chpbk.)
> THE COLLECTED LETTERS OF ROBERT E. HOWARD, VOLUME 1: 1923-1929

**To Tevis Clyde Smith, August 21, 1926, Bohut salaam, sahib: / I think you owe me one, two, three . . .**
> Also contains *Twilight on Stonehenge (v); Ocean-Thoughts (v)*

First appeared in THE LAST OF THE TRUNK OCH BREV I URVAL (Chpbk.)
> THE COLLECTED LETTERS OF ROBERT E. HOWARD, VOLUME 1: 1923-1929
> "Twilight on Stonehenge" has been published separately

**To Tevis Clyde Smith, late Aug-early September 1927, ARE YOU THE YOUNG MAN TO WHOM . . .**
> Also contains *Revenge; Legend; Where Strange Gods Squall (part 1); Untitled ("Take some honey from a cat") (v); The Mottoes of the Boy Scouts (v); Untitled ("Against the blood red moon . . .") (v); Untitled ("Toast to the British! . . .") (v)*

First appeared in THE LAST OF THE TRUNK OCH BREV I URVAL (Chpbk.)
> THE COLLECTED LETTERS OF ROBERT E. HOWARD, VOLUME 1: 1923-1929
> "Revenge" has been published separately

**To Tevis Clyde Smith, ca. fall 1927, Salaam: / Then the little boy said to Goofus Gorilla . . .**
> Also contains *Where Strange Gods Squall (part 2); Untitled ("What became of Waring?") (v); The Robes of the Righteous (v); Untitled ("After the trumps are sounded") (v)*

First appeared in THE LAST OF THE TRUNK OCH BREV I URVAL (Chpbk.)
> THE COLLECTED LETTERS OF ROBERT E. HOWARD, VOLUME 1: 1923-1929

**To Tevis Clyde Smith, ca. September 1927, Salaam: / Having just got your letter I'll write now . . .**
> Also contains *The Road to Hell (early version, only lines 1-4, 24-28) (v); Flight (early version, incomplete) (v); Untitled ("The Baron of Fenland . . .") (v)*

First appeared in AMERICAN AND EUROPEAN MANUSCRIPTS AND PRINTED BOOKS, December 19, 1986 (facsimile reproduction of the second page only, the one containing the poetry)
> ROBERT E. HOWARD: SELECTED LETTERS: 1923-1930 (Chpbk., complete letter, but without the verse)
> MANUSCRIPTS FROM GOWER-PENN, VOLUME 2, #3 (Chpbk., facsimile reproduction of the second page only, includes the poetry)
> THE COLLECTED LETTERS OF ROBERT E. HOWARD, VOLUME 1: 1923-1929
> Untitled ("The Baron of Fenland") and "Flight" have both been published separately

**To Tevis Clyde Smith, ca. October 1927, Salaam: / Seeking cognizance of things looked after . . .**
> Also contains *The Fastidious Fooey Mancucu; Lilith (v); The Gods Remember (1) (v); The Dreams of Men (v); The Builders (2) (v); The Road to Babel (v); Memories (2) (v); Untitled ("Tell me not in coocoo numbers")*

First appeared in ROBERT E. HOWARD: SELECTED LETTERS: 1923-1930 (Chpbk., story and verse not included)
> THE COLLECTED LETTERS OF ROBERT E. HOWARD, VOLUME 1: 1923-1929
> "Lilith", "The Dreams of Men", "The Road to Babel", and "Memories" (2) have all been published separately

**To Tevis Clyde Smith, ca. January 1928, Salaam: / Listen, you crumb, I think you already owe me a letter.**
> Also contains *Wolfsdung; Untitled ("Keep women, thrones and kingly lands") (v); Untitled ("The world goes back to the primitive, yea") (v); Untitled ("I do not sing of a paradise") (v); Untitled ("Mother Eve, Mother Eve, . . .") (v); Untitled ("The east is red and I am dead") (v)*

First appeared in ROBERT E. HOWARD: SELECTED LETTERS: 1923-1930 (Chpbk., story and verse not
     included)
     THE COLLECTED LETTERS OF ROBERT E. HOWARD, VOLUME 1: 1923-1929
     "Wolfsdung" has also been published separately

**To Tevis Clyde Smith, ca. January 1928, I wasn't lying to you Saturday evening when . . .**
     Also contains *King Hootus; Symbols (v); Romany Road (v); Love (v); The Chant Demoniac (v); A Man (v);*
          *The Grey Lover (v); Life (1) (v)*
First appeared in ROBERT E. HOWARD: SELECTED LETTERS: 1923-1930 (Chpbk., only "Symbols" is included,
     the story and the rest of the verse not included)
     THE COLLECTED LETTERS OF ROBERT E. HOWARD, VOLUME 1: 1923-1929
     "Symbols", "Romany Road", "Love", "The Chant Demoniac", and "A Man" have all been published separately

**To Tevis Clyde Smith, week of February 20, 1928, The fellow who wrote The Kasidah strung . . .**
     Also contains *Untitled ("A typical small town drugstore . . .")*
     First appeared in ROBERT E. HOWARD: SELECTED LETTERS: 1923-1930 (Chpbk., story not included)
     THE LAST OF THE TRUNK OCH BREV I URVAL (first complete appearance)
     THE COLLECTED LETTERS OF ROBERT E. HOWARD, VOLUME 1: 1923-1929

**To Tevis Clyde Smith, ca. March 1928, The only reason for writing this letter . . .**
     Also contains *Keresa, Keresita (v)*
First appeared in ROBERT E. HOWARD: SELECTED LETTERS: 1923-1930 (Chpbk., verse not included)
     THE COLLECTED LETTERS OF ROBERT E. HOWARD, VOLUME 1: 1923-1929
     "Keresa, Keresita" has been published separately

**To Tevis Clyde Smith, ca. March 1928, Salaam: / Not having much of anything specially to say . . .**
     Also contains *How to Select a Successful Evangelist (v); The Choir Girl (v); A Song of Cheer (v);*
          *Repentance (v); Untitled ("I am MAN from the primal . . .") (v)*
First appeared in THE LAST OF THE TRUNK OCH BREV I URVAL (Chpbk.)
     THE COLLECTED LETTERS OF ROBERT E. HOWARD, VOLUME 1: 1923-1929

**To Tevis Clyde Smith, ca. March 1928, Salaam: / Glad you're writing these days . . .**
     Also contains *Untitled ("The spiders of weariness . . .") (v); The Dust Dance (various portions from (2)) (v);*
          *Untitled ("Moses was our leader . . .") (v); Secrets (v); The Dust Dance (portions from (1)) (v); The*
          *Chinese Gong (v)*
First appeared in ROBERT E. HOWARD: SELECTED LETTERS: 1923-1930 (Chpbk., only "The Odyssey of
     Israel" is included, the remaining verse is not included)
     THE COLLECTED LETTERS OF ROBERT E. HOWARD, VOLUME 1: 1923-1929
     "The Dust Dance" (2), Untitled ("Moses was our leader . . ."), and "The Dust Dance" (1) have all been
          published separately

**To Tevis Clyde Smith, ca. May 1928, Salaam: / So Klatt has gone West.**
First appeared in ROBERT E. HOWARD: SELECTED LETTERS: 1923-1930 (Chpbk.)
     ZARFHAANA #35 (Chpbk.)
     THE DARK MAN #1 (Chpbk.)
     THE COLLECTED LETTERS OF ROBERT E. HOWARD, VOLUME 1: 1923-1929

**To Tevis Clyde Smith, ca. June 1928, Salaam: / Ho, ho, the long lights lift amain . . .**
   Also contains *Untitled ("Ho, ho, the long lights lift amain . . .") (v); The Rump of Swift; A Young Wife's*
      *Tale (v); Lesbia (1) (v); A Roman Lady (v); Untitled ("They matched me up that night . . .") (v);*
      *Song of a Fugitive Bard (v); Untitled ("A cringing woman's lot . . .") (v); Nights to Both of Us*
      *Known (v)*
First appeared in THE LAST OF THE TRUNK OCH BREV I URVAL (Chpbk.)
   THE COLLECTED LETTERS OF ROBERT E. HOWARD, VOLUME 1: 1923-1929
   "A Young Wife's Tale", "Song of a Fugitive Bard", and "Nights to Both of Us Known" have all been
      published separately

**To Tevis Clyde Smith, ca. July 1928, Salaam: / A Warning to Orthodoxy**
   Also contains *A Warning to Orthodoxy (v)*
First appeared in THE LAST OF THE TRUNK OCH BREV I URVAL (Chpbk.)
   THE COLLECTED LETTERS OF ROBERT E. HOWARD, VOLUME 1: 1923-1929
   "A Warning to Orthodoxy" has been published separately

**To Tevis Clyde Smith, ca. October 1928, Salaam: / I could have gone with you for dinner if . . .**
   Also contains *The Ecstasy of Desolation (v)*
First appeared in WRITER OF THE DARK
   ROBERT E. HOWARD: SELECTED LETTERS: 1923-1930 (Chpbk., verse not included)
   THE COLLECTED LETTERS OF ROBERT E. HOWARD, VOLUME 1: 1923-1929
   "The Ecstasy of Desolation" has been published separately

**To Tevis Clyde Smith, ca. October 1928, Salaam: / The reason I'm sending The Junto to you . . .**
First appeared in THE LAST OF THE TRUNK OCH BREV I URVAL (Chpbk.)
   THE COLLECTED LETTERS OF ROBERT E. HOWARD, VOLUME 1: 1923-1929

**To Tevis Clyde Smith, ca. November 1928, Salaam: / Listen you goddamn so forth . . .**
   Also contains *A Song of the Anchor Chain (v); The Ballad of Abe Slickemmore (v)*
First appeared in THE LAST OF THE TRUNK OCH BREV I URVAL (Chpbk.)
   THE COLLECTED LETTERS OF ROBERT E. HOWARD, VOLUME 1: 1923-1929
   "A Song of the Anchor Chain" has been published separately

**To Tevis Clyde Smith, ca. November 1928, Salaam: / I'll swear you're the only galoot I ever heard of**
   **. . .**
   Also contains *Song from an Ebony Heart (v); Untitled ("Swords glimmered up the pass") (v); Rebellion (v);*
      *A Great Man Speaks (v); Yodels of Good Cheer to the Pipple, Damn Them (v); Untitled ("He*
      *clutched his . . .") (v); Untitled ("Noah was my applesauce") (v); Untitled ("Let me live as I was*
      *born to live") (v); Untitled ("Adam's loins were mountains") (v); The Ballad of Monk Kickawhore*
      *(v); A Ballad of Insanity (v); Untitled ("I hate the man . . .") (v); A Far Country (v)*
First appeared in ROBERT E. HOWARD: SELECTED LETTERS: 1923-1930 (Chpbk.)
   THE COLLECTED LETTERS OF ROBERT E. HOWARD, VOLUME 1: 1923-1929
   "Song from an Ebony Heart", "Rebellion", and "A Far Country" have all been published separately

**To Tevis Clyde Smith, ca. November 1928, Salaam: / I got such a laugh . . .**
   Also contains *Nancy Hawk – A Legend of Virginity (v); Untitled ("Drawers that a girl . . .") (v); Untitled*
      *("Tumba Hooey"); To a Nameless Woman (v)*
First appeared in THE LAST OF THE TRUNK OCH BREV I URVAL (Chpbk.)
   THE COLLECTED LETTERS OF ROBERT E. HOWARD, VOLUME 1: 1923-1929
   "To a Nameless Woman" has been published separately

**To Tevis Clyde Smith, ca. November 1928, Heh heh! / At last I've sold a story to Ghost Stories.**

Also contains *Untitled ("Scarlet and gold are the stars tonight") (v); Untitled ("Old Faro Bill was a man of might") (v); Untitled ("Rebel souls from the falling dark") (v); The Call of Pan (v); Untitled ("A sappe ther wos and that a crumbe manne") (v)*

First appeared in ROBERT E. HOWARD: SELECTED LETTERS: 1923-1930 (Chpbk., verse not included)

THE COLLECTED LETTERS OF ROBERT E. HOWARD, VOLUME 1: 1923-1929

"The Call of Pan" has been published separately


**To Tevis Clyde Smith, ca. November-December 1928, Heh heh! / Sappho, the Grecian . . .**

Also contains *Untitled ("Sappho, the Grecian hills are gold") (v); Untitled ("Romona! Romona!") (v); A Fable for Critics (v); Untitled ("My brother he was an auctioneer") (v); Flaming Marble (v)*

First appeared in THE LAST OF THE TRUNK OCH BREV I URVAL (Chpbk.)

THE COLLECTED LETTERS OF ROBERT E. HOWARD, VOLUME 1: 1923-1929

"A Fable for Critics" and "Flaming Marble" have both been published separately


**To Tevis Clyde Smith, ca. December 1928, Salaam: / Out in front of Goldstein's . . .**

Also contains *Untitled ("Out in front of Goldstein's . . .") (v); The Deed Beyond the Deed (v); An American (v); Untitled ("There's an isle far away . . .") (v); Shadow of Dreams (v); My Children (v); Untitled ("The women come and . . .") (v); Silence Falls on Mecca's Walls (v); The Last Words He Heard (v); Untitled ("Flappers flicker . . .") (v); Untitled ("I hold all women . . .") (v); Untitled ("Love is singing soft and low") (v)*

First appeared in ROBERT E. HOWARD: SELECTED LETTERS: 1923-1930 (Chpbk., none of the verse is included, this version starts with "The rattle of the keys . . .")

THE LAST OF THE TRUNK OCH BREV I URVAL (first complete appearance)

THE COLLECTED LETTERS OF ROBERT E. HOWARD, VOLUME 1: 1923-1929

"Silence Falls on Mecca's Walls" and "The Last Words He Heard" have both been published separately


**To Tevis Clyde Smith, ca. late 1928, Salaam: / I'll swear, if I'd laughed much more . . .**

Also contains *The People of the Winged Skulls; Untitled ("Oh, we are little children . . ."); Untitled ("The tall man answered: . . ."); Untitled ("The tall man rose and said: . . ."); Untitled ("The tall man said: . . ."); Untitled ("Moonlight and shadows barred the land")*

First appeared in THE LAST OF THE TRUNK OCH BREV I URVAL (Chpbk.)

THE COLLECTED LETTERS OF ROBERT E. HOWARD, VOLUME 1: 1923-1929

The poems are contained in the story


**To Tevis Clyde Smith, ca. February 1929, Salaam: / Ancient English Balladel**

Also contains *Ancient English Balladel (v); Untitled ("At the Inn of the Gory Dagger") (v)*

First appeared in ROBERT E. HOWARD: SELECTED LETTERS: 1923-1930 (Chpbk., verse not included, starts with "Looks like I'm not going . . .")

THE LAST OF THE TRUNK OCH BREV I URVAL (first complete appearance)

THE COLLECTED LETTERS OF ROBERT E. HOWARD, VOLUME 1: 1923-1929

"Ancient English Balladel" has been published separately


**To Tevis Clyde Smith, ca. February 1929, Salaam: / Last night the Sunday School class had a party . . .**

Also contains *The Case of the College Toilet; Untitled ("And there were lethal women . . .") (v); Untitled ("A haunting cadence . . .") (v); Untitled ("Through the mists of silence . . .") (v); The Mysteries (v)*

First appeared in ROBERT E. HOWARD: SELECTED LETTERS: 1923-1930 (Chpbk., the story and verse not included)

YESTERYEAR #4 (Chpbk.)

THE COLLECTED LETTERS OF ROBERT E. HOWARD, VOLUME 1: 1923-1929

"The Case of the College Toilet" has been published separately

**To Tevis Clyde Smith, ca. March 1929, Salaam: / Black Dawn**
> Also contains *Black Dawn (v); The Path of Strange Wanderers (v); At the Bazaar (v); Untitled ("Hatrack!"); Untitled ("By old Abe Goldstein's . . .") (v); Bastards All!; Songs of Bastards; Untitled ("A beggar, singing without . . .")*
First appeared in THE LAST OF THE TRUNK OCH BREV I URVAL (Chpbk.)
> THE COLLECTED LETTERS OF ROBERT E. HOWARD, VOLUME 1: 1923-1929
"Black Dawn", "The Path of Strange Wanderers", "Bastards All!", and "Songs of Bastards" have all been published
> separately

**To Tevis Clyde Smith, ca. early to mid 1929, Salaam: / Life is a yellow mist among the stars . . .**
> Also contains *To a Roman Woman (v); Ivory in the Night (v)*
First appeared in THE LAST OF THE TRUNK OCH BREV I URVAL (Chpbk.)
> THE COLLECTED LETTERS OF ROBERT E. HOWARD, VOLUME 1: 1923-1929

**To Tevis Clyde Smith, ca. April 1929, Salaam: / The iron harp that Adam christened life . . .**
> Also contains *Untitled ("The iron harp that Adam christened Life") (v); To the Contended (v); High Blue Halls (v); An American Epic (v)*
First appeared in ROBERT E. HOWARD: SELECTED LETTERS: 1923-1930 (Chpbk., verse not included, this
> version starts with "I enjoyed your letter highly and roared . . .")
> THE COLLECTED LETTERS OF ROBERT E. HOWARD, VOLUME 1: 1923-1929 (first complete
> publication)

**To Tevis Clyde Smith, ca. June 1929, Salaam: / I received an announcement from Chicago . . .**
> Also contains *Black Seas (v)*
First appeared in ROBERT E. HOWARD: SELECTED LETTERS: 1923-1930 (Chpbk., verse not included)
> THE COLLECTED LETTERS OF ROBERT E. HOWARD, VOLUME 1: 1923-1929
> "Black Seas" has been published separately

**To Tevis Clyde Smith, ca. July 1929, Salaam: / The main reason I'm writing this letter is . . .**
> Also contains *Irony*
First appeared in ROBERT E. HOWARD: SELECTED LETTERS: 1923-1930 (Chpbk., story not included)
> THE COLLECTED LETTERS OF ROBERT E. HOWARD, VOLUME 1: 1923-1929

**To Tevis Clyde Smith, ca. late December 1929, Well: / Here I am doing business at the old stand . . .**
First appeared in ROBERT E. HOWARD: SELECTED LETTERS: 1923-1930 (Chpbk.)
> THE COLLECTED LETTERS OF ROBERT E. HOWARD, VOLUME 1: 1923-1929

**To Tevis Clyde Smith, ca. January 1930, Many thanks for the letter you wrote Farnsworth . . .**
First appeared in ROBERT E. HOWARD: SELECTED LETTERS: 1923-1930 (Chpbk.)
> THE COLLECTED LETTERS OF ROBERT E. HOWARD, VOLUME 2: 1930-1932

**To Tevis Clyde Smith, ca. February 1930, Well, here is the letter.**
First appeared in ROBERT E. HOWARD: SELECTED LETTERS: 1923-1930 (Chpbk.)
> THE COLLECTED LETTERS OF ROBERT E. HOWARD, VOLUME 2: 1930-1932

**To Tevis Clyde Smith, ca. February 1930, Salaam, Fear Ohghruagach: / Life is a cynical, romantic pig . . .**
> Also contains *Untitled ("Life is a cynical, romantic pig") (v)*
First appeared in ROBERT E. HOWARD: SELECTED LETTERS: 1923-1930 (Chpbk., verse not included, excerpt
> starts with "I owe Hink a letter.")
First appeared in THE LAST OF THE TRUNK OCH BREV I URVAL (first complete appearance)
> THE COLLECTED LETTERS OF ROBERT E. HOWARD, VOLUME 2: 1930-1932

**To Tevis Clyde Smith, ca. March 1930, Well, Fear Finn, tell Cuchullain the Dutchess . . .**
　　Also contains *The Autumn of the World (v); A Tribute to the Sportsmanship of the Fans (v); Aw Come On and Fight (v); The Song of the Sage (v)*
First appeared in ROBERT E. HOWARD: SELECTED LETTERS: 1923-1930 (Chpbk., verse not included)
　　THE COLLECTED LETTERS OF ROBERT E. HOWARD, VOLUME 2: 1930-1932
　　"The Autumn of the World" has been published separately

**To Tevis Clyde Smith, ca. March 1930, Well, Fear Finn: / I trust you are in good healthel . . .**
　　Also contains *Whispers (v)*
First appeared in ROBERT E. HOWARD: SELECTED LETTERS: 1923-1930 (Chpbk., verse not included)
　　THE COLLECTED LETTERS OF ROBERT E. HOWARD, VOLUME 2: 1930-1932
　　"Whispers" has been published separately

**To Tevis Clyde Smith, ca. early April 1930, Well, Fear Finn, you mention being in a lethargic . . .**
　　Also contains *Ambition (v); Whispers on the Nightwind (v); The Gladiator and the Lady (v)*
First appeared in ROBERT E. HOWARD: SELECTED LETTERS: 1923-1930 (Chpbk., verse not included)
　　THE COLLECTED LETTERS OF ROBERT E. HOWARD, VOLUME 2: 1930-1932
　　"Whispers on the Nightwind" and "The Gladiator and the Lady" have both been published separately

**To Tevis Clyde Smith, ca. April 1930, Salaam: / Well, Fear Finn, I believe in days gone yore . . .**
　　Also contains *The Mutiny of the Hellroarer; The Return of the Sea-Farer (v)*
First appeared in THE LAST OF THE TRUNK OCH BREV I URVAL (Chpbk.)
　　THE COLLECTED LETTERS OF ROBERT E. HOWARD, VOLUME 2: 1930-1932
　　"The Return of the Sea-Farer" has been published separately

**To Tevis Clyde Smith, ca. May 1930, Salaam: / Well, Fear Finn, I hope this letter finds you o.k. . . .**
First appeared in THE LAST OF THE TRUNK OCH BREV I URVAL (Chpbk.)
　　THE COLLECTED LETTERS OF ROBERT E. HOWARD, VOLUME 2: 1930-1932

**To Tevis Clyde Smith, ca. May 1930, Well, Fear Finn, I was in Brownwood yesterday . . .**
　　Also contains *A Stirring of Green Leaves (v); The Rhyme of the Viking Path (v); A Marching Song of Connacht (v)*
First appeared in ROBERT E. HOWARD: SELECTED LETTERS: 1923-1930 (Chpbk., verse not included)
　　THE COLLECTED LETTERS OF ROBERT E. HOWARD, VOLUME 2: 1930-1932
　　"A Stirring of Green Leaves", "The Rhyme of the Viking Path" and "A Marching Song of Connacht" have all been published separately

**To Tevis Clyde Smith, ca. week of June 9, 1930, Well, Fear Finn: / The pictures came at last and here they are.**
First appeared in ROBERT E. HOWARD: SELECTED LETTERS: 1923-1930 (Chpbk.)
　　THE COLLECTED LETTERS OF ROBERT E. HOWARD, VOLUME 2: 1930-1932

**To Tevis Clyde Smith, ca. July 1930, Salaam, Fear Finn: / Then Stein the peddler . . .**
　　Also contains *Untitled ("Then Stein the peddler . . .") (v); A Ballad of Beer (v)*
First appeared in THE LAST OF THE TRUNK OCH BREV I URVAL (Chpbk.)
　　THE COLLECTED LETTERS OF ROBERT E. HOWARD, VOLUME 2: 1930-1932
　　"A Ballad of Beer" has been published separately

**To Tevis Clyde Smith, ca. July 1930, Salaam, Fear Finn: / Well, me bauld buccaneer . . .**
　　Also contains *Lives and Crimes of Notable Artists*
First appeared in THE LAST OF THE TRUNK OCH BREV I URVAL (Chpbk.)
　　THE COLLECTED LETTERS OF ROBERT E. HOWARD, VOLUME 2: 1930-1932
　　"Lives and Crimes of Notable Artists" has been published separately

**To Tevis Clyde Smith, May 9, 1931, Fear Finn: / Have youse heard anything more . . .**
First appeared in ROBERT E. HOWARD: SELECTED LETTERS: 1931-1936 (Chpbk.)
    THE COLLECTED LETTERS OF ROBERT E. HOWARD, VOLUME 2: 1930-1932

**To Tevis Clyde Smith, ca. mid-May 1931, Well Fear Finn: / I got a letter from Bradford saying that . . .**
First appeared in ROBERT E. HOWARD: SELECTED LETTERS: 1931-1936 (Chpbk.)
    THE COLLECTED LETTERS OF ROBERT E. HOWARD, VOLUME 2: 1930-1932

**To Tevis Clyde Smith, week of May 18, 1931, Fear Finn: / I should have answered your letter . . .**
First appeared in THE LAST OF THE TRUNK OCH BREV I URVAL (Chpbk.)
    THE COLLECTED LETTERS OF ROBERT E. HOWARD, VOLUME 2: 1930-1932

**To Tevis Clyde Smith, ca. early June 1931, Fear Finn: / Thanks very much for the Frontier . . .**
First appeared in THE LAST OF THE TRUNK OCH BREV I URVAL (Chpbk.)
    THE COLLECTED LETTERS OF ROBERT E. HOWARD, VOLUME 2: 1930-1932

**To Tevis Clyde Smith, ca. August 1931, Fear Finn: / Well, I doubt if this missile will be very scintillant . . .**
First appeared in ROBERT E. HOWARD: SELECTED LETTERS: 1931-1936 (Chpbk.)
    THE COLLECTED LETTERS OF ROBERT E. HOWARD, VOLUME 2: 1930-1932

**To Tevis Clyde Smith, ca. September 1931, Fear Finn: / Lizzen my children and you shall be told . . .**
    Also contains *Untitled ("Lizzen my children and you shall be told") (v)*
First appeared in ROBERT E. HOWARD: SELECTED LETTERS: 1931-1936 (Chpbk.)
    THE LAST OF THE TRUNK OCH BREV I URVAL (Chpbk.)
    THE COLLECTED LETTERS OF ROBERT E. HOWARD, VOLUME 2: 1930-1932

**To Tevis Clyde Smith, ca. September 1931, Fear Finn: / I've been waiting for a letter from you . . .**
First appeared in THE LAST OF THE TRUNK OCH BREV I URVAL (Chpbk.)
    THE COLLECTED LETTERS OF ROBERT E. HOWARD, VOLUME 2: 1930-1932

**To Tevis Clyde Smith, ca. October 1931, Fear Finn: / The reason I haven't written you sooner . . .**
First appeared in THE LAST OF THE TRUNK OCH BREV I URVAL (Chpbk.)
    THE COLLECTED LETTERS OF ROBERT E. HOWARD, VOLUME 2: 1930-1932

**To Tevis Clyde Smith, ca. November 1931, Fear Finn: / I wrote Bradford a coarse rude letter . . .**
    Also contains *Who is Grandpa Theobold? (v); Untitled ("Let me rest with the ages")*
    THE HOWARD COLLECTOR #6
First appeared in ROBERT E. HOWARD: SELECTED LETTERS: 1931-1936 (Chpbk.)
    THE COLLECTED LETTERS OF ROBERT E. HOWARD, VOLUME 2: 1930-1932
    "Who is Grandpa Theobold" has been published separately

**To Tevis Clyde Smith, November 1931, Fear Finn: / Here are the blasted verses.**
    Also contains *The Last Day (v); Moonlight on a Skull (v)*
First appeared in MANUSCRIPTS FROM GOWER-PENN, VOLUME 2, #3 (Chpbk.)
    THE LAST OF THE TRUNK OCH BREV I URVAL (Chpbk.)
    THE COLLECTED LETTERS OF ROBERT E. HOWARD, VOLUME 2: 1930-1932
    Both poems previously sold to WEIRD TALES but not published yet at the time of this letter

**To Tevis Clyde Smith, ca. November 1931, Fear Finn: / Have you heard anything from the Christopher?**

Also contains *Untitled ("Many fell at the grog-shop walls") (v)*
First appeared in ROBERT E. HOWARD: SELECTED LETTERS: 1931-1936 (Chpbk.)
  THE COLLECTED LETTERS OF ROBERT E. HOWARD, VOLUME 2: 1930-1932

**To Tevis Clyde Smith, ca. early January 1932, Dear Clyde: / I only learned of your uncle's death today.**
First appeared in THE LAST OF THE TRUNK OCH BREV I URVAL (Chpbk.)
  THE COLLECTED LETTERS OF ROBERT E. HOWARD, VOLUME 2: 1930-1932

**To Tevis Clyde Smith, ca. February 1932, Fear Finn: / Well, how runs the world these days?**
First appeared in THE LAST OF THE TRUNK OCH BREV I URVAL (Chpbk.)
  THE COLLECTED LETTERS OF ROBERT E. HOWARD, VOLUME 2: 1930-1932

**To Tevis Clyde Smith, ca. March 1932, Fear Finn: / Sorry to hear you've been carved on again.**
First appeared in THE LAST OF THE TRUNK OCH BREV I URVAL (Chpbk.)
  THE COLLECTED LETTERS OF ROBERT E. HOWARD, VOLUME 2: 1930-1932

**To Tevis Clyde Smith, ca. March 1932, Fear Finnel: / When I wzs a kie in East Texas . . .**
First appeared in THE LAST OF THE TRUNK OCH BREV I URVAL (Chpbk.)
  THE COLLECTED LETTERS OF ROBERT E. HOWARD, VOLUME 2: 1930-1932

**To Tevis Clyde Smith, ca. April 1932, Fear Finn: / I heard from that bone-crushing man-eater . . .**
Also contains *A Weird Ballad (v); Little Brown Man of Nippon (v)*
First appeared in ROBERT E. HOWARD: SELECTED LETTERS: 1931-1936 (Chpbk., verse not included)
  THE COLLECTED LETTERS OF ROBERT E. HOWARD, VOLUME 2: 1930-1932
  "A Weird Ballad" and "Little Brown Man of Nippon" have both been published separately

**To Tevis Clyde Smith, ca. May 1932, Fear Finn: / Just a bit of press-agenting . . .**
First appeared in THE LAST OF THE TRUNK OCH BREV I URVAL (Chpbk.)
  THE COLLECTED LETTERS OF ROBERT E. HOWARD, VOLUME 2: 1930-1932
  Hand-written, on stationary from the Worth Hotel in Fort Worth, Texas

**To Tevis Clyde Smith, ca. May 1932, Fear Finn: / Well, here I am back at the old home town . . .**
First appeared in THE LAST OF THE TRUNK OCH BREV I URVAL (Chpbk.)
  THE COLLECTED LETTERS OF ROBERT E. HOWARD, VOLUME 2: 1930-1932

**To Tevis Clyde Smith, ca. May 1932, Fear Finn: / Thank you very much for going to all the trouble . . .**
Also contains *The Toy Rattle Murder Case*
First appeared in ROBERT E. HOWARD: SELECTED LETTERS: 1931-1936 (Chpbk., story not included)
  THE COLLECTED LETTERS OF ROBERT E. HOWARD, VOLUME 2: 1930-1932

**To Tevis Clyde Smith, ca. May 1932, Fear Finn: / Lo, friend, I approach thee with a liver . . .**
Also contains *John Brown (v); Abe Lincoln (v); John Kelley (v); The Tom Thumb Moider Mystery; Authorial Version of Doona (v)*
First appeared in ROBERT E. HOWARD: SELECTED LETTERS: 1931-1936 (Chpbk., only Authorial Version of Doona included, not the story or other verse)
  THE COLLECTED LETTERS OF ROBERT E. HOWARD, VOLUME 2: 1930-1932
  "John Brown" and "Abe Lincoln" have both been published separately

**To Tevis Clyde Smith, ca. very late May 1932, Fear Finn: / Let us tool forth to Australia . . .**
First appeared in THE LAST OF THE TRUNK OCH BREV I URVAL (Chpbk.)
  THE COLLECTED LETTERS OF ROBERT E. HOWARD, VOLUME 2: 1930-1932

**To Tevis Clyde Smith, ca. August 1932, Fear Finn: / I don't know when I've enjoyed a pome . . .**
> Also contains *Dreaming in Israel (v); Samson's Broodings (v)*
First appeared in THE LAST OF THE TRUNK OCH BREV I URVAL (Chpbk.)
> THE COLLECTED LETTERS OF ROBERT E. HOWARD, VOLUME 2: 1930-1932
> "Dreaming in Israel" and "Samson's Broodings" have both been published separately

**To Tevis Clyde Smith, ca. September 1932, Fear Finn: / You owe me a letter, you louse, he said . . .**
> Also contains *A Glass of Vodka; One Blood Strain (v)*
First appeared in ROBERT E. HOWARD: SELECTED LETTERS: 1931-1936 (Chpbk., story and verse not
> included)
> THE COLLECTED LETTERS OF ROBERT E. HOWARD, VOLUME 2: 1930-1932

**To Tevis Clyde Smith, ca. November 1932, Fear Finn: / Well, I finally get around to answering . . .**
> Also contains *Lines to G.B. Shaw (v); A Mick in Israel (v); Musings (2) (v); Envoy (v)*
First appeared in THE LAST OF THE TRUNK OCH BREV I URVAL (Chpbk.)
> THE COLLECTED LETTERS OF ROBERT E. HOWARD, VOLUME 2: 1930-1932
> "Musings" (2) has been published separately

**To Tevis Clyde Smith, ca. May 1933, Fear Finn: / I was in Brownwood yesterday . . .**
First appeared in THE LAST OF THE TRUNK OCH BREV I URVAL (Chpbk.)
> THE COLLECTED LETTERS OF ROBERT E. HOWARD, VOLUME 3: 1933-1936

**To Tevis Clyde Smith, ca. October 1933, Fear Finn: / The Galleon Press has just brought out . . .**
First appeared in THE LAST OF THE TRUNK OCH BREV I URVAL (Chpbk.)
> THE COLLECTED LETTERS OF ROBERT E. HOWARD, VOLUME 3: 1933-1936

## *UNDATED LETTERS to TCS*

**To Tevis Clyde Smith, Undated, Salaam / Again glancing over your last letter . . .**
> Also contains *Surrender (2) (v); I Praise My Nativity (v); Dreaming (v)*
First appeared in THE LAST OF THE TRUNK OCH BREV I URVAL (Chpbk.)
> THE COLLECTED LETTERS OF ROBERT E. HOWARD, VOLUME 3: 1933-1936
> "Surrender" (2) and "I Praise My Nativity" have both been publish separately

**To Tevis Clyde Smith, Undated, Ha ha! Your not going to get off so easily . . .**
> Also contains *The Coming of Bast (v)*
First appeared in THE LAST OF THE TRUNK OCH BREV I URVAL (Chpbk.)
> THE COLLECTED LETTERS OF ROBERT E. HOWARD, VOLUME 3: 1933-1936

**To Tevis Clyde Smith, Undated, Salaam: / I have forgotten whether you or Truett . . .**
> Also contains *A Song of College (v); That Women May Sing of Us (v); Sighs in the Yellow Leaves (v); A
> Song of Greenwich (v); Ballade (v)*
First appeared in THE LAST OF THE TRUNK OCH BREV I URVAL (Chpbk.)
> THE COLLECTED LETTERS OF ROBERT E. HOWARD, VOLUME 3: 1933-1936
> "Ballade" has been published separately

**To Tevis Clyde Smith, Undated, The Seeker thrust . . .**
 Also contains *Untitled ("The Seeker thrust . . .")); To a Certain Cultured Woman (v); The Winds of the Sea (2) (v); The Iron Harp (a cycle of five poems, including Out of the Deep; Babel; Laughter in the Gulf; Moon Shame; A Crown for a King)*
First appeared in THE LAST OF THE TRUNK OCH BREV I URVAL (Chpbk.)
 THE COLLECTED LETTERS OF ROBERT E. HOWARD, VOLUME 3: 1933-1936
 "The Winds of the Sea" (2), "Out of the Deep", "Babel", "Laughter in the Gulf", "Moon Shame", and "A Crown for a King" have all been published separately

**To Tevis Clyde Smith, Undated, Not even a movie in this godforsaken town . . .**
First appeared in THE LAST OF THE TRUNK OCH BREV I URVAL (Chpbk.)
 THE COLLECTED LETTERS OF ROBERT E. HOWARD, VOLUME 3: 1933-1936

**To Tevis Clyde Smith, Undated, Well, Fear Finn, I read your story . . .**
 Also contains *The Cuckoo's Revenge (v); The Madness of Cormac (v); A Challenge to Bast (v)*
First appeared in THE LAST OF THE TRUNK OCH BREV I URVAL (Chpbk.)
 THE COLLECTED LETTERS OF ROBERT E. HOWARD, VOLUME 3: 1933-1936
 "The Cuckoo's Revenge" and "A Challenge to Bast" have both been published separately

**To Tevis Clyde Smith, Undated, Fear Finn: / I'm damned if I can think of anything . . .**
 Also contains *A Poet's Skull (v)*
First appeared in THE LAST OF THE TRUNK OCH BREV I URVAL (Chpbk.)
 THE COLLECTED LETTERS OF ROBERT E. HOWARD, VOLUME 3: 1933-1936
 "A Poet's Skull" has been published separately

**To Tevis Clyde Smith, Undated, Salaam: / Shadows of Dreams**
 Also contains *Shadows of Dreams (v)*
First appeared in THE LAST OF THE TRUNK OCH BREV I URVAL (Chpbk.)
 THE COLLECTED LETTERS OF ROBERT E. HOWARD, VOLUME 3: 1933-1936
 "Shadows of Dreams" has been published separately

**To Tevis Clyde Smith, Undated, Salaam: / There once was a wicked . . .**
 Also contains *Untitled ("There once was a wicked old elf") (v); Untitled ("There are grim things did, . . .") (v); To Lyle Saxon (v)*
First appeared in THE LAST OF THE TRUNK OCH BREV I URVAL (Chpbk.)
 THE COLLECTED LETTERS OF ROBERT E. HOWARD, VOLUME 3: 1933-1936
 "To Lyle Saxon" has been published separately

**To Tevis Clyde Smith, Undated, If you dont publish this . . .**
 Also contains *The Viking of the Sky (v)*
First appeared in AUSTIN, VOLUME 3, #3 (Chpbk.)
 THE LAST OF THE TRUNK OCH BREV I URVAL (Chpbk.)
 THE COLLECTED LETTERS OF ROBERT E. HOWARD, VOLUME 3: 1933-1936
 "The Viking of the Sky" has been published separately

**To Tevis Clyde Smith, Undated, Salaam: / As my dear public . . .**
 Also contains *Untitled ("As my dear public remembers . . .")*
First appeared in THE LAST OF THE TRUNK OCH BREV I URVAL (Chpbk.)
 THE COLLECTED LETTERS OF ROBERT E. HOWARD, VOLUME 3: 1933-1936

**To Tevis Clyde Smith, Undated, "King Bahthur's Court"**
      Also contains *King Bahthur's Court*
First appeared in THE LAST OF THE TRUNK OCH BREV I URVAL (Chpbk.)
      THE COLLECTED LETTERS OF ROBERT E. HOWARD, VOLUME 3: 1933-1936

**To Tevis Clyde Smith, Undated, Ahatou noyon, Fear Finn: / Thinking of nothing . . .**
      Also contains *The Werewolf Murder Case*
First appeared in THE LAST OF THE TRUNK OCH BREV I URVAL (Chpbk.)
      THE COLLECTED LETTERS OF ROBERT E. HOWARD, VOLUME 3: 1933-1936

**To Tevis Clyde Smith, Undated, Salaam / Skulls against the Dawn**
      Also contains *Skulls Against the Dawn (v); Drummings on an Empty Skull (v)*
First appeared in THE LAST OF THE TRUNK OCH BREV I URVAL (Chpbk.)
      THE COLLECTED LETTERS OF ROBERT E. HOWARD, VOLUME 3: 1933-1936

## *DOCUMENTS ENCLOSED with TCS LETTERS*

**"The Adventurer's Mistress" (2) (v)**
      Also contains *The Adventurer's Mistress (2) (v)*
First appeared in THE LAST OF THE TRUNK OCH BREV I URVAL (Chpbk.)
      THE COLLECTED LETTERS OF ROBERT E. HOWARD, VOLUME 3: 1933-1936
      The verse has been published separately

**I've done my part in writing it.**
      Also contains *Untitled ("There were three lads . . .") (v)*
First appeared in THE LAST OF THE TRUNK OCH BREV I URVAL (Chpbk.)
      THE COLLECTED LETTERS OF ROBERT E. HOWARD, VOLUME 3: 1933-1936

**Poem penned by Akbar Ali . . .**
      Also contains *Untitled ("Match a toad with a far-winged hawk") (v)*
First appeared in THE LAST OF THE TRUNK OCH BREV I URVAL (Chpbk.)
      THE COLLECTED LETTERS OF ROBERT E. HOWARD, VOLUME 3: 1933-1936

**"Crusade" (v)**
      Also contains *Crusade (v)*
First appeared in THE LAST OF THE TRUNK OCH BREV I URVAL (Chpbk.)
      THE COLLECTED LETTERS OF ROBERT E. HOWARD, VOLUME 3: 1933-1936
      The verse has been published separately

**"Sang the King of Midian" (v)**
      Also contains *Sang the King of Midian (v)*
First appeared in THE COLLECTED LETTERS OF ROBERT E. HOWARD, VOLUME 3: 1933-1936
      The verse has been published separately

**"Renunciation" (v)**
      Also contains *Renunciation (v)*
First appeared in THE LAST OF THE TRUNK OCH BREV I URVAL (Chpbk.)
      THE COLLECTED LETTERS OF ROBERT E. HOWARD, VOLUME 3: 1933-1936
      The verse has been published separately

**"Thoughts of an Afghan on a raid"**
First appeared in THE LAST OF THE TRUNK OCH BREV I URVAL (Chpbk.)
    THE COLLECTED LETTERS OF ROBERT E. HOWARD, VOLUME 3: 1933-1936
    This is a cartoon

**"Relentless Reginald . . ."**
First appeared in THE NEW HOWARD READER #1 (Chpbk.)
    THE LAST OF THE TRUNK OCH BREV I URVAL (Chpbk.)
    THE COLLECTED LETTERS OF ROBERT E. HOWARD, VOLUME 3: 1933-1936
    This is a cartoon

**Drawing of a strange cow**
First appeared in THE LAST OF THE TRUNK OCH BREV I URVAL (Chpbk.)
    THE COLLECTED LETTERS OF ROBERT E. HOWARD, VOLUME 3: 1933-1936
    This is a cartoon

## *TO SWANSON, CARL (3)*

**To Carl Swanson, ca. March 1932 I am sending you . . .**
First appeared in THE LAST OF THE TRUNK OCH BREV I URVAL (Chpbk.)
    THE COLLECTED LETTERS OF ROBERT E. HOWARD, VOLUME 2: 1930-1932

**To Carl Swanson, ca. April 1932 I am interested in . . .**
First appeared in THE LAST OF THE TRUNK OCH BREV I URVAL (Chpbk.)
    THE COLLECTED LETTERS OF ROBERT E. HOWARD, VOLUME 2: 1930-1932

**To Carl Swanson, ca. late May1932 I'm sorry you had . . .**
First appeared in THE LAST OF THE TRUNK OCH BREV I URVAL (Chpbk.)
    THE COLLECTED LETTERS OF ROBERT E. HOWARD, VOLUME 2: 1930-1932

## *TO TALMAN, WILFRED BLANCH (7)*

**To Wilfred Blanch Talman, ca. February 1931, I can hardly find words to express . . .**
First appeared in RUNES OF AHRH EIH ECHE (Chpbk.)
    THE COLLECTED LETTERS OF ROBERT E. HOWARD, VOLUME 2: 1930-1932

**To Wilfred Blanch Talman, ca. April 1931, I'm glad you liked "Kings of the Night."**
First appeared in RUNES OF AHRH EIH ECHE (Chpbk.)
    THE COLLECTED LETTERS OF ROBERT E. HOWARD, VOLUME 2: 1930-1932

**To Wilfred Blanch Talman, ca. July 1931, I should have answered your letter . . .**
First appeared in RUNES OF AHRH EIH ECHE (Chpbk.)
    THE COLLECTED LETTERS OF ROBERT E. HOWARD, VOLUME 2: 1930-1932

**To Wilfred Blanch Talman, ca. September 1931, Thank you very much for the letter you wrote . . .**
First appeared in REH (Chpbk.)
    WHISPERS, June 1975
    THE SECOND BOOK OF ROBERT E. HOWARD
    RUNES OF AHRH EIH ECHE (Chpbk.)
    ROBERT E. HOWARD: SELECTED LETTERS: 1931-1936 (Chpbk.)
    ROBERT E. HOWARD: THE POWER OF THE WRITING MIND
    THE COLLECTED LETTERS OF ROBERT E. HOWARD, VOLUME 2: 1930-1932

**To Wilfred Blanch Talman, ca. October 1931, I'm returning herewith your stories . . .**
First appeared in RUNES OF AHRH EIH ECHE (Chpbk.)
    THE COLLECTED LETTERS OF ROBERT E. HOWARD, VOLUME 2: 1930-1932

**To Wilfred Blanch Talman, ca. March 1932, I've finally gotten around to answering . . .**
First appeared in RUNES OF AHRH EIH ECHE (Chpbk.)
    THE COLLECTED LETTERS OF ROBERT E. HOWARD, VOLUME 2: 1930-1932

**To Wilfred Blanch Talman, ca. July 1932, Thanks very much for "De Halve Maen."**
First appeared in THE HOWARD COLLECTOR #13
    RUNES OF AHRH EIH ECHE (Chpbk.)
    THE COLLECTED LETTERS OF ROBERT E. HOWARD, VOLUME 2: 1930-1932

## *TO THRILLS OF THE JUNGLE MAGAZINE (1)*

**To Thrills of the Jungle Magazine, ca. June to late 1929, I enclose herewith a short story . . .**
First appeared in THE NEW HOWARD READER #1 (Chpbk.)
    THE COLLECTED LETTERS OF ROBERT E. HOWARD, VOLUME 1: 1923-1929

## *TO TORBETT, FRANK THURSTON (2)*

**To Frank Thurston Torbett, April 28, 1936, I'm sorry I have not . . .**
First appeared in THE LAST OF THE TRUNK OCH BREV I URVAL (Chpbk.)
    THE COLLECTED LETTERS OF ROBERT E. HOWARD, VOLUME 3: 1933-1936

**To Frank Thurston Torbett, June 3, 1936, My mother is very low . . .**
First appeared in ROBERT E. HOWARD: SELECTED LETTERS: 1931-1936 (a reproduction of the original
    postcard)
    THE COLLECTED LETTERS OF ROBERT E. HOWARD, VOLUME 3: 1933-1936

## *TO WANDREI, DONALD (1)*

**To Donald Wandrei, ca. February 21, 1933, I've been intending to write to you . . .**
First appeared in THE LAST OF THE TRUNK OCH BREV I URVAL (Chpbk.)
    THE COLLECTED LETTERS OF ROBERT E. HOWARD, VOLUME 3: 1933-1936
    Available at the Minnesota Historical Society, in the Donald Wandrei papers

## *TO WEIRD TALES (8)*

**To Weird Tales, ca. December 1925, These are sheer masterpieces. . . .**
First appeared in WEIRD TALES, February 1926
    THE WEIRD WRITINGS OF ROBERT E. HOWARD, VOLUME ONE
    THE COLLECTED LETTERS OF ROBERT E. HOWARD, VOLUME 1: 1923-1929

**To Weird Tales, ca. May 1927, Your last three issues . . .**
First appeared in WEIRD TALES, June 1927
    THE NEW HOWARD READER #2 (Chpbk.)
    WEST IS WEST AND OTHERS
    THE WEIRD WRITINGS OF ROBERT E. HOWARD, VOLUME ONE
    THE COLLECTED LETTERS OF ROBERT E. HOWARD, VOLUME 1: 1923-1929

## *TO WESTERN STORY (1)*

## TO WRIGHT, FARNSWORTH (4)

**To Farnsworth Wright, January 23, 1926 I have no carbon copy of Wolfshead . . .**
First appeared in POST OAKS AND SAND ROUGHS
    RAUHER SAND UND WILDE EICHEN
    THE COLLECTED LETTERS OF ROBERT E. HOWARD, VOLUME 1: 1923-1929

**To Farnsworth Wright, ca. June 1930, I have long looked forward to reading . . .**
First appeared in THE HOWARD COLLECTOR #11
    ZARFHAANA #1 (Chpbk.)
    RUNES OF AHRH EIH ECHE (Chpbk.)
    ROBERT E. HOWARD: SELECTED LETTERS: 1923-1930 (Chpbk.)
    THE COLLECTED LETTERS OF ROBERT E. HOWARD, VOLUME 2: 1930-1932
    MOICHANIE IDOLA (Russian)

**To Farnsworth Wright, ca. June-July 1931, In your last letter you asked me to give you . . .**
First appeared in THE GHOST, May 1945
    THE LAST CELT
    CROSS PLAINS #6
    PIGEONS FROM HELL (Embodied in the Introduction)
    ROBERT E. HOWARD: SELECTED LETTERS: 1931-1936 (Chpbk.)
    ROBERT E. HOWARD: THE POWER OF THE WRITING MIND
    WEST IS WEST AND OTHERS
    THE COLLECTED LETTERS OF ROBERT E. HOWARD, VOLUME 2: 1930-1932

**To Farnsworth Wright, May 6, 1935, I always hate to write a letter like this . . .**
First appeared in THE HOWARD COLLECTOR #9
    RUNES OF AHRH EIH ECHE (Chpbk.)
    THE HOWARD COLLECTOR, Ace
    THE LAST OF THE TRUNK OCH BREV I URVAL (Chpbk.)
    THE COLLECTED LETTERS OF ROBERT E. HOWARD, VOLUME 3: 1933-1936

## TO UNKNOWN RECEPIENTS (3)

**To an unknown recepient, ca. September 1928, Salaam: Tunney sure gave Heeney . . .**
First appeared in THE LAST OF THE TRUNK OCH BREV I URVAL (Chpbk.)
    THE COLLECTED LETTERS OF ROBERT E. HOWARD, VOLUME 1: 1923-1929
    Likely either to Preece or TCS, Glenn Lord thinks Preece

**To an unknown recepient, Salaam: Not much to say . . .**
First appeared in THE LAST OF THE TRUNK OCH BREV I URVAL (Chpbk.)
    THE COLLECTED LETTERS OF ROBERT E. HOWARD, VOLUME 3: 1933-1936

**Draft ?**
Unpublished

# BOOKS IN ENGLISH

This list is for English-language books that contain all or mostly all REH-written material. Books that contain only a relatively small amount actually written by REH (e.g., anthologies, critical works about REH) are to be found in the ANTHOLOGIES list. For purposes of this bibliography, I define "book" as being any publication that has a spine, either hard or soft, the exception being periodicals, especially pulps such as Weird Tales, which indeed have a printed spine, but are still listed under PERIODICALS. Items that are staple-bound, or utilizing other novel binding methodologies, are under CHAPBOOKS. Books in languages other than English are listed under the index titled as such, that index following this one.

This listing is in ALPHABETIC ORDER BY TITLE. If more than one edition of a book is known, the later editions are listed below the first. If books from different publishers have the same title but differing contents, the books are given separate listings, with the oldest work being listed first. All contents solely by REH unless otherwise noted. All publishers US unless otherwise noted. If there is other non-REH content, I have not listed it.

Additional information beyond contents and basic publisher information, such as cover artist, illustrator, who wrote the introduction, editor, limitations on number of copies, etc., are presented in the Notes, if known. Works shown in **BOLD** are first appearance of the work anywhere, and there will be a mention in the Notes for that book that it **Contains a First Appearance**. Poetry is indicated by (v).

Abbreviations used in this list include:
PB – paperback; HB – hardback; TPB – trade paperback;
nd – no date shown on book

## *Form of Entry:*
**Title**
> Contents
> 1$^{st}$ edition [publisher, format, date]
>> Notes
> Other editions
>> Notes

## Almuric
> Contains *Almuric*
> 1$^{st}$ Edition, Ace, PB (40c, F-305), 1964
> Ace, PB, 2$^{nd}$ printing (60c, different cover), 1970
> New English Library ("NEL", UK), PB, 1971
>> Cover art by Richard Clifton-Dey
> Grant, HB, 1975
>> Limited to 3500 copies; illustrated by David Ireland
> Sphere (UK), PB, 1977
>> Cover art by Chris Achilleos
> Berkley, PB, December 1977
>> Based on the Grant edition, included a fold out poster by Ken Kelly
> Berkley, PB, 2$^{nd}$ printing, nd (January 1978)

## Almuric

Contains *Almuric*
1st Edition, Pulpville Press, HB and TPB, August 2006
> Cover and interior artwork by David Burton; published via lulu.com

## Almuric

Contains *Almuric*
1st Edition, Paizo Press, TPB, November 2007
> Introduction by Joe R. Lansdale

## Always Comes Evening

Contains *Always Comes Evening; The Poets; The Singer in the Mist; Solomon Kane's Homecoming; Futility ("Golden Goats . . ."); The Song of the Bats; The Moor Ghost; Recompense; The Hills of Kandahar; Which Will Scarcely Be Understood; Haunting Columns; The Last Hour; Ships; The King and the Oak; The Riders of Babylon; Easter Island; Moon Mockery; Shadows on the Road; The Soul-Eater; The Dream and the Shadow; The Ghost Kings; Desert Dawn; An Open Window; The Song of the Mad Minstrel; The Gates of Ninevah; Fragment; The Harp of Alfred; Remembrance; Crete; Forbidden Magic; Black Chant Imperial; A Song Out of Midian; Arkham; The Voices Waken Memory; Babel; Song At Midnight; The Ride of Falume; Autumn; Dead Man's Hate; One Who Comes at Eventide; To a Woman ("Though fathoms . . ."); Emancipation; Retribution; Chant of the White Beard; Rune; Song of the Pict; Prince and Beggar; Hymn of Hatred; Invective; Men of the Shadows; Babylon; Niflheim; The Heart of the Sea's Desire; Laughter in the Gulfs; A Song of the Don Cossacks; The Gods of Easter Island; Nisapur; Moon Shame; The Tempter; Lines Written in the Realization That I Must Die;* plus chapter headings from **The Road of Azrael**; *The Pool of the Black One, Kings of the Night, Red Blades of Black Cathay, The Phoenix on the Sword (all 4 chapters, 2-5), The Scarlet Citadel (chapters 1, 2, 3, and 5), and Queen of the Black Coast (all v)*
1st Edition, Arkham House, HB, 1957
> **Contains a First Appearance**; cover art by Frank Utpatel; introduction and Foreword by Dale Hart; selected by Glenn Lord; limited to 636; all but approximately 100 copies have the spine lettering upside down

## Always Comes Evening

Contains *Always Comes Evening; The Poets; The Singer in the Mist; Solomon Kane's Homecoming; Futility ("Golden goats . . ."); The Song of the Bats; The Moor Ghost; Recompense; The Hills of Kandahar; Which Will Scarcely Be Understood; Haunting Columns; The Last Hour; Ships; The King and the Oak; The Riders of Babylon; Easter Island; Moon Mockery; Shadows on the Road; The Soul-Eater; The Dream and the Shadow; The Ghost Kings; Desert Dawn; An Open Window; The Song of the Mad Minstrel; The Gates of Ninevah; Fragment; The Harp of Alfred; Remembrance; Crete; Forbidden Magic; Black Chant Imperial; A Song Out of Midian; Arkham; The Voices Waken Memory; Babel; Song At Midnight; The Ride of Falume; Autumn; Dead Man's Hate; One Who Comes at Eventide; To a Woman ("Though fathoms . . ."); Emancipation; Retribution; Chant of the White Beard; Rune; Song of the Pict; Prince and Beggar; Hymn of Hatred; Invective; Men of the Shadows; Babylon; Niflheim; The Heart of the Sea's Desire; Laughter in the Gulfs; A Song of the Don Cossacks; The Gods of Easter Island; Nisapur; Moon Shame; The Tempter; Lines Written in the Realization That I Must Die; Parody; A Crown for a King;* **The Song of Yar Ali Khan (deluxe edition only)**; *plus chapter headings from The Road of Azrael; The Pool of the Black One, Kings of the Night, Red Blades of Black Cathay, The Phoenix on the Sword (all 4 chapters, 2-5), The Scarlet Citadel (chapters 1, 2, 3, and 5), and Queen of the Black Coast (all v)*
1st Edition, Underwood-Miller, HB, 1977
Underwood-Miller, Limited edition, HB, 1977
> **Contains a First Appearance**; based on the Arkham House Edition, but adds three additional poems; illustrated by Keiko Nelson; new introduction by Glenn Lord; came out in two different jackets, the original in 1977 by Keiko Nelson (a colorful stylized dragon), a new one in 1980 by Mara Murray (black and white with red lettering, photo of skulls piled on skulls); "The Song of Yar Ali Khan" came as a loose insert in the deluxe edition, and in a few regular editions, copy of original holographic version; "Parody"

is printed on the front endleaves, in both print and original holographic; the limited edition is leather bound and slipcased, limited to 206 copies, signed by Keiko Nelson

## Beyond the Black River: The Weird Works of Robert E. Howard, Volume 7
Contains *The Grisly Horror; Jewels of Gwahlur; Beyond the Black River; The Challenge from Beyond; Shadows in Zamboula*
1ˢᵗ Edition, Wildside Press, HB, August 2007
> Cover art by Stephen Fabian; introduction by Damon Sasser; all based on original pulp pages with minimal editing; first printing is Smythe sewn, on acid free paper, limited to 1400 copies

## Beyond the Borders
Contains *The Voice of El-Lil; The Cairn on the Headland; Casonetto's Last Song; The Cobra in the Dream; Dig Me No Grave; The Haunter of the Ring; Dermod's Bane; King of the Forgotten People; The Children of the Night; The Dream Snake; The Hyena; People of the Black Coast; The Fire of Asshurbanipal*
1ˢᵗ Edition, Baen, PB, October 1996
> Cover art by Ken Kelly; introduction by TKF Weisskopf

## Black Canaan
Contains *Black Canaan; Delenda Est; The Haunter of the Ring; The House in the Oaks (completed by August Derleth); Arkham (v);An Open Window (v); the verse heading from The Black Stone; The Cobra in the Dream; Dermod's Bane; People of the Black Coast; The Dwellers Under the Tomb; The Noseless Horror; Moon of Zambebwei*
1ˢᵗ Edition, Berkley, PB, May 1978
> Introduction by Gehan Wilson; the poetry is slightly different from original, and incorporated into "The House in the Oaks"

## Black Colossus
Contains *Black Colossus; Shadows in the Moonlight*
1ˢᵗ Edition, Grant, HB, 1979
> Illustrated by Ned Dameron; a traycase MAY have been offered via Gray Parrot

## The Black Stranger and Other American Tales
Contains *The Black Stranger; Marchers of Valhalla; The Gods of Bal-Sagoth; Nekht Semerkeht; Black Vulmea's Vengeance; The Strange Case of Josiah Wilbarger; The Valley of the Lost; Kelly the Conjure-Man; Black Canaan; Pigeons from Hell; Old Garfield's Heart; The Horror from the Mound; The Thunder-Rider; The Grim Land (v); plus excerpts from two REH letters,one to August Derleth, ca. January 1933 ("I was much interested in your accounts . . ."), and the other to HPL, December 5, 1935 ("A rather belated reply to your interesting . . .")*
1ˢᵗ Edition, Bison Books, HB and TPB, April 2005
> Cover art by Mike Mignola; introduction and edited by Steve Tompkins; HB and TPB being offered at the same time

## Black Vulmea's Vengeance
Contains *Black Vulmea's Vengeance;* **Swords of the Red Brotherhood***; The Isle of Pirates' Doom*
1ˢᵗ Edition, Grant, HB, 1976
> **Contains a First Appearance**; illustrated by Robert James Pailthorpe; limited to 2600 copies; text used as basis for all later editions
Baronet, TPB, 1977
> New cover by Stephen Fabian; uses loose pages from the Grant HB edition
Zebra, PB, March 1977
Berkley, PB, 1979
Ace, PB, June 1987

## Blood of the Gods and Other Stories

Contains *The Country of the Knife; Hawk of the Hills; The Daughter of Erlik Khan; Blood of the Gods; Swords of Shahrazar*

1st Edition, Girasol Collectables, TPB, Spring 2005

> Cover art by Joseph Clement Coll; edited by Paul Herman; all stories edited back to match original pulp appearance

## Bloodstar

Contains *Bloodstar (Valley of the Worm)*

1st Edition, Morningstar Press, HB, 1976

> Graphic novel adaptation of "Valley of the Worm", written by John Jakes; limited to 5000 copies, all numbered; illustrated by Richard Corben; first 1000 signed and numbered (as "XXX/1000") by Corben

Ariel, TPB, September 1979

> The entire story is rewritten by John Pocsik (aka Simon Revelstroke)

## The Bloody Crown of Conan

Contains *People of the Black Circle; The Hour of the Dragon; A Witch Shall be Born; synopsis for People of the Black Circle; synopsis for The Hour of the Dragon; synopsis for A Witch Shall be Born; untitled synopsis and draft ("Drums of Tombalku"); plus various REH notes related to the stories*

1st Edition, Del Rey, TPB, November 2004

> Edited by Patrice Louinet and Rusty Burke; includes all the line art from ROBERT E. HOWARD'S COMPLETE CONAN OF CIMMERIA, VOLUME 2, by Wandering Star, as well as black and white versions of the color plates; this edition MAY include further corrections, and hence may be better text than the Wandering Star edition

SFBC Fantasy (Science Fiction Book Club), HB, November 2004

> The plates in this book and the Del Rey TPB are both in B&W, not color as in the original Wandering Star version

## The Book of Robert E. Howard

Contains *Pigeons from Hell; Recompense (v); The Pit of the Serpent; Empire (v); Etchings in Ivory (*which includes *Flaming Marble; Skulls and Orchids; Medallions in the Moon; The Gods that Men Forgot; Bloodstones and Ebony); Thor's Son (v); Cimmeria (v); A Sonnet of Good Cheer (v); Red Blades of Black Cathay; The Dust Dance (v); The Bar By the Side of the Road (v); Knife, Bullet and Noose; The Gold and the Grey (v); Gents on the Lynch; A Song Out of Midian (v); She Devil; The Day that I Die (v); The Voice of El-Lil; Black Wind Blowing; The Curse of the Golden Skull; Black Talons*

1st Edition, Zebra, PB, February 1976

Zebra, PB, 2nd printing, April 1976

> Cover and illustrated by Jeff Jones; introduction by Glenn Lord, with comments at the start of each story

Berkley, PB, February 1980

> Cover by Ken Kelly

## Boxing Stories

Contains *In the Ring (v); The Pit of the Serpent; The Bull Dog Breed; The Champion of the Forecastle; Waterfront Law; Texas Fists; The Fightin'est Pair; Vikings of the Gloves;* **Cultured Cauliflowers (Costigan version)**; *A New Game for Costigan; Hard-Fisted Sentiment; When You Were a Set-Up and I Was a Ham (v); The Spirit of Tom Molyneaux; Crowd-Horror;* **Iron Men**; *Kid Galahad; Fists of the Desert; They Always Come Back; Kid Lavigne Is Dead (v)*

1st Edition, Bison Books, HB and TPB, April 2005

> **Contains a First Appearance**; cover art by Gary Gianni; edited by Chris Gruber; HB and TPB being offered at the same time; "Cultured Cauliflowers" is the original Costigan version, from the Cross Plains Public Library typescript

## Bran Mak Morn

Contains ***Foreword by REH, discussing Picts (Excerpted from a letter to HPL, ca. early January 1932 ("Yes I enjoyed the postcards.", the excerpt beginning with "There is one hobby of mine . . .")***; *The Drums of Pictdom (v)*; *The Lost Race*; ***Men of the Shadows***; *Kings of the Night*; ***A Song of the Race (v)***; *Worms of the Earth*; ***Fragment ("A gray sky arched . . .")***; ***The Night of the Wolf***; *The Dark Man*; ***Chant of the White Beard (v); Rune (v); Song of the Pict (v)***

1st Edition, Dell, PB, September 1969

Dell, PB, 2nd, printing, September 1969 (Canada)

> **Contains a First Appearance**; cover art by Frank Frazetta; the last three listed poems are all contained as untitled verse in the story "Men of the Shadows"

## Bran Mak Morn

Contains *Foreword by REH, discussing Picts (Excerpted from a letter to HPL, ca. early January 1932 ("Yes I enjoyed the postcards.", the excerpt beginning with "There is one hobby of mine . . ."); The Drums of Pictdom (v); The Lost Race; Men of the Shadows; Kings of the Night; A Song of the Race (v); Worms of the Earth; Fragment ("A gray sky arched . . ."); The Dark Man; The Gods of Bal-Sagoth; Chant of the White Beard (v); Rune (v); Song of the Pict (v)*

1st Edition, Baen, PB, January 1996

> Cover art by Ken Kelly; introduction by David Weber; the last three listed poems are all contained as untitled verse in the story "Men of the Shadows"

## Bran Mak Morn - The Last King

Contains *Men of the Shadows; Kings of the Night; A Song of the Race (v); Worms of the Earth; The Dark Man; The Lost Race; The Drums of Pictdom (v); The Little People; The Little People - facsimile of original typescript; Children of the Night; Bran Mak Morn (aka Bran Mak Morn: A Play); Bran Mak Morn - facsimile of original manuscript; Bran Mak Morn (Synopsis); Worms of the Earth - draft version; Fragment ("A grey sky arched...");* ***The Bell of Morni (v)***; *Chant of the White Beard (v); Rune (v); Song of the Pict (v)*

1st Edition, Wandering Star, Trade HB, 2001

1st Edition, Wandering Star, Limited HB, 2001

1st Edition, Wandering Star, Leatherbound HB, 2001

> **Contains a First Appearance**; also contains "Robert E. Howard and the Picts: A Chronology" (excerpts from letters, etc., in chronological order); "Robert E. Howard, Bran Mak Morn and the Picts" by Rusty Burke and Patrice Louinet; notes on the Original Howard Texts; foreword by Gary Gianni; introduction by Rusty Burke; includes a CD dramatic reading of *Worms of the Earth* by former members of The Royal Shakespeare Company; limited printing limited to 850 copies, and includes some extra artwork, slipcase, and signed and numbered; leatherbound limited edition is only 50 copies, similar to limited edition, but also with leather binding and slipcase; the last three listed poems are all contained as untitled verse in the story "Men of the Shadows"

## Bran Mak Morn - The Last King

Contains *Men of the Shadows; Kings of the Night; A Song of the Race (v); Worms of the Earth; The Dark Man; The Lost Race; The Drums of Pictdom (v); The Little People; The Little People - facsimile of original typescript; Children of the Night; Bran Mak Morn (aka Bran Mak Morn: A Play); Bran Mak Morn - facsimile of original manuscript; Bran Mak Morn (Synopsis); Worms of the Earth - draft version; Fragment ("A grey sky arched...");The Bell of Morni (v);* ***Untitled fragment ("Men have had visions ere now. . .")***; *Chant of the White Beard (v); Rune (v); Song of the Pict (v)*

1st Edition, Del Rey, TPB, June 2005

> **Contains a First Appearance**; also contains "Robert E. Howard and the Picts: A Chronology" (excerpts from letters, etc., in chronological order); "Robert E. Howard, Bran Mak Morn and the Picts" by Rusty Burke and Patrice Louinet; notes on the Original Howard Texts; foreword by Gary Gianni; introduction by Rusty Burke; includes the last item, which was not in the WS edition; the last three listed poems are all contained as untitled verse in the story "Men of the Shadows"

SFBC, HB, May 2005

Del Rey, TPB, November 2005

## Chants de Guerre et de Mort ("Poems of War and Death")

Contains *Always Comes Evening; The Poets; The Singer in the Mist; Futility; The Song of the Bats; The Moor Ghost; Recompense; The Hills of Kandahar; Which Will Scarcely Be Understood; Haunting Columns; The Last Hour; Ships; The Riders of Babylon; Easter Island; Moon Mockery; Shadows on the Road; The Soul-Eater; The Dream and the Shadow; The Ghost Kings; Desert Dawn; The Song of the Mad Minstrel; The Gates of Ninevah; Fragment; The Harp of Alfred; Remembrance; Crete; Forbidden Magic; Black Chant Imperial; A Song Out of Midian; The Voices Waken Memory; Babel; Song At Midnight; The Ride of Falume; Autumn; Dead Man's Hate; One Who Comes at Eventide; To a Woman; Emancipation; Retribution; Prince and Beggar; Hymn of Hatred; Invective; Babylon; Niflheim; The Heart of the Sea's Desire; Laughter in the Gulfs; A Song of the Don Cossacks; The Gods of Easter Island; Nisapur; Moon Shame; The Tempter; Lines Written in the Realization That I Must Die; A Crown for a King (all v)*

1ˢᵗ Edition, NeO, TPB, January 1987

> Cover and color plates by Jean-Michel Nicollet; edited by Francois Truchaud; this is a French edition of Underwood-Miller's ALWAYS COMES EVENING, with the contents rearranged, and some deleted; bilingual edition (French and English); the first edition is limited to 500 copies, and is numbered

NeO, TPB, 2ⁿᵈ Edition, 1988

> The 2ⁿᵈ only has an illustration on the cover, a much larger print run of 4264 copies, and is a smaller physical size

## The Collected Letters of Robert E. Howard, Volume 1: 1923-1929

Contains *letters to the following:*

*To TCS (handwritten), June 8, 1923 ("Hello Clyde, / May the blessings . . .")*
*To TCS, June 22, 1923 ("Clyde sahib, greeting: / I found your letter . . .)*
*To TCS, July 7, 1923 ("To Clyde bahadur-sahib, greeting: / I got your letter.")*
*To TCS, July 30, 1923 ("Clyde sahib, bohut salaam, bahadur; / The picnic has come . . .")*
*To TCS, August 4, 1923 ("Clyde sahib; / You say I'll be in . . .")*
*To TCS, August 24, 1923 ("Bohut salaam, Clyde sahib; / I was all ready to . . .")*
*To TCS, September 9, 1923 ("Clyde sahib; / First off I must apologize . . .")*
*To TCS, October 5, 1923 ("Salaam, Clyde; / Maybe you think I've moved . . .")*
*To TCS, November 4, 1923 ("Bohut salaam, Clyde bahadur; / It's been quite a while . . .")*
*To Adventure, ca. February 1924 ("I am writing for information . . .")*
*To TCS, April 21, 1924 ("Salaam, Clyde sahib; / I should have written . . .")*
*To TCS, June 19, 1924 ("Salaam, Clyde sahib; / I suppose you think I'm rather slow . . .")*
*To Adventure, ca. July 1924 ("1. At what period did the feudal . . .")*
*To TCS (handwritten), September 7, 1924 ("Salaam, Clyde, / You ought to be here.")*
*To Western Story, ca. fall 1924 ("-And I am not one of those . . .")*
*To TCS, January 7, 1925 ("Salaam, Clyde sahib; / I was in Brownwood the . . .")*
*To TCS, January 30, 1925 ("Salaam, sahib; / I'm sending you a lot of junk.")*
*To Robert W. Gordon, February 4, 1925 ("Dear Sir; / I am sending you a few songs.")*
*To TCS, February 25, 1925 ("Salaam, sahib; / Chapter XIX / Writers of the Bunkorian Age")*
*To TCS, March 17, 1925 ("The top o' the marnin' O'Clydo; / Faith and bejabbers!")*
*To TCS, April 1925 (Salaam, sahib; / What Ho!")*
*To TCS, May 24, 1925 ("Salaam; / Hot zowie, old topper, . . .")*
*To TCS, July 7, 1925 ("Salaam, Sahib; / I believe you owe me a letter.")*
*To TCS, July 16, 1925 ("Salaam, sahib; / What ho, milord!")*
*To TCS, July 1925 ("Salaam; Clyde; / Old boy, I got your letter.")*
*To TCS, ca. July 1925 ("Salaam, Clyde sahib, / I haven't got any answer . . .")*
*To TCS, August 6, 1925 ("Salaam; I'm glad you passed the exams.")*
*To TCS, August 26, 1925 ("Salaam; / I've been thinking.")*
*To TCS, August 28, 1925 ("Salaam; / I've been thinking.")*
*To TCS, October 9, 1925 ("Salaam, sahib; Say, bo, you're developing into a real poet.")*
*To Herbert Klatt, ca. fall 1925 ("Bohut salaam, bahadur; / Again I write you, . . .")*
*To Weird Tales, ca. January 1926 ("These are sheer masterpieces.")*
*To TCS, January 14, 1926 ("Salaam, bahadur, bohut salaam; / By Baal I am joyed . . .")*

*To TCS, January 14, 1926 ("Salaam; / This is a habit of mine, always was.")*
*To Farnsworth Wright, January 23, 1926 ("Dear Sir; / I have no carbon copy of 'Wolfshead'.")*
*To Robert W. Gordon, February 15, 1926 ("Dear Mr. Gordon; / I was delighted to receive your letter, . . .")*
*To The Ring, ca. early 1926 ("Here is my opinion on the greatest heavyweights of all time:")*
*To Robert W. Gordon, April 9, 1926 ("Dear Sir; / I must really ask your pardon . . .")*
*To TCS, April 14, 1926 ("Salaam; / Being in an (un)poetical mood, . . .")*
*To TCS, May 7, 1926 ("Salaam; / I'm sending you a flock of poetry.")*
*To TCS, June 23, 1926 ("Salaam; / I'm trying to write again, . . .")*
*To TCS, August 6, 1926 ("Salaam, sahib; / In the first place, . . .")*
*To TCS, August 21, 1926 ("Bohut salaam, sahib; / I think you owe me one, two, . . .")*
*To Edna Mann, October 30, 1926 ("Dear Friend; / As usual I have to start my letter with an apology, . . .")*
*To Robert W. Gordon (handwritten), January 2, 1927 ("My dear Mr. Gordon; / Upon seeing a request . . .")*
*To Robert W. Gordon, March 17, 1927 ("Dear Mr. Gordon; / This time I have an excuse . . .")*
*To Weird Tales, ca. May 1927 ("Your last three issues have been very fine.")*
*To TCS, ca. late August / early September 1927 ("ARE YOU THE YOUNG MAN . . .")*
*To TCS, ca. fall 1927 ("Salaam: / Then the little boy said to Goofus Gorilla, . . .")*
*To TCS, ca. September 1927 ("Salaam: / Having just got your letter . . .")*
*To TCS, ca. October 1927 ("Salaam: / Seeking cognizance of thing . . .")*
*To TCS, ca. January 1928 ("Salaam: / Listen, you crumb, I think you owe me . . .")*
*To TCS, ca. January 1928 ("I was lying to you Saturday evening when I said . . .")*
*To Harold Preece, ca. January-February 1928 ("Salaam: / Say, listen, tramp, you owe me a letter . . .")*
*To TCS, week of February 20, 1928 ("The fellow who wrote The Kasidah . . .")*
*To TCS, ca. March 1928 ("The only reason for writing this letter . . .")*
*To TCS, ca. March 1928 ("Salaam: / Not having much of anything specially . . .")*
*To TCS, ca. March 1928 ("Salaam: / Glad you're writing these days.")*
*To Harold Preece, ca. early 1928 ("Salaam: / You'll have to pardon me for not . . .")*
*To Weird Tales, ca. April 1928 ("Mr. Lovecraft's latest story, 'The Call of Cthulhu', . . .")*
*To Robert W. Gordon, postmarked May 14, 1928 ("Dear Mr. Gordon: / Many thanks for the letter, . . .")*
*To TCS, ca. May 1928 ("Salaam: / So Klatt has gone West.")*
*To TCS, ca. June 1928 ("Salaam; / Ho, ho, the long lights lift amain . . .")*
*To Harold Preece, ca. June 1928 ("Salaam: / No, I was not trying to catch flies.")*
*To Harold Preece, postmarked June 4, 1928 (postcard with drawing only)*
*To The Fort Worth Record, ca. July 1928 ("Tunney can't win.")*
*To The Brownwood Bulletin, July 18, 1928 ("Arthur 'Kid' Dula is due . . .")*
*To TCS, ca. July 1928 ("Salaam: / A Warning to Orthodoxy")*
*To Harold Preece, ca. August 1928 ("Salaam: / Glad you enjoyed our reunion . . .")*
*To Harold Preece, postmarked September 5, 1928 ("Salaam: / ("Yes, I like the idea of Eldorado . . .")*
*To Harold Preece, ca. September 1928 ("Salaam: / Tunney sure gave Heeney a tough beating . . .")*
*To Harold Preece, postmarked September 23, 1928 ("Salaam: / The tang of winter is in the air . . .")*
*To TCS, ca. October 1928 ("Salaam; / I could have gone with you . . .")*
*To Harold Preece, received October 20, 1928 ("Salaam: / Your stationery is alright.")*
*To TCS, ca. October 1928 ("Salaam: / The reason I'm sending The Junto to you . . .")*
*To TCS, ca. November 1928 ("Salaam: / Listen you goddamn so forth and so on, . . .")*
*To TCS, ca. November 1928 ("Salaam: / I'll swear you're the only galoot . . .")*
*To TCS, ca. November 1928 ("Salaam: THIS IS A LETTER I STARTED . . .")*
*To TCS, ca. November 1928 ("Salaam: / I got such a laugh out of your parody . . .")*
*To TCS, ca. November 1928 ("Heh heh! At last I've sold a story . . .")*
*To TCS, ca. November-December 1928 ("Salaam: / Heh heh! Sappho, the Grecian hills . . .")*
*To TCS, ca. December 1928 ("Salaam: / Out in front of Goldstein's, . . .")*
*To Harold Preece, ca. December 1928 ("Salaam: / You're right; women are great actors.")*
*To TCS, ca. late 1928 ("Salaam: / I'll swear, if I'd laughed much more . . .")*
*To Weird Tales (unmailed), ca. January 1929 (". . . whatever to do with beetles, except . . .")*
*To TCS, ca. February 1929 ("Salaam: / Ancient English Balledel")*
*To TCS, ca. February 1929 ("Salaam: / Last night the Sunday School class . . .")*
*To TCS, ca. March 1929 ("Salaam: / Black Dawn")*

*To TCS, ca. early to mid 1929 ("Salaam: / Life is a yellow mist among the stars.")*
*To Harold Preece, ca. March 1929 ("Salaam: / I've been very neglectful of my correspondence lately.")*
*To Argosy All-Story Weekly, ca. Spring 1929 ("I was born in Texas about twenty-three . . .")*
*To TCS, ca. April 1929 ("The iron harp that Adam christened Life")*
*To Thrills of the Jungle Magazine, ca. June to late 1929 ("Editor Thrills of the Jungle Magazine,")*
*To TCS, ca. June 1929 ("Salaam: / I received an announcement from Chicago: . . .")*
*To TCS, ca. July 1929 ("Salaam: / The main reason I'm writing this letter . . .")*
*To Harold Preece, ca. September 1929 ("Salaam: / I've been reading Destiny Bay . . .")*
*To Harold Preece, postmarked September 18, 1929 ("I don't remember saying anything . . .")*
*To Weird Tales, ca. October 1929 ("I have just been reading the September Weird Tales, . . .)*
*To TCS, ca. late December 1929 ("Well: / Here I am doing . . .")*
as well as the following stories and poems contained in the letters: The Campus at Midnight (v); Untitled ("When Napoleon down in Africa . . .") (v); Neolithic Love Song (v); Untitled ("The helmsman gaily, rode down the rickerboo . . .") (v); Untitled ("Now bright, now red, the sabers sped among the racing horde . . .") (v) The Dook of Stork; Untitled ("Bill Boozy was a pirate bold") (v); Untitled ("Out of Asia the tribesmen came") (v); Untitled ("A clash of steel, a thud of hoofs") (v); Untitled ("A hundred years the great war raged") (v); Untitled ("Palm-trees are waving in the Gulf breeze") (v); Untitled ("Hills of the North! Lavender hills") (v); Untitled ("Dark are your eyes") (v); Slugger's Vow (v); Untitled ("I am the spirit of War!") (v); Untitled ("I lay in Yen's opium joint") (v) The Bombing of Gon Fanfew (v); The Sappious Few Menchew; The Post of the Sappy Skipper; The Bored of the Cow; When You Were a Set-Up and I Was a Ham (v); **Untitled ("And Dempsey climbed into the ring . . .") (v)**; Untitled ("I tell you this my friend") (v); **Untitled ("Mingle my dust with the burning brand") (v); Untitled ("Roses laughed in her pretty hair") (v)**; Untitled ("All the crowd") (v); The Dancer (v); Destiny (2) (v); Laughter (v); Untitled ("We are the duckers of crosses") (v); Untitled ("The shades of night were falling faster") (v); Untitled ("Give ye of my best . . .") (v); Untitled ("Early in the morning I gazed . . .") (v); Eternity (v); Serpent (v); Shadows (3) (v); Destiny (3) (v); Adventure (2) (v); Libertine (v); Nun (v); Prude (v); Adventurer (v); Poet (v); Dancer (v); Dreamer (v); Sailor (v); Cowboy (v); Toper (v); Girl (v); Deeps (v); Thor (v); Mystic (v); Orientia (v); The Mountains of California (v); Monarchs (v); Lust (v); The Alamo (v); San Jacinto (1) (v); Romance (2) (v); Arcadian Days (v); Twilight on Stonehenge (v); Ocean-Thoughts (v); Revenge; Legend; Where Strange Gods Squall (part 1); Untitled ("Take some honey from a cat") (v); The Mottoes of the Boy Scouts (v); Untitled ("Against the blood red moon . . .") (v); Untitled ("Toast to the British! . . .") (v); Where Strange Gods Squall (part 2); Untitled ("What's become of Waring?") (v); The Robes of the Righteous (v); Untitled ("After the trumps are sounded") (v); The Road to Hell (early version, only lines 1-4, 24-28) (v); Flight (early version, incomplete) (v); Untitled ("The Baron of Fenland . . .") (v); **The Fastidious Fooey Mancucu**; Lilith (v); **The Gods Remember (1) (v)**; The Dreams of Men (v); **The Builders (2) (v)**; The Road to Babel (v); Memories (2) (v); Wolfsdung; **Untitled ("Keep women, thrones and kingly lands") (v); Untitled ("The world goes back to the primitive, yea") (v); Untitled ("I do not sing of a paradise") (v); Untitled ("Mother Eve, Mother Eve, . . .") (v); Untitled ("The east is red and I am dead") (v); King Hootus**; Symbols (v); Romany Road (v); Love (v); The Chant Demoniac (v); A Man (v); **The Grey Lover (v); Life (1) (v)**; Untitled ("A typical small town drugstore . . ."); Keresa, Keresita (v); How to Select a Successful Evangelist (v); The Choir Girl (v); A Song of Cheer (v); Repentance (v); Untitled ("I am MAN from the primal . . .") (v); **Untitled ("The spiders of weariness . . .") (v)**; The Dust Dance (various portions from (2)) (v); Untitled ("Moses was our leader . . .") (v); **Secrets (v)**; The Dust Dance (portions from (1)) (v); **The Chinese Gong (v)**; Untitled ("Ho, ho, the long lights lift amain . . .") (v); The Rump of Swift; A Young Wife's Tale (v); Lesbia (1) (v); A Roman Lady (v); Untitled ("They matched me up that night . . .") (v); Song of a Fugitive Bard (v); Untitled ("A cringing woman's lot . . .") (v); Nights to Both of Us Known (v); A Warning to Orthodoxy (v); The Ecstasy of Desolation (v); A Song of the Anchor Chain (v); The Ballad of Abe Slickemmore (v); Song from an Ebony Heart (v); **Untitled ("Swords glimmered up the pass") (v)**; Rebellion (v); **A Great Man Speaks (v); Yodels of Good Cheer to the Pipple, Damn Them (v); Untitled ("He clutched his . . .") (v); Untitled ("Noah was my applesauce") (v); Untitled ("Let me live as I was born to live") (v); Untitled ("Adam's loins were mountains") (v); The Ballad of Monk Kickawhore (v); A Ballad of Insanity (v); Untitled ("I hate the man . . .") (v)**; A Far Country (v); Nancy Hawk – A Legend of Virginity (v); Untitled ("Drawers that a girl . . .") (v); Untitled ("Tumba Hooey"); To a Nameless Woman (v); **Untitled ("Scarlet and gold are the stars tonight") (v); Untitled ("Old Faro Bill was a man of might") (v); Untitled ("Rebel souls from the falling dark") (v)**; The Call of Pan (v); **Untitled ("A sappe ther wos and that a crumbe manne") (v)**; Untitled ("Sappho, the Grecian hills are gold") (v); Untitled ("Romona! Romona!") (v); A Fable for Critics

*(v); Untitled ("My brother he was an auctioneer") (v); Flaming Marble (v); Untitled ("Out in front of Goldstein's . . .") (v); The Deed Beyond the Deed (v); An American (v); Untitled ("There's an isle far away . . .") (v); Shadow of Dreams (v); My Children (v); Untitled ("The women come and . . .") (v); Silence Falls on Mecca's Walls (v); The Last Words He Heard (v); Untitled ("Flappers flicker . . .") (v); Untitled ("I hold all women . . .") (v); Untitled ("Love is singing soft and low") (v); The People of the Winged Skulls; Ancient English Balladel (v); Untitled ("At the Inn of the Gory Dagger") (v); The Case of the College Toilet; Untitled ("And there were lethal women . . .") (v); Untitled ("A haunting cadence . . .") (v); Untitled ("Through the mists of silence . . .") (v); The Mysteries (v); Black Dawn (v); The Path of Strange Wanderers (v); At the Bazaar (v); Untitled ("Hatrack!"); Untitled ("By old Abe Goldstein's . . .") (v); Bastards All!; Songs of Bastards; To a Roman Woman (v); Ivory in the Night (v);* **Untitled ("The iron harp that Adam christened Life") (v); To the Contended (v); High Blue Halls (v); An American Epic (v);** *Black Seas (v);* **Irony;** *Untitled ("A beggar, singing without");* **Untitled ("Tell me not in coocoo numbers");** *Untitled ("Oh, we are little children . . ."); Untitled ("The tall man answered: . . ."); Untitled ("The tall man rose and said: . . ."); Untitled ("The tall man said: . . ."); Untitled ("I knocked upon her lattice – soft!"); Untitled ("Let us up in the hills . . ."); Untitled ("Life is a lot of hooey"); Untitled ("Men are toys . . ."); Untitled ("Moonlight and shadows barred the land")*

1st Edition, REH Foundation Press, HB, expected May 2007

> **Contains a First Appearance**; cover by Jim & Ruth Keegan; limited to 300 copies; edited by Rob Roehm; introduction and annotations by Rusty Burke; all 99 letters thought to have been written from 1923 through 1929; first of a three volume set attempting to publish all of REH's letters; several of these letters had previously been published in REH: SELECTED LETTERS, but those often were truncated, heavily edited, or missing poetry or stories; at time of publication this became the largest REH poetry collection, with 165 poems

## The Collected Letters of Robert E. Howard, Volume 2: 1930-1932

Contains *letters to the following:*

*To Robert H. Barlow, ca. December 1932, Price tells me you are interested . . .*
*To Robert H. Barlow, ca. December 1932, I'll be glad to sign the title . . .*
*To Harry Bates June 1, 1931, You may, or you may not . . .*
*To August Derleth, ca. December (15?) 1932, I had intended answering . . .*
*To August Derleth, ca. December (29?) 1932, I read your recent letter with the greatest interest . . .*
*To Carl Jacobi, pm, March 22, 1932, I found your recent letter very interesting . . .*
*To H.P. Lovecraft, ca. July 1, 1930, I am indeed highly honored to have received . . .*
*To H.P. Lovecraft, ca. August 1930, Let me first thank you for the opportunity . . .*
*To H.P. Lovecraft, ca. September 1930, I envy you your sojourn to Quebec.*
*To H.P. Lovecraft, ca. September 1930, I am very glad that you enjoyed your visit . . .*
*To H.P. Lovecraft, ca. October 1930, It is with greatest delight that I learn . . .*
*To H.P. Lovecraft, ca. December 1930, As always, your letter proved highly . . .*
*To H.P. Lovecraft, ca. January 1931, As always I found your recent letter . . .*
*To H.P. Lovecraft, ca. January 1931, This is rather a belated letter thanking . . .*
*To H.P. Lovecraft, ca. February 1931, I highly appreciate . . .*
*To H.P. Lovecraft, ca. February 1931, I'm writing this letter . . .*
*To H.P. Lovecraft, ca. June 1931, I didn't take much of a trip after all.*
*To H.P. Lovecraft, July 14, 1931, Just a line . . .*
*To H.P. Lovecraft, ca. August 1931, You must indeed . . .*
*To H.P. Lovecraft, ca. October 1931, Thanks for the post-card views.*
*To H.P. Lovecraft, ca. October 1931, I intended to answer . . .*
*To H.P. Lovecraft, ca. October 1931, Many thanks for the opportunity . . .*
*To H.P. Lovecraft, December 9, 1931, I would have answered . . .*
*To H.P. Lovecraft, ca. January 1932, Yes, I enjoyed the postcards . . .*
*To H.P. Lovecraft, ca. February 1932, This isn't to flaunt my homely countenance, . . .*
*To H.P. Lovecraft, March 2, 1932, I'm finally getting around . . .*
*To H.P. Lovecraft, May 24, 1932, Glad you liked the Oriental story . . .*
*To H.P. Lovecraft, July 13, 1932, It is with the utmost humiliation . . .*
*To H.P. Lovecraft, August 9, 1932, I am very sorry to hear of your recent . . .*

*To H.P. Lovecraft, September 22, 1932, I read, as always, your comments on . . .*
*To H.P. Lovecraft, ca. October 1932, I hope you decide . . .*
*To H.P. Lovecraft, November 2, 1932, I want to begin this letter by an apology.*
*To H.P. Lovecraft, ca. November 1932, Here's a clipping . . .*
*To H.P. Lovecraft, ca. December 1932, Having read your latest letter . . .*
*To Kirk Mashburn, ca. March 1932, I am writing to express my appreciation for . . .*
*To Kirk Mashburn, ca. Sept 1932, Just a line to congratulate . . .*
*To Oriental Stories, Summer 1932, Brundage did a fine job . . .*
*To Harold Preece, pm, January 4, 1930, Yes, we fade from youth swiftly.*
*To Harold Preece, ca. February 1930, Go manee jeea git. You're in Kansas now, eh?*
*To Harold Preece, pm, March 24, 1930, Thanks for the picture.*
*To Harold Preece, ca. early Apr 1930 Thanks for the Saint Padraic's card.*
*To Harold Preece, ca. October 1930, Well, Harold, how did you like my story . . .*
*To Harold Preece, ca. October or early November 1930 Well, Harold, I'm sorry to hear your . . .*
*To Harold Preece, pm, November 24, 1930, I hope you'll pardon my negligence . . .*
*To Tevis Clyde Smith, ca. January 1930, Many thanks for the letter you wrote Farnsworth . . .*
*To Tevis Clyde Smith, ca. February 1930, Well, here is the letter.*
*To Tevis Clyde Smith, ca. February 1930, Salaam, Fear Ohghruagach: / Life is a cynical, . . .*
*To Tevis Clyde Smith, ca. March 1930, Well, Fear Finn, tell Cuchullain the Dutchess . . .*
*To Tevis Clyde Smith, ca. March 1930, Well, Fear Finn, / I trust you are in good healthel . . .*
*To Tevis Clyde Smith, ca. early April 1930, Well, Fear Finn, you mention being in a lethargic . . .*
*To Tevis Clyde Smith, ca. April 1930, Salaam: / Well, Fear Finn, I believe in days gone yore . . .*
*To Tevis Clyde Smith, ca. May 1930, Salaam: / Well, Fear Finn, I hope this letter finds you o.k. . . .*
*To Tevis Clyde Smith, ca. May 1930, Well, Fear Finn, I was in Brownwood yesterday . . .*
*To Tevis Clyde Smith, ca. week of June 9, 1930, Well, Fear Finn: / The pictures came at last . . .*
*To Tevis Clyde Smith, ca. July 1930, Salaam, Fear Finn: / Then Stein the peddler . . .*
*To Tevis Clyde Smith, ca. July 1930, Salaam, Fear Finn: / Well, me bauld buccaneer . . .*
*To Tevis Clyde Smith, late July or early August 1930, Well, Fear Finn: / I haven't heard from . . .*
*To Tevis Clyde Smith, ca. September 1930, Well, Fear Finn, me bauld braw Hieland bully . . .*
*To Tevis Clyde Smith, ca. early September 1930, Well, Fear Finn: / I hope you'll sell the . . .*
*To Tevis Clyde Smith, ca. Nov 1930, Well, Fear Finn: / I read your article . . .*
*To Tevis Clyde Smith, probably ca. December 1930, I'm not surprized that Byrne . . .*
*To Tevis Clyde Smith, ca. Dec 1930, Well, Fear Finn: / I don't know when I'll be able . . .*
*To Tevis Clyde Smith, ca. January 1931, Well, Fear Finn: / You owe me a letter, but . . .*
*To Tevis Clyde Smith, ca. February 1931, Fear Finn: / I've delayed writing you, hoping I'd . . .*
*To Tevis Clyde Smith, ca. March 1931, Well, Fear Finn: / Congratulations on your history . . .*
*To Tevis Clyde Smith, ca. March 1931, Fear Finn: / I don't have to tell you how sorry I am . . .*
*To Tevis Clyde Smith, ca. March 14, 1931, Well, Fear Finn: / Heigho for sunny San Antonio.*
*To Tevis Clyde Smith, May 9, 1931, Fear Finn: / Have youse heard anything more . . .*
*To Tevis Clyde Smith, ca. mid-May 1931, Well Fear Finn: / I got a letter from Bradford saying . . .*
*To Tevis Clyde Smith, week of May 18, 1931, Fear Finn: / I should have answered your letter . . .*
*To Tevis Clyde Smith, ca. early June 1931, Fear Finn: / Thanks very much for the Frontier . . .*
*To Tevis Clyde Smith, ca. August 1931, Fear Finn: / Well, I doubt if this missile will be . . .*
*To Tevis Clyde Smith, ca. September 1931, Fear Finn: / Lizzen my children and you shall . . .*
*To Tevis Clyde Smith, ca. September 1931, Fear Finn: / I've been waiting for a letter from you . . .*
*To Tevis Clyde Smith, ca. October 1931, Fear Finn: / The reason I haven't written you sooner . . .*
*To Tevis Clyde Smith, ca. November 1931, Fear Finn: / I wrote Bradford a coarse rude letter . . .*
*To Tevis Clyde Smith, November 1931, Fear Finn: / Here are the blasted verses.*
*To Tevis Clyde Smith, ca. November 1931, Fear Finn: / Have you heard anything from . . .*
*To Tevis Clyde Smith, ca. early January 1932, Dear Clyde: / I only learned of your uncle's . . .*
*To Tevis Clyde Smith, ca. February 1932, Fear Finn: / Well, how runs the world these days?*
*To Tevis Clyde Smith, ca. March 1932, Fear Finn: / Sorry to hear you've been carved on again.*
*To Tevis Clyde Smith, ca. March 1932, Fear Finnel: / When I wzs a kie in East Texas . . .*
*To Tevis Clyde Smith, ca. April 1932, Fear Finn: / I heard from that bone-crushing man-eater . . .*
*To Tevis Clyde Smith, ca. May 1932, Fear Finn: / Just a bit of press-agenting . . .*

*To Tevis Clyde Smith, ca. May 1932, Fear Finn: / Well, here I am back at the old home town . . .*
*To Tevis Clyde Smith, ca. May 1932, Fear Finn: / Thank you very much for going to all the . . .*
*To Tevis Clyde Smith, ca. May 1932, Fear Finn: / Lo, friend, I approach thee with a liver . . .*
*To Tevis Clyde Smith, ca. very late May 1932, Fear Finn: / Let us tool forth to Australia . . .*
*To Tevis Clyde Smith, ca. August 1932, Fear Finn: / I don't know when I've enjoyed a pome . . .*
*To Tevis Clyde Smith, ca. September 1932, Fear Finn: / You owe me a letter, you louse, he said . . .*
*To Tevis Clyde Smith, ca. November 1932, Fear Finn: / Well, I finally get around to answering . . .*
*To Carl Swanson, ca. March 1932 I am sending you . . .*
*To Carl Swanson, ca. April 1932 I am interested in . . .*
*To Carl Swanson, ca. late May1932 I'm sorry you had . . .*
*To Wilfred Blanch Talman, ca. February 1931, I can hardly find words to express . . .*
*To Wilfred Blanch Talman, ca. April 1931, I'm glad you liked "Kings of the Night."*
*To Wilfred Blanch Talman, ca. July 1931, I should have answered your letter . . .*
*To Wilfred Blanch Talman, ca. September 1931, Thank you very much for the letter you wrote . . .*
*To Wilfred Blanch Talman, ca. October 1931, I'm returning herewith your stories . . .*
*To Wilfred Blanch Talman, ca. March 1932, I've finally gotten around to answering . . .*
*To Wilfred Blanch Talman, ca. July 1932, Thanks very much for "De Halve Maen."*
*To Weird Tales, ca. March 1930, "Thirsty Blades" is fine . . .*
*To Weird Tales, ca. December 1930, I was particularly fascinated . . .*
*To Weird Tales, ca. February 1932, Congratulations on the appearance . . .*
*To Farnsworth Wright, ca. June 1930, I have long looked forward to reading . . .*
*To Farnsworth Wright, ca. June-July 1931, In your last letter you asked me to give you . . .*
*As well as the following poetry and stories contained in the letters: Reuben's Brethren (v); Arkham (v); Untitled ("Slow shifts the sands of time . . .") (v);* **Untitled ("Life is a cynical, romantic pig") (v)**; *The Autumn of the World (v);* **A Tribute to the Sportsmanship of the Fans (v); Aw Come On and Fight (v); The Song of the Sage (v)**; *Whispers (v);* **Ambition (v)**; *Whispers on the Nightwind (v); The Gladiator and the Lady (v); The Mutiny of the Hellroarer; The Return of the Sea-Farer (v); A Stirring of Green Leaves (v); The Rhyme of the Viking Path (v); A Marching Song of Connacht (v); Untitled ("Then Stein the peddler . . .") (v); A Ballad of Beer (v); Lives and Crimes of Notable Artists;* **Voyages with Villains**; *Daughter of Evil (v); Untitled ("Lizzen my children and you shall be told") (v); Who is Grandpa Theobold? (v); The Last Day (v); Moonlight on a Skull (v); Untitled ("Many fell at the grog-shop walls") (v); A Weird Ballad (v); Little Brown Man of Nippon (v);* **The Toy Rattle Murder Case**; *John Brown (v); Abe Lincoln (v);* **John Kelley (v); The Tom Thumb Moider Mystery**; *Authorial Version of Doona (v); Dreaming in Israel (v); Samson's Broodings (v);* **A Glass of Vodka; One Blood Strain (v)**; *Lines to G.B. Shaw (v); A Mick in Israel (v); Musings (2) (v); Envoy (v);* **Untitled ("Let it rest with the ages")**; *The Grim Land (v); Mihiragula (v); Song Before Clontarf (v); Belshazzar (v); portions of The Ballad of King Geraint (v); A Peasant on the Euphrates (v); Untitled ("Thomas Fitzgerald, Shane O'Neill") (v)*

1st Edition, REH Foundation Press, HB, expected July 2007

> **Contains a First Appearance**; cover by Jim & Ruth Keegan; limited to 300 copies; edited by Rob Roehm; introduction and annotations by Rusty Burke; all 107 letters thought to have been written from 1930 through 1932; second of a three volume set attempting to publish all of REH's letters; several of these letters had previously been published in REH: SELECTED LETTERS, but those often were truncated, heavily edited, or missing poetry or stories

**The Collected Letters of Robert E. Howard, Volume 3: 1933-1936**

Contains *letters to the following:*

*To Robert H. Barlow, ca. April 2, 1933, Here are some notes . . .*
*To Robert H. Barlow, June 1, 1934, Concerning the illustrations you . . .*
*To Robert H. Barlow, June 14, 1934, If I ever decide to dispose . . .*
*To Robert H. Barlow, July 5, 1934, Here, at last, is the last . . .*
*To Robert H. Barlow, Dec 17, 1935, Thank you very much for the copy . . .*
*To Robert H. Barlow, February 14, 1936, This is to express, somewhat belatedly . . .*
*To The Californian Magazine, 1936, Thank you very much . . .*
*To The Claytons Magazines, June 13, 1933, A few weeks ago . . .*
*To Denis Archer, May 20, 1934, As you doubtless remember . . .*
*To Denis Archer, May 22, 1934, As you doubtless remember . . .*
*To Jack Byrne, April 21, 1936, My agent, O.A. Kline, tells me . . .*
*To August Derleth, ca. January 1933, I was much interested in your accounts . . .*
*To August Derleth, ca. February 1933, After so long a time, I'm getting around to answering . . .*
*To August Derleth, ca. March 1933, I should have told you that I meant to keep . . .*
*To August Derleth, ca. March 13, 1933, Many thanks for FRONTIER GENERATIONS . . .*
*To August Derleth, ca. March (23?) 1933, I quite agree with you regarding . . .*
*To August Derleth, ca. May 1933, As a starter, I must apologize . . .*
*To August Derleth, July 3, 1933, Please accept my belated thanks . . .*
*To August Derleth, ca. July 1933, Thanks immensely for the opportunity of reading . . .*
*To August Derleth, ca. August 1933, Yes, I certainly did enjoy "Five Alone" . . .*
*To August Derleth, September 4, 1933, Glad you liked the rhyme I sent you.*
*To August Derleth, ca. October 1933, Thanks very much for the opportunity of reading . . .*
*To August Derleth, ca. October 1933, By all means use the hawk incident . . .*
*To August Derleth, ca. November 1933, I enjoyed reading your "Hawk on the Blue" very much . . .*
*To August Derleth, ca. December 1933, I think Scribner's was nuts to turn down "Hawk on . . .*
*To August Derleth, ca. December 1933, Hope you had a good Christmas . . .*
*To August Derleth, ca. January 1934, I note with sympathy your remarks . . .*
*To August Derleth, ca. late March 1934, Pardon this belated letter . . .*
*To August Derleth, May 30 1934, I have a feeling that I've been owing . . .*
*To August Derleth, ca. June 1934, Having completed several weeks of . . .*
*To August Derleth, ca. mid-October 1934, I haven't yet gotten a copy . . .*
*To August Derleth, December 11, 1934, I recently found your letter of October 18 in my file . . .*
*To August Derleth, ca. February 1935, I would have written you long ago . . .*
*To August Derleth, ca. June 1935, I reckon you've wondered at times . . .*
*To August Derleth, June 20, 1935, This card was purchased in Lincoln . . .*
*To August Derleth, July 4, 1935, Thanks very much for the article, "Afternoon in June." . . .*
*To August Derleth, November 1, 1935, I should have written you months ago . . .*
*To August Derleth, November 28, 1935, Thanks for the opportunity of reading . . .*
*To August Derleth, April 15, 1936, Just a hurried line to let you know . . .*
*To August Derleth, May 9, 1936, I am indeed sorry to learn of the deaths . . .*
*To The Fantasy Fan, ca. 1933, I find the Fantasy Fan . . .*
*To The Fantasy Fan, ca. late 1933, I liked the November issue . . .*
*To The Fantasy Fan, ca. 1934, Smith's poem in the March issue . . .*
*To R. Fowler Gafford, May 20, 1934, This answer to your last letter . . .*
*To Charles D. Hornig, November 1, 1933, Thanks for the copy . . .*
*To Charles D. Hornig, November 10, 1933, Here is a short story, "The Frost-King's Daughter" . . .*
*To Charles D. Hornig, August 10, 1934, Glad you liked the verses . . .*
*To Charles D. Hornig, May 3, 1935, I'm very sorry . . .*
*To Carl Jacobi, March 17, 1933, I am glad to write to Wright, commenting . . .*
*To Carl Jacobi, ca. Summer 1934, Thank you for the kind comments . . .*
*To Otis Adelbert Kline, May 13, 1935, I'm writing this to ask . . .*
*To Otis Adelbert Kline, January 8, 1936, A belated acknowledgment . . .*
*To Otis Adelbert Kline, January 13, 1936, Just read yours of the 11th.*

*To Otis Adelbert Kline, January 18, 1936, Just read your letter of the 15th.*
*To William Kofoed, Jan 8, 1935, Glad that Bloomfield can use "Fists of the Desert."*
*To August Lenniger, February 20, 1933, Here are the copies of "The Shadow Kingdom" . . .*
*To August Lenniger, March 8, 1933, This is to inform you that I have . . .*
*To August Lenniger, Dec 27, 1935, I have received your letter of the 17ᵗʰ.*
*To H.P. Lovecraft, March 6, 1933, I have just read your recent letter . . .*
*To H.P. Lovecraft, April 23, 1933, I'm enclosing some of the latest views . . .*
*To H.P. Lovecraft, ca. July 1933, Glad we got the physical-mental question . . .*
*To H.P. Lovecraft, ca. August 1933, I am sending on to you the enclosed manuscript . . .*
*To H.P. Lovecraft, ca. September or October 1933, I was very sorry to hear . . .*
*To H.P. Lovecraft, November 3, 1933, Glad you liked the rattles.*
*To H.P. Lovecraft, ca. November 1933, I am so submerged in work . . .*
*To H.P. Lovecraft, ca. January 1934, I enjoyed very much . . .*
*To H.P. Lovecraft, ca. January 1934, I deeply appreciate . . .*
*To H.P. Lovecraft, March 24, 1934, Here's a little item . . .*
*To H.P. Lovecraft, ca. May 1934, Glad you're having a good time in Florida.*
*To H.P. Lovecraft, ca. June 1934, Glad you're finding . . .*
*To H.P. Lovecraft, ca. July 1934, I started writing this months ago . . .*
*To H.P. Lovecraft, ca. September 1934, Thanks very much for the postcards . . .*
*To H.P. Lovecraft, ca. December 1934, I read your account . . .*
*To H.P. Lovecraft, December 3, 1934, Glad you found the cat article of some . . .*
*To H.P. Lovecraft, ca. January 1935, I have finally found time . . .*
*To H.P. Lovecraft, ca. May 1935, The reason I haven't answered . . .*
*To H.P. Lovecraft, ca. July 1935, Thanks very much for the fine post-cards . . .*
*To H.P. Lovecraft, October 3, 1935, Here are some clippings . . .*
*To H.P. Lovecraft, December 5, 1935, A rather belated reply to your interesting . . .*
*To H.P. Lovecraft, February 11, 1936, Glad you enjoyed the dream write-up I sent you.*
*To H.P. Lovecraft, May 11, 1936, (partial draft of May 13)*
*To H.P. Lovecraft, May 13, 1936, I am indeed sorry to hear . . .*
*To Magic Carpet Magazine, January 1933, Thanks very much for the remarks . . .*
*To Magic Carpet Magazine, April 1933, Congratulations on the quality . . .*
*To P. Schuyler Miller, SM, March 10, 1936, I feel indeed honored that you and Dr. Clark . . .*
*To Alvin Earl Perry, ca. early 1935, The first character I ever created . . .*
*To Emil Petaja, December 17, 1934, Thank you very much for the splendid sonnet.*
*To Emil Petaja, March 6, 1935, Glad the ms. proved satisfactory.*
*To Emil Petaja, July 23, 1935, Please believe my delay in answering . . .*
*To Emil Petaja, September 6, 1935, Yes, I did like . . .*
**To Harold Preece, date unknown, Salaam: Say, listen, tramp . . .**
*To E. Hoffmann Price, February 15, 1936, I have eventually found time to answer your cards.*
*To E. Hoffmann Price, April 21, 1936, Glad you-all liked "She-Devil."*
*To E. Hoffmann Price, June 3, 1936, Sorry to hear Pawang Ali has been banished.*
*To Novalyne Price, September 27, 1934, How about going to the show . . .*
*To Novalyne Price, ca. December 1934, Like my meal-ticket, Conan the Cimmerian . . .*
*To Novalyne Price, June 19, 1935, The weather is good . . .*
*To Novalyne Price, June 19, 1935, Dear Novalyne . . . cordially . . .*
*To Novalyne Price, July 4, 1935, I take my typewriter . . .*
*To Novalyne Price, July 8, 1935, Thank you for your invitation to call . . .*
*To Novalyne Price, February 14, 1936, I heard yesterday you had . . .*
*To Novalyne Price, February 15, 1936, I'm sorry but I won't be able . . .*
*To Novalyne Price, March 5, 1936, I just now read the letter . . .*
*To Novalyne Price, May 27, 1936, You needn't have bothered . . .*
*To Hugh G. Schonfield, June 15, 1933, As I promised, in answer to your letter . . .*
*To Clark Ashton Smith, pm, March 15, 1933, I hardly know how to thank you for the copy . . .*
*To Clark Ashton Smith, ca. July 1933, I really must apologize for not having . . .*
*To Clark Ashton Smith, pm, July 22, 1933, I can hardly find words to express . . .*

*To Clark Ashton Smith, ca. October 1933, Thanks very much for the kind things . . .*
*To Clark Ashton Smith, pm, December 14, 1933, Only the fact that I have been sick . . .*
*To Clark Ashton Smith, December 20, 1933 [no text]*
*To Clark Ashton Smith, ca. January 1934, Thanks again for the drawing of the wizard.*
*To Clark Ashton Smith, ca. March 1934, I am sorry to hear you have been indisposed . . .*
*To Clark Ashton Smith, pm, May 21 1934, My delay in answering your last letter . . .*
*To Clark Ashton Smith, July 23, 1935, I'm ashamed of my long delay in answering . . .*
*To Tevis Clyde Smith, ca. May 1933, Fear Finn: / I was in Brownwood yesterday . . .*
*To Tevis Clyde Smith, ca. October 1933, Fear Finn: / The Galleon Press has just brought out . . .*
*To Tevis Clyde Smith, Undated, Salaam / Again glancing over your last letter . . .*
*To Tevis Clyde Smith, Undated, Ha ha! Your not going to get off so easily . . .*
*To Tevis Clyde Smith, Undated, Salaam: / I have forgotten whether you or Truett . . .*
*To Tevis Clyde Smith, Undated, The Seeker thrust . . .*
*To Tevis Clyde Smith, Undated, Not even a movie in this godforsaken town . . .*
*To Tevis Clyde Smith, Undated, Well, Fear Finn, I read your story . . .*
*To Tevis Clyde Smith, Undated, Fear Finn: / I'm damned if I can think of anything . . .*
*To Tevis Clyde Smith, Undated, Salaam: / Shadows of Dreams*
*To Tevis Clyde Smith, Undated, Salaam: / There once was a wicked . . .*
*To Tevis Clyde Smith, Undated, If you dont publish this . . .*
*To Tevis Clyde Smith, Undated, Salaam: / As my dear public . . .*
*To Tevis Clyde Smith, Undated, "King Bahthur's Court"*
*To Tevis Clyde Smith, Undated, Ahatou noyon, Fear Finn: / Thinking of nothing . . .*
*To Tevis Clyde Smith, Undated, Salaam / Skulls against the Dawn*
*To Tevis Clyde Smith, undated, enclosed document, The Adventurer's Mistress*
*To Tevis Clyde Smith, undated, enclosed document, I've done my part in writing it.*
*To Tevis Clyde Smith, undated, enclosed document, Poem penned by Akbar Ali . . .*
*To Tevis Clyde Smith, undated, enclosed document, Crusade*
*To Tevis Clyde Smith, undated, enclosed document, Sang the King of Midian*
*To Tevis Clyde Smith, undated, enclosed document, Renunciation*
*To Tevis Clyde Smith, undated, enclosed document, Thoughts of an Afghan on a raid*
*To Tevis Clyde Smith, undated, enclosed document, Relentless Reginald . . .*
*To Tevis Clyde Smith, undated, enclosed document, Drawing of a strange cow*
*To Frank Thurston Torbett, April 28, 1936, I'm sorry I have not . . .*
*To Frank Thurston Torbett, June 3, 1936, My mother is very low . . .*
*To Donald Wandrei, ca. February 21, 1933, I've been intending to write to you . . .*
*To Weird Tales, ca. May 1936, Enthusiasm impels me . . .*
*To Farnsworth Wright, May 6, 1935, I always hate to write a letter like this . . .*
*To an unknown recepient, Salaam: Not much to say . . .*
*As well as the following poetry and stories contained in the letters: Untitled ("You have built a world of paper and wood") (v); Untitled ("They were there, in the distance dreaming") (v) and Untitled ("Under the grim San Saba hills") (v); Cimmeria (v); Surrender (2) (v); I Praise My Nativity (v); Dreaming (v); The Coming of Bast (v); A Song of College (v); That Women May Sing of Us (v); Sighs in the Yellow Leaves (v); A Song of Greenwich (v); Ballade (v); Untitled ("The Seeker thrust . . ."); To a Certain Cultured Woman (v); The Winds of the Sea (2) (v); The Iron Harp (a cycle of five poems, including Out of the Deep; Babel; Laughter in the Gulf; Moon Shame; A Crown for a King); The Cuckoo's Revenge (v); The Madness of Cormac (v); A Challenge to Bast (v); A Poet's Skull (v); Shadows of Dreams (v); Untitled ("There once was a wicked old elf") (v); Untitled ("There are grim things did, . . .") (v); To Lyle Saxon (v); The Viking of the Sky (v); **Untitled ("As my dear public remembers . . .")**; King Bahthur's Court; The Werewolf Murder Case; Skulls Against the Dawn (v); The Adventurer's Mistress (2) (v); Untitled ("There were three lads . . .") (v); Untitled ("Match a toad with a far-winged hawk") (v); Crusade (v); Sang the King of Midian (v); Renunciation (v); Drummings on an Empty Skull (v); The Diablos Trail (synopsis)*

1st Edition, REH Foundation Press, HB, expected late 2007

> **Contains a First Appearance**; cover by Jim & Ruth Keegan; limited to 300 copies; edited by Rob Roehm; introduction and annotations by Rusty Burke; all 146 letters thought to have been written from 1933 through 1936; third of a three volume set attempting to publish all of REH's letters; several of these

letters had previously been published in REH: SELECTED LETTERS, but those often were truncated, heavily edited, or missing poetry or stories

## The Coming of Conan

Contains *The Hyborian Age, part 1; The Shadow Kingdom; The Mirrors of Tuzun Thune; The King and the Oak (v); The Tower of the Elephant; The God in the Bowl (modified by LSDC); Rogues in the House; The Frost Giant's Daughter (modified by LSDC); Queen of the Black Coast;* **plus a letter to P. Schuyler Miller, March 10, 1936 ("I feel indeed honored that you and Dr. Clark . . .")**
1st Edition, Gnome Press, HB, 1953
> **Contains a First Appearance**; cover by Frank Kelly Freas; limited to 4000 copies; introduction by REH, HPL and John Clark; edited by LSDC

## The Coming of Conan the Cimmerian

Contains *The Phoenix on the Sword; The Frost-Giant's Daughter; The God in the Bowl; The Tower of the Elephant; The Scarlet Citadel; Queen of the Black Coast; Black Colossus; Iron Shadows in the Moon; Xuthal of the Dusk; Pool of the Black One; Rogues in the House; The Vale of Lost Women; The Devil in Iron; Untitled (The Hall of the Dead); Untitled (The Hand of Nergal); The Hyborian Age; Cimmeria (v); Notes on various Peoples of the Hyborian Age*
1st Edition, Del Rey, TPB, November 2003
> Based on the Wandering Star's ROBERT E. HOWARD'S COMPLETE CONAN OF CIMMERIA, VOLUME 1; also contains REH's two maps of the Hyborian Age and a Hyborian Names page; also contains excerpts from drafts and other miscellanea; used original typescripts for "Frost-Giant's Daughter", "The God in the Bowl", "The Scarlet Citadel", "Vale of Lost Women", plus lots of the unfinished stuff and marginalia, including unpublished synopses, and the first-submitted version of "The Phoenix on the Sword"; includes all the line art from ROBERT E. HOWARD'S COMPLETE CONAN OF CIMMERIA, VOLUME 1, as well as black-and-white versions of the color plates; artwork by Mark Schultz; this has gone to multiple printings, the first is on a very white paper, the rest on a more common-looking cream or off-white paper; according to the editor, this may be THE MOST PREFERRED SOURCE, as Del Rey had their own pro editors go through the document, and found some mistakes Patrice and Rusty had missed, likely be the same answer for the other volumes as well

SFBC Fantasy (Science Fiction Book Club), HB, December 2004
> This is a HB reprint of the Del Rey PB edition, with the color plates done in B&W

Del Rey, HB, November 2005
> The color plates are restored

## The Complete Action Stories

Contains *The TNT Punch; The Sign of the Snake; Blow the Chinks Down!; Breed of Battle; Dark Shanghai; Mountain Man; Guns of the Mountains; The Scalp Hunter; A Gent from Bear Creek; The Road to Bear Creek; The Haunted Mountain; War on Bear Creek; The Feud Buster; Cupid from Bear Creek; The Riot at Cougar Paw; The Apache Mountain War; Pilgrims to the Pecos; Pistol Politics; Evil Deeds at Red Cougar; High Horse Rampage; "No Cowherders Wanted"; The Conquerin' Hero of the Humbolts; Sharp's Gun Serenade*
1st Edition, Hermanthis, PB, November 2001
> Introduction and edited by Paul Herman; contains the original artwork that was published with the original pulps; first printing limited to 50 copies, sold out in a week; first has little color bleed on cover into artwork, and says "Robert E.Howard" on cover, no space between E. and Howard, both errors corrected on later printings; total printed less than 350, around 321

Wildside Press, HB, November 2003
Wildside Press, TPB, January 2005

## The Complete Chronicles of Conan

Contains *The Hyborian Age; Cimmeria (v); The Phoenix on the Sword; The Scarlet Citadel; The Tower of the Elephant; Black Colossus; The Slithering Shadow; The Pool of the Black One; Rogues in the House; Shadows in the Moonlight; Queen of the Black Coast; The Devil in Iron; The People of the Black Circle; A Witch Shall Be Born; Jewels of Gwahlur; Beyond the Black River; Shadows in Zamboula; Red Nails; The Hour of the Dragon (with all verse headings); The God in the Bowl; The Black Stranger; The Frost-Giant's Daughter; Drums of Tombalku (draft); The Vale of Lost Women; Wolves Beyond the Border (draft); The Snout in the Dark (draft); The Hall of the Dead (synopsis); The Hand of Nergal (fragment); Notes on Various Peoples of the Hyborian Age*

1$^{st}$ Edition, Gollancz, HB, January 2006

2$^{nd}$ printing, Gollancz, HB, du

> Edited and Afterword by Stephen Jones; two page map of the Hyborian Age by Dave Senior; collects The Conan Chronicles Volume 1 and Volume 2 published by Gollancz/Millennium into one edition; the cover is leather-style with Les Edwards' art embossed in gold; the binding material has the exact feel of leather, but is a synthetic; full color frontispiece, full page illustrations, and spot illustrations; no jacket, as issued; the second printing has the frontispiece in B&W instead of color

## The Complete Yellow Jacket

Contains *Halt! Who Goes There?; After the Game; Sleeping Beauty; Weekly Short Story; Private Magrath of the A.E.F. (v); The Thessalians; Ye College Days; Cupid v. Pollux; The Reformation: A Dream*

2$^{nd}$ Edition, Hermanthis, PB, October 2001

> Edited by Paul Herman; first printing limited to 50 copies; first edition was printed as a staple-bound chapbook (see Chapbook listings); 2$^{nd}$ edition is formatted significantly differently from 1$^{st}$, perfectbound instead of staples, slightly larger size, yellow cover, two small changes in two footnotes; additional printings for a total of 350 copies of 2$^{nd}$ edition; first printing of 50 copies of 2$^{nd}$ edition actually had a white cover, then all later printings were with yellow cover

## Conan

Contains *The Hyborian Age (Part 1); The Tower of the Elephant; The Hall of the Dead (completed by LSDC); The God in the Bowl; Rogues in the House; The Hand of Nergal (completed by Lin Carter) plus a letter to P. Schuyler Miller, March 10, 1936 ("I feel indeed honored that you and Dr. Clark . . .")*

1$^{st}$ Edition, Lancer, PB, 1968 (60c)

> Cover art by Frank Frazetta; edited by LSDC; it is quite possible that over one million copies of this book are in print; the early Lancer printings have purple-edged pages

Lancer, PB, 2$^{nd}$ printing, 1968 (Canada)

Lancer, PB, 3$^{rd}$ printing, 1968 (75c)

Lancer, PB, 4$^{th}$, printing, 1968 (Canada)

Lancer, PB, 5$^{th}$ printing, 1969

Lancer, PB, 6$^{th}$ printing, nd (1970, #75-104)

Lancer, PB, 7$^{th}$ printing, nd (1970, #75104-095)

Lancer, PB, 8$^{th}$ printing, nd (Canada)

Lancer, PB, 9$^{th}$ printing, nd (1971)

> Pages are now yellow-edged starting with this printing

Lancer, PB, 10$^{th}$ printing, April 1972

Lancer, PB, 11$^{th}$ printing, September 1972

Lancer, PB, 12$^{th}$ printing, 1973

> Lancer went backrupt in 1973, but there were numerous later printings by Prestige and Ace, perhaps 20 or more printings total; Prestige books have ACE on the cover, but are stamped with "Prestige" on the copyright page; also editions by Sphere and Orbit; this series continued up to the late 1980's; also the basis for numerous licensed as well as bootleg non-English editions; by far the most reproduced REH series in the world; it is quite possible that over one million copies of this book are in print

## The Conan Chronicles 1

Contains *The Hyborian Age (Part 1); The Tower of the Elephant; The Hall of the Dead (completed by LSDC); The God in the Bowl; Rogues in the House; The Hand of Nergal (completed by Lin Carter); The Bloodstained God (with LSDC); The Frost Giant's Daughter; Queen of the Black Coast; Vale of Lost Women; The Snout in the Dark (completed by LSDC and Lin Carter); Hawks Over Shem (with LSDC); Black Colossus; Shadows in the Moonlight; The Road of the Eagles (with LSDC); A Witch Shall Be Born*

1st Edition, Sphere (UK), PB, 1989

> Combines the first three Lancer editions, CONAN, CONAN OF CIMMERIA, and CONAN THE FREEBOOTER; cover art by Blas Gallego

Orbit (UK), PB, 1989 (may be the Sphere edition)

Orbit (UK), PB, 2nd printing, 1990

Orbit (UK), PB, 3rd printing, 1991

Orbit (UK), PB, 4th printing, 1992

## The Conan Chronicles I: The People of the Black Circle

Contains *The Hyborian Age; The Tower of the Elephant; The Hall of the Dead; The God in the Bowl; Rogues in the House; The Hand of Nergal; The Frost-Giant's Daughter; Queen of the Black Coast; The Vale of Lost Women; The Snout in the Dark; Black Colossus; Shadows in the Moonlight; A Witch Shall be Born; Shadows in Zamboula; The Devil in Iron; The People of the Black Circle; The Slithering Shadow; Drums of Tombalku; The Pool of the Black One*

1st Edition, Millenium (UK), PB, August 2000

> Part 1 of two-part "complete" Conan set; supposedly based mostly on original WEIRD TALES text, few LSDC-edited versions; the second volume was published by Gollancz without Millenium

## The Conan Chronicles 2

Contains *The People of the Black Circle; The Slithering Shadow; The Drums of Tombulku; The Pool of the Black One; Shadows in Zamboula; The Devil in Iron; The Flame Knife (with LSDC)*

1st Edition, Orbit (UK), PB, September 1990

> Cover art by Blas Gallego; collects three of the Lancer editions, CONAN THE ADVENTURER, CONAN THE WANDERER, and CONAN THE BUCCANEER

## The Conan Chronicles II: Hour of the Dragon

Contains *Notes on Various Peoples of the Hyborian Age; Red Nails; Jewels of Gwahlur; Beyond the Black River; The Black Stranger;* **Wolves Beyond the Border (original draft)**; *The Phoenix on the Sword; The Scarlet Citadel; The Hour of the Dragon, with verse headings; Cimmeria (v)*

1st Edition, Gollancz (UK), PB, 2001

> **Contains a First Appearance**; part 2 of two part complete Conan set, mostly based on original WEIRD TALES text, few LSDC-edited versions; "Wolves Beyond the Border" is first appearance of draft; VOLUME ONE was published by Millenium

## Conan of Cimmeria

Contains *The Bloodstained God (with LSDC); The Frost Giant's Daughter; Queen of the Black Coast; Vale of Lost Women;* **The Snout in the Dark (completed by LSDC and Lin Carter)**

1st Edition, Lancer, PB, 1969

> Cover art by Frank Frazetta; edited by LSDC; the early Lancer printings have purple-edged pages

Lancer, PB, 2nd printing, nd (1970)

Lancer, PB, 3rd printing, nd (Canada)

Lancer, PB, 4th printing, nd (1971)

> Pages are now yellow-edged starting with this printing

Lancer, PB, 5th printing, April 1972

Lancer, PB, 6th printing, September 1972

Lancer, PB, 7th printing, 1973

> Lancer went backrupt in 1973, but there were numerous later printings by Prestige and Ace, perhaps 20 or more printings total; Prestige books have ACE on the cover, but are stamped with "Prestige" on the

copyright page; also editions by Sphere and Orbit; this series continued up to the late 1980's; also the basis for numerous licensed as well as bootleg non-English editions; by far the most reproduced REH series in the world; it is quite possible that over one million copies of this book are in print

## Conan the Adventurer

Contains *The People of the Black Circle; The Slithering Shadow;* **Drums of Tombulku (completed by LSDC);** *The Pool of the Black One*

1st Edition, Lancer, PB, November 1966

> **Contains a First Appearance**; cover art by Frank Frazetta; introduction by LSDC, edited by LSDC; the early Lancer printings have purple-edged pages

Lancer, PB, 2nd printing, 1967

Lancer, PB, 3rd printing, 1967 (Canada)

Lancer, PB, 4th printing, 1968

Lancer, PB, 5th printing, 1969

Lancer, PB, 6th printing, nd (1970)

Lancer, PB, 7th printing, nd (1971)

> Pages now yellow-edged starting with this printing

Lancer, PB, 8th printing, April 1972

Lancer, PB, 9th printing, September 1972

Lancer, PB, 10th printing, 1973

Sphere, PB, 1973

> Lancer went backrupt in 1973, but there were numerous later printings by Prestige and Ace, perhaps 20 or more printings total; Prestige books have ACE on the cover, but are stamped with "Prestige" on the copyright page; also editions by Sphere and Orbit; this series continued up to the late 1980's; by far the most reproduced REH series in the world; it is quite possible that over one million copies of this book are in print; the original Sphere edition used the Frazetta cover, by October 1988 Sphere was using a Blas Gallego cover

## Conan the Avenger

Contains *The Hyborian Age (part 2)*

1st Edition, Lancer, PB, 1968

> Cover art by Frank Frazetta; edited by LSDC; the early Lancer printings have purple-edged pages

Lancer, PB, 2nd printing, 1968 (Canada)

Lancer, PB, 3rd printing, 1969

Lancer, PB, 4th printing, 1969 (Canada)

Lancer, PB, 5th printing, nd (1970)

Lancer, PB, 6th printing, nd (1971)

> Pages now yellow-edged starting with this printing

Lancer, PB, 7th printing, April 1972

Lancer, PB, 8th printing, September 1972

Lancer, PB, 9th printing, 1973

> Lancer went backrupt in 1973, but there were numerous later printings by Prestige and Ace, perhaps 20 or more printings total; Prestige books have ACE on the cover, but are stamped with "Prestige" on the copyright page; also editions by Sphere and Orbit; this series continued up to the late 1980's; also the basis for numerous licensed as well as bootleg non-English editions; by far the most reproduced REH series in the world; it is quite possible that over one million copies of this book are in print

## Conan the Barbarian

Contains *Black Colossus; Shadows in the Moonlight; A Witch Shall Be Born; Shadows in Zamboula; The Devil in Iron*

1st Edition, Gnome Press, HB, 1954

> Cover by Ed Emshwiller; limited to 3000 copies, edited by LSDC

## Conan the Conqueror

Contains *Conan the Conqueror* (aka *The Hour of the Dragon*)
>1$^{st}$ Edition, Gnome Press, HB, 1950

Cover by John Forte; edited by John D. Clark; limited to 5000 copies

Ace, PB, 1953 (D-36)
>Based on the Gnome Press edition; an "Ace Double", with "The Sword of Rhiannon", by Leigh Brackett, as the other side

Boardman (UK), HB, 1954
>Photo-offset from the Gnome Press edition

Lancer, PB, March 1967
>Cover art by Frank Frazetta; edited and introduction by LSDC; the early Lancer printings have purple-edged pages

Lancer, PB, 2$^{nd}$ printing, 1967 (Canada)

Lancer, PB, 3$^{rd}$ printing, 1968

Lancer, PB, 4$^{th}$ printing, 1968 (Canada)

Lancer, PB, 5$^{th}$ printing, 1969

Lancer, PB, 6$^{th}$ printing, 1969 (Canada)

Lancer, PB, 7$^{th}$ printing, nd (1970)

Lancer, PB, 8$^{th}$ printing, nd (Canada)
>Pages now yellow-edged starting with this printing

Lancer, PB, 9$^{th}$ printing, nd (1971)

Lancer, PB, 10$^{th}$ printing, August 1972

Lancer, PB, 11$^{th}$ printing, January 1973
>Used as the basis for all subsequent PB editions; Lancer went backrupt in 1973, but there were numerous later printings by Prestige and Ace, perhaps 20 or more printings total; Prestige books have ACE on the cover, but are stamped with "Prestige" on the copyright page; also editions by Sphere and Orbit; this series continued up to the late 1980's; also the basis for
>numerous licensed as well as bootleg non-English editions; by far the most reproduced REH series in the world; it is quite possible that over one million copies of this book are in print

## Conan the Freebooter

Contains *Hawks Over Shem (with LSDC); Black Colossus; Shadows in the Moonlight; The Road of the Eagles (with LSDC); A Witch Shall Be Born*

1$^{st}$ Edition, Lancer, PB, 1968
>Cover art by John Duillo; edited by LSDC; the early Lancer printings have purple-edged pages

Lancer, PB, 2$^{nd}$ printing, 1968 (Canada)

Lancer, PB, 3$^{rd}$ printing, 1969

Lancer, PB, 4$^{th}$ printing, nd (1970)

Lancer, PB, 5$^{th}$ printing, nd (Canada)

Lancer, PB, 6$^{th}$ printing, nd (1971)
>Pages now yellow-edged starting with this printing

Lancer, PB, 7$^{th}$ printing, January 1973
>Lancer went backrupt in 1973, but there were numerous later printings by Prestige and Ace, perhaps 20 or more printings total; Prestige books have ACE on the cover, but are stamped with "Prestige" on the copyright page; also editions by Sphere and Orbit; this series continued up to the late 1980's; also the basis for numerous licensed as well as bootleg non-English editions; by far the most reproduced REH series in the world; it is quite possible that over one million copies of this book are in print

## Conan the Usurper

Contains *The Treasure of Tranicos; The Phoenix on the Sword; The Scarlet Citadel;* **Wolves Beyond the Border (completed by LSDC)**

1$^{st}$ Edition, Lancer, PB, May 1967
>**Contains a First Appearance**; cover art by Frank Frazetta; edited and introduction by LSDC; the early Lancer printings have purple-edged pages

Lancer, PB, 2$^{nd}$ printing, 1967 (Canada)
Lancer, PB, 3$^{rd}$ printing, 1969
Lancer, PB, 4$^{th}$ printing, nd (1970)
Lancer, PB, 5$^{th}$ printing, nd (1971)
>   Pages now yellow-edged starting with this printing

Lancer, PB, 6$^{th}$ printing, August 1972
Lancer, PB, 7$^{th}$ printing, January 1973
>   Lancer went backrupt in 1973, but there were numerous later printings by Prestige and Ace, perhaps 20 or more printings total; Prestige books have ACE on the cover, but are stamped with "Prestige" on the copyright page; also editions by Sphere and Orbit; this series continued up to the late 1980's; also the basis for numerous licensed as well as bootleg non-English editions; by far the most reproduced REH series in the world; it is quite possible that over one million copies of this book are in print

## Conan the Wanderer

Contains *Shadows in Zamboula; The Devil in Iron; The Flame Knife (with LSDC)*
1$^{st}$ Edition, Lancer, PB, 1968
>   Cover art by John Duillo; edited by LSDC; the early Lancer printings have purple-edged pages

Lancer, PB, 2$^{nd}$ printing, 1968 (Canada)
Lancer, PB, 3$^{rd}$ printing, 1969
Lancer, PB, 4$^{th}$ printing, 1969 (Canada)
Lancer, PB, 5$^{th}$ printing, nd (1970)
Lancer, PB, 6$^{th}$ printing, nd (Canada)
Lancer, PB, 7$^{th}$ printing, nd (1971)
>   Pages now yellow-edged starting with this printing

Lancer, PB, 8$^{th}$ printing, May 1972
Lancer, PB, 9$^{th}$ printing, September 1972
Lancer, PB, 10$^{th}$ printing, 1973
>   Lancer went backrupt in 1973, but there were numerous later printings by Prestige and Ace, perhaps 20 or more printings total; Prestige books have ACE on the cover, but are stamped with "Prestige" on the copyright page; also editions by Sphere and Orbit; this series continued up to the late 1980's; also the basis for numerous licensed as well as bootleg non-English editions; by far the most reproduced REH series in the world; it is quite possible that over one million copies of this book are in print

## Conan the Warrior

Contains *Red Nails; Jewels of Gwahlur; Beyond the Black River*
1$^{st}$ Edition, Lancer, PB, January 1967
>   Cover art by Frank Frazetta; edited and introduction by LSDC; the early Lancer printings have purple-edged pages

Lancer, PB, 2$^{nd}$ printing, 1968
Lancer, PB, 3$^{rd}$ printing, 1969
Lancer, PB, 4$^{th}$ printing, nd (1970)
Lancer, PB, 5$^{th}$ printing, nd (1971)
>   Pages now yellow-edged starting with this printing

Lancer, PB, 6$^{th}$ printing, April 1972
Lancer, PB, 7$^{th}$ printing, September 1972
Lancer, PB, 8$^{th}$ printing, 1973
Sphere, PB, 1973
>   Lancer went backrupt in 1973, but there were numerous later printings by Prestige and Ace, perhaps 20 or more printings total; Prestige books have ACE on the cover, but are stamped with "Prestige" on the copyright page; also editions by Sphere and Orbit; this series continued up to the late 1980's; also the basis for numerous licensed as well as bootleg non-English editions; by far the most reproduced REH series in the world; it is quite possible that over one million copies of this book are in print

## The Conquering Sword of Conan

Contains *The Servants of Bit-Yakin (Jewels of Gwahlur); Beyond the Black River; The Black Stranger; The Man-Eaters of Zamboula (Shadows in Zamboula); Red Nails; Untitled Notes;* **Wolves Beyond the Border (early draft); Wolves Beyond the Border (later draft); The Black Stranger (early synopsis); The Black Stranger (later synopis); The Man-Eaters of Zamboula (synopis); Red Nails (draft)***; letter to P. Schuyler Miller, March 10, 1936; plus a map of the Hyborian Age*

1<sup>st</sup> Edition, Del Rey, TPB, December 2005

> Edited by Patrice Louinet and Rusty Burke; based on the Wandering Star ROBERT E. HOWARD'S COMPLETE CONAN OF CIMMERIA, VOLUME 3, which may or may not see publication; cover and extensive interior artwork by Greg Manchess; the original color plates are reproduced here in B&W

SFBC, HB, December 2005

> The color plates are again in B&W

## Cormac Mac Art

Contains *Tigers of the Sea (completed by David Drake); Swords of the Northern Sea; The Night of the Wolf; The Temple of the Abomination (long version); The Temple of Abomination (Outline)*

1<sup>st</sup> Edition, Baen, PB, March 1995

> Cover art by Ken Kelly; edited by David Drake

## Crimson Shadows: The Best Of Robert E. Howard, Volume 1

Contains *The Shadow Kingdom; The Ghost Kings (v); The Curse of the Golden Skull; Red Shadows; The One Black Stain (v); The Dark Man; The Marching Song of Connacht (v); Kings of the Night; Recompense (v); The Black Stone; The Song of a Mad Minstrel (v); The Fightin'est Pair; The Grey God Passes; The Song of the Last Briton (v); Worms of the Earth; An Echo from the Iron Harp (v); Lord of the Dead; Untitled ("You have built a world of paper and wood") (v); "For the Love of Barbara Allen"; The Tide (v); The Valley of the Worm; The Dust Dance: Selections, Version II (v); The People of the Black Circle; Beyond the Black River; A Word from the Outer Dark (v); Hawk of the Hills; Sharp's Gun Serenade; Lines Written in the Realization That I Must Die (v)*

1<sup>st</sup> Edition, Del Rey, TPB, July 2007

> Cover and interior art by Jim & Ruth Keegan; selected, edited and introduction by Rusty Burke; first of a two-volume set

## Cthulhu the Mythos and Kindred Horrors

Contains *Arkham (v); The Black Stone; The Fire of Asshurbanipal; The Thing on the Roof; Dig Me No Grave;* **Silence Falls on Mecca's Walls (v)***; The Valley of the Worm; The Shadow of the Beast; Old Garfield's Heart; People of the Dark; Worms of the Earth; Pigeons from Hell; An Open Window (v)*

1<sup>st</sup> Edition, Baen, PB, May 1987

Baen, PB, 2<sup>nd</sup> printing, 1989

Baen, PB, 3<sup>rd</sup> printing, 1992

> **Contains a First Appearance**; introduction by David Drake

## The Dark Man and Others

Contains *The Voice of El-Lil; Pigeons from Hell; The Dark Man; The Gods of Bal-Sagoth; People of the Dark; The Children of the Night; The Dead Remember; The Man on the Ground; The Garden of Fear; The Thing on the Roof; The Hyena; Dig Me No Grave; The Dream Snake; In the Forest of Villefere; Old Garfield's Heart*

1<sup>st</sup> Edition, Arkham House, HB, 1963

> Limited to 2029 copies; "The Dead Remember" was accidentally printed incomplete; cover art by Frank Utpatel; edited and introduction by August Derleth

Lancer, PB, 1972

## The Dark Man Omnibus, Volume 1

Contains *The Voice of El-Lil; Pigeons from Hell; The Dark Man; The Gods of Bal-Sagoth; The Man on the Ground; In the Forest of Villefere*
1st Edition, Panther (UK), PB, 1978
> Cover by PAJ (Peter Jones); edited and introduction by August Derleth; based on the Arkham House edition of THE DARK MAN AND OTHERS

## The Dark Man Omnibus, Volume 2

Contains *People of the Dark; The Children of the Night; The Dead Remember; The Garden of Fear; The Thing on the Roof; The Hyena; Dig Me No Grave; The Dream Snake; Old Garfield's Heart*
1st Edition, Panther (UK), PB, 1979
> Cover by PAJ (Peter Jones); edited and introduction by August Derleth; based on the Arkham House edition of THE DARK MAN AND OTHERS

## The Daughter of Erlik Khan

Contains *The Daughter of Erlik Khan*
1st Edition, Medusa Expressions, HB, 2007
> Limited to 150 copies; illustrated by Serge Jacques; edited by Michael Hranek; had to be ordered directly from Michael Hranek; an extra print copy of the cover is tipped in

## The Devil in Iron

Contains *The Devil in Iron; Shadows in Zamboula*
1st Edition, Grant, HB, 1976
> Limited to 3500 copies; illustrated by Dan Green; a traycase was offered via Gray Parrot, not common
1st Edition, Grossett and Dunlap, TPB, 1978
> Trade paperback binding using loose pages from the original Grant version

## The Devil in Iron

Contains *The Devil in Iron; The Moon of Skulls; The Valley of the Worm*
1st Edition, Incarna Publishing, TPB, 2005
> Artwork by Newton Burcham; printed via Lulu.com

## Echoes from an Iron Harp

Contains *Age Comes to Rabelais; Belshazzar*; *But the Hills Were Ancient Then; Cimmeria; A Dawn in Flanders; The Day That I Die; Dreams of Ninevah; The Dust Dance (1); The Dust Dance (2) (lines 1-80); The Dweller in Dark Valley; Earth-Born; Fables for Little Folks; "Feach Air Muir Lionadhi Gealach Buidhe Mar Or"; Futility ("Time races . . ."); Heritage ("My people came . . ."); Illusion; John Ringold; Kid Lavigne is Dead; The Kissing of Sal Snooboo; A Lady's Chamber; The Last Day; Lost Altars; Memories ("I rose . . ."); A Moment; Moonlight on a Skull; Not Only in Death They Die; Private Magrath of the A.E.F.; Reuben's Brethren; Roundelay of the Roughneck; The Sands of Time; The Sea; The Skull in the Clouds; Skulls and Dust; Skulls over Judah; Slumber; A Song of Defeat; The Song of Horsa's Galley; A Song of the Legions; A Song for Men That Laugh; A Sonnet of Good Cheer; Sonora to Del Rio; Surrender ("I will rise . . ."); Tarantella; Thor's Son; Timur-lang; To Certain Orthodox Brethren; A Vision;* **A Warning (first complete version)**; *Where Are Your Knights, Donn Othna?; Who is Grandpa Theobold?; The Years Are as a Knife*; And Headings From: *The Black Stone; The Blood of Belshazzar; Death's Black Riders; The Fearsome Touch of Death; The Grey God Passes; The Hour of the Dragon; Kelly the Conjure-Man; The Lion of Tiberias (Chapter 3 only); Something About Eve; The Sowers of the Thunder; The Thing on the Roof (all v)*
1st Edition, Grant, HB, 1972
> **Contains a First Appearance**; limited to 1079 copies; illustrated by Alicia Austin; there are two distinctly different shades of red used for the binding

## The 'El Borak' Stories - Blood of The Gods; The Daughter of Erlik Khan; Hawk of the Hills; Son Of The White Wolf; The Country of The Knife

Contains *Blood of The Gods; The Daughter of Erlik Khan; Hawk of the Hills; Son Of The White Wolf; The Country of The Knife*
1st Edition, The Echo Library (UK), TPB, March 2007
> Texts from Project Gutenberg Australia

## The End of the Trail: Western Stories

Contains *"Golden Hope" Christmas; Drums of the Sunset; The Extermination of Yellow Donory; The Judgment of the Desert; Gunman's Debt; The Man on the Ground; The Sand-Hill's Crest (v); The Devil's Joker; Knife, Bullet and Noose; Law-Shooters of Cowtown; The Last Ride; John Ringold (v); The Vultures of Wahpeton (both endings); Vultures' Sanctuary; The Dead Remember; The Ghost of Camp Colorado; The Strange Case of Josiah Wilbarger; The Ballad of Buckshot Roberts (v); and select excerpts from the following letters to HPL, August 1931 ("You must indeed . . ."); October 1931 ("I intended to answerd . . ."); January 1931 ("As always I found your recent letter . . ."); February 1931 ("I highly appreciate . . ."); July 1935 ("Thanks very much for the fine post-cards . . .")*
1st Edition, Bison Books, HB and TPB, April 2005
> **Contains a First Appearance**; introduction and edited by Rusty Burke; cover art by Jim and Ruth Keegan; HB and TPB being offered at the same time

## Eons of the Night

Contains *The House of Arabu; The Garden of Fear; The Twilight of the Grey Gods; Spear and Fang; Delenda Est; Marchers of Valhalla; Sea Curse; Out of the Deep; In the Forest of Villefere; Wolfshead; plus one letter to HPL, July 1933 ("Glad we got the physical-mental question . . .") (excerpt only)*
1st Edition, Baen, PB, March 1996
> Cover art by Ken Kelly; introduction by SM Sterling

## The Essential Conan

Contains *The verse heading from the original draft of The Hour of the Dragon; The Hour of the Dragon; The Devil in Iron; The People of the Black Circle; A Witch Shall be Born; Jewels of Gwahlur; Beyond the Black River; Shadows in Zamboula; Red Nails; The Hyborian Age*
1st Edition, SFBC Fantasy (Science Fiction Book Club), HB, June 1998
> Cover by Ken Kelly; introductions by Karl Edward Wagner, combines the previous Putnam HB editions from 1977, with most of the errors cleaned up

## The Exotic Writings of Robert E. Howard

Contains *The Voice of El-Lil; Red Blades of Black Cathay; Hawks of Outremer; The Blood of Belshazzar; The Sowers of the Thunder; Lord of Samarcand; The Lion of Tiberias; Alleys of Darkness; The Shadow of the Vulture; The Treasures of Tartary; Son of the White Wolf; Black Vulmea's Vengeance; Gates of Empire; People of the Dark; The Cairn on the Headland; The Garden of Fear; The Dead Remember; Black Talons; The Tomb's Secret; Fangs of Gold; Names in the Black Book; Graveyard Rats; Black Wind Blowing; She Devil; Desert Blood; The Dragon of Kao Tsu; The Purple Heart of Erlik; Murderer's Grog; Letter to Magic Carpet Magazine, January 1933 ("Thanks very much for the remarks . . ."); letter to Magic Carpet Magazine, April 1933 ("Congratulations on the quality . . ."); letter to Oriental Stories, Summer 1932 ("Brundage did a fine job . . .")*
1st Edition, Girasol Press, HB, October 2006
> Cover by Doug Klauba; introductions by Neil and Leigh Meachem; facsimile reprint of all the original pulp pages of these stories; combined with the two earlier volumes of Weird Writings, this now includes all the pulp pages with REH works, excepting boxing and western, both humorous and straight

## Five Tales of Conan the Barbarian

Contains *The Phoenix on the Sword; Queen of the Black Coast; Rogues in the House; The Scarlet Citadel; The Tower of the Elephant*

1st Edition, The Echo Library (UK), TPB, March 2007

> Texts from Project Gutenberg Australia; cover says edited by Grace Isabel Colbron, an error, and will supposedly be corrected on later editions

## Flight

Contains *Flight; Flint's Passing (both v)*

1st Edition, Stolte, HB, 1992

> Limited to 20 copies, all hand-made; cover art is a needleblock based on REH portrait; interior illustrations by Marcus Boas and MT Colleen Nielsen; one or two copies were bound in leather instead of cloth

## The Garden of Fear: The Weird Works of Robert E. Howard, Volume 6

Contains *Queen of the Black Coast; The Haunter of the Ring; The Garden of Fear; The Devil in Iron; The Voices Waken Memory (v); The People of the Black Circle; A Witch Shall Be Born*

1st Edition, Wildside Press, HB, December 2006

> Cover by Stephen Fabian; edited by Paul Herman; introduction by Ben Szumskyj; all based on original pulp pages with minimal editing; first printing is Smythe sewn, on acid free paper, limited to 1400 copies

## Gates of Empire and Others

Contains *Red Blades of Black Cathay; Hawks of Outremer; The Blood of Belshazzar; Lord of Samarcand; The Sowers of the Thunder; The Lion of Tiberias; The Shadow of the Vulture; Gates of Empire*

1st Edition, Wildside Press, HB, March 2004

Wildside Press, HB, 2nd printing, 2004

Wildside Press, TPB, September 2006

> Edited by Paul Herman; introduction by Fred Blosser; all based on original pulp pages with minimal editing; first printing is Smythe sewn, on acid free paper, limited to 600 copies; the second printing is regular POD, glued spine; 1st edition is marked "First Edition", don't know if the 2nd is as well

## A Gent from Bear Creek

Contains **A Gent from Bear Creek (novel)**

1st Edition, Jenkins (UK), HB, 1937

Jenkins (UK), HB, 2nd Edition, 1938

> **Contains a First Appearance; this is the first REH book ever produced**; 1st edition priced at 7/6 (7 shilling / 6 pence), the 2nd edition is known as "The Cheap Edition", only 2/6 (2 shilling, 6 pence); only a dozen or so copies combined of the editions known to exist, only Glenn Lord's known to have the first edition dust jacket; The V&A Museum in London has a copy of the Cheap edition dust jacket; the Cheap edition may have been on thinner paper, but measurements of all available copies have not shown any significant differences; a copy without a dust jacket sold on eBay for $2500 in 12/02; allegedly another copy sold in London in 2004 for around $8000; in September 2006 a rather beat up ex-lib copy with no jacket sold on eBay as a Buy It Now for $8500, and was subsequently resold a few days later for over $10K

Grant, HB, 1965

Grant, HB, 2nd Edition, 1975

> 1st Edition limited to 732 copies, 2nd edition limited to 1500 copies; the first edition is photo-offset from the Jenkins edition; the second Grant edition was re-typeset by hand on a typewriter, all italics removed, and that was carried over into later editions; 2nd illustrated by Tim Kirk

Zebra, PB, September 1975

Zebra, PB, 1st Canadian printing, September 1975

Zebra, PB, 2nd printing, February 1976

Zebra, PB, 3rd printing, April 1976

## A Gent from Bear Creek and Others

Contains *A Gent from Bear Creek (novel); While Smoke Rolled; Texas John Alden*
Wildside Press, 1st Edition, HB, July 2005
> Restored texts, to original publications; cover by David Burton; edited by Paul Herman

## The Ghost Ocean and Other Poems of the Supernatural

Contains **The Isle of Hy-Brasil**; *The One Black Stain*; **Viking's Vision; To All Sophisticates; Man Am I; Never Beyond the Beast; Shadows from Yesterday; The Ghost Ocean; The Song of the Last Briton; The Gates of Babylon; Lilith; Two Men; Memories of Alfred; To a Woman ("Ages ago . . ."); When the Glaciers Rumbled South**; *Candles*; **Shadow Thing**; *Song of the Pict*; **The Flood; The Adventurer's Mistress** *(all v)*
1st Edition, Gibbelins Gazette Press, HB, 1982
> **Contains a First Appearance**; limited to 360 copies, the first 50 are hardback; the rest are staples, and listed in the CHAPBOOKS section; many of these poems have never been reprinted; cover by Charles E. Williams, Jr., interior illustrations by Rick McCollum, Charles E. Williams, Jr., and Steve Trout; the publisher also distributed some of these in REHUPA #60

## The Gods of Bal-Sagoth

Contains *The Gods of Bal-Sagoth; Casonetto's Last Song; King of the Forgotten People; Usurp the Night; The Curse of the Golden Skull; The Shadow of the Beast; Nekht Semerkeht; Restless Waters;* **The Isle of the Eons**
1st Edition, Ace, PB, April 1979
> **Contains a First Appearance**; edited by Glenn Lord

## Graveyard Rats and Others

Contains *Black Talons; Fangs of Gold; The Tomb's Secret; Names in the Black Book; Graveyard Rats; Black Wind Blowing*
1st Edition, Wildside Press, HB, August 2003
Wildside Press, TPB, December 2004
> Edited by Paul Herman, introduction by Don Herron; a collection of detective stories, all edited back to original pulp appearance

## The Grim Lands: The Best Of Robert E. Howard, Volume 2

Contains *By This Axe I Rule!; The King and the Oak (v); The Mirrors of Tuzun Thune; The Tower of the Elephant; Which Will Scarcely Be Understood (v); Wings in the Night; Solomon Kane's Homecoming (v); Lord of Samarcand; Timur-lang (v); A Song of the Naked Lands (v); The Shadow of the Vulture; Echoes from an Anvil (v); The Bull Dog Breed; Black Harps in the Hills (v); The Man on the Ground; Old Garfield's Heart; The Vultures of Wahpeton; Gents on the Lynch; The Grim Land (v); Pigeons From Hell; Never Beyond the Beast (v); Wild Water; Musings ("The little poets . . .) (v); Son of the White Wolf; Black Vulmea's Vengeance; Flint's Passing (v); Red Nails; Cimmeria (v)*
1st Edition, Del Rey, TPB, December 2007
> Cover and interior art by Jim & Ruth Keegan; selected, edited and introduction by Rusty Burke; second of a two-volume set

## The Hand of Kane

Contains *The Hills of the Dead; Hawk of Basti; Wings in the Night; The Children of Asshur*
1st Edition, Centaur, PB, October 1970
Centaur, PB, 2nd printing, nd (1976), "The Illustrated Edition"
> Cover art by Jeff Jones; "Hawk of Basti" and "The Children of the Night" are fragments, and published as such; 1st Edition is 75c, the 2nd is $1.50; the Illustrated Edition includes a frontispiece and 6 interior illustrations by Ned Dameron
Haddock (unauthorized, Hungary), PB, nd (1972)

## Hawks of Outremer

Contains *Hawks of Outremer; Blood of Belshazzar;* **The Slave-Princess (completed by Richard Tierney)**
1st Edition, Grant, HB, 1979

>  **Contains a First Appearance**; edited and introduction by Richard L. Tierney; illustrated by Rob MacIntyre and Chris Pappas

## Heroes of Bear Creek

Contains *A Gent from Bear Creek (novel);The Riot at Cougar Paw; Pilgrims to the Pecos; High Horse Rampage; The Apache Mountain War; Pistol Politics; The Conquerin' Hero of the Humbolts; A Ringtailed Tornado; "No Cowherders Wanted"; Mayhem and Taxes; Evil Deeds at Red Cougar; Sharp's Gun Serenade; The Peaceful Pilgrim; While Smoke Rolled; A Elkins Never Surrenders* (All Breckinridge Elkins)
1st Edition, Ace, PB, November 1983

>  Collects the three Grant Breckinridge Elkins HB Books: GENT FROM BEAR CREEK, PRIDE OF BEAR CREEK, and MAYHEM ON BEAR CREEK

## The Hour of the Dragon

Contains *The verse heading from the original draft of The Hour of the Dragon; The Hour of the Dragon; letters to Denis Archer, May 20, 1934 ("As you doubtless remember . . ."); to August Derleth, May 9, 1936 ("I am indeed sorry to learn of the deaths . . .") (excerpt only);* **to HPL, May 13, 1936 ("I am indeed sorry to hear . . .") (excerpt only)**; *to P. Schuyler Miller, SM, March 10, 1936 ("I feel indeed honored that you and Dr. Clark . . ."); to Harold Preece, pm, March 24, 1930 ("Thanks for the picture.") (excerpt only); to Hugh G. Schonfield, June 15, 1933 ("As I promised, in answer to your letter . . ."); to Alvin Earl Perry, ca. early 1935 ("The first character I ever . . .") (excerpt only); to Clark Ashton Smith, July 23, 1935 ("I'm ashamed of my long delay . . .") (excerpt only); to Clark Ashton Smith, July 22, 1933 ("I can hardly find words . . .") (excerpt only); to Clark Ashton Smith, December 14, 1933 ("Only the fact that I have been sick . . .") (excerpt only); To E. Hoffmann Price, February 15, 1936 ("I have eventually found time to answer your cards.") (excerpt only)*
1st Edition, Berkley, HB, 1977

>  **Contains a First Appearance**; cover art by Ken Kelly; foreword and afterword by Karl Edward Wagner; all the letters are in the foreword or afterword; this was the first time that the verse heading had been published with the story

Berkley, PB, August 1977

>  Includes a fold-out poster by Ken Kelly

Putnam (Science Fiction Book Club), HB, 1977

>  Retypeset, introduced several errors

Berkley, PB, 2nd printing, August 1977
Berkley, PB, 3rd printing, date unknown
Berkley, PB, 4th printing, October 1980

>  This printing has no poster, and can be spotted as the cover does not mention the poster

## The Hour of the Dragon

Contains *The Hour of the Dragon*
1st Edition, Grant, HB, 1989

>  Illustrated by Ezra Pound; no traycase was offered, though Grant did refer buyers to someone who could make one, if they asked

## Hours of the Dragon: The Weird Works of Robert E. Howard, Volume 8

Contains *The Hour of the Dragon; The Hyborian Age*
1st Edition, Wildside Press, HB, May 2007

>  Edited by Paul Herman, based on original publication texts

## The Howard Collector

Contains Stories: *Two Against Tyre; Sea Curse; The Curse of the Golden Skull; Death's Black Riders; Untitled Fragment ("Beneath the glare of the sun, . . ."); Spanish Gold on Devil Horse; The Heathen; The Thessalians; Ye College Days; Cupid v Pollux; Musings of a Moron; Sunday in a Small Town; West Is West; Knife, Bullet and Noose; Sentiment; Midnight; Kelly the Conjure-Man; With a Set of Rattlesnake Rattles; The Beast from the Abyss;* Poetry: *Hope Empty of Meaning; Life; Solomon Kane's Homecoming (variant version); Visions; Harvest; On with the Play; Roads; The Bar By the Side of the Road; Marching Song of Connacht; The Legacy of Tubal-Cain;* Letters: *to R.H. Barlow, June 14, 1934 ("If I ever decide to dispose . . ."); to R. H. Barlow, June 1, 1934 ("Concerning the illustrations you . . ."); to August Derleth, ca. July 1933 ("Thanks immensely for the opportunity of reading . . ."); to August Derleth, May 9, 1936 ("I am indeed sorry to learn of the deaths . . ."); to HPL, ca. August 1933 ("I am sending on to you the enclosed manuscript . . ."); to Emil Petaja, December 17, 1934 ("Thank you very much for the splendid sonnet."); to Clark Ashton Smith, pm, March 15, 1933 ("I hardly know how to thank you for the copy . . ."); to Clark Ashton Smith, July 23, 1935 (" I'm ashamed of my long delay in answering . . ."); to Farnsworth Wright, May 6, 1935 ("I always hate to write a letter like this . . .")*
1st Edition, Ace, PB, April 1979
> Edited by Glenn Lord; was originally suppose to be a FAX hardback, didn't happen

## The Howard Collector Anthology

Edited by Glenn Lord; announced by FAX, but never issued

## The Incredible Adventures of Dennis Dorgan

Contains *The Alleys of Singapore; The Jade Monkey; The Mandarin Ruby; **The Yellow Cobra; In High Society; Playing Journalist; The Destiny Gorilla; A Knight of the Round Table; Playing Santa Claus; The Turkish Menace***
1st Edition, FAX, HB, 1974
> **Contains a First Appearance**; cover art and illustrations by Tom Foster; introduction by Darrell C. Richardson

Zebra, PB, December 1975
Zebra, PB, 2nd printing, February 1976
Zebra, PB, 3rd printing, April 1976
> Cover by Jeff Jones

## The Iron Man

Contains ***Men of Iron**; The Iron Man; **They Always Come Back**; Fists of the Desert*
1st Edition, Zebra, PB, March 1976
Zebra, PB, 2nd printing, October 1976
> **Contains a First Appearance**; cover by Jeff Jones; photo-offset from Grant HB edition, 1976; introduction by Donald Grant; even though photo-offset from the Grant pages, was actually published before the Grant edition by about a month, due to delays at Grant, per Grant himself in an interview in FANTASY CROSSROADS #10/11

Grant, HB, 1976
> Illustrated by David Ireland

## The Iron Man, with the Adventures of Dennis Dorgan

Contains *Men of Iron; The Iron Man; They Always Come Back; Fists of the Desert; The Alleys of Singapore; The Jade Monkey; The Mandarin Ruby; The Yellow Cobra; In High Society; Playing Journalist; The Destiny Gorilla; A Knight of the Round Table; Playing Santa Claus; The Turkish Menace*
1st Edition, Ace, PB, October 1983
> Combines the earlier published THE IRON MAN, by Grant, 1974, and THE ADVENTURES OF DENNIS DORGAN, by Fax, in 1974

## Jewels of Gwahlur

Contains *Jewels of Gwahlur;* ***The Snout in the Dark (unfinished)***
1st Edition, Grant, HB, 1979; MAYBE a traycase was offered via Gray Parrot
    **Contains a First Appearance**; illustrated by Dean Morrissey; limited to 3000 copies

## King Conan

Contains *Jewels of Gwahlur; Beyond the Black River; The Treasure of Tranicos (with LSDC); The Phoenix on the Sword; The Scarlet Citadel*
1st Edition, Gnome Press, HB, 1953
    Cover by David Kyle; edited by LSDC; limited to 4000 copies

## King Kull

Contains *The Hyborian Age (portions);* ***Exile of Atlantis****; The Shadow Kingdom;* ***The Altar and the Scorpion; Black Abyss (completed by Lin Carter); Delcardes' Cat; The Skull of Silence; Riders Beyond the Sunrise (completed by Lin Carter); By This Axe I Rule!; The Striking of the Gong; Swords of the Purple Kingdom; Wizard and Warrior (completed by Lin Carter);*** *The Mirrors of Tuzun Thune; The King and the Oak (v)*
1st Edition, Lancer, PB, September 1967
Lancer, PB, 2nd printing, September 1969
Lancer, PB, 3rd printing, August 1972
    **Contains a First Appearance**; cover art by Roy Krenkel; edited by Lin Carter
Lancer, PB, 4th printing, 1972 (Canada)
Lancer, PB, 5th printing, June 1973
Sphere (UK), PB, 1976
    Based on the Lancer edition; Cover art by Chris Achilleos

## Kull

Contains *Prolog (a portion of "The Hyborian Age"); Exile of Atlantis; The Shadow Kingdom; The Altar and the Scorpion; Delcardes' Cat; The Skull of Silence; By This Axe I Rule!; The Striking of the Gong; Swords of the Purple Kingdom; The Mirrors of Tuzun Thune; The King and the Oak (v); The Black City (fragment); Untitled ("'Thus', said Tu, . . ."); Untitled ("Three men sat at a table . . ."); Epilog (more of "The Hyborian Age")*
1st Edition, Grant, HB, 1985
    Illustrated by Ned Dameron
1st Limited Edition, Grant, HB, 1985
    Limited edition is 400 copies; illustrated by Ned Dameron; based on the earlier Bantam edition, KULL: THE FABULOUS WARRIOR KING

## Kull

Contains *Prolog (a portion of "The Hyborian Age"); Exile of Atlantis; The Shadow Kingdom; The Altar and the Scorpion; Delcardes' Cat; The Skull of Silence; By This Axe I Rule!; The Striking of the Gong; Swords of the Purple Kingdom; The Mirrors of Tuzun Thune; The King and the Oak (v); The Black City (fragment); Untitled ("'Thus', said Tu, . . ."); Untitled ("Three men sat at a table . . ."); Epilog (more of "The Hyborian Age"); The Curse of the Golden Skull*
1st Edition, Baen, PB, July 1995
    Cover art by Ken Kelly; edited by David Drake; adds the last story to the earlier Bantam/Grant editions

## Kull: Exile of Atlantis

Contains *Exile of Atlantis; The Shadow Kingdom; The Mirrors of Tuzan Thune; Untitled ("'Thus' said Tu . . ."); Delcardes' Cat; The Skull of Silence; The Striking of the Gong; Altar and the Scorpion; The Curse of the Golden Skull; The Black City; Untitled ("Three men sat at a table . . ."); By This Axe I Rule!; Swords of the Purple Kingdom; The King and the Oak (v); Kings of the Night; Summer Morn (v); Am-ra the Ta-an (v); The Tale of Am-ra;* ***Untitled ("A land of wild . . ."); Untitled (" . . . determined. So I set out up of . . ."); The Shadow Kingdom (incomplete draft); Delcardes' Cat (draft);*** *The King and the Oak (v) (draft)*
1st Edition, Del Rey, PB, October 2006

Science Fiction Book Club, HB, November 2006
> **Contains a First Appearance**; illustrated by Justin Sweet; edited by Patrice Louinet; introduction by Steve Tompkins

## Kull: The Fabulous Warrior King

Contains *Prolog (a portion of "The Hyborian Age"); Exile of Atlantis; The Shadow Kingdom; The Altar and the Scorpion; Delcardes' Cat; The Skull of Silence; By This Axe I Rule!; The Striking of the Gong; Swords of the Purple Kingdom; The Mirrors of Tuzun Thune; The King and the Oak (v); The Black City (fragment); Untitled ("'Thus', said Tu, . . ."); Untitled ("Three men sat at a table . . ."); Epilog (more of "The Hyborian Age")*

1$^{st}$ Edition, Bantam, PB, September 1978
> **Contains a First Appearance**; edited by Andrew J Offutt; deletes all the Lin Carter material found in the earlier KING KULL books; cover by Lou Feck

## Lair of the Hidden Ones

Announced by Grant in the 1970's, but never published, supposedly a rewrite by Darrell Crombie of "Three-Bladed Doom" to add a weird element, don't know if a manuscript exists

## The Last Cat Book

Contains *The Beast from the Abyss*

1$^{st}$ Edition, Dodd, Mead, TPB, 1984
> Illustrated by Peter Kuper

## The Last of the Trunk

Contains *Blue River Blues; The Battling Sailor; The Drawing Card; The Jinx; The Wildcat and the Star; Fistic Psychology; Untitled ("Huh?" I was so dumbfounded . . .); Fighting Nerves; The Atavist; A Man of Peace; The Weeping Willow; The Right Hook; A Tough Nut to Crack; The Trail of the Snake; The Folly of Conceit; The Fighting Fury; Night Encounter; The Ferocious Ape; The Ghost Behind the Gloves; Misto Dempsey; The Brand of Satan; Incongruity; The Slayer; The Man Who Went Back; Untitled Synopsis (Hunwulf, an American . . .); Untitled (Thure Khan gazed out . . .); Untitled (As he approached . . .); A Room in London (outline); The Shadow in the Well (draft); Fate is the Killer; The Grove of Lovers; The Drifter; The Lion Gate; Untitled (Franey was a fool.); The Ivory Camel; Wolves – and a Sword; Untitled (I'm a man of few words . . .); Untitled Synopsis (First Draft: James Norris . . .); The Dominant Male; The Paradox; Untitled (Mike Costigan, writer and self avowed futilist . . .); The Splendid Brute; Circus Charade; The Influence of the Movies; Untitled (William Aloysius McGraw's father . . .); A Man and a Brother; Man; Pigskin Scholar; The Recalcitrant; Untitled ("Arrange, Madame, arrange!"); Untitled ("Yessah!" said Mrs. . . .); The Question of the East; In His Own Image; The Punch; The Female of the Species; The Last Man; The Treasure of Henry Morgan; Untitled (The lazy quiet of the mid-summer day . . .); Through the Ages; The White Jade Ring; The Roving Boys on a Sandburg; Westward, Ho!; The Wild Man; What the Deuce?; The Land of Forgotten Ages; The Funniest Bout; The Red Stone; A Unique Hat; Untitled ("A man," said my friend Larry Aloysius O'Leary . . .); Untitled (. . . that is, the artistry is but a symbol . . .); Untitled (I met him first in the Paradise saloon . . .); Untitled (Maybe it don't seem like anything interesting . . .); Untitled (So there I was.); Untitled (Trail led through dense jungle . . .); Untitled (Two men were standing in the bazaar at Delhi . . .); Untitled (When Yar Ali Khan crept . . .); Untitled (Who I am it matters little . . .); A Twentieth Century Rip Van Winkle; The Ghosts of Jacksonville; A Boy, a Beehive, and a Chinaman; Mr. Dowser Buys a Car; A Faithful Servant; A South Sea Storm; The Ghost of Bald Rock Ranch; A Fishing Trip; Friends; Ten Minutes on a Street Corner; The Wings of the Bat*

1$^{st}$ Edition, The Robert E. Howard Foundation, HB, expected June 2007
> Edited and introduction by Patrice Louinet; an attempt to publish all the remaining prose that was unpublished at this point in time; all content preceded a month earlier by the Swedish released THE LAST OF THE TRUNK OCH BREV I URVAL, see this under Chapbooks.

**The Last Ride**

Contains *The Last Ride; The Extermination of Yellow Donory; Knife, Bullet and Noose; The Devil's Joker; Vultures' Sanctuary; Law-Shooters of Cowtown;* ***Gunman's Debt***
1$^{st}$ Edition, Berkley, PB, June 1978
> **Contains a First Appearance**; cover art by Ken Kelly

**The Legend of Solomon Kane**

Contains *Skulls in the Stars; The Right Hand of Doom; Red Shadows; Rattle of Bones; The Castle of the Devil (completed by Ramsey Campbell); Death's Black Riders (fragment); The Moon of Skulls; The One Black Stain (v); Blades of the Brotherhood; The Hills of the Dead; Hawk of Basti (completed by Ramsey Campbell); The Return of Sir Richard Grenville (v); Wings in the Night; The Footfalls Within; The Children of Asshur (completed by Ramsey Campbell); Solomon Kane's Homecoming (v)*
1$^{st}$ Edition, Night Hag Productions (AU), TPB, 2006
> Collects together the contents from the three Centaur Solomon Kane books, THE HAND OF KANE, THE MOON OF SKULLS, and SOLOMON KANE

**Lord of Samarcand and Other Adventure Stories of the Old Orient**

Contains *Red Blades of Black Cathay; Hawks of Outremer; The Blood of Belshazzar; The Sowers of the Thunder; Lord of Samarcand; Timur-Lang (v); The Lion of Tiberias; The Shadow of the Vulture; Gates of Empire; The Road of the Eagles; Hawks Over Egypt; The Road of Azrael; The Slave-Princess (synopsis and unfinished draft); Two Against Tyre; The Track of Bohemond; The Shadow of the Hun;* ***Untitled ("He knew de Bracy . . .");*** *Untitled ("The wind from the Mediterranean . . .");* ***Recap of Harold Lamb's The Wolf Chaser; Untitled ("The Persians had all fled . . .")***
1$^{st}$ Edition, Bison Books, HB and TPB, April 2005
> **Contains a First Appearance**; cover art by Sindy Bell; introduction by Patrice Louinet; edited by Rusty Burke; HB and TPB being offered at the same time

**Lord of the Dead**

Contains *Lord of the Dead; Names in the Black Book;* ***The Mystery of Tannernoe Lodge (completed by Fred Blosser)***
1$^{st}$ Edition, Grant, HB, 1981
> **Contains a First Appearance**; introduction by Robert E. Briney; illustrated by Duncan Eagleson

**The Lost Valley of Iskander**

Contains *The Daughter of Erlik Khan;* ***The Lost Valley of Iskander;*** *Hawk of the Hills*
1$^{st}$ Edition, FAX, HB, 1974
> **Contains a First Appearance**; illustrated by Michael Kaluta
Zebra, PB, January 1976
Zebra, PB, 2$^{nd}$ printing, March 1976
Zebra, PB, 3$^{rd}$ printing, October 1976
> Cover by Jeff Jones; interior illustrations by Mike Kaluta; photo-offset from the Fax HB edition, 1974; contains a full page drawing not in the Fax edition; the Fax edition has three color plates that don't show up in the PB editions; used as basis for all the PB editions
Orbit (UK), PB, 1976
Berkley, PB, September 1979
Berkley, PB, 2$^{nd}$ printing, 1979
Ace, PB, November 1986

## Marchers of Valhalla

Contains *Marchers of Valhalla; The Thunder-Rider; The Grey God Passes (2nd Edition only)*
1st Edition, Grant, HB, 1972
2nd Edition, Grant, HB, 1977

**Contains a First Appearance**; first edition limited to 1654 copies, second edition is an enlarged edition, contains extra story; first edition illustrated by Robert Bruce Acheson, second by Marcus Boas

## Marchers of Valhalla

Contains *The Grey God Passes; A Thunder of Trumpets; Marchers of Valhalla; Sea Curse; Out of the Deep; The Thunder-Rider; "For the Love of Barbara Allen"; The Valley of the Lost (2)*
1st Edition, Sphere (UK), PB, 1977
Berkley, PB, January 1978
Berkley, PB, 2nd Edition, date unknown

Berkley 1st has red background on spine and title strip, 2nd has blue background; introduction by Fritz Leiber; includes a pull-out poster

## Mayhem on Bear Creek

Contains *"No Cowherders Wanted"; Mayhem and Taxes; Evil Deeds at Red Cougar; Sharp's Gun Serenade; The Peaceful Pilgrim; While Smoke Rolled; A Elkins Never Surrenders*
1st Edition, Grant, HB, 1979

Illustrated by Tim Kirk

## The Moon of Skulls

Contains *The Moon of Skulls; Skulls in the Stars; The Footfalls Within*
1st Edition, Centaur, PB, November 1969 (60c)
Haddock (unauthorized, Hungary), PB, nd (1972)
Centaur, PB, 2nd printing, nd (1974) ($1.25)
Centaur, PB, 3rd printing ("The Illustrated Edition"), nd (1976) ($1.50)

Cover art by Jeff Jones; interior illustrations by David Wentzel; the Illustrated Edition includes seven new drawings from Marcus Boas

## Moon of Skulls: The Weird Works of Robert E. Howard, Volume 2

Contains *Skull-Face; Dead Man's Hate (v); The Fearsome Touch of Death; A Song Out of Midian (v); Shadows on the Road (v); The Moon of Skulls; The Hills of the Dead; Black Chant Imperial (v); The Voice of El-Lil*
1st Edition, Wildside Press, HB, March 2005
Wildside Press, TPB, January 2006

Cover by Stephen Fabian; introduction by Mark Finn; edited by Paul Herman; first edition is Smythe-sewn, limited to 1000 copies, later editions will be POD glue-bound

## Nameless Cults

Contains *The Black Stone; Worms of the Earth; The Little People; People of the Dark; The Children of the Night; The Thing on the Roof; The Abbey (completed by C.J. Henderson); The Fire of Asshurbanipal; The Door to the World (completed by Joseph S. Pulver); The Hoofed Thing; Dig Me No Grave; The House in the Oaks (completed by August Derleth); The Black Bear Bites; The Shadow Kingdom; The Gods of Bal-Sagoth; Skull-Face; Black Eons (completed by Robert M. Price); The Challenge from Beyond*
1st Edition, Chaosium, TPB, October 2001
Chaosium, TPB, 2nd printing, December 2004

Cover art by Harry Fassl; interior art by David Carson; edited by Robert M Price; also includes numerous articles on REH; was suppose to be published in 1998

## Night Images

Contains *The King and the Oak; The Cats of Anubis; Musings; No More the Serpent Prow; Haunting Columns; Black Dawn; Visions; **Echoes from an Anvil**; Altars and Jesters; The Ghost Kings; Egypt; The Heart of the*

*Sea's Desire; The Day Breaks Over Simla; The Tide;* **A Song Out of the East***; Tiger Girl; The Sea Girl;* **A Thousand Years Ago***; The Gold and the Grey; Marching Song of Connacht; Black Harps in the Hills; The Legacy of Tubal-Cain;* **Victory***; Viking's Trail; The Phoenix on the Sword; Kings of the Night; The King and the Mallet; Song Before Clontarf; To Harry the Oliad Man; And Beowulf Rides Again; Always Comes Evening (lines 1-14 only); Solomon Kane's Homecoming;* **The Master-Drum***; The Kiowa's Tale; Flight; Adventure;* **The Song of the Jackal***; Empire; Singing Hemp;* **Days of Glory***; Mark of the Beast; The Road to Rome;* **Roar, Silver Trumpets; The King of the Ages Comes***; The Jackal; The Campus at Midnight; When the Gods Were Kings;* **Oh Babylon, Lost Babylon***; A Word from the Outer Dark; Age; Swamp Murder; To a Friend; The Dead Slaver's Tale;* **A Buccaneer Speaks***; Hope Empty of Meaning; Hopes of Dreams;* **A Song for All Women (deluxe edition only)** *(all v)*

1st Edition, Morningstar Press, HB, 1976
1st Edition, limited, Morningstar Press, HB, 1976
>    **Contains a First Appearance**; cover by Frank Frazetta; interior art by Richard Corben; limited to 1000 copies, 250 of a "Special Edition", and 750 of a "Regular Edition"; the regular edition has a blue binding, the special edition has a black binding with slipcase and an extra full color Frazetta illustration; signed by Corben; foreword by John Pocsik; introduction by Armand Eisen; this version of "Oh Babylon, Lost Babylon" is the first complete appearance

## The People of the Black Circle

Contains *The People of the Black Circle*
1st Edition, Grant, HB, September 1974; a traycase was offered via Gray Parrot, not common
>    Limited to 3000 copies; illustrated by David Ireland

## The People of the Black Circle

Contains *The Devil in Iron; The People of the Black Circle; A Witch Shall be Born; Jewels of Gwahlur*
1st Edition, Berkley, HB, 1977
>    Cover art by Ken Kelly; introduction by Karl Edward Wagner; illustrated by Hugh Rankin
Berkley, PB, 1977
>    Comes with a fold-out poster; cover art and poster by Ken Kelly
Putnam (Science Fiction Book Club), HB, 1977
>    Retypeset, introduce several errors
Berkley, PB, 2nd printing, 1977
>    This printing has no poster, and can be spotted as the cover does not mention the poster

## People of the Black Circle

Contains *The People of the Black Circle; Jewels of Gwalhur; Beyond the Black River; A Witch Shall Be Born; Gods Of The North*
1st Edition, AudioRealms, 5 CD set, expected August 2007
>    Cover by Dalmazio Frau; edited by Paul Herman; all works edited back to match original pulp pages; 5 CD audio set, 5.5 hours; uses texts from Wildside Press' WEIRD WORKS OF ROBERT E. HOWARD series, to start a new four audio book series of Conan stories

## People of the Dark: The Weird Works of Robert E. Howard, Volume 3

Contains *Kings of the Night; Song of a Mad Minstrel (v); The Children of the Night; The Footfalls Within; The Gods of Bal-Sagoth; The Black Stone; The Dark Man; The Thing on the Roof; The Last Day (v); The Horror from the Mound; People of the Dark*
1st Edition, Wildside Press, HB, July 2005
Wildside Press, HB, 2nd printing, July 2005
Wildside Press, TPB, July 2006
>    Cover by Stephen Fabian; introduction by Joe R. Lansdale; edited by Paul Herman; all works edited back to match original pulp pages; 1st printing Smythe sewn, limited to 1200 copies, 2nd printing regular POD, glued spine

## Pigeons from Hell

Contains *Pigeons from Hell; The Gods of Bal-Sagoth; People of the Dark; The Children of the Night; The Dead Remember; The Man on the Ground; The Garden of Fear; The Hyena; Dig Me No Grave; The Dream Snake; In The Forest of Villefere; Old Garfield's Heart; The Voice of El-Lil; and a letter to Farnsworth Wright, ca. June 1930 ("I have long looked forward to reading...")*
1st Edition, Zebra, PB, June 1976
> Illustrated by Jeff Jones; introduction and story comments by Glenn Lord
Ace, PB, July 1979
> Cover art by Esteban Maroto

### The Pool of the Black One

Contains *The Pool of the Black One;* **Drums of Tombulku (fragment)**
1st Edition, Grant, HB, 1986; MAYBE a traycase was offered via Gray Parrot
> **Contains a First Appearance**; illustrated by Hank Jankus

### Post Oaks and Sand Roughs

Contains **Post Oaks and Sand Roughs;** *The Seven-Up Ballad (v); Dula Due to be Champion;* **a letter to Western Story, ca. late fall, 1924 ("—And I am not one of those writers..."); a letter to Farnsworth Wright, January 23, 1926 ("I have no carbon copy of Wolfshead..."); a letter to Herbert Klatt, ca. Fall 1925 ("Again I write you...")**
1st Edition, Grant, HB, 1990
> **Contains a First Appearance**; cover art by Phil Hale; WESTERN STORY letter is a brief excerpt, pp. 16-17, letter presumably lost; Klatt letter is paraphrased on p. 79, presumably lost

### The Pride of Bear Creek

Contains *The Riot at Cougar Paw; Pilgrims to the Pecos; High Horse Rampage; The Apache Mountain War; Pistol Politics; The Conquerin' Hero of the Humbolts; A Ringtailed Tornado*
1st Edition, Grant, HB, 1966
Grant, HB, 2nd Edition, 1977
> First edition limited to 812 copies; illustrated by Tim Kirk; 2nd edition ("1st Illustrated Edition") adds extra illustrations by Tim Kirk; was retypeset by typewriter, all italics removed, which was carried over in all later printings; second edition limited to 1600 copies

### Queen of the Black Coast

Contains *Queen of the Black Coast; The Vale of Lost Women*
1st Edition, Grant, HB, 1978; a traycase was offered via Gray Parrot, not common
> Illustrated by Michael R. Hague; limited to 2750 copies

### Rauher Sand Und Wilde Eichen

Contains *Post Oaks and Sand Roughs; Spear and Fang;* **A Man (v); a letter to TCS, July 1925 ("Salaam Clyde; / Old boy, I got your letter.");** *a letter to Farnworth Wright, January 23, 1926 ("I have no carbon copy of Wolfshead..."); a letter to Western Story, ca. late fall, 1924 ("—And I am not one of those writers..."); plus some drawings from various REH letters*
1st Edition, Erster Deutscher (Germany), TPB, 1993
> **Contains a First Appearance**; all in German except for the poem and the letter to Farnworth Wright, 1926, both of which are printed in both English and German; WESTERN STORY letter is a brief excerpt only, letter presumably lost

### Red Blades of Black Cathay

Contains *Red Blades of Black Cathay;* **Diogenes of Today; Eighttoes Makes a Play**
1st Edition, Grant, HB, 1971
> **Contains a First Appearance**; co-written with TCS; limited to 1091 copies; most copies have carmine binding, some have a distinctly much lighter shade

## Red Nails

Contains *Red Nails; The Hyborian Age*
1st Edition, Grant, HB, 1975; a traycase was offered via Gray Parrot, not common
> Limited to 3500 copies; illustrated by George Barr

## Red Nails

Contains *Beyond the Black River; Shadows in Zamboula; Red Nails; The Hyborian Age*
1st Edition, Berkley, HB, 1977
> Introduction by Karl Edward Wagner; Cover art by Ken Kelly

Berkley, PB, October 1977
> Comes with a fold-out poster; cover art and poster by Ken Kelly

Putnam (Science Fiction Book Club), HB, 1977
> Retypeset, added several errors

Berkley, PB, 2nd printing, 1978
> This printing has no poster, and can be spotted as the cover does not mention the poster

## Red Nails

Contains *Red Nails*
1st Edition, Incarna Publishing, TPB, 2005
> Cover and artwork by Newton Burcham; printed via lulu.com

## Red Shadows

Contains *Skulls in the Stars;* **The Right Hand of Doom;** *Red Shadows; Rattle of Bones;* **The Castle of the Devil;** *The Moon of Skulls; The One Black Stain (v);* **Blades of the Brotherhood;** *The Hills of the Dead;* **Hawk of Basti; The Return of Sir Richard Grenville (v);** *Wings in the Night; The Footfalls Within;* **The Children of Asshur;** *Solomon Kane's Homecoming (v)*
1st Edition, Grant, HB, 1968
> **Contains a First Appearance**; 1st Edition limited to 896 copies; all editions illustrated by Jeff Jones; introduction by Glenn Lord; edited by Donald Grant

Grant, HB, 2nd Edition, 1971
> 2nd edition limited to 741 copies; the 2nd corrects the order of the plates and a different colored binding, else the same as the 1st

Grant, HB, 3rd Edition, 1978
> The 3rd edition is a larger format version

## The Return of Skull-Face

Contains **The Return of Skull-Face (completed by Richard Lupoff)**
1st Edition, FAX, HB, 1977
1st Edition, FAX, HB, Limited, 1977
> **Contains a First Appearance**; cover and interior illustrations by Stephan E. Leialoha; introduction by Frank Belknap Long; limited restricted to 150 copies, with special binding and signed by Lupoff and Leialoha; regular edtion limited to 1350 copies

## A Rhyme of Salem Town and Other Poems

Contains *Ace High; The Affair at the Tavern; The Actor; The Ages Stride on Golden Feet; And So I Sang; Artifice; Another Hymn of Hate; As I Rode Down to Lincoln Town; Astarte's Idol Stands Alone; Baal-Pteor; The Bandit; The Baron and the Wench; The Broken Walls of Babel; The Builders; The Call of the Sea (first complete publication of this poem); A Calling to Rome; The Cells of the Coliseum; The Chief of the Matabeles; Code; Cornish Jack; The Cry Everlasting; The Desert; The Desert Hawk; Devon Oak; The Drum; A Dull Sound as of Knocking; Echoes from an Anvil; Edgar Guest; Eric of Norway; Escape; Exhortation; Far in the Gloomy Northland; Farewell, Proud Munster; Freedom; The Gods I Worshipped; An Incident of the Muscovy-Turkish War; King of the Sea; Krakorum; The Ladder of Life; Land of the Pioneer; The Lies; Longfellow Revised; Little Bell of Brass; Little Brown Man of Nippon; The Lost San Saba Mine; Lunacy Chant; Mahomet; Man, the Master; Mankind; Mine but to Serve; A Misty Sea; Mihiragula; Modest Bill; Native Hell; No Man's*

*Land; Now and Then; O the Brave Sea-Rover; The Oaks; On with the Play; Over the Old Rio Grandey; Only a Shadow on the Grass; The Open Window; The Passing of the Elder Gods; Perspective; The Phantoms Gather; The Phases of Life; The Pirate; The Plains of Gilban; Prelude; The Primal Urge; Rattle of Drums; A Quatrain of Beauty; A Rhyme of Salem Town; Romance; The Road to Bliss; The Road to Freedom; The Road to Yesterday; Roads; Roar, Silver Trumpets; The Rover; The Rulers; San Jacinto (II, "Red fields of glory . . ."); The Sea and the Sunrise; Sea-Chant; Senor Zorro; The Sign of the Sickle; The Slayer; A Song of Bards; The Stralsund; The Sword of Lal Singh; Swings and Swings; The Tartar Raid; Time, the Victor; To a Kind Missionary Woiker; To Moderns; To the Stylists; The Tower of Zukala; The Trail of Gold; Trail's End; Untamed Avatars; Untitled ("Murky the night"); The Wanderer; Was I There?; West; The Wheel of Destiny; When I Was a Youth; When I Was in Africa; When Men Were Bold; Who Shall Sing of Babylon?; The Winds of the Sea; The Winds That Walk the World; The Worshippers; Zululand; Untitled ("For what is a maid to the shout of kings?"); Untitled ("As you dance upon the air."); Yesterdays; Baal; Down the Ages; The House of Gael; Ju-Ju Doom; Mystic Lore; The King of Trade; The Peasant on the Euphrates; Am-ra the Ta-an (all v)*
The Robert E. Howard Foundation, HB, February 2007
Introduction by Paul Herman; limited to 300 numbered editions; there is an earlier, very limited, Kinko's bound
    version, only six copies of it, listed under "Chapbooks"; this version has been resorted and retypeset

## The Right Hand of Doom and Other Tales of Solomon Kane

Contains *Solomon Kane; Skulls in the Stars; The Right Hand of Doom; Rattle of Bones; The Moon of Skulls; The Hills of the Dead; The Footfalls Within; Wings in the Night; Blades of the Brotherhood; Death's Black Riders; The Return of Sir Richard Grenville (v); The One Black Stain (v); Solomon Kane's Homecoming*
1st Edition, Wordsworth (UK), PB, 2007
    Introduction by M.J. Elliott

## The Riot at Bucksnort and Other Western Tales

Contains *Mountain Man; Meet Cap'n Kidd; Guns of the Mountains; The Peaceful Pilgrim; War on Bear Creek; The Haunted Mountain; The Feud Buster; The Riot at Cougar Paw; Pistol Politics; "No Cowherders Wanted"; The Conquerin' Hero of the Humbolts; A Gent from the Pecos; Gents on the Lynch; The Riot at Bucksnort; Knife-River Prodigal; A Man-Eating Jeopard*
1st Edition, Bison Books, HB and TPB, April 2005
    Introduction and edited by David Gentzel; cover art by Scott Gustafson; HB and TPB being offered at the
    same time

## The Road of Azreal

Contains *The Road of Azrael; **The Track of Bohemund; The Way of the Swords; Hawks Over Egypt**; Gates of Empire*
1st Edition, Grant, HB, 1979
1st Limited Edition, Grant, HB, 1979
    **Contains a First Appearance**; illustrated by Roy Krenkel; limited edition is slipcased, limited to 310
    copies, signed by Krenkel; "The Way of the Swords" is one of two versions of the story by REH
Bantam, PB, July 1980
    New introduction by Gordon R Dickson

## Robert E. Howard Omnibus

Contains *The Footfalls Within; The Pool of the Black One; The Good Knight; Hawks of Outremer; Gates of Empire; The Grey God Passes; The Secret of Lost Valley; Dermod's Bane; Knife-River Prodigal; Drums of the Sunset; Black Vulmea's Vengeance; The House of Arabu*
1st Edition, Orbit (UK), PB, 1977
Orbit (UK), PB, 2nd printing, August 1978
    Cover art by "PAJ" (Peter Jones)

## Robert E. Howard Selected Letters
Planned by Grant but then dropped, Necronomicon ended up publishing this as a two chapbook series

## Robert E. Howard—The Power of the Writing Mind
Contains *The Door to the Garden (as "untitled"); The Devil's Woodchopper; Double Cross; Some People Who Have Had Influence Over Me; letter to Argosy All-Story Weekly, July 20, 1929 ("I was born about twenty-three . . ."); letter to Wilfred Blanch Talman, ca. September 1931 ("Thank you very much for the letter you wrote . . ."); letter to Farnsworth Wright, ca. June-July 1931 ("In your last letter you asked me to give you . . ."); Twentieth Century Slave Trade; The Great Munney Ring; Bookmen and Books; Puritans; Sisters; L'Envoi (1) (v) ; Vengeance of a Woman; miscellaneous boxing commentary*
1ˢᵗ Edition, Mythos Books, December 2003
> TPB, edited by Ben Szumskyj, also includes an interview with Glenn Lord, and articles by Ben Szumskyj, Joe Marek, Patrice Louinet, Rusty Burke, Leo Grin, Scott Sheaffer, Tom Munnerlyn, and artwork by Gary Gianni, Rick Cortes, Mark Schultz, Rick McCollum, David Burton; 8.5x11; the last eight works are contained in a facsimile reproduction of THE RIGHT HOOK, VOLUME 1, #1 (Chpbk.), one of REH's self-published little newsletters

## Robert E. Howard's Complete Conan of Cimmeria, Volume 1
Contains *The Phoenix on the Sword; The Frost-Giant's Daughter; The God in the Bowl; The Tower of the Elephant; The Scarlet Citadel; Queen of the Black Coast; Black Colossus; Iron Shadows in the Moon; Xuthal of the Dusk; Pool of the Black One; Rogues in the House; The Vale of Lost Women; The Devil in Iron; Untitled (The Hall of the Dead); Untitled (The Hand of Nergal); The Hyborian Age; Cimmeria (v); Notes on Various Peoples of the Hyborian Age*
1ˢᵗ Edition, Wandering Star, HB, March 2003
> Edited by Patrice Louinet and Rusty Burke; also contains REH's two maps of the Hyborian Age and a Hyborian Names page; used original typescripts for "Frost-Giant's Daughter", "The God in the Bowl", "The Scarlet Citadel", "Vale of Lost Women", plus of course all the unfinished stuff and marginalia, including unpublished synopses, REH's original maps of the Hyborian world and the first-submitted version of "The Phoenix on the Sword"; artwork by Mark Schultz; very expensive, "Limited edition" sold for $195 (1950 copies), Artist's edition sold for $270 (only 100 copies), and Ultra Limited Deluxe (i.e., Leather) sold for $390 (only 100 copies); all slip-cased; used as the basis for Del Rey's PB THE COMING OF CONAN, as well as the SFBC HB edition of THE COMING OF CONAN; the Del Rey text is considered superior, corrected a couple errors

## Robert E. Howard's Complete Conan of Cimmeria, Volume 2
Contains *People of the Black Circle; The Hour of the Dragon; A Witch Shall be Born;* **People of the Black Circle (synopsis); The Hour of the Dragon (synopsis); A Witch Shall be Born (synopsis);** *untitled synopsis and draft ("Drums of Tombalku"); plus various REH notes related to the stories*
1ˢᵗ Edition, Wandering Star, HB, July 2004
> **Contains a First Appearance**; edited by Patrice Louinet and Rusty Burke; Very expensive, limited edition for $195 (limited to 1950 copies); Ultra Limited, for $270, only 100 copies; and Leather, for $390, only 100 copies; all slip-cased; artwork by Gary Gianni; "People of the Black Circle" and "A Witch Shall Be Born" are both from typescripts; reprinted by Del Rey and SFBC as THE BLOODY CROWN OF CONAN

## Robert E. Howard's Complete Conan of Cimmeria, Volume 3
Announced by Wandering Star, and used as the basis for THE CONQUERING SWORD OF CONAN, but may or may not be published

## Robert E. Howard's Heroic Creation: Conan
Contains the entire Ace Conan 12 volume set, as a boxed set
1ˢᵗ Edition, Ace, PB, September 1984

## Robert E. Howard's Poems on the Edge

Contains *Cimmeria; Slumber; Black Chant Imperial; Rune; The Return of Sir Richard Grenville; Ghost Dancers; verse heading for The Thing on the Roof; Bride of Chuchulain; Niflheim; The Dweller of Dark Valley (all v)*
1st Edition, Panther's Cage (Kovacs), HB, December 2005
> Illustrated by Hubert Schweizer; no DJ, gold binding; limited to only five copies

## Robert E. Howard's Strange Tales

Contains *The Fearsome Touch of Death; The Voice of El-Lil; Gods of the North; The Garden of Fear; The Cairn on the Headland; The People of the Dark; A Thunder of Trumpets; Black Canaan*
1st Edition, McHaney, TPB, January 2005
McHaney, HB, December 2005
> Most are based on original appearance texts; published as POD via lulu.com; edited by Dennis McHaney; HB edition limited to 100 copies

## Robert E. Howard's World of Heroes

Contains *The Valley of the Worm; The Shadow Kingdom; Jewels of Gwahlur; Worms of the Earth; Kings of the Night; The Gods of Bal-Sagoth; Wings in the Night; Swords of Shahrazar; The Daughter of Erlik Khan; Hawks of Outremer*
1st Edition, Robinson (UK), PB, 1989
> Cover by Chris Achilleos; introduction by Mike Ashley titled "From Conan to Indiana Jones"; "Wings in the Night" is a bowdlerized version

## Rogues in the House

Contains *Rogues in the House;* **The Frost-Giant's Daughter**
1st Edition, Grant, HB, 1976; a traycase was offered via Gray Parrot, not common
> **Contains a First Appearance**; illustrated by Marcus Boas; this is the first appearance of the original Conan version of "The Frost-Giant's Daughter", based on the original manuscript; limited to 3500 copies

## Savage Adventures

Contains *Beyond the Black River; The Devil in Iron; Jewels of Gwahlur; Rogues in the House; Shadows in Zamboula; Skulls in the Stars; The Moon of Skulls; The Hills of the Dead; Wings in the Night; The Footfalls Within; The Valley of the Worm; Pigeons from Hell*
1st Edition, Wildcat Books, TPB, 2004
> Edited by Ron Hanna; sold via lulu.com, very short lived, stopped when they received an infringement letter; inferior texts, from some online PD source; maybe less than 10 copies, perhaps

## The Savage Tales of Solomon Kane

Contains *Skulls in the Stars; The Right Hand of Doom; Red Shadows; Rattle of Bones; The Castle of the Devil; Death's Black Riders; The Moon of Skulls; The One Black Stain (v); The Blue Flame of Vengeance; The Hills of the Dead; Hawk of Basti; The Return of Sir Richard Grenville (v); Wings in the Night; The Footfalls Within; The Children of Asshur; Solomon Kane's Homecoming (v); Solomon Kane's Homecoming (v) (variant)*
1st Edition, Wandering Star, HB, 1998
> Extensively illustrated and signed by Gary Gianni; "The Blue Flame of Vengeance" is just a retitling of "Blades of the Brotherhood", it is NOT the Pocsik version; supposedly the most perfectly clean text ever printed; cost $160 new, came with a CD with dramatic readings of the three poems by former members of the Royal Shakespeare Company, and extra copies of the color plates; there was also an unboxed "publisher's edition", as well as a leather bound version, both of which included an extra plate; 50 of the leatherbound, and maybe 50 of the unboxed; also supposedly 50 other boxed and unnumbered with an additional plate that were given out to movie folks; details vary according to whom you ask
Del Rey, TPB, July 2004
> Supposedly the most perfectly clean text ever printed, even better than the original WS hardback, corrected a couple errors
Del Rey (SFBC), HB, November 2004

**The Scarlet Citadel**
Announced by Grant in the 1980's, but never published

**The Second Book of Robert E. Howard**
Contains *Sword Woman; Which Will Scarcely Be Understood (v); The Striking of the Gong; The Song of Horsa's Galley (v); The Good Knight; A Word from the Outer Dark (v); Black Canaan; The Song of a Mad Minstrel (v); Kelly the Conjure-Man; Surrender ("I will rise . . .") (v); The Footfalls Within; Knife-River Prodigal; Musings ("The little poets . . .") (v); Life (v);* **The House of Suspicion**; *Reuben's Brethren (v); Two Against Tyre; The Guise of Youth (v); "For the Love of Barbara Allen"; Guns of Khartoum; Lines Written in the Realization that I Must Die (v); and a letter to Wilfred B. Talman, ca. September 1931 ("Thank you very much for the letter you wrote . . .")*
1<sup>st</sup> Edition, Zebra, PB, May 1976
Zebra, PB, 2<sup>nd</sup> printing, February 1977
> **Contains a First Appearance**; illustrated by Jeff Jones; introduction and comments by Glenn Lord; letter included in the introduction
Berkley, PB, May 1980

**Shadow Kingdoms: The Weird Works of Robert E. Howard, Volume 1**
Contains *Spear and Fang; In the Forest of Villefere; Wolfshead; The Lost Race; The Song of the Bats (v); The Ride of Falume (v); The Riders of Babylon (v); The Dream Snake; The Hyena; Remembrance (v); Sea Curse; The Gates of Nineveh (v); Red Shadows; The Harp of Alfred (v); Easter Island (v); Skulls in the Stars; Crete (v); Moon Mockery (v); Rattle of Bones; Forbidden Magic (v); The Shadow Kingdom; The Mirrors of Tuzun Thune; The Moor Ghost (v); Red Thunder (v)*
1<sup>st</sup> Edition, Wildside Press, HB, November 2004
Wildside Press, HB, 2<sup>nd</sup> printing, November 2004
Wildside Press, TPB, November 2005
Wildside Press, PB, 2<sup>nd</sup> edition, October 2006
> Cover by Stephen Fabian; introduction by Mark Finn; edited by Paul Herman; all works edited back to match original pulp pages; 1<sup>st</sup> printing Smythe sewn, limited to 1200 copies, 2<sup>nd</sup> printing regular POD, glued spine; the TPB edition had a first print run of 3000 copies; the 2<sup>nd</sup> edition switches the book size to a more typical paperback size, and has a new cover design with art by Ken Kelly

**Shadow Kingdoms: The Weird Works of Robert E. Howard, Volume 1**
Contains *The Lost Race; The Song of the Bats (v); The Ride of Falume (v); The Riders of Babylon (v); The Dream Snake; The Hyena; The Gates of Nineveh (v); Red Shadows; The Harp of Alfred (v); Easter Island (v); Skulls in the Stars; Crete (v); Moon Mockery (v); Rattle of Bones; Forbidden Magic (v); The Shadow Kingdom; The Mirrors of Tuzun Thune; The Moor Ghost (v); Red Thunder (v); Skull-Face; Dead Man's Hate (v); The Fearsome Touch of Death; The Moon of Skulls; The Hills of the Dead; The Voice of El-Lil*
1<sup>st</sup> Edition, Cosmos Books, PB, June 2007
> Cover by Ken Kelly; no introduction; edited by Paul Herman; all works edited back to match original pulp pages; mass market PB edition; combines some of the content of the first two volumes of Wildside Press' WEIRD WORKS OF ROBERT E. HOWARD series, to start a new five book series; printed by Dorchester Publishing on behalf of Wildside Press, who owns Cosmos Books

**Shadow Kingdoms: The Weird Works of Robert E. Howard, Volume 1**
Contains *The Lost Race; The Dream Snake; The Hyena; Red Shadows; Skulls in the Stars; Rattle of Bones; The Mirrors of Tuzun Thune; Red Thunder (v); The Voice of El-Lil*
1<sup>st</sup> Edition, AudioRealms, 5 CD set, June 2007
> Cover by Ken Kelly; introduction by Mark Finn; edited by Paul Herman; all works edited back to match original pulp pages; 5 CD audio set, combines some of the content of the first two volumes of Wildside Press' WEIRD WORKS OF ROBERT E. HOWARD series, to start a new five audio book series; vocal performances by Brian Holsopple, Bob Souer, Bob Barnes, and Charles McKibben; produced and directed by Fred Godsmark

## Shadows of Dreams

Contains **Shadows of Dreams**; *Flaming Marble; Shadow of Dreams;* **A Weird Ballad; A Warning to Orthodoxy; Whispers**; *A Riding Song;* **Castaway**; *Black Seas; Silence Falls on Mecca's Walls;* **Keresa, Kerasita; Whispers on the Night Winds; Nights to Both of Us Known; To Lyle Saxon; Symbols; A Stirring of Green Leaves; The Gladiator and the Lady; A Song of the Anchor Chain; The Path of the Strange Wanderers**; *I Praise My Nativity;* **Ballade; Destiny ("What is there . . ."); Stay Not from Me; The Last Word He Heard; The Ecstasy of Desolation; Musings ("To every man . . .")**; *Dreaming of Israel; The Dust Dance (2) (lines 81-96); A Challenge to Bast;* **The Odyssey of Israel; Romany Road; Twilight on Stonehenge; The Call of Pan; Samson's Broodings; The Road to Babel; The Dreams of Men; A Far Country; To a Nameless Woman; Song of a Fugitive Bard; A Poet's Skull; A Fable for Critics; Love; Song from an Ebony Heart; Love's Young Dream; A Ballad of Beer; John Brown; Abe Lincoln; Surrender ("Open the window . . .")** *(all v)*
1ˢᵗ Edition, Grant, HB, 1989
> **Contains a First Appearance**; artwork by Richard Berry; limited to 750 copies and signed by Richard Berry; introduction by Glenn Lord; these poems all came from the TCS papers, mostly from letters from REH to TCS

## The She Devil

Contains *She Devil; Ship in Mutiny; The Purple Heart of Erlik; The Dragon of Kao Tsu; Murderer's Grog; Desert Blood; Guns of Khartum; Daughters of Feud*
1ˢᵗ Edition, Ace, PB, December 1983
> Cover art by Jodi Penalva; a fairly scarce book, can be pricey to obtain

## Singers in the Shadows

Contains **Zukala's Hour; Night Mood; The Sea-Woman; The Bride of Cuchulain; The Stranger; Shadows; Rebel; White Thunder; The Men That Walk with Satan; Thus Spake Sven the Fool; Sacrifice; The Witch; The Lost Galley; Hadrian's Wall; Attila Rides No More; The Fear That Follows**; *Destination;* **The Tavern; The Road to Hell; The Twin Gates** *(all v)*
1ˢᵗ Edition, Grant, HB, 1970
> **Contains a First Appearance**; cover art by Dave Karbonik, eight interior illustrations by Robert Bruce Acheson; limited to 549 copies; was originally presented to Albert and Charles Boni in 1928, rejected
Science Fiction Graphics, HB, 1977
> Limited to 1500 copies; illustrated by Marcus Boas

## Skull-Face

Contains *Skull-Face;* **Lord of the Dead**; *Names in the Black Book; Taverel Manor (completed by Richard Lupoff)*
1ˢᵗ Edition, Berkley, PB, February 1978
Berkley, PB, 2ⁿᵈ printing, nd (March 1979)
> **Contains a First Appearance**; introduction by Richard Lupoff titled "Pictures in the Flames"

## Skull-Face

Contains *Skull-Face*
1ˢᵗ Limited Edition, Medusa Expressions, PB, March 2006
1ˢᵗ Regular Edition, Medusa Expressions, PB, March 2006
> Cover and interior art by Hannibal King; edited by Michael Hranek; the Artist's Edition of 100 signed and numbered copies with no cover text except on the spine, less than 90 actually sold; regular edition of 500 copies with full cover text, including title and credits, less than 490 sold; there is also an alternate cover, with all the cover verbage at the top in a black bar, very limited, maybe five total

## Skull-Face and Others

Contains *Which Will Scarcely Be Understood (v); Wolfshead; The Black Stone; The Horror from the Mound; The Cairn on the Headland; Black Canaan; The Fire of Asshurbanipal; A Man-Eating Jeopard; Skull-Face; The Hyborian Age; Worms of the Earth; The Valley of the Worm; Skulls in the Stars; Rattle of Bones; The Hills of the Dead; Wings in the Night; The Shadow Kingdom; The Mirrors of Tuzun Thune; Kings of the Night; The Phoenix on the Sword; The Scarlet Citadel; The Tower of the Elephant; Rogues in the House; Shadows in Zamboula; Lines Written in the Realization That I Must Die (v)*

1st Edition, Arkham House, HB, 1946

> Limited to 3004 copies; cover art by Hannes Bok; edited and introduction by August Derleth; includes a Memorial from HPL

## Skull-Face Omnibus

Contains *Which Will Scarcely Be Understood (v); Wolfshead; The Black Stone; The Horror from the Mound; The Cairn on the Headland; Black Canaan; The Fire of Asshurbanipal; A Man-Eating Jeopard; Skull-Face; The Hyborian Age; Worms of the Earth; The Valley of the Worm; Skulls in the Stars; Rattle of Bones; The Hills of the Dead; Wings in the Night; The Shadow Kingdom; The Mirrors of Tuzun Thune; Kings of the Night; The Phoenix on the Sword; The Scarlet Citadel; The Tower of the Elephant; Rogues in the House; Shadows in Zamboula; Lines Written in the Realization That I Must Die (v)*

1st Edition, Neville-Spearman (UK), HB, 1974 (£2.50)

Neville-Spearman (UK), HB, 2nd printing, May 1975 (£3.75)

> Cover art by Reg Boorer; photo-offset from Arkham House's SKULL-FACE AND OTHERS

## Skull-Face Omnibus, Volume 1, Skull-Face and Others

Contains *Which Will Scarcely Understood (v); Skull-face; Wolfshead; The Black Stone; The Horror from the Mound; The Cairn on the Headland; Black Canaan*

1st Edition, Panther (UK), PB, 1976

> Cover by Chris Achilleos; part one of a three-volume set reprinting Arkham House's SKULL-FACE AND OTHERS

## Skull-Face Omnibus, Volume 2, The Valley of the Worm and Others

Contains *The Fire of Asshurbanipal; A Man-Eating Jeopard; Worms of the Earth; Kings of the Night; The Valley of the Worm; Skulls in the Stars; Rattle of Bones; The Hills of the Dead; Wings in the Night; Which Will Scarcely Be Understood (v)*

1st Edition, Panther (UK), PB, 1976

> Cover by Chris Achilleos; part two of a three-volume set reprinting Arkham House's SKULL-FACE AND OTHERS

## Skull-Face Omnibus, Volume 3, The Shadow Kingdom and Others

Contains *The Hyborian Age; The Shadow Kingdom; Mirrors of Tuzun Thune; The Phoenix on the Sword; The Scarlet Citadel; The Tower of the Elephant; Rogues in the House; Shadows in Zamboula; Lines Written in Realization That I Must Die (v); Which Will Scarcely Be Understood*

1st Edition, Panther (UK), PB, 1976

> Cover by Chris Achilleos; part three of a three-volume set reprinting Arkham House's SKULL-FACE AND OTHERS

## The 'Soloman Crane' Stories

Contains *Skulls in the Stars; The Footfalls Within; The Moon of Skulls; The Hills of the Dead; Wings in the Night; Rattle of Bones; Red Shadows*

1st Edition, The Echo Library (UK), TPB, March 2007

> Texts from Project Gutenberg Australia; erroneously listed as editced by Grace Isabel Colbron, and error that may be fixed in later editions, hopefully along with the title

## Solomon Kane

Contains *The Right Hand of Doom; Red Shadows; Rattle of Bones; The Castle of the Devil (unfinished fragment); Blades of the Brotherhood; The Return of Sir Richard Grenville (v); Solomon Kane's Homecoming (v)*

1st Edition, Centaur, PB, February 1971 (60c)
> Cover art by Jeff Jones; introduction by Albert E Gechter

Haddock (unauthorized, Hungary), PB, nd (February 1972)

Centaur, PB, 2nd printing, nd (1974) ($1.25, "Third Big Edition")
> Cross Plains Public Library has an edition called "The Third Big Edition", priced at $1.25, but there is no record of a "Second" edition before it

Centaur, PB, 3rd printing, nd (1976) ($1.50, "The Illustrated Edition")
> Interior illustrations by David Wenzel

## Solomon Kane

Contains *Skulls in the Stars; The Right Hand of Doom; Red Shadows; Rattle of Bones; The Castle of the Devil (completed by Ramsey Campbell); Death's Black Riders; The Moon of Skulls; The One Black Stain (v); Blades of the Brotherhood; The Hills of the Dead; Hawk of Basti (completed by Ramsey Campbell); The Return of Sir Richard Grenville (v); Wings in the Night; The Footfalls Within; The Children of Asshur (completed by Ramsey Campbell); Solomon Kane's Homecoming (v)*

1st Edition, Baen, PB, November 1995
> Attempts to go back to the original text, where available; "The Footfalls Within" is expurgated, maybe from Grant; cover art by Ken Kelly; introduction by Ramsey Campbell

## Solomon Kane: Skulls in the Stars

Contains *Skulls in the Stars; The Right Hand of Doom; Red Shadows; Rattle of Bones;* **The Castle of the Devil (completed by Ramsey Campbell)***; The Moon of Skulls; The One Black Stain (v); Blades of the Brotherhood*

1st Edition, Bantam, PB, December 1978
> **Contains a First Appearance**; introduction by Ramsey Campbell; first appearance of the Ramsey Campbell completions

## Solomon Kane: The Hills of the Dead

Contains *The Hills of the Dead;* **The Hawk of Basti (completed by Ramsey Campbell)***; The Return of Sir Richard Grenville (v); Wings in the Night; The Footfalls Within;* **The Children of Asshur (completed by Ramsey Campbell)***; Solomon Kane's Homecoming (v)*

1st Edition, Bantam, PB, March 1979
> **Contains a First Appearance**; introduction by Ramsey Campbell; first appearance of the Ramsey Campbell completions

## Son of the White Wolf

Contains *Blood of the Gods; The Country of the Knife; Son of the White Wolf*

1st Edition, FAX, HB, 1977
> Illustrated by Marcus Boas

Orbit (UK), PB, 1977
> Cover art by Chris Archilleos; likely based on FAX edition

Futura (UK), PB, July 1977

Berkley, PB, April 1978

Futura (UK), PB, 2nd printing, August 1978

Ace, PB, January 1987

## The Sowers of the Thunder

Contains *The Lion of Tiberias; The Sowers of the Thunder; Lord of Samarcand; The Shadow of the Vulture; and the verse heading from Chapter 2 of Phoenix on the Sword*

1st Edition, Grant, HB, 1973
> Limited to 2509 copies; illustrated by Roy Krenkel; 1st and 2nd are the same, except 2nd has heavier paper, making the dust jacket not fit quite right, also maybe black page edges on the first, white on the second; the verse heading is in the introduction by Roy Krenkel

Zebra, PB, March 1975
> Cover by Jeff Jones, interior Illustrations by Roy Krenkel; photo-offset from Grant HB edition

Zebra, PB, 2nd printing, August 1975
Grant, HB, 2nd Edition, 1976
Zebra, PB, 3rd printing, February 1976
Zebra, PB, 4th printing, October 1976
Zebra, PB, 5th printing, 1977
Sphere (UK), PB, 1977
Ace, PB, July 1979
> Photo-offset from the Grant HB edition

## The Sword of Conan

Contains *The People of the Black Circle; The Slithering Shadow; The Pool of the Black One; Red Nails*
1st Edition, Gnome Press, HB, 1952
> Cover by David Kyle, edited by John D. Clark; limited to 4000 copies

## Sword Woman

Contains *Sword Woman; Blades for France; Mistress of Death (with Gerald W. Page); The King's Service; The Shadow of the Hun*
1st Edition, Zebra, PB, May 1977
> Illustrated by Stephen Fabian; introduction by Leigh Brackett

Berkley, PB, December 1979
Ace, PB, October 1986

## Swords of Shahrazar

Contains *Swords of Shahrazar; The Treasures of Tartary;* **The Curse of the Crimson God**
1st Edition, Futura (or Orbit, UK), PB, February 1976
> **Contains a First Appearance**; cover art by Chris Achilleos; appeared virtually simultaneously with the FAX HB edition on which it is based; other PB editions also contain "The Brazen Peacock" and "The Black Bear Bites"

FAX, HB, 1976
> Heavily illustrated by Michael Kaluta; introduction by Frederic Cook; this edition is actually titled THE SWORDS OF SHAHRAZAR, an error

Futura (or Orbit, UK), PB, 2nd printing, September 1976

## Swords of Shahrazar

Contains *The Treasures of Tartary; Swords of Shahrazar; The Curse of the Crimson God; The Brazen Peacock; The Black Bear Bites*
1st Edition, Berkley, PB, March 1978
Ace, PB, November 1987
> Adds "The Brazen Peacock" and "The Black Bear Bites" to the earlier edition of this book

## Tales of Conan

Contains *The Bloodstained God; Hawks Over Shem; The Road of the Eagles; The Flame Knife (all with LSDC)*

1st Edition, Gnome Press, HB, 1955

Cover by Ed Emshwiller, limited to 4000 copies; generally red with black binding, though several other lesser variations exist; all these stories are non-Conan stories turned into Conan stories by LSDC

## Three Tales of Conan the Barbarian

Contains *A Witch Shall Be Born; Black Colossus; The People of the Black Circle*

1st Edition, The Echo Library (UK), TPB, March 2007

Texts from Project Gutenberg Australia; erroneously listed as editced by Grace Isabel Colbron, and error that may be fixed in later editions

## Three-Bladed Doom

Contains *Three-Bladed Doom*

1st Edition, Zebra, PB, July 1977

Cover by "Enrich"

Orbit (UK), PB, 1977

Futura (UK), PB, July 1977

Futura (UK), PB, 2nd printing, August 1978

Ace, PB, December 1979

Cover art by Sanjulian; text considered superior to the Zebra edition

Ace, PB, 2nd printing, March 1987

## Tigers of the Sea

Contains *Tigers of the Sea (completed by Richard Tierney); Swords of the Northern Sea; The Night of the Wolf; The Temple of Abomination (completed by Richard Tierney)*

1st Edition, Grant, HB, 1974

**Contains a First Appearance**; edited by Richard Tierney; introduction by Glenn Lord; illustrated by Tim Kirk

Zebra, PB, May 1975

New cover by Jeff Jones, otherwise photo-offset from the Grant HB edition, 1974

Zebra, PB, 2nd printing, August 1975

Zebra, PB, 3rd printing, February 1976

Zebra, PB, 4th printing, April 1976

Zebra, PB, 5th printing, 1977

Sphere (UK), PB, 1977

Ace, PB, June 1979

New cover by "Sanjulian", otherwise photo-offset from Grant HB edition, 1974

Ace, PB, 2nd printing, April 1984

## Tower of the Elephant

Contains *Tower of the Elephant; God in the Bowl*

1st Edition, Grant, HB, 1975; a traycase was offered via Gray Parrot, not common

Limited to 3100 copies; illustrated by R. Robertson

Grossett and Dunlap, TPB, 1978

Trade paperback binding up loose pages from the original Grant version

## Trails in Darkness

Contains *The Dead Remember; Black Canaan; Kelly the Conjure-Man; The Valley of the Lost (2); The Man on the Ground; Black Hound of Death; "For the Love of Barbara Allen"; The Hoofed Thing; Moon of Zambebwei; The Horror from the Mound*
1st Edition, Baen, PB, June 1996
> Cover art by Ken Kelly; introduction by SM Sterling

## Treasures of Tartary and Others

Contains *Treasures of Tartary; Son of the White Wolf; Black Vulmea's Vengeance; Boot-Hill Payoff; The Vultures of Wahpeton*
1st Edition, Wildside Press, HB, July 2004
Wildside Press, HB, 2nd printing, 2004
Wildside Press, TPB, 2006
> Edited and introduction by Paul Herman; all stories based on original pulp pages with minimal editing; first printing is Smythe sewn, on acid-free paper, limited to 600 copies, no notation in the book; the second printing is regular POD, glued spine; TPB has a reworked cover

## The Ultimate Triumph: The Heroic Fantasy of Robert E. Howard

Contains stories: *Beyond the Black River;* **The House of Arabu***; Spears of Clontarf; The Night of the Wolf; Spear and Fang; The Valley of the Worm; Lord of Samarcand;* poetry: **An Echo from the Iron Harp***; A Word from the Outer Dark; The Song of the Last Briton; A Song of the Naked Lands; Viking's Trail; plus excerpts from some letters*
1st Edition, Wandering Star, HB, 2000
> **Contains a First Appearance**; "The House of Arabu" is restored text, the poem is a later version never before published; contains more than 120 Frazetta sketches, 30-45% of those previously unpublished; there is a leather bound version, limited slipcase version, and a regular version

## The Valley of the Worm: The Weird Works of Robert E. Howard, Volume 5

Contains *Black Colossus; The Man on the Ground; The Slithering Shadow; The Pool of the Black One; Old Garfield's Heart; One Who Comes at Eventide (v); To a Woman (Though fathoms deep . . .") (v); Rogues in the House; The Valley of the Worm; Gods of the North; Shadows in the Moonlight*
1st Edition, Wildside Press, HB, June 2006
> Cover by Stephen Fabian; introduction by James Reasoner; edited by Paul Herman; all works edited back to match original pulp pages; 1st printing Smythe sewn, limited to 1200 copies, 2nd printing regular POD, glued spine

## The Vultures

Contains *The Vultures;* **Showdown at Hell's Canyon; letter to HPL, September 1934 ("Thanks very much for the postcards . . .") (excerpt only)**
1st Edition, Fictioneer, HB, 1973
Fictioneer, HB, 2nd Edition, 1975
> **Contains a First Appearance**; afterword by Glenn Lord, letter is quoted there; 1st edition limited to 1100 copies; there are 3 distinctive jackets: 1 a "hard-toned" one on coated paper, and 2 "soft-toned" ones, one on uncoated paper and one on coated, the last is by far the most common; 1st edition has black binding, gilt lettering, prices at $5.95; 2nd edition has maroon binding, silver lettering, priced at $6.95, and the price was increased to $8.50 later

## The Vultures of Whapeton

Contains *The Vultures of Whapeton; Showdown at Hell's Canyon; Drums of the Sunset; Wild Water; letter to HPL, September 1934 ("Thanks very much for the postcards . . .") (excerpt only)*
1st Edition, Zebra, PB, November 1975
    Cover by Jeff Jones; afterword by Glenn Lord, letter is quoted there
Zebra, PB, 2nd printing, March 1976
Zebra, PB, 3rd printing, October 1976
Berkley, PB, January 1980

## Waterfront Fists and Others

Contains *Letter to the Ring, April 1926 ("Here is my opinion on the greatest heavyweights . . ."); Kid Lavigne Is Dead (v); Dula Due to Be Champion; Apparition in The Prize Ring; The Pit of the Serpent; The Bull Dog Breed; Sailor's Grudge; Fist and Fang; The Iron Man; Winner Take All; Waterfront Fists; Champ of the Forecastle; Alleys of Peril; Texas Fists; Circus Fists; Vikings of the Gloves; Night of Battle; The Slugger's Game; General Ironfist; Sluggers on the Beach; Alleys of Darkness*
1st Edition, Wildside Press, HB, May 2003
Wildside Press, TPB, December 2004
    Introduction by Mark Finn; edited by Paul Herman; a collection of boxing works; includes original artwork from stories, all restored to original pulp appearance

## The Weird Writings of Robert E. Howard, Volume One

Contains *Spear and Fang; In the Forest of Villefère; a letter to The Eyrie, February 1926 ("These are sheer masterpieces. . . ."); Wolfshead; The Lost Race; The Song of the Bats (v); Letter to the Eyrie, June 1927 ("Your last three issues . . ."); The Ride of Falume (v); The Riders of Babylon (v); The Dream Snake; The Hyena; Remembrance (v); Sea Curse; Letter to the Eyrie, May 1928 ("Mr. Lovecraft's latest story . . ."); The Gates of Nineveh (v); Red Shadows; The Harp of Alfred (v); Easter Island (v); Skulls in the Stars; Crete (v); Moon Mockery (v); Rattle of Bones; Forbidden Magic (v); The Shadow Kingdom; The Moor Ghost (v); The Mirrors of Tuzun Thune; Skull-Face; Letter to the Eyrie, November 1929 ("I have just been reading . . ."); Dead Man's Hate (v); The Fearsome Touch of Death; A Song out of Midian (v); Letter to the Eyrie, April 1930 ("'Thirsty Blades' is fine . . ."); Shadows on the Road (v); The Moon of Skulls; The Hills of the Dead; Black Chant Imperial (v); Kings of the Night; The Song of a Mad Minstrel (v); The Children of the Night; Letter to the Eyrie, January 1931 ("I was particularly fascinated . . ."); The Footfalls Within; The Gods of Bal-Sagoth; The Black Stone; The Dark Man; The Thing on the Roof; The Last Day (v); Letter to the Eyrie, March 1932 ("Congratulations on the appearance . . ."); The Horror from the Mound; Wings in the Night; Arkham (v); An Open Window (v); Worms of the Earth; The Phoenix on the Sword; The Scarlet Citadel; The Tower of the Elephant; Autumn (v); Moonlight on a Skull (v); Black Colossus; The Man on the Ground; The Slithering Shadow; The Pool of the Black One; Old Garfield's Heart; Rogues in the House; The Valley of the Worm; Shadows in the Moonlight; Queen of the Black Coast; The Haunter of the Ring*
1st Edition, Girasol Press, HB, February 2006
1st Limited Edition, Girasol Press, HB, February 2006
    Facsimile reproduction of all original WEIRD TALES pages containing REH material, in a two volume set; includes all original artwork from stories; cover art by Rudy Nebres; the limited includes a frontispiece by Roy Krenkel, limited to 50 copies total

## The Weird Writings of Robert E. Howard, Volume Two

Contains *The Devil in Iron; The People of the Black Circle; A Witch Shall Be Born; The Grisly Horror; Jewels of Gwahlur; Beyond the Black River; Shadows in Zamboula; The Hour of the Dragon; Black Caanan; Letter to The Eyrie, June 1936 ("Enthusiasm impels me . . ."); Red Nails; Black Hound of Death; The Fire of Asshurbanipal; Dig Me No Grave; The Soul-Eater (v); The Dream and the Shadow (v); Which Will Scarcely Be Understood (v); Futility ("Golden goats . . .") (v); Fragment (v); Haunting Columns (v); The Poets (v); The Singer in the Mist (v); Pigeons From Hell (two versions); The Last Hour (v); Ships (v); Lines Written in the Realization That I Must Die (v); A Thunder of Trumpets; Recompense (v); The Ghost Kings (v); The King and the Oak (v); Desert Dawn (v); Almuric; The Hills of Kandahar (v); The Black Stone; The Dark Man*
1st Edition, Girasol Press, HB, March 2006
1st Limited Edition, Girasol Press, HB, March 2006

Facsimile reproduction of all original WEIRD TALES pages containing REH material, in a two volume set; includes all original artwork from stories; cover art by Neal Adams; the limited includes a frontispiece by Neil Mechem, limited to 50 copies total; "The Black Stone" and "The Dark Man" are facsimiles from WT reprints in the 1950s, as well as the second version of "Pigeons from Hell" in this volume

## West is West and Others

Contains *West Is West; "Golden Hope" Christmas; Unhand Me, Villain; Aha! or The Mystery of the Queen's Necklace; The Sheik; The Sea (v); What the Nation Owes to the South; Halt! Who Goes There?; The Kissing of Sal Snooboo (v); The Ideal Girl; The Maiden of Kercheezer (v); The Rules of Etiquette (v); Illusion (v); Fables for Little Folks (v); Roundelay of the Roughneck (v); Futility ("Time races on . . .") (v); Tarantella (v); After the Game; Sleeping Beauty; Weekly Short Story; Private Magrath of the A.E.F. (v); The Thessalians; Ye College Days; Cupid vs. Pollux; The Reformation: A Dream; Flaming Marble (v); Rebellion (v); A Lady's Chamber (v); Dreaming on Downs (v); Skulls and Dust (v); Empire's Destiny (v); Shadow of Dreams (v); Red Thunder (v); Tides (v); To a Woman ("Though fathoms deep . . .") (v); One Who Comes at Eventide (v); letter to Adventure, ca. 1924 ("Questions? I am writing . . .", with response); letter to Adventure, 1924 ("At what period . . .", with response); letter to The Ring, ca. 1926 ("Here is my opinion . . ."); letter to Weird Tales, ca. May 1927 ("Your last three issues . . ."); letter to Weird Tales, ca. April 1928 ("Mr. Lovecraft's latest . . ."); letter to Weird Tales, ca. October 1929 ("I have just been . . ."); letter to Weird Tales, ca. March 1930 ("'Thirsty Blades' is fine . . ."); letter to Weird Tales, ca December 1930 ("I was particularly fascinated . . ."); letter to Weird Tales, ca. February 1932 ("Congratulations on the appearance . . ."); letter to Weird Tales, ca. May 1936 ("Enthusiasm impels me . . ."); Dula Due to be Champ; letter to The Fort Worth Record, ca. July 1928 ("Tunney can't win . . ."); letter to The Californian, 1936 ("Thank you very much . . ."); letter to The Fantasy Fan, ca. 1933 ("I find the Fantasy Fan . . ."); letter to The Fantasy Fan, ca. late 1933 ("I liked the November issue . . ."); letter to The Fantasy Fan, ca. 1934 ("Smith's poem in the March issue . . ."); The Voices Waken Memory (v); Babel (v); The Ghost of Camp Colorado; The Tempter (v); With a Set of Rattlesnake Rattles; letter to Farnsworth Wright, ca. June-July 1931 ("In your last letter . . ."); Some People Who Have Had Influence Over Me; The Wandering Years; letter to E. Hoffmann Price, February 15, 1936 ("I have eventually . . ."); letter to E. Hoffmann Price, April 21, 1936 ("Glad you-all liked 'She-Devil' . . ."); letter to E. Hoffmann Price, June 3, 1936 ("Sorry to hear Pawang Ali . . ."); Untitled ("The wind from the Mediterranean . . ."); But the Hills Were Ancient Then (v); letter to August Derleth, ca. January 1933 ("I was much interested . . .", excerpt only, discussing Astounding); Dreams of Ninevah (v); The Sands of Time (v); Sonora to Del Rio (v); Midnight; The One Black Stain (v); letter to Harold Preece, ca. October 1930 ("Well, Harold, how did you like . . ."); The Skull in the Clouds (v); Surrender ("I will rise . . .") (v); letter to Harold Preece, October 20, 1928 ("Your stationery is alright."); plus some interesting non-REH commentary including Robert E. Howard as a Boy, by Mrs. T.A. Burns; Robert Howard, Short Story Writer, by The Tattler Editor; Jacket to Have Short Story Writer, by Yellow Jacket Editor; Unusual Stories (advertisement); commentary on REH in The Fantasy Fan (4 items); Miscellany in The Fantasy Fan; Under Our Reading Lamp, by The Republic Editor; The Adventure Story, by Natalie H. Wooley; and all contents for The Howard Collector, #1, #2 and #3*

1st Edition, Rob Roehm and "Alex Runions", HB & TPB, February 2006

Roehm's Room Press, HB & TPB, April 2007

Edited by Rob Roehm and Joe Marek; published via lulu.com; a collection of non-commercial works, including juvenilia, newspaper, letters to the editor, and poetry journals; first HB appearance for a lot of this material, some first reprinting since first publication; "Alex Runions" is a pseudonym for Joe Marek

## Winds of Time

Contains *Cimmeria; Skull in the Clouds; The Return of Sir Richard Grenville; Black Chant Imperial; Always Comes Evening; Solomon Kane's Homecoming; The One Black Stain; Lines Written in the Realization That I Must Die; The Song of a Mad Minstrel; The Dweller in Dark Valley; Where Are Your Knights, Donn Othna?; The Dance With Death; Ghost Dancers; Recompense; Candles; The Thing on the Roof (story heading); The Bride of Cuchulain; Babel; A Moment; The Men That Walk With Satan; The Hour of the Dragon (chapter headings); The Tempter; The Sands of Time; Earth-Born; Marching Song of Connacht; Roads; To a Woman ("Though fathoms deep . . ."); Rune; On with the Play; Visions; Niflheim; An Open Window; "Feach Air Muir*

*Lionadhi Gealach Buidhe Mar Or"; Queen of the Black Coast (verse heading); The Road of Azreal (verse heading); The Ghost Ocean; Slumber; Roundelay of the Roughneck (all v)*

1st Edition, Tom Kovacs, HB, 2007

> Cover and numerous interior illustrations by Hubert Schweizer; blue binding with silver lettering, with wraparound dust jacket; foreword by Glenn Lord; essays by Hugh Walker and Bernd Karwath; all poems in English and German; limited to 1000 copies

## Wings in the Night: The Weird Works of Robert E. Howard, Volume 4

Contains *Wings in the Night; Arkham (v); An Open Window (v); Worms of the Earth; The Phoenix on the Sword; The Scarlet Citidel; The Cairn on the Headland; The Tower of the Elephant; Autumn (v); Moonlight on a Skull (v)*

1st Edition, Wildside Press, HB, November 2005

Wildside Press, HB, 2nd printing, November 2005

Wildside Press, PB, January 2007

> Cover by Stephen Fabian; introduction and editing by Paul Herman; all works edited back to match original pulp pages; 1st printing Smythe sewn, limited to 1200 copies, 2nd printing regular POD, glued spine

## A Witch Shall Be Born

Contains *A Witch Shall be Born*

1st Edition, Grant, HB, 1975; a traycase was offered via Gray Parrot, not common

> Limited to 3100 copies; illustrated by Alicia Austin

## Wolfshead

Contains *The Black Stone; The Valley of the Worm; Wolfshead; The Fire of Asshurbanipal; The House of Arabu; The Horror from the Mound; The Cairn on the Headland; plus an small excerpt from a letter to HPL, ca. July 1933 ("Glad you got the physical-mental . . .")*

1st Edition, Lancer, PB, 1968 (60c)

Lancer, PB, 2nd printing, 1968 (Canada)

Lancer, PB, 3rd printing, nd (1972)

Lancer, PB, 4th printing, nd (Canada)

> Cover art by Frank Frazetta; letter excerpt is used as an introduction, and begins with "I was eighteen when I wrote 'Spear and Fang'."

## Wolfshead

Contains *The Black Stone; The Valley of the Worm; Wolfshead; The Fire of Asshurbanipal; The House of Arabu; The Horror from the Mound*

1st Edition, Bantam, PB, September 1979

> New introduction by Robert Bloch; cover artist unidentified; "The Cairn on the Headland" is not included in this volume, nor the REH letter excerpt

## Worms of the Earth

Contains *Foreword by REH, discussing Picts (excerpted from a letter to HPL, ca. early January 1932 ("Yes I enjoyed the postcards.", the excerpt beginning with "There is one hobby of mine . . ."); The Drums of Pictdom (v); The Lost Race; Men of the Shadows; Kings of the Night; A Song of the Race (v); Worms of the Earth; Fragment ("A gray sky arched . . ."); The Dark Man; Chant of the White Beard (v); Rune (v); Song of the Pict (v)*

1st Edition, Grant, HB, 1974

> Limited to 2500 copies; cover and interior illustrations by David Ireland; the last three listed poems are all contained as untitled verse in the story "Men of the Shadows"; interior illustrations included in all later editions as well

Zebra, PB, July 1975

> Cover by Jeff Jones

Zebra, PB, 1st Canadian printing, 1975

Zebra, PB, 2^nd printing, August 1975
Orbit (UK), PB, 1976
> Cover art by Chris Achilleos

Zebra, PB, 3^rd printing, April 1976
Zebra, PB, 4^th printing, January 1977
Ace, PB, June 1979
> Cover art by Sanjulian

Ace, PB, 2^nd printing, September 1987

## Writer of the Dark

Contains Poetry: *Skulls;* ***Ghost Dancers;*** ***Long Ago****; Tiger Girl; Let the Gods Die; Swamp Murder;* ***The Cooling of Spike McRue****; A Legend; The Song of the Gallows Tree; Song Before Clontarf;* Stories: ***The Ghost with the Silk Hat****; Graveyard Rats; Teeth of Doom;* ***The Mark of a Bloody Hand****; Spears of Clontarf; A Gent from the Pecos*; ***plus a letter to TCS, ca. October 1928 ("Salaam: / I could have gone with you for dinner . . .")***

1^st Edition, Dark Carneval (Switzerland), TPB, 1986
> **Contains a First Appearance**; illustrated by Bodo Schafer; introduction by Glenn Lord; Kovacs originally printed up 500 sets of pages, 200 were bound in red/orange paper cover with a rat illo, 120 more in a plain tan cover, after he lost the first cover design, 80 were lost in a flood, and 100 still to be bound, hopefully as hardcovers, someday; "The Ecstasy of Desolation" is included in the letter

# PERIODICALS CONTAINING REH MATERIAL

This index is sorted by title of periodical, then by date or number. I have tried to be consistent in choosing which publications go in this PERIODICALS list, and which go in the CHAPBOOKS list. In general, if it looks like a professional publication or I am not sure, it is in this list.

Items in **BOLD** are **First Appearance** of that work anywhere, of which there are many, as REH sold over 100 stories to the pulps during his lifetime, and much of his later discovered works were first published in various magazines of the 1960's and 1970's.

Non-English periodicals are noted in the title heading. Poetry is indicated by (v).

*Form of Entry:*
**Title**
Issue ID (Date or Number)
    Contents
        Notes

**Action Stories**
January 1931
    Contains *The TNT Punch*
June 1931
    Contains *The Sign of the Snake*
October 1931
    Contains *Blow the Chinks Down*
November 1931
    Contains *Breed of Battle*
January 1932
    Contains *Dark Shanghai*
March-April 1934
    Contains *Mountain Man*
May-June 1934
    Contains *Guns of the Mountains*
August 1934
    Contains *The Scalp Hunter*
October 1934
    Contains *A Gent from Bear Creek*
December 1934
    Contains *The Road to Bear Creek*
February 1935
    Contains *The Haunted Mountain*
April 1935
    Contains *War on Bear Creek*
June 1935
    Contains *The Feud Buster*
August 1935
    Contains *Cupid from Bear Creek*
October 1935
    Contains *The Riot at Cougar Paw*

December 1935
> Contains **The Apache Mountain War**

February 1936
> Contains **Pilgrims to the Pecos**

April 1936
> Contains **Pistol Politics**

June 1936
> Contains **Evil Deeds at Red Cougar**

August 1936
> Contains **High Horse Rampage**

September 1936
> Contains **"No Cowherders Wanted"**

October 1936
> Contains **The Conquerin' Hero of the Humbolts**

January 1937
> Contains **Sharp's Gun Serenade**

## Adventure
March 20, 1924
> Contains *a letter to the editor ("Question? I am writing . . .")*
>> **This is the first time that Robert E. Howard's name appeared in a professional magazine**

August 20, 1924
> Contains *a letter to the editor ("At what period . . .")*

## Adventure Tales (by Wildside Press)
#1, December 2004
> Contains *The Skull in the Clouds; An Open Window; The Singer in the Mist (all v)*

#4, January 2007
> Contains *Son of the White Wolf*

## Amazing Science Fiction Stories
January 1985
> Contains **Buccaneer Treasure (v)**

## Amazing Stories
March 1986
> Contains **All Hallows Eve (v)**

## American and European Manuscripts and Printed Books
December 19, 1986
> Contains **Untitled poem ("The Baron of Fenland . . .", lines 1-4)**; *Flight (v) (lines 1-2, 5-8, 15-20, 23-24); The Road to Hell (lines 1-4, 24-28)*
>> An advertisement for a Christie's auction that included a facsimile reproduction of the second page from a letter to TCS, ca. September 1927 ("Salaam:/ Then the little boy said . . ."); a large stack of TCS letters were being offered at auction; they did not sell

## American Poet
April 1929
> Contains *A Lady's Chamber (v)*
>> Author listed as "Patrick Howard"

May 1929
    Contains *Skulls and Dust (v)*
        Author listed as "Patrick Howard"

## Amra

Volume 2, #7, November 1959
    Contains *Untitled ("The wind from the Mediterranean . . .")*
Volume 2, #8, November-December 1959
    Contains *But the Hills Were Ancient Then (v)*
Volume 2, #9, January 1960
    Contains *an excerpt from a letter to August Derleth, ca. December 1933 ("I think Scribners . . .")*
Volume 2, #29, August 1964
    Contains *a letter to Harold Preece, ca. October 1930 ("Well, Harold, I'm sorry to hear your nose . . .")*
Volume 2, #30, September 1964
    Contains a letter to August Derleth, ca. January 1933 ("I was much interested in your accounts . . .")
        Lengthy letter discussing the Indians of Texas as well as the stories of Cynthia Ann Parker and Quanah Parker
Volume 2, #36, September 1965
    Contains *a letter to Clark Ashton Smith, ca. March 1934 ("I am sorry to hear you have been indisposed . . .")*
Volume 2, #39, March 1966
    Contains *six letters to Clark Ashton Smith, July 22, 1933 ("I can hardly find words to express . . ."); December 14, 1933 ("Only the fact that I have been sick . . ."); January 20, 1934 ("Thanks very much for the kind things . . ."); ca. January 1934 ("Thanks again for the drawing of the wizard."); July 23, 1935 ("I'm ashamed of my long delay . . .")*
Volume 2, #47, August 1968
    Contains *Something About Eve*

## Ariel

#1, Autumn 1976
    Contains *The Symbol (v); A Crown for a King (v)*; *plus excerpts from Bloodstar*
        Back cover is painting "Conan of Cimmeria" by Frazetta; lots of artwork by Frazetta and Corben
#3, April 1978
    Contains *Musings ("The little poets . . .") (v)*
        Poem illustrated by Jack Kirby

## Argosy

August 15, 1936
    Contains *The Dead Remember*
October 3, 1936
    Contains *A Gent from the Pecos*
October 17, 1936
    Contains *Gents on the Lynch*
October 31, 1936
    Contains *The Riot at Bucksnort*
November 28, 1936
    Contains *Vultures' Sanctuary*

## Argosy All-Story Weekly

July 20, 1929
    Contains *Crowd-Horror; a letter to the editor ("I was born in Texas about twenty-three . . .")*

**Avon Fantasy Reader**

#2, 1947

> Contains *The Mirrors of Tuzun Thune*

#7, 1948

> Contains *The Cairn on the Headland*

#8, 1948

> Contains *Queen of the Black Coast*
>> Cover based on REH story

#10, 1949

> Contains *A Witch Shall Be Born*
>> Cover based on REH story

#12, 1950

> Contains *The Blond Goddess of Bal-Sagoth*

#14, 1950

> Contains *Temptress of the Tower of Torture and Sin*
>> Bizarre alternate title to "The Voice of El-Lil"

#18, 1952

> Contains **The Witch from Hell's Kitchen**

**The Baylor United Statement**

Spring 1923

> Contains **The Sea (v)**
>> No known copies exist; a publication of the Baylor College for Women, now University of Mary Hardin-Baylor; mentioned by REH in a letter to TCS, June 22, 1923 ("Clyde sahib greeting: / I found your first letter . . .")

**Brownwood Bulletin**

May 26, 1923

> Contains **What the Nation Owes the South**

July 18, 1928

> Contains **Dula Due to Be Champion**
>> Only known copy is Glenn Lord's, which is only a clipping that was included in REH's papers

**The Californian**

> Summer 1936
>
> Contain **a letter to the editor ("Thank you very much . . .")**
>> In response to a nice article written about him in that magazine

**CAS - Nyctalops**

#7, August 1972

> Contains *a letter to Clark Ashton Smith, pm, July 22, 1933 ("I can hardly find words to express . . .")*
>> Silver Scarab Press, limited to 1000 copies

**Chacal**

#1, Winter 1976

> Contains **The Road of Azrael; The Ballad of Singapore Nell (v)**; *Futility ("Time races on . . .") (lines 23-30 only)*
>> Artwork by Hannes Bok, Richard Corben, Frank Frezetta, Stephen Fabian, and Marcus Boas; cover by Jeff Easley, based on "Queen of the Black Coast"; "Futility" is used as a heading for the David C. Smith story

#2, Spring 1977

> Contains **Daughter of Evil (v); The Palace of Bast (v)**

**Coleman Democrat-Voice**
May 28, 1931
    Contains *The Ghost of Camp Colorado*
September 27, 1934
    Contains *The Ghost of Camp Colorado*
November 12, 1936
    Contains *The Ghost of Camp Colorado*

**Comic Forum (Austrian)**
#15, September 1982
    Contains *Cimmeria (v)*

**Complete Stories**
August 1936
    Contains ***The Country of the Knife***

**Contemporary Verse**
September 1929
    Contains ***Tides (v)***
        Produced by Benjamin Musser

**Coven 13**
January 1970, #3
    Contains ***The Little People***
March 1970
    Contains ***"Feach Air Muir Lionadhi Gealach Buidhe Mar Or" (v)***

**Cowboy Stories**
July 1936
    Contains ***A Man-Eating Jeopard***
July 1937
    Contains ***Knife-River Prodigal***

**Crit-Q**
#1, 1951
    Contains *Recompense (v); the verse heading from Chapter 5 of The Phoenix on the Sword*
        Published by Robert E. Briney

**Cross Plains**
#1, January 1974
    Contains *Golden Hope Christmas*
#2, March 1974
    Contains *The Sign of the Snake*
#3, March 1974
    Contains ***A Horror in the Night***
        Dated March, but was actually suppose to be May-June
#4, Summer 1974
    Contains ***Law Shooters of Cowtown***
#5, September/November 1974
    Contains ***Under the Baobab Tree***; *The Vultures of Whapeton (alternate ending)*

#6, 1975

> Contains ***The Devil's Joker, a letter to Harold Preece, pm, January 4, 1930 ("Yes, we fade from youth swiftly."), with a lengthy discussion of the evolution of the Celts;*** *a letter to E. Hoffmann Price, February 15, 1936 ("I have eventually found time to answer your cards."); and a letter to Farnsworth Wright, ca. June 1930 ("I have long looked forward to reading . . .")*

#7, September 1975

> Contains ***Wild Water; The Road to Freedom (v)***

## Cross Plains Review

June 29, 1923

> Contains *The Sea (v)*

November 2, 1928

> Contains ***Drums of the Sunset (part 1 of 9)***

November 9, 1928

> Contains ***Drums of the Sunset (part 2 of 9)***

November 16, 1928

> Contains ***Drums of the Sunset (part 3 of 9)***

November 23, 1928

> Contains ***Drums of the Sunset (part 4 of 9)***

November 30, 1928

> Contains ***Drums of the Sunset (part 5 of 9)***

December 7, 1928

> Contains ***Drums of the Sunset (part 6 of 9)***

December 14, 1928

> Contains ***Drums of the Sunset (part 7 of 9)***

December 21, 1928

> Contains ***Drums of the Sunset (part 8 of 9)***

January 4, 1929

> Contains ***Drums of the Sunset (part 9 of 9)***
>
> > Thought to have been, and should have been, printed in this issue, but no copy exists

June 19, 1936

> Contains *A Man-Eating Jeopard*

August 14, 1936

> Contains *What the Nation Owes the South*

June 18, 1937

> Contains ***The Tempter (v)***

July 6, 1990

> Contains *The Tempter (v)*

June 8, 2000

> Contains *The Sea (v)*
>
> > Print run of 1500

## Dallas Morning News

February 24, 1980

> Contains *The Tempter (v) (lines 31-40)*
>
> > In article by Bob St. John titled "A Paradox Within Himself"

## Daniel Baker Collegian
March 15, 1926
>Contains ***Illusion; Fables for Little Folks (both v)***
>>School paper for Daniel Baker College, no known copies exist, Glenn Lord has clippings from REH papers

April 12, 1926
>Contains ***Roundelay of the Roughneck (v)***

May 25, 1926
>Contains ***Futility ("Time races on . . ."); Tarantella (both v)***

## The Dark Man
#6, Summer 2001
>Contains *Hate's Dawn (v)*; ***A Son of Spartacus (v)***
>>A critical anthology, by "Mind's Eye HyperPublishing (Frank Coffman) / Iron Harp Publications"

Volume 3, #1, 2006
>Contains *Isle of the Eons; **Tallyho!***

## Different Worlds
#42, May-June 1986
>Contains *Dagon Manor*
>>UK publication

## Dime Sports Magazine
April 1936
>Contains ***Iron-Jaw***

## Double Action Western
December 1956
>Contains ***While Smoke Rolled***

## Famous Fantastic Mysteries
December 1952
>Contains *Skull-Face*
>>Cover based on REH story

June 1953
>Contains *Worms of the Earth*

## Fanciful Tales
Fall 1936
>Contains ***Solomon Kane's Homecoming (v)***
>>There is a facsimile reprint done by Marc Michaud in 1977, listed here under Chapbooks, the way to tell them apart is the reprint has a new intro that makes clear its recent state, as well as a copyright notice dated 1977

## Fantastic Adventure Stories
Volume 1, #2, August 2007
>Contains *Sea Curse*

## Fantastic
May 1961
>    Contains *The Garden of Fear*

December 1961
>    Contains *The Dead Remember*

January 1967
>    Contains *The People of the Black Circle*

## Fantastic Stories
Volume 24, #4, June 1975
>    Contains **The Tower of Time**
>    > Completed by Lin Carter

## Fantastic Universe
October 1955
>    Contains **Hawks over Shem (with LSDC)**
>    > A LSDC rewrite of an original REH story, "Hawks over Egypt", to turn it into a Conan story

December 1955
>    Contains **Conan, Man of Destiny (with LSDC)**
>    > A LSDC rewrite of an original REH story, "The Road of the Eagles", to turn it into a Conan story

April 1956
>    Contains **The Bloodstained God (with LSDC)**
>    > A LSDC rewrite of an original REH story, "The Curse of the Crimson God", to turn it into a Conan story

December 1956
>    Contains *Gods of the North (with LSDC)*

## Fantasy Book
Volume 3, #2 (whole number 12), June 1984
>    Contains *Death's Black Riders (completed by Fred Blosser)*
>    > Only appearance of this particular collaboration

Volume 3, #3 (whole number 13), September 1984
>    Contains **Skulls (v)**

Volume 4, #2 (whole number 16), June 1985
>    Contains *Black Eons (completed by Robert M. Price)*
>    > Complete story based on a fragment published in THE HOWARD COLLECTOR, Ace

Volume 5, #3 (whole number 21), September 1986
>    Contains **For Man Was Given the Earth to Rule (v); A Challenge to Bast (v)**
>    > Second poem illustrated by Walt Davis

Volume 5, #5 (whole number 23), March 1987
>    Contains **Black Seas (v); I Praise My Nativity (v)**

## Fantasy Commentator
#43, Fall 1990
>    Contains *The Tavern (v)*

#45/46, Winter 1993/94
>    Contains *Arkham (v); An Open Window (v)*
>    > Both are just the first four lines, used as a basis for a 14 line sonnet by Lee Baker

## Fantasy Crossroads

#1, November 1, 1974

Contains **The Hall of the Dead**; *Delenda Est; Recompense (v); The Singer in the Mist (v); The Song of a Mad Minstrel (v)*

Limited to 890 copies

#2, February 1975

Contains **Heritage ("Saxon blood . . .") (v)**; *Heritage ("My people came . . ."); Always Comes Evening (v); The Poets (v); and two letters to Harold Preece, received October 20, 1928 ("Your stationery is alright."), and ca. October 1930 ("Well, Harold, how did you like my story . . ."); Drums of the Sunset; The Curse of the Golden Skull*

Limited to 450 copies; there are indeed two versions of "Heritage" in this issue

#3, May 1975

Contains **Flint's Passing (v)**; *The Ghost Kings (v); The Good Knight; a letter to Harold Preece, ca. December 1928 ("You're right; women are great actors."); and* **a letter to Novalyne Price, July 8, 1935 ("Thank you for your invitation to call . . .")**

Limited to 520 copies; the names of Miss Price and Truett Vinson were masked out of the letters

#4/5, August 1975

Contains **War to the Blind (v); The Day Breaks Over Simla (v); The Abbey**; *Man with the Mystery Mitts*

Limited to 565 copies

#6, November 1975

Contains **The Gondarian Man**; *Hope Empty of Meaning (v); and a letter to Harold Preece, ca. February 1930 ("You're in Kansas now, eh?")*

Limited to 980 Copies

Special Edition #1, January 1976

Contains *More Evidence of the Inate Divinity of Man*; **Fists of the Revolution**; *Visions (v)*

Limited to 535 copies; announced as FANTASY CROSSROADS ANNUAL in THE HOWARD REVIEW #4

#7, February 1976

Contains *College Socks;* **Untitled ("The night was damp . . ."); Madam Goose's Rhymes (v); plus a letter to Harold Preece, ca. August 1928 ("Glad you enjoyed our reunion at Fort Worth.")**

Limited to 985 copies

#8, May 1976

Contains **Miser's Gold (v)**; **Daughters of Feud**

Limited to 1000 copies; art by Corben, Fabian, and Coye; a portfolio based on "God in the Bowl"

#9, August 1976

Contains **The Last Laugh**

Limited to 1200 copies; cover by Richard Corben

#10/11, March 1977

Contains **Genseric's Fifth Born Son**

Limited to 1200 copies

#13, June 1978

Contains **The Feud (v)**

#14, September 1978

Contains *Oh Babylon, Lost Babylon (v)*

## Fantasy Crosswinds

#1, January 1977

Contains **The Curse of Greed; The Kiowa's Tale (v)**; *The Outcast (v)*

Limited to 300 copies

#2 1977

Contains **The Door to the Garden**

Limited to 300 copies

#3, February 1977

Contains *Roar, Silver Trumpets (v)*

## Fantasy Fan

December 1933
> Contains *a letter to the editor ("I find the Fantasy Fan . . .")*

January 1934
> Contains *a letter to the editor ("I liked the November issue . . .")*

March 1934
> Contains **Gods of the North**

May 1934
> Contains *a letter to the editor ("Smith's poem in the March issue . . .")*

September 1934
> Contains **The Voices Waken Memory (v)**

January 1935
> Contains **Babel (v)**

## Fantasy Fiction

#1, August 1953
> Contains *The Frost Giant's Daughter*
>> Edited by LSDC; likely an LSDC rewrite of the Amra version

## Fantasy Magazine

July 1935
> Contains *a letter to Alvin Earl Perry, ca. early 1935 ("The first character I ever created . . .")*
>> Contains the comment that Conan stalked full grown out of oblivion, while REH was in a Rio Grande border town; the letter is quoted piecemeal throughout a biographical article on REH by Alvin Earl Perry

September 1935
> Contains **The Challenge from Beyond**

## Fantasy Magazine

March 1953
> Contains **The Treasure of Tranicos (with LSDC)**

## Fantasy Tales (UK)

#11, Winter 1982
> Contains **Seven Kings (v)**

Winter 1983
> Contains **The Zulu Lord (v)**

Summer 1987
> Contains **An Outworn Story (v)**

Autumn 1988
> Contains **Memories ("Shall we remember . . .") (v)**

## Fiction (French)

#233, May 1973
> Contains *Pour l'Amour de Barbara Allen (For the Love of Barbara Allen)*
>> Published by Opta; translation by R. Lathière

## Fight Stories

July 1929
> Contains **The Pit of the Serpent**

February 1930
> Contains **The Bull Dog Breed**

March 1930
> Contains *Sailor's Grudge*

May 1930
> Contains *Fist and Fang*

June 1930
> Contains *The Iron Man*

July 1930
> Contains *Winner Take All*

September 1930
> Contains *Waterfront Fists*

November 1930
> Contains *Champ of the Forecastle*

January 1931
> Contains *Alleys of Peril*

May 1931
> Contains *Texas Fists*

December 1931
> Contains *Circus Fists*

February 1932
> Contains *Vikings of the Gloves*

March 1932
> Contains *Night of Battle*

Fall 1937
> Contains *Manila Manslaughter*
>> A reprint of "The Pit of the Serpent", author listed as "Mark Adam"

Winter 1937-38
> Contains *You Got to Kill a Bulldog*
>> A reprint of "The Bull Dog Breed", author listed as "Mark Adam"

Spring 1938
> Contains *Costigan v. Kid Camera*
>> A reprint of "Sailor's Grudge", author listed as "Mark Adam"

June-July 1938
> Contains *Champ of the Seven Seas*
>> A reprint of "Champ of the Forecastle"; author listed as "Mark Adam"

Fall 1938
> Contains *Fall Guy*
>> A reprint of "The Iron Man", with a few edits, author listed as "John Starr"

Winter 1938-39
> Contains *Cannibal Fists*
>> A reprint of "Fist and Fang", author listed as "Mark Adam"

Summer 1939
> Contains *Shanghaied Mitts*
>> A reprint of "Texas Fists", author listed as "Mark Adam"

Winter 1939-40
> Contains *Sucker!*
>> A reprint of "Winner Take All", author listed as "Mark Adam"

Summer 1940
> Contains *Stand Up and Slug!*
>> A reprint of "Waterfront Fists", author listed as "Mark Adam"

Fall 1940
> Contains *". . . Including the Scandinavian!"*
>> A reprint of "Vikings of the Gloves", author listed as "Mark Adam"

Winter 1940
>  Contains *Leather Lightning*
>> A reprint of "Alleys of Peril", author listed as "Mark Adam"

Fall 1941
>  Contains *The Waterfront Wallop*
>> A reprint of "The TNT Punch", author listed as "Mark Adam"

Spring 1942
>  Contains *Sampson Had a Soft Spot*
>> A reprint of "Breed of Battle", author listed as "Mark Adam"

Summer 1942
>  Contains *Slugger Bait*
>> A reprint of "Circus Fists", author listed as "Mark Adam"

Fall 1942
>  Contains *Shore Leave for a Slugger*
>> A reprint of "Night of Battle", author listed as "Mark Adam"

## Fort Worth Record

July 20, 1928
>  Contains ***a letter to the editor ("Tunney can't win.")***

## From Beyond the Dark Gateway

#3, April 1974
>  Contains ***The Black Bear Bites***
>> By Silver Scarab Publishing, limited to 550 copies

## Frontier Times

June 1931
>  Contains *The Ghost of Camp Colorado*
>> The original has a tan cover, 48 pages, 7X10.5 size, published by J. Martin Hunter of Bandera, TX; much of FRONTIER TIMES was apparently reprinted in the 1970s by Hunter's Frontier Times of Iola, WI, the reprint having a blue cover, and being only 6.75" wide

May 1936
>  Contains a new article about Camp Colorado, and cites the earlier REH article as a secondary source

## Gargoyle

#1, 1950
>  Contains *Arkham (v)*

## Gensou Bungaku (Japanese)

#19, July 1987
>  Contains *Yamu No Teiou (Kings of the Night)*

## Gensou To Kaiki (Japanese)

#12, October 1974
>  Contains *Kyoufu No Niwa (The Garden of Fear)*

## The Ghost

May 1945
>  Contains ***The Wandering Years; Some People Who Have Had Influence Over Me; a letter to Farnsworth Wright, ca. June 1930 ("I have long looked forward to reading . . ."); and three letters to E Hoffmann Price, February 15, 1936 ("I have eventually found time to answer your cards."), April 21 1936 ("Glad you-all liked 'She-Devil.'"), and June 3, 1936 ("Sorry to hear Pawang Ali has been banished.")***

## Ghost Stories

April 1929

> Contains ***The Apparition in the Prize Ring***
>
>> Author listed as John Taverel

## Golden Atom

1959-60, 20th Anniversary Issue

> Contains ***Dreams of Ninevah (v)***

## Golden Fleece

November 1938

> Contains ***Black Vulmea's Vengeance***

January 1939

> Contains ***Gates of Empire***

## The Haunt of Horror

June 1973

> Contains *Usurp the Night*

## Hayakawa Mystery Magazine (Japanese)

August 1967

> Contains *Shinin Wa Oboete Iru (The Dead Remember)*

April 1969

> Contains *Itsurakukyou No Gen-Ei (The Slithering Shadow)*

October 1969

> Contains *Hyoushin No Musume (The Frost-Giant's Daughter); Kokkaiwan No Jo'ou (Queen of the Black Coast)*

November 1969

> Contains *Kamigami No Nemuri (The Cairn on the Headland); Mubatama Kaigann No Jo-Ou (Queen of the Black Coast); Youma Ga Tani (The Valley of the Worm)*

July 1970

> Contains *Metsubou No Tami (The Lost Race)*

November 1971

> Contains *Ankoku No Tami (The Children of the Night)*

November 1973

> Contains *Ankoku No Shuzoku (The People of the Dark)*

December 1974

> Contains *Arikhu No Shinhu No Shinzou (The Purple Heart of Erlik)*

## Heavy Metal

#3, June 1977

> Contains *Night Images; The Ghost Kings; The Heart of the Sea's Desire; A Word from the Outer Dark (all v)*
>
>> Artwork by Frank Frazetta and Richard Corben

December 1980

> Contains *Bloodstar (part 1)*
>
>> A graphic novel by Richard Corben, based on "Valley of the Worm"

January 1981

> Contains *Bloodstar (part 2)*

February 1981

> Contains *Bloodstar (part 3)*

March 1981

> Contains *Bloodstar (part 4)*

April 1981
> Contains *Bloodstar (part 5)*

May 1981
> Contains *Bloodstar (part 6)*

June 1981
> Contains *Bloodstar (part 7)*

July 1981
> Contains *Bloodstar (part 8)*


## Hopalong Cassidy's Western Magazine

Fall 1950
> Contains *Texas John Alden*


## The Howard Collector (edited and sold by Glenn Lord)

#1, Summer 1961
2nd printing, October 1975
> Contains *With a Set of Rattlesnake Rattles; Midnight;* **The Sands of Time (v); Sonora to Del Rio (v)**
> Limited to 250 copies of 1st edition

#2, Spring 1962
> Contains **The One Black Stain (v);** *The Skull in the Clouds (v);* and **a letter to Harold Preece, ca. October 1930 ("Well, Harold, how did you like my story . . .")**
> Limited to maybe 250 copies

#3, Fall 1962
> Contains *West is West;* **Surrender ("I will rise . . .") (v);** and **a letter to Harold Preece, received October 20, 1928 ("Your stationery is alright.")**
> Limited to 150 copies

#4, Summer 1963
> Contains *Aha! or The Mystery of the Queen's Necklace; Sea Curse; Skulls and Dust (v); Futility ("Time races on . . .") (v)*
> Limited to 150 copies

#5, Summer 1964
> Contains **Kelly the Conjure-Man; The Last White Man; Belshazzar (v); A Dawn at Flanders (v); Timur-lang (v); John Ringold (v); A Warning (partial v); a letter to Clark Ashton Smith, July 23, 1935 ("I'm ashamed of my long delay in answering . . .") and a letter to August Derleth, May 9, 1936 ("I am indeed sorry to learn of the deaths . . .")**
> Limited to 150 copies; "A Warning" is contained in the Derleth letter

#6, Spring 1965
> Contains *The Thessalians; Knife, Bullet and Noose; Who is Grandpa Theobold? (v);* and **a letter to TCS, ca. November 1931 ("Fear Finn: / I wrote Bradford a coarse rude letter . . .")**
> Limited to 150 copies

#7, Winter 1965
> Contains *Spear and Fang; Cupid v. Pollux;* **The Dust Dance (I) (v); Cimmeria (v);** *the short version of Cimmeria(v);* **a letter to Kirk Mashburn, ca. March 1932 ("I am writing to express my appreciation for . . ."), and two letters to Harold Preece, ca. March 1929 ("I've been very neglectful of my correspondence . . ."), and pm, March 24, 1930 ("Thanks for the picture."); a letter to Emil Petaja, December 17, 1934 ("Thank you very much for the splendid sonnet.")**
> Limited to 150 copies

#8, Summer 1966
> Contains **Alleys of Treachery; The Shadow of Doom; Age Comes to Rabelais (v);** *Roundelay of the Roughneck (v);* **plus a letter to Harold Preece, pm, September 23, 1928 ("The tang of winter is in the air . . .")**
> Limited to 150 copies

#9, Spring 1967

Contains *The Curse of the Golden Skull; Sentiment; Untitled ("Beneath the glare . . ."); The Day That I Die (v); A Sonnet of Good Cheer (v); Skulls over Judah (v);* a letter to Harold Preece, pm, September 5, 1928 ("Yes, I like the idea of Eldorado . . ."); and a letter to Farnsworth Wright, May 6, 1935 ("I always hate to write a letter like this . . .")

Limited to 150 copies, though there are an unknown number of later printed ones

#10, Spring 1968

Contains *Musings of a Moron; Death's Black Riders; The Dust Dance (2) (lines 1-80) (v);* Heritage ("My people came . . .") (v); and **a letter to Harold Preece, ca. February 1930 ("You're in Kansas now, eh?")**

Limited to 300 copies

#11, Spring 1969

Contains *The Ghost in the Doorway; Thor's Son (v); Sunday in a Small Town;* Ye College Days; *Reuben's Brethren (v); Where Are Your Knights, Donn Othna? (v);* the verse heading from The Hour of the Dragon; a letter to Farnsworth Wright, ca. June 1930 ("I have long looked forward to reading . . ."); and two letters to Clark Ashton Smith, pm, March 15, 1933 ("I hardly know how to thank you for the copy . . ."), and ca. July 1933 ("I really must apologize for not having . . .")

Limited to somewhere between 300-500 copies

#12, Spring 1970

Contains *Two Against Tyre; To Certain Orthodox Brethren (v); A Song of the Legions (v);* plus a letter to Carl Jacobi, ca. Summer 1934 ("Thank you for the kind comments . . ."), and a letter to Harold Preece, ca. September 1929 ("I've been reading DESTINY BAY and in . . .")

Limited to somewhere between 300-500 copies

#13, Fall 1970

Contains *The Heathen; The Song of Horsa's Galley (v); A Moment (v);* a letter to Wilfred B. Talman, ca. July 1932 ("Thanks very much for 'De Halve Maen.'") and two letters to Harold Preece, ca. December 1928 ("You're right; women are great actors."), and pm, November 24, 1930 ("I hope you'll pardon my negligence . . .")

Limited to somewhere between 300-500 copies; the last letter only includes the last paragraph of a 5-paragraph letter

#14, Spring 1971

Contains *Sailor Dorgan and the Jade Monkey; A Dream; A Pledge (v);* Singing in the Wind (v); *No More the Serpent Prow (v);* Age (v); Postcard to Harold Preece, June 4, 1928 (No words)

Limited to somewhere between 300-500 copies

#15, Fall 1971

Contains *The Beast from the Abyss;* Eighttoes Makes a Play (alternate ending); *Solomon Kane's Homecoming (variant version, v); Hope Empty of Meaning (v);* a letter to HPL, August 1933 ("I am sending on to you the enclosed manuscript . . ."); and a letter to August Derleth, ca. July 1933 ("Thanks immensely for the opportunity of reading . . .")

Limited to somewhere between 300-500 copies

#16, Spring 1972

Contains *The Fire of Asshurbanipal;* Visions (v); *Marching Song of Connacht (v);* plus a letter to Harold Preece, ca. early April 1930 ("Thanks for the Saint Padraic's card.")

Limited to somewhere between 300-500 copies

#17, Fall 1972

Contains *Spanish Gold on Devil Horse (part 1); The Bar By the Side of the Road (v); Harvest (v); On with the Play (v); Roads (v)*

Limited to somewhere between 300-500 copies

#18, Fall 1973

*Contains **Spanish Gold on Devil Horse (part 2); Life (v); The Legacy of Tubal-Cain (v),** plus two letters to R.H. Barlow, June 1, 1934 ("Concerning the illustrations you . . ."); June 14, 1934 ("If I ever decide to dispose . . .")*

Limited to 500 copies

**Inside & SF Advertiser**

September 1956

Contains the Heading from *The Black Stone (v)*

## Jack Dempsey's Fight Magazine
May 1934
    Contains ***The Slugger's Game***
June 1934
    Contains ***General Ironfist***
August 1934
    Contains ***Sluggers of the Beach***

## JAPM: The Poetry Weekly ("Just Another Poetry Magazine", Produced by Benjamin Musser)
September 16, 1929
    Contains ***Red Thunder (v)***

## Lands of Wonder (German, later retitled "Magira")
#1, 1967
    Contains *Chant of the White Beard (v)*
#2, 1967
    Contains *Riders of Babylon (v); plus the heading to Red Blades of Black Cathay*
#3, November 1967
    Contains *Babylon (v); Laughter in the Gulfs (v)*

## Leaves
#1, Summer 1937
    Contains ***With a Set of Rattlesnake Rattles***

## L'Herne
#12, October 15, 1969
    Contains *The Dream and the Shadow(v)*

## Los Cuentos Fantasticos (Mexican)
#8, October 1948
    Contains *The Mirrors of Tuzun Thune*

## Lost Fantasies
#4, 1976
    Contains ***The Dwellers Under the Tomb***

## Magazine of Fantasy & Science Fiction
August 1966
    Contains ***"For the Love of Barbara Allen"***
February 1967
    Contains ***The Hall of the Dead (completed by LSDC)***

## Magazine of Horror
#9, June 1965
    Contains *Skulls in the Stars*
#11, November 1965
    Contains ***The Dweller in Dark Valley (v)***; *Rattle of Bones*

#12, Winter 1965/66
  Contains **Destination (v)**
    Cover by Gray Morrow
#13, Summer 1966
  Contains **Valley of the Lost ("Jim Brill licked his parched lips, . . .")**
    Lengthy intro to the story by Robert A.W. Lowndes explaining source for story
#15, Spring 1967
  Contains **The Vale of Lost Women**
    Cover by Virgil Finlay
#16, Summer 1967
  Contains **A Song for Men That Laugh (v)**
#17, Fall 1967
  Contains **Dermod's Bane**
#18, November 1967
  Contains **Out of the Deep**
#19, January 1968
  Contains **The Years Are As a Knife (v)**
#21, May 1968
  Contains *Kings of the Night*
#22, July 1968
  Contains *Worms of the Earth*
#28, July 1969
  Contains **Not Only in Death They Die (v)**
#30, December 1969
  Contains **Slumber (v)**
#31, February 1970
  Contains **The Noseless Horror**
#34, Fall 1970
  Contains **A Song of Defeat (v)**
#36, April 1971
  Contains *The Grisly Horror*

## The Magic Carpet Magazine (previously titled Oriental Stories)
July 1933
  Contains **The Lion of Tiberias**
January 1934
  Contains **Alleys of Darkness; The Shadow of the Vulture**

## Magira (German)
#11, February 1972
  Contains *Nisapur (v)*
#21, June/July 1975
  Contains *Moonlight on a Skull (v)*
#23/24, December 1975
  Contains *A Song of the Race (v); the verse heading from Red Blades of Black Cathay*
#27, December 1976
  Contains *Futility ("Golden goats . . .") (v)*
#31, December 1978
  Contains *Solomon Kane's Homecoming (v)*
#32, Fall 1979
  Contains *the verse heading from Red Blades of Black Cathay*

#33, Fall 1980
> Contains *Chant of the White Beard (v); The Return of Sir Richard Grenville (v)*

#38, Spring 1992
> Contains **The Dance with Death (v)**

## Marvel Tales

Volume 1, #2, July-August 1934
> Contains **The Garden of Fear**
>> Comes in two different covers, a white with green design version, with ghostly woman, and an orange with green design with a skull-headed snake, titles listed in different order on the covers, the orange and green one includes extra content, including a TOC, a contest, and some editorial content. Maybe more versions?

## Masked Rider Western

May 1944
> Contains **Texas John Alden**

## Max Brand's Western Magazine

January 1950
> Contains *Shave That Hawg!*

June 1950
> Contains *Vultures' Sanctuary*

## Max Brand's Western Magazine (UK)

#2, 1949
> Contains *Shave That Hawg!*

## Mediascene

#20, July-August 1976
> Contains *On Reading – And Writing*
>> Embodied in an autobiographical essay by REH, titled "I Created Conan", created by cutting down "On Reading – And Writing", specifically pages 49-58 from THE LAST CELT; artwork by Barry Smith, Jim Steranko, and Neal Adams

## The New Hieroglyph

March 1944
> Contains *Babel (v); The Voices Waken Memory (v); Song at Midnight (v)*

## ORB

Volume 3 #1 (whole number 10) (1952)
> Contains *Song at Midnight (v)*
>> 8 1/2 x 11, 36 pages, published by Bob Johnson, editorial logo by Hannes Bok

## Oriental Stories (later retitled The Magic Carpet Magazine)

October-November 1930
> Contains **The Voice of El-Lil**

February-March 1931
> Contains **Red Blades of Black Cathay**

April-May-June 1931
> Contains **Hawks of Outremer**

Autumn 1931
> Contains **The Blood of Belshazzar**

Winter 1932
> Contains **The Sowers of the Thunder**

Spring 1932
> Contains **Lord of Samarcand**

## The Phantagraph

February 1936
> Contains **The Hyborian Age (part 1 of 3)**

August 1936
> Contains **The Hyborian Age (part 2 of 3); Always Comes Evening (v)**

October-November 1936
> Contains **The Hyborian Age (part 3 of 3)**

August 1940
> Contains **Song at Midnight (v)**

## Planète (French)

#24, September-October 1965
> Contains *Le Phénix sur l'Epée (The Phoenix on the Sword)*
>> Translation by M. Bergier; a shortened version

## Poet's Scroll

January 1929
> Contains **Flaming Marble (v)**
>> Author listed as "Patrick Howard"

February 1929
> Contains **Rebellion (v)**

April 1929
> Contains **Dreaming on Downs (v)**
>> Author listed as "Patrick Howard"

June 1929
> Contains **Empire's Destiny (v)**
>> Author listed as "Patrick Howard"

August 1929
> Contains **Shadow of Dreams (v)**

## Portti (Finnish, put out by the Tampere SF Society)

January 1990
> Contains *The Valley of the Worm*

April 1993
> Contains *The Garden of Fear*

## The Progress

Volume 1, #2, February 1, 1924
> Contains **The Maiden of Kercheezer (v); Rules of Etiquette (v)**
>> A Cross Plains High School publication

## Pulp Review (Pulp Collector Press, John Gunnison, all facsimile reprints)

#5, July 1992
> Contains *Black Wind Blowing*

#13, 1994
> Contains *Black Talons*

#15, May 1994
   Contains *Fangs of Gold*
#17, September 1994
   Contains *The Tomb's Secret (The Teeth of Doom)*

## REH: Lone Star Fictioneer (Arnie Fenner & Byron Roark)

#1, Spring 1975
   Contains **The Loser**; *Knife-River Prodigal; Death's Black Riders; and a photo of REH & Dave Lee*
      Wraparound cover of Solomon Kane by Stephen Fabian; also includes artwork by Roy Krenkel, Arnie Fenner, John Severin, Stan Dresser, Herb Arnold, and Stephen Fabian, plus a center-spread by Tim Conrad
#2, Summer 1975
   Contains **Sword Woman**; *plus a photo of REH*
      Wraparound cover of Conan by Stephen Fabian; artwork by Howard Chaykin, Frank Brunner, center-spread of Solomon Kane by Alan Weiss, Walt Simonson, Rosella Carson, John & Mary Severin, and Carl Potts
#3, Fall 1975
   Contains **Guns of Khartoum; The Brazen Peacock**
      Wraparound cover by Alan Weiss, colored by Richard Corben; artwork by Stephen Fabian, Arnie Fenner, Alex Nino, Howard Chaykin, Steve Leialoha, Roy Krenkel, Craig Russell, Tim Kirk, Alfredo Alcala, Walt Simonson
#4, Spring 1976
   Contains **Three-Bladed Doom (short version)**; *plus a photo of REH*
      Front cover by Marcus Boas; artwork by Howard Chaykin, Arnie Fenner, Jim Steranko, John Severin, Marie Severin, George Barr, Walt Simonson, Nestor Redondo, Frank Frazetta; research revealed that the editor rewrote the beginning and ending, plus added 1100 words of his own creation, all without notice; this certainly raises questions about the rest of the REH material he published

## REH: Two-Gun Raconteur (by "Black Coast Press" (Damon Sasser))

#2, Summer 1976
   Contains *a letter to Clark Ashton Smith, pm, March 15, 1933 ("I hardly know how to thank you for the copy . . .")*
      Front cover by Gene Day; interior artwork by numerous others
#3, 1976
   Contains *The Devil's Joker*
      Limited to 500 copies; artwork by numerous artists, including Stephen Fabian, Gene Day, and Arnie Fenner
#4, Summer 1977
   Contains *Golden Hope Christmas; Untitled ("The Dane came in with a rush . . .")*
      Artwork by Marcus Boas and Stephen Fabian
#5, Winter 2003
   Contains *A Horror in the Night*
      Artwork by Stephen Fabian, Arnie Fenner, Ken Ramey, Gene Day, Don Herron, Jeff Easley, Fred Bobb and Greg Vander Leon; limited to 250 copies
#6, Fall 2004
   Contains *Under the Baobab Tree*
      Artwork by Stephen Fabian, Gene Day, Charles Keegan, and Bill Cavalier
#7, Winter 2004
   Contains *The Haunted Hut*
      Artwork by Charles Keegan, Newton Burcham, Bill Cavalier, Joe Wehrle, David Burton, and Stephen Fabian; limited to 250 copies
#8, Summer 2005
   Contains *Black Country*
      Artwork by Gene Day, Bill Cavalier, Esteban Maroto, Greg Ruth, Stephen Fabian, and David Burton

#9, February 2006
>> Contains *Shadow of Doom*

#10, October 2006
>> Contains *Voice of Death*

#11, June 2007
>> Contains *A Touch of Color*

## The Ring

April 1926
>> Contains **a letter to the editor ("Here is my opinion of the greatest heavyweights . . .")**

June 1928
>> Contains **Kid Lavigne is Dead (v)**

## The Riverside Quarterly

June 1966
>> Contains *The Dust Dance (I) (lines 5-20 only)*
>>> Poem contained in a review of THE HOWARD COLLECTOR

## The Robert E. Howard Foundation Newsletter

Volume 1, #1, June 2007
>> Contains **Rattle of Bones (early draft)**
>>> Facsimile reproduction of original typescript; a giveaway to Legacy Circle and Friends of REH members of REHF; very limited quantities, less than 100 total

Volume 1, #2, November 2007
>> Contains *Untitled ("The Seeker thrust . . .")*; **The Slugger's Game (synopsis); A Knight of the Round Table (synopsis); General Ironfist (synopsis); Sluggers on the Beach (synopsis); Dark Shanghai (synopsis); The Silver Heel (synopsis); Untitled ("Hernando de Guzman: . . .")**; *A Boy, a Beehive, and a Chinaman*; **Untitled ("Fill up my goblet . . .") (v); The Builders (3) (v); Untitled ("Brazen thewed giant . . ."); a sheet of drawings**; *Nekht Semerkeht (one page only)*
>>> The various synopses are facsimile reproduction of original typescript pages, as is the Hernando de Guzman item, the sheet of drawings, and the one page of "Nekht Semerkeht"; "The Silver Heel" is page 5 only, the only surviving page of this synopsis; "A Boy, a Beehive and a Chinaman" is a facsimile reproduction of a holographic REH high school paper; the page for "Nekht Semerkeht" is in color, to show the yellow paper REH used late in his life; very limited, less than 100 total

## Robert E. Howard: World's Greatest Pulpster

#1, September 2001
>> Contains *The Tomb's Secret; Black Talons; The Harp of Alfred (v); The Gates of Ninevah (v); Easter Island (v); The Riders of Babylon (v); The Song of the Bats (v); Dead Man's Hate (v)*
>>> A proposed magazine by Dennis McHaney, the publisher changed its mind; only five copies created

## Rod Serling's The Twilight Zone Magazine

Volume 4, #2, August 1984
>> Contains *The Feline Mystique*
>>> A few page excerpt from THE LAST CAT BOOK, based on "Beast from the Abyss"; cover states "Robert E. Howard's Wild Pussycats!"

## S-F Magazine (Japanese)

April 1969
>> Contains *Gekka No Kaiei (Shadows in the Moonlight)*

October 1969
>> Contains *Kuroi Kawa No Kanata (Beyond the Black River)*

November 1970
>   Contains *Kyozo No Tou (The Tower of the Elephant)*

October 1971
>   Contains *Tuzun Thune No Kagami (The Mirrors of Tuzun Thune)*

September 1972
>   Contains *Kuroi Ishi (The Black Stone)*

## Shangri L'Affaires

#72, April 1, 1968
>   Contains **Memories ("I rose . . .") (v)**

## Smashing Novels Magazine

December 1936
>   Contains **Vultures of Whapeton**

## Soutwest Airlines Magazine

November 1980
>   Contains *The Tempter (v) (lines 31-40)*
>   >   In article titled "The Tortured Genius of Cross Plains, Texas", possibly the same as a Dallas Morning News article

## Space Science Fiction

September 1952
>   Contains **The God in the Bowl**
>   >   Introduction and edited by LSDC; including comments from a letter from HPL

## Space Science Fiction (UK)

Volume 1, #1, December 1952
>   Contains *The God in the Bowl*
>   >   Reprinting the US version listed above

## Spaceway Science Fiction

Volume 4, #3, October 1969
>   Contains **People of the Black Coast**

## Spectrum

Super Special #2, June 2004
>   Contains *Always Comes Evening (lines 5-8, 10-12); Song from an Ebony Heart (lines 5-8); The Guise of Youth (lines 13-20); Surrender ("Open the window . . .", lines 3-4); The Sands of Time (lines 11-12); Love's Young Dream (lines 21-28) (all v)*

## Spicy-Adventure Stories

April 1936
>   Contains **She-Devil**

June 1936
>   Contains **Desert Blood**

September 1936
>   Contains **The Dragon of Kao Tsu**

November 1936
>   Contains **The Purple Heart of Erlik**

January 1937
>   Contains **Murderer's Grog**

September 1942
>Contains *Revenge by Proxy*
>>A reprint of "Desert Blood", author listed as "William Decatur"

October 1942
>Contains *Nothing to Lose*
>>A reprint of "The Purple Heart of Erlik", author listed as "R.T. Maynard"

November 1942
>Contains *Outlaw Working*
>>A reprint of "Murderer's Grog", author listed as "Max Neilson"

## Sport Story Magazine

September 25, 1931
>Contains **College Socks**

October 25, 1931
>Contains **Man with the Mystery Mitts**

December 25, 1931
>Contains **The Good Knight**

## Star Western

September 1936
>Contains **The Curly Wolf of Sawtooth**

## Startling Mystery Stories

#4, Spring 1967
>Contains **Secret of Lost Valley ("As a wolf spies . . .")**

#6, Fall 1967
>Contains *A Vision (v)*

Volume 2, #5 (whole number 11), Winter 1968-69
>Contains *The Haunter of the Ring*

## Stirring Science Stories

February 1941
>Contains *Always Comes Evening (v)*

## Strange Detective Stories

December 1933
>Contains **Black Talons**

February 1934
>Contains **Fangs of Gold; The Tomb's Secret**

## Strange Tales

June 1932
>Contains **People of the Dark**

January 1933
>Contains **The Cairn on the Headland**

## Strange Worlds

#12, Fall 2003
>Contains Red *Nails; The Devil in Iron*
>>Facsimile reproduction of pulp pages for "Devil in Iron"; tape binding, clear cover over color inkjet work

**The Summit County Journal (all supposedly with artwork by Jeff Jones)**
June 9, 1967; June 16, 1967; June 23, 1967; June 30, 1967

July 7, 1967; July 14, 1967; July 21, 1967; July 28, 1967; August 11, 1967; August 18, 1967; August 25, 1967; September 1, 1967
> Contains *Evil Deeds at Red Cougar (8 part serial)*
>> August 11 was a reprint of August 4, which was incomplete

September 8, 1967; September 15, 1967; September 22, 1967; September 29, 1967
> Contains *Mayhem and Taxes (4 part serial)*

October 6, 1967; October 13, 1967; October 20, 1967; October 27, 1967; November 3, 1967; November 10, 1967; November 17, 1967
> Contains *While Smoke Rolled (7 part serial)*

November 24, 1967; December 1, 1967; December 8, 1967; December 15, 1967; December 22, 1967; December 29, 1967; January 5, 1968
> Contains *"No Cowherders Wanted" (7 part serial)*
>> Mistitled as "While Smoke Rolled" in first installment

January 12, 1968; January 19, 1968; January 26, 1968; February 2, 1968; February 9, 1968
> Contains *A Elkins Never Surrenders (5 part serial)*

February 16, 1968; February 23, 1968; March 1, 1968; March 8, 1968; March 15, 1968; March 22, 1968; March 29, 1968
> Contains **The Peaceful Pilgrim (7 part serial)**

April 5, 1968; April 12, 1968; April 19, 1968; April 26, 1968; May 3, 1968; May 10, 1968
> Contains *Striped Shirts and Busted Hearts (Six part serial)*
>> The May 10 issue has the last part of "The Peaceful Pilgrim", and the first part of "Mountain Man"

May 10, 1968; May 17, 1968; May 24, 1968; May 31, 1968; June 7, 1968; June 14, 1968; June 21, 1968; June 28, 1968; July 5, 1968; July 12, 1968; July 19, 1968
> Contains *Mountain Man (11 part serial)*
>> The July 19 issue has the last part of "Mountain Man", and the first part of "Meet Cap'n Kidd"

July 19, 1968; July 26, 1968; August 2, 1968; August 9, 1968; August 16, 1968; August 23, 1968; August 30, 1968; September 6, 1968; September 13, 1968; September 20, 1968; September 27, 1968; October 4, 1968
> Contains *Meet Cap'n Kidd (12 part serial)*
>> The issue of October 4 contains the last part of "Meet Cap'n Kidd", and the first part of "Guns of the Mountains"

October 4, 1968; October 11, 1968; October 18, 1968; October 25, 1968; November 1, 1968; November 8, 1968; November 15, 1968; November 22, 1968; November 29, 1968; December 6, 1968; December 13, 1968
> Contains *Guns of the Mountains (11 part serial)*

December 20, 1968; December 27, 1968; January 3, 1969; January 10, 1969; January 17, 1969; January 24, 1969; January 31, 1969; February 7, 1969; February 14, 1969; February 21, 1969; February 28, 1969; March 7, 1969; March 14, 1969; March 21, 1969; March 28, 1969
> Contains *A Gent from Bear Creek (15 part serial)*

April 4, 1969; April 11, 1969; April 18, 1969; April 25, 1969; May 2, 1969; May 9, 1969; May 16, 1969; May 23, 1969; May 30, 1969; June 6, 1969; June 13, 1969; June 20, 1969; June 27, 1969; July 4, 1969; July 11, 1969; July 18, 1969

>  Contains *The Feud Buster (16 part serial)*
>
>  The July 18 issue contains the last part of "The Feud Buster", and the first part of "The Road to Bear Creek"

July 18, 1969; July 25, 1969; August 7, 1969; August 14, 1969; August 21, 1969; August 28, 1969; September 4, 1969; September 11, 1969; September 18, 1969; September 25, 1969; October 2, 1969; October 9, 1969; October 16, 1969; October 23, 1969; October 30, 1969; November 6, 1969

>  Contains *The Road to Bear Creek (16 part serial)*

November 13, 1969; November 20, 1969; November 27, 1969; December 4, 1969; December 11, 1969; December 18, 1969; December 25, 1969; January 1, 1970; January 8, 1970; January 15, 1970; January 22, 1970; January 29, 1970; February 5, 1970; February 12, 1970; February 26, 1970; March 5, 1970; March 12, 1970; March 19, 1970

>  Contains *The Scalp Hunter (18 part serial)*

March 26, 1970; April 2, 1970; April 9, 1970; April 16, 1970; April 23, 1970; April 30, 1970; May 7, 1970; May 14, 1970; May 21, 1970; May 28, 1970; June 4, 1970; June 11, 1970; June 18, 1970; June 25, 1970

>  Contains *Cupid from Bear Creek (14 part serial)*

July 3, 1970; July 10, 1970; July 17, 1970; July 24, 1970; July 31, 1970; August 7, 1970; August 14, 1970; August 21, 1970; August 28, 1970; September 4, 1970; September 11, 1970; September 18, 1970

>  Contains *The Haunted Mountain (12 part serial)*

September 25, 1970; October 2, 1970; October 9, 1970; October 16, 1970; October 23, 1970; October 30, 1970; November 6, 1970; November 13, 1970; November 20, 1970; November 27, 1970

>  Contains *Educate or Bust (Part 10 of 10)*

December 4, 1970; December 11, 1970; December 18, 1970; December 25, 1970; January 1, 1971; January 8, 1971; January 15, 1971; January 22, 1971; January 29, 1971; February 5, 1971; February 12, 1971; February 19, 1971; February 26, 1971; March 5, 1971; March 12, 1971

>  Contains *War on Bear Creek (15 part serial)*

March 19, 1971; March 26, 1971; April 2, 1971; April 9, 1971; April 16, 1971; April 23, 1971; April 30, 1971; May 7, 1971; May 14, 1971; May 21, 1971; May 28, 1971; June 4, 1971; June 11, 1971; June 18, 1971; June 25, 1971; July 2, 1971; July 9, 1971; July 16, 1971; July 23, 1971; July 30, 1971; August 6, 1971; August 13, 1971; August 20, 1971; August 27, 1971; September 3, 1971; September 10, 1971; September 17, 1971

>  Contains *When Bear Creek Came to Chawed Ear (27 part serial)*

September 24, 1971; October 1, 1971; October 8, 1971; October 15, 1971; October 22, 1971; October 29, 1971; November 5, 1971; November 12, 1971; November 19, 1971; November 26, 1971; December 3, 1971; December 10, 1971; December 17, 1971; December 24, 1971; December 31, 1971; January 7, 1972; January 14, 1972; January 21, 1972

>  Contains *The Riot at Cougar Paw (18 part serial)*

January 28, 1972; February 4, 1972; February 11, 1972; February 18, 1972; February 25, 1972; March 3, 1972; March 10, 1972; March 17, 1972; March 24, 1972; March 31, 1972; April 7, 1972; April 14, 1972; April 21, 1972; April 28, 1972; May 5, 1972; May 12, 1972; May 19, 1972; May 26, 1972; June 2, 1972; June 9, 1972

>  Contains *Pilgrims to the Pecos (20 part serial)*

June 16, 1972; June 23, 1972; June 30, 1972; July 7, 1972; July 14, 1972; July 21, 1972; July 28, 1972; August 4, 1972; August 11, 1972; August 18, 1972; August 25, 1972; September 1, 1972; September 8, 1972; September 15, 1972; September 22, 1972; September 29, 1972; October 6, 1972; October 13, 1972

> Contains *High Horse Rampage (18 part serial)*

October 20, 1972; October 27, 1972; November 3, 1972; November 10, 1972; November 17, 1972; November 24, 1972

> Contains *The Apache Mountain War (incomplete) (6 part serial)*

## Super-Detective Stories
May 1934
> Contains **Names in the Black Book**

## Sword (Spanish)
#4, 1989
> Contains *Autumn; A Crown for a King; Niflheim; The Ride of Falume; Shadows on the Road; The Song of the Don Cossocks; Which Will Scarcely Be Understood (all v)*
> > All poetry in both Spanish and English

## Sword and Fantasy
#4, October 2005
> Contains *The Challenge from Beyond*
> > This is a facsimile reproduction of the original appearance of this story from FANTASY MAGAZINE

## Sword and Sorcery Annual
1975
> Contains *Queen of the Black Coast*
> > Uses the text from AVON FANTASY READER #8; cover and interior illustrations by Stephen Fabian

## Tähtivaeltaja (Finnish, put out by the Helsinki SF Society)
April 1991
> Contains *The Devil in Iron*

## Tales from the Pulps
Volume 1, #3, November 2007
> Contains *Mountain Man*

## The Tattler (school paper for Brownwood High School)
December 22, 1922
> Contains **"Golden Hope" Christmas; West is West**
February 15, 1923
> Contains **Unhand Me Villian**
March 1, 1923
> Contains **Aha! or The Mystery of the Queen's Necklace**
March 15, 1923
> Contains **The Sheik; and a short commentary by the editor titled "Robert E. Howard, Short Story Writer"**
January 6, 1925
> Contains **The Ideal Girl; The Kissing of Sal Snooboo (v)**

## Texaco Star
April 1931
> Contains **The Ghost of Camp Colorado**

**Thrilling Adventures**
January 1935
    Contains ***The Treasures of Tartary***
December 1936
    Contains ***Son of the White Wolf***

**Thrilling Mystery**
February 1936
    Contains ***Graveyard Rats***
June 1936
    Contains ***Black Wind Blowing***

**Top-Notch**
October 1934
    Contains ***Swords of Shahrazar***
December 1934
    Contains ***The Daughter of Erlik Khan***
June 1935
    Contains ***Hawk of the Hills***
July 1935
    Contains ***Blood of the Gods***

**Top Western Fiction Annual**
1952
    Contains *Texas John Alden*

**Trumpet**
#7, May 1968
    Contains *Ambition in the Moonlight;* ***To a Man Whose Name I Never Knew;*** *Musings;* ***Etched in Ebony;*** *The Galveston Affair; Surrender – Your Money or Your Vice; Them*
        Mostly reprinted from THE JUNTO

**Uncanny Tales (Canadian)**
September-October 1943
    Contains *Always Comes Evening*

**Wayfarer**
#4, 1969
    Contains ***Lost Altars (v)***

**Weird Tales**
July 1925
    Contains ***Spear and Fang***
August 1925
    Contains ***In the Forest of Villefere***
February 1926
    Contains ***a letter to The Eyrie ("These are sheer masterpieces. . . .")***
April 1926
    Contains ***Wolfshead***
January 1927
    Contains ***The Lost Race***
May 1927
    Contains ***The Song of the Bats (v)***

June 1927
    Contains *a letter to The Eyrie ("Your last three issues . . .")*
October 1927
    Contains **The Ride of Falume (v)**
January 1928
    Contains **The Riders of Babylon (v)**
February 1928
    Contains **The Dream Snake**
March 1928
    Contains **The Hyena**
April 1928
    Contains **Remembrance (v)**
May 1928
    Contains **Sea Curse; plus a letter to The Eyrie ("Mr. Lovecraft's latest story . . .")**
July 1928
    Contains **The Gates of Nineveh (v)**
August 1928
    Contains **Red Shadows**
September 1928
    Contains **The Harp of Alfred (v)**
December 1928
    Contains **Easter Island (v)**
January 1929
    Contains **Skulls in the Stars**
February 1929
    Contains **Crete (v)**
April 1929
    Contains **Moon Mockery (v)**
June 1929
    Contains **Rattle of Bones**
July 1929
    Contains **Forbidden Magic (v)**
August 1929
    Contains **The Shadow Kingdom**
September 1929
    Contains **The Mirrors of Tuzun Thune; The Moor Ghost (v)**
October 1929
    Contains **Skull-Face (part 1 of 3)**
November 1929
    Contains **Skull-Face (part 2 of 3); plus a letter to The Eyrie ("I have just been reading . . .")**
December 1929
    Contains **Skull-Face (part 3 of 3)**
January 1930
    Contains **Dead Man's Hate (v)**
February 1930
    Contains **The Fearsome Touch of Death**
April 1930
    Contains **A Song Out of Midian (v); plus a letter to The Eyrie ("'Thirsty Blades' is fine . . .")**
May 1930
    Contains **Shadows (v)**
June 1930
    Contains **The Moon of Skulls (part 1 of 2)**
July 1930
    Contains **The Moon of Skulls (part 2 of 2)**
August 1930

Contains *The Hills of the Dead*
September 1930
    Contains *Black Chant Imperial (v)*
November 1930
    Contains *Kings of the Night*
January 1931
    Contains *a letter to the Eyrie ("I was particularly fascinated . . .")*
February-March 1931
    Contains *The Song of a Mad Minstrel (v)*
April-May 1931
    Contains *The Children of the Night*
September 1931
    Contains *The Footfalls Within*
October 1931
    Contains *The Gods of Bal-Sagoth*
November 1931
    Contains *The Black Stone*
December 1931
    Contains *The Dark Man*
February 1932
    Contains *The Thing on the Roof*
March 1932
    Contains *The Last Day (v); plus a letter to the Eyrie ("Congratulations on the appearance . . .")*
May 1932
    Contains *The Horror from the Mound*
July 1932
    Contains *Wings in the Night*
August 1932
    Contains *Arkham (v)*
September 1932
    Contains *An Open Window (v)*
        Cover by Margaret Brundage
November 1932
    Contains *Worms of the Earth*
December 1932
    Contains *The Phoenix on the Sword*
January 1933
    Contains *The Scarlet Citadel*
March 1933
    Contains *The Tower of the Elephant*
        Cover by Margaret Brundage
April 1933
    Contains *Autumn (v)*
May 1933
    Contains *Moonlight on a Skull (v)*
June 1933
    Contains *Black Colossus*
July 1933
    Contains *The Man on the Ground*
        Cover by Margaret Brundage

September 1933
>     Contains ***The Slithering Shadow***
>     >     Cover by Margaret Brundage

October 1933
>     Contains ***The Pool of the Black One***
>     >     Cover by Margaret Brundage

December 1933
>     Contains ***Old Garfield's Heart***
>     >     Cover by Margaret Brundage

January 1934
>     Contains ***Rogues in the House***
>     >     Cover by Margaret Brundage

February 1934
>     Contains ***The Valley of the Worm***
>     >     Cover by Margaret Brundage

April 1934
>     Contains ***Shadows in the Moonlight***
>     >     Cover by Margaret Brundage

May 1934
>     Contains ***Queen of the Black Coast***
>     >     Cover by Margaret Brundage

June 1934
>     Contains ***The Haunter of the Ring***
>     >     Cover by Margaret Brundage

August 1934
>     Contains ***The Devil in Iron***
>     >     Cover by Margaret Brundage

September 1934
>     Contains ***The People of the Black Circle (part 1 of 3)***
>     >     Cover by Margaret Brundage

October 1934
>     Contains ***The People of the Black Circle (part 2 of 3)***
>     >     Cover by Margaret Brundage

November 1934
>     Contains ***The People of the Black Circle (part 3 of 3)***
>     >     Cover by Margaret Brundage

December 1934
>     Contains ***A Witch Shall be Born***
>     >     Cover by Margaret Brundage

February 1935
>     Contains ***The Grisly Horror***
>     >     Cover by Margaret Brundage

March 1935
>     Contains ***Jewels of Gwahlur***
>     >     Cover by Margaret Brundage

May 1935
>     Contains ***Beyond the Black River (part 1 of 2)***
>     >     Cover by Margaret Brundage

June 1935
>     Contains ***Beyond the Black River (part 2 of 2)***
>     >     Cover by Margaret Brundage

November 1935
>    Contains **Shadows in Zamboula**
>>    Cover by Margaret Brundage

December 1935
>    Contains **The Hour of the Dragon (part 1 of 5)**
>>    Cover by Margaret Brundage

January 1936
>    Contains **The Hour of the Dragon (part 2 of 5)**
>>    Cover by Margaret Brundage

February 1936
>    Contains **The Hour of the Dragon (part 3 of 5)**
>>    Cover by Margaret Brundage

March 1936
>    Contains **The Hour of the Dragon (part 4 of 5)**
>>    Cover by Margaret Brundage

April 1936
>    Contains **The Hour of the Dragon (part 5 of 5)**
>>    Cover by Margaret Brundage

June 1936
>    Contains **Black Canaan; plus a letter to the Eyrie ("Enthusiasm impels me . . .")**
>>    Cover by Margaret Brundage

July 1936
>    Contains **Red Nails (part 1 of 3)**
>>    Cover by Margaret Brundage

August-September 1936
>    Contains **Red Nails (part 2 of 3)**
>>    Cover by Margaret Brundage

October 1936
>    Contains **Red Nails (part 3 of 3)**
>>    Also contains RH Barlow's poetry tribute to REH

November 1936
>    Contains **The Black Hound of Death**
>>    Cover by Margaret Brundage

December 1936
>    Contains **The Fire of Asshurbanipal**
>>    Cover by J. Allen St. John, based on "The Fire of Asshurbanipal"

February 1937
>    Contains **Dig Me No Grave**

August 1937
>    Contains **The Soul-Eater (v)**
>>    Cover by Margaret Brundage

September 1937
>    Contains **The Dream and the Shadow (v)**
>>    Cover by Margaret Brundage

October 1937
>    Contains **Which Will Scarcely Be Understood (v)**
>>    Cover by Margaret Brundage

November 1937
>    Contains **Futility ("Golden goats . . .") (v)**
>>    Cover by Margaret Brundage

December 1937
>    Contains **Fragment ("And so his boyhood . . .") (v)**

February 1938
>    Contains **Haunting Columns (v)**

March 1938

Contains ***The Poets (v)***
April 1938
Contains ***The Singer in the Mist (v)***
May 1938
Contains ***Pigeons from Hell***
     Cover by Margaret Brundage
June 1938
Contains ***The Last Hour (v)***
July 1938
Contains ***Ships (v)***
August 1938
Contains ***Lines Written in the Realization that I Must Die (v)***
September 1938
Contains ***A Thunder of Trumpets***
     Cover by Margaret Brundage
November 1938
Contains ***Recompense (v)***
December 1938
Contains ***The Ghost Kings (v)***
February 1939
Contains ***The King and the Oak (v)***
March 1939
Contains ***Desert Dawn (v)***
May 1939
Contains ***Almuric (part 1 of 3)***
June-July 1939
Contains ***Almuric (part 2 of 3); The Hills of Kandahar (v)***
August 1939
Contains ***Almuric (part 3 of 3)***
October 1939
Contains *Worms of the Earth*
November 1951
Contains *Pigeons from Hell*
November 1953
Contains *The Black Stone*
September 1954
Contains *The Dark Man*
Summer 1973
Contains *Spear and Fang*
Fall 1973
Contains *The Man on the Ground*
Winter 1973
Contains *Sea Curse*
Fall 1989 (#294)
Contains ***Universe (v)***
     Also released as a hardback and limited edition hardback
Winter 1989-90 (#295)
Contains ***The Chant Demoniac (v)***
     Also released as a hardback and limited edition hardback
Summer 1990 (#297)
Contains ***Memories ("Shall we remember . . .") (v)***
     Also released as a hardback and limited edition hardback

Fall 1991 (#302)
>     Contains ***Zukala's Love Song (v)***
>>     Also released as a hardback and limited edition hardback

Winter 1991-1992 (#303)
>     Contains *The Zulu Lord (v)*
>>     Also released as a hardback and limited edition hardback

## Weird Tales (Canadian)

November 1936
>     Contains *Shadows in Zamboula*
>>     Exactly the same as US, except says "Printed in Canada" on cover, and has a blue and white box covering the nude woman, which says "Magazine of the Bizarre and Unusual, November, 25c"; perhaps all WTs were this way for a while in Canada?

September 1944
>     Contains *The Ghost Kings (v)*

November 1944
>     Contains *Recompense (v)*

January 1945
>     Contains *Desert Dawn (v)*

March 1945
>     Contains *The King and the Oak (v)*

September 1947
>     Contains *Recompense (v)*

## Weirdbook (edited by W. Paul Ganley)

#1
>     1st printing, 1968
>     2nd printing, 1973
>     Contains ***The Cobra in the Dream***
>>     Cover by Ralph Rayburn Phillips

#2, 1969
>     Contains ***The Haunted Hut***

#3, 1970
>     Contains ***Usurp the Night***

#6, 1973
>     Contains ***Black Country***

#8
>     1st printing, 1974
>     2nd printing, 1987
>     Contains ***The Dead Slaver's Tale (v)***

#9
>     1st printing, 1975
>     2nd printing, 1999
>     Contains ***Mark of the Beast (v)***

#10
>     1st printing, 1976
>     2nd printing, 1999
>     Contains ***Let the Gods Die (v)***

#11, 1977
>     Contains ***Nocturne (v)***
>>     Cover by Roy Krenkel, interior artwork by numerous others, including Gene Day and Stephen Fabian

#12, 1977
>     Contains ***Dance Macabre (v)***

#13, 1978
>Contains ***Only a Shadow on the Grass (v); The Return of the Sea-Farer (v)***
>>Second poem has a full page illustration by Stephen Fabian

#15, 1981
>Contains ***Drake Sings of Yesterday (v)***

## The West
September 1967
>Contains ***Apparition of Josiah Wilbarger***

## Western Aces
October 1935
>Contains ***Boot-Hill Payoff***

## Whispers
#1, July 1973
>Contains ***The Cats of Anubis (v)***

#2, December 1973
>Contains ***Egypt (v)***

#4, July 1974
>Contains ***The Sea-Girl (v)***

Volume 2, #1, November 1974 (whole number 5)
>Contains ***Zukala's Jest (v)***

Volume 2, #2/3, June 1975 (whole number 6/7)
>Contains ***a letter to W.B. Talman, ca. September 1931 ("Thank you very much for the letter you wrote Street and Smith.")***

## White Wolf Magazine
#9, date unknown
>Contains *The Moon of Skulls (Chapters 1-3)*

#10, date unknown
>Contains *The Moon of Skulls (Chapters ???)*

#11, date unknown
>Contains *The Moon of Skulls (Chapters ???)*

## Witchcraft & Sorcery
#5, January-February 1971
>Contains ***Mistress of Death; Musings ("The little poets . . .") (v)***
>>The story was completed by Gerald W. Page

#6, May 1971
>Contains ***Flight (v)***

#7, 1972
>Contains ***Hopes of Dreams (v)***

#10, 1974
>Contains ***Restless Water***

## Worlds of Fantasy
#1, 1968
>Contains ***Delenda Est***

## Xenophile
#18, October 1975
> Contains *letters to Hugh G. Schonfield, June 15, 1933 ("As I promised, in answer to your letter . . ."); to Denis Archer, May 20, 1934 ("As you doubtless remember . . .")*
>> Published by Nils Harden

## The Yellow Jacket (school paper for Howard Payne College, only one original copy of each known to exist, at Howard Payne University)
September 24, 1924
> Contains *Halt! Who Goes There?*
>> Discovered by Tim Arney and Rusty Burke in recent times, the actual paper disappeared shortly thereafter

October 27, 1926
> Contains *After the Game; Sleeping Beauty*

November 3, 1926
> Contains *Weekly Short Story*

January 13, 1927
> Contains *The Thessalians; Private Magrath of the A.E.F. (v)*

January 20, 1927
> Contains *Ye College Days*

February 10, 1927
> Contains *Cupid v. Pollux*

April 21, 1927
> Contains *The Reformation a Dream*

November 8, 1934
> Contains *Private Magrath of the A.E.F. (v)*

## Yorick (Italian)
#32/33, December 2001/January 2002
> Contains *The Shadow of Doom*
>> As "L'ombra del destino", translated by Luca Manini and illustrated by Raoul Perazzi

## Zane Grey Western Magazine
June 1970
> Contains *The Extermination of Yellow Donory*

# ANTHOLOGIES
## and other bound books that contains at least some Robert E. Howard material, in English

These books contain at least some REH material. This listing does not include critical or other scholarly works relating to REH, unless they are known to in fact also contain REH material.

Works in **BOLD** are **First Appearance** of that work.

Non-English items are under the listing for NON-ENGLISH BOOKS, infra.

Abbreviations used herein include:
PB – paperback; HB – hardback; TPB – trade paperback;
nd – no date shown on book

*Form of Entry:*
**Title**
>Contents
>1<sup>st</sup> edition [publisher, format, date]
>>Notes
>Other editions
>>Notes

**13 Tales of Terror**
>Contains *The Tower of the Elephant*
>1<sup>st</sup> Edition, Scribner's Sons, TPB, 1977
>>Edited by Les Daniels and Diane Thompson; part of the "Scribner Student Paperback Series, SSP 38"

**The 14th Fontana Book of Great Ghost Stories**
>Contains *The Man on the Ground*
>1<sup>st</sup> Edition, Fontana, PB, 1978
>>Edited by R. Chetwynd-Hayes

**American Supernatural Tales**
>Contains *Old Garfield's Heart*
>1<sup>st</sup> Edition, Penguin Classics, PB, October 2007
>>Edited by ST Joshi

**Ancient Ruins and Archeology**
>Contains *Easter Island (v) (lines 1-4, 9-14 only)*
>1<sup>st</sup> Edition, Doubleday, HB, 1964
>>By LSDC; later reprinted as CITADELS OF MYSTERY

**Arkham's Masters of Horror: A 60th Anniversary Anthology Retrospective of the First 30 Years of Arkham House**
>Contains *The Secret of Lost Valley (titled "The Valley of the Lost")*
>1<sup>st</sup> Edition, Arkham House, HB, 2000
>>Edited by Peter Ruber; limited to 4000 copies

## The Avon Fantasy Reader
Contains *Witch from Hell's Kitchen*
1st Edition, Avon, PB, January 1969
Cover art by Gray Morrow; edited by Donald A. Wollheim and George Ernsberger

## Baker's Dozen: 13 Short Fantasy Novels
Contains *Red Nails*
1st Edition, Greenwich House, HB, 1984
Cover art by Morris Taub; edited by Isaac Asimov, Martin Greenberg and Charles Waugh; reprinted as THE MAMMOTH BOOK OF SHORT FANTASY NOVELS

## The Barbarian Swordsmen
Contains *The Tower of the Elephant; Brachen the Kelt; plus a small excerpt from a letter to HPL, June 1934 ("Glad you're finding . . ."), the excerpt starting with "Thank you for the kind things you said about my 'Shadows in the Moonlight'."*
1st Edition, Star (UK), PB, 1981
**Contains a First Appearance**; edited by Sean Richards (aka Peter Haining)

## Barbarians
Contains *Beyond the Black River*
1st Edition, Signet, PB, January 1986
Cover by Ken Kelly; edited by Robert Adams, Martin H. Greenberg, and Charles C. Waugh

## Barbarians II
Contains *The Valley of the Worm*
1st Edition, Signet, PB, February 1988
Cover by Ken Kelly; edited by Robert and Pamela Adams, and Martin H. Greenberg

## Beyond Midnight
Contains *The Gray God Passes*
1st Edition, Berkley, PB, November 1976
Cover by "Vicent DiFate"; story introductions by TED Klein; edited by Kirby McCauley

## Beyond the Gate of Dream
Contains *The Hand of Nergal (completed by Lin Carter)*
1st Edition, Leisure Books, PB, 1977
Edited by Lin Carter; identical to Belmont edition, except for cover, and error in name (GATE should be GATES); the title is correct on the title page

## Beyond the Gates of Dream
Contains *The Hand of Nergal (completed by Lin Carter)*
1st Edition, Belmont Tower, PB, August 1969
Edited by Lin Carter; also see BEYOND THE GATE OF DREAM listed above
Belmont Tower, PB, November 1972
Different jacket from the Belmont 1st edition
Five Star (PBS Ltd), PB, 1973
Dorchester, PB, 1982
Wildside Press, TPB, 1999

## Beyond the Walls of Sleep
Contains *The Challenge from Beyond*
1st Edition, Arkham House, HB, 1943
Edited by August Derleth

## The Book of Madness: Whispers Without, Chaos Within
Contains the first four lines of *Black Chant Imperial (lines 1-4 only); The Dust Dance (1) (lines 69-72 only); An Open Window; The Song of a Mad Minstrel (lines 1-10, 29-32) (all v)*
1st Edition, White Wolf, TPB, 1995

## The Caller of the Black
Contains *the verse heading from The Black Stone*
1st Edition, Arkham House, HB, 1971
> By Brian Lumley; the verse is contained in a story titled "In the Vaults Beneath"

## Christopher Lee's "X" Certificate No 1
Contains *The Black Stone*
1st Edition, Star, PB, 1975
WH Allen, HB, 1976
> Cover includes photo from UA film THE MAN WITH THE GOLDEN GUN; introduction by Christopher Lee; edited by Christopher Lee and Michel Parry; later US version of this book titled FROM THE ARCHIVES OF EVIL

## Citadels of Mystery
Contains *Easter Island (v) (lines 1-4, 9-14 only)*
1st Edition, Fontana, PB, 1972
Ballantine, PB, 1973
> By LSDC; reprint of ANCIENT RUINS AND ARCHEOLOGY

## The Complete Oriental Stories
Contains Contains *The Voice of El-Lil; Red Blades of Black Cathay; Hawks of Outremer; The Blood of Belshazzar; The Sowers of the Thunder; Lord of Samarcand*
1st Edition, Girasol Collectables, HB, Fall 2007
> Facsimile reproduction of all 9 issues of ORIENTAL STORIES in a 3-volume set

## The Conan Grimoire
Contains *Untitled fragment ("The wind from the Mediterranean . . ."); Something About Eve; plus six letters to Clark Ashton Smith, including: pm, July 22, 1933 ("I can hardly find words to express . . ."); ca. October 1933 ("Thanks very much for the kind things . . ."); pm, Dec 14, 1933 ("Only the fact that I have been sick . . ."); ca. January 1934 ("Thanks again for the drawing of the wizard."); ca. March 1934 ("I am sorry to hear you have been indisposed . . ."); July 23, 1935 ("I'm ashamed of my long delay in answering . . .")*
1st Edition, Mirage Press, HB, 1972
> Cover art by Berni Wrightson; edited by LSDC and George Scithers; limited to 1500 copies

## The Conan Swordbook
Contains *a letter to August Derleth, ca. Jan 1933 ("I was much interested in your accounts . . ."), and a letter to Harold Preece, ca. Oct or early Nov 1930 ("Well, Harold, I'm sorry to hear your nose . . .")*
1st Edition, Mirage Press, HB, 1969
> Includes 14 illustrations, including 3 by Frazetta; edited by LSDC and George Scithers; limited to 1500 copies

## The Dark Barbarian
Contains *Age Comes to Rabelais (lines 7-8, 11-12); A Dawn in Flanders; Crete (lines 13-16); Dreams of Ninevah (lines 1-8); The Dust Dance (1) (lines 9-12); The Dust Dance (2) (lines 1-4 only); Echoes from an Iron Anvil (lines 13-16, 19, 22); Hope Empty of Meaning (lines 1, 7-8); The King and the Oak (lines 1-3); A Lady's Chamber (lines 3-4, 10-11); Lines Written in the Realization that I Must Die (lines 5, 23-24); The Outgoing of Sigurd the Jerusalem-Farer (lines 6-7, 9-10); Reuben's Brethren (lines 1-2, 13-14);The Riders of Babylon (lines 15-17); The Road of Azrael (lines 1-4); Roads; The Sands of Time (lines 5-6, 11-12); Solomon Kane's*

*Homecoming (lines 13, 16, 31); A Song of Defeat (lines 7-8, 27-28); The Song of Horsa's Galley (lines 7, 11, 15-16); A Song of the Naked Lands (lines 25-28, 51-52); Surrender ("I will rise . . .") (lines 7-8, 35-36); The Tempter (lines 35-36, 40); Timur-lang; Today (line 10, 18-20); Which Will Scarcely Be Understood (lines 1, 7-9, 13, 19-26); Zukala's Hour (lines 37-44);* **Zukala's Love Song (lines 42, 54-55, 80)** *(all v);* also a critical anthology, includes a number of photos, as well as a bibliography and story index

1st Edition, Greenwood Press, HB, 1984

> **Contains a First Appearance**; no jacket, as issued; edited by Don Herron

Wildside Press, TPB, September 2000

Wildside Press, HB, 2003

## The Dark Horse Book of the Dead

Contains *Old Garfield's Heart*

1st Edition, HB, June 2005

> No DJ, as issued; mostly a collection of comic work, the REH story is straight text with a few Gary Gianni illustrations mixed in

## Dark Imaginings: A Collection of Gothic Fantasy

Contains *The Mirrors of Tuzun Thune*

1st Edition, Delta (Dell), TPB, April 1978

Delta (Dell), TPB, July 1978

> Cover art by "Schick"; edited by Robert H. Boyer and Kenneth J. Zahorski

## Dark Mind, Dark Heart

Contains ***The Grey God Passes***

1st Edition, Arkham House, HB, 1962

> **Contains a First Appearance**; cover art by Dale Mann; edited by August Derleth

Mayflower, PB, 1963

Mayflower, PB, 1966

## Dark of the Moon

Contains *Always Comes Evening; Arkham; Futility ("Golden goats . . ."); The Ghost Kings; The Harp of Alfred; The King and the Oak; The Last Hour; Lines Written in the Realization that I Must Die; Moon Mockery; Recompense; Solomon Kane's Homecoming; Which Will Scarcely Be Understood; The Singer in the Mist (all v)*

1st Edition, Arkham House, HB, 1947

> Edited by August Derleth

1st Edition, Books for Libraries Press, HB, 1969

> No jacket, as issued

## The Dark of the Soul

Contains *The Horror from the Mound*

1st Edition, Tower, PB, 1970

> Cover is an unidentified special effects photograph; edited by Don Ward

## Dark Things

Contains ***The House in the Oaks (completed by August Derleth)***; *Arkham (v); An Open Window (v); the verse heading from The Black Stone*

1st Edition, Arkham House, HB, 1971

> **Contains a First Appearance**; edited by August Derleth; a slightly different version of the poem, incorporated into the story

## Dark Valley Destiny

Contains *Lines Written in the Realization that I Must Die (lines 5-10); The Singer in the Mist (lines 1-8); The Dweller in Dark Valley (lines 9-12, 17-20); The Dust Dance (2); A Moment (lines 13-16); The Grim Land (lines 1-8 only); Fragment ("And so his boyhood . . .") (lines 1-4, 19-28); Hymn of Hatred; Slumber; The Heart of the Sea's Desire (lines 1-8); The Road of Kings; A Song Out of Midian (lines 1-3, 7-9); The Tempter; Recompense (lines 1-4, 17-24); Cimmeria; Adventure; The Bride of Cuchulain (lines 18-24);* **The Call of the Sea (lines 1-6)**; *Emancipation (lines 18-20); Crete (lines 1-4); The Ghost Kings (lines 1-3); Invective; The Sea (lines 1-6); The Tempter (lines 11-20, 31-40); A Warning (lines 9-12 of Howard Collector version); the verse heading from Chapter 5 of The Phoenix on the Sword (all v, mostly incomplete);* plus numerous excerpts from stories and letters

1st Edition, Blue Jay, HB, 1983

> **Contains a First Appearance**; by LSDC; cover art by Kevin Eugene Johnson; the complete version of "Cimmeria"

## The Dead Man's Kiss

Contains *the verse heading from The Fearsome Touch of Death*

1st Edition, Pocket Books, PB, 1992

> By Robert Weinberg

## Echoes of Valor

Contains ***The Black Stranger***

1st Edition, TOR, PB, February 1987

> **Contains a First Appearance**; this is the true original Conan version of "The Black Stranger", see Prose Index for details; cover art by Ken Kelly; introduction and edited by Karl Edward Wagner

## Echoes of Valor II

Contains *The Frost-King's Daughter; The Frost-Giant's Daughter;* **a letter to Charles Hornig, Nov 10, 1933 ("Here is a short story, 'The Frost-King's Daughter' . . .")**

1st Edition, TOR, HB, August 1989

TOR, PB, 1991

> **Contains a First Appearance**; cover art by Sam Rakeland (aka Rich Berry); explanatory introduction and edited by Karl Edward Wagner

## Echoes of Valor III

Contains *The Shadow of the Vulture*

1st Edition, TOR, PB, September 1991

> Cover art by Sam Rakeland (aka Rich Berry); edited by Karl Edward Wagner

## Eight Strange Tales

Contains *Dig Me No Grave*

1st Edition, Fawcett (Gold Medal), PB, October 1972

> Edited by Vic Ghidalia

## The Eternal City

Contains *Kings of the Night; first 4 lines of The Song of Bran (v)*

1st Edition, Baen, PB, January 1990

> Cover art by John Rheaume; edited by David Drake, Martin H. Greenberg, and Charles G. Waugh

## Famous Fantastic Mysteries

Contains *Worms of the Earth*

1st Edition, Gramercy, HB, August 1991

> Illustrated by Virgil Finlay; edited by Stefan Dziemianowicz, Robert Weinberg and Martin H. Greenberg

## Fancyclopedia
Contains *Recompense (v)*
1st Edition, The Fantasy Foundation, PB, 1944
>    Edited by John Bristol and Forrest J. Ackerman; limited to 250 copies; attempts to be an encyclopeadia for all words used in fantasy or science fiction

## The Fantastic Civil War
Contains *"For the Love of Barbara Allen"*
1st Edition, Baen, PB, June 1991
>    Cover art by Ken Kelly; edited by Frank McSherry, Jr.

## The Fantastic Swordsmen
Contains *The Drums of Tombalku (completed by LSDC)*
1st Edition, Pyramid, PB, May 1967
Pyramid, PB, 2nd printing, 1967
>    Cover art by Jack Gaughan; edited by LSDC; 1st Edition is R-1621, 2nd printing is X-1621

## The Fantastic Worlds of Robert E Howard
Contains *the verse heading from The Queen of the Black Coast*
1st Edition, Jim Van Hise, TPB, June 1997
Jim Van Hise, 2nd printing, 2002
>    Edited by Jim Van Hise; first edition limited to 1200 copies, second to 2000 copies; the second edition includes a replacement drawing by Gary Gianni

## The Fantasy Hall of Fame
Contains *The Valley of the Worm*
1st Edition, Arbor House, HB, October 1983
>    Cover art by E.T. Steadman, edited by Robert Silverberg and Martin Greenberg

## Far Below and Other Horrors
Contains *Out of the Deep*
1st Edition, FAX, HB, 1974
FAX, PB, 1974
>    Cover art by Lee Brown Coye; edited by Robert Weinberg; HB limited to 1000 copies; the TPB edition by FAX may have come out first
Starmont House, HB, 1985
Starmont, PB, February 1987
Wildside Press, HB, 2003
Wildside Press, TPB, 2003

## Feast of Fear
Contains *The Cobra in the Dream*
1st Edition, Manor, PB, 1977
>    Edited by Vic Ghidalia

## Fire and Sleet and Candlelight
Contains **Earth-Born;** *The Sands of Time (all v)*
1st Edition, Arkham House, HB, 1961
>    **Contains a First Appearance**; cover art by Gary Gore; edited by August Derleth
1st Edition, Books for Libraries Press, HB, 1973
>    No jacket, as issued

## The First Book of Unknown Tales of Horror
Contains *The Little People*
1st Edition, Sidgwick and Jackson (UK), PB, 1976
> Edited by Peter Haining
1st Edition, Mews, PB, October 1976

## From the Archives of Evil
Contains *The Black Stone*
1st Edition, Warner Books, PB, January 1976
> Photo of Christopher Lee on cover; introduction by Christopher Lee; edited by Christopher Lee and Michel Parry; same as CHRISTOPHER LEE'S "X" CERTIFICATE #1

## A Gazetteer of the Hyborian World of Conan and an Ethnogeographical Dictionary of Principle Peoples of the Era
Contains *Notes on Various Peoples of the Hyborian Age*
1st Edition, Starmont, HB and PB, 1977
> **Contains a First Appearance**; by Lee N. Falconer (pseudonym for Julian May, famed female SF writer)
1st Edition, Borgo Press, HB and PB, date unknown
> Borgo Press bought out Starmont, and sold out the rest of the books, may or may not have any indication of that on the books

## Getting Even
Contains *The Man on the Ground*
1st Edition, Bobbs-Merrill, HB, 1978
> Edited by Diana King

## Ghor, Kin-Slayer
Contains *Ghor, Kin-Slayer*
1st Edition, Necronomicon Press, TPB, 1997
> By Robert E. Howard, Karl Edward Wagner, Joseph Brennan, Richard L. Tierney, Michael Moorcock, Charles R. Saunders, Andrew J. Offutt, Manly Wade Wellman, Darrell Schwietzer, A.E. Van Vogt, Brian Lumley, Frank Belknap Long, Adrian Cole, Ramsey Campbell, H. Warner Munn, Marion Zimmer Bradley, and Richard A. Lupoff; cover art by Robert H. Knox; a round robin effort, the first chapter is by REH, the remaining 16 chapters are by the authors shown, in order; twelve of the 17 chapters were published in FANTASY CROSSROADS; this is the first complete copy of the story published

## The Giant Book of Fantasy Tales
Contains *Memories ("Shall we remember . . .") (v)*
1st Edition, The Book Company (AU), TPB, May 1996
> Edited by Stephen Jones and David Sutton

## Glenn Lord's Ultima Thule
Contains *letters to Hugh G. Schoenfield, June 15, 1933 ("As I promised, . . ."); to Denis Archer, May 20, 1934 ("As you doubtless remember, . . .")*
2nd Edition, Rob Roehm (via lulu.com), TPB, 2006
> A reprinting of the entire ULTIMA THULE series, all six issues; also contains several rejection letters to REH, some foreign publication listings, the contents of REH's library, and how much REH was paid for his stories during his lifetime; the first printing was only 15 copies, and is listed in the CHAPBOOKS lists

## Golden Fleece
Contains *Gates of Empire*
1st Edition, Odyssey Publications, TPB, 1975
> Cover art by Harold S. Delay; edited by William H. Desmond, Diane M. Howard, John R. Howard, and Robert K. Weiner; facsimile reproductions of original pulp pages

## Gooseflesh!
Contains *The Black Country*
1st Edition, Berkley, PB, December 1974
> Edited by Vic Ghidalia
1st Edition, Manor, PB, 1977

## Great Cities of the Ancient World
Contains *Babylon (v) (lines 1-8); Oh Babylon, Lost Babylon (v) (lines 19-24)*
1st Edition, Doubleday, HB, 1972
> By LSDC

## Grim Death
Contains *The Black Stone*
1st Edition, Selwyn and Blount (UK), HB, 1932
> Edited by Christine Campbell Thomson; **first hardback appearance ever of an REH story**

## Haunted America
Contains *The Dead Remember*
1st Edition, Barnes and Noble, HB, 1994
Barnes and Noble, HB, 2nd printing, date unknown
Barnes and Noble, TPB, 1994
> Cover art by Edward Gorey; edited by Marvin Kaye; this reprinted HAUNTED AMERICA: STAR-SPANGLED SUPERNATURAL STORIES

## Haunted America: Star-Spangled Supernatural Stories
Contains *The Dead Remember*
1st Edition, Doubleday (SFBC), HB, 1991
> Cover art by Edward Gorey; Edited by Marvin and Saralee Kaye; later editions, just titled HAUNTED AMERICA

## Horror! 100 Best Books
Contains *Something About Eve*
1st Edition, Xanadu, HB, 1988
> Edited by Stephen Jones and Kim Newman; a collection of articles by horror authors writing about various movies
NEL, HB, 1988
Carroll and Graf, HB, June 1998
Hodder and Stoughton, TPB, 1992

## The Horror Hall of Fame
Contains *Pigeons from Hell*
1st Edition, Carroll and Graf, HB, July 1991
> Edited by Robert Silverberg and Martin Greenberg
Doubleday (Book of the Month Club), HB, 1991
Carroll and Graf, PB, 1992
Robert Hale, Ltd. (UK), HB, 1992

## Horror Hunters

Contains *The Thing on the Roof*
1st Edition, McFadden, PB, 1971
    Edited by Roger Elwood and Vic Ghidalia
Manor Books, PB, 1975

## Horror Times Ten

Contains *The Dead Remember*
1st Edition, Berkley, PB, June 1967
    Edited by Alden H Norton
Berkley, PB, 2nd printing, June 1968
Berkley, PB, 3rd printing, December 1968
Berkley, PB, 4th printing, July 1969
Berkley, PB, 5th printing, September 1969
Berkley, PB, 6th printing, September 1970
Berkley, PB, 7th printing, November 1970
Berkley, PB, 8th printing, December 1971
Berkley, PB, 9th printing, February 1972
Berkley, PB, 10th printing, date unknown
Berkley, PB, 11th printing, date unknown
Berkley, PB, 12th printing, date unknown
Berkley, PB, 13th printing, date unknown

## Horrors Unknown

Contains *The Challenge from Beyond*
1st Edition, Ryerson Press, HB, June 1971
    Edited by Sam Moskowitz
Walker and Co., HB, June 1971
Kaye and Ward (UK), HB, May 1972
Berkley, PB, February February 1976

## Howard's Haunts

Contains *Cimmeria (v)*
Rob Roehm, TPB, 1st Edition, January 2007
    A travelogue with extensive color photography of REH's Texas stops and the three big events of 2006:
    the REH Birthday Bash in Fort Worth, Howard Days in Cross Plains, and World Fantasy Con in Austin;
    first edition was sold for only ONE DAY on lulu, all later printings listed as second editions; published
    via lulu.com

## The Howard Review #1

Contains *The Fearsome Touch of Death*
Dennis McHaney, HB, 1st Edition, December 1974
    Limited to 25 copies of this edition, there was also a staples 1st edition, limited to 204 copies; staples
    edition listed in the CHAPBOOKS lists; artwork by Tom Foster; introduction by McHaney; a copy sold
    on eBay for $877 in 2007

## The Howard Review #12

Contains *The Tomb's Secret; Black Talons; The Song of the Bats (v); The Riders of Babylon (v); The Harp of
Alfred (v); The Gates of Nineveh (v)*
1st Edition, Dennis McHaney, TPB, 2004
    Both a color and a B&W edition; POD via Lulu.com; also contains repros of all the JACK DEMPSEY
    FIGHT MAGAZINE covers in which an REH stories appeared

## The Howard Review #13

Contains *The Dark Man; The Voice of El-Lil; The Fire of Asshurbanipal; The Voices Waken Memory (v); Babel (v)*

1st Edition, Dennis McHaney, TPB, December 2004
> POD via Lulu.com; "The Dark Man", "The Voice of El-Lil" and "The Fire of Asshurbanipal" are all facsimile reprints of original pulp pages

## The Hyborian Age

Contains *The Hyborian Age*

1st Edition, LANY Coop, staples, 1938
> **Contains a First Appearance**; first complete publication

## Imaginary Worlds

Contains *The Singer in the Mist (v) (lines 9-14)*

1st Edition, Ballantine, PB, June 1973
> Cover art by Gervasio Gallardo; edited by Lin Carter; non-fiction discussion of various fantasy writers, including a section on REH, including LSDC's involvement

## In Lands That Never Were

Contains *The Hall of the Dead*

1st Edition, Thunder's Mouth Press, PB, September 2004
> Edited by Gordon Van Gelder

## In Lovecraft's Shadow

Contains *The House in the Oaks (completed by August Derleth)*

1st Edition, Mycroft and Moran, HB, 1998
> Edited by Joseph Wrzos; a collection of Derleth-completed stories, mostly HPL

## Isaac Asimov's Magical Worlds of Fantasy: Witches and Wizards

Contains *The People of the Black Circle*

1st Edition, Bonanza, HB, 1985
> Edited by Isaac Asimov, Martin H. Greenberg, Charles G. Waugh; reprint that includes ISAAC ASIMOV'S MAGINCAL WORLDS OF FANTASY #1: WIZARDS

## Isaac Asimov's Magical Worlds of Fantasy #1: Wizards

Contains *The People of the Black Circle*

1st Edition, Signet, PB, October 1983
> Edited by Isaac Asimov; later reprinted in ISAAC ASIMOV'S MAGICAL WORLDS OF FANTASY: WITCHES AND WIZARDS

## Isaac Asimov's Magical Worlds of Fantasy #9: Atlantis

Contains *The Shadow Kingdom*

1st Edition, Signet, PB, January 1988
> Introduction by Isaac Asimov; edited by Isaac Asimov, Martin H. Greenberg, and Charles G. Waugh

## Keep on the Light

Contains *Worms of the Earth*

1st Edition, Selwyn and Blount (UK), HB, 1933
> Edited by Christine Campbell Thomson

## The Last Celt

Contains *The Hall of the Dead (synopsis); The Hand of Nergal (unfinished); The Wandering Years;* **An Autobiography; A Touch of Trivia**; *Untitled poem* (**"When wolf meets wolf, . . ."**); *Untitled story* (**"A Cossack and a Turk . . ."**); **Kublai Khan (v); Jazz Music; The Sword; The Follower (v); Young Lockanbars (v); Spears of the East**; *plus full and portions of several letters, including:* **to Charles Hornig, Aug 10, 1934** (**"Glad you liked the verses . . .", excerpt only, begins "Yes, I received a copy of 'The Battle That . . ."**); *to Denis Archer, 20 May 1934 ("As you doubtless remember, in your letter . . ."); to Farnsworth Wright, ca. June 1930 ("I have long looked forward to reading . . ."); and portions of several letters put together to create something called* **On Reading – And Writing**, *as well as several photos of REH*

1st Edition, Grant, HB, 1976

> **Contains a First Appearance**; cover includes a photograph of REH; compiled and edited by Glenn Lord; the standard bibliography for REH prior to this book; eight of these works appeared in a facsimile reproduction of THE GOLDEN CALIPH (Chpbk.), of which only one copy is known; limited to 2600 copies; letter to Denis Archer is a facsimile reproduction

1st Edition, Berkley, PB, November 1977

> Cover art by Ken Kelly

## Literary Swordsmen and Sorcerers

Contains *The Singer in the Mist (v) (lines 1-8); The Ghost Kings (v) (lines 7-9); The Tempter (v) (lines 1-8)*

1st Edition, Arkham House, HB, 1976

> By LSDC; cover art by Tim Kirk; poem used as chapter heading for "The Miscast Barbarian: Robert E. Howard"

## Lone Star Universe

Contains **The Coming of Bast (v)**

1st Edition, Heidelberg, HB, 1976

**Contains a First Appearance**; cover art by Mike Presley; introduction by Harlan Ellison; edited by George Proctor and Steven Utley

## Lost Continents

Contains *the verse heading from The Pool of the Black One*

1st Edition, Gnome Press, HB, 1954

> By LSDC

Dover, PB, 1970

Peter Smith Publishing, HB, 1970

Remploy, PB, 1971

Ballantine, PB, 1975

## Lost in the Rentharpian Hills

Contains **two letters to Carl Jacobi: pm, March 22, 1932 ("I found your recent letter very interesting . . ."), and March 17, 1933 ("I am glad to write to Wright, commenting . . .")**

1st Edition, Bowling Green University Popular Press, HB, 1985

> **Contains a First Appearance**; by R. Dixon Smith

## Lost Worlds

Contains *Riders Beyond the Sunrise (completed by Carter)*

1st Edition, DAW, PB, August 1980

> Cover art by "Enrich"; edited by Lin Carter; introduction to story by Carter

## Lovecraft: A Biography
Contains *The Tempter (v) (lines 17-20)*
1st Edition, Doubleday, HB, 1975
New English Library ("NEL", UK), PB, 1975
Ballantine, PB, 1976
    By LSDC

## Lovecraft: A Look Behind the Cthulhu Mythos
Contains *the verse heading from The Black Stone*
1st Edition, Ballantine, PB, 1972
    By Lin Carter

## Lurking Shadows
Contains *The Valley of the Worm*
1st Edition, Star (UK), PB, 1979
    Edited by Michel Parry and Christopher Lee

## The Macabre Reader
Contains *The Cairn on the Headland*
1st Edition, Ace, PB, 1959
Brown, Watson Ltd (UK) ("Digit Books"), PB, June 1960
    Cover art by Ed Emsh; edited by Donald Wollheim

## The Magic of Atlantis
Contains *The Mirrors of Tuzun Thune*
1st Edition, Lancer, PB, 1970
    Cover art by Walotsky; edited by Lin Carter

## The Magic Carpet Magazine
Contains *Alleys of Darkness*
1st Edition, Odyssey Publications, TPB, 1977
    Cover by Margaret Brundage; edited by William H. Desmond, Diane M. Howard, John R. Howard,
    Robert K. Wiener "Odyssey Publications #9"; facsimile reproductions of original pulp pages

## The Mammoth Book of Fantasy
Contains *Valley of the Worm*
1st Edition, Robinson, TPB, September 2001
Carroll & Graf, TPB, November 2001
    Edited by Isaac Mike Ashley

## The Mammoth Book of Monsters
Contains *The Horror from the Mound*
1st Edition,Carroll & Graf, TPB, May 2007
Robinson, TPB, June 2007
    Edited by Isaac Stephen Jones; cover art by Les Edwards; illustrations by Randy Broecker

## The Mammoth Book of Short Fantasy Novels
Contains *Red Nails*
1st Edition, Robinson, TPB, 1986
    Edited by Isaac Asimov, Martin H. Greenberg, and Charles G. Waugh; same as BAKER'S DOZEN

## The Man from Cross Plains
Contains *Ghost with the Silk Hat*
1ˢᵗ Edition, Dennis McHaney, TPB, 2006
Dennis McHaney, HB, 2006
> Edited by Dennis McHaney; cover is modified photo of REH at Fort McKavitt; sold as a fundraiser for the Cross Plains Fire Relief Fund, with numerous articles concerning REH and Cross Plains; published via lulu.com

## Midnight Sun
Contains *Flight (v, lines 17-24)*
1ˢᵗ Edition, Night Shade Books, HB, 2003
SFBC Fantasy (Science Fiction Book Club), HB, 2003 or 2004
> Edited by Karl Edward Wagner

## The Mighty Barbarians
Contains *A Witch Shall be Born*
1ˢᵗ Edition, Lancer, PB, 1969
> Cover art by James Steranko; edited by Hans Stefan Santesson

## The Mighty Swordsmen
Contains *Beyond the Black River*
1ˢᵗ Edition, Lancer, PB, 1970
> Cover art by James Steranko; edited by Hans Stefan Santesson

## Modern American Poetry
Contains **One Who Comes At Eventide; To a Woman ("Though fathoms . . .") (both v)**
1ˢᵗ Edition, Galleon Press, HB, 1933
> **Contains a First Appearance**; edited by Gerta Aison; **first appearance of REH poetry in hardback**

## More Not at Night
Contains *Rogues in the House*
1ˢᵗ Edition, Arrow (UK), PB, 1961
Arrow (UK), PB, 2ⁿᵈ printing, 1963
> Edited by Christine Campbell Thomson; reprint of TERROR BY NIGHT; later NEVER AT NIGHT is the same thing with different cover

## More Tales of Unknown Horror
Contains *Delenda Est*
1ˢᵗ Edition, New English Library ("NEL"), PB, 1979
> Edited by Peter Haining

## Never at Night
Contains *Rogues in the House*
1ˢᵗ Edition, Arrow (UK), PB, 1972
> Edited by Christine Campbell Thomson; cover has photo of a hand; same as MORE NOT AT NIGHT, just new name; reprint of TERROR BY NIGHT

## The Neverending Hunt
Contains **Over the Rockies in a Ford**
1ˢᵗ Edition, Hermanthis Press, HB, 2006
> **Contains a First Appearance**; edited by Paul Herman; first printing limited to 100 signed and numbered copies

## New Worlds for Old
Contains *The Garden of Fear*
1st Edition, Ballantine, PB, September 1971
    Cover art by David Johnston; edited by Lin Carter

## Night Chills
Contains *People of the Black Coast*
1st Edition, Avon, PB, November 1975
    Edited by Kirby McCauley

## The Nyarlathotep Cycle: Stories about the God of a Thousand Forms
Contains *Silence Falls on Mecca's Walls (v)*
1st Edition, Chaosium, TPB, May 1997
    Cover art by HE Fassl; interior illustrations by Dave Carson; edited by Robert M. Price; title page is
    different, TALES instead of STORIES

## One Who Walked Alone
Contains *To a Woman (v); One Who Comes at Eventide (v);* **and some letters to Novalyne Price, including:**
**September 27, 1934 ("How about going to the show . . .")**
**ca. December 1934 ("Like my meal-ticket, Conan the Cimmerian . . .")**
**June 19, 1935 ("The weather is good . . .")**
**June 19, 1935 ("Dear Novalyne . . . cordially . . .")**
**July 4, 1935 ("I take my typewriter . . .")**
*July 8, 1935 ("Thank you for your invitation to call . . .")*
**February 14, 1936 ("I heard yesterday you had . . .")**
**February 15, 1936 ("I'm sorry but I won't be able . . .")**
**March 5, 1936 ("I just now read the letter . . .")**
**May 27, 1936 ("You needn't have bothered . . .")**
1st Edition, Grant, HB, October 1986
Grant, HB, 2nd printing, 1988
Grant, HB, 3rd printing, December 1998
    **Contains a First Appearance**; by Novalyne Price Ellis; cover art on 1st and 2nd by Richard Berry; 3rd
    printing has photo of Rene Zellwiger on cover; first printing was 600 copies, second was 550, third
    unknown

## Operation: Phantasy – The Best from the Phantagraph
Contains *Song at Midnight (v)*
1st Edition, Phantagraph (Donald Wollheim), HB, 1967
    Edited by Donald Wollheim; produced and distributed by Donald Grant; 420 signed copies with 400 of
    them for sale; blue cloth cover with illustrated jacket

## Oriental Stories
Contains *The Voice of El-Lil*
1st Edition, Odyssey Publications, TPB, 1975
    Cover by Margaret Brundage; edited by William H. Desmond, Diane M. Howard, John R. Howard,
    Robert K. Weiner; all facsimile reproductions of original pulp pages

## Oriental Stories, The Magic Carpet Magazine and The Souk
Contains *The Voice of El-Lil*
1st Edition, McHaney, TPB, June 2005
    Edited by Dennis McHaney; printed via lulu.com; the story was deleted from the book after the first year
    of publication, so all later editions do NOT include it

## Over the Edge
Contains ***The Blue Flame of Vengeance (with John Pocsik)***
1st Edition, Arkham House, HB, 1964
Gollancz, HB, 1967
Gollance, HB, 2nd printing, 1967 (not sure if this really exists)
Arrow, PB, 1976

> **Contains a First Appearance**; edited by August Derleth; basically a completely new story, with just a few excerpts from REH's story, plus using the setting, characters, etc.; Pocsik is listed as "completing" the story, though of course it was already complete to start with

## The Oxford Book of Fantasy Stories
Contains *The Tower of the Elephant*
1st Edition, Oxford, HB, 1994
1st Edition, Oxford, TPB, 1995
Oxford, TPB, 2nd printing, 2003

> Cover by Pete Lyon; edited by Tom Shippey

## The Prentice Hall Anthology of Science Fiction and Fantasy
Contains *The Tower of the Elephant*
1st Edition, Prentice Hall, TPB, 2000

> Cover art by Frank R. Paul; edited by Garyn G. Roberts

## Pulp Fiction Classics #1: Hour of the Dragon
Contains *The Hour of the Dragon*
1st Edition, Wildcat Books, PB, 2004

> Very short lived production via lulu.com

## The Pulps: Fifty Years of American Pop Culture
Contains *The Valley of the Worm; The Purple Heart of Erlik*
1st Edition, Chelsea House, HB, September 1970
1st Edition, Chelsea House, TPB, 1970
1st Edition, Bonanza, HB, 1971
Chelsea House, TPB, 1976

> Edited by Tony Goodstone; cover has reproduction photo of MAMMOTH ADVENTURE pulp magazine; distributed by Random House in USA and Canada

## Realms of Wizardry
Contains *Swords of the Purple Kingdom*
1st Edition, Doubleday, HB, 1976

> Cover design by Robert Aulicino; edited by Lin Carter; introduction to REH story by Lin Carter

## Rivals of Weird Tales
Contains *The Cairn on the Headland*
1st Edition, Bonanza, HB, 1990

> Cover art by John Rosato (adapted from an original by Wesso (aka Hans Wessoloski)); edited by Robert Weinberg, Stefan Dziemianowicz and Martin Greenberg

## Robert E. Howard—The Power of the Writing Mind
Contains *The Door to the Garden (as "untitled"); The Devil's Woodchopper; Double Cross; Vengeance of a Woman; L'Envoi(1) (v); Some People Who Have Had Influence Over Me; letter to Argosy All-Story Weekly, July 20, 1929 ("I was born about twenty-three . . ."); letter to Wilfred Blanch Talman, ca. September 1931 ("Thank you very much for the letter you wrote . . ."); letter to Farnsworth Wright, ca. June-July 1931 ("In your last letter you asked me to give you . . .")*

1ˢᵗ Edition, Mythos Books, TPB, December 2003
> Artwork by Gary Gianni, Rick Cortes, Mark Schultz, Rick McCollum, and David Burton; edited by Ben Szumskyj; also includes an interview with Glenn Lord, and articles by Ben Szumskyj, Joe Marek, Patrice Louinet, Rusty Burke, Leo Grin, Scott Sheaffer, and Tom Munnerlyn; 8.5x11

## Savage Heroes: Tales of Magical Fantasy
Contains *The Temple of Abomination (completed by Richard Tierney)*
1ˢᵗ Edition thus, Taplinger, HB, 1980
> Cover design by Roy Thomas; cover art and interior illustrations by Jim Pitts; edited and introduction by Michel Parry; this appears to be a reprint of SAVAGE HEROES, TALES OF SORCERY AND BLACK MAGIC, with just a title change; this is listed as 1st American edition so either the 1975 edition is UK or this is a second edition

## Savage Heroes, Tales of Sorcery and Black Magic
Contains *The Temple of Abomination (completed by Richard Tierney)*
1ˢᵗ Edition, Taplinger, HB, 1975
Star, PB, 1977
> Interior illustrations by Jim Pitts; edited and introduction by Eric Pendragon (pseudonym for Michel Parry); later edition is titled SAVAGE HEROES: TALES OF MAGICAL FANTASY

## Savage Pulp #1
Contains *Rogues in the House*
1ˢᵗ Edition, Incarna Publishing, HB & TPB, 2005
> Sold on lulu.com

## Science-Fantasy Correspondent #1
Contains **The Guise of Youth (v)**
1ˢᵗ Edition, Carrollton Clark, HB, December 1975
> **Contains a First Appearance**; edited by Willis Conover; lasted only one issue; limited to 100 numbered copies; issued at the first World Fantasy Convention, in hardback

## Sea-Cursed
Contains *Sea Curse*
1ˢᵗ Edition, Barnes and Noble, HB, 1994
> Cover art by Lynn J. Binder; edited by T. Lian McDonald, Stefan Dziemianowicz and Martin Greenberg

## The Second Avon Fantasy Reader
Contains *The Blonde Goddess of Bal-Sagoth*
1ˢᵗ Edition, Avon, PB, February 1969
> Cover art by Gray Morrow; edited by Donald A. Wollheim and George Ernsberger

## The Second Mayflower Book of Black Magic Stories
Contains *Dig Me No Grave*
1ˢᵗ Edition, Mayflower, PB, 1974
> Edited by Michel Parry

## The Shuttered Room
Contains *the verse heading from The Black Stone*
1ˢᵗ Edition, Arkham House, HB, 1959
> By HPL and "Divers Hands"; in a Lin Carter article called "HPL: The Books"

## The Sixth Mayflower Book of Black Magic Stories
Contains *The Thing on the Roof*
1st Edition, Mayflower, PB, 1977
> Cover art by Les Edwards; edited by Michel Parry

## Sleep No More: Twenty Masterpieces of Horror for the Connoisseur
Contains *The Black Stone*
1st Edition, Farrar and Rinehart, HB, 1944
> Cover art by Lee Brown Coye; edited by August Derleth; brief REH bio included, with illustration

Farrar and Rinehart, HB, 2nd printing, 1944
Farrar and Rinehart, HB, 3rd printing, 1944
Farrar and Rinehart, HB, 4th printing, 1944
Armed Services, HB, ~1945
Panther (UK), PB, 1964
> New cover, artist unknown

Panther (UK), PB, 2nd printing, 1966

## The Spawn of Cthulhu
Contains *The Children of the Night*
1st Edition, Ballantine, PB, October 1971
> Cover art by Gervasio Gellardo; edited by Lin Carter; introduction by Lin Carter

## The Spell of Conan
Contains *The Ghost of Camp Colorado; Untitled fragment ("The wind from the Mediterranean wafted . . ."); Something About Eve*
1st Edition, Ace, PB, July 1980
> Edited by LSDC

## The Spell of Seven
Contains *Shadows in Zamboula*
1st Edition, Pyramid, PB, June 1965
> Cover and interior illustrations by Virgil Finlay; introduction and edited by LSDC

Pyramid, PB, 2nd printing, December 1969
> New cover art by Gail Burwen

## Starmont Reader's Guide #35: Robert E. Howard
Contains *Always Comes Evening (lines 5-12 only)*
1st Edition, HB and PB, 1987
Borgo Press, HB and PB, date unknown
> By Marc Cerasini and Charles Hoffman; cover has a photo of REH; includes a "primary reference"; Borgo Press bought out Starmont, and sold out the rest of the books, may or may not have any indication of that on the books

## Stories of Ghosts
Contains *The Apparition in the Prize Ring*
1st Edition, Opar Press, PB, 1973
> Edited by Camille E. Cazedessus, Jr.

## A Strange Glory
Contains *The Dweller in Dark Valley (v)*
1st Edition, McClelland and Stewart (CA), TPB, 1975
> Cover art by Rene Zamic; edited by Gerry Goldberg

## Strange Tales of Mystery and Terror
Contains *People of the Dark*
1st Edition, Odyssey Publications, PB, 1976
> Cover art by HW Wesso (pseudonym for Hans Wessoloski); edited by William H. Desmond, Diane M. Howard, John R. Howard, and Robert K. Weiner; "Odyssey Publications #6"; facsimile reproductions of original pulp pages

## Strange Worlds
Contains *Red Nails*
1st Edition, Wildcat Books, PB, 2004
> Sold via lulu.com

## Swords Against Darkness
Contains ***Nekht Semerkeht (completed by Andrew J. Offutt)***
1st Edition, Zebra, PB, February 1977
> **Contains a First Appearance**, cover art by Frank Frazetta; edited by Andrew J. Offutt

## Swords and Sorcery
Contains *Shadows in the Moonlight*
1st Edition, Pyramid, PB, December 1963
> Cover art by Virgil Finlay; introduction and edited by LSDC

## Swordsmen and Supermen
Contains *Meet Cap'n Kidd*
1st Edition, Centaur, PB, February 1972
> Cover art by Virgil Finlay; edited by Lawan Chomchalow

## Tales of Dungeons and Dragons
Contains *The People of the Black Coast*
1st Edition, Century Hutchinson (UK), HB, November 1986
> Edited by Peter Haining
Book Club Associates (aka Guild Publishing, UK), HB, 1986
Century Hutchinson (UK), HB, 2nd printing, June 1987

## Tales of the Cthulhu Mythos
Contains *The Black Stone*
1st Edition, Arkham House, HB, 1969
> Edited and introduction by August Derleth; used as basis for a two-volume PB series with the same title
Grafton, TPB, September 1988
> Cover artist Tim White
Arkham House, HB, 2nd Edition, 1989
> Re-edited by James Turner
Harper-Collins, PB, 1994
Del Rey, PB, October 1998

## Tales of the Cthulhu Mythos, Volume 1
Contains *The Black Stone*
1st Edition, Beagle, PB, May 1971
> Edited and introduction by August Derleth; based off the Arkham House TALES OF THE CTHULHU MYTHOS
Ballantine, PB, 1973
> Cover art by John Holmes
Ballantine, PB, 2nd printing, 1973

Ballantine, PB, 3<sup>rd</sup> printing, 1974
Ballantine, PB, 4<sup>th</sup> printing, 1975
Ballantine, PB, 5<sup>th</sup> printing, 1975
Panther, PB, 1975

## Tales of the Lovecraft Mythos
Contains *The Fire of Asshurbanipal; The Thing on the Roof*
1<sup>st</sup> Edition, Fedogan and Bremer, HB, 1992
    Cover art by Gahan Wilson; edited by Robert Price; limited to 3500 copies; this version of "The Fire of Asshurbanipal" is the non-supernatural version
Del Rey, TPB, 2002

## A Taste for Blood
Contains *The Hills of the Dead*
1<sup>st</sup> Edition, Dorset, HB, 1992
    Cover by "Humungus Illustration"; edited by Martin H. Greenberg, Stefan Dziemianowicz, and Robert E. Weinberg
Barnes and Noble, PB, 1993
    Cover by Charles Ziga

## Terror by Night
Contains *Rogues in the House*
1<sup>st</sup> Edition, Selwyn and Blount, HB, 1934
    Edited by Christine Campbell Thomson; **first hardback appearance of a Conan story**; reprinted as MORE NOT AT NIGHT

## Third Book of Unknown Tales of Horror
Contains *Delenda Est*
1<sup>st</sup> Edition, Sidgwick and Jackson, HB, 1980
    Edited by Peter Haining

## Time Warps
Contains *"For the Love of Barbara Allen"*
1<sup>st</sup> Edition, Raintree, PB, 1984
    Edited by Isaac Asimov, Martin Greenberg and Charles Waugh

## To Sleep Perchance to Dream . . . Nightmare
Contains *The Black Stone*
1<sup>st</sup> Edition, Barnes and Noble, HB, 1993
1<sup>st</sup> Edition, Barnes and Noble, TPB, 1993
    Cover art by Kevin Kelly; edited by Stefan Dziemianowicz, Robert E. Weinberg and Martin H. Greenberg

## Tough Guys and Dangerous Dames
Contains *Names in the Black Book*
1<sup>st</sup> Edition, Barnes and Noble, HB, 1993
Barnes and Noble, TPB, 1995
    Cover art by E.T. Steadman; edited by Robert E. Weinberg, Stefan Dziemianowicz, and Martin H. Greenberg

## A Treasury of Fantasy

Contains *Swords of the Purple Kingdom*
1st Edition, Avenel, HB, 1981
Chatham River Press, TPB, 1984
    Cover art by Russ Hoover; edited by Cary Wilkins
Gramercy, HB, 1995
    Cover art by "Romas"

## Vampire

Contains *The Horror from the Mound*
1st Edition, Severn House, HB, 1985
1st Edition, WH Allen and Co. (Target Books), PB, 1985
    Edited by Peter Haining

## Warlocks and Warriors

Contains *The Hills of the Dead*
1st Edition, Putnam (Science Fiction Book Club), HB, 1970
    Cover art by Jim Steranko; edited and introduction by LSDC; short bio at start of story
Berkley, PB, January 1971
Tower, PB, 1971

## Waves of Terror

Contains *Sea Curse*
1st Edition, Victor Gollancz Ltd, HB, 1976
    Edited by Michel Parry

## Weird Legacies

Contains *Skulls in the Stars*
1st Edition, Star, PB, 1977
    Edited by Mike Ashley; cover art by Peter Andrew Jones

## Weird Tales

Contains *Pigeons from Hell*
1st Edition, Pyramid, PB, May 1964
Pyramid, PB, 2nd printing, April 1977
    Cover art by Virgil Finlay; edited by Leo Margulies

## Weird Tales

Contains *The Black Hound of Death; Haunting Columns (v)*
1st Edition, Neville-Spearman (UK), HB, 1976
    Edited by Peter Haining; cover is reproduction of a 30's WT cover; facsimile of original pages, with original artwork
Carroll and Graf, HB, 1990
    Cover art by Harold S. DeLay and Lee Brown Coye
Xanadu, HB, 1990
    Same cover as Carroll and Graf

## Weird Tales #1
Contains *Scarlet Tears (with Lin Carter); Red Thunder (v)*
1st Edition, Zebra, PB, 1980
Zebra, PB, 2nd printing, 1981
> **Contains a First Appearance**; cover art by Tom Barber; introduction by Lin Carter, with extensive comments from numerous others; edited by Lin Carter; "Scarlet Tears" is extensively rewritten by Lin Carter, yet Carter does not mention this anywhere; this version of "Red Thunder" is slightly different from its original appearance

## Weird Tales #2
Contains *The Song of the Gallows Tree (v)*
1st Edition, Zebra, PB, 1981
> **Contains a First Appearance**; cover art by Tom Barber; edited by Lin Carter

## Weird Tales #3
Contains *The Guardian of the Idol (with Gerald W. Page)*
1st Edition, Zebra, PB, August 1981
> **Contains a First Appearance**; cover art by Tom Barber; edited by Lin Carter; an unfinished 700 word manuscript, with a synopsis, completed by Gerald W. Page

## Weird Tales #4
Contains *The Doom-Chant of Than-Kul (v)*
1st Edition, Zebra, PB, 1983
> **Contains a First Appearance**; edited by Lin Carter

## Weird Tales #294
Contains *Universe (v)*
1st Edition, Terminus Publishing, HB, Fall 1989
Terminus Publishing, Limited HB, Fall 1989
Terminus Publishing, TPB, Fall 1989
> **Contains a First Appearance**; all editions published simultaneously

## Weird Tales #295
Contains *The Chant Demoniac (v)*
1st Edition, Terminus Publishing, HB, Winter 1989-90
Terminus Publishing, Limited HB, Winter 1989-90
Terminus Publishing, TPB, Winter 1989-90
> **Contains a First Appearance**; all editions published simultaneously

## Weird Tales #297
Contains *Memories (v)*
1st Edition, Terminus Publishing, HB, Summer 1990
Terminus Publishing, Limited HB, Fall 1989
Terminus Publishing, TPB, Fall 1989
> **Contains a First Appearance**; all editions published simultaneously

## Weird Tales #302
Contains *Zukala's Love Song (v)*
1st Edition, Terminus Publishing, HB, Fall 1991
Terminus Publishing, Limited HB, Fall 1989
Terminus Publishing, TPB, Fall 1989
> **Contains a First Appearance**; all editions published simultaneously

## Weird Tales #303
Contains *The Zulu Lord (v)*
1st Edition, Terminus Publishing, HB, Winter 1991-1992
Terminus Publishing, Limited HB, Fall 1989
Terminus Publishing, TPB, Fall 1989
    All editions published simultaneously

## Weird Tales: 32 Unearthed Tales
Contains *The Shadow Kingdom*
1st Edition, Bonanza, HB, 1988
    Edited by Stefan Dziemianowicz, Robert Weinberg and Martin Greenberg

## Weird Tales: Seven Decades of Terror
Contains *Sea Curse*
1st Edition, Barnes and Noble, HB, 1997
    Edited by John Betancourt and Robert Weinberg; "Published by arrangement with Wildside Press"

## Weird Tales: The Magazine That Never Dies
Contains *Skulls in the Stars*
1st Edition, Doubleday (SFBC), HB, 1988
    Cover art by Richard Kriegler; edited by Marvin Kaye and Saralee Kaye; cover art is based on "Skulls in the Stars"
Barnes and Noble, HB, 1996

## Weird Tales, Volume 1
Contains *The Black Hound of Death; Haunting Columns (v)*
1st Edition, Sphere, PB, 1978
    Edited by Peter Haining; reprint of WEIRD TALES, Neville-Spearman, which was converted to a 2-PB set

## Weird Vampire Tales
Contains *The Horror from the Mound*
1st Edition, Gramercy, HB, 1992
    Cover art by Harold de Lay and Jim Campbell, based on an original WEIRD TALES cover; edited by Robert Weinberg, Stefan Dziemianowicz and Martin Greenberg

## Werewolf: Horror Stories of the Man-Beast
Contains *Wolfshead*
1st Edition, Severn House, HB, 1987
    Cover art by Trevor Newman; edited and introduction by Peter Haining

## Worlds of Weird
Contains *The Valley of the Worm*
1st Edition, Pyramid, PB, January 1965
    Cover art by Virgil Finlay; edited by Leo Margulies; introduction by Sam Moskowitz
Pyramid, PB, 2nd printing, April 1977
Jove, PB, October 1978

## WT 50: A Tribute to Weird Tales
Contains *The Devil of Dark Lake; Serpent Vines*
1st Edition, Weinburg, PB, 1974
    **Contains a First Appearance**; cover art by John Mayer, interior art by numerous artists, including Frank Frazetta; edited by Robert Weinberg; also includes a copy of a REH signature in the back

## The Year's Best Fantasy Stories

Contains *The Temple of Abomination (completed by Richard L. Tierney)*
1<sup>st</sup> Edition, DAW, PB, October 1975
    Cover art by George Barr; introduction and edited by Lin Carter

## The Year's Best Fantasy Stories: 4

Contains *Nekht Semekeht (completed by Andrew J. Offutt)*
1<sup>st</sup> Edition, DAW, PB, Decmeber 1978
    Cover art by Esteban Maroto; edited by Lin Carter

## The Year's Best Fantasy Stories: 5

Contains *Lord of the Dead*
1<sup>st</sup> Edition, DAW, PB, January 1980
    Cover art by "Penalva"; introduction and edited by Lin Carter

## Young Blood

Contains *Pigeons from Hell*
1<sup>st</sup> Edition, Zebra, PB, March 1994
    Cover has photo of long-haired man with a knife; edited by Mike Baker

## The Young Magicians

Contains *The Valley of the Worm*
1<sup>st</sup> Edition, Ballantine, PB, October 1969
    Cover art by Sheryl Slavitt; edited by Lin Carter
1<sup>st</sup> Edition, Pan (Ballantine), PB, 1971

# CHAPBOOKS, amateur works, non-print media, and other esoterica

This section includes all the various publications that do not fall appropriately under any of the other categories. This list includes staple-bound chapbooks, audio publications, single sheets, and other unusual and different formats. Many of these are rare to very rare, with publication runs as small as 3-10 copies.

Note that REHupa is the Robert E. Howard United Press Association, an "apa", which has been in existence for decades, and has been limited to a maximum of 30 members throughout its tenure. Each member provides 32 copies of his own "zine" to the editor-in-chief, who in turn binds and redistributes the material every other month. Each zine is typically named by its contributor, though occasionally one will find a contributed untitled zine. In general, REHupa zines are limited to 30-35 copies, though some items are occasionally printed in larger quantities.

This list is sorted in ALPHABETIC ORDER BY TITLE OF WORK. Non-English items are noted in the title heading.

Works shown in **BOLD** are **First Appearance** in that publication. Poetry is indicated by (v).

## *Form of Entry:*
**Title**
> Contents
> Publisher, format, date
>> Notes


## 4<sup>th</sup> World Fantasy Convention Program
> Contains *Cimmeria (v)*
> Michael Templin, staples, 1977
>> This convention was to honor Robert E. Howard, and was organized by Michael Templin; also contains a "Pigeons from Hell" portfolio by Gary Templin, and drawings of Conan, Bran Mak Morn, Solomon Kane and Francis X. Gordon by Paul Schliesser

## Absinthe Pie #14
> Contains *Visions (v)*
> Bo Cribbs, staples, November 1992
>> Distributed in REHUPA #117

## Absinthe Pissed
> Contain *The Haunted Hut*
> Bo Cribbs, staples, February 1993
>> Distributed in REHUPA #119

## The Adventures of Lal Singh
> Contains **The Tale of the Rajah's Ring; The Further Adventures of Lal Singh; Lal Singh, Oriental Gentleman**
> Cryptic Publications, staples, 1985
>> **Contains a First Appearance**; edited by Robert M. Price

## All Fled, All Done
Contains *The Song of Yar Ali Khan(v)*
Glenn Lord, staples, February 1996
> Distributed in REHUPA #137, a one-shot that contained copies of articles from the CROSS PLAINS REVIEW following REH's death

## All-Around Magazine #3
Contains *Under the Great Tiger (Part 1 of 2)*
Tevis Clyde Smith, staples, May-June 1923
> Produced by TCS while in high school, only 3 copies of each known to exist; a combined issue

## All-Around Magazine #4
Contains *Under the Great Tiger (Part 2 of 2)*
Tevis Clyde Smith, staples, July 1923
> Produced by TCS while in high school, only 3 copies of each known to exist; story concluded in this issue; a set of this magazine sold on Ebay in April 1999 for $378.88; another set sold on eBay in October 2005, a complete run of all five issues, fetched over $900

## Altars and Jesters
Contains *Altars and Jesters (v)*
Roy Squires, small booklet, 1974
> **Contains a First Appearance**; limited to 218 copies

## Aquila Nidus #6
Contains *Song Before Clontarf (v)*
Tim Arney, staples, November 1990
> Distributed in REHUPA #106

## Aquila Nidus #29
Contains *Halt! Who Goes There?*
Tim Arney, staples, October 1998
> Distributed in REHUPA #153

## Aquila Nidus [no number, April 2006]
Contains *The Ghost Behind the Gloves (first two pages of typescript)*
Tim Arney, staples, April 2006
> **Contains a First Appearance**; distributed in REHUPA #198

## The Auburn Circle
Contains *An Open Window (v)*
Unknown publisher, unknown format, Spring 1976
> Contained in a story called "Dark Shapes Rising", by James Shoffner

## Austin, Volume 3, #1
Contains *two letters to TCS, June 8, 1923 ("Hello Clyde, / May the blessing of Allah rest upon you . . ."); September 7, 1924 ("Salaam, Clyde, / You ought to be here."); Untitled ("When Napoleon down in Africa . . .") (v); Neolithic Love Song (v)*
Tom Munnerlyn, staples, May 1992
> **Contains a First Appearance**; distributed in REHUPA #115

**Austin, Volume 3, #2**

Contains *Twentieth Century Slave Trade; The Great Munney Ring; Bookmen and Books; Puritans; Sisters; Vengeance of a Woman; John L. Sullivan (v); L'Envoi(1), (2) and (3) (v); Untitled ("And Bill, he looks . . .") (v); Untitled ("Ho, merry bark, . . .") (v); My Sentiments Set to Jazz (v); What is Love? (v); Untitled ("This is a young world . . .") (v); untitled article ("MUNN! MUNN! . . ."); Le Gentil Homme le Diable; Jack Dempsey (v); A Pirut Story; Untitled ("My name is San Culotte."); Ringside Tales; miscellaneous boxing commentary*

Tom Munnerlyn, staples, September 1992

> Distributed in REHUPA #117; reprints all three issues of THE RIGHT HOOK

**Austin, Volume 3, #3**

Contains **A letter to TCS, undated ("If you dont publish . . ."); The Viking of the Sky (v)**; *Le Gentil Homme le Diable*

Tom Munnerlyn, staples, November 1992

> **Contains a First Appearance**; distributed in REHUPA #118; the untitled poem was originally handwritten on the endpapers of REH's copy of P.C. Wren's BEAU GESTE; facsimile reproduction of original letter and an issue of THE TOREADOR, June 1925

**The Ballad of King Geraint**

Contains **The Ballad of King Geraint (v)**

Gibbelins Gazette Press, staples, 1989

> **Contains a First Appearance**; limited to 70 copies; distributed in REHUPA #100

**The Ballad of Red Sonja**

Contains *Side 1 -"The Ballad of Red Sonja" by Kurt Gresham; Side 2 –"Red Sonja in the Words of Robert E. Howard" - Aural Theatre, by Frank Thorne*

Unknown publisher, 45 record, 1976

> May possibly contain some REH material on side 2

**Barbarian Scroll #6**

Contains *Out of the Deep*

Alfonso DJ Alfonso, staples, February 1989

**Barbarian Scroll #7**

Contains *Dermod's Bane*

Alfonso DJ Alfonso, staples, April 8, 1989

**Barbarian Scroll #12**

Contains *The Little People*

Alfonso DJ Alfonso, staples, April 1, 1990

**Barnswoggle #1**

Contains *Neolithic Love Song (v)*

Thomas Kovacs, staples, November 1987

> Distributed in REHUPA #88

**Beltric Writes #39**

Contains *the verse headings from The Queen of the Black Coast*

Steve Trout, staples, January 1988

> Distributed in REHUPA #89

**Beltric Writes #56**
    Contains *The Legacy of Tubal-Cain (v)*
    Steve Trout, staples, November 1991
        Distributed in REHUPA #112

**Bicentennial Tribute to REH**
    Contains **The Return of the Sorcerer***;* plus several rejection letters to REH
    George Hamilton, staples with DJ, 1976
        **Contains a First Appearance**; artwork by George Hamilton; limited to 194 copies

**Bimbos and Barbarianettes**
    Contains *Love (v)*
    Unknown publisher, staples, June 1996
        Distributed in REHUPA #139, unknown contributor

**Black Dawn**
    Contains **Black Dawn (v)**
    Roy Squires, small booklet, 1972
    **Contains a First Appearance**; limited to 234 copies; a series of five sequential untitled poems

**The Black Stranger**
    Contains *The Black Stranger*
    Wandering Star, loose pages, 2002
        A limited reproduction of the original typescript from Cross Plains Public Library, loose pages, in a folder decorated by Gary Gianni; limited to 250 numbered copies, plus 26 lettered copies to be sold by Cross Plains Public Library; penciled in editing likely by LSDC

**Blades for France**
    Contains **Blades for France**
    George Hamilton, staples with DJ, 1975
        **Contains a First Appearance**; limited to 300 copies; introduction by E. Hoffmann Price

**Blades of the Brotherhood**
    Contains **Blades of the Brotherhood (Malachi Grim version)**
    REH Foundation, loose pages in a folder, 2007
        **Contains a First Appearance**; facsimile reproduction of an original typescript; not sold, but a giveaway to Legacy Circle members of the REHF; printed on buff paper with "REHF" hand-initialed in red ink on each page

**Blufftown Barbarian #6**
    Contains *The Song of the Bats (v)*
    Dennis McHaney, staples, February 2001

**Blufftown Barbarian #8**
    Contains *Easter Island; The Gates of Ninevah; The Harp of Alfred (all v)*
    Dennis McHaney, staples, February 2001

**Boys Own Fantasy Annual**
    Contains *The Apparition in the Prize Ring*
    Graeme Flanagan, staples, November 1982
        Distributed in REHUPA #60

## Bran Mak Morn: A Play and Others
Contains ***Bran Mak Morn: A Play; The Diablos Trail; The Black Moon; Hand of the Black Goddess; Double Cross***; *Ship in Mutiny*
Cryptic Publications, staples, 1983
> **Contains a First Appearance**; title on cover is "Bran Mak Morn: A Play and Other"; 400 unnumbered copies, plus 25 numbered copies, signed by Glenn Lord, Bob Price, and Stephen Fabian; edited by Robert M. Price

## Breed of Battle
Contains *Breed of Battle*
Violet Crown Radio Players, CD, February 2005
> A CD of an actual radio play, performed live before a studio audience in Austin

## Bunyips in the Mulga #19
Contains ***a letter to Emil Petaja, March 6, 1935 ("Glad the ms. proved satisfactory.")***
Graeme Flanagan, staples, September 1984
> **Contains a First Appearance**; distributed in REHUPA #71

## The Burkburnett Papers [no number, February 2004]
Contains *Something About Eve*
Carl Osman, staples, February 2004
> Distributed in REHUPA #185

## Busted Ribs and Broken English, Volume 6, #2
Contains *The King and the Oak (v)*
David Gentzel, staples, December 2002
> Distributed in REHUPA #178

## The Cairn on the Headland
Contains *The Cairn on the Headland*
Television script, date unknown
> A television script based on the REH story; suppose to be on the list of stories, according to Karl Edward Wagner; don't know if a script was ever written; Glenn Lord has never seen one, so likely doesn't exist

## Candles
Contains ***Candles (v)***
Curmudgeon Press (Michael Horvat), staples, Late 1974 or early 1975
> **Contains a First Appearance**; limited to 45 copies, in a special envelope; unauthorized; supposedly all but 3-5 were accidentally destroyed prior to distribution, blowing out of a boat as it was going across a lake to the post office; one showed up on eBay in 12/99; Glenn Lord questions whether this is really an REH poem; poem was apparently discovered by Horvat in a book, in the Library of Amateur Journalism, claiming it was written down in a dedication in a book to or by Samuel Loveman, possibly in REH's own hand, or at least ascribed to him

Charles Garvin, staples, 1979
> Limited to 50 copies

Glenn Lord, staples, date unknown
John Melville, staples, November 1979
> Distributed as an extra with his contribution to REHUPA, HYBORIAN CHUNTERINGS #11, in mailing 42

## Certiorari Accepted #1

Contains *After the Game*
Paul Herman, staples, August 1999
    Distributed in REHUPA #158

## The Challenge from Beyond

Contains *The Challenge from Beyond*
Fantasy Amateur Press Association (Pennsylvania Dutch Cheese Press), staples, 1954
    Limited to 65 mimeographed copies

## The Challenge from Beyond

Contains *The Challenge from Beyond*
1st Edition, Necronomicon Press, staples, 1978
2nd Edition, Necronomicon Press, staples, March 1990
2nd Edition, Necronomicon Press, staples, 2nd printing, October 1997
    1st is different from 2nd and 3rd, which are the same, the 1st edition has wavy edges and the cover is made
    from a heavier stock; cover art by Robert H. Knox

## The Chronicler of Cross Plains #1

Contains *The Sign of the Snake; Casonetto's Last Song*
Damon Sasser, staples, 1978
    Includes lots of artwork, including Gene Day and a portfolio on REH characters by Arnold Fenner

## The Chronicler of Cross Plains #2

Contains *Desert Blood*
Damon Sasser (Black Coast Press), staples, June 2006
    Includes artwork by Rafael Kayanan, David Burton, Bill Cavalier, Robert Sankner, Michael L. Peters, and
    Joe Wehrle

## The Cimmerian Scroll #1

Contains *The Haunter of the Ring*
Alfonso DJ Alfonso, staples, May 1, 1988
    Allegedly CPI had a discussion with the publisher about this title, and it was changed for subsequent
    issues to THE BARBARIAN SCROLL

## Cold Steel #10

Contains *Untitled ("The baron of Fenland . . ."); Flight (lines 1-2, 5-8, 15-20, 23-24); Untitled ("The Baron of Fenland . . .")*
Indiana Bill Cavalier, staples, November 1987
    Distributed in REHUPA #88; poetry is included in a facsimile reproduction of the second page of a letter
    to TCS, ca. September 1927 ("Salaam:/ Then the little boy said . . ."); this page is in turn included in
    AMERICAN AND EUROPEAN MANUSCRIPTS AND PRINTED BOOKS, a copy of which is included
    in this zine

## Cold Steel #16

Contains *The Dust Dance (2) (lines 81-96)*
Indiana Bill Cavalier, staples, November 1988
    Distributed in REHUPA #94

## Cold Steel #119

Contains *Recompensei (v)*
Indiana Bill Cavalier, staples, February 2006
    Distributed in REHUPA #197

**Cold Steel #121**
 Contains *The Bell of Morni (v)*
 Indiana Bill Cavalier, staples, June 2006
  Distributed in REHUPA #199

**The Coming of El Borak**
 Contains *The Coming of El Borak; Khoda Khan's Tale; The Iron Terror; Untitled ("Gordon, the American . . ."); El Borak ("I emptied my revolver . . .")*
 Cryptic Publications, staples, September 1987
  **Contains a First Appearance**; cover by Stephen Fabian; introduction by Robert M. Price; edited by Robert M. Price

**The Complete Yellow Jacket**
 Contains *Halt! Who Goes There?; After the Game; Sleeping Beauty; Weekly Short Story; Private Magrath of the A.E.F. (v); The Thessalians; Ye College Days; Cupid v. Pollux; The Reformation: A Dream*
 Hermanthis Press (Paul Herman), staples, December 1999
  Limited to 99 copies, though listed as 100; on acid-free paper, with acid-free jacket, no artwork; off-white cover; also a very limited set of Presentation Copies, only 8 lettered copies, using Turkish Marbled Paper, Spanish Marine design; 2<sup>nd</sup> edition is formatted significantly differently, perfect bound instead of staples, slightly larger size, yellow cover, two small changes in two footnotes, and is listed in the BOOKS list

**Conan and the Big Isle**
 Contains *the verse heading from The Pool of the Black One*
 Unknown publisher, staples, November 1989
  Distributed in REHUPA #100, unknown contributor

**Conan: Queen of the Black Coast**
 Contains *The Song of Belit (v)*
 Stephen Fabian, portfolio, 1976
  Seven plates; limited to 1000 copies

**Costigan #19**
 Contains *Notes for A Gent from Bear Creek*
 Glenn Lord, staples, July 1978
  Distributed in REHUPA #47

**Costigan #24**
 Contains *The Tempter (v) (lines 31-40)*
 Glenn Lord, staples, September 1980
  Reprint of DALLAS MORNING NEWS article, distributed in REHUPA #47

**Costigan Special #1**
 Contains *The Seven-Up Ballad (v)*
 Glenn Lord, staples, November 1982
  **Contains a First Appearance**; distributed in REHUPA #60

**The Count of Thirty: A Tribute to Ramsey Campbell**
 Contains *Which Will Scarcely Be Understood (v) (lines 42-45)*
 Necronomicon Press, staples, 1993

## CromLech #1

Contains *Spectres in the Dark*
Marc A. Cerasini, staples, Spring 1985
> **Contains a First Appearance**; cover art by Stephen Fabian; later possibly distributed by Cryptic Publications

## CromLech #2

Contains *Shadow in the Well (synopsis only)*
Marc A. Cerasini, staples, Fall 1987
> **Contains a First Appearance**; edited by Marc A. Cerasini; in the introduction Cerasini acknowledges that this volume is being published via Robert M. Price, who was Cryptic Publications, but not a Cryptic book

## CromLech #3

Contains *Snout in the Dark (synopsis)*; *Drums of Tombulku (synopsis)*; *Bran Mak Morn: A Play*; **Bran Mak Morn (synopsis) ("The story of a forgotten age . . .")**; *The Diablos Trail;* **Wolfsdung**; *The Vultures of Whapeton (alternate ending)*
Cryptic Publications, staples, 1988
> **Contains a First Appearance**; also contains a thorough listing of REH stories; "The Diablos Trail" has a sentence left out, on page 14, the fifth line down should read: "'Not if you tries the Diablos,' says he, pessimistic.", that sentence should follow "I'll be seein' you.", but it is gone in this printing; edited by Robert M. Price

## The Cross Plainsman [no number, October 2003]

Contains *Roads (v); Adventurer (v)*
Frank Coffman, staples, October 2003
> Distributed in REHUPA #183

## The Cross Plainsman [no number, August 2004]

Contains **Untitled ("Out of Asia the tribesmen came . . .")**; *Destiny ("What is there real . . .")*; **Adventure ("I am the spur . . .")**; **Nun**; *Adventurer;* **Poet; Monarchs; The Ballad of Abe Slickenmore; Untitled ("Scarlet and gold are the stars tonight", last four lines only)** *(all v)*
Frank Coffman, staples, August 2004
> **Contains a First Appearance**; distributed in REHUPA #188

## The Cross Plainsman [no number, December 2005]

Contains *The Challenge from Beyond*
Frank Coffman, staples, December 2005
> Distributed in REHUPA #196

## The Cross Plainsman [no number, April 2006]

Contains *The Soul-Eater (v); The Dream and the Shadow (v); The Last Hour (v); Haunting Columns (v); The Singer in the Mist (v)*
Frank Coffman, staples, April 2006
> Distributed in REHUPA #298

## The Cross Plainsman [no number, August 2006]

Contains *Ocean-Thoughts (v)*
Frank Coffman, staples, August 2006
> **Contains a First Appearance**; distributed in REHUPA #200

**The Cross Plainsman [no number, December 2006]**
> Contains *The Ghost King" (v); The One Black Stain (v); Marching Song of Connacht (v); The Song of the Mad Minstrel (v); The Song of the Last Briton (v); An Echo From an Iron Harp (v)*
> Frank Coffman, staples, December 2006
> > Distributed in REHUPA #202

**The Cross Plainsman, Volume 2003, #1**
> Contains *The Harp of Alfred (v)*
> Frank Coffman, staples, April 2003
> > Distributed in REHUPA #180

**Crypt of Cthulhu #3**
> Contains *the verse heading from The Black Stone*
> Cryptic Publications, staples, Candlemas 1982
> > Edited by Robert M. Price; verse appears in two different articles

**Crypt of Cthulhu #16**
> Contains ***The Hand of Obeah***
> Cryptic Publications, staples, Michaelmas (September) 1983
> > **Contains a First Appearance**; edited by Robert M. Price

**Crypt of Cthulhu #22**
> Contains ***The Fear-Master***
> Cryptic Publications, staples, Roodmas 1984
> > **Contains a First Appearance**; edited by Robert M. Price

**Crypt of Cthulhu #25**
> Contains ***The Supreme Moment***
> Cryptic Publications, staples, Michaelmas 1984
> > **Contains a First Appearance**; edited by Robert M. Price

**Crypt of Cthulhu #31**
> Contains ***Golnor the Ape***
> Cryptic Publications, staples, Roodmas 1985
> > **Contains a First Appearance**

**Crypt of Cthulhu #39**
> Contains ***The Voice of Doom***
> Cryptic Publications, staples, April 1986
> > **Contains a First Appearance**

**Crypt of Cthulhu #47**
> Contains ***The Mark of a Bloody Hand***
> Cryptic Publications, staples, April 1987
> > **Contains a First Appearance**

**Crypt of Cthulhu #105**
> Contains *Death's Black Riders*
> Mythos Books, staples, 2002

**Dark Fantasy #9**
> Contains *The Road to Yesterday*
> Unknown publisher, unknown format, September 1976
>> Illustrated by Stephen Fabian, Roy Krenkel, and Gene Day; published in Canada

**Dark Fantasy #11**
> Contains *Visions (v)*
> Unknown publisher, unknown format, 1977
>> A Canadian fanzine

**Dark Fantasy #16**
> Contains *The Ghost Kings*
> Unknown publisher, unknown format, June 1978
>> Published in Canada

**The Dark Man #1**
> Contains ***The Frost-Giant's Daughter (early draft)****; and a letter to TCS, ca. May 1928 ("Salaam: / So Klatt has gone West.")*
> Necronomicon Press, staples, August 1990
>> **Contains a First Appearance**; cover by Indiana Bill Cavalier

**The Dark Man #2**
> Contains ***Bill Smalley and the Power of the Human Eye***
> Necronomicon Press, staples, July 1991
>> **Contains a First Appearance**; cover by Robert H. Knox

**The Dark Man #3**
> Contains *What the Nation Owes the South*
> Necronomicon Press, staples, April 1993
>> Cover art by Jason Eckhardt

**Dark Phantasms #1**
> Contains *The Black Hound of Death*
> VW Studios (Gary Dolmorn), staples, Summer 1976
>> Artwork by Roy Krenkel and others; edited by Bill Whitcomb; limited to 1600 copies

**Dear August: Letters, Robert E. Howard to August Derleth, 1932-1936**
> Contains *several letters to August Derleth, including:*
> ***ca. December (15?) 1932 ("I had intended answering . . .")***
> *ca. December (29?) 1932 ("I read your recent letter with the greatest interest . . .")*
> *ca. January 1933 ("I was much interested in your accounts . . .")*
> *ca. February 1933 ("After so long a time, I'm getting around to answering . . .")*
> *ca. March 1933 ("I should have told you that I meant to keep . . .")*
> ***ca. March 13, 1933 ("Many thanks for FRONTIER GENERATIONS . . .")***
> *ca. May 1933 ("As a starter, I must apologize . . .")*
> ***July 3, 1933 ("Please accept my belated thanks . . .")***
> *ca. July 1933 ("Thanks immensely for the opportunity of reading . . .")*
> ***ca. August 1933 ("Yes, I certainly did enjoy 'Five Alone' . . .")***
> ***September 4, 1933 ("Glad you liked the rhyme I sent you.")***
> *ca. October 1933 ("Thanks very much for the opportunity of reading . . .")*
> ***ca. October 1933 ("By all means use the hawk incident . . .")***
> *ca. November 1933 ("I enjoyed reading your 'Hawk on the Blue' very much . . .")*
> *ca. December 1933 ("I think Scribner's was nuts to turn down 'Hawk on . . .")*

*ca. December 1933 ("Hope you had a good Christmas . . .")*
*ca. January 1934 ("I note with sympathy your remarks . . .")*
*ca. late March 1934 ("Pardon this belated letter . . .")*
*May 30 1934 ("I have a feeling that I've been owing . . .")*
*ca. June 1934 ("Having completed several weeks of . . .")*
*ca. mid-October 1934 ("I haven't yet gotten a copy . . .")*
*December 11, 1934 ("I recently found your letter of October 18 in my file . . .")*
*ca. February 1935 ("I would have written you long ago . . .")*
*ca. June 1935 ("I reckon you've wondered at times . . .")*
*July 4, 1935 ("Thanks very much for the article, 'Afternoon in June.' . . .")*
*November 1, 1935 ("I should have written you months ago . . .")*
*November 28, 1935 ("Thanks for the opportunity of reading . . .")*
*April 15, 1936 ("Just a hurried line to let you know . . .")*
*May 9, 1936 ("I am indeed sorry to learn of the deaths . . .")*
REH Properties, tape binding, 2002

> **Contains a First Appearance**; texts are Glenn Lord's transcriptions from the original letters; this collection includes all the letter to August Derleth, except for a postcard REH sent to August Derleth; each of these books were cheaply created, tape bound with card stock covers, likely copied down at a copy shop, to try and create a publication for US copyright purposes, no information on number of copies created, likely less than ten actually distributed

## Dear HPL: Letters, Robert E. Howard to H.P. Lovecraft, 1930-1936

Contains *several letters to HPL, including:*
*ca. July 1, 1930 ("I am indeed highly honored to have received . . .")*
*August 1930 ("Let me first thank you for the opportunity . . .")*
*September 1930 (1) ("I envy you your sojourn to Quebec.")*
*September 1930 (2) ("I am very glad that you enjoyed your visit . . .")*
*October 1930 ("It is with greatest delight that I learn . . .")*
*December 1930 ("As always, your letter proved highly . . .")*
**January 1931 ("As always, I found your recent letter . . .")**
*January 1931 ("This is rather a belated letter thanking . . .")*
**February 1931 ("I highly appreciate . . .")**
**February 1931 ("I'm writing this letter . . .")**
*June 1931 ("I didn't take much of a trip after all.")*
**July 14 1931 ("Just a line . . .")**
**August 1931 ("You must indeed . . .")**
*October 1931 ("Thanks for the post-card views.")*
**October 1931 ("I intended to answer . . .")**
**December 9, 1931 ("I would have answered . . .")**
**January 1932 ("Yes, I enjoyed the postcards . . .")**
**ca. March 2, 1932 ("I was extremely interested in your comment . . .")**
**April 1932 ("At last I've gotten around . . .")**
**May 24, 1932 ("Glad you liked the Oriental story . . .")**
**July 13, 1932 ("It is with the utmost humiliation . . .")**
**August 9, 1932 ("I am very sorry to hear of your recent . . .")**
*September 22, 1932 ("I read, as always, your comments on . . .")*
**ca. October 1932 ("I hope you decide . . .")**
**November 1932 ("Here's a clipping . . .")**
**December 1932 ("Having read your latest letter . . .")**
**March 6, 1933 ("I have just read your recent letter . . .")**
**April 23, 1933 ("I'm enclosing some of the latest views . . .")**
*July 1933 ("Glad we got the physical/mental question . . .")*
**September & October 1933 ("I was very sorry to hear . . .")**
*November 3, 1933 ("Glad you liked the rattles.")*
**November 1933 ("I am so submerged in work . . .")**

*January 1934 ("I enjoyed very much . . .")*
*January 1934 ("I deeply appreciate . . .")*
*March 24, 1934 ("Here's a little item . . .")*
*May 1934 ("Glad you're having a good time in Florida.")*
*June 1934 ("Glad you're finding . . .")*
*July 1934 ("I started writing this months ago . . .")*
*September 1934 ("Thanks very much for the postcards . . .")*
*December 1934 ("I read your account . . .")*
*December 1934 ("Glad you found the cat article . . .")*
*October 3, 1935 ("Here are some clippings . . .")*
*February 11, 1936 ("Glad you enjoyed the dream write-up I sent you.")*
*May 13, 1936 ("I am indeed sorry to hear . . .") (first complete publication)*
REH Properties, tape binding, 2002

> **Contains a First Appearance**; most are copies of original documents, others are Glenn Lord's transcriptions, may or may not be edited; only contains 44 of the original 53 letters to HPL, so still some unpublished; several pages have words cut off at right or bottom; each of these books were cheaply created, tape bound with card stock covers, likely copied down at a copy shop, to try and create a publication for US copyright purposes, no information on number of copies created, likely less than ten actually distributed

## Deeper Than You Think #1

Contains *Untitled article (". . . which has characterized . . .")*; ***The Celtica Notes of Robert E. Howard***
Joel Frieman, staples, January 1968

> **Contains a First Appearance**; published by Joel Frieman, edited by Frieman and Bob Weinberg, 8.5X11, apparently pretty scholarly; limited to 100 copies; "The Celtica Notes of Robert E. Howard" is a facsimile reproduction of REH's original notes

## Delirium Tremens #1 (Spanish)

Contains *A Song of the Race (v)*
Unknown publisher, staples, November 1986

## Delirium Tremens #3 (Spanish)

Contains *Tarantella (v) (lines 32-37)*
Unknown publisher, staples, November 1, 1992

## Desire and Other Erotic Poems

Contains ***Desire***; *Lilith; The Dust Dance (1) (lines 53-72 only, untitled); A Challenge to Bast; Palace of Bast;* ***A Negro Girl; Limericks to Spank By;*** *The Harlot; The Ballad of Singapore Nell;* ***Good Mistress Brown; The Myth***; *A Song for All Women; Strange Passion;* ***Lesbia***; *Daughter of Evil*
Charles Hoffman, staples, 1989

> **Contains a First Appearance**; extensive illustrations by Frank Frazetta, distributed in REHUPA #100, in his zine ADEQUATE ADVENTURE STORIES #4

## The Destiny Gorilla

Contains *Sailor Dorgan and the Destiny Gorilla*
Violet Crown Radio Players, CD, February 2004

> A CD of an actual radio play, performed live before a studio audience in Austin; available in both a regular CD case as well as advance copy in a black-and-white paper sleeve; cover is from JACK DEMPSEY'S FIGHT MAGAZINE, August 1934

## The Diversifier, Volume 3, #4 (whole #20)

Contains *Sea Curse*
Castle Publications, staples, May 1977
70 page chapbook, artwork by Allen Koszowski, Mark Gelotte, A. B. Cox, Gary Kato, and Stephen Riley

## Dragonfields #3

Contains *The Sands of the Desert (v)*
Charles L. Saunders ("Triskell Press"), staples, Summer 1980
Canadian semi-pro zine

## Dreams from Yohaneth-Lahai #38

Contains *a letter to Denis Archer, May 20, 1934 ("As you doubtless remember, in your letter . . .")*
Unknown publisher, staples, January 1988
Distributed in REHUPA #89, unknown contributor

## The Eastern Kingdom Songbook

Contains *the verse heading from Chapters 2 and 5 of The Phoenix on the Sword; the verse heading from Chapter 2 of The Scarlet Citadel*
Unknown publisher, unknown format, 1980
Goes at least through a 3$^{rd}$ edition

## Echoes from the Black Stone #12

Contains *Easter Island (v) (Lines 9-14)*
Crispin Burnham, staples, July 1979
Distributed in REHUPA #40

## Ein Traumer Aus Texas (German)

Contains ***A Dungeon Opens***; *The Rhyme of the Three Slavers; Always Comes Evening; The Bride of Cuchulain; Candles; Cimmeria (lines 27-32); Crete (lines 1-4); Fragment ("And so his boyhood . . .") (lines 1-28 only); The Ghost Ocean; A Hairy-Chested Idealist Sings; The Heart of the Sea's Desire (lines 1-12, 17-24, embodied in article titled "Ein Traumer Aus Texas"); Hope Empty of Meaning; Invective; Lines Written in the Realization that I Must Die (lines 5-8, 13-16, 21-24); verse headings from Men of the Shadows; The Men That Walk with Satan; Moon Mockery; Moonlight on a Skull; Musings ("The little poets . . ."); Niflheim; The One Black Stain; Recompense; The Return of Sir Richard Grenville; The Rhyme of the Three Slavers; The Ride of Falume; Rune; Shadows; The Skull in the Clouds; Slumber; Solomon Kane's Homecoming; The Song of the Bats; A Song of the Race; A Song Out of Midian; The Stranger; The Tempter; A Warning (lines 1-4 of Howard Collector version); Where Are Your Knights, Donn Othna?; Which Will Scarcely Be Understood; White Thunder; Zukala's Hour; the verse headings from The Queen of the Black Coast (all v)*
Unknown publisher, HB and PB, 1987
**Contains a First Appearance**

## A Elkins Never Surrenders

Contains ***A Elkins Never Surrenders***
David Gentzel, staples, August 2006
Produced for REHupa #200; a booklet that contains an early draft of this story

## Etchings and Odysseys #1

Contains ***Casanetto's Last Song***; *Babel (v); Rune (v)*
Eric Carlson, staples, 1973
**Contains a First Appearance**

## Etchings and Odysseys #9
Contains *Drum Gods (v); The Gods Remember (v)*
Randy Everts, staples, 1986
**Contains a First Appearance**

## Etchings and Odysseys #10
Contains *A Song of the Werewolf Folk (v)*
Randy Everts, staples, 1987
**Contains a First Appearance**

## Etchings in Ivory
Contains *Proem; Flaming Marble; Skulls and Orchids; Medallions in the Moon; The Gods that Men Forgot; Bloodstones and Ebony*
Glenn Lord, staples, 1968
> **Contains a First Appearance**; limited to 268 copies; all these are "prose poetry"; there is a second forgery edition, which can be spotted in that the forgery has REH's name on the jacket in upper and lowercase letters, while the original has REH's name in uppercase only; introduction by Donald Fryer

Hall Publications (Wayne Warfield), staples, 1975
> Reprint of Glenn Lord's original chapbook; limited to 500 copies

## Expecting the Barbarians, #8
Contains *The King and the Oak (v) (lines 4-24)*
Steve Tompkins, staples, February 1997
> Distributed in REHUPA #143

## Fanciful Tales, Volume 1, #1
Contains *Solomon Kane's Homecoming (v)*
Necronomicon, staples, 1977
> This is a facsimile reprint done by Marc Michaud in 1977 of the original 1936 magazine; the way to tell them apart is this reprint has a new intro that makes clear its recent state, as well as a copyright notice dated 1977

## Fantasia #11/12 (German)
Contains *The Men That Walk with Satan; The Skull in the Clouds; The Song of the Bats; The Tempter (all v)*
Unknown publisher, staples, November 1981
> A fanzine

## Fantome #1
Contains *The Hashish Land*
David Parsons, staples, October 1978
**Contains a First Appearance**

## Fear Dunn #1
Contains *A Song for All Women (v)*
Glenn Lord, staples, March 1984
> Distributed in REHUPA #68, Glenn Lord

## The Flaming Circle of Troglis #8
Contains *The Tempter (v) (lines 17-20)*
Unknown publisher, staples, January 1983
> Distributed in REHUPA #61, unknown contributor

## The Flaming Circle of Troglis #14
Contains *the verse heading from Chapter 4 of The Phoenix on the Sword*
Unknown publisher, staples, January 1984
> Distributed in REHUPA #67, unknown contributor

## From the Hells Beneath the Hells
Contains *The Song of a Mad Minstrel (v); The Curse of the Golden Skull; Altars and Jesters - An Opium Dream (v); The Mirrors of Tuzun Thune*
Alternate World Recordings, LP record, 1975
> First (and possibly only) pressing limited to 1050 copies; dramatic readings by Ugo Toppo; Jeff Jones cover; there is also a booklet in the album with the complete text of the recording

## The Garden of Fear and Other Stories of the Bizarre and Fantastic
Contains *The Garden of Fear*
William L. Crawford, staples, 1945
> Cover art by Alva Rogers; edited by William L. Crawford; cover comes in numerous different colors, including at least green, blue and yellow; allegedly Crawford had a deal to get these distributed in magazines, and produced 15,000, but the deal fell through, and he spent the rest of his life trying to unload them

## The Ghost Ocean and Other Poems of the Supernatural
Contains **The Isle of Hy-Brasil**; *The One Black Stain;* **Viking's Vision; To All Sophisticates; Man Am I; Never Beyond the Beast; Shadows from Yesterday; The Ghost Ocean; The Song of the Last Briton; The Gates of Babylon; Lilith; Two Men; Memories of Alfred; To a Woman ("Ages ago . . ."); When the Glaciers Rumbled South;** *Candles;* **Shadow Thing**; *Song of the Pict;* **The Flood; The Adventurer's Mistress** (all v)
Gibbelins Gazette Press, staples, 1982
> **Contains a First Appearance**; limited to 360 copies, the first 50 are hardback, and listed in the BOOKS section; many of these poems have never been reprinted; cover by Charles E. Williams, Jr., interior illustrations by Rick McCollum, Charles E. Williams, Jr., and Steve Trout; the publisher also distributed some of these in REHUPA #60

## Glenn Lord's Ultima Thule
Contains *letters to Hugh G. Schoenfield, June 15, 1933 ("As I promised, . . ."); to Denis Archer, May 20, 1934 ("As you doubtless remember, . . .")*
Joe Marek, staples, 2001
> A reprinting of the entire ULTIMA THULE series, all six issues; also contains several rejection letters to REH, some foreign publication listings, the contents of REH's library, and how much REH was paid for his stories during his lifetime; the first printing was only 15 copies; a 2nd edition by Rob Roehm is listed in the ANTHOLOGIES section

## The Gold and the Grey
Contains **The Gold and the Grey (v)**
Roy Squires, small booklet, 1974
> **Contains a First Appearance**; limited to 218 copies

## The Golden Caliph
Contains **Untitled poem ("When wolf meets wolf, . . ."); Untitled story ("A Cossack and a Turk . . ."); Kublai Khan (v); Jazz Music; The Sword; The Follower (v); Young Lockanbars (v); Spears of the East (fragment)**
Robert E. Howard, staples, ca. 1922 or 1923
> **Contains a First Appearance**; REH's own amateur magazine; apparently only one issue; reprinted in THE LAST CELT

## Golden Fleece (November 1938)
Contains *Black Vulmea's Vengeance*
Girasol Collectables, pulp format, September 2006
> Replica of original pulp magazine

## "Golden Hope" Christmas
Contains *"Golden Hope" Christmas*
Shirt Pocket Press (Dennis McHaney), staples, Christmas 2002
> Limited to 100 copies, some for REHUPA; cover and frontispiece by J. Allen St. John

## The Grey God Passes
Contains *The Grey God Passes*
Charles F. Miller, staples, 1975
> Art by Walter Simonson

## The Grim Land & Others
Contains ***The Devil's Woodchopper (completed by TCS); Nectar; The Grim Land; The Gods of the Jungle Drums; De Ole River Ox; The Road to Yesterday; The Adventurer; To an Earthbound Soul; The Outcast; Today; A Pirate Remembers (all v except for the first piece)***
Stygian Isle Press (Jonathan Bacon), staples, 1976
> **Contains a First Appearance**; limited to 450 copies; front cover by Lee Brown Coye, back cover by Broc Sears, illustrations by Randall Spurgin, KW Raney III, Gene Day, Stephen Fabian, Frank A. Circocco, Broc Sears, Robert K. Oermann, Richard Huber, Jr.; introduction by TCS, edited by Jonathan Bacon

## Hardwired Hinterland #6
Contains *The Song of Horsa's Galley (v); A Word from the Outer Dark (v)*
Rich Jervis, staples, Spring 1989

## Hardwired Hinterland #7
Contains *The Heart of the Sea's Desire (v, lines 1-8 only); verse headings from Men of the Shadows (v); Solomon Kane's Homecoming (v) (lines 21-32); The Tempter (v) (lines 27-40); the verse heading from Red Blades of Black Cathay*
Rich Jervis, staples, June 1994
> Distributed in REHUPA #127

## Hardwired Hinterland #8
Contains *Cimmeria (v); Recompense (v)*
Rich Jervis, staples, Ca. 1991
> Distributed in REHUPA

## Hardwired Hinterland, Volume 2, #7
Contains *Always Comes Evening (v); The Song of a Mad Minstrel (v)*
Rich Jervis, staples, December 1994
> Distributed in REHUPA #130

## The Horror from the Mound
Contains *The Horror from the Mound*
Television script, date unknown
> Written by Karl Edward Wagner and based on the REH story, for the television show Darkroom; likely around 1980 or 1981; never produced

## The Howard Reader #8

Contains Stories: *The Slave-Princess; Taverel Manor; The Mystery of Tannernoe Lodge; The House; Sailor Dorgan and the Turkish Menace; The Guardian of the Idol*; Poetry: *Ecstacy; Men Build Them Houses; A Hairy-Chested Idealist Sings; The Adventurer; To a Woman ("Ages ago . . ."); The Grim Land; Shadows from Yesterday; The Gods of the Jungle Drums; When the Glaciers Rumbled South; Nectar; To the Evangelists; The Outgoing of Sigurd the Jerusalem-Farer; The Ghost Ocean; De Ole River Ox; The Road to Yesterday; Man Am I; Alien*; Essays: *A Touch of Trivia; An Autobiography*; plus letters to: *Weird Tales, June 1936 ("Enthusiasm impels me . . ."); Emil Petaja, December 17, 1934 ("Thank you very much for the splendid sonnet."); Novalyne Price, February 15, 1936 ("I'm sorry but I won't be able . . .")*

Joe Marek, staples, August 2003

> This series was formerly titled THE NEW HOWARD READER; quantity printed unknown, likely less than 200

## The Howard Review #1

Contains *The Fearsome Touch of Death*

Dennis McHaney, staples, 1st Edition, December 1974

> 1st limited to 204 copies, described as "poorly mimeographed"; artwork by Tom Foster; introduction by McHaney; there is also a limited HB set of 25 copies of this edition, listed in the ANTHOLOGIES

Dennis McHaney, staples, 2nd Edition, October 1975

> 2nd is significantly modified from 1st edition; 2nd edition adds *Dead Man's Hate (v); A Thunder of Trumpets; Moon Mockery (v)*; additional artwork included from Stephen Fabian and Roy Krenkel; limited to 600 copies

Dennis McHaney, staples, 2nd Edition, 2nd printing, January 1976

> An additional 500 copies

## The Howard Review #2

Contains *Vikings of the Glove; The Riot at Bucksnort;* **Riding Song (v); Song Before Clontarf (v); Untitled ("It was the end . . ."); Untitled ("The night Sailor Steve . . ."); Untitled ("I had just hung . . .")**

Dennis McHaney, newspaper format, March 1975

> **Contains a First Appearance**; printed on newsprint, very large format, lots of art by Tom Foster; limited to 1790 copies

## The Howard Review #3

Contains *The Beast from the Abyss; The Reformation: A Dream; The Soul-Eater (v)*

Dennis McHaney, staples, June 1975

> Cover is a REH photo that first appeared in an insert in Fantasy Magazine, September 1936; physically a small book, limited to 500 copies

## The Howard Review #4

Contains *The TNT Punch; Singing in the Wind (v)*

Dennis McHaney, staples, September 1975

> Sent out in a decorated envelope, along with a collection of Roy Krenkel material; illustrations by Stephen Fabian, Frank Frazetta and Tom Foster

## The Howard Review #5

Contains *The Noseless Horror;* **The Passionate Typist (v)**

Dennis McHaney, staples, November 1976

> **Contains a First Appearance**; artwork by Roy Krenkel, Frank Frazetta, Arnold Fenner, and Marcus Boas

## The Howard Review #7
Contains **Sailor Costigan and the Swami**
Dennis McHaney, staples, April 1977
**Contains a First Appearance**

## The Howard Review #11
Contains **Thoroughbreds; Lives and Crimes of Notable Artists**
Dennis McHaney, staples, February-May 1995
**Contains a First Appearance**; artwork by Rick McCollum; while the pub date on the book is in 1995, it was actually published in July 1998

## HPL: A Magazine of Tribute to Howard Phillips Lovecraft (1890-1937)
Contains *Who Is Grandpa Theobold? (v)*
Meade & Penny Frierson, staples, March 28, 1972
Published by Meade and Penny Frierson, limited to 1000 copies of first printing, 500 of second, a tribute magazine for HPL, only one issue, staple bound

## The Hyborian Age
Contains *The Hyborian Age*
LANY Cooperative, staples, 1938

## The Hyborian Age
Contains **a letter to Emil Petaja, September 6, 1935 ("Yes, I did like . . .")**
Unknown publisher, staples, April 1977
**Contains a First Appearance**; distributed in THE HYPERBOREAN LEAGUE #7, unknown contributor

## Hyborian Chunterings #6
Contains *Candles (v)*
John Melville, staples, September 1978
Distributed in REHUPA 35

## The Illustrated Gods of the North
Contains *Gods of the North*
Necronomicon Press, staples, 1977
Illustrated by Mark King; limited to 750 copies; tipped in REH photo

## In Memorium: Conan the Barbarian, 1970-1993
Contains *Futility ("Golden goats . . .") (lines 28-30)*
Unknown publisher, staples, October 1993
In REHUPA #123, unknown contributor

## In the Tombs of Khemi
Contains *a letter to Argosy All-Story Weekly, ca. Spring 1929 ("I was born in Texas about twenty-three . . .")*
Bill Whitaker, staples, July 1976
For REHUPA #22

## Incredible Adventures #1
Contains *Desert Blood*
Weinburg, staples, 1977
Edited by Gene Marshall and Carl F. Waedt

## The Iron Harp
Contains *The Song of a Mad Minstrel (v)*
Unknown publisher, staples, September 1978
> Distributed in REHUPA #35, unknown contributor

## Iron Legions, Volume 3, #3
Contains *The Man with the Mystery Mitts*
Chris Gruber, staples, December 2004
> Distributed in REHUPA #190

## Iron Legions, Volume 5, #2
Contains *a letter to The Ring Magazine, ca. 1926 ("Here is my opinion . . .")*
Chris Gruber, staples, June 2006
> Distributed in REHUPA #199

## Is #6
Contains *A Warning (partial v); plus* **nine letters to August Derleth including:**
*ca. December (29?) 1932 ("I read your recent letter with the greatest interest . . .")*
*ca. February 1933 ("After so long a time, I'm getting around to answering . . .")*
*ca. March 1933 ("I should have told you that I meant to keep . . .")*
*ca. October 1933 ("Thanks very much for the opportunity of reading . . .")*
*ca. November 1933 ("I enjoyed reading your 'Hawk on the Blue' very much . . .")*
*ca. December 1933 ("I think Scribner's was nuts to turn down 'Hawk on . . .")*
*December 11, 1934 ("I recently found your letter of October 18 in my file . . .")*
*July 4, 1935 ("Thanks very much for the article, 'Afternoon in June.'")*
*May 9, 1936 ("I am indeed sorry to learn of the deaths . . .")*
Unknown publisher, staples, September 1972
> **Contains a First Appearance**; one or more of these are facsimile reproductions of original letters; the poem is in the last letter

## Isaacson's Legacy, Volume 1, #20
Contains *a letter to HPL, ca. July 1934 ("I started writing . . . ")*
Danny Street, staples, June 2006
> Distributed in REHUPA #199

## Isle of Pirates' Doom
Contains *Isle of Pirates' Doom*
George Hamilton, staples with DJ, 1975
> **Contains a First Appearance**; limited to 302 copies; artwork by Stephen Fabian; introduction by Fred Blosser

## Ixion Unbound #5
Contains *a reprint of an issue of "Reina de la Costa Negra", a Mexican comic book about The Queen of the Black Coast*
Stygian Isle Press (Jonathan Bacon), staples, May 1976
> Distributed in REHUPA #21

## Jack Dempsey's Fight Magazine (May 1934)
Contains *The Slugger's Game*
Adventure House, pulp style, 2005
> A facsimile reproduction of the original pulp

## The Junto, September 1928

Contains *Surrender! Your Money or Your Vice; Them; Age (v)*

The Junto, single sheet, September 1928

> **Contains a First Appearance**; a circular mailing that went between several people who called themselves The Junto, each adding some content; only one original copy of each; several are currently lost, including those held by Lenore Preece, and those held by TCS; Glenn Lord has copies of all or most; all works are first appearance

## The Junto, October 1928

Contains *More Evidences of the Innate Divinity of Man; A Hairy-Chested Idealist Sings (v)*

The Junto, single sheet, October 1928

> **Contains a First Appearance**; a circular mailing that went between several people who called themselves The Junto, each adding some content; only one original copy of each; several are currently lost, including those held by Lenore Preece, and those held by TCS; Glenn Lord has copies of all or most; all works are first appearance

## The Junto, December 1928

Contains *The Galveston Affair; A Song for Men that Laugh (v); To the Evangelists (v)*

The Junto, single sheet, December 1928

> **Contains a First Appearance**; a circular mailing that went between several people who called themselves The Junto, each adding some content; only one original copy of each; several are currently lost, including those held by Lenore Preece, and those held by TCS; Glenn Lord has copies of all or most; all works are first appearance

## The Junto, January 1929

Contains *Ambition by Moonlight*

The Junto, single sheet, January 1929

> **Contains a First Appearance**; a circular mailing that went between several people who called themselves The Junto, each adding some content; only one original copy of each; several are currently lost, including those held by Lenore Preece, and those held by TCS; Glenn Lord has copies of all or most; all works are first appearance

## The Junto, July 1929

Contains *Hate's Dawn; The King and the Mallet; Singing in the Wind (all v)*

The Junto, single sheet, July 1929

> **Contains a First Appearance**; a circular mailing that went between several people who called themselves The Junto, each adding some content; only one original copy of each; several are currently lost, including those held by Lenore Preece, and those held by TCS; Glenn Lord has copies of all or most; all works are first appearance

## The Junto, August 1929

Contains *Heritage ("My people . . .") (v); Surrender ("I will rise . . .") (v)*

The Junto, single sheet, August 1929

> **Contains a First Appearance**; a circular mailing that went between several people who called themselves The Junto, each adding some content; only one original copy of each; several are currently lost, including those held by Lenore Preece, and those held by TCS; Glenn Lord has copies of all or most; all works are first appearance

## The Junto, September 1929

Contains *Midnight; Sentiment; Musings; Nectar (v)*

The Junto, single sheet, September 1929

> **Contains a First Appearance**; a circular mailing that went between several people who called themselves The Junto, each adding some content; only one original copy of each; several are currently lost, including

those held by Lenore Preece, and those held by TCS; Glenn Lord has copies of all or most; all works are first appearance

## The Junto, January 1930
Contains *The Skull in the Clouds (v); Feach Air Muir Lionadhi Gealach Buidhe Mar Or (v)*
The Junto, single sheet, January 1930
> **Contains a First Appearance**; a circular mailing that went between several people who called themselves The Junto, each adding some content; only one original copy of each; several are currently lost, including those held by Lenore Preece, and those held by TCS; Glenn Lord has copies of all or most; all works are first appearance

## The Junto, unknown date
Contains *Swings and Swings (v)*
The Junto, single sheet, date unknown
> **Contains a First Appearance**; a circular mailing that went between several people who called themselves The Junto, each adding some content; only one original copy of each; several are currently lost, including those held by Lenore Preece, and those held by TCS; Glenn Lord has copies of all or most; all works are first appearance; Glenn Lord does NOT have a copy of this one, instead, the poem was found in the LSDC papers at the Harry Ransom Center at the University of Texas, Austin, listing it as being from THE JUNTO

## Kadath #1
Contains *A Word from the Outer Dark (v)*
Lin Carter, staples, 1974
> **Contains a First Appearance**; 24 page booklet, very rare, was suppose to be a new magazine, subscription money taken, then never came out, though a few were apparently handed out at a convention

## The Keltic Journal, Volume 21
Contains *Recompense (v)*
Scotty Henderson, staples, October 2004
> Distributed in REHUPA #189

## The King's Service
Contains *The King's Service*
George Hamilton, staples with DJ, 1975
> **Contains a First Appearance**; limited to 310 copies; artwork by Stephen Fabian; introduction by Richard Tierney

## The Last of the Trunk Och Brev I Urval
Contains *Blue River Blues; The Battling Sailor; **The Drawing Card; The Jinx; The Wildcat and the Star; Fistic Psychology; Untitled ("Huh?" I was so dumbfounded . . .); Fighting Nerves; The Atavist; A Man of Peace**; The Weeping Willow; The Right Hook; **A Tough Nut to Crack; The Trail of the Snake; The Folly of Conceit; The Fighting Fury; Night Encounter; The Ferocious Ape**; The Ghost Behind the Gloves; **Misto Dempsey; The Brand of Satan; Incongruity; The Slayer; The Man Who Went Back; Untitled Synopsis (Hunwulf, an American . . .); Untitled (Thure Khan gazed out . . .); Untitled (As he approached . . .); A Room in London (outline); The Shadow in the Well (draft); Fate is the Killer; The Grove of Lovers; The Drifter; The Lion Gate; Untitled (Franey was a fool.); The Ivory Camel; Wolves – and a Sword; Untitled (I'm a man of few words . . .); Untitled Synopsis (First Draft: James Norris . . .); The Dominant Male; The Paradox; Untitled (Mike Costigan, writer and self avowed futilist . . .); The Splendid Brute; Circus Charade; The Influence of the Movies; Untitled (William Aloysius McGraw's father . . .); A Man and a Brother; Man; Pigskin Scholar; The Recalcitrant; Untitled ("Arrange, Madame, arrange!"); Untitled ("Yessah!" said Mrs. . . .); The Question of the East; In His Own Image; The Punch; The Female of the Species; The Last Man; The Treasure of Henry Morgan; Untitled (The lazy quiet of the mid-summer day . . .);***

*Through the Ages; The White Jade Ring; The Roving Boys on a Sandburg; Westward, Ho!; The Wild Man; What the Deuce?; The Land of Forgotten Ages; The Funniest Bout; The Red Stone; A Unique Hat; Untitled ("A man," said my friend Larry Aloysius O'Leary . . .); Untitled ( . . . that is, the artistry is but a symbol . . .); Untitled (I met him first in the Paradise saloon . . .); Untitled (Maybe it don't seem like anything interesting . . .); Untitled (So there I was.); Untitled (Trail led through dense jungle . . .); Untitled (Two men were standing in the bazaar at Delhi . . .); Untitled (When Yar Ali Khan crept . . .); Untitled (Who I am it matters little . . .); A Twentieth Century Rip Van Winkle; The Ghosts of Jacksonville; A Boy, a Beehive, and a Chinaman; Mr. Dowser Buys a Car; A Faithful Servant; A South Sea Storm; The Ghost of Bald Rock Ranch; A Fishing Trip; Friends; Ten Minutes on a Street Corner; The Wings of the Bat;* plus letters to TCS, June 8, 1923 *("May the blessings of Allah . . ."); to TCS, June 22, 1923 ("Clyde sahib, greeting:/ I found your letter . . ."); to TCS, July 7, 1923 ("To Clyde bahadur-sahib . . ."); to TCS, July 30, 1923 ("Clyde, sahib, bohut salaam, . . ."); to TCS, August 4, 1923 ("Clyde sahib;/ You say I'll . . ."); to TCS, October 5, 1923 ("Salaam, Clyde;/ Maybe you think . . ."); to TCS, November 4, 1923 ("Bohut salaam, Cyde bahadur;/ It's been quite a . . . ."); to TCS, April 21, 1924 ("Salaam, Clyde sahib;/ I should have written . . ."); to TCS, June 19, 1924 ("Salaam Clyde sahib;/ I suppose you . . .");* to *TCS, September 7, 1924 ("Salaam, Clyde,/ You ought to be here.");* to TCS, January 7, 1925 *("Salaam, Clyde sahib;/ I was in Brownwood . . ."); to TCS, January 30, 1925 (Salaam, sahib;/ I'm sending you . . ."); to TCS, February 25, 1925 ("Salaam, sahib;/Chapter XIX"); to TCS, March 17, 1925 ("The top o' the mornin', O'Clyde"); to TCS, April 6, 1925 ("Salaam, sahib;/ What ho!"); to TCS, May 24, 1925 ("Salaam;/ Hot zowie, . . ."); to TCS, July 7, 1925 ("Salaam, sahib;/ I believe you . . .");* to TCS, ca. July 1925 *("Salaam; Clyde;/ Old boy, . . .");* to TCS, ca. July 1925 *("Salaam, Clyde sahib,/ I haven't got any . . ."); to TCS, August 6, 1925 ("Salaam;/ I'm glad you . . ."); to TCS, October 9, 1925 ("Salaam, sahib;/ Say, bo, . . ."); to TCS, January 14, 1926 ("Salaam, bahadur, bohut salaam; . . ."); to TCS, January 14, 1926 ("Salaam;/ This is a habit . . ."); to TCS, April 14, 1926 ("Salaam;/ Being in an . . ."); to TCS, May 7, 1926 (Salaam;/ I'm sending you . . ."); to TCS, June 23, 1926 ("Salaam;/I'm trying to write . . ."); to TCS, August 6, 1926 ("Salaam, sahib;/ In the first place, . . ."); to TCS, August 21, 1926 ("Bohut salaam, sahib;/ I think you owe . . .");* to Edna Mann, October 30, 1926 *("As usual I . . .");* to TCS, ca. late August 1927 *("ARE YOU THE YOUNG . . ."); to TCS, ca. fall 1927 ("Salaam:/ Then the little boy . . ."); to Harold Preece, ca. early 1928 ("Salaam:/ You'll have to pardon . . ."); to TCS, week of February 20, 1928 ("The fellow who wrote . . ."); to TCS, ca. March 1928 ("Salaam:/ Not having much of . . ."); to TCS, ca. June 1928 ("Salaam:/ Ho, ho, the long . . ."); to Harold Preece, ca. June 1928 ("Salaam:/ No, I was not . . ."); to TCS, ca. July 1928 ("Salaam:/ A Warning to Orthodoxy"); to unknown recipient, ca. September 1928 ("Salaam:/ Tunney sure gave . . ."); to TCS, ca. October 1928 ("Salaam:/ The reason I'm sending . . ."); to TCS, ca. November 1928 ("Salaam:/ Listen you goddamn . . ."); to TCS, ca. November 1928 ("Salaam:/ I got such a laugh . . ."); to TCS, ca. November-December 1928 ("Salaam:/ Heh heh!"); to TCS, ca. December 1928 ("Salaam:/ Out in front . . ."); to TCS, ca. late 1928 ("Salaam:/ I'll swear, . . ."); to TCS, ca. February 1929 ("Salaam:/ Ancient English Balladel"); to TCS, ca. March 1929 ("Salaam:/ Black Dawn"); to TCS, ca. early to mid 1929 ("Salaam:/ Life is a yellow . . ."); to TCS, ca. February 1930 ("Salaam; Fear Orghruagach;"); to TCS, ca. April 1930 ("Salaam:/ Well, Fear Finn, I believe . . ."); to TCS, ca. May 1930 ("Well, Fear Finn, I hope . . ."); to TCS, ca. July 1930 ("Salaam, Fear Finn:/ Then Stein the . . ."); to TCS, ca. July 1930 ("Salaam, Fear Finn;/ Wel, me bauld . . ."); to TCS, ca. November 1930 ("Well, Fear Finn:/ I read your article . . ."); to TCS, ca. December 1930 ("Fear Finn:/ I'm not surprised . . ."); to TCS, ca. December 1930 ("Well, Fear Finn:/ I don't know . . ."); to TCS, ca. January 1931 ("Well, Fear Finn:/ You owe me a . . ."); to TCS, ca. February 1931 ("Fear Finn:/ I've delayed writing . . ."); to TCS, ca. March 1931 ("Well, Fear Finn:/ Congratulations on your . . ."); to TCS, ca. March 14, 1931 ("Well, Fear Finn:/ Heigho for sunny . . ."); to TCS, week of May 18, 1931 ("Fear Finn:/ I should have answered . . ."); to TCS, ca. early June 1931 ("Fear Finn:/ Thanks very much . . .");* to TCS, ca. September 1931 *("Fear Finn:/ Lizzen my children . . ."); to TCS, ca. September 1931 ("Fear Finn:/ I've been waiting . . ."); to TCS, ca. October 1931 ("Fear Finn:/ The reason I haven't . . ."); to H.P. Lovecraft, ca. October 1931 ("Many thanks for the . . .");* to TCS, ca. *November 1931 ("Fear Finn:/ Here are the blasted . . ."); to TCS, ca. early January 1932 ("Dear Clyde:/ I only learned . . ."); to TCS, ca. February 1932 ("Fear Finn:/ Well, how runs . . ."); to H.P.*

Lovecraft, ca. February 1932 ("This isn't to flaunt . . ."); to TCS, ca. March 1932 ("Fear Finn:/ Sorry to hear . . ."); to TCS, ca. March 1932 (Fear Finnel:/ When I was a kie . . ."); to Carl Swanson, ca. March 1932 ("I was sending . . ."); to Carl Swanson, ca. April 1932 ("I am interested . . ."); to TCS, ca. May 1932 ("Fear Finn:/ Just a bit . . ."); to TCS, ca. May 1932 ("Fear Finn:/ Well, here I am . . ."); to Carl Swanson, ca. late May 1932 ("I'm sorry you had . . ."); to TCS, ca. very late May 1932 ("Fear Finn:/ Let us tool . . ."); to TCS, ca. August 1932 ("Fear Finn:/ I don't know when . . ."); to Kirk Mashburn, ca. September 1932 ("Just a line . . ."); to TCS, ca. November 1932 ("Fear Finn:/ Well, I finally . . ."); to Donald Wandrei, ca. February 21, 1933 ("I've been intending . . ."); to TCS, ca. May 1933 ("Fear Finn:/ I was in Brownwood . . ."); to The Claytons Magazines, June 13, 1933 ("A few weeks ago . . ."); to TCS, ca. October 1933 ("Fear Finn:/ The Galleon Press . . ."); to Charles D. Hornig, November 1, 1933 ("Thanks for the copy . . ."); to Clark Ashton Smith, December 20, 1933 (a signed Christmas card); to R. Fowler Gafford, May 20, 1934 ("This answer to your . . ."); to Denis Archer, May 22, 1934 ("As you doubtless . . ."); to William Kofoed, January 8, 1935 ("Glad the Bloomfield . . ."); to H.P. Lovecraft, ca. January 1935 ("I have finally found . . ."); to Charles D. Hornig, May 3, 1935 ("I'm very sorry . . ."); to Farnsworth Wright, May 6, 1935 ("I always hate . . ."); to Otis Adelbert Kline, May 13, 1935 ("I'm writing this . . ."); to H.P. Lovecraft, ca. May 1935 ("The reason I haven't . . ."); to August Derleth, June 20, 1935 ("This postcard was . . ."); to H.P. Lovecraft, ca. July 1935 ("Thanks very much for . . ."); to Robert H. Barlow, December 17, 1935 ("Thank you very much . . ."); to August Lenniger, December 27, 1935 ("I have received . . ."); to Otis Adelbert Kline, January 8, 1936 ("A belated acknowledgement . . ."); to Otis Adelbert Kline, January 13, 1936 ("Just read yours . . ."); to Otis Adelbert Kline, January 18, 1936 ("Just read your letter . . ."); to Novalyne Price, February 14, 1936 ("I heard yesterday . . ."); to Frank Thurston Torbett, April 28, 1936 ("I'm sorry I have . . ."); to August Derleth, May 9, 1936 ("I am indeed . . ."); to H.P. Lovecraft, May 11, 1936 ("I am indeed sorry . . ."); to Weird Tales, ca. May 1936 ("Enthusiasm impels me . . ."); to The Californian, summer 1936 ("Thank you very much . . ."); to TCS, undated ("King Bahthur's Court"); to TCS, undated ("Ha ha! You're . . ."); to TCS, undated ("Again glancing at your . . ."); to TCS, undated ("The Seeker thrust . . ."); to TCS, undated ("If you dont publish . . ."); to TCS, undated ("Skulls Against the Dawn"); to TCS, undated ("Shadows of Dreams"); to TCS, undated ("I have forgotten . . ."); to TCS, undated ("As my dear public . . ."); to TCS, undated ("There once was a . . ."); to TCS, undated ("I'm damned if . . ."); to TCS, undated ("Not even a movie . . ."); to TCS, undated ("Ahatou noyon, Fear Finn:/ Thinking of nothing . . ."); to TCS, undated ("Well, Fear Finn, I read your story . . ."); to TCS, undated ("The Adventurer's Mistress"); to TCS, undated ("I've done my part . . ."); to TCS, undated ("Poem penned by . . ."); to TCS, undated ("Crusade"); to TCS, undated ("Renunciation"); to TCS, undated ("Thoughts of an Afghan . . ."); to TCS, undated ("Relentless Reginald . . ."); to TCS, undated (drawing of a strange cow); to unknown recipient, undated ("Not much to say . . ."); as well as the following prose and poetry contained in these letters: Untitled ("When Napoleon down in Africa . . .") (v); Neolithic Love Song (v); Untitled ("The helmsman gaily, rode down the rickerboo . . .") (v); Untitled ("Now bright, now red, the sabers sped among the racing horde . . .") (v); The Dook of Stork; Untitled ("Bill Boozy was a pirate bold") (v); Untitled ("Out of Asia the tribesmen came") (v); Untitled ("A clash of steel, a thud of hoofs") (v); Untitled ("A hundred years the great war raged") (v); Untitled ("Palm-trees are waving in the Gulf breeze") (v); Untitled ("Hills of the North! Lavender hills") (v); Untitled ("Dark are your eyes") (v); Slugger's Vow (v); Untitled ("I am the spirit of War!") (v); Untitled ("I lay in Yen's opium joint") (v); The Bombing of Gon Fanfew (v); The Sappious Few Menchew; The Post of the Sappy Skipper; The Bored of the Cow; When You Were a Set-Up and I Was a Ham (v); Untitled ("I tell you this my friend") (v); Untitled ("All the crowd") (v); The Dancer (v); Destiny (2) (v); Laughter (v); Untitled ("We are the duckers of crosses") (v); Untitled ("The shades of night were falling faster") (v); Untitled ("Give ye of my best . . .") (v); Untitled ("Early in the morning I gazed . . .") (v); Eternity (v); Serpent (v); Shadows (3) (v); Destiny (3) (v); Adventure (2) (v); Libertine (v); Nun (v); Prude (v); Adventurer (v); Poet (v); Dancer (v); Dreamer (v); Sailor (v); Cowboy (v); Toper (v); Girl (v); Deeps (v); Thor (v); Mystic (v); Orientia (v); The Mountains of California (v); Monarchs (v); Lust (v); The Alamo (v); San Jacinto (1) (v); Romance (2) (v); Arcadian Days (v); Twilight on Stonehenge (v); Ocean-Thoughts (v); Revenge; Legend; Where Strange Gods Squall (part 1); Untitled ("Take some honey from a cat") (v); The Mottoes of the Boy Scouts (v); Untitled ("Against *the blood red moon . . .") (v); Untitled ("Toast to the British! . . .") (v); Where Strange Gods Squall (part 2); Untitled ("Whats become of Waring?") (v); The Robes of the Righteous (v); Untitled ("After the trumps are sounded") (v); Untitled ("A typical small town drugstore . . ."); How to Select a Successful Evangelist (v); The Choir Girl (v); A Song of Cheer (v); Repentance (v); Untitled ("I am MAN from the primal . . .") (v); Untitled ("Ho, ho, the long lights lift amain . . .") (v); The Rump of Swift; A Young Wife's Tale (v); Lesbia (1) (v); A Roman Lady (v); Untitled ("They matched me up that night . . .") (v); Song of a Fugitive Bard (v); Untitled ("A cringing woman's lot . . .") (v); Nights to Both of Us Known (v); A Warning to Orthodoxy (v); A Song of the Anchor Chain (v); The Ballad of Abe Slickemmore (v); Nancy Hawk, A Legend of Virginity (v); Untitled ("Drawers that a girl . . .") (v); Untitled ("Tumba Hooey"); To a Nameless Woman (v); Untitled ("Sappho, the Grecian hills are gold") (v); Untitled ("Romona! Romona!") (v); A Fable for Critics (v); Untitled ("My brother he was an auctioneer") (v); Flaming Marble (v); Untitled ("Out in front of Goldstein's . . .") (v); The Deed Beyond the Deed (v); An American (v); Untitled ("There's an isle far away . . .") (v); Shadow of Dreams (v); My Children (v); The Slayer (v); Silence Falls on Mecca's Walls (v); The Last Words He Heard (v); Untitled ("Flappers flicker . . .") (v); Untitled ("I hold all women . . .") (v); Untitled ("Love is singing soft and low") (v); The People of the Winged Skulls; Ancient English Balladel (v); Untitled ("At the Inn of the Gory Dagger") (v); Black Dawn (v); The Path of Strange Wanderers (v); At the Bazaar (v); Untitled ("Hatrack!"); Untitled ("By old Abe Goldstein's . . .") (v); Bastards All!; Songs of Bastards; To a Roman Woman (v); Ivory in the Night (v); The Mutiny of the Hellroarer; The Return of the Sea-Farer (v); Untitled ("Then Stein the peddler . . .") (v); A Ballad of Beer (v); Lives and Crimes of Notable Artists; Untitled ("Lizzen my children and you shall be told") (v); The Last Day (v); Moonlight on a Skull (v); Dreaming in Israel (v); Samson's Broodings (v); Lines to G.B. Shaw (v); A Mick in Israel (v); Musings (2) (v); Envoy (v); Surrender (2) (v); I Praise My Nativity (v); Dreaming (v); The Coming of Bast (v); A Song of College (v); That Women May Sing of Us (v); Sighs in the Yellow Leaves (v); A Song of Greenwich (v); Ballade (v); Untitled ("The Seeker thrust . . ."); To a Certain Cultured Woman (v); The Winds of the Sea (2) (v); The Iron Harp (a cycle of five poems, including Out of the Deep; Babel; Laughter in the Gulf; Moon Shame; A Crown for a King); The Cuckoo's Revenge (v); The Madness of Cormac (v); A Challenge to Bast (v); A Poet's Skull (v); Shadows of Dreams (v); Untitled ("There once was a wicked old elf") (v); Untitled ("There are grim things did, . . .") (v); To Lyle Saxon (v); The Viking of the Sky (v); Untitled ("As my dear public remembers . . ."); King Bahthur's Court; The Werewolf Murder Case; Skulls Against the Dawn (v); The Adventurer's Mistress (2) (v); Untitled ("There were three lads . . .") (v); Untitled ("Match a toad with a far-winged hawk") (v); Crusade (v); Renunciation (v); The Campus at Midnight (v); Untitled ("You have built a world of paper and wood") (v); Untitled ("Oh, we are little children . . ."); Untitled ("The tall man answered: . . ."); Untitled ("The tall man rose and said: . . ."); Untitled ("The tall man said: . . ."); Untitled ("I knocked upon her lattice – soft!"); Untitled ("Let us up in the hills . . ."); Untitled ("Life is a lot of hooey"); Untitled ("Men are toys . . ." ); Drummings on an Empty Skull (v); Untitled ("A beggar, singing without"); Untitled ("Moonlight and shadows barred the land")*

1st Edition, Paradox Entertainment, comb binding, March 2007

**Contains a First Appearance**; introduction by Patrice Louinet; edited by Patrice Louinet and Rob Roehm; limited to 14 copies, two of which are now in national libraries in Sweden, which is the location of publication in Europe; an attempt to publish all the remaining prose and letters (as well as the prose and poetry contained in those letters) that was unpublished at this point in time, to secure a "publication right" under the Berne Covention, throughout Europe; for many of these letters it is the first time they are being published complete

## Le Fulmer #25 (French)

Contains *Solomon Kane's Homecoming (v) (lines 1-4, 29-36)*
Unknown publisher, staples, March 1985

## Lewd Tales

Contains *Songs of Bastards; Bastards All!; Ancient English Ballade (v); Untitled ("I knocked upon her lattice – soft!"); Untitled ("Let us up in the hills . . ."); Untitled ("Life is a lot of hooey"); Untitled ("Men are toys . . .")*
Cryptic Publications, staples, 1987
> **Contains a First Appearance**; cover by Stephen Fabian; the first two items are plays; edited by Robert M. Price; the last four poems are contained in the play "Songs of Bastards"

## Lhork Extra #3 (Spanish)

Contains *The King and the Oak (v)*
Unknown publisher, staples, 1992
> Spanish amateur journal

## Lurid Confessions #1

Contains *The Curse of Greed; A Matter of Age; The Voice of the Mob; The Devil in His Brain*
Cryptic Publications, staples, June 1986
> **Contains a First Appearance**; edited by Robert M. Price

## Magic Carpet Magazine (July 1933)

Contains *The Lion of Tiberias*
Girasol Collectables, pulp format, July 2007
> Replica of original pulp magazine

## Magira #25 (German)

Contains *the verse heading from Men of the Shadows*
Unknown publisher, unknown format, Summer 1976
> German amateur fanzine

## Magira #33 (German)

Contains *Chant of the White Beard (v)*
Unknown publisher, unknown format, Fall 1980
> German amateur fanzine

## Magira #38 (German)

Unknown publisher, unknown format, Spring 1992
Contains *The Dance with Death (v)*
> **Contains a First Appearance**

## A Man-Eating Jeopard

Contains *A Man-Eating Jeopard*
Alla Ray Morris, staples, 1994
Alla Ray Morris, 2nd printing, staples, 1998
> Sold at the Howard House only, in Cross Plains, TX, to raise money for Project Pride; facsimile copy of the original story; the first printing has a brown one, the second printing is more of a light beige

## Manuscripts from Gower-Penn, Volume 2, #3

Contains *a letter to TCS, ca. November 1931 ("Here are the blasted verses."); The Last Day (v); Moonlight on a Skull (v); Untitled ("The baron of Fenland . . ."); a letter to TCS, ca. September 1927 (Having just got your letter . . .") (second page only)*
Benjamin Szumskyj, staples, December 2002
> **Contains a First Appearance**; distributed in REHUPA #178; the poetry is contained in the letters

**Mesmeridian #3**
>Contains *Dermod's Bane; Valley of the Lost; Devil in his Brain*
>Dennis McHaney, staples, 1976
>>Never issued, instead was seized by the IRS(!)

**The Midtown Downtown Special Trestler: The Illustrators of R.E.H.: Tom Foster**
>Contains *Futility ("Golden goats . . .") (v)*
>Tom Foster, staples, March 2003
>>Sold at the Mid-South Con; collection of Tom Foster illustrations of REH material

**Mirror of Fantasy #3 (German)**
>Contains *the verse heading from The Hour of the Dragon*
>Unknown publisher, staples, September 1978
>>German fanzine

**Mirror of Fantasy #4 (German)**
>Contains *The Ghost Kings (v)*
>Unknown publisher, staples, November 1978
>>German fanzine

**Mirror of Fantasy #5 (German)**
>Contains *A Word from the Outer Dark (v)*
>Unknown publisher, staples, 1979
>>German fanzine

**The Miskatonic (unknown number)**
>Contains *Musings ("The little poets . . .") (v)*
>Dirk Mosig, staples, February 1974
>>Distributed in EOD #5

**The Miskatonic #15**
>Contains *An Open Window (v)*
>Dirk Mosig, staples, August 1, 1976
>>Distributed in EOD

**Morgan Visits Pulp-Con**
>Contains *a letter to Harry Bates, June 1, 1931 ("You may, or you may not . . .")*
>Morgan Holmes, staples, October 1993
>>Distributed in REHUPA #123

**Musings #2**
>Contains *Lines Written in the Realization that I Must Die (v); The Tempter (v)*
>Unknown publisher, staples, March 1991
>>Distributed in REHUPA #108, unknown contributor

**Mystero #22 (Italian)**
>Contains *With a Set of Rattlesnake Rattles*
>Mondo Ignoto Srl, staples, March 2002

## Neolithic Love Song

Contains *Neolithic Love Song (v)*

Thomas Kovacs, single piece of cardstock, 1987

> **Contains a First Appearance**; limited to 36 copies, signed and numbered; illustrated by Thomas Geissmann; "Published . . . for the occasion of the 13th WORLD FANTASY CONVENTION in Nashville, Tennessee on October 29 - November 1, 1987"; was included in REHUPA #88

## The New Howard Reader #1

Contains Stories: *The Devil of Dark Lake; Brachen the Kelt (restored version); Ambition in the Moonlight; The Last Laugh; The Shadow of Doom; Untitled ("The night was damp . . ."); The Supreme Moment; Untitled ("The wind from . . ."); *Poetry: *Cimmeria ("pure text"); Drake Sings of Yesterday; Rebellion; The Sand-Hill's Crest; Only a Shadow on the Grass; All Hallow's Eve; John L. Sullivan; The Sword of Mohammed; Flint's Passing; The King and the Oak ("pure text"); Untitled ("A Chinese washer, Ching-Ling . . ."); The Maiden of Kercheezer; Untitled ("This is a young world"); The Whoopansat of Humorous Kookooyam; The Cuckoo's Revenge; Candles; *Synopsis: *The Shadow in the Well; The House of Om;* Articles: *Something About Eve; Them;* letters: **to Thrills of the Jungle, ca. June to late 1929 ("I enclose herewith a short story . . .")**; to E. Hoffmann Price, June 3, 1936 ("Sorry to hear Pawang Ali has been . . ."); to Carl Jacobi, March 17, 1933 ("I am glad to write to Wright, commenting . . ."); to August Derleth, December 11, 1934 ("I recently found your letter . . ."); to Emil Petaja, March 6, 1935 ("Glad the ms. proved satisfactory."); to Novalyne Price, September 27, 1934 ("How about going to the show . . ."); to R. H. Barlow, ca. December 1932 ("I'll be glad to sign the title . . ."); to Robert W. Gordon, April 9, 1926 ("I must really ask your pardon, having . . ."); to Harold Preece, ca. November 1930 ("Well, Harold, I'm sorry to hear . . .")*

Joe Marek, staples, 1998

Joe Marek, staples, "2nd State of 1st printing", 1998

> **Contains a First Appearance**; first printing limited to around 30 copies, all numbered; 2nd State includes some corrections, especially to the copyright notices; 2nd State has perhaps 100 or more copies extant; all printings limited to one year of distribution

## The New Howard Reader #2

Contains Stories: *The Touch of Death; The Tower of Time; The Ghost in the Doorway; Spectres in the Dark; Golnor the Ape; A Dream; The Heathen; Miss High-Hat; **The Tale of Am-Ra**; Aha! or the Mystery of the Queen's Necklace; Musings; Mountain Man;* Poetry: *A Song of the Naked Lands; Zukala's Love Song; Red Thunder; For Man Was Given the Earth to Rule; Buccaneer Treasure; The Sands of the Desert; Custom; Memories; A Dungeon Opens; The Symbol; The Viking of the Sky; Dreaming on Downs; An Outworn Story; A Young Wife's Tale; L'Envoi (1); Untitled ("And Bill, he looked . . ."); A Man;* Essay: *To a Man Whose Name I Never Knew;* plus letters to *Weird Tales, June 1927 ("Your last three issues . . ."); to Carl Jacobi, pm, March 22, 1932 ("I found your recent letter very interesting . . ."); to August Derleth, ca. March 1933 ("I should have told you that . . ."), to Emil Petaja, July 23, 1935 ("Please believe my delay in answering . . ."); R.H. Barlow, ca. December 1932 ("Price tells me you are interested . . ."); Harold Preece, pm, September 5, 1928 ("Yes, I like the idea . . ."); Novalyne Price, ca. December 1934 ("Like my meal-ticket, Conan the Cimmerian . . ."); Robert W. Gordon, February 15, 1926 ("I was delighted to receive your letter . . ."); Hugh G. Schonfield, June 15, 1933 ("As I promised, in answer . . ."); and Argosy All-Story Weekly Magazine, July 20, 1929 ("I was born in Texas about twenty-three . . .")*

Joe Marek, staples, August 1998

Later state of 1st Edition, Joe Marek, staples, 1998

> **Contains a First Appearance**; very limited first printing, total unknown, maybe 30; later state is maybe another 50 or more copies, correcting some typographical errors; first state has the 24 line version of "Red Thunder" from WEIRD TALES #1, Zebra, while the later state, likely any after #33, have the original JAPM version

## The New Howard Reader #3

Contains Stories: *Untitled ("The Dane came in with a rush . . .");Serpent Vines; Etched in Ebony; The Jade God; The Return of the Sorcerer; The Devil in his Brain; The Hand of Obeah; Dagon Manor; Guns of the Mountains;* Poetry: *The Rhyme of the Three Slavers; Zukala's Jest; Dance Macabre; The Chant Demoniac;*

*Miser's Gold; These Things Are Gods; War to the Blind; Seven Kings; Empire's Destiny; L'Envoi (2); Drowned; Girls; Untitled ("Ho, Merry Bark . . ."); Up, John Kane!;* Essays: *Hashish Land; The Galveston Affair; The Ghost of Camp Colorado;* Synopsis: *Bran Mak Morn;* letters: *to Weird Tales, May 1928 ("Mr Lovecraft's latest story, THE CALL OF CTHULHU . . ."); to Clark Ashton Smith, pm, July 22, 1933 ("I can hardly find words . . ."); to Fort Worth Record (erroneously called Fort Worth Star-Telegram), ca. July 1928 ("Tunney can't win."); to August Derleth, ca. January 1933 ("I was much interested in your accounts . . ."); to Emil Petaja, September 6, 1935 ("Yes, I did like . . ."); to R. H. Barlow, February 14, 1936 ("This is to express, somewhat belatedly . . ."); to Novalyne Price, June 19, 1935 ("The weather is good . . ."); to August Lenniger, February 20, 1933 ("Here are the copies of 'The Shadow Kingdom' . . ."); to Robert W. Gordon p.m. May 14, 1928 ("Many thanks for the letter, also the paper."); to Harold Preece, January 4, 1930 ("Yes, we fade from youth swiftly.")*

Joe Marek, staples, November 1998

> Cover by Indiana Bill Cavalier; very limited, likely less than 100; "The Ghost of Camp Colorado" is a Facsimile reproduction of the original publication in the Texaco Star

## The New Howard Reader #4

Contains Stories: *Under the Baobab Tree; The Gondarian Man; Guests of the Hoodoo Room; The Voice of the Mob; She-Cats of Samarcand; Stones of Destiny; The Haunted Hut; The Thessalians; The Spell of Damballah; Golden Hope Christmas; A Gent from Bear Creek;* Poetry: *The Return of the Sea-Farer; Drum Gods; The Coming of Bast; The Gods Remember; A Pledge; The Road to Freedom; Mad Meg Gill; The Phases of Life; A Dying Pirate Speaks of Treasure; The Weakling; L'Envoi (3); My Sentiments, Set to Jazz; The Zulu Lord; Untitled ("The baron of Fenland . . ."); The Song of Yar Ali Khan;* Essays: *With a Set of Rattlesnake Rattles; The Celtica Notes of Robert E. Howard;* plus letters to: *Weird Tales, November 1929 ("I have just been reading . . ."); August Derleth ca. February 1933 ("After so long a time . . ."); E. Hoffmann Price, April 21, 1936 ("Glad you-all liked 'She-Devil'."); R.H. Barlow, ca. April 2, 1933 ("Here are some notes of Price's . . ."); August Lenniger, March 8, 1933 ("This is to inform you that I have . . ."); Robert W. Gordon, March 17, 1927 ("This time I have an excuse for not having . . ."); Novalyne Price, June 19, 1935 ("Dear Novalyne . . . cordially . . ."); Harold Preece, pm, March 24, 1930 ("Thanks for the picture."); and TCS, June 8, 1923 ("Hello Clyde, / May the blessing of Allah rest upon you . . .")*

Joe Marek, staples, January 1999

Joe Marek, staples, 2nd printing, January 1999

> **Contains a First Appearance**; the first printing is limited to 13 copies, and has a white cover with hand-colored inks, and a insert containing the table of contents for #5; the second printing has a pink cover; "The Gent from Bear Creek" is the original magazine version; more than 60 of the second printing

## The New Howard Reader #5

Contains Stories: *Redflame; Black Country; Intrigue in Kurdistan; Halt! Who Goes There?; The People of the Serpent; Wolfsdung; The Fear-Master; The Feud Buster;* Poetry: *The Dance with Death; When Death Drops Her Veil; Heritage ("Saxon blood . . ."); Nocturne; The Doom Chant of Than-Kul; Counterspells; A Song of the Werewolf Folk; Dreams; Universe; The Feud; Madam Goose's Rhymes; What Is Love?; Rules of Etiquette; Tides;* **Untitled ("The times, the times . . .")**; *and a facsimile reproduction copy of Verses in Ebony, by Glenn Lord, which includes the poems Black Dawn; The Road to Rome; The Gold and the Grey; A Song of the Naked Lands; Essays: The Strange Case of Josiah Wilbarger; The Vicar of Wakefield;* and letters to: *Weird Tales, April 1930 ("'Thirsty Blades' is fine . . ."); E. Hoffmann Price, February 15, 1936 ("I've eventually found time . . ."); August Derleth, ca. November 1933 ("I enjoyed reading your 'Hawk on the Blue' . . ."); Kirk Mashburn, ca. March 1932 ("I am writing to express . . ."); Robert W. Gordon, January 2, 1927 ("Upon seeing a request of yours in a late . . ."); R. H. Barlow July 5, 1934 ("Here, at last, is the last . . ."); Novalyne Price, July 4, 1935 ("I take my typewriter . . ."); Robert W. Gordon, February 4, 1925 ("I am sending you a few songs . . ."); Carl Jacobi, ca. Summer 1934 ("Thank you for the kind comments . . ."); The Ring Magazine, April 1926 ("Here is my opinion on the greatest heavyweights . . ."); TCS, September 7, 1924 ("Salaam, Clyde, / You ought to be here.")*

Joe Marek, staples, March 1999

> **Contains a First Appearance**; very limited, likely less than 50; signed by Joe Marek; "Verses in Ebony" is a facsimile of the original "dummy" prototype

## The New Howard Reader #6

Contains Stories: *Genseric's Son; Black Eons; Musings of a Moron; The Spirit of Brian Boru; The Vultures of Whapeton (with the alternate endings); Unhand Me, Villain; Le Gentil Homme le Diable; A Matter of Age; The Weaker Sex; Eighttoes Makes a Play (with the alternate ending); The Road to Bear Creek;* Poetry: *The Ballad of King Geraint; Harvest; On with the Play*; Essays: *More Evidence of the Innate Divinity of Man; The Ideal Girl;* plus letters to *Weird Tales, January 1931 ("I was particularly fascinated by the poem . . ."); Adventure Magazine, March 20, 1924 ("Question? I am writing for information in regard . . ."); August Derleth, ca. October 1933 ("Thanks very much for the opportunity . . ."); and Novalyne Price, July 8, 1935 ("Thank you for your invitation . . .")*
Joe Marek, staples, Autumn 1999
> Cover art by Bob Barger; very limited, likely less than 60

## The New Howard Reader #7

Contains Stories: *Three-Bladed Doom (short version); Spanish Gold on Devil Horse; Sunday in a Small Town; Age Lasting Love; The Fire of Asshurbanipal (straight adventure version); The Sheik; Midnight; The Curse of Greed; Pictures in the Fire; West is West; The Last White Man; A Stranger in Grizzly Claw;* Poetry: *Always Comes Evening; Roads; Destiny ("I think I was born . . .");* Essays: *Sentiment; Surrender: Your Money or Your Vice;* plus letters to: *Weird Tales, March 1932 ("Congratulations on the appearance and excellence . . ."); Adventure Magazine, August 20, 1924 ("At what period did the feudal system flourish most . . ."); Charles D. Hornig, November 10, 1933 ("Here is a short story, 'The Frost-King's Daughter' . . ."); and Novalyn Price, 14 Feb 1936 ("I heard yesterday you had . . .")*
Joe Marek, staples, Spring 2000
> Cover art by Joe Marek; very limited, likely less than 60; this series was continued as THE HOWARD READER #8

## No Refuge

Contains *a letter to HPL, December 1930 ("As always, your letter proved highly . . .")*
Steve Trout, staples, November 1989
> Distributed in REHUPA #100

## North of Khyber

Contains **North of Kyber; The Land of Mystery; El Borak ("Were you ever stranded . . ."); The Shunned Castle; A Power Among the Islands**
Cryptic Publications, staples, 1987
> **Contains a First Appearance**; these are El Borak – Sonora Kid team-ups; introduction by Robert M. Price; edited by Robert M. Price

## Odds and Ends #1

Contains *The Maiden of Kercheezer (v); Rules of Etiquette (v)*
Unknown publisher, staples, August 1986
> Distributed in REHUPA #81, unknown contributor; facsimile reproduction of the original appearance in THE PROGRESS, 1924

## Odes at the Black Dog

Contains *Always Comes Evening; Autumn; Dreams of Ninevah; Fables for Little Folks; The Ghost Kings; The Harp of Alfred; Kid Lavigne is Dead; The King and the Oak; The Kissing of Sal Snooboo; Lines Written in the Realization That I Must Die; The Poets; Recompense; Remembrance; Ships; The Singer in the Mist; Solomon Kane's Homecoming; The Song of the Mad Minstrel; The Tempter; To a Woman ("Though fathoms deep . . .")(all v)*
Paul Herman, staples, January 2006
> Distributed at the Robert E. Howard 100th Birthday Celebration, January 21, 2006; all layout by Dennis McHaney; cover illustration by Tom Foster; was originally schedule to be held at a tavern called the Black Dog, and hence the title, but was moved at the last second to a place called The Torch, in Fort Worth

## Omniumgathum

Contains **Black Harps in the Hills; To Harry the Oliad Men; Adventure; The Tide; The Jackal; The Campus at Midnight; Tiger Girl (all v)**

Stygian Isle Press (Jonathan Bacon), staples, 1976

> **Contains a First Appearance**; cover art by Clyde Caldwell; edited by Jonathan Bacon and Steve Troyanovich; limited to 1000 copies

## One More Barbarian #13

Contains *Candles (v)*

Joe Marek, staples, January 1980

> Distributed in REHUPA #43

## Onion Tops #3

Contains *Fables for Little Folks (v)*

Rob Roehm, staples, April 2005

> Distributed in REHUPA #192

## Onion Tops #9

Contains *The Kissing of Sal Snooboo (v); To a Woman ("Though fathoms deep . . .") (v)*

Rob Roehm, staples, April 2006

> Distributed in REHUPA #198

## Onion Tops #12

Contains *The Sea (v)*

Rob Roehm, staples, October 2006

> Distributed in REHUPA #201

## Onion Tops #15

Contains *Zukala's Jest (v); The Tower of Zukala (v); Zukala's Love Song (v); Zukala's Hour (v)*

Rob Roehm, staples, April 2007

> Distributed in REHUPA #204

## Oriental Stories (October-November 1930)

Contains *The Voice of El-Lil*

Girasol Collectables, pulp format, 2003

> Replica of original pulp magazine

## Oriental Stories (February-March 1931)

Contains *Red Blades of Black Cathay*

Girasol Collectables, pulp format, April 2005

> Replica of original pulp magazine

## Oriental Stories (Spring 1931)

Contains *Hawks of Outremer*

Girasol Collectables, pulp format, 2006

> Replica of original pulp magazine

## Oriental Stories (Autumn 1931)

Contains *The Blood of Belshazzar*

Girasol Collectables, pulp format, 2006

> Replica of original pulp magazine

## Oriental Stories (Spring 1932)

Contains *Lord of Samarcand*
Girasol Collectables, pulp format, October 2006
    Replica of original pulp magazine

## Oriental Stories (Winter 1932)

Contains *The Sowers of the Thunder*
Girasol Collectables, pulp format, July 2006
    Replica of original pulp magazine

## The Ossuary of Acheron

Contains *The Song of a Mad Minstrel (v) (lines 1-10); Which Will Scarcely Be Understood (v) (lines 42-45)*
Rick McCollum, staples, August 1995
    Distributed in REHUPA #134

## Outnumbered and Alone, Volume 4, #4

Contains *An excerpt from a letter to HPL, August 9, 1932 ("I am very sorry to hear . . .")*
Mark Finn, staples, August 2005
    Distributed in REHUPA #194

## Pale Horse

Contains *Autumn; Emancipation; Lines Written in the Realization that I Must Die; Moon Shame; One Who Comes at Eventide; The Poets; The Song of a Mad Minstrel; Which Will Scarcely Be Understood (all v)*
Unknown publisher, staples, March 1992
    Distributed in REHUPA #114, creator unknown

## Pay Day

Contains ***A Touch of Color***; *The Loser; A Horror in the Night;* ***Nerve; The Sophisticate; The Block; The Nut's Shell; Pay Day***
Cryptic Publications, staples, 1986
    **Contains a First Appearance**; introduction by Robert Price; edited by Robert M. Price

## Pfade ins Fantastique, Book 1 (German)

Contains *Always Comes Evening; Black Chant Imperial; The Bride of Cuchulain; Candles; Recompense; The Road to Hell; Rune; Slumber; The Tempter; Where Are Your Knights, Donn Othna? (all v)*
Erster Deutscher Fantasy Club, staples, 1996
    Verse published in both German and English

## Pfade ins Fantastique, Book 2 (German)

Contains *The Dance with Death; Earth-Born; A Moment; The Song of a Mad Minstrel (all v)*
Erster Deutscher Fantasy Club, staples, 1996
    Verse published in both German and English

## Phantasy Digest #1

Contains *Graveyard Rats*
Wayne Warfield, staples, 1976
    Artwork by various artists

## Phantasy Digest #2

Contains *People of the Serpent*
Wayne Warfield, staples, 1977
    Artwork by various artists

## The Phoenix on the Sword

Contains *The Phoenix on the Sword; The Scarlet Citadel; The Tower of the Elephant; Black Colossus; Gods of the North*

Wildside Press, audio book, March 2007

> Based on the Weird Works texts; a five-CD set

## Pigeons from Hell

Contains *Pigeons from Hell*

Script City, television script, December 4, 1981

> Based on REH's "Pigeons from Hell", this script is for an episode of "Darkroom", a very short-lived TV show, only 3 or 4 episodes; this episode was never produced; makes the primary character female ("Tina"), she has to kill Johnny in the end, Buckner gets killed, very different

## Prizraki Zambul

Contains *Shadows in Zamboula*

Journalist Fund of Byelorussia, staples, 1990

> Russian

## Pulp Magazine #1

Contains ***Stones of Destiny***

Cryptic Publications, staples, March 1989

> **Contains a First Appearance**; edited by Robert M. Price

## Pulse Pounding Adventure Stories #1

Contains *Intrigue in Kurdistan*

Cryptic Publications, staples, December 1986

> Edited by Robert M. Price

## Queen of the Black Coast

Contains ***Queen of the Black Coast (early draft)***

REH Foundation, loose pages in a folder, 2007

> **Contains a First Appearance**; facsimile reproduction of an original typescript; not sold, but a giveaway to Legacy Circle members of the REHF; printed on buff paper with "REHF" hand-initialed in red ink on each page; this early draft features "Taramis" instead of "Belit"

## Queen of the Black Coast portfolio

Contains *The Song of Belit,* as well as a collection of seven plates by Stephen Fabian

House of Fantasy, portfolio, 1976

> Limited to 1000 copies

## The Raven #1

Contains *Musings of a Moron; The Man on the Ground; Cimmeria (v); Death's Black Riders; Hope Empty of Meaning (v); Kublai Khan (v); Lines Written in the Realization that I Must Die (v); Visions (v); the verse heading from The Black Stone; the verse heading from The Thing on the Roof*

Thomas Kovacs, staples, December 1981

> Stories in German, poems in English and German, and two poems in Hungarian, don't know which two; less than 200 copies printed

## Razored Zen #39

Contains *The Dead Remember*

Charles Gramlich, staples, April 1999

> A facsimile reproduction of the 1961 appearance in FANTASTIC MAGAZINE; distributed in REHUPA #156

## Razored Zen #82
Contains *The Devil's Woodchopper; Recompense (v)*
Charles Gramlich, staples, August 2006
>> The story completed by Charles Gramlich; distributed in REHUPA #200

## Redflame #3
Contains **Redflame**
Mark Kimes, staples, November 1987
>> Distributed in REHUPA #88

## Red Ruins #1
Contains *The Gold and the Grey (v)*
Unknown publisher, staples, August 1997
>> Distributed in REHUPA #146, unknown contributor

## REH
Contains **a letter to Wilfred B. Talman, ca. September 1931 ("Thank you very much ...")**
Randy Everts, staples, May 1975
>> **Contains a First Appearance**; distributed in REHUPA #15; lengthy excerpt, beginning with "My ancestors were among . . ."

## REHupa #117
Contains *Girls; The Sword of Mohammed; Untitled ("A Chinese washer . . .") (all v)*
Glenn Lord, staples, September 1992
>> An untitled letter from Glenn Lord that was published in this issue included a copy of THE TOREADOR, July 5, 1925, which contained these poems

## REHupa #118
Contains **The Vicar of Wakefield**
Glenn Lord, staples, November 1992
>> An untitled letter from Glenn Lord that was published in this issue included a copy of this original school paper from REH

## Report on a Writing Man
Contains *Under the Great Tiger*, also several photos of REH, including cover
Necronomicon Press, staples, 1991
>> "Under the Great Tiger" is a facsimile of the original appearance

## The Return of the Seafarer
Contains *The Return of the Seafarer (v)*
Thomas Kovacs, folded heavy stock, 1988
>> Limited to 25 copies; illustration by Bodo Schafer; "Published by Thomas Kovacs for the occasion of the 46th World Science Fiction Convention in New Orleans, 1 to 5 September, 1988."

## Revelations from Yuggoth #1
Contains **The Spell of Damballah**
Cryptic Publications, staples, November 1987
>> **Contains a First Appearance**; edited by Robert M. Price

## Revelations from Yuggoth #2
Contains *Slumber (v)*
Cryptic Publications, staples, May 1988
>> Edited by Robert M. Price

**Revelations from Yuggoth #3**
Contains *Destination (v)*
Cryptic Publications, staples, February 1989
    Edited by Robert M. Price


**A Rhyme of Salem Town and Other Poems**
Contains ***Ace High; The Affair at the Tavern; The Actor; The Ages Stride on Golden Feet; And So I Sang; Artifice; Another Hymn of Hate; As I Rode Down to Lincoln Town; Astarte's Idol Stands Alone; Baal-Pteor; The Bandit; The Baron and the Wench; The Broken Walls of Babel; The Builders; The Call of the Sea** (first complete publication of this poem); **A Calling to Rome; The Cells of the Coliseum; The Chief of the Matabeles; Code; Cornish Jack; The Cry Everlasting; The Desert; The Desert Hawk; Devon Oak; The Drum; A Dull Sound as of Knocking;* Echoes from an Anvil; *Edgar Guest; Eric of Norway; Escape; Exhortation; Far in the Gloomy Northland; Farewell, Proud Munster; Freedom; The Gods I Worshipped; An Incident of the Muscovy-Turkish War; King of the Sea; Krakorum; The Ladder of Life; Land of the Pioneer; The Lies; Longfellow Revised; Little Bell of Brass; Little Brown Man of Nippon; The Lost San Saba Mine; Lunacy Chant; Mahomet; Man, the Master; Mankind; Mine but to Serve; A Misty Sea; Mihiragula; Modest Bill; Native Hell; No Man's Land; Now and Then; O the Brave Sea-Rover; The Oaks;* On with the Play; **Over the Old Rio Grandey;* Only a Shadow on the Grass; **The Open Window; The Passing of the Elder Gods; Perspective; The Phantoms Gather;* The Phases of Life; **The Pirate; The Plains of Gilban; Prelude;* The Primal Urge; **Rattle of Drums; A Quatrain of Beauty** ("Quattrain" on title page); **A Rhyme of Salem Town; Romance; The Road to Bliss;* The Road to Freedom; The Road to Yesterday; Roads; Roar, Silver Trumpets; **The Rover; The Rulers; San Jacinto** (II, "Red fields of glory . . ."); **The Sea and the Sunrise; Sea-Chant; Senor Zorro; The Sign of the Sickle; The Slayer; A Song of Bards; The Stralsund; The Sword of Lal Singh;* Swings and Swings; **The Tartar Raid; Time, the Victor; To a Kind Missionary Woiker; To Moderns; To the Stylists; The Tower of Zukala; The Trail of Gold; Trail's End; Untamed Avatars; Untitled** ("Murky the night") ("Untitled" on Table of Contents page); **The Wanderer; Was I There?; West; The Wheel of Destiny; When I Was a Youth; When I Was in Africa; When Men Were Bold; Who Shall Sing of Babylon?; The Winds of the Sea; The Winds That Walk the World; The Worshippers; Zululand; Untitled** ("For what is a maid to the shout of kings?"); **Untitled** ("As you dance upon the air."); **Yesterdays; Baal; Down the Ages; The House of Gael; Ju-Ju Doom; Mystic Lore; The King of Trade; The Peasant on the Euphrates; Am-ra the Ta-an** (all v)*
REH Properties, tape binding, 2002
    **Contains a First Appearance**; allegedly all the poetry still remaining unpublished as of the end of 2002, though appears to be missing all the poetry from the TCS letters; each of these books were cheaply created, tape bound with card stock covers, likely copied down at a copy shop, to try and create a publication for US copyright purposes, no information on number of copies created, likely less than ten actually distributed; there is a later HB edition by The Robert E. Howard Foundation


**The Rhyme of the Three Slavers**
Contains ***The Rhyme of the Three Slavers (v)***
Thomas Kovacs, folded cardstock, October 1983
    **Contains a First Appearance**; limited to 250 copies, signed and numbered; published for The Raven's Club


**Rhymes of Death**
Contains *An Open Window; Arkham; Which Will Scarcely Be Understood; Fragment* ("And so his boyhood . . ."); *The Tempter; Niflheim; Emancipation; Ecstasy; A Hairy-Chested Idealist Sings;* **The Ballad of Bucksnort Roberts**; *Futility* ("Golden goats . . ."); **The End of the Glory Trail** (all v)
Dennis McHaney, staples, 1975
    **Contains a First Appearance**; limited to 600 numbered copies, there are also 268 unnumbered copies; illustrated by Tom Foster; signed by Tom Foster; one title in error, actually "Buckshot" Roberts

## Rhymes of Texas and the Old West

Contains *But the Hills Were Ancient Then; Cimmeria; The Lost San Saba Mine; The Dweller in Dark Valley; Ghost Dancers; The Kiowa's Tale; The Grim Land; Sonora to Del Rio; Cowboy; Over the Old Rio Grandey; The Bandit; Roundelay of the Roughneck; John Ringold; The Ballad of Buckshot Roberts; Untitled ("Old Faro Bill . . ."); Modest Bill; The Alamo; San Jacinto (I); San Jacinto (II); The Feud; End of the Glory Trail; The Sand-Hill's Crest (all v)*

The Robert E. Howard Foundation Press, staples, June 2007

> Cover art by Jim & Ruth Keegan; introduction by James Reasoner; edited by Paul Herman; a giveaway to Legacy Circle members of REHF, first handed out at the REH Days luncheon on June 8, 2007

## The Right Hook, Volume 1, #1

Contains **Twentieth Century Slave Trade; The Great Munney Ring; Bookmen and Books; Puritans; Sisters; L'Envoi (1) (v) ; Vengeance of a Woman; miscellaneous boxing commentary**

Robert E. Howard, staples (maybe), Spring 1925

> **Contains a First Appearance**; Introduction by REH; only one copy known, though may have originally been four of each; this issue was six pages; a facsimile reproduction of this can be seen in AUSTIN, VOLUME 3, #2 (Chpbk.) and ROBERB E. HOWARD—THE POWER OF THE WRITING MIND

## The Right Hook, Volume 1, #2

Contains **L'Envoi (2) (v); Untitled ("And Bill, he looks at me . . .") (v); Untitled ("Ho, Merry bark, . . .") (v); What is Love? (v); untitled article ("MUNN! MUNN!"); Le Gentil Homme le Diable; John L. Sullivan (v); Jack Dempsey (v); A Pirut Story; miscellaneous boxing commentary**

Robert E. Howard, staples (maybe), 1925

> **Contains a First Appearance**; only one copy known, though may have originally been four of each; this issue is seven pages; a facsimile reproduction of this can be seen in AUSTIN, VOLUME 3, #2

## The Right Hook, Volume 1, #3

Contains **Untitled ("This is a young world . . .") (v); Untitled ("My name is Sam Culotte."); My Sentiments, Set to Jazz (v);Ringside Tales; L'Envoi (3) (v); miscellaneous boxing and other commentary**

Robert E. Howard, staples (maybe), 1925

> **Contains a First Appearance**; only one copy known, though may have originally been four of each; this issue is twelve pages; a facsimile reproduction of this can be seen in AUSTIN, VOLUME 3, #2

## Risque Stories #1

Contains **She-Cats of Samarcand; Strange Passion (v)**; *Lesbia (v); Desire (v)*; **Untitled ("John Gorman found himself . . .")**

Cryptic Publications, staples, March 1984

> **Contains a First Appearance**; the author for "She-Cats" is listed as "Sam Walser", but is actually a story written by Charles Hoffman and Marc A. Cerasini based on the untitled synopsis; edited by Robert M. Price; "Desire" not listed in the table of contents

## Risque Stories #2

Contains **The Whoopansat of Humorous Kookooyam (v)**

Cryptic Publications, staples, October 1984

> **Contains a First Appearance**; edited by Robert M. Price

## Risque Stories #3

Contains **The Harlot (v)**

Cryptic Publications, staples, July 1985

> **Contains a First Appearance**; cover by Stephen Fabian; edited by Robert M. Price

## Risque Stories #4
Contains ***Miss High-Hat***
Cryptic Publications, staples, October 1986
**Contains a First Appearance**

## Risque Stories #5
Contains ***A Young Wife's Tale (v); The Cuckoo's Revenge (v)***
Cryptic Publications, staples, March 1987
**Contains a First Appearance**; edited by Robert M. Price

## The Road to Rome
Contains ***The Road to Rome (v)***
Roy Squires, small booklet, 1972
**Contains a First Appearance**; limited to 217 copies;

## The Road to Velitrium #25
Contains *The Devils of Dark Lake*
Jim Van Hise, staples, April 1998
Distributed in REHUPA #150

## The Road to Velitrium #30
Contains *Ambition in the Moonlight; To a Man Whose Name I Never Knew; Musings; Etched in Ebony; The Galveston Affair; Surrender – Your Money or Your Vice; Them*
Jim Van Hise, staples, August 1999
A facsimile reproduction of these works original appearance in Trumpet #7; distributed in REHUPA #156

## The Road to Velitrium #49
Contains *The Challenge from Beyond*
Jim Van Hise, staples, February 2003
Distributed in REHUPA #179; a facsimile reproduction of the original appearance in FANTASY MAGAZINE, September 1935

## The Road to Velitrium #50
Contains *Song at Midnight (v)*
Jim Van Hise, staples, August 2003
Distributed in REHUPA #182; a facsimile reproduction of the original appearance in THE PHANTAGRAPH, August 1940

## Robert E. Howard and Weird Tales #3
Contains *a letter to Weird Tales, June 1936 ("Enthusiasm impels me . . .")*
Dennis McHaney, staples, August 2002
Distributed in REHUPA #176, as well as some extra copies; contains various letters to The Eyrie relating to REH, July 1935 to July 1936; also full page color reproductions of various REH WEIRD TALES covers, and several interior illustrations for REH stories in WEIRD TALES

## Robert E. Howard and Weird Tales #4
Contains *People of the Dark*
Dennis McHaney, staples, December 2002
Limited to 100 copies, some distributed in REHUPA #178; also contains letters to The Eyrie about REH, July 1936 to February 1937; plus artwork by J. Allen St. John, Virgil Finlay, Harold Delay, and Roy Krenkel

## Robert E. Howard at the Black Dog
Contains *Recompense (v); and a small excerpt from Beyond the Black River*
Bill Cavalier, folded paper, January 2006
> Very limited, maybe 50 copies; illustrated by Bill Cavalier; the contents were read by Bill Cavalier at the REH 100th Birthday Celebration at The Torch (it was suppose to be the Black Dog) in Fort Worth

## Robert E. Howard in The Fantasy Fan
Contains **letter to Charles Hornig, ca. November 1, 1933 ("Thanks for the copy . . .")**; *letter to Charles Horning, ca. November 10, 1933 ("Here is a short story . . ."); letter to The Fantasy Fan, December 1933 ("I find the Fantasy Fan . . ."); letter to The Fantasy Fan, January 1934 ("I liked the November issue . . ."); Gods of the North; letter to The Fantasy Fan, May 1934 ("Smith's poem in the March issue . . ."); letter to Charles Hornig, August 10, 1934 ("Glad you liked the verses."); The Voices Waken Memory (v); Babel (v);* **letter to Charles Hornig, May 3, 1935 ("I'm very sorry to hear . . .")**
Rob Roehm, staples, 2006
> **Contains a First Appearance**; limited to 40 copies; collection of all letters and contents by or about REH in The Fantasy Fan, and correspondence with the editor; includes the announcement of "The Garden of Fear" in Unusual Stories, which never actually came out; first complete publication of the August 10, 1934 letter to Hornig; for REHupa 200

## A Robert E. Howard Memorial: June 13-15, 1986
Contains **The Sand-Hills' Crest; The Weakling**; *The One Black Stain; the verse headings from The Black Stone and The Thing on the Roof (all v)*
Unknown publisher, staples, 1986
> **Contains a First Appearance**; cobbled together by the folks that made the first Cross Plains get-together in 1986, likely something like 10-20 copies in existence

## Robert E. Howard: Selected Letters: 1923-1930
Contains *Symbols; Daughter of Evil; The Odyssey of Israel; Reuben's Brethren;* **Untitled ("Lizzen my children and you shall be told"); Untitled ("Many fell at the grog-shop wall");** *Untitled ("Slow shifts the sands of time . . .") (all v); plus 49 letters by REH to various people, including:*
*H.P. LOVECRAFT:*
**Ca. July 1, 1930 ("I am indeed highly honored to have received . . .")**
**August 1930 ("Let me first thank you for the opportunity . . .")**
**September 1930 (1) ("I envy you your sojourn to Quebec.")**
**September 1930 (2) ("I am very glad that you enjoyed your visit . . .")**
**October 1930 ("It is with greatest delight that I learn . . .")**
**December 1930 ("As always, your letter proved highly . . .")**
*HAROLD PREECE:*
*pm, September 23, 1928 ("The tang of winter is in the air . . .")*
*Received October 20, 1928 ("Your stationery is alright.")*
*ca. December 1928 ("You're right; women are great actors.") ( First complete publication)*
*ca. March 1929 ("I've been very neglectful of my correspondence . . .")*
*ca. September 1929 ("I've been reading DESTINY BAY and in . . .")*
*ca. February 1930 ("You're in Kansas now, eh?")*
*ca. October 1930 ("Well, Harold, how did you like my story . . .")*
*pm, November 24 1930 ("I hope you'll pardon my negligence . . .")*
*TEVIS CLYDE SMITH:*
**August 24, 1923 ("Bohut Salaam, Clyde sahib: / I was all ready to come over to Brownwood . . .")**
**September 9, 1923 ("Clyde sahib: / First off I must apologize for not having . . .")**
**July 16,1925 ("Salaam, sahib: / What ho, milord!")**
**August 26, 1925 ("Salaam: / I've been thinking. What is reality . . .")**
**August 28, 1925 ("Salaam: / I've been thinking. Did you ever stop . . .")**
**ca. September 1927 ("Salaam: / Having just got your letter . . .")**
**ca. October 1927 ("Salaam: / Seeking cognizance of things . . .")**

*ca. January 1928 ("Salaam: / Listen, you crumb, . . .")*
*ca. January 1928 ("I wasn't lying to you Saturday evening when . . .")*
*week of February 20, 1928 ("The fellow who wrote The Kasidah . . .")*
*ca. March 1928 ("The only reason for writing this letter . . .")*
*ca. March 1928 ("Salaam: / Glad you're writing these days . . .")*
*ca. May 1928 ("Salaam: / So Klatt has gone West.")*
*ca. October 1928 ("Salaam: / I could have gone with you . . .")*
*ca. November 1928 ("Salaam: / I'll swear you're the only galoot . . .")*
*ca. November 1928 ("Heh, heh! / At last I've sold a story to Ghost Stories.")*
*ca. December 1928 ("The rattle of the keys sounds good under my . . .") (leaves out the opening poetry ("Out in front of Goldstein's . . ."))*
*ca. February 1929 ("Looks like I'm not going to make it over . . .") (leaves out the opening poetry ("Ancient English Balladel"))*
*ca. February 1929 ("Salaam: / Last night the Sunday School class . . .")*
*ca. April 1929 ("I enjoyed your letter highly and roared . . .") (leaves out the opening poem ("The iron harp that Adam christened . . ."))*
*ca. June 1929 ("Salaam: / I received an announcement . . .")*
*ca. July 1929 ("Salaam: / The main reason I'm writing this letter is . . .")*
*ca. late December 1929 ("Well: / Here I am doing business . . .")*
*ca. January 1930 ("Many thanks for the letter . . .")*
*ca. February 1930 ("Well, here is the letter.")*
*ca. March 1930 ("I owe Hink a letter.") (leaves out opening poetry ("Life is a cynical . . ."))*
*ca. March 1930 ("Well, Fear Finn, tell Cuchullain the Dutchess . . .")*
*ca. March 1930 ("Well, Fear Finn: / I trust you are in good healthel . . .")*
*ca. early April 1930 ("Well, Fear Finn, you mention being in . . .")*
*ca. May 1930 ("Well, Fear Finn, I was in Brownwood yesterday . . .")*
*ca. week of June 9, 1930 ("Well, Fear Finn: / The pictures came at last . . .")*
*late July or early August 1930 ("Well, Fear Finn: / I haven't heard from our story, but that's . . .")*
*ca. September 1930 ("Well, Fear Finn, me bauld braw Hieland . . .")*
*ca. early September 1930 ("Well, Fear Finn: / I hope you'll sell the duelling story.")*
*FARNSWORTH WRIGHT:*
*ca. June 1930 ("I have long looked forward to reading . . .")*
Necronomicon Press, staples, October 1989

> **Contains a First Appearance**; cover art by Robert H. Knox; leaves out almost all of the stories and verse included in the various letters by REH

## Robert E. Howard: Selected Letters: 1931-1936

Contains *Authorial Version of "Doona" (v); A Warning (same as The Howard Collector version); Who Is Grandpa Theobold?; 30 letters to various people, including:*
*AUGUST DERLETH:*
*ca. December (29?), 1932 ("I read your recent letter with the greatest interest . . .")*
*ca. December 1933 ("I think Scribner's was nuts to turn down 'Hawk on . . .")*
*July 4, 1935 ("Thanks very much for the article, 'Afternoon in June.' . . .")*
*May 9, 1936 ("I am indeed sorry to learn of the deaths . . .")*
*H.P. LOVECRAFT:*
*June 1931 ("I didn't take much of a trip after all.")*
*September 22, 1932 ("I read, as always, your comments on . . .")*
*November 2, 1932 ("I want to begin this letter by an apology.")*
*July 1933 ("Glad we got the physical/mental question . . .")*
*November 3, 1933 ("Glad you liked the rattles.")*
*December 5, 1935 ("A rather belated reply to your interesting . . .")*
*February 11, 1936 ("Glad you enjoyed the dream write-up I sent you.")*
*CLARK ASHTON SMITH:*
*ca. October 1933 ("Thanks very much for the kind things . . .")*
*pm, December 14, 1933 ("Only the fact that I have been sick . . .")*

*ca. January 1934 ("Thanks again for the drawing of the wizard.")*
*ca. March 1934 ("I am sorry to hear you have been indisposed . . .")*
**pm, May 21 1934 ("My delay in answering your last letter . . .")**
*TEVIS CLYDE SMITH:*
**ca. March 1931 ("Fear Finn: / I don't have to tell you . . .")**
**May 9, 1931 ("Fear Finn: / Have youse heard anything more . . .")**
**ca. mid-May 1931 ("Well Fear Finn: / I got a letter from Bradford saying that . . .")**
**ca. August 1931 ("Fear Finn: / Well, I doubt if this missile . . .")**
**ca. September 1931 ("Fear Finn: / Lizzen my children and . . .")**
*ca. November 1931 ("Fear Finn: / I wrote Bradford a coarse . . .")*
**ca. November 1931 ("Fear Finn: / Have you heard anything . . .")**
**ca. April 1932 ("Fear Finn: / I heard from that bone-crushing . . .")**
**ca. May 1932 ("Fear Finn: / Thank you very much for going . . .")**
**ca. May 1932 ("Fear Finn: / Lo, friend, I approach thee . . .")**
**ca. September 1932 ("Fear Finn: / You owe me a letter, you louse . . .")**
*WILFRED BLANCH TALMAN:*
*ca. September 1931 ("Thank you very much for the letter you wrote . . .")*
*FRANK THURSTON TORBETT:*
**June 3, 1936 ("My mother is very low . . .")**
*FARNSWORTH WRIGHT:*
*ca. June-July 1931 ("In your last letter you asked me to give you . . .")*
Necronomicon Press, staples, March 1991
> **Contains a First Appearance**; cover art by Robert H. Knox; poems imbedded in letters to TCS

## Robert E. Howard's Bran Mak Morn: A Sketchbook

Contains *Men of the Shadows (v); plus a few excerpts from Kings of the Night*
Wandering Star, staples, July 2000
> Limited to 3000 copies; artwork by Gary Gianni

## Robert E. Howard's Conan

Contains *The Tower of the Elephant; The Frost Giant's Daughter*
1st Pressing, Moondance Records, 33rpm LP record, 1975
2nd Pressing, Moondance Records, 33rpm LP record, 1975
> Dramatizations, with a number of actors and background music; two pressings, first was 1500 copies, second was 1000 copies; the second has a Tim Conrad cover; there is also a poster based on the Tim Conrad cover

## Robert E. Howard's Fight Magazine #1

Contains *Pit of the Serpent; The Bull Dog Breed; Sailors' Grudge; Fist and Fang; Winner Take All; Waterfront Fists*
Necronomicon Press, staples, March 1990
> Cover art and interior restorations by Robert H. Knox; banner by Stephen Fabian

## Robert E. Howard's Fight Magazine #2

Contains *The Champion of the Forecastle; Alleys of Peril; Waterfront Law; Texas Fists; The Fightin'est Pair;* **The Champ (v); When You Were a Set-Up and I Was a Ham (v)**
Necronomicon Press, staples, September 1990
> **Contains a First Appearance**; cover art and interior restorations by Robert H. Knox; banner by Stephen Fabian

## Robert E. Howard's Fight Magazine #3

Contains *Circus Fists; Vikings of the Gloves; Night of Battle; The Slugger's Game; General Ironfist; Sluggers of the Beach*
Necronomicon Press, staples, September 1991
> Cover art and interior restorations by Robert H. Knox; banner by Stephen Fabian

## Robert E. Howard's Fight Magazine #4

Contains *Sailor Costigan and the Swami;* **By the Law of the Shark; Flying Knuckles; Hard-Fisted Sentiment; The Honor of the Ship***; Fragment ("It was the end of the fourth round."); Fragment ("The night Sailor Steve Costigan fought Battlin' O'Rourke, . . .");* **In the Ring (v); Slugger's Vow (v)**
Necronomicon Press, staples, October 1996
> **Contains a First Appearance**; interior art by Jason Eckhardt & Robert Knox; banner by Stephen Fabian

## Runes of Ahrh-Eih-Eche

Contains *The Ghost of Camp Colorado;* plus letters to the following people:
*R.H. BARLOW:*
*June 1, 1934 ("Concerning the illustrations you mentioned . . .")*
**June 14, 1934 ("If I ever decide to dispose of the Rankin . . .")**
*AUGUST DERLETH:*
*May 9, 1936 ("I am indeed sorry to learn of the deaths . . .")*
*ca. July 1933 ("Thanks immensely for the opportunity of reading . . .")*
*CARL JACOBI:*
*ca. Summer 1934 ("Thank you for the kind comments . . .")*
*H.P. LOVECRAFT:*
*ca. July 1933 ("I am sending on to you the enclosed manuscript . . .")*
*HAROLD PREECE:*
*ca. September 1928 ("Glad you enjoyed our reunion at Fort Worth.")*
**pm, September 18, 1929 ("I don't remember saying anything against . . .")**
**pm, November 24, 1930 ("I hope you'll pardon my negligence . . .") (first appearance of all except last paragraph)**
*ca. early Apr, 1930 ("Thanks for the Saint Padraic's card.")*
*ca. October 1930 ("Well, Harold, how did you like my story . . .")*
*ca. February 1930 ("You're in Kansas now, eh?")*
*ca. December 1928 ("You're right; women are great actors.")*
*rec'd October 20, 1928 ("Your stationery is alright.")*
*ca. September 1929 ("I've been reading DESTINY BAY and in . . .")*
*CLARK ASHTON SMITH:*
*pm, March 15, 1933 ("I hardly know how to thank you for the copy . . .")*
*ca. Summer 1933 ("I really must apologize for not having . . .")*
*July 23, 1935 ("I'm ashamed of my long delay in answering . . .")*
*WILFRED BLANCH TALMAN:*
**ca. March 1931 ("I can hardly find words to express . . .")**
**ca. July 1931 ("I should have answered your letter . . .")**
**ca. May 1931 ("I'm glad you liked 'Kings of the Night.'")**
**ca. October 1931 ("I'm returning herewith your stories . . .")**
*ca. October 1931 ("Thank you very much for the letter you wrote . . .")*
**ca. March 1932 ("I've finally gotten around to answering . . .")**
*ca. July 1932 ("Thanks very much for 'De Halve Maen.'")*
*FARNSWORTH WRIGHT:*
*May 6, 1935 ("I always hate to write a letter like this.")*
*August 1930 ("I have long looked forward to reading . . .")*
Stygian Isle Press (Jonathan Bacon), staples, June 1976
> **Contains a First Appearance**; magazine size

## Savage Tales of Solomon Kane

Contains *Solomon Kane's Homecoming; The One Black Stain; The Return of Sir Richard Grenville (all v)*
Wandering Star, CD, 1998
> A CD containing dramatic readings by former members of the Royal Shakespeare Company; included with the SAVAGE TALES OF SOLOMON KANE book from Wandering Star

## Seanchai #46

Contains *Never Beyond the Beast (v); Untitled ("Men are toys . . .") (v)*
Rusty Burke, staples, November 1988
> Distributed in REHUPA #94

## Seanchai #47

Contains *The Road to Yesterday (v)*
Rusty Burke, staples, January 1989
> Distributed in REHUPA #95

## Seanchai #51

Contains *The Road to Yesterday (v)*
Rusty Burke, staples, September 1989
> Distributed in REHUPA #99

## Seanchai #60

Contains ***three letters to Robert W. Gordon, including:***
***February 4, 1925 ("I am sending you a few songs . . .")***
***February 15, 1926 ("I was delighted to receive your letter . . .")***
***January 2, 1927 ("Upon seeing a request of yours in a late . . .")***
Rusty Burke, staples, March 1991
> **Contains a First Appearance**; distributed in REHUPA #108

## Seanchai #64

Contains ***three letters to Robert W. Gordon, including:***
***April 9, 1926 ("I must really ask your pardon, having . . .")***
***March 17, 1927 ("This time I have an excuse for not having . . .")***
***May 14, 1928 ("Many thanks for the letter, also the paper.")***
Rusty Burke, staples, November 1991
> **Contains a First Appearance**; distributed in REHUPA #112

## Seanchai #71

Contains *Red Thunder (v)*
Rusty Burke, staples, April 1993
> The 24 line version of this poem; distributed in REHUPA #120

## Seanchai #74

Contains *Love's Young Dream (v); Never Beyond the Beast (v) (lines 13-16)*
Rusty Burke, staples, February 1994
> Distributed in REHUPA #125

## Seanchai #82

Contains *the verse heading from The Skull of Silence*
Rusty Burke, staples, August 1997
> Distributed in REHUPA #146

**Seanchai #112**
Contains *a letter to Edna Mann, October 30, 1926 ("As usual I have to . . .")*
Rusty Burke, staples, August 2006
**Contains a First Appearance**; distributed in REHUPA #200

**Servant of the Warsman #2**
Contains *Lines Written in the Realization that I Must Die (v)*
Unknown publisher, staples, December 1994
Distributed in REHUPA #130, unknown contributor

**Servant of the Warsman #8**
Contains *The Gold and the Grey (lines 29-32 only); The Tempter (lines 37-40); To All Sophisticates (lines 4-7) (all v)*
Publisher known, staples, February 1996
Distributed in REHUPA #137, unknown contributor

**Shadow of the Beast**
Contains ***The Shadow of the Beast; The Tomb of the Dragon***
George Hamilton, staples with DJ, 1977
**Contains a First Appearance**; limited to 280 copies

**Shadow of the Hun**
Contains ***Shadow of the Hun; Untitled ("The Dane came in with a rush . . .")***
George Hamilton, staples with DJ, 1975
**Contains a First Appearance**; limited to 318 copies; artwork by Stephen Fabian; introduction by TCS

**Shayol #1**
Contains *Flight (v) (lines 17-24)*
Arney Fenner, staples, November 1977
A slick semi-prozine, 64 pages

**Shudder Stories #1**
Contains ***Guests of the Hoodoo Room***
Cryptic Publications, staples, June 1984
**Contains a First Appearance**; edited by Robert M. Price

**Shudder Stories #2**
Contains ***The House of Om (synopsis)***
Cryptic Publications, staples, December 1984
**Contains a First Appearance**; edited by Robert M. Price

**Shudder Stories #4**
Contains ***Dagon Manor (completed by C.J. Henderson)***
Cryptic Publications, staples, March 1986
**Contains a First Appearance**; cover by Stephen Fabian; edited by Robert M. Price

**Simba #2**
Contains *To Harry the Oliad Man (v)*
Cliff Bird, magazine format, September 1978
Limited to 500 copies

## The Slithering Shadow
Contains *The Slithering Shadow*
Real Conan Press (Dennis McHaney), staples, 1997
> Limited to 11 copies, cover is the same as on the WEIRD TALES issue, and also includes interior art

## Solomon Kane's Homecoming
Contains *Solomon Kane's Homecoming (v)*
Wandering Star, brochure, 1998
> An advertisement for THE SAVAGE TALES OF SOLOMON KANE

## Solomon Kane's Homecoming
Contains *Solomon Kane's Homecoming (v)*
Pinnacle, card stock page, August 2008
> A two-sided color 8.5X11 card stock piece, with the poem running over both sides, with lots of color illustrations; was included in a limited-edition bonus pack, cost $100, to go with the new Savages Worlds of Solomon Kane RPG; limited to 50 copies

## A Song of the Naked Lands
Contains *A Song of the Naked Lands (v)*
Roy Squires, small booklet, 1973
> **Contains a First Appearance**; limited to 230 copies

## The Sonora Kid
Contains ***The West Tower; Brotherly Advice; Desert Rendezvous; Red Curls and Bobbed Hair; The Sonora Kid – Cowhand; The Sonora Kid's Winning Hand; Untitled ("A blazing sun in a blazing sky...");  Untitled ("The Hades Saloon..."); Untitled ("The hot Arizona sun..."); Untitled ("Madge Meraldson..."); Untitled ("Steve Allison settled himself..."); Untitled ("The way it came about...") (alternate titled "The Mountains of Thibet")***
Cryptic Publications, staples, June 1988
> **Contains a First Appearance**; cover by Stephen Fabian; edited by Robert M. Price

## Spears of Clontarf
Contains ***Spears of Clontarf; plus a letter to Harry Bates, June 1, 1931 ("You may, or you may not...")***
George Hamilton, staples with DJ, 1978
> **Contains a First Appearance**; limited to 152 copies

## Spears of Clontarf
Contains *Spears of Clontarf*
Dark Carneval (Tom Kovacs), perfect bound, May 1986
> Limited to 80 copies; a preprint from THE WRITER OF THE DARK; comes in at least two color of covers, gray and ivory; 20 of the gray-covered copies also include "The Rhyme of the the Three Slavers"

## Spicy-Adventure Stories (April 1936)
Contains *She Devil*
Girasol Collectables, pulp format, 2004
> Replica of original pulp magazine

## Spicy-Adventure Stories (June 1936)
Contains *Desert Blood*
Girasol Collectables, pulp format, 2004(?)
> Replica of original pulp magazine

**Spicy-Adventure Stories (September 1936)**
Contains *The Dragon of Kao Tsu*
Girasol Collectables, pulp format, June 2006
Replica of original pulp magazine

**Spicy-Adventure Stories (November 1936)**
Contains *The Purple Heart of Erlik*
Girasol Collectables, pulp format, 2003
Replica of original pulp magazine

**Spicy-Adventures (January 1937)**
Contains *Murderer's Grog*
Girasol Collectables, pulp format, June 2005
Replica of original pulp magazine

**Spoor Anthology #1**
Contains ***And Beowulf Rides Again (v); When the Gods Were Kings (v)***
Fort Necessity Press (Fred Adams), staples, 1974
**Contains a First Appearance**

**Strange Tales**
Contains *The Harp of Alfred (v); Easter Island (v); The Gates of Nineveh (v); excerpts from The Cairn on the Headland and The People of the Dark*
Dennis McHaney, staples, August 2001
A REHUPA contribution, contained in BLUFFTOWN BARBARIAN #8; also contains an index to all the issues of STRANGE TALES

**Strange Tales (June 1932)**
Contains *People of the Dark*
Girasol Collectables, pulp format, 2003
Replica of original pulp magazine

**Strange Tales (January 1933)**
Contains *The Cairn on the Headland*
Wildside Press, pulp format, September 2004
A facsimile reprint of the original pulp

**Strange Tales (January 1933)**
Contains *The Cairn on the Headland*
Girasol Collectables, pulp format, March 2003
Replica of the original pulp magazine

**Terminal Eyes #8**
Contains *The Dust Dance (v)*
Tim Marion, staples, November 2002
Distributed in FAPA #261 (November 2002) and REHUPA #178 (December 2002); don't know which version of this poem

**Thriller, Episode #14140**
Contains *Pigeons from Hell*
Unknown producer, TV show, 1961
TV show which did an episode based on "Pigeons from Hell"

## To Yith and Beyond

Contains *The Voices Waken Memory (v) (lines 1-18)*

Mohassuck Press, hole punch and fasteners, 1990

Facsimile reproductions of various items by Mr. Rimel; included is a facsimile reproduction of a page from THE FANTASY FAN, September 1934, that has some of Mr. Rimel's work, the page also includes the first 18 lines of "The Voices Waken Memory"; this item was limited to 125 copies, was bound via hole punched and metal prong fasteners, around 100 unnumbered pages, and was distributed in EOD

## Toadstool Wine

Contains **Drowned (v)**

W. Paul Ganley, staples, 1975

**Contains a First Appearance**; cover by Lee Brown Coye; this is an odd publication, as it is a "sampler" of material from six different small circulation fantasy/horror magazines; both WEIRDBOOK and WHISPERS are represented; the Howard poem is in the WEIRDBOOK section, but was never actually published in WEIRDBOOK (or anywhere else); W. Paul Ganley was the coordinating editor, and was also the editor for WEIRDBOOK

## The Toreador, July 5, 1925

Contains **The Sword of Mohammed (v); Girls (v); Untitled ("A Chinese washer . . .") (v)**

Truett Vinson, stapled pages, July 5, 1925

**Contains a First Appearance**; only one copy known

## The Toreador, July 25, 1925

Contents unknown, MAY contain some REH works

Truett Vinson, stapled pages, July 25, 1925

## Two Against Tyre

Contains *Two Against Tyre*

Dennis McHaney, staples, 1975

Artwork by Stephen Fabian; limited to 1500 copies total, 900 unnumbered on cheaper paper, 600 numbered on 70 lb. Strathmore Artlaid paper

## Two-Fisted Detective Stories

Contains **The Silver Heel; The Voice of Death; Untitled synopsis ("Steve Harrison received . . ."); The Sons of Hate**

Cryptic Publications, staples, May 1984

**Contains a First Appearance**; limited to 500 unnumbered copies, of which 50 are numbered and signed by Fabian and Price, 26 are lettered, and 20 are presentation copies; cover by Stephen Fabian; introduction by Robert Price; edited by Robert M. Price; "CromLech Series #2"

## Ultima Thule #1

Contains *letters to Hugh G. Schonfield, June 15, 1933 ("As I promised, . . ."); to Denis Archer, May 20, 1934 ("As you doubtless remember, . . .")*

Glenn Lord, staples, October 1975

Distributed in THE HYPERBORIAN LEAGUE #1

## Unaussprechlichen Kulten #1 (French and English)

Contains Stories: **Vengeance (Revenge)**; *Bran Mak Morn: Une Piece de Theatre (Bran Mak Morn: A Play)*; Poetry: **Custom; Counterspells**; Synopsis: *Bran Mak Morn*

Les Grande Anciens, staples, October 1990

**Contains a First Appearance**; all translations by Patrice Louinet

## Unaussprechlichen Kulten #2 (French and English)

Contains Stories: *Sans titre ("Le Danois arriva soudain . . .") (Untitled, "The Dane came in a rush . . ."); Le Dieu de Jade (The Jade God);* Poetry: *These Things Are Gods; The Phases of Life*
Les Grande Anciens, staples, July 1992
**Contains a First Appearance**; all translations by Patrice Louinet

## [Untitled zine]

Contains *a letter to Emil Petaja, July 23, 1935 ("Please believe my delay in answering . . .")*
The Strange Company (Randy Everts), staples, September 1976
**Contains a First Appearance**; for REHUPA #23; a photocopy of the original letter, in Everts' untitled contribution to this apa
The Strange Company (Randy Everts), staples, October 1976
For THE HYPERBOREAN LEAGUE 5, October 1976, again as an untitled contribution to the apa

## [Untitled zine]

Contains *two postcards to Novalyne Price, both June 19, 1935 ("Dear Novalyne . . . Cordially") and ("The weather is good . . .")*
Novalyne Price Ellis, staples, May 1991
A contribution from her to REHUPA #109, as an untitled zine

## Up, John Kane and Other Poems

Contains *Up, John Kane!; When Death Drops Her Veil; A Dying Pirate Speaks of Treasure; Mad Meg Gill; Dreams (all v)*
Roy Squires, small booklet, 1977
**Contains a First Appearance**; limited to 353 copies, numbers 1 through 297 have dark blue cover, numbers 298 through 353 have bisque cover; there are perhaps six or so of each cover that are unnumbered

## Valley of the Lost

Contains *Secret of Lost Valley (as "Valley of the Lost")*
Charles F. Miller, staples, 1975
Limited to 777 copies, at least some signed by the artist, Bot Roda

## Verses in Ebony

Contains *Empire; A Legend of Faring Town; Echoes from an Iron Anvil; The Night Winds; Men Build Them Houses; Viking's Trail; Swamp Murder; Alien; Singing Hemp; The Outgoing of Sigurd the Jerusalem-Farer; To a Friend; Revolt Pagan; To All Lords of Commerce (all v)*
George Hamilton, staples with DJ, 1975
**Contains a First Appearance**; limited to 263 copies; this edition has a black and white jacket; there was a prototype in 1974 that was somewhat smaller, different contents, and featured a color version of the same cover used in this version; there was also a few of this regular edition that came with color covers, only 20 of those produced

## Verses in Ebony (dummy prototype)

Contains *Black Dawn; The Road to Rome; The Gold and the Grey; A Song of the Naked Lands (all v)*
George Hamilton, staples with DJ, 1975
Limited to 50(?) copies; this is a prototype in 1974 that was somewhat smaller, that contained just the four poems first used by Roy Squires for his chapbooks, and featured a color version of the same black and white cover used in the final VERSES IN EBONY

## Voices of the Night and Other Poems
Contains *The Voices Waken Memory; Babel; Song at Midnight; Always Comes Evening (all v);* plus one REH photo
Necronomicon Press, staples, 1977
> Limited to 500 copies

## Warriors of the Glenn
Contains *Rune (v) (lines 27-30)*
Vern Clark, staples, May 1985
> Distributed in REHUPA #75

## Waterfront Fists and Others Promo Postcard
Contains *Kid Lavigne is Dead (v)*
Paul Herman, postcard, June 2003
> Limited to 100 copies, handed out at REH Days in Cross Plains, 2003; front had a color reproduction of book WATERFRONT FISTS AND OTHERS, and the reverse had the poem

## Weird Tales (July 1925)
Contains *Spear and Fang*
Girasol Collectables, pulp format, 2004
> Replica of original pulp magazine

## Weird Tales (April 1926)
Contains *Wolfshead*
Girasol Collectables, pulp format, November 2005
> Replica of original pulp magazine

## Weird Tales (October 1933)
Contains *The Pool of the Black One*
Girasol Collectables, pulp format, April 2005
> Replica of original pulp magazine

## Weird Tales (August 1934)
Contains *The Devil in Iron*
Girasol Collectables, pulp format, May 2007
> Replica of original pulp magazine

## Weird Tales in the Thirties
Contains *Black Chant Imperial (v) (lines 1-4 only)*
Reg Smith, staples, 1966

## Which Will Scarcely Be Understood #3
Contains *Reuben's Brethren (v)*
Rich Jervis, staples, March 1990
> Distributed in REHUPA #102

## Which Will Scarcely Be Understood (unknown number)
Contains *Symbols (v)*
Rich Jervis, staples, March 1991
> Distributed in REHUPA #108

**Whispers at Night**
Contains *Musings ("The little poets . . .")*
May 1985
>   Distributed in REHUPA #75, unknown contributor

**Whistler in the Dark**
Contains *Pigeons from Hell*
Spencer Smith, film, 2000
>   An independent film by this Memphis person, based on "Pigeons from Hell"

**Wild Water**
Contains *Wild Water*
REH Foundation, loose pages in a folder, 2007
>   **Contains a First Appearance**; facsimile reproduction of an original typescript; not sold, but a giveaway to Legacy Circle members of the REHF; printed on buff paper with "REHF" hand-initialed in red ink on each page

**Windy City Pulp and Paperback Show 2ⁿᵈ Annual**
Contains *Gates of Empire*
Pulp Vault & Black Dog Books, staples, March 2002

**Windy City Pulp Stories #7**
Contains *Alleys of Darkness*
Black Dog Books, staples, May 2007

**Wolfsdung**
Contains *Wolfsdung*
Barnswoggle Press (Thomas Kovacs), staples, 1988
>   Only three copies made; publisher listed as Barnswoggle Press

**Wolfshead: The Demon of the Full Moon #0 (Swiss)**
Contains *Musings ("The little poets . . .") (v); The One Black Stain (v); In the Forest of Villefere*
Thomas Kovacs, staples, 1981
>   Limited to 250, the poetry is in English, the story in German

**Worms of the Earth**
Contains *Worms of the Earth*
Wandering Star, CD, 2001
>   A CD containing a dramatic reading by former members of the Royal Shakespeare Company; included with the BRAN MAK MORN – THE LAST KING book from Wandering Star

**Wurg 77**
Contains *The Return of the Sea-Farer (v)*
Thomas Kovacs, staples, October 1988
>   Distributed in REHUPA #93

**Xuthol**
Contains *a letter to Emil Petaja, September 6, 1935 ("Yes, I did like . . .")*
George Hamilton, staples, May 1977
>   Distributed in REHUPA #27

**Yesteryear #4**
> Contains *a letter to TCS, ca. February 1929 ("Salaam: / Last night the Sunday School class . . ."*); **The Case of the College Toilet; Untitled ("And there were lethal women . . .") (v); Untitled ("A haunting cadence . . .") (v); Untitled ("Through the mists of silence . . .") (v); The Mysteries (v)**
> Unknown publisher, staples, October 1989
>> Distributed in PEAPS 9 (Pulp Era Amateur Press Society); first complete publication of the letter, including a short story and several verses, all of which were part of the original letter

**Yggdrasil, Volume 1, #1**
> Contains *The Mirrors of Tuzun Thune*
> Scott Sheaffer, staples, May 1992
>> Perhaps printed in a print run of a few hundred, but very rare nonetheless

**Zarfhanna #1**
> Contains *a letter to Farnsworth Wright, ca. June 1930 ("I have long looked forward to reading . . .")*
> Glenn Lord, staples, May 1974
>> Distributed in EOD

**Zarfhanna #7**
> Contains **two letters to August Lenniger, February 20, 1933 ("Here are the copies of 'The Shadow Kingdom' . . ."), and March 8, 1933 ("This is to inform you that I have . . .")**
> Glenn Lord, staples, August 1976
>> **Contains a First Appearance**; For EOD 15

**Zarfhanna #20**
> Contains *The Tempter (v) (lines 31-40)*
> Glenn Lord, staples, August 1980
>> Reprint of Dallas Morning News article

**Zarfhaana #22**
> Contains **two letters to HPL, December 3, 1934 ("Glad you found the cat article of some . . ."), and May 1934 ("Glad you're having a good time in Florida.")**
> Glenn Lord, staples, August 1981
>> **Contains a First Appearance**; distributed in EOD 35

**Zarfhanna #33**
> Contains **a letter to HPL, January 1931 ("This is rather a belated letter thanking . . .")**
> Glenn Lord, staples, August 1988
>> **Contains a First Appearance**; distributed in EOD 63

**Zarfhanna #34**
> Contains **a letter to HPL, October 1931 ("Thanks for the post-card views.")**
> Glenn Lord, staples, February 1989
>> **Contains a First Appearance**; distributed in EOD 65

**Zarfhanna #35**
> Contains *a letter to TCS, ca. May 1928 ("Salaam: / So Klatt has gone West.")*
> Glenn Lord, staples, August 1988
>> Distributed in EOD 67 (November 1989) and REHUPA #101 (January 1990)

**Zarfhanna #38**
   Contains *a letter to Weird Tales, ca. January 1929 (". . . whatever to do with beetles, . . .")*
   Glenn Lord, staples, August 1991
      For EOD; the letter was never mailed

**Zarfhanna #42**
   Contains *seven letters to RH Barlow:*
   *ca. December 1932 ("Price tells me you are interested . . .")*
   *ca. December 1932 ("I'll be glad to sign the title . . .")*
   *ca. April 2, 1933 ("Here are some notes . . .")*
   *June 1, 1934 ("Concerning the illustrations you . . .")*
   *June 14, 1934 ("If I ever decide to dispose . . .")*
   *July 5, 1934 ("Here, at last, is the last . . .")*
   *February 14, 1936 ("This is to express, somewhat belatedly . . .")*
   Glenn Lord, staples, May 1993
      **Contains a First Appearance**; distributed in EOD 82

**Zhivuschie Pod Uspya Initsami**
   Contains *The Dwellers under the Tomb*
   Lenizdat, staples, 1993
      Russian

# A SAMPLING OF NON-ENGLISH REH BOOKS AND ANTHOLOGIES

It would be most challenging to list ALL the non-English REH books. The greatest problem is the bootlegging. REH is SO popular worldwide, his works have been published in more than 20 languages, quite often simply by fans, though still published as true hardback or paperback books. The expense and difficulties in pursuing copyright lawsuits in other countries has kept the copyright owners from going after the various scofflaws. Even becoming aware of such books is exceedingly difficult, though occasionally the stray anonymous package lands on Glenn Lord's doorstep from Lithuania or Brazil.

This list is SORTED FIRST BY LANGUAGE, THEN BY BOOK TITLE. As I am not pristinely familiar with the subtleties of non-English articles in language usage, all titles are sorted by first word, period. This list also includes anthologies that contain any REH work. Works shown in **BOLD** are **First Appearance** of the work anywhere, and there will be a corresponding note in the Notes for that book that it **Contains a First Appearance**. If I know the translation of the book or story title, it is included after the title. Poetry is indicated by (v).

Abbreviations used herein include:
PB – paperback; HB – hardback; TPB – trade paperback;
nd – no date shown on book

## *Form of Entry:*
**Title**
>    Contents [foreign title listed first, if known]
>    1st edition [publisher, format, date]
>        Notes
>    Other editions
>        Notes

# BULGARIAN

**Brat Boury**
>    Contains *Brat Boury (seven unspecified Breckinridge Elkins stories); Golos Tmuy (Taverel Manor), plus 11 unspecified letters to Tevis Clyde Smith, and four to Harold Preece*
>    1st Edition, Severe Zapad, HB, 1999

**Bury Nad Orienta**
>    Contains *Tiberiyskiyat Luv (The Lion of Tiberias); Seyachi na Bury (The Sowers of the Thunder); Gospodaryat na Samarcand (The Lord of Samarcand); Syankata na Leshoyada (The Shadow of the Vulture); Plamuka na Ashurbanipali (The Fire of Asshurbanipal)*
>    1st Edition, ELF, PB, 2001
>        Translated by Stamta Strahilov

**Chernyat Kolos**
>    Contains *Pluzgashtata se Syanka (The Slithering Shadow); Cernyat Kolos (Black Colossus); Pheniks Vurhou Metcha (The Phoenix on the Sword); Choudovishteto na Pokriva (The Thing on the Roof); Proklyatieto na Moreto (Sea Curse); Gulubi ot Ada (Pigeons from Hell)*
>    1st Edition, Beva Press, PB, 1992
>        Cover by Ivalio Nenov; translated by Ivan Zlatursky & Ana Pereclijska

## Conan Zavoevatelya

Contains *Conan the Conqueror*
1st Edition, Bard, PB, 1998
  Translated by Georgy Stoyanov

## Ise Rodi Veshica

Contains *A Witch Shall Be Born*
1st Edition, Izdatelska Kusha "Plyada", PB, 1991
  Cover art by Petur Stanimirov; illustrations by Evgeniy Yordanov

## Konan Avanturista

Contains *Khorata ot Cherniya Krag (The People of the Black Circle); Prokradvasca se Syanka (The Slithering Shadow); Barabanite na Tombalku (Drums of Tombalku); Basejnat na Cherniya (The Pool of the Black One)*
1st Edition, Bard, PB, 1997
  Translated by Georgy Stoyanov

## Konan: Chasut Na Drakona

Contains *The Hour of the Dragon*
1st Edition, Beva Press, PB, 1992
  Translated by Ana Pererliyska

## Konan Skitnika

Contains *Senki v Zambula (Shadows in Zamboula); Zhelezniyat Dyavol (The Devil in Iron); Ogneniyat Kinzhal (The Flame Knife)*
1st Edition, Bard, PB, 1998
  Translated by Dimitar Dobrev

## Konan Unishtozhitelya

Contains *Khiborijskata Era (The Hyborian Age, Part 1); Kralitsata na Cherniya Briyag (Queen of the Black Coast); Prizratcite na Zamboula (Shadows in Zamboula); Chervenite Gvozdei (Red Nails); Otvad Chernata Reka (Beyond the Black River); Khiborijskata Era (The Hyborian Age, Pt. 2)*
1st Edition, Ofir, PB, 1996
  Translated by Silvana Milanova

## Konan Varvaryna

Contains *Chorata ot Chernya Krug (The People of the Black Cricle); Valshebnyat Prusten (Shadows in Zamboula); Dashteryata na Stouda (The Frost Giant's Daughter); "Surdechno Vasht: Robert Howard" (Letter to P.Schuyler Miller, March 10, 1936 ("I feel honored . . ."))*
1st Edition, Orphia, PB, 1991
  Cover art by Dariush Hoinatsky; translated by Rumyana Boshkova & Lyudmil Martinov

# CROATIAN

## Monolith 002

Contains *Zvlier iz Bezdana (The Beast from the Abyss)*
1st Edition, Zagrebacka Naklada, HB, 1999
  Edited by Davorin Horak; an anthology

## Conan

Contains *Hyborysko Doba (The Hyborian Age), Pt. 1 / Slonova Kula (The Tower of the Elephant); Dvorana Smrti (The Hall of the Dead); Bozanstvo u Kugli (The God in the Bowl); Nasilnia u Kuci (Rogues in the House); Nergalova Ruka (The Hand of Nergal)*
1st Edition, KZ Zagrebacka Naklada, PB, 1998
> Cover art by Esad T. Ribic; translated by Blanka Hrvat

# CZECH

## Bran Mak Morn

Contains *Ztracena Rasa (The Lost Race); Lide Stinu (Men of the Shadows); Kralove Noci (Kings of the Night); Pisen Jednoho Naroda (A Song of the Race) (v); Pomsta ze Zeme (Worms of the Earth); Fragment ("A gray sky arched . . ."); Temny Muz (The Dark Man); Bohove Bal-Sagoth (The Gods of Bal-Sagoth); Chant of the White Beard (v); Rune (v); Song of the Pict (v); The Drums of Pictdom (v)*
1st Edition, Laser, PB, 2000
> Reprint and translation of the Baen edition of the same title, including David Drake introduction and cover by C.W. Kelly

## Conan Barbar

Contains *Nemedijské Kriniky (The Hyborian Age), Pt. 1; Věž Slona (The Tower of the Elephant); Brih v Mise (The God in the Bowl); Darebáci v Domě (Rogues in the House); Dcera Pána Mrazu (The Frost Giant's Daughter); Královna Cerného Pobřeži (Queen of the Black Coast); Udoli Ztracených (Vale of Lost Women); Černý Kolos (Black Colossus); Stiny Měsični Záře (Shadows in the Moonlight); A Zrodi se Carodějkę (A Witch Shall Be Born); Zamboulské Stiny (Shadows in Zamboula); Dábel v Zelezo Vtělený (The Devil in Iron); Lidé Cerného Kruhu (People of the Black Circle); Pliživý Stin (The Slithering Shadow); Jezirko Toho Cerného (The Pool of the Black One)*
1st Edition, AFSF, HB, 1997
> Cover art by Petr Proksik; translated by Jan Kantûrek

## Conan Barbar

Identical to Muz Z Cimmerie; q.v.
1st Edition, AFSF, PB, 1991
> Translated by Jan Kantûrek

## Conan Dobyvatel

Contains *Rudé Hřeby (Red Nails); Gwahluruv Pokland (Jewels of Gwahlur); Za Cernou Rekou (Beyond the Black River); Meč s Fénixem (The Phoenix on the Sword); Scarlatou Citadela (Scarlet Citadel); Hodina Draka (The Hour of the Dragon); Nemedijske Kroniky (The Hyborian Age), pt. 2*
1st Edition, AFSF, HB, 1997
> Cover art by Petr Proksik; translated by Jan Kantûrek and Bedřich Možuchi

## Conan: Meč S Fénixem

Contains *Stiny v Zamboule (Shadows in Zamboula); Sloni Věž (The Tower of the Elephant); Ďáblova Dcera (A Witch Shall Be Born); Sněhová Princezna (The Frost-Giant's Daughter)*
1st Edition, Nezavisly Novinar II, PB, 1991
> Cover art by Jan Kys; translated by Petr Kachna

## Conan Barbar A Jiné Povídky

Contains *Nemeḍyské Kroniky (The Hyborian Age), pt. 1; Mihotavý Stin (The Slithering Shadow); Údoli Ztracených Žen (The Vale of Lost Women); Touto Sekyrou Vládnu Já (By This Axe I Rule!); Temná Socha (The Dark Man)*
1st Edition, Klub Julese Vernea, PB, 1991
> Cover art by Kâja Saudek

## Conan – Hodina Draka

Contains *Conan the Conqueror*
1st Edition, Winston Smith v Praze, PB, 1991
    Cover art by Joska Skalnik; translated by Jan Kantûrek

## Conan

Contains *Nemedijské Kriniky (The Hyborian Age), Pt. 1; Věž Slona (The Tower of the Elephant); Brih v Mise (The God in the Bowl); Darebáci v Domě (Rogues in the House); Dcera Pána Mrazu (The Frost Giant's Daughter); Královna Cerného Pobřeži (Queen of the Black Coast); Černý Kolos (Black Colossus); Stiny Měsični Zárě (Shadows in the Moonlight); A Zrodi se Carodějkę (A Witch Shall Be Born); Zamboulské Stiny (Shadows in Zamboula); Dábel v Zelezo Vtělený (The Devil in Iron); Lidé Cerného Kruhu (People of the Black Circle); Pliživý Stin (The Slithering Shadow); Jezirko Toho Cerného (The Pool of the Black One); Rudé Hřeby (Red Nails); Gwahluruv Pokland (Jewels of Gwahlur); Za Cernou Rekou (Beyond the Black River); Meč s Fénixem (The Phoenix on the Sword); Šarlatová Citadela (The Scarlet Citadel); Nemedijské Kroniky (The Hyborian Age), pt. 2*
1st Edition, AFSF, HB, 1994
    Cover art by Petr Proksik; translated by Jan Kantûrek

## Sarlatova Citadela

Contains *Sarlatova Citadela (The Scarlet Citadel)*
1st Edition, Nova Vina, PB, 1992
    Translated by Michael Bronec

## Tygři Moře

Contains *Temný Muž (The Dark Man); Bohové Bal-Sagoth (The Gods of Bal-Sagoth); Lidé Stinů (Men of the Shadows); Ztracená Rasa (The Lost Race); Aššurbanipalův Plamen (The Fire of Asshurbanipal); Svatyně Odpornosti (The Temple of Abomination); Meče Serverniho Moře (Swords of the Northern Sea); Noc Vlka (Night of the Wolf); Tygři Moře (Tigers of the Sea)*
1st Edition, Laser, PB, 1993
    Cover art by Boris Vallejo; translated by Michael Bronec

## Vez Slona A Jine Povidky

Contents unknown
1st Edition, Zlaty Kun, PB, 1989
Nakladatelstvi BB Art, PB, 2000

# DUTCH

## Almuric

Contains *Almuric*
1st Edition, Scala SF, PB, 1977

## Conan

Contains *Het Hyboriaanse Tijdperk (The Hyborian Age), Pt. 1; De Toren van de Olifant (The Tower of the Elephant); De Zaal der Doden (The Hall of the Dead); De God in de Schaal (The God in the Bowl); Schurken in Huis (Rogues in the House); De Hand van Nergal (The Hand of Nergal)*
1st Edition, A. W. Bruna & Zoon, PB, 1976
    Cover art by Julius de Goede; translated by F. Lancel (The Tower of the Elephant and The Hyborian Age) and Pon Ruiter (remainder); reprint of Lancer CONAN book

## Conan De Avonturier (Conan the Adventurer)

Contains *De Priesters van de Zwarte Kring (The People of the Black Circle); De Glijdende Schaduw (The Slithering Shadow); De Tom-Toms van Tombalku (Drums of Tombalku); De Poel van het Groene Verderf (The Pool of the Black One)*
1st Edition, A. W. Bruna & Zoon, PB, 1978
> Cover art by L. Ashton Fisher; translated by Pon Ruiter; reprint of Lancer's CONAN THE ADVENTURER

## Conan De Barbaar

Contains *Het Hyboriaanse Tijdperk (The Hyborian Age), Pt. 1; De Toren van de Olifant (The Tower of the Elephant); De Zaal der Doden (The Hall of the Dead); De God in de Schaal (The God in the Bowl); Schurken in Huis (Rogues in the House); De Hand van Nergal (The Hand of Nergal)*
1st Edition, W & L Boeken, PB, 1983
> Cover art by Bosis Vallejo; translated by F. Lancel (The Tower of the Elephant and The Hyborian Age) Pon Ruiter (remainder); a reprint of the Lancer CONAN book

## Conan De Barbaar: Het Uur Van De Draak (Conan the Barbarian: Hour of the Dragon)

Contains *The Hour of the Dragon; verse heading from Hour of the Dragon; Cimmeria (lines 2-5, 18)*
1st Edition, Uitgeverij Gradivus B.V., PB, 1982
> Translated from WEIRD TALES; cover art by Oliviero Berni; translated by Pon Ruiter

## Conan De Krijger (Conan the Warrior)

Contains *Rode Spijkers (Red Nails); Juwelen van Gwahlur (Jewels of Gwahlur); Aan de Overkant van de Zwarte Rivier (Beyond the Black River)*
1st Edition, A. W. Bruna & Zoon, PB, 1978
> Cover art by L. Ashton Fisher; translated by Pon Ruiter and Frits Lancel (Red Nails); reprint of CONAN THE WARRIOR

## Conan De Overweldiger (Conan the Usurper)

Contains *De Schat van Tranicos (The Treasure of Tranicos); Wolven Over de Grens (Wolves Beyond the Border); De Feniks op het Zwaard (The Phoenix on the Sword); Scharlaken Citadel (The Scarlet Citadel)*
1st Edition, A. W. Bruna & Zoon, PB, 1979
> Cover art by L. Ashton Fisher; translated by Pon Ruiter; reprint of CONAN THE USURPER

## Conan Der Vrijbuiter

Contains *Haviken boven Shem (Hawks Over Shem); De Zwarte Kolos (Black Colossus); Schaduwen in het Maanlicht (Shadows in the Moonlight); Het Pad der Adelaars (The Road of the Eagles); Zal u een Heks Geboren Worden (A Witch Shall be Born)*
1st Edition, A. W. Bruna & Zoon, PB, 1977
> Cover art by Julius de Goede; translated by Pon Ruiter; reprint of CONAN THE FREEBOOTER

## Conan Der Zwerver

Contains *Schaduwen in Zamboula (Shadows in Zamboula); De Duivel van Ijzer (The Devil in Iron); Het Vlammende Mes (The Flame Knife)*
1st Edition, A. W. Bruna & Zoon, PB, 1977
> Cover art by Julius de Goede; translated by C.A.G. van den Broek (Shadows in Zamboula) and Pon Ruiter (remainder); reprint of CONAN THE WANDERER

## Conan En De Koningin Van De Zwarte Kust

Contains *De Bloedbevlekte God (The Bloodstained God); De Dochter van de Ijsreus (The Frost Giant's Daughter); De Koningin van de Zwarte Kust (Queen of the Black Coast); Het dal der Verloren Vrouwen (The Vale of Lost Women); De Muil in het Duister (The Snout in the Dark)*
1st Edition, W & L Boeken, PB, 1983
    Cover art by Bosis Vallejo; translated by Pon Ruiter

## Conan En De Scharlaken Citadel

Contains *De Schat van Tranicos (The Treasure of Tranicos); Wolven over de Grens (Wolves Beyond the Border); De Feniks op het Zwaard (The Phoenix on the Sword); Scharlaken Citadel (The Scarlet Citadel)*
1st Edition, W & L Boeken, PB, 1984
    Translated by Pon Ruiter

## Conan En Het Vlammende Mes

Contains *Schaduwen in Zamboula (Shadows in Zamboula); De Duivel van Ijzer (The Devil in Iron); Het Vlammende Mes (The Flame Knife)*
1st Edition, W & L Boeken, PB, 1983
    Cover art by Bosis Vallejo; translated by Pon Ruiter; reprint of CONAN THE WANDERER

## Conan Van Cimmerie (Conan of Cimmeria)

Contains *The Bloodstained God; The Frost Giant's Daughter; Queen of the Black Coast; Vale of Lost Women; The Snout in the Dark*
1st Edition, Bruna, PB, 1976
    Reprint of Lancer's CONAN OF CIMMERIA

## De Bewoner Van Het Meer (The Inhabitants of the Lake)

Contains *Dig Me No Grave*
1st Edition, Bruna, PB, 1968
    Book #1225

## De Stem Van El-Lil (The Voice of El-Lil)

Contains *De Heuvels van de Doden (The Hills of the Dead); De Vergissing van Esau Brill (The Man on the Ground); De Toren van de Olifant (The Tower of the Elephant); De Stem van El-Lil (The Voice of El-Lil); De Grijze God (The Grey God Passes); De Verschrikking van het Graf (The Horror from the Mound); Koningen der Duisternis (Kings of the Night); Rode Spijkers (Red Nails); De Terugkeer van Solomon Kane (Solomon Kane's Homecoming) (v); Het Hyboriaanse Tijdperk (The Hyborian Age)*
1st Edition, A.W. Bruna & Zoon, 1972
    Cover art by Dick Bruna; edited by A.C. Prins; translated by Frits Lancel; Book #FEH 5

## De Zwarte Steen (The Black Stone)

Contains *De Zwarte Steen (The Black Stone); Koninkrijk der Schaduwen (The Shadow Kingdom); Vleugels in de Nacht (Wings in the Night); Het Vuur van Assoerbanipal (The Fire of Asshurbanipal); Schimmen in Zamboela (Shadows in Zamboula); Het Binnenste der Aarde (Worms of the Earth)*
1st Edition, A.W. Bruna & Zoon, PB, 1969
    Cover art by Dick Bruna; interior heading by Frank Utpatel; translated by C.A.G. van den Broek; Book #1272; illustrated by Aart C. Prins

# ESTONIAN

## Conan Ja Varelev Vari

Contains *Musta Ringi Rahvas (The People of the Black Circle); Varelev Vari (The Slithering Shadow); Musta Olevuse Tuk (The Pool of the Black One); Punased Naeled (Red Nails); Gwahluri Kalliskivid (Jewels of Gwahlur)*
1st Edition, Elmatar, HB, 2000
    Translated by Jaana Peetersoo

## Conan Ja Punane Kants

Contains *Teisel Pool Musta Jöge (Beyond the Black River); Fööniks Möögateral (Phoenix on the Sword); Punane Kants (The Scarlet Citadel); Draakoni Tund (The Hour of the Dragon)*
1st Edition, Elmatar, HB, 2000
    Translated by Jaana Petterson

## Conan Ja Musta Ranniku Kuninganna

Contains *Elevanditorn (The Tower of the Elephant); Maja Tais Kurjategijaid (Rogues in the House); Musta Ranniku Kuninganna (Queen of the Black Coast); Must Koloss (Black Colossus); Varjud Kuuvalguses (Shadows in the Moonlight); Noid on Sundinud (A Witch Shall Be Born); Varjud Zambulas (Shadows in Zamboula); Kurat Raudses Ihus (The Devil in Iron)*
1st Edition, Elmatar, HB, 1999
    Translated by Jaana Peetersoo

## Draakoni Tund

Contains *The Hour of the Dragon*
1st Edition, Fantaasia, PB, 1999

## Pimeduse Rahvas

Contains *Villefere'i Metsas (In the Forest of Villefere); Hundipea (Wolfshead); Must Kanaan (Black Canaan); Huaan (The Hyena); Vana Garfieldi Suda (Old Garfield's Heart); Kivikaime Neemel (The Cairn on the Headland); Pimeduse Rahvas (People of the Dark)*
1st Edition, Fantaasia, HB, 2002

# FINNISH

## Conan Taistelija

Contains *Musta Kolossi (Black Colossus); Noita on Syntyvä (A Witch Shall Be Born); Punaiset Naulat (Red Nail); Feeniks-lintu Miekassa (The Phoenix on the Sword); Tulipunainen Linnoitus (The Scarlet Citadel)*
1st Edition, Kustanus Oy Jalava, PB, 1990
    Cover art by Petri Hiltunen; translated by Ulla Selkälä

## Kadotussen Kuilu

Contains *Pimeyden Kansa (The People of the Dark); Pako Atlantiksesta (Exile of Atlantis); Hil jaisuuden Kallo (The Skull of Silence); Valtakunnan Miekat (Swords of the Purple Kingdom); Käärme Paratiisissa (The Vale of Lost Women); Harmaan Jumalan Tuho (The Grey God Passes); Korppikotkan Varjo (The Shadow of the Vulture); Pääkallokuu (The Moon of Skulls); Askeleita Hautaholvissa (The Footfalls Within); Kadotettujen Laakso (The Valley of the Lost)*
1st Edition, Werner Soders rom Osakeyhtio, PB, 1993
    Translated by Ulla Selkälä

## Kauhupokkari 1 (Horror-Collection 1)
Contains *Dig Me No Grave*
1$^{st}$ Edition, Javala, PB, 1991
>   Artwork by Petri Hiltunen; edited by Markku Sadelehto

## Musta Kivi (The Black Stone)
Contains *The Black Stone*
1$^{st}$ Edition, WSOY, PB, 1995
>   A collection of horror/fantasy-stories; edited by Markku Sadelehto

## Mustan Jumalan Suudelma (Kiss of the Black God)
Contains *The Black Stranger*
1$^{st}$ Edition, WSOY, PB, 1993
>   A collection of horror/fantasy-stories; edited by Markku Sadelehto

## Outoja Tarinoita 1 (Weird Tales 1)
Contains *Pigeons from Hell*
1$^{st}$ Edition, Javala, PB, 1990
>   One of six volumes; artwork by Petri Hiltunen; edited by Markku Sadelehto

## Outoja Tarinoita 4 (Weird Tales 4)
Contains *Black Canaan*
1$^{st}$ Edition, Javala, PB, 1992
>   One of a six volume set; artwork by Petri Hiltunen; edited Markku Sadelehto

## Outoja Tarinoita 5 (Weird Tales 5)
Contains *The Horror from the Mound*
1$^{st}$ Edition, Javala, PB, 1993
>   One of a six volume set; artwork by Petri Hiltunen; edited by Markku Sadelehto

## Pimeyden Linnake (Fortress of Darkness)
Contains *The Gods of Bal-Sagoth*
1$^{st}$ Edition, Javala, PB, 1991
>   A collection of fantasy stories; artwork by Petri Hiltunen; edited by Markku Sadelehto

## REH: Conan Cimmerialainen (REH: Conan of Cimmeria)
Contains *Cimmeria (v); The Frost Giant's Daughter; Shadows in the Moonlight; Slithering Shadows; The Pool of the Black One; Jewels of Gwahlur*
1$^{st}$ Edition, Javala, PB, 1991
Javala, PB, 2$^{nd}$ printing, 2000
>   Edited and artwork by Petri Hiltunen

## REH: Conan Ja Demonit (REH: Conan and Demons)
Contains *The Tower of the Elephant; Rogues in the House; Queen of the Black Coast; The People of the Black Circle; Beyond the Black River*
1$^{st}$ Edition, Javala, PB, 1990
>   Artwork by Petri Hiltunen; edited by Markku Sadelehto

## REH: Conan Taistelija (REH: Conan the Warrior)
Contains *Black Colossus; A Witch Shall Be Born; Red Nails; The Phoenix on the Sword; The Scarlet Citadel*
1$^{st}$ Edition, Javala, PB, 1990
>   Artwork by Petri Hiltunen; edited by Markku Sadelehto

## REH: Conan Voittaja (REH: Conan Victorious)

Contains *The Hour of the Dragon*

1st Edition, Javala, PB, 1991

> Suppose to be "Conan the Conqueror", but actually it translates more like "Conan Victorious"; artwork by Petri Hiltunen

## REH: Kadotuksen Kuilu (Abyss of Damnation)

Contains *People of the Dark; Exile of Atlantis; The Skull of Silence; Swords of the Purple Kingdom; The Vale of Lost Women; The Grey God Passes; The Shadow of the Vulture; The Moon of Skulls; The Footfalls Within; The Valley of the Lost*

1st Edition, WSOY, PB, 1993

> Edited by Markku Sadelehto

## REH: Yön Kuninkaat (REH: Kings of the Night)

Contains *The Shadow Kingdom; The Mirrors of Tuzun Thune; By This Axe I Rule!; Kings of the Night; Worms of the Earth; The Dark Man; Red Shadows; The Hills of the Dead; Wings in the Night*

1st Edition, WSOY, PB, 1992

> Edited by Markku Sadelehto

## Velhojen Valtakunta (Realms of Sorcerers)

Contains *Shadows in Zamboula*

1st Edition, Javala, PB, 1987

> A collection of fantasy stories; artwork by Petri Hiltunen; edited by Juhani Hinkkanen

# FRENCH

## Admirations

Contains *the verse heading from Chapter 4 of The Phoenix on the Sword; the verse heading from Chapter 2 and 5 of The Scarlet Citadel*

Christian Bourgois, PB, 1970

Les Editions de l'Oeil du Sphinx, PB, 2000

> In French, authored by Jacques Bergier, one of the earliest and most famous REH fan in France, this book is a collection of ten articles about his favorite authors, including one on REH; the original version is quite difficult to locate; the later edition is POD

## Agnes De Chastillon

Contains *Agnès la Noire (Sword Woman); Des Epées pour la France (Blades for France); La Maîtresse de la Mort (Mistress of Death); Au Service du Roi (The King's Service); L'Ombre du Hun (Shadow of the Hun)*

1st Edition, NeO, PB, June 1983

NeO, PB, 2nd printing, September 1985(?)

> Cover by Jean-Michel Nicollet; translated by Francois Truchaud; Book #78

Fleuve Noir, PB, 1993

> Cover art by Gilles Francescano ; Book #21

## Almuric

Contains *Almuric*

1st Edition, NeO, PB, June 1986

> Cover by Jean-Michel Nicollet; translated by Francois Truchaud; Book #174

Fleuve Noir, PB, 1991

> Cover art by Gilles Francescano; Book #8

## Atlantides

Contains *La Lune des Crânes (The Moon of Skulls); Le Royaume des Chimères (The Shadow Kingdom)*
1st Edition, Presses de la Cite ("Omnibus"), HB, 1989

Presses de la Cite ("Omnibus"), HB, 2nd printing, expected in 2000(?)
    Translation by Francois Truchaud

## Bran Mak Morn

Contains *La Race Oubliée (The Lost Race); Les Hommes des Ténèbres (Men of the Shadows); Les Rois de la Nuit (Kings of the Night); Les Vers de la Terre (Worms of the Earth); Fragment; Le Crépuscule du Dieu Gris (The Grey God Passes)*
1st Edition, NeO, PB, November 1982
NeO, PB, 2nd printing, January 1985
NeO, PB, 3rd printing, 1986(?)
    Cover by Jean-Michel Nicollet; translated by Francois Truchaud; Book #60
Fleuve Noir, PB, 1992
    Cover art by Gilles Francescano; Book #18

## Chants de Guerre et de Mort (Poems of War and Death)

Contains *Always Comes Evening; The Poets; The Singer in the Mists; Solomon Kane's Homecoming; Futility; The Song of the Bats; The Moor Ghost; Recompense; The Hills of Kandahar; Which Will Scarcely Be Understood; Haunting Columns; The Last Hour; Ships; The King and the Oak; The Riders of Babylon; Easter Island; Moon Mockery; Shadows on the Road; The Soul-Eater; The Dream and the Shadow; The Ghost Kings; Desert Dawn; An Open Window; The Song of the Mad Minstrel; The Gates of Ninevah; Fragment; The Harp of Alfred; Remembrance; Crete; Forbidden Magic; Black Chant Imperial; A Song Out of Midian; Arkham; The Voices Waken Memory; Babel; Song At Midnight; The Ride of Falume; Autumn; Dead Man's Hate; One Who Comes at Eventide; To a Woman; Emancipation; Retribution; Chant of the White Beard; Rune; The Road of Azrael; Song of the Pict; Prince and Beggar; Hymn of Hatred; Invective; Men of the Shadows; Babylon; Nifheim; The Heart of the Sea's Desire; Laughter in the Gulfs; A Song of the Don Cossacks; The Gods of Easter Island; Nisapur; Moon Shame; The Tempter; Lines Written in the Realization That I Must Die; A Crown for a King; plus chapter headings from The Pool of the Black One, Kings of the Night, Red Blades of Black Cathay, The Phoenix on the Sword, The Scarlet Citadel, and Queen of the Black Coast (all v)*
1st Edition, NeO, PB, January 1987
    Cover and color plates by Jean-Michel Nicollet; edited by Francois Truchaud; this is a French edition of Underwood-Miller's ALWAYS COMES EVENING, with the contents rearranged, and some deleted; bilingual edition (French and English); the first edition is limited to 500 copies, and is numbered
NeO, PB, 2nd Edition, 1988
    The 2nd only has an illustration on the cover, a much larger print run of 4264 copies, and is a smaller physical size

## Conan

Contains *The Hyborian Age (Part 1); La Tour de L'Eléphant (The Tower of the Elephant); La Chambre des Morts (The Hall of the Dead); Le Dieu dans L'Urne (The God in the Bowl); Le Rendez-vous des Bandits (Rouges in the House); La Main de Nergal (The Hand of Nergal)*
1st Edition, Edition Spéciale, PB, 1972
    Cover art by Philippe Druillet; translated by Anne Zribi; based on Lancer/Ace editions
Editions J.-C. Lattes, PB, 1980
    Cover art by Keleck; translated by Anne Zribi
Editions J'ai Lu, PB 1980
    Translation by Anne Zribi; Book Code #1754; cover art by Frank Frazetta
Editions J'ai Lu, PB, 1984

# Conan

Contains *The Hyborian Age (Part 1); The Tower of the Elephant; The Hall of the Dead (completed by LSDC); The God in the Bowl; Rogues in the House; The Hand of Nergal (completed by Lin Carter) plus a letter to P. Schuyler Miller, March 10, 1936 ("I feel indeed honored that you and Dr. Clark . . ."); The Bloodstained God (with LSDC); The Frost Giant's Daughter; Queen of the Black Coast; Vale of Lost Women; The Snout in the Dark (completed by LSDC and Lin Carter); Hawks Over Shem (with LSDC); Black Colossus; Shadows in the Moonlight; The Road of the Eagles (with LSDC); A Witch Shall Be Born; Shadows in Zamboula; The Devil in Iron; The Flame Knife (with LSDC)*

1st Edition, Claude Lefroncq Editeur s.a., PB, 1998
> Cover art by Doug Beekmann; reprints the first four Lancer Conan books

# Conan la Fin de L'Atlantide

Contains *Le Peuple du Cercle Noir (The People of the Black Circle); L'Ombre de Xuthal (The Slithering Shadow); Les Tambours de Tombalku (Drums of Tombalku); Le Bassin de L'Ile aux Géants (The Pool of the Black One)*

1st Edition, Edition Speciale, 1972
> Cover art by Philippe Druillet; translated by Francois Truchaud

# Conan La Naissance Du Monde

Contains *Les Clous Rouges (Red Nails); Les Joyaux de Gwahlur (Jewels of Gwahlur); Au-delá de la Rivière Noire (Beyond the Black River)*

1st Edition, Édition Spéciale, PB, 1972
> Covert art by Philippe Druillet; translated by Francois Truchaud

# Conan L'Aventurier

Contains *Le Peuple du Cercle Noir (The People of the Black Circle); L'Ombre de Xuthal (The Slithering Shawdow); Les Tambours de Tombalku (Drums of Tombalku); Le Bassin de L'Ile aux Géants (The Pool of the Black One)*

1st Edition, Editions J.-C. Lattés, PB, 1980
> Translated by Francois Truchaud; cover art by Frank Frazetta; based on Lancer's CONAN THE ADVENTURER

Éditions J'ai lu, PB, 1986

# Conan Le Cimmérien

Contains *Le Dieu Taché de Sang (The Bloodstained God); La Fille du Géant du Gel (The Frost-Giant's Daughter); La Reine de la Côte Noire (Queen of the Black Coast); la Vallée des Femmes Perdues (The Vale of Lost Women); Le Groin dans les Ténèbres (The Snout in the Dark)*

1st Edition, Editions J.-C. Lattés, PB, 1982
> Cover art by Keleck; translated by Francois Truchaud

Editions J'Ai Lu, PB
> Cover art by Frank Frazetta; translated by Francois Truchaud

# Conan Le Conquerant (Conan the Conqueror)

Contains *The Hour of the Dragon (as Conan the Conqueror)*

1st Edition, J'ai Lu, PB, 1980
> Translation by Francois Truchaud; new cover by Frank Frazetta; Book Code #2468

Editions J.-C. Lattés, PB, 1980
Éditions J'ai Lu, PB, 1988

# Conan Le Flibustier

Contains *Des Esperviers sur Shem (Hawks over Shem); Le Colosse Noir (Black Colossus); Des Ombres dans la Clarté Lunaire (Shadows in the Moonlight); La Route des Aigles (The Road of the Eagles); Une Sorciere Viendra au Monde! (A Witch Shall Be Born)*

1st Edition, Editions J.-C. Lattés, PB, 1982

Cover art by Jean-Michel Nicollet; translated by Francois Truchaud
Éditions J'ai Lu, PB, 1985
Cover art by Frank Frazetta; translated by Francois Truchaud

## Conan Le Guerrier

Contains *Les Clous Rouges (Red Nails); Les Joyaux de Gwahlur (Jewels of Gwahlur); Au-dela de la Riviére Noire (Beyond the Black River)*
1st Edition, Éditions J.-C. Lattés, PB, 1981
Cover art by Jean-Michel Nicollet; translated by Francois Truchaud
Éditions J'ai Lu, PB, 1986
Cover art by Frank Frazetta; translated by Francois Truchaud

## Conan Le Vagabond

Contains *Les Ombres de Zamboula (Shadow in Zamboula); Le Diable d'Airain (The Devil in Iron); Le Kriss (The Flame-Knife)*
1st Edition, Éditions J.-C. Lattés, PB, 1982
Cover art by Jean-Michel Nicollet; translated by Eric Chédaille
Éditions J'ai Lu, PB, 1985
Cover art by Frank Frazetta; translated by Francois Truchaud

## Conan L'Usurpateur

Contains *Le Trésor de Tranicos (The Treasure of Tranicos); Des Loups sur la Frontiere (Wolves Beyond the Border); Le Phénix sur l'Épée (The Phoenix on the Sword); La Citadelle Écarlate (The Scarlet Citadel)*
1st Edition, Éditions J.-C. Lattés, PB, 1982
Cover art by Jean-Michel Nicollet; translated by Eric Chédaille
Editions J'Ai Lu, PB, 1986
Editions J'Ai Lu, PB, 1987

## Cormac Fitzgeoffrey

Contains *Les Aigles d'Outremer (Hawks of Outremer); Le Sang de Belshazzar (The Blood of Belshazzar); La Princesse Esclave (The Slave Princess); Les Epées Rouges de Cathay la Noire (Red Blades of Black Cathay); Les Morts se Souviennent (The Dead Remember)*
1st Edition, NeO, PB, November 1984
Cover by Jean-Michel Nicollet; translated by Francois Truchaud; Book #123

## Cormac Mac Art

Contains *Les Tigres de la Mer (Tigers of the Sea); Les Epées de Mers Nordiques (Swords of the Northern Sea); La Nuit du Loup (The Night of the Wolf); Le Temple de l'Abomination (The Temple of Abomination); La Maison d'Arabu (The House of Arabu)*
1st Edition, NeO, PB, January 1983
NeO, PB, 2nd printing, date unknown
Cover by Jean-Michel Nicollet, translated by Francois Truchaud; Book #66
Fleuve Noir, PB, 1992
Cover by Gilles Francescano; Book #14

## Dennis Dorgan

Contains **Un Poing Capital (Hard-Fisted Sentiment)**; *La Nuit où Steve Costigan . . . (Untitled ("The night Steve Costigan . . .")); C'était la fin du quatrième round . . . (Untitled ("It was the end of the fourth round . . .")); **Marin et Boxeur (The Battling Sailor); Pour l'Honneur du Navire (The Honor of the Ship)**; Les Ruelles de Singapour (Alleys of Darkness); Le Singe de Jade (Sailor Dorgan and the Jade Monkey); Le Rubis Mandarine (Alleys of Treachery); Le Cobra Jaune (The Yellow Cobra); Dans la Haute Société (In High Society); Dennis Joue les Journalistes (A New Game for Dorgan); Le Gorille du Destin (The Destiny Gorilla); Un Chevalier de la Table Ronde (A Knight of the Round Table); Un Père Noël Musclé (A Two-Fisted Santa Claus); La Menace Turque (The Turkish Menace)*

NeO, PB, July 1987
> **Contains a First Appearance**; cover by Jean-Michel Nicollet; translated by Francois Truchaud; Book #192

## Des Spectres dans la Ténèbres, (Spectres in the Dark)
Contains *Des Spectres Dans la Ténèbres, (Spectres in the Dark)*
1<sup>st</sup> Edition, La Clef D'Argent, PB, 1989
> Translation by P. Gindre

## El Borak le Magnifique (El Borak the Magnificent)
Contains *Shalizahr la Mystérieuse (Three-Bladed Doom (long version)); L'Horreur Sans Nez (The Noseless Horror); La Malédiction du Crâne d'Or (The Curse of the Golden Skull)*
1<sup>st</sup> Edition, NeO, PB, March 1984
> Cover by Jean-Michel Nicollet, translated by Francois Truchaud; Book #102
Fleuve Noir, PB, 1992
> Cover by Gilles Francescano; Book #13

## El Borak le Redoutable (El Borak the Redoubtable)
Contains *Le Sang des Dieux (Blood of the Gods); Le Pays du Couteau (Country of the Knife); Le Fils du Loup Blanc (Son of the White Wolf)*
1<sup>st</sup> Edition, NeO, PB, February 1984
> Cover art by Jean-Michel Nicollet; translated by Francois Truchaud; based on SON OF THE WHITE WOLF; Book #99
Fleuve Noir, PB, 1992
> Cover by Gilles Francescano; Book #11

## El Borak l'Eternel (El Borak the Eternal)
Contains ***El Borak (El Borak ("I emptied my revolver . . .")); La Venue d'El Borak (The Coming of El Borak); Un Certain Frank Gordon (El Borak ("Were you ever . . .")); Intrigues au Kurdistan (Intrigue in Kurdistan); La Terreur d'Acier (The Iron Terror); Le Récit de Khoda Khan (Khoda Khan's Tale); Le Pays du Mystère (The Land of Mystery); Au Nord de la Passe de Khaïbar (North of Khyber); Aventure Dans les Iles (A Power Among the Isles); Le Château Maudit (The Shunned Castle); Gordon l'Américain (Untitled ("Gordon the American . . ."))***
1<sup>st</sup> Edition, NeO, PB, May 1984
> **Contains a First Appearance**; cover by Jean-Michel Nicollet, translated by Francois Truchaud; Book #108
Fleuve Noir, PB, 1992
> > Cover by Gilles Francescano; Book #15

## El Borak l'Invincible (El Borak the Invincible)
Contains *La Fille d'Erlik Khan (The Daughter of Erlik Khan); La Vallée Perdue d'Iskander (The Lost Valley of Iskander); L'Aigle des Collines (Hawk of the Hills)*
1<sup>st</sup> Edition, NeO, PB, August 1983
> Cover by Jean-Michel Nicollet, translated by Francois Truchaud; Book #87
Fleuve Noir, PB, 1992
> Cover by Gilles Francescano; Book #9

## Fureur Noirs
Contains *Magie Noire á Canaan (Black Canaan); Le Feu d'Asshurbanipal (The Fire of Asshurbanipal); Les Guerriers du Valhalla (Marchers of Valhalla); La Vallée du Ver (The Valley of the Worm); La Voix d'El-Lil (The Voice of El-lil)*
1st Edition, Nouvelles Éditions Marabout, PB, 1981
> Cover art by Jean Alessandrini; translated by Francois Truchaud

## Histoires Anglo-Saxonnes de Vampires (Anglo-Saxon Stories of Vampires)

Contain *Le Tertre Maudit (The Horror from the Mound)*
1$^{st}$ Edition, Libraries des Champ-Elysees, PB, 1978
>> Translation by J. Marigny

## Histoires de Cauchemars

Contains *Le Serpent du Rêve (The Dream Snake)*
1$^{st}$ Edition, Presses Pocket, PB, 1977
>> Translated by J. Papy

## Histoires d'Outre-Monde (Stories of the Outer World)

Contains *Coup Double (The Man on the Ground)*
1$^{st}$ Edition, Casterman, HB, 1966
>> Translation by J. Papy

## Kirby O'Donnell

Contains *Le Trésor des Tartares (The Treasures of Tartary); Les Epees de Shahrazar (Swords of Shahrazar); La Malédiction du Dieu Pourpre (Trail of the Bloodstained God); Les Adorateurs du Diable (The Brazen Peacock); La Vengeance de l'Ours Noir (The Black Bear Bites); La Hyène (The Hyena)*
1$^{st}$ Edition, NeO, PB, September 1984
>> Cover by Jean-Michel Nicollet; translated by Francois Truchaud; Book #117

## Kull le Roi Barbare (Kull the Barbarian King)

Contains *Exilé d'Atlantis (Exile of Atlantis); Le Royaume des Chimères (The Shadow Kingdom); L'Autel et le Scorpion (The Altar and the Scorpion); Noirs Abysses (Black Abyss); Le Chat de Delcardes (Delcardes' Cat); Le Crâne du Silence (The Skull of Silence); Ceux qui allèrent au-delà du soleil levant (Untitled ("'Thus,' said Tu . . .")); Par Cette Hache Je Règne! (By This Axe I Rule!); Le Coup de Gong (The Striking of the Gong); Les Epées du Royaume Pourpre (Swords of the Purple Kingdom); Magicien et Guerrier (Wizard and Warrior); Les Miroirs de Tuzun Thune (The Mirrors of Tuzun Thune)*
1$^{st}$ Edition, NeO, PB, 1980
>> Cover by Jean-Michel Nicollet; translated by Francois Truchaud; based on Lancer KING KULL; Book #10
NeO, PB, 2$^{nd}$ printing, May 1983
NeO, PB, 3$^{rd}$ printing, September 1984
Euredif, PB, 1984
>> Book #35
NeO, PB, 4$^{th}$ printing, April 1988
Fleuve Noir, PB, 1992
>> Cover by Gilles Francescano; Book #10

## La Citadelle Ecarlate (The Scarlet Citadel)

Contains *Le Crane du Silence (The Skull of Silence); Clair de Lune sur un Krane (Moonlight on a Skull) (v); Niniv (Dreams of Ninevah) (v); Mais ou Sont tes Reves d-Autrefois (But the Hills Were Ancient Then?) (v); Cimmerie (Cimmeria) (v); La Citadelle Ecarlate (The Scarlet Citadel)*
1$^{st}$ Edition, Presses Pocket, PB, 1979
>> Translator unknown; Book Code #5055 (possibly Jeff Jones, but doesn't look like his work), edited by Marc Duveau

## La Flamme De La Vengeance (The Flame of Vengeance)

Contains *Le Moment Suprême (The Supreme Moment); Les Cavaliers Noirs de la Mort (Death's Black Riders); Les Souterrains de l'Horreur (Dagon Manor); L'Apparition Sur le Ring (The Apparition in the Ring); La Grande Combine (Double Cross); Le Fantôme au Chapeau de Soie (The Ghost with the Silk Hat); plus a history of Solomon Kane by Fred Blosser*

1st Edition, NeO, PB, April 1988

Cover by Jean-Michel Nicollet, translated by Francois Truchaud; Book #206

## La Grande Anthologie Du Fantastique (The Big Anthology of Fantasy)

Contains *Le Serpent du Rêve (The Dream Snake)*

1st Edition, Casterman, HB, 1967

Presses Pocket, PB, 1977

Presses de la Cite, PB, February 1996

Translation by J. Papy

## La Main De La Deesse Noire (Hand of the Black Goddess)

Contains *La Main de la Déesse Noire (Hand of the Black Goddess); Le Collier de Balkis (Sons of Hate); Les Invités de la Chambre Maudite (Guests of the Hoodoo Room)*

1st Edition, NeO, PB, March 1986

Cover by Jean-Michel Nicollet, translated by Francois Truchaud; Book #164

Fleuve Noir, PB, 1993

Cover by Gilles Francescano; Book #20

## La Route D'azrael (The Road of Azrael)

Contains *Des Eperviers Sur l'Egypte (Hawks Over Egypt); Sur les Traces de Bohémond (The Track of Bohemund); Les Portes de l'Empire (Gates of Empire); La Route d'Azrael (The Road of Azrael)*

1st Edition, NeO, PB, May 1986

Cover by Jean-Michel Nicollet, translated by Francois Truchaud; Book #170

Fleuve Noir, PB, 1993

Cover by Gilles Francescano; Book #19

## La Tombe du Dragon (Tomb of the Dragon)

Contains *La Tombe du Dragon (Tomb of the Dragon);* **Le Roi des Iles (Shackled Mitts);** *Le Bûcheron du Diable (The Devil's Woodchopper); Sous le Baobab (Under the Baobab Tree);* **Un Amour Eternel (Age Lasting Love);** *Les Dieux du Nord (The Frost-King's Daughter); Le Sortilège de Damballah (The Spell of Damballah);* **L'Esprit de Brian Boru (The Spirit of Brian Boru);** *Le Retour du Sorcier (The Return of the Sorcier); La Porte du Monde (The Door of the World); le Maître de la Peur (The Fear-Master); La Voix d'Obi (The Hand of Obeah);* **Un Couple Racé (Thoroughbreds);** *Miss Pimbêche (Miss High-Hat);* **Le Sexe Faible (The Weaker Sex);** *Les Pierres du Destin (The Stones of Destiny); La Malédiction de la Cupidité (The Curse of Greed); Une Question d'Age (A Matter of Age); La Voix de la Foule Déchaînée (The Voice of the Mob); Le Démon Dans Son Esprit (The Devil in His Brain); Un Peu de Couleur (A Touch of Color); Le Perdant (The Loser); Le Courage (Nerve); Un Homme Courtois (The Sophisticate); Le Billot (The Block); Une Histoire de Fous (The Nut's Shell); Jour de Paie (Pay Day); Le Fils Prodigue de Knife-River (Knife-River Prodigal); Un Putois Putride (A Man-Eating Jeopard)*

1st Edition, NeO, PB, February 1990

**Contains a First Appearance**; "NeO Omnibus #1"; cover by Jean-Michel Nicollet; translated by Francois Truchaud

## Le Chien de la Mort (The Hound of Death)

Contains *Le Dernier Chant de Casonetto (Casonetto's Last Song); Le Roi du Peuple Oublié (King of the Forgotten People); Que Vienne la Nuit (The Hoofed Thing); L'Ombre de la Bête (The Shadow of the Beast); Nekht Semerkeht; En Eau Trouble (Restless Waters); Des Griffes Dans la Nuit (Talons in the Dark); Le Chien de la Mort (Black Hound of Death)*

1<sup>st</sup> Edition, NeO, PB, January 1986

> Cover by Jean-Michel Nicollet; translated by F. Truchaud; Book #158

Fleuve Noir, PB, 1992

> Cover art by Gilles Francescano; Book #16

## Le Manoir de la Terreur (The Manor of Terror)

Contains *Un Rêve (A Dream); **Images Dans le Feu (Pictures in the Fire);** L'Ombre de la Mort (The Shadow of Doom); Le Fantôme sur le Seuil (The Ghost in the Doorway); Les Plantes de l'Enfer (Serpent Vines); L'Horreur dans la Nuit (A Horror in the Night); La Voix de l'Au-Delà (The Voice of Doom); L'Empreinte Sanglante (The Mark of the Bloody Hand); L'Or du Cheval du Diable (Spanish Gold on Devil Horse); Le Manoir de la Terreur (Taveral Manor)*

1<sup>st</sup> Edition, NeO, PB, September 1987

> **Contains a First Appearance**; cover by Jean-Michel Nicollet, translated by Francois Truchaud; first complete appearance of "Pictures in the Fire", the first page of that story had previously appeared in THE LAST CELT; Book #196

## Le Manoir des Roses

Contains *La Chambre de Belle-Dame (The Lady's Chamber) (v)*

1<sup>st</sup> Edition, Opta, PB, 1968

> Translator unknown; edited by Marc Duveau; English and French side by side

Presses Pocket, PB, 1978

> Book Code #5035; cover art possibly by Jeff Jones, though certainly doesn't look like his work

## Le Pacte Noir (The Dark Pact)

Contains *Le Loup-Garou (Wolfshead); Le Cairn de l'Homme Gris (The Cairn on the Headland); L'Horreur des Abîmes (Skull-Face); La Vallée du Ver (The Valley of the Worm); Le Peuple des Ténèbres (People of the Dark)*

1<sup>st</sup> Edition, NeO, PB, 1<sup>st</sup> Trimester 1979

> Cover by Jean-Michel Nicollet, translated by Francois Truchaud; Book #2

NeO, PB, 2<sup>nd</sup> printing, December 1983

Marabout, PB, 1981

NeO, PB, 3<sup>rd</sup> printing, January 1988

## Le Pacte Noir, Volume 1 (The Dark Pact)

Contains *Le Loup-Garou (Wolfshead); Le Cairn de l'Homme Gris (The Cairn on the Headland); Magie Noire à Canaan (Black Canaan); Le Feu d'Asshurbanipal (The Fire of Asshurbanipal); L'Horreur des Abîmes (Skull-Face); Les Guerriers du Valhalla (Marchers of Valhalla); La Vallée du Ver (The Valley of the Worm); La Voix d'El-Lil (The Voice of El-Lil); Le Peuple des Ténèbres (People of the Dark)*

1<sup>st</sup> Edition, Fleuve Noir, PB, 1991

> Cover by Gilles Francescano, translated by Francois Truchaud; Book #5; this book together with #6 came from the NeO LE PACTE NOIR; am not sure which stories are in which volume

## Le Pacte Noir, Volume 2 (The Dark Pact)

Contains *Le Loup-Garou (Wolfshead); Le Cairn de l'Homme Gris (The Cairn on the Headland); Magie Noire à Canaan (Black Canaan); Le Feu d'Asshurbanipal (The Fire of Asshurbanipal); L'Horreur des Abîmes (Skull-Face); Les Guerriers du Valhalla (Marchers of Valhalla); La Vallée du Ver (The Valley of the Worm); La Voix d'El-Lil (The Voice of El-Lil); Le Peuple des Ténèbres (People of the Dark)*

1<sup>st</sup> Edition, Fleuve Noir, PB, 1991

> Cover by Gilles Francescano, translated by Francois Truchaud; Book #6; this book together with #5 came from the NeO LE PACTE NOIR; am not sure which stories are in which volume

## Le Rebelle (The Rebel)

Contains *Le Rebelle (Post Oaks and Sand Roughs)*
1st Edition, NeO, PB, January 1989
> **Contains a First Appearance**; cover by Jean-Michel Nicollet, translated by Francois Truchaud; Book #215

## Le Retour de Kane (The Return of Kane)

Contains *Les Collines de la Mort (The Hills of the Dead); L'Epervier de Basti (The Hawk of Basti); Des Ailes dans la Nuit (Wings in the Night); Des Bruits de Pas à l'Intérieur! (The Footfalls Within); Les Enfants d'Assur (Children of Asshur); Solomon Kane's Homecoming (v, original); The Return of Sir Richard Grenville (v)*
1st Edition, NeO, PB, March 1982
NeO, PB, 2nd printing, August 1983
NeO, PB, 3rd printing, June 1988
> Cover by Jean-Michel Nicollet, translated by Francois Truchaud; Book #38

Fleuve Noir, PB, 1991
> Cover by Gilles Francescano; Book #3

## Le Seigneur De Samarcande (Lord of Samarcand)

Contains *Le Petit Peuple (The Little People); La Cabane Hantée (The Haunted Hut); Noirs Sortilèges (Black Country); Les Doigts de la Mort (The Touch of Death); Les Démons du Lac Noir (The Devils of Dark Lake); Le Vol des Aigles (The Road of the Eagles); Le Seigneur de Samarcande (Lord of Samarcand)*
1st Edition, NeO, PB, September 1986
> Cover by Jean-Michel Nicollet, translated by Francois Truchaud; Book #179

## Le Tertre Maudit (Horror from the Mound)

Contains *Lance et Croc (Spear and Fang); La Malédiction de la Mer (Sea Curse); Du Fond des Abîmes (Out of the Deep); En Replis Tortueux (The Dream Snake); Coup Double (The Man on the Ground); Le Coeur de Jim Garfield (Old Garfield's Heart); Pour l'Amour de Barbara Allen (For the Love of Barbara Allen); Le Tertre Maudit (Horror from the Mound); Le Monolithe Noir (The Black Stone); Une Sonnerie de Trompettes (A Thunder of Trumpets); Le Cavalier-Tonnerre (The Thunder-Rider); La Vallée Perdue (The Valley of the Lost (2))*
1st Edition, NeO, PB, November 1985
> Cover by Jean-Michel Nicollet, translated by several, most by F. Truchaud, the exceptions being "En Replis Tortueux" and "Coup Double" (J. Papy), "Le Coeur de Jim Garfield" (M. Deutsch), "Pour l'Amour de Barbara Allen" (R. Lathière), and "Le Tertre Maudit" (J. Marigny)); Book #154

Fleuve Noir, PB, 1991
> Cover by Gilles Francescano; Book #4

## Légendes du Mythe de Cthulhu (Legends of the Cthulhu Mythos)

Contains *La Pierre Noir (The Black Stone)*
1st Edition, France Loisirs, PB, 1975
Christian Bourgois, PB, 1975
J'ai Lu, PB, 1975
> Translator unknown; don't know which edition came first

## Les Habitants des Tombes (The Dwellers of the Tomb)

Contains *Delenda Est; Celui Qui Hantait la Bague (The Haunter of the Ring); La Maison Parmi les Chênes (The House in the Oaks); Le Cobra du Rêve (The Cobra in the Dream); Le Fléau de Dermod (Dermod's Bane); Le Peuple de la Côte Noire (People of the Black Coast); Les Habitants des Tombes (Dwellers Under the Tomb); La Lune de Zambebwei (The Moon of Zambebwei); Les Adorateurs d'Ahriman (Black Wind Blowing)*
1st Edition, NeO, PB, September 1985
> Cover by Jean-Michel Nicollet, translated by Francois Truchaud; Book #148

Fleuve Noir, PB, 1991

Cover by Gilles Francescano; Book #2

## Les Meilleurs Récits de Weird Tales, Volume 1
Contains *Les Miroirs de Tuzun Thune (The Mirrors of Tuzun Thune)*
1ˢᵗ Edition, J'ai Lu, PB, 1975
Translation by France-Marie Watkins; the three WEIRD TALES volumes were combined and reissued in 1989 as a single hardback, edited by Jacques Sadoul, title unknown

## Les Meilleurs Récits de Weird Tales, Volume 2
Contains *La Citadelle Ecarlate (The Scarlet Citadel)*
1ˢᵗ Edition, J'ai Lu, PB, 1975
Translation by France-Marie Watkins; the three WEIRD TALES volumes were combined and reissued in 1989 as a single hardback, title unknown

## L'Homme Noir (The Dark Man)
Contains *L'Homme Noir (The Dark Man); Les Pigeons de l'Enfer (Pigeons from Hell); Les Dieux de Bal-Sagoth (The Gods of Bal-Sagoth); Les Enfants de la Nuit (Children of the Night); Le Jardin de la Peur (The Garden of Fear); La Chose Ailée Sur le Toit (The Thing on the Roof); Ne Me Creusez Pas de Tombe (Dig Me No Grave); Dans la Forêt de Villefère (In the Forest of Villefere)*
1ˢᵗ Edition, Libraries des Champ-Elysees, PB, 1976
Cover by Pascal Vercken, translated by Francois Truchaud; Book #1
NeO, PB, April 1982
NeO, PB, 2ⁿᵈ printing, February 1984
NeO, PB, 3ʳᵈ printing, February 1988
Cover by Jean-Michel Nicollet; Book #40
Fleuve Noir, PB, 1991
Cover by Gilles Francescano; Book #7

## L'Ile des Epouvantes (Isle of the Eons)
Contains *Le Fils de Genséric (Genseric's Fifth Born Son); Brachan le Celte (Brachen the Kelt); La Tour du Temps (The Tower of Time); Le Gardien de l'Idole (The Guardian of the Idol); Eithriall le Barbare (Two Against Tyre); Les Lances de Clontarf (The Spears of Clontarf); l'Ile des Epouvantes (Isle of the Eons)*
1ˢᵗ Edition, NeO, PB, November 1987
Cover by Jean-Michel Nicollet, translated by Francois Truchaud; Book #199

## Nouvelles Histoires d'Outre-Monde (New Stories of the Outer World)
Contains *En Replis Tortueux (The Dream Snake)*
1ˢᵗ Edition, Casterman, HB, 1967
Translated by J. Papy
Presses Pocket, PB, 1977
Omnibus, PB, 1996

## Orbites 4
Contains *Lance et Croc (Spear and Fang)*
1ˢᵗ Edition, NeO, PB, December 1982
An anthology; translated by Francois Truchaud

## Poings d'Acier (Fists of Iron)

Contains *Les Hommes de Fer (Men of Iron); Iron Mike Brennon (Iron Men); Ils Remontent Toujours Sur le Ring (They Always Come Back); Les Poings du Désert (Fists of the Desert); La Peur de la Foule (Crowd-Horror);* **Le Saule Pleureur (Weeping Willow); Le Crochet du Droit (The Right Hook)**
1st Edition, NeO, PB, June 1989
> **Contains a First Appearance**; cover by Jean-Michel Nicollet, translated by Francois Truchaud; Book #217

## Solomon Kane

Contains *Des Crânes Dans les Etoiles (Skulls in the Stars); La Main Droite du Destin (The Right Hand of Doom); Ombres Rouges (Red Shadows); Bruits d'Ossements (Rattle of Bones); Le Château du Diable (The Castle of the Devil); La Lune des Crânes (The Moon of Skulls); Les Epées de la Fraternité (Blue Flame of Vengeance); The One Black Stain (v)*
1st Edition, NeO, PB, March 1981
NeO, PB, 2nd printing, July 1983
NeO, PB, 3rd printing, July 1985
NeO, PB, 4th printing, May 1988
> Cover by Jean-Michel Nicollet, translated by Francois Truchaud; Book #26

Fleuve Noir, PB, 1991
> Cover by Gilles Francescano, translated by Francois Truchaud; Book #1

## Sonya La Rouge (Sonya the Red)

Contains *Sonya la Rouge (The Shadow of the Vulture); Le Lion de Tibériade (The Lion of Tiberias); Les Cavaliers de l'Armaguédon (Sowers of the Thunder)*
1st Edition, NeO, PB, July 1985
> Cover by Jean-Michel Nicollet, translated by Francois Truchaud; Book #144

Fleuve Noir, PB, 1992
> Cover by Gilles Francescano; Book #12

## Steve Costigan

Contains *La Fosse aux Serpents (The Pit of the Serpent); La Race du Bouledogue (The Bulldog Breed); La Rancune du Marin (Sailor's Grudge); Poing et Croc (Fist and Fang); Le Vainqueur Empoche Tout (Winner Take All); Les Poings du Marin (Waterfront Fists); Le Champion des Sept Mers (Champ of the Seven Seas); Un Punch au T.N.T. (The TNT Punch)*
1st Edition, NeO, PB, November 1986
> Cover by Jean-Michel Nicollet, translated by Francois Truchaud; Book #180

## Steve Costigan et le Signe du Serpent (Steve Costigan and the Sign of the Snake)

Contains *Les Ruelles du Danger (Alleys of Peril); Les Poings du Texas (Texas Fists); Le Signe du Serpent (The Sign of the Snake); Casse-Tête Chinetoque (House of Peril); La Race des Bagarreurs (The Fighin'est Pair); Les Poings du Cirque (Circus Fists); Intrigues à Shangaï (One Shanghai Night)*
1st Edition, NeO, PB, November 1986
> Cover by Jean-Michel Nicollet, translated by Francois Truchaud; Book #183

## Steve Costigan Le Champion (Steve Costigan – The Champion)

Contains *Les Vikings du Ring (Vikings of the Gloves); La Nuit de la Bataille (Night of Battle); Match Contre la Montre! (The Slugger's Game); Le Général Poing d'Acier (General Ironfist); La Pêche au Trésor (Sluggers on the Beach);* **Blue River Blues; La Loi du Requin (By the Law of the Shark); Un Cocktail Explosif (Flying Knuckles);** *Steve Costigan et le Fakir (Sailor Costigan and the Swami)*
1st Edition, NeO, PB, March 1987
> **Contains a First Appearance**; cover by Jean-Michel Nicollet; translated by Francois Truchaud; Book #187

### Steve Harrison et le Maitre des Morts (Steve Harrison and the Lord of the Dead)

Contains *Le Peuple du Serpent (People of the Serpent); Le Maître des Morts (Lord of the Dead); Les Noms du Livre Noir (Names in the Black Book); Les Dents de la Mort (Teeth of Doom); Le Mystère de Tannernoe Lodge (The Mystery of Tanneroe Lodge)*

1st Edition, NeO, PB, January 1985

    Cover by Jean-Michel Nicollet; translated by Francois Truchaud; Book #127

### Steve Harrison et le Talon d'Argent (Steve Harrison and the Silver Heel)

Contains *La Lune Noire (The Black Moon); La Maison du Soupçon (The House of Suspicion); Le Talon d'Argent (The Silver Heel); La Voix de la Mort (The Voice of Death); Steve Harrison . . . (Untitled Synopsis, "Steve Harrison . . ."); Les Rats du Cimetière (Graveyard Rats)*

1st Edition, NeO, PB, March 1985

    Cover by Jean-Michel Nicollet; translated by Francois Truchaud; Book #132

### Univers 01 (Universe 1)

Contains *Le Défi de l'Au-Dela (The Challenge from Beyond)*

1st Edition, J'ai Lu, PB, 1975

    Translator unknown

### Vingt Pas Dans L'au-Delà (Twenty Not in the Beyond(?))

Contains *Le Coeur de Jim Garfield (Old Garfield's Heart)*

1st Edition, Casterman, HB, 1970

    Translation by M. Deutsch

### Vulmea Le Pirate Noir (Vulmea – The Black Pirate)

Contains *Les Epées de la Fraternité Rouge (Swords of the Red Brotherhood); La Vengeance de Vulméa le Noir (Black Vulmea's Vengeance); Les Pirates du Temple Maudit (The Isle of Pirates' Doom)*

1st Edition, NeO, PB, May 1985

    Cover by Jean-Michel Nicollet, translated by Francois Truchaud; Book #138

Fleuve Noir, PB, 1992

    Cover by Gilles Francescano; Book #17

### Wild Bill Clanton

Contains *Le Démon des Mers du Sud (The She-Devil); Mutinerie à Bord (Ship in Mutiny); Le Coeur Pourpre d'Erlik (The Purple Heart of Erlik); Le Dragon de Kao Tsu (The Dragon of Kao Tsu); Le Grog du Meurtrier (Murderer's Grog); Le Sang du Désert (Desert Blood); Les Canons de Khartoum (Guns of Khartoum); Les Filles de la Haine (Daughters of Feud)*

1st Edition, NeO, PB, July 1984

    Cover by Jean-Michel Nicollet, translated by Francois Truchaud; Book #114

# GERMAN

### Almuric

Contains *Almuric*

1st Edition, Wilhem Heyen Verlag, PB, 1973

    Translated by Yoma Cap

### Atlantis Ist Uberall

Contents unknown

1st Edition, William Goldmann Verlag; Germany, PB, 1988

    Edited by Andrew Offutt

### Conan

Contains *Der Elefantenturm (The Tower of the Elephant); Im Saal der Toten (The Hall of the Dead); Der Gott in der Schale (The God in the Bowl); Der Rote Priester (Rogues in the House); Nergals Hand (The Hand of Nergal)*
1st Edition, Wilhem Heyen Verlag, PB, 1970
    Cover art by Herbert Bruck; translated by Fritz Moeglich

## Conan

Contains *A letter to P.S. Miller, March 10, 1936 ("I am indeed . . ."); Das Hyborische Zeitalter (The Hyborian Age), Pt. 1; In Der Turm des Elefanten (The Tower of the Elephant); In der Halle der Toten (The Hall of the Dead); Der Gott in der Schale (The God in the Bowl); Der Rote Priester (Rogues in the House); Nergals Hand (The Hand of Nergal)*
2nd Edition, Wilhem Heyen Verlag GmbH, PB, 1982
    Translated by Lore Strassl and Hubert Strassl

## Conan

Contains *Cimmerien (Cimmeria) (v); Im Zeichen des Phonix (The Phoenix on the Sword); Ymirs Tochter (The Frost-Giant's Daughter); Der Gott in der Schale (The God in the Bowl); Der Turm des Elefanten (The Tower of the Elephant); Die Scharlachrote Zitadelle (The Scarlet Citadel); Die Konigin der Schwarzen Kuste (Queen of the Black Coast); Natohk, der Zauberer (Black Colossus); Schatten im Mundlicht (Shadows in the Moonlight); Der Wandelnde Schatten (The Slithering Shadow); Der Teich der Riesen (The Pool of the Black One); Der Rote Priester (Rogues in the House); Das Tal der Verlorenen Frauen (The Vale of Lost Women); Der Eiserne Teufel (The Devil in Iron); Im Zeichen des Phonix (The Phoenix on the Sword - first submitted draft); Ammerkungen zu Verschiedernen Volkern des Hyborischen Zeitalters (Notes on the Various Peoples of the Hyborian Age); Das Hyborische Zeitalter (The Hyborian Age); Ohne Titel (Untitled Synopsis); Ohne Titel (Untitled Synopsis - The Scarlet Citadel); Ohne Titel (Untitled Synopsis - Black Colossus); Ohne Titel (Untitled Fragment); Ohne Titel (Untitled Synopsis); Ohne Titel (Untitled Draft)*
1st Edition, Wilhelm Heyne Verlag, PB, 2003
    A reprint of ROBERT E. HOWARD'S COMPLETE CONAN OF CIMMERIA, VOLUME 1; cover by Charles Keegan, texts translated by Jurgen Langowski, "Cimmeria" translated by Erik Simon

## Conan Der Abenteurer

Contains *Dre Schwarze Kreis (The People of the Black Circle); Der Wandernde Schatten (The Slithering Shadow); Die Trommeln von Tombalku (Drums of Tombalku); Der Teich der Riesen (The Pool of the Black One)*
1st Edition, Wilhelm Heyne Verlag, PB, 1971
    Cover art by Herbert Bruck; translated by Fritz Moeglich
2nd Edition, Wilhelm Heyne Verlag GmbH & Co., PB, 1983
    Cover art by Thomas Thiemeyer; translated by Lore Strassl

## Conan Der Eroberer

Contains *Conan the Conqueror*
1st Edition, Wilhelm Heyne Verlag, PB, 1972
    Cover by Johnny Bruck
2nd Edition, Wilhelm Heyne Verlag GmbH & Co., PB, 1984
    Translated by Lore Strassl

## Conan Der Freibeuter

Contains *Der Wahnsinnige Konig (Hawks Over Shem); Natohk, der Zauberer (Black Colossus); Schatten im Mondlicht (Shadows in the Moonlight); Die Strasse der Adler (The Road of the Eagles); Salome, die Hexe (A Witch Shall Be Born)*
1st Edition, Wilhelm Heyne Verlag, PB, 1970
    Cover art by Herbert Bruck; translated by Fritz Moeglich

## Conan Der Thronräuber

Contains *Der Schatz des Tranicos (The Treasure of Tranicos); Wolfe Jenseits der Grenze (Wolves Beyond the Border); Im Zeichen des Phonix (The Phoenix on the Sword); Die Scharlachrote Zitadelle (The Scarlet Citadel)*
1st Edition, Wilhelm Heyne Verlag GmbH & Co., PB, 1984
Translated by Lore Strassl

## Conan Der Usurpator

Contains *Der Schatz des Tranicos (The Treasure of Tranicos); Wölfe jenseits der Grenze (Wolves Beyond the Border); Im Zeichen des Phönix (The Phoenix on the Sword); Die Scharlachrote Zitadelle (The Scarlet Citadel)*
1st Edition, Wilhelm Heyne Verlag, PB, 1971
Cover art by Herbert Bruck; translated by Fritz Moeglich

## Conan Der Wanderer

Contains *Die Menschenfresser von Zamboula (Shadows in Zamboula); Der Eiserne Teufel (The Devil in Iron); Der Flammendolch (The Flame Knife)*
1st Edition, Wilhelm Heyne Verlag, PB, 1971
Cover art by Herbert Bruck; translated by Fritz Moeglich
2nd Edition Wilhelm Heyne Verlag GmbH & Co., PB, 1982
Cover by Thomas Theimeyer; translated by Lore Strassl

## Conan Und Der Falmmendolch

Contains *The Flame Knife*
1st Edition Wilhelm Heyne Verlag GmbH & Co., PB, 1992
Cover by Thomas Thiemeyer; translated by Lore Strassl

## Conan Und Der Schatz Des Tranicos

Contains *The Treasure of Tranicos*
1st Edition Wilhelm Heyne Verlag GmbH & Co., PB, 1992
Translated by Lore Strassl

## Conan Von Cimmeria

Contains *Der Blutbefleckte Gott (The Bloodstained God); Die Tochter des Frostriesen (The Frost Giant's Daughter); Die Koenig der Schwarzen Kuste (Queen of the Black Coast); Das Tal der Verlorenen Frauen (The Vale of Lost Women); Damon aus der Nacht (The Snout in the Dark)*
1st Edition, Wilhelm Heyne Verlag, PB, 1970
Cover art by Herbert Bruck; translated by Fritz Moeglich

## Das Grosse Lesebuch Der Fantasy

Contains *Die Gefahr aus dem Jenseits (The Challenge from Beyond)*
1st Edition, Wilhelm Goldmann Verlag, unknown format, 1995
Edited by Melissa Andersson; an anthology

## Das Haus Des Grauens

Contains *Brief von Howard an HPL (from a letter to HPL, 1933); Der Grabhugel (The Cairn on the Headland); Im Forst von Villefere (In the Forest of Villefere); Der Wolsdamon (Wolfshead); Der Schwarze Stein (The Black Stone); Das Ding auf dem Dach (The Thing on the Roof); Das Haus des Grauens (Pigeons from Hell)*
1st Edition, Erich Pabel Verlag KG, PB, December 1976
Erich Pabel Verlag, PB, 2nd printing, August 1979
"Vampir Horror Stories #52"; translated by Eduard Luskchandl; Foreword by Hugh Walker

## Degen Der Gerechtigkeit

Contains *Auf dem Pfad der Rache (Blades of the Brotherhood); Das Skelett des Magiers (Rattle of Bones); Der Moorgeist (Skulls in, the Stars); Schatten des Todes (Red Shadows); Der Ruf des Dschungels (The Hills of the Dead); Schritte in der Gruft (The Footfalls Within)*
1st Edition, Erich Pabel Verlag KG, PB, August 1975
Erich Pabel Verlag KG, PB, 2nd printing, April 1978
    "Terra Fantasy #11"; translated by Eduard Lukschandl; introduction by Hugh Walker

## Der Lovecraft-Zirkel

Contains *Die Bedrohung aus dem Weltraum (The Challenge from Beyond); Im Wold von Villefere (In the Forest of Villefere)*
1st Edition, Blitz-Verlag, PB, 2000
    Edited by Frank Festa; translated by Michael Siefener; an anthology

## Der Schatz Der Tataren

Contains *Der Fluch der Roten Gottes (The Curse of the Crimson God); Der Schatz der Tataren (The Treasure of Tartary); Die Schwerter von Shahrazar (Swords of Shahrazar); Der Bronzene Pfau (The Brazen Peacock); Der Schwarze Lama (The Black Bear Bites)*
1st Edition, Erich Pabel Verlag KG, PB, 1980
    Cover art by Nikolai Lutohin; translated by Martin Thau

## Die Besten Fantasy-Stores 4

Contains *Nekht Semerkeht*
1st Edition, Verlag Arthur Moewig GMBH, PB, 1988
    Edited by Lin Carter

## Die Bestie Von Bal-Sagoth

Contains *Der Lowe von Tiberias (The Lion of Tiberias); Die Den Wind Saen (The Sowers of the Thunder); Die Bestie von Bal-Sagoth (The Gods of Bal-Sagoth); verse heading for Chapter 2 of The Phoenix on the Sword*
1st Edition, Erich Pabel Verlag KG, Rastatt, PB, December 1977
Erich Pabel Verlag KG, Rastatt, PB, 2nd printing, August 1980
    "Terra Fantasy No. 42"; cover by Ken Kelly; three illustrations by Pierangelo Hoog; translated by Eduard Lukschandl; Foreword by Hugh Walker; Foreword contains the verse heading

## Die Krieger Von Assur

Contains *Die Starasse Azraels (The Road of Azrael); Die Burg des Teufels (The Castle of the Devil); Die Stadt des Mondgotts (Hawk of Basti); Die Krieger von Assur (The Children of Asshur); Sir Richard Grenville Kehrt Zurüch (The Return of Sir Richard Grenvillie) (v)*
1st Edition, Erich Pabel Verlag KG, PB, 1982
    Cover art by Stephen Fabian; translated by Lore Strassl; Helmutt Pesch ("The Return of Sir Richard Grenville")

## Geister Der Nacht

Contains *Der Garten des Grauens (The Garden of Fear); Das Ende des Grauen Gottes (The Grey God Passes); Geister der Nacht (The House of Arabu); Herr von Samarkand (Lord of Sanarcand); Des Traumers Lohn (Recompense) (v)*
1st Edition, Erich Pabel Verlag KG, PB, August 1978
Erich Pabel Verlag KG, PB, 2nd printing, April 1981
    "Terra Fantasy No. 50"; cover by Ken Kelly; two illustrations by Pierangelo Boog; translated by Helmut Pesch (Recompense); Lore Strassi (the remaining works); Foreword by Hugh Walker

## Gespenster Der Vergangenheit

Contains *Solomon Kanes Heimkehr (Solomon Kane's Homecoming) (v); Der Grosse Treck (Marchers of Valhalla); Das Tal des Hollenwurms (The Valley of the Worm); Der Donnerreiter (The Thunder-Rider); Zwei Gegen Tyrus (Two Against Tyre); Das Wlk der Finsternis (People of the Dark)*
1$^{st}$ Edition, Erich Pabel Verlag KG, PB, December 1978
Erich Pabel Verlag KG, PB, 2$^{nd}$ printing, 1981
      "Terra Fantasy No. 55"; cover by Esteban Marota; translated by Ludwig Rief (Solomon Kane's Homecoming).; Lore Strassi (remainder); Foreword by Hugh Walker

## Herr Von Valusien

Contains *Der Koenig und die Eiche (The King and the Oak); Jagd im Land der Schatten (Riders Beyond the Sunrise); Herr von Valusien (By This Axe I Rule!); Verrat am Koenig (Swords of the Purple Kingdom); Die Spiegel des Tuzun Thune (The Mirrors of Tuzun Thune); Epilogue (The Hyborian Age: Epilog); Rotaths Fluch (The Curse of the Golden Skull)*
1$^{st}$ Edition, Erich Pabel Verlag KG, PB, December 1976
Erich Pabel Verlag KG, PB, 2$^{nd}$ printing, August 1979
      "Terra Fantasy #29"; cover art by Nikolai Lutohin; "The King and the Oak" translated by Ludwig Rief, the rest by Eduard Lukschandl; Foreword by Hugh Walker; first six lines of "The King and the Oak" which were discarded by Howard before the final version are embodied in the Foreword

## Herrscher Der Nacht

Contains *Vorwort (Foreword by REH, discussing Picts (Excerpted from a letter to HPL, ca. early January 1932 ("Yes I enjoyed the postcards.", the excerpt beginning with "There is one hobby of mine . . .")); Das Verschwundene Volk (The Lost Race); Die im Dunkein Wohnen . . . (Men of the Shadows); Herrscher der Nacht (Kings of the Night); Fragment ("A grey sky . . ."); Wurmer der Erde (Worms of the Earth); The Drums of Pictdom (v); A Song of the Race (v); The Dark Man; Chant of the White Beard (v); Rune (v); Song of the Pict (v)*
1$^{st}$ Edition, Erich Pabel Verlag KG, PB, January 1975
Erich Pabel Verlag KG, PB, 2$^{nd}$ printing, August 1977
      "Terra Fantasy #3"; translated by Eduward Luks-chandl; introduction by Hugh Walker; also includes a map of Bran Mak Morn's world, and five interior illustrations, four by David Ireland; "The Drums of Pictdom" (Die Trommein der Pikten) embodied in the Foreword; the last three poems listed are incorporated in "Men of the Shadows"; based on the Grant WORMS OF THE EARTH

## Horde Aus Dem Morgenland

Contains *Die Schwarze Agnes (Sword Woman); Degen fur Frankreich (Blades for France); Braut des Todes (Mistress of Death); Horde aus dem Morgen-land (The Shadow of the Vulture)*
1$^{st}$ Edition, Erich Pabel Verlag KG, PB, August 1977
Erich Pabel Verlag KG, PB, 2$^{nd}$ printing, April 1980
      "Terra Fantasy #37"; cover by Chris Achilleos; four interior illustrations by Pierangelo Boog; translated by Eduard Lukschandl; Foreword by Hugh Walker; verse heading of Chapter 4 of Sword Woman is embodied in the Foreword

## Im Land Der Messer

Contains *Das Blut der Gotter (Blood of the Gods); Im Land der Messer (The Country of the Knife); Der Sohn des Weiben Wolfs (Son of the White Wolf)*
1st Edition, Erich Pabel Verlag KG, PB, 1980
      Cover art by Boris Vallejo; translated by Dagmar Hartmann

## Im Schatten Der Geier

Contains *Vultures of Whapeton*
1st Edition, Wilhelm Heyne Verlag GmbH & Co., KG, PB
      Translated by Rainer M. Schröder

## Krieger Des Nordens

Contains *Krieger des Nordens (Tigers of the Sea); Die Nacht der Schwerter (Swords of the Northern Sea); Die Rache der Pikten (The Night of the Wolf); Tempel des Grauens (The Temple of Abomination)*
1st Edition, Erich Pabel Verlag KG, PB, July 1976
Erich Pabel Verlag KG, PB, 2nd printing, March 1979
"Terra Fantasy #23"; cover art by Chris Achilleos; translated by Eduard Lukschandl; Foreword by Hugh Walker; based on the Grant TIGERS OF THE SEA

## Kull

Contains *Die Hyborische Epoche (The Hyborian Age), Prolog; Kull von Atlantis (The Shadow Kingdom)*
1st Edition, Fantasy Club FOLLOW, PB, 1974
Cover by Roy G. Krenkel; translated by Lore Matthaey

## Kull Von Atlantis

Contains *Die Hyborische Epoche (The Hyborian Age), Prolog; Flucht aus Atlan-tis (Exile of Atlantis); Das Schattenkoenigreich (The Shadow Kingdom); Der Altar und der Skorpion (The Altar and the Scorpion); Schwarzer Abgrund (Black Abyss); Delcardes' Katze (Delcardes' Cat); Der Schaedel der Stille (The Skull of Silence); Zauberer und Krieger (Wizard and Warrior); Nur Einen Gongschlag Lang (The Striking of the Gong)*
1st Edition, Erich Pabel Verlag KG, PB, November 1976
Erich Pabel Verlag KG, PB, 2nd printing, July 1979
"Terra Fantasy #28"; translated by Lore Strassl; Foreword by Hugh Talker; apparently drawn from the Lancer KING KULL

## Kull Von Atlantis

Contains *Prolog (portions of The Hyborian Age); Flucht aus Atlantis (Exile of Atlantis); Das schattenkönigreich (The Shadow Kingdom); Der Altar und der Skorpion (The Altar and the Scorpion); Delcardes' Katze (Delcardes' Cat); Der Schädel der Stille (The Skull of Silence); Diese Axt ist Mein Zepter! (By This Axe I Rule!); Nur Einen Gongschlag Lang (The Striking of the Gong); Verschwörung bei Nacht (Swords of the Purple Kingdom); Der König und die Eiche (The King and the Oak) (v); Untitled ("'Thus,' said Tu, . . ."); Die Spiegel des Tuzun Thune (The Mirrors of Tuzun Thune); Die Schwarze Stadt (The Black City); Untitled ("Three men sat at a table . . ."); Epilog (more portions from The Hyborian Age)*
1st Edition, Bastei-Verlag Gustav H. Lubbe GmbH & Co., PB, 1989
Cover art by Frank Frazzetta; translated by Hubert Strassl; based on the Bantam KULL

## Racher Der Verdammten

Contains *Die Hand des Rachers (The Right Hand of Doom); Konigreich des Sch-reckens (The Moon of Skulls); Schwarze Schwingen (Wings in the Night); Das Idol (The Dark Man)*
1st Edition, Erich Pabel Verlag KG, PB, January 1976
Erich Pabel Verlag KG, PB, 2nd printing, Fall 1978
"Terra Fantasy #17"; translated by Eduard Lukschandl; Foreword by Hugh Walker

## Rauher Sand Und Wilde Eichen

Contains *Post Oaks and Sand Roughs; Spear and Fang; **A Man (v); a letter to TCS, July 1925 ("Salaam Clyde; / Old boy, I got your letter.");** a letter to Farnworth Wright, January 23, 1926 ("I have no carbon copy of Wolfshead . . ."); a letter to Western Story, ca. late fall, 1924 ("—And I am not one of those writers . . ."); plus some drawings from various REH letters*
1st Edition, Erster Deutscher (Germany), PB, 1993
**Contains a First Appearance**; all in German except for the poem and the letter to Farnworth Wright, 1926, both of which are printed in both English and German; WESTERN STORY letter is a brief excerpt only, letter presumably lost

# GREEK

**Almourik**
> Contains *Almuric*
> 1st Edition, Selefais, PB, 1981

**Almuric**
> Contains *Almuric*
> 1st Edition, Orora, PB, 1981
>> Translated by G. Balanos

**Anthologia Epistimonikis Fantasias - Istories Apo Efialtikous Cosmous, Volume 10**
> Contains *To Plasma sti Stegi (The Thing on the Roof)*
> 1st Edition, Orora, PB, 1986
>> Translated by G. Balanos

**Anthologia Epistimonikis Fantasias - Istories Apo Fantastikous Cosmous, Volume 1**
> Contains *To Vasilio ton Skion (The Shadow Kingdom)*
> 1st Edition, Orora, PB, 1989
>> Translated by Makis Panorios

**Anthologia Epistimonikis Fantasias - Istories Apo Paraxenes Thalases / 2, Volume 55**
> Contains *Skies sto Feggarofoto (Shadows in the Moonlight)*
> 1st Edition, Orora, PB, 1997
>> Translated by Thomas Mastakouris

**Anthologia Epistimonikis Fantasias - Istories Apo Paraxenous Topous, Volume 18**
> Contains *Nekht Semerkeht*
> 1st Edition, Orora, PB, 1992
>> Translated by Thomas Mastakouris

**Anthologia Epistimonikis Fantasias - Istories Apo Veloudo Ke Atsali, Volume 20**
> Contains *I Kilada tou Skolika (The Valley of the Worm)*
> 1st Edition, Orora, PB, 1992
>> Translated by Thomas Mastakouris

**Anthologia Epistimonikis Fantasias - Istories Ematos Ke Pathous, Volume 49**
> Contains *I Vasilisa tis Mavris Aktis (Queen of the Black Coast)*
> 1st Edition, Orora, PB, 1996
>> Translated by Thomas Mastakouris

**Anthologia Epistimonikis Fantasias - Istories Iroikis Fantasias, Volume 12**
> Contains *O Laos tou Skotadiou (People of the Dark)*
> 1st Edition, Orora, PB, 1989
>> Translated by G. Balanos

**Anthologia Epistimonikis Fantasias - Istories Magias Ke Tromou, Volume 7**
> Contains *I Fotia tou Asshurbanipal (The Fire of Asshurbanipal); To Kefali tou Likou (Wolfshead)*
> 1st Edition, Orora, PB, 1987
>> Translated by G. Balanos

## Anthologia Epistimonikis Fantasias - Istories Me Magous Ke Magises, Volume 28

Contains *O Pirgos tou Elephanta (The Tower of the Elephant)*
1st Edition, Orora, PB, 1993
Translated by Thomas Mastakouris

## Anthologia Epistimonikis Fantasias - Istories Me Theous Ke Demones /2, Volume 60

Contains *I Kori tou Giganta ton Pagon (The Frost-Giant's Daughter)*
1st Edition, Orora, PB, 1999
Translated by Thomas Mastakouris

## Anthologia Epistimonikis Fantasias - Istories Tis Mithologias Chtulhu, Volume 17

Contains *Mi Skapsete Tafo gia Mena (Dig Me No Grave)*
1st Edition, Orora, PB, 1990
Translated by G. Balanos

## Conan Pera Apo Ton Mavro Potamo

Contains *Conan Pera Apo Ton Mavro Potamo (Beyond the Black River)*
1st Edition, Alien, PB, 1996
Translator unknown

## Conan O Pirgos Tou Erpetou

Contains *Conan O Pirgos Tou Erpetou (Red Nails)*
1st Edition, Alien, PB, 1996
Translated by Thomas Mastakouris; cover art by Boris

## Conan Pera Apo Ton Mavro Potamo

Contains *Beyond the Black River*
1st Edition, Alien, PB, 1996

## I Lofi Ton Nekron Kai Alla Diegemata

Contains *L Lofi Ton Nekron (The Hills of the Dead); Fterouges Stin Nykta (Wings in the Night); I Galazia Floga Tis Ekdikisis (The Blue Flame of Vengeance); Krotalisma Apo Kokala (Rattle of Bones); Krania Sta Asteria (Skulls in the Stars)*
1st Edition, Ekdoseis Orora, PB, 1989
Translated by Giorgos Balanos

## I Vasilisa Tis Mavris Aktis

Contains *O Pirgos tou Elephanta (The Tower of the Elephant); I Kori tou Giganta ton Pagon (The Frost-Giant's Daughter); O Theos sto Doheia (The God in the Bowl); Parisactoi sto Spiti (Rogues in the House); I Vasilisa tis Mavris Aktis (Queen of the Black Coast); H Koilada tou Homenon Gynaikon (The Vale of Lost Women)*
1st Edition, Aiolos, PB, 2002

## Istories Frikis

Contains *I Mavri Petra (The Black Stone)*
1st Edition, Selefais, PB, 1981
Translated by G. Balanos

## Konan Ho Kataktetes

Contains *Conan the Conqueror*
1st Edition, Publications Space EPE, PB, 1986
Cover art by V. Karayannis; translated by Mina Cheimona

## Konan Ho Tykhodioktes

Contains *Ta Onta tou Maurou Kyklos (The People of the Black Circle); He Glistere Skia (The Slithering Shadow); He Limen tou Maurou Giganta (Pool of the Black One); Ta Tympana tou Tompalkou (Drums of Tombalku)*
1st Edition, Publications Space EPE, PB, 1986
    Cover art by V. Karayannis; translated by Damianos Mikides

## Kull

Contains *The Hyborian Age (portions); Exile of Atlantis; The Shadow Kingdom; The Altar and the Scorpion; Black Abyss; Delcardes' Cat; The Skull of Silence; Riders Beyond the Sunrise; By This Axe I Rule!; The Striking of the Gong; Swords of the Purple Kingdom; Wizard and Warrior; The Mirrors of Tuzun Thune; The King and the Oak (v)*
1st Edition, Patakis, PB, 1967
    Based on the Lancer KING KULL book; translator unknown

## O Archontas Ton Necron (Lord of the Dead)

Contains *O Archontas Ton Necron (Lord of the Dead); Names in the Black Book*
1st Edition, Alien, PB, 1995

## O Kipos Tou Fovou

Contains *Gerakia Pano apo tin Egypto (Hawks Over Egypt); O Kipos Tou Fovou (The Garden of Fear); I Xanthi Thea tou Bal-Sagoth (The Gods of Bal-Sagoth); Lolitou (The House of Arabu)*
1st Edition, Dragon, PB, 1982
Locus-7, PB, 2000
    Translated by G. Balanos

## O Magos Apo Tin Atlantida

Contains *Skull-Face*
1st Edition, Alien, PB, 1994

## O Pirgos Tou Erpetou - Pera Apo Ton Mavro Potamo

Contains *O Pirgos tou Erpetou (Red Nails); Pera apo tou Mavro Potamo (Beyond the Black River)*
1st Edition, Aiolos, PB, 2000

## Oi Mavroi Prophites

Contains *Skies stin Zamboula (Shodows in Zamboula); O Siderenios Daimonas (The Devil in Iron); Oi Anthropoi tou Mavrou (The People of the Black Circle)*
1st Edition, Aiolos, PB, 2005

## Skies Sto Feggarofoto

Contains *Mia Magissa Tha Gennithei (A Witch Shall Be Born); O Mavros Kolossos (Black Colossus); Skies sto Feggarofoto (Shadows in the Moonlight)*
1st Edition, Aiolos, PB, 2003

## To Antro Tis Frikis

Contains unknown
1st Edition, Alien, PB, 1996
    No idea of contents, but suppose to be an REH book

## To Likofos Ton Gkrizon Theon (The Grey God Passes)

Contains *To Likofos Ton Gkrizon Theon (The Grey God Passes)*; and maybe other REH material
1st Edition, Alien, PB, 1996

# HUNGARIAN

## A Koponyak Holdja

Contains *Vörös Árnyak (Red Shadows); Zörgő Csontok (Rattle of Bones); A Testvériség Péngéi (Blades of the Brotherhood); Koponyák Holdja (The Moon of Skulls); Koponyák A Csillagfényben (Skulls in the Stars); A Vámpirok Hegye (The Hills of the Dead)*
1st Edition, Cherubion Konyvkiadó, PB, 1993
    Translated by Nemes István, Békési József, Tóth Attila & Jónás János

## Almuria

Contains *A Fekete Idegen (The Black Stranger); Almuria (Almuric)*
1st Edition, Cherubion Konyvkiado, PB, 2002
    Translated by Nemes Istvan

## A Szoldas Barbár

Contains *Vörös Szögek (Red Nails); Gwahlur Fogai (Jewels of Gwahlur); Túl a Fekete Folyón (Beyond the Black River)*
1st Edition, Phoenix Konyvkiado, PB, 1991
    Cover by Tibor Szendrei

## Árnykirályok

Contains *A Kígyó Jegyében (The Shadow Kingdom); Árnkirályok (Kings of the Night); A Föld Férgei (Worms of the Earth); A Sötét Bálvány (The Dark Man); Bal-Sagoth Istenei (The Gods of Bal-Sagoth)*
1st Edition, Cherubion Kft, PB, 1992
    Cover art by Tibor Szendrei; translated by Zsolt Kornya

## Az Alkony Kiralyai

Contains *Holtak Csarnoka (The Hall of the Dead); Nergal Keze (The Hand of Nergal)*
1st Edition, Cherub Ion Kdnyvkiado, HB, 1998
    Translated by Jonas Janos

## Barbar Pokol

Contains *Remseg a Sotetben (The Snout in the Dark)*
1st Edition, Cherub Ion Kdnyvkiado, HB, 2000
    Translated by Erdei Palma

## Barbarok Es Varazslok

Contains *Az Elefant Tornya (The Tower of the Elephant); Isten a Szarkofagban (The God in the Bowl); Zsivanyok a Hazban (Rogues in the House); Fonix a Kardon (The Phoenix on the Sword); A Voros Citadella (The Scarlet Citadel)*
1st Edition, Phoenix Konyvkiado, 1991
    Edited and translated by Istvan Nemes

## Conan A Barbár

Contains *A Fekete Kolosszus (Black Colossus); Szulessen Boszorkány! (A Witch Shall Be Born); Árnyak Zambulában (Shadows in Zamboula); A Vasördög (The Devil in Iron); Árnyak a Holdfényben (Shadows in the Moonlight)*
1st Edition, Csokonai Kiado Vállalat, PB, 1989
    Cover art by László Kathy; translated by István Nemes

## Conan, A Bosszúálló

Contains *The Hour of the Dragon*
1st Edition, Cherubion Kft, PB, 1992
> Cover art by Tibor Szendrei; translated by Istvan Nemes

## Conan A Kimmériai

Contains *Ymir leánya (The Frost-Giant's Daughter); Az elefánt tornya (The Tower of the Elephant); Ist en a szarkofágban (The God in the Bowl); Zsiványok a házban (Rogues in the House); A Fekete Tengerpart királynoje (Queen of the Black Coast); Elveszett asszonyok völgye (The Vale of Lost Women); A fekete kolosszus (Black Colossus); Szülessen boszorkany! (A Witch Shall Be Born); Árnyak Zambulában (Shadows in Zamboula); A vasördög (The Devil in Iron); Árnyak a holdfényben (Shadows in the Moonlight); A Fekete Kör népe (The People of the Black Circle); A végzet árnyéka (The Slithering Shadow); Vörös szegek (Red Nails); Gwahlur fogai (The Jewels of Gwahlur); Túl a fekete folyón (Beyond the Black River); Fönix a kardon (The Phoenix on the Sword); A vörös citadella (The Scarlet Citadel)*
1st Edition, Phoenix Konyvex, HB, 1993
> Cover art by Szendrei Tibor; translated by Nemes István & Kornya Zsolt

## Hösök Kora

Contains *Atlantiszi Álom (Exile of Atlantis); A Bárd Jogán (By This Axe I Rule!); A Skorpió Oltára (The Altar and the Scorpion); Delcardes Macskája (Delcardes' Cat); A Csend Koponyája (The Skull of Silence); Egyetlen Gongütés (The Striking of the Gong); Kardok az Éjszakában (Swords of the Purple Kingdom); Tuzun Thune Tukre (The Mirrors of Tuzun Thune); Az Elveszett Nép (The Lost Race); Ködböl és Homályból (Men of the Shadows); Becsületbeli Ugy (Hawks of Outremer); A Végzet Jobb Keze (The Right Hand of Doom); Sötét Szárnyak Suhogása (Wings in the Night)*
1st Edition, Valhalla Páholy Könyvklub, PB, 1997
> Cover art by Jim Burns; translated by Kornya Zsolt

## Jegmagia

Contains *A Verfoltos Balvany (The Bloodstaind God)*
1st Edition, Cherub Ion Kdnyvkiado, HB, 1999
> Translated by Erdei Palma

## Ne Assatok Nekem Sirt

Contents unknown
1st Edition, Cherubion Konyvkiado, PB, date unknown

## Osszes Conan, Tortenete 1

Contains *Kimmeria (Cimmeria) (v); A Hyboriai Kor (The Hyborian Age); Ymir Leanya (The Frost-Giant's Daughter); Az Elefant Tornya (The Tower of the Elephant); Nergal Keze (The Hand of Nergal - fragment); Holtak Csarnoka ( The Hall of the Dead - synopsis); Isten a Szarkofagban (The God in the Bowl); Zsivanyok a Hazban (Rogues in the House) ; A Fekete Tengerpart Kiralynoje (Queen of the Black Coast); Elveszett Asszonyok Volgye (The Vale of Lost Women); A Fekete Idegen (The Black Stranger); Ormany a Sotetben (The Snout in the Dark); A Fekete Kolosszus (Black Colossus); Szulessen Boszorkanyl (A Witch Shall Be Born); Arnyak Zambulaban (Shadows in Zamboula); A Vasordog (The Devil in Iron); Arnyak a Holdfenyben (Shadows in the Moonlight); A Fekete Kor Nepe (The People of the Black Circle); Tombalku Dobjai (Drums of Tombalku - unfinished); A Vegzet Aryyeke (The Slithering Shadow)*
1st Edition, Szukitz Konyvkiado, HB, 2004
> This is a translation of Millenium's THE CONAN CHRONICLES, VOLUME 1 and has the John Howe cover art

# ITALIAN

## Almuric
Contains *il Pianeta Selvaggio (Almuric)*
1st Edition, Editrice Nord, HB, 1982
>> Cover art by Frank Frazetta; blue binding, white lettering

## Almuric
Contains *Pianeti Per Tutti (Almuric)*
1st Edition, Arnoldo Mondadori S.p.A., PB, 2001

## Chi Di Vampiro Ferisce: H.P. Lovecraft & Others
Contains *L Orrore Dalla Collina (The Horror from the Mound)*
1st Edition, Casa Editrice La Tribuna, HB, 1972
>> Trans. by G. Cossato & Sandro Sandrelli

## Chiodi Rossi
Contains *Red Nails*
1st Edition, Compagnia del Fantastico (Gruppo Newton), PB, 1995
>> Cover art by Marco Sani; translated by Gianni Pilo

## Conan!
Contains *La Torre dell 'Elefante (The Tower of the Elephant); Il Palazzo dei Morti (The Hall of the Dead); Il Dio nell 'Urna (The God in the Bowl); Gli Intrusi a Palazzo (Rogues in the House); La Mano di Nergal (The Hand of Nergal); a letter to P. Schuyler Miller, March 10, 1936 ("I am indeed . . .")*
1st Edition, Editrice Nord, HB, 1976
>> Cover art by Frank Frazetta; translated by Giusi Riverso

## Conan Di Cimmeria
Contains *Il Dio Insanguinato (The Bloodstained God); La Figlia del Gigante del Ghiacci (The Frost Giant's Daughter); La Regina della Perdute Costa Nera (Queen of the Black Coast); La Valle delle Donne Perdute (The Vale of Lost Women); Il Muso nel Buio (The Snout in the Dark)*
1st Edition, Editrice Nord Sdf, HB, 1978
>> Cover art by Frank Frazetta; translated by G. L. Staffilano

## Conan Il Cimmero
Contains *A letter to P. Schuyler Miller, March 10, 1936 ("I am indeed . . ."); L'Era Hyboriana (The Hyborian Age) pt. 1; La Torre dell 'Elefante (The Tower of the Elephant); Il Palazzo dei Morti (The Hall of the Dead); Il Dio nell 'Urna (The God in the Bowl); Gli Intrusti a Palazzo (Rogues in the House); La Mano di Nergal (The Hand of Nergal); Il Dio Insanguinato (The Bloodstained God); La Figlia del Gigante dei Ghiacci (The Frost Giant's Daughter); La Regina della Costa Nera (Queen of the Black Coast); La Valle Delle Donne Perdute (The Vale of Lost Women); Il Muso nel Buio (The Snout in the Dark); Falchi su Shem (Hawks over Shem); Colosso Nero (Black Colossus); Ombre al Chiaro di Luna (Shadows in the Moonlight); La Strada dell Aquile (The Road of the Eagles); Nascera una Strega (A Witch Shall Be Born)*
1st Edition, Casa Editrice Nord, PB, 1993
>> Translators by Guisi Riverso, G.L. Staggilano & Riccardo Valla, and Roberta Rambelli; collects the first three Lancer books

## Conan Il Pirata

Contains *Falchi su Shem (Hawks Over Shem); Colosso Nero (Black Colossus); Ombre al Chiaro di Luna (Shadows in the Moonlight); La Strada Delle Aquile (The Road of the Eagles); Nascera una Strega (A Witch Shall Be Born)*
1st Edition, Editrice Nord Sdf, HB, 1979
    Cover art by Frank Frazetta; translated by Roberta Rambelli

## Conan L'Usurpatore

Contains *Il Tesoro di Tranicos (The Treasure of Tranicos); Lupi Oltre la Frontiera (Wolves Beyond the Border); La Fenice Sull a Lama (The Phoenix on the Sword); La Cittadella Scarlatta (The Scarlet Citadel)*
1st Edition, Editrice Nord Sdf, HB, 1977
    Cover art by Frank Frazetta; translated by Giusi Riverso based on the Lancer CONAN THE USURPER

## Conan Lo Zingaro

Contains *Ombre a Zamboula (Shadows in Zamboula); Il diavolo di Ferro (The Devil in Iron); Il Pugnale di Fiamma (The Flame Knife)*
1st Edition, Editrice Nord Sdf, HB, 1980
    Cover art by Maurizio Mantero; translated by Roberta Rambelli

## Culti Innominabili

Contains *La Pietra Nera (The Black Stone); Non Scavarmi la Fossa (Dig Me No Grave); La Casa sul Tetto (The Thing on the Roof); Il Fuoco di Assurbanipal (The Fire of Asshurbanipal); La Casa fra le Querce (The House in the Oaks)*
1st Edition, Nexus Editrice Srl, PB
    Cover art by Roberto Gigli; translated by Roberto Cecchini & Roberto Di Meglio

## I Figli Di Asshur

Contains *I Passi all'Interno (The Footfalls Within); Le Colline dei Morti (The Hills of the Dead); I Figli di Asshur (The Children of Asshur); Il Castello del Diavolo (The Castle of the Devil)*
1st Edition, Compagnia del Fantastico (Gruppo Newton), PB 1994
    Translated by Gianni Pilo

## I Signori Della Spada

Contains *Il Tempio dell 'Abominio (The Temple of Abomination); I Vermi della Terra (Worms of the Earth); Re delle Tenebre (Kings of the Night); Il Crepuscolo del Dio Grigio (The Grey God Passes); Turlogh, il Nero (The Dark Man)*
1st Edition,Compagnia del Fantastico (Gruppo Newton), PB, 1994
    Translated by Gianni Pilo

## I Veggenti Neri

Contains *The People of the Black Circle*
1st Edition, Compagnia del Fantastico (Gruppo Newton), PB, 1995
    Cover art by Marco Sani; translated by Gianni Pilo

## Il Regno Di Conan

Contains *Red Nails; Jewels of Gwahlur; Beyond the Black River; The Treasure of Tranicos; The Phoenix on the Sword; The Scarlet Citadel; Wolves Beyond the Border (completed by LSDC); The Hour of the Dragon*
1st Edition, Casa Editrice Nord s.r.l., PB,1994
    Cover art by Ken Kelly; based on the Lancer CONAN THE WARRIOR, CONAN THE USURPER, AND CONAN THE CONQUEROR

## Il Regno Di Conan Il Grande

Contains *Red Nails; Jewels of Gwahlur; Beyond the Black River; The Treasure of Tranicos; The Phoenix on the Sword; The Scarlet Citadel; Wolves Beyond the Border (completed by LSDC); The Hour of the Dragon*

1st Edition, Casa Editrice Nord S.r.l., HB, 1989

> Cover art by Oliviero Berni; dark blue binding, silver lettering; based on the last six Lancer volumes

## Il Segno del Serpente (The Sign of the Snake)

Contains *Il Segno del Serpente (The Sign of the Snake); Un Canto Della Stirpe (A Song of the Race) (v); Acque Selvagge (Wild Water); Tutti Bastardi! (Bastards All!)*

1st Edition, Yorick Fantasy Magazine, PB, 1992

> Cover art by Raoul Perazzi; interior art by Raoul Perazzi (14), Alexandro Bani (1), Pompeo De Vito (4), Lorenzo Grassi (1) and Nicola Mari (1); translated by Massimo Tassi and Massimo Davoli (The Sign of the Serpant), Massimo Tassi (A Song of the Race), Lorenzo Mussini (Wild Water) and Leonardo Chiesi (Bastards All!); introduzione by G. de Turris; produced as a supplemental book for the Italian Yorick fantasy magazine, focusing exclusively on the work of Robert E. Howard; includes translated older articles from Glenn Lord and LSDC, among others

## Kull Di Valusia

Contains *Prologo (Prolog); Esilo da Atlantide (Exile of Atlantis); Il Regno Fantasma (The Shadow Kingdom); L'Altare e lo Scorpione (The Altar and the Scorpion); L'Abisso Tenebroso (Black Abyss); Il Gatto di Delcardes (Delcardes' Cat); Il Teschio del Silenzio (The Skull of Silence); Cavalieri Oltre il Sorgere del Sole (Riders Beyond the Sunrise); Quest Ascia e il Mio Scettrol (By This Axe I Rule!); Un Colpo di Gong (The Striking of the Gong); Le Spade del Regno Purpureo (Swords of the Purple Kingdom); Mago e Guerriero (Wizard and Warrior); Gli Specchi di Tuzun Thune (The Mirrors of Tuzun Thune); Il Re e la Quercia (The King and the Oak) (v)*

1st Edition, Editrice Nord, HB 1975

Casa Editrice Nord, PB, 1993

> Cover art by Karel Thole; translated by G.L. Staffilano; based on the Lancer KING KULL; blue binding with white lettering

## La Leggenda Di Conan Il Cimmero

Contains *L'Era Hyboriane (The Hyborian Age), Pt. 1; The Tower of the Elephant; The Hall of the Dead (completed by LSDC); The God in the Bowl; Rogues in the House; The Hand of Nergal (completed by Lin Carter); a letter to P. Schuyler Miller, March 10, 1936 ("I feel indeed honored ); The Bloodstained God (with LSDC); The Frost Giant's Daughter; Queen of the Black Coast; Vale of Lost Women; The Snout in the Dark (completed by LSDC and Lin Carter); The People of the Black Circle; The Slithering Shadow; Drums of Tombulku (completed by LSDC); The Pool of the Black One; Hawks Over Shem (with LSDC); Black Colossus; Shadows in the Moonlight; The Road of the Eagles (with LSDC); A Witch Shall Be Born*

1st Edition, Casa Editrice Nord S.r.l., HB, 1989

> Cover art by Oliviero Berni; blue binding, silver lettering; based on the first six Lancer Conan editions

## La Luna Dei Teschi

Contains *La Luna dei Teschi (The Moon of Skulls); Il Retorno di Solomon Kane (Solomon Kane's Homecoming) (v); Le Lame della Fratellanza (Blades of the Brotherhood); Una Sola Macchia Scura (The One Black Stain) (v)*

1st Edition, Compagnia del Fantastico (Gruppo Newton), PB, 1994

> Cover by Marco Sani; translated by Gianni Pilo

## La Maschera Di Cthulhu

Contains *I Figli della Notte (The Children of the Night)*

1st Edition, Fanucci Editore, format unknown, 1987

> Translated by Gianni Pilo, Daniela Galdo & Daniela Consiglio; edited by Gianni Pilo; an anthology

## Le Ali Notturne

Contains *Le Ali Notturne (Wings in the Night); Ombre Rosse (Red Shadows); La Mano Destra del Giudizio (The Right Hand of Doom); Il Retorno di Sir Richard Grenville (The Return of Sir Richard Grenville) (v); Hawk di Basti (Hawk of Basti); Lo Scricchiolio delle Ossa (Rattle of Bones); I Neri Cavalieri della Morte (Death's Black Riders); Teschi Sulle Stelle (Skulls in the Stars)*
1st Edition, Compagna del Fantastico (Newton), PB, 1995
Translated by Gianni Pilo

## L'Era Di Conan

Contains *La Fenice Sulla Lama (The Phoenix on the Sword); La Rocca Scarlatta (The Scarlet Citadel); La Torre dell 'Elefante (The Tower of the Elephant); Colosso Nero (Black Colossus); L'Ombra che Scivola (The Slithering Shadow)*
1st Edition, Arnoldo Mondadori Ediotore, PB, 1989
Cover art by Frank Frazetta; translated by Giuseppe Lippi
Oscar fantasy Gennaio, PB, 1989
Don't know which edition was first, of if the OFG version has the same artwork, or is indeed the same book

## L'Era Hyboriana Di Conan

Contains *La Fine dell 'Era Hyboriana (The Hyborian Age, Part 2 of 2)*
1st Edition, Casa Editrice Nord s.r.l., PB, 1994
Cover by Ken Kelly; based on the last three Lancer volumes

## L'Era Hyboriana Di Conan Il Cimmero

Contains *Introduzione (Letter, Howard to P. Schuyler Miller, 3/11/36); L'Era Hyboriana (The Hyborian Age), Pt. 1; L'Era Hyboriana (The Hyborian Age), Pt. 2*
1st Edition, Editrice Nord, HB, 1981
Cover art by Frank Frazetta; translated by Gianpaolo Cossato & Sandro Sandrelli; blue binding; white lettering

## L'Ira Di Conan

Contains *Lo Stagno dei Neri (The Pool of the Black One); Malfattori a Palazzo (Rogues in the House); Ombre al Chiaro di Luna (Shadows in the Moonlight); La Regina della Costa Nera (Queen of the Black Coast); Il Demone di Ferro (The Devil in Iron); Il Cerchio Nero (The People of the Black Circle); Nascera una Strega (A Witch Shall Be Born); I Giorelli di Gwahlur (Jewels of Gwahlur)*
1st Edition, Arnoldo Mondadori Editore, PB, 1990
Cover art by Frank Frazetta; translated by Diane Georgiacodis and Lidia Lax

## L'Ora Del Dragone

Contains *The Hour of the Dragon*
1st Edition, Compagnia del Fantastico (Gruppo Newton), PB, 1994
Cover art by Ken Kelly; translated by R. Valla & G.L. Staffilano

## L'Ora Di Conan

Contains *The Hour of the Dragon*
1st Edition, Arnoldo Mondadori Editore S.p.A., PB, 1992
Cover by Frank Frazetta; translated by Lidia Lax

## L'Ultimo Uomo Bianco

Contains *L'Ultimo Uomo Bianco (The Last White Man)*
1st Edition, Edizioni di Ar s.a.s., PB, 1991
Translated by Marcella D'Urso; claimed by some to be the "long version", only in Italian, but Glenn Lord says its just the synopsis

## L'Urlo Di Conan

Contains *Al di la del Fiume Nero (Beyond the Black River); Ombre su Zambuola (Shadows in Zambuola); Chiodi Rossi (Red Nails); Il Dio nel Sarcofago (The God in the Bowl); 11 Tesoro di Tranicos (The Treasure of Tranicos); La Figlia del Gigante del Gelo (The Frost Giant's Daughter); La Vallata delle Donne Perdute (The Vale of Lost Women)*
1st Edition, Arnoldo Mondadori Editore, PB, 1991
    Cover art by Richard Hescox; translated by Diana Georgiacodis & Lidia Lax

## Orrore A Faring Town

Contents unknown
1st Edition, Il Cerchio Iniziative Editoriali, 1999, Italy, PB

## Ombre Dal Tempo

Contents unknown
1st Edition, Fanucci Editore, 1994, Italy, PB

## Solomon Kane

Contains *Teschi fra le Stelle (Skulls in the Stars); La Mano Destra del Demonio (The Right Hand of Doom); Ombre Rosse (Red Shadows); Gli Oscuri Cavalieri Della Morte (Death's Black Riders); Un Rumore d'Ossa (Rattle of Bones); Il Castello del Diavolo (The Castle of the Devil; completed by Gianluigi Zuddas); La Luna dei Teschi (The Moon of Skulls); La Macchia Nera (The One Black Stain) (v); L'Azzurra Fiamma Della Vendetta (The Blue Flame of Vengeance: w / John Pocsik); Le Colline dei Morti (The Hills of the Dead); Hawk di Basti (Hawk of Basti; completed by Gianluigi Zuddas); Il Retorno di Sir Richard Grenville (The Return of Sir Richard Grenville) (v); Ali Nella Notte (Wings in the Night); I Passi nel Mausoleo (The Footfalls Within); I Figli di Asshur (The Children of Asshur; completed by Gianluigi Zuddas); Il Retorno a Casa di Solomon Kane (Solomon Kane's Homecoming) (v)*
1st Edition, Fanucci Editore, HB, 1979
    Cover art by Frank Frazetta; translated by Roberta Rambelli; blue binding, gilt lettering; poems published both in Italian and English

## Solomon Kane Il Giustiziere

Contains *Teschi Sotto le Stelle (Skulls in the Stars); La Mano Destra della Vendetta (The Right Hand of Doom); Ombre Rosse (Red Shadows); Un Rumore d'Ossa (Rattle of Bones); Il Castello del Diavola (with Zuddas) (The Castle of the Devil); La Luna dei Teschi (The Moon of Skulls); La Macchia Nera (The One Black Stain) (v); L'Azzurra Fiamma della Vendetti (The Blue Flame of Vengeance); Le Colline dei Morti (The Hills of the Dead); Hawk di Basti (w/ Zuddas) (Hawk of Basti); Il Ritorno di Sir Richard Grenville (The Return of Sir Richard Grenville) (v); Ali Nella Notte (Wings in the Night); I Passi nel Mauseleo (The Footfalls Within); I Figli di Asshur (w/ Zuddas) (The Children of Asshur); Il Ritorno a Casa di Solomon Kane (Solomon Kane's Homecoming) (v)*
1st Edition, Editrice Nord, PB, 2002

## Tutti I Cicli Fantastici, Volume 1: Il Ciclo Di Conan

Contents unknown
1st Edition, Grandi Tascabili Economici Newton, 1995, Italy, TPB

## Tutti I Cicli Fantastici, Volume 2: Il Ciclo di Conan, Volume 2

Contains *Chiodi Roddi (Red Nails); Le Gemme di Gwahlur (Jewels of Gwahlur); Oltre il Fiume Nero (Beyond the Black River); Il Tesoro di Tranicos (The Treasure of Tranicos); Le Fenice Sulla Lama (The Phoenix on the Sword); La Cittadella Scarlatta (The Scarlet Citadel); L'Ora del Dragone (The Hour of the Dragon)*
1st Edition, Grande Economici Newton, PB, 1995
    Cover art by Marco Sani

## Tutti I Cicli Fantastici, Volume 3: I Cicli Celta E Di Faccia Di Teschio

Contents unknown

1st Edition, Grandi Tascabili Economici Newton, 1995, Italy, TPB

## Tutti I Cicli Fantastici, Volume 4: I Cicli Di Solomon Kane E Kirby Buckner

Contents unknown

1st Edition, Grandi Tascabili Economici Newton, 1995, Italy, TPB

## Tutti I Cicli Fantastici, Volume 5: I Cicli Di Kull, Di Valusia, Di James Allison, Di Cthulhu, Di Almuric

Contents unknown

1st Edition, Grandi Tascabili Economici Newton, 1995, Italy, TPB

# JAPANESE

## Akuma No Yume, Tenshi No Tameiki

Contains *Daichi No Youso (Worms of the Earth)*

1st Edition, Sheishinsha, PB, 1980

Edited by Keisuke Otaki

## Ankoku No Saiki

Contains *Hato Wa Jigoku Kara Kuru (Pigeons from Hell)*

1st Edition, Shinjinbutsu Ouraisha, PB, 1969

Edited by Teiichi Hirai, Kawatarou Nakajima & Jun-Ichirou Kirou

## Arajishi Conan

Contains *Chinurareta Jashin (The Bloodstained God); Kaen-Ken No Makyo (The Flame Knife); Kyoran No Miyako (Hawks Over Shem); Arawashi No Michi (Road of the Eagles)*

1st Edition, Hayakawa Shobo, PB, 1973

Cover art by Motoichiro Takebe; translated by Masa'aki Sato; priced at 270 Yen; same story list as the Gnome Press TALES OF CONAN, based on it? In any case, the remaining stories are LSDC rewrites of non-Conan REH stories

## Bokensha Conan

Contains *Hyojin No Musume (The Frost Giant's Daughter); Enkei No Hitsugi (God in the Bowl); Kokkaiwan No Jo'ou (Queen of the Black Coast); Gunto No Miyako (Rogues in the House); Kyozo No Tou (The Tower of the Elephant)*

1st Edition, Hayakawa Shobo, PB, 1971

Priced at 210 Yen; based on Lancer CONAN and CONAN OF CIMMERIA, using only the complete REH-only stories

## Bokeno Conan

Contains *The Hour of the Dragon*

1st Edition, Asahi Sonolama, HB, 1974

Jacket and interior illustrations by Takashi Minamiyama; edited and rewritten slightly by Hiroshi Aramata; the translator toned it down to make it a juvenile book; translator listed as "Sieji D", as Sieji Dan is Hiroshi's pen name

## Conan To Arawashi No Michi

Contains *Kuroi Kaiju (Black Colossus); Shem No Hagetaka (Hawks Over Shem); Arawashi No Michi (Road of the Eagles); Gekka No Kage (Shadows in the Moonlight); Majo No Tanjo (A Witch Shall Be Born)*
1st Edition, Tokyo Sogensha Ltd, PB, 1971
> Priced at 200 Yen; based on CONAN THE FREEBOOTER

## Conan To Dokuro No Miyako

Contains *Sekikan No Naka No Kami (The God in the Bowl); Shi No Hiroma (The Hall of the Dead); Nergal No Te (The Hand of Nergal); Hyboria-Jidai (The Hyborian Age, Part 1); Yakata No Uchi No Kyokan-Tachi (Rogues in the House); Zo No Tou (The Tower of the Elephant)*
1st Edition, Tokyo Sogensha Ltd, PB, 1971
Tokyo Sogensha Ltd, PB, later printing, 2001
> Priced at 200 Yen; based on CONAN

## Conan To Hono'o No Tamken

Contains *Koutetsu No Akuma (The Devil in Iron); Hono-O No Tanken (The Flame Knife); Zamboula No Kage (Shadows in Zamboula)*
1st Edition, Tokyo Sogensha Ltd, PB, 1972
> Priced at 200 Yen; based on CONAN THE WANDERER

## Conan To Kodai-Ohkoku No Hihou

Contains *Kokuga Wo Koete (Beyond the Black River); Kodai-Ohkoku No Hihou (Jewels of Gwahlur); Chi No Tsume (Red Nails)*
1st Edition, Tokyo Sogensha Ltd, PB, 1974
> Cover art by Shuji Yanagi; translated by Toshiyasu Uno; based on CONAN THE WARRIOR

## Conan To Kuroi Yogensha

Contains *Tombalku No Taiko (Drums of Tombalku); Kuroi Yogensha (The People of the Black Circle); Kokuma No Izumi (The Pool of the Black One); Shinobi-Yoru Kage (The Slithering Shadow)*
1st Edition, Tokyo Sogensha Ltd, PB, date unknown
> Based on CONAN THE ADVENTURER

## Conan To Sekihi No Nori

Contains *Chi-Nurareta Shinzo (The Bloodstained God); Hyojin No Musume (The Frost Giant's Daughter); Kuroi Kaigan No Jo'o (Queen of the Black Coast); Yami No Naka No Kai (The Snout in the Dark); Kieuseta On'natachi No Tani (The Vale of Lost Women)*
1sst Edition, Tokyo Sogensha Ltd, PB, 1971
> Priced at 200 Yen; based on CONAN OF CIMMERIA

## Dai-Teio Conan

Contains *Hyboria-Jidai (The Hyborian Age, Part 2); Fushicho No Ken (The Phoenix on the Sword); Shinku No Toride (The Scarlet Citadel); Tranicos No Takara (The Treasure of Tranicos)*
1st Edition, Hayakawa Shobo, PB, 1972
> Priced at 260 Yen; likely based on CONAN THE USURPER and CONAN THE AVENGER, leaving out the LSDC material, except "The Treasure of Tranicos"

## Fusicho Conan

Contains *Ankoku No Kawa Wo Koete (Beyond the Black River); Gwahlur No Hiho (Jewels of Gwahlur); Akai Fudo (Red Nails)*
1st Edition, Hayakawa Shobo, PB, 1971
> Priced at 230 Yen; likely based on CONAN THE ADVENTURER

## Fu'unji Conan

Contains *Makai No Junin (The People of the Black Circle); Kokuma No Izumi (The Pool of the Black One); Genei No Miyako (The Slithering Shadow)*
1st Edition, Hayakawa Shobo, PB, 1970
> Priced at 210 Yen; likely based on CONAN THE ADVENTURER, leaving out the LSDC material

## Hora Ando Fantazi Kessakusen #1

Contains *Yume No Hebi (The Dream Snake)*
1st Edition, Sheishinsha, PB, 1984
> Edited by Keisuke Otaki

## Hora Ando Fantazi Kessakusen #2

Contains *Shiryou No Oka (The Hills of the Dead)*
1st Edition, Sheishinsha, PB, 1985
> Edited by Keisuke Otaki

## Kaiki To Gensou #1

Contains *Youchuu No Tani (The Valley of the Worm)*
1st Edition, Kadokawa Shoten, PB, 1975
> Edited by Kouzaburou Yano

## Ken To Mahou No Monogatari

Contains *Budukyou no Hangyojin (Black Canaan); Kijin No Ishizuka (The Cairn on the Headland); Sabaku No Mato (The Fire of Asshurbanipal); Kyuuketsuki No Haka (The Horror from the Mound); Akuryou No Yakata (The House of Arabu); Mitsurin No Jinrou (Wolfshead)*
1st Edition, Asahi Sonorama, PB, 1986
> Priced at 580 Yen; maybe based from the Lancer WOLFSHEAD book

## Ku Ritoru Ritoru Shinwashu

Contains *Hafu No Ue No Mono (The Thing on the Roof)*
1st Edition, Kokusho Kankoukai, PB, 1976
> Edited by Hiroshi Aramata

## Kuro No Ishibumi

Contains *Arkham (v); The Black Stone; The Fire of Asshurbanipal; The Thing on the Roof; Dig Me No Grave; Silence Falls on Mecca's Walls (v); The Valley of the Worm; The Shadow of the Beast; Old Garfield's Heart; People of the Dark; Worms of the Earth; Pigeons from Hell; An Open Window (v)*
1st Edition, Tokyo Sogensha Ltd, PB, 1991
> Japanese edition of CTHULHU THE MYTHOS AND KINDRED HORRORS; cover art by Hitoshi Yoneda; translated by Kenji Natsuki
Tokyo Sogensha Ltd, PB, 2nd printing, August 2000

## Kuthuru #4

Contains *Haka Wa Iranai (Dig Me No Grave)*
1st Edition, Sheishinsha, HB, 1983
Sheishinsha, PB, 1989
> Edited by Keisuke Otaki

**Kuthuru #5**
> Contains *Kuroi Ishi (The Black Stone)*
> 1st Edition, Sheishinsha, HB, 1983
> Sheishinsha, PB, 1992
>> Edited by Keisuke Otaki

**Kuthuru #7**
> Contains *Asshubaniparu No Hono-O (The Fire of Asshurbanipal)*
> 1st Edition, Sheishinsha, PB, 1989
>> Edited by Keisuke Otaki

**Kuthuru #8**
> Contains *Yane No Ue Ni (The Thing on the Roof)*
> 1st Edition, Sheishinsha, PB, 1990
>> Edited by Keisuke Otaki

**Kyosenshi Conan**
> Contains *Sabaku no Mao (Black Colossus); Koutetsu No Akuma (Devil in Iron); Gekka No Kaiei (Shadows in the Moonlight); Zamboula No Kage (Shadows in Zamboula); Majo No Tanjo (A Witch Shall Be Born)*
> 1st Edition, Hayakawa Shobo, PB, 1971
>> Priced at 240 Yen; possibly based on CONAN THE WANDERER and CONAN THE FREEBOOTER, using only the complete REH-only stories

**Kyoufu Tsushin #2**
> Contains *Okiyou No Jashim (The Thing on the Roof)*
> 1st Edition, Kawada Shobo Shinsha, PB, 1973
>> Edited by Kouji Nakata

**Majo No Tanjo**
> Contains *Majo No Tanjo (A Witch Shall Be Born)*
> 1st Edition, Shinjinbutsu Ouraisha, PB, 1970
>> Edited by Michio Tsuzuki

**Makyo-Wakusei Almuric**
> Contains *Makyo-Sakusei Almuric (Almuric)*
> 1st Edition, Hayakawa Shobo, PB, 1972
>> Priced at 200 Yen

**Seifuku-O Conan**
> Contains *Seifuku-O Conan (Conan the Conqueror)*
> 1st Edition, Hayakawa Shobo, PB, 1970
>> Priced at 220 Yen; possibly based on Lancer CONAN THE CONQUEROR

**Shin Ku Ritoru Ritoru Sihwa Taikei #3**
> Contains *Yami Ni Hisomu Agito (Usurp the Night)*
> 1st Edition, Kokusho Kankoukai, PB, 1982
>> Edited by Nachi Shirou

**Shin Ku Ritoru Ritoru Sihwa Taikei #9**
> Contains *Kuro No Shizin (The House in the Oaks)*
> 1st Edition, Kokusho Kankoukai, PB, 1983
>> Edited by Nachi Shirou

**Sukaru Feisu**
> Contains *Ashabaruparu No Empou (The Fire of Asshurbanipal); Kyoufu No Niwa (The Garden of Fear); Sukaru Feisu (Skull Face); Routou Kidari (Wolfshead); Daichi No Youso (Worms of the Earth)*
> 1st Edition, Kokusho Kankoukai, PB, 1977
>> Priced at 980 Yen

**Waido #3**
> Contains *Yoru No Matsuei (The Children of the Night)*
> 1st Edition, Sheishinsha, PB, 1990
>> Edited by Keisuke Otaki

**Weird Tales #2**
> Contains *Kage No Ohkoku (The Shadow Kingdom)*
> 1st Edition, Kokusho Kankoukai, PB, 1984
>> Edited by Shiro Nachi and Sadao Miyakabe

**Weird Tales #3**
> Contains *Habataku Akki (Wings in the Night)*
> 1st Edition, Kokusho Kankoukai, PB, 1984
>> Edited by Shiro Nachi and Sadao Miyakabe

# LITHUANIAN

**Konanas**
> Contains *Dramblio Bokstas (The Tower of the Elephant); Raudonasis Zynys (Rogues in the House); Numireliu Meneje (The Hall of the Dead); Negralo Ranka (The Hand of Nergal); Dievas is Taures (The God in the Bowl); Raganos Zenklas (A Witch Shall Be Born)*
> 1st Edition, Eridanas, PB, 2000
>> Cover by Luis Royo; translated by Neringa Butkiene

# NORWEGIAN

**Conan**
> Contains *Letter to P. Schuyler Miller, March 19, 1936 (I feel indeed . . .); Den Hyboriske Tidsalder (The Hyborian Age), Part 1; Elefanttårnet (The Tower of the Elephant); De Dødes Hall (The Hall of the Dead); Guden i Bollen (The God in the Bowl); Kjeltringer i Huset (Rogues in the House); Negals Hånd (The Hand Of Nergal)*
> 1st Edition, SEMIC/Nordisk Forlog AS, PB, 1994
>> Cover art by Boris Vallejo; translated by G. Hvidsten & Egil Stenseth Haraldsson

**Conan Eventyreren**
> Contains *Den Svarte Sirkelens Folk (The People of the Black Circle); En Fiende i Mørket (The Slithering Shadow); Trommer over Tombalku (Drums of Tombalku); De Svarte Kjempenes Brønn (The Pool of the Black One)*
> 1st Edition, SEMIC/Nordisk Forlag AG, PB, 1995
>> Cover art by Boris Vallejo; translated by Lars Finsen

**Conan Fribytteren**
> Contains *Hauker over Shem (Hawks Over Shem); Svarte Koloss (Black Colossus); Skygger i Manelyset (Shadows in the Moonlight); Ørneveien (The Road of the Eagles); En Heks Skal Bli Født (A Witch Shall Be Born)*
> 1st Edition, SEMIC/Nordisk Forlag AG, PB, 1995
>> Cover art by Boris Vallejo; translated by Lars Finsen

## Conan Krigeren
Contains *De Gales By (Red Nails); Gwahlurs Skatt (Jewels of Gwahlur); Tapt Land (Beyond the Black River)*
1st Edition, SEMIC/Nordisk Forlag AG, PB
> Cover art by Boris Vallejo; translated by Lars E. Finsen

## Conan Snikmordernes By
Contains *Skygger i Zamboula (Shadows in Zamboula); Djevelen i Lenker (The Devil in Iron); Flamme-kniven (The Flame Knife)*
1st Edition, SEMIC/Nordisk Forlag AG, PB, 1995
Cover art by Boris Vallejo; translated by Per G. Hvidsten

## Conan Tronraneren
Contains *Tranicos Skatt (The Treasure of Tranicos); Ulvene Utenfor (Wolves Beyond the Border); Den Gamle i Fjellet (The Phoenix on the Sword); Det Røde Citadellet (The Scarlet Citadel)*
1st Edition, Bonnier Publications, PB, 1995
> Cover art by Boris Vallejo; translated by Lars E. Finsen

# POLISH

## Almuric
Contains *Almuric*
1st Edition, Wydawnictwa ANDOR, PB, 1992
> Cover art by Luis Royo; translated by Katarzyna Pawlak

## Almurik I Inne Opowiadania
Contains *Almurik (Almuric); Król Zapomnianego Ludu (King of the Forgotten People); Grzmienie Trąb (A Thunder of Trumpets); Ludzie Czarnego Wybrzeża (People of the Black Coast)*
1st Edition, Wydawnictwo PiK, HB, 1994
> Cover art and illustrations by Artur Przebindowski; translated by Anna Reszka (Almuric, "People of the Black Coast") & Piotr Leszczyński (remainder)

## Barbarzyńca
Contains *Letter to P.S. Miller, March 10, 1936 ("I feel indeed honored . . ."); Dolina Zaginionych Kobiet (The Vale of Lost Women); Czarny Kolos (Black Colossus); Feniks na Mieczu (The Phoenix on the Sword)*
1st Edition, Versus Spolka zo.o, PB, 1990
> Cover art by Andrzej Janicki; translated by Zbigniew A. Królicki & Pawel Kruk

## Bogowie Bal-Sagoth
Contains *Piemny Posąg(The Dark Man); Bogowie Bal-Sagoth (The Gods of Bal-Sagoth)*
1st Edition, Wydawnictwo Iskry, PB, 1987
> Cover art by Tadeusz Luczejko; translated by Piotr R. Cholowa

## Bramy Imperium
Contains *Droga Azraela (The Road of Azrael); Męskie Sny (The Dreams of Men) (v); Szlak Boemunda (The Track of Bohemund); Droga Mieczy (The Way of the Swords); Rozkosz Samotności (The Ecstasy of Desolation) (v); Jastrzębie nad Egiptem (Hawks Over Egypt); Bramy Imperium (Gates of Empire)*
1st Edition, Wydawnictwo GEA, HB, 1994
> Cover art by Melvyn Grant; interiors by Piotr Gancewski; translated by Piotr Ogorzałek, Dariusz Pal, Aleksander Sokołowski & Agata Wierzbicka

## Cien Bestii

Contains *Wąz ze Snu (The Dream Snake); Serce Starego Garfielda (Old Garfield's Heart); Delenda Est / Cień Bestii (The Shadow of the Beast); Hiena (The Hyena); Zguba Dermoda (Dermod's Bane); Czlowiek na Ziemi (The Man on the Ground); Bestia z Otchlani (The Beast from the Abyss); Prožna Nadzieja (Hope Empty of Meaning) (v); Umarty Pamięta (The Dead Remember); Upiór Piersćienia (The Haunter of the Ring); Beznosy Horror (The Noseless Horror); Czarny Kamień (The Black Stone); Horror z Kurhanu (The Horror from the Mound)*

1st Edition, Wydawnictwo PiK, HB, 1994
> Cover art by Dariusz Rzontkowski

## Conan

Contains *Skarby Gwalhura (Jewels of Gwahlur); Tajemnica Swiatyni Kalliana (The God in the Bowl); Dolina Zaginionych Kobiet (The Vale of Lost Women); Cienie w Blashu Ksiezyca (Shadows in the Moonlight); Cienie w Zambouli (Shadows in Zamboula); Szmaragdowa Ton (The Pool of the Black One); Feniks na Mieczu (The Phoienix on the Sword); Stalowy Demon (The Devil in Iron); Reka Nergala (The Hand of Nergal); Straznicy Larsha (The Hall of the Dead); Okrwawiony Bog (The Bloodstained God)*

1st Edition, Wydawnictwo Atlantis, PB, 1990
> Translated by Zbigniew A. Krolicki

## Conan

Contains *Letter to P.S. Miller, March 10, 1936 ("I feel indeed honored . . ."); Era Hyboryjska (The Hyborian Age); Wieża Slonie (The Tower of the Elephant); Komnata Smierci (The Hall of the Dead); Bög w Pucharze (The God in the Bowl); Dom Pelen Lotrów (Rogues in the House); Reka Nergala (The Hand of Nergal)*

1st Edition, Wydawnictwo PiK, HB, 1991
> Cover art by Frank Frazetta; illustrations by Zbigniew Mielnik; translated by Zbigniew A. Królicki; black pictorial boards

## Conan: Czerwone Cwieki

Contains *Red Nail*
1st Edition, n.p., PB, 1984

## Conan: Droga Do Tronu

Contains *Czerwone Cwieki (Red Nails); Za Czarną Rzeką (Beyond the Black River); Szkarlatna Cytadela (The Scarlet Citadel); Era Hyboryjska (Pt. II) (The Hyborian Age)*

1st Edition, Wydawnictwa Alfa, PB, 1988
> Cover art by Robert Bury; translated by Stanislaw Czaja, Lukasz Piother, and Stanislaw Plebański

## Conan: Godzina Smoka

Contains *The Hour of the Dragon*
1st Edition, Wydawnictwo Alfa, PB, 1988
> Cover art by Robert Bury; translated by Stanislaw Czaja

## Conan Najemnik

Contains *Szmaragdowa Toń (The Pool of the Black One); Stalowy Demon (The Devil in Iron); Cienie w Blasku Księżyca (Shadows in the Moonlight); Skarby Gwahlura (Jewels of Gwahlur)*

1st Edition, Wydawnictwo Nakom, PB, 1990
> Translated by Zbigniew A. Krolicki

## Conan Obieżyświat

Contains *Cienie W Zambouli (Shadows in Zamboula); Stalowy Demon (The Devil in Iron); Płomienny Nóż (The Flame Knife)*

> 1st Edition, Wydawnictwo PiK, HB, 1991
> Cover art by Frank Frazetta; illustrations by Zbigniew Mielnik; translated by Robert P. Lipski ("The Flame Knife") & Zbigniew A. Królicki (remainder)

## Conan Ognisty Wicher

Contains *Dzieci Nocy (A Elkins Never Surrenders) (???)*
1st Edition, Wydawnictwo, PB, 1994
> Cover art by Navarro; translated by Katarzyna Pawlak

## Conan Pirat

Contains *Jastrzębie nad Shemen (Hawks over Shem); Czarny Kolos (Black Colossus); Cienie w Blasku Księzyca (Shadows in the Moonlight); Dorga Orłów (The Road of the Eagles); Narodzi się Czarownica (A Witch Shall Be Born)*
1st Edition, Wydawnictwo PiK, HB, 1991
Cover art by Frank Frazetta; illustrations by Zbigniew Mielnik

## Conan: Reka Nergala/Stalowy Demon

Contains *Reka Nergala (The Hand of Nergal); Stalowy Demon (The Devil in Iron)*
1st Edition, Wroclaw, PB, 1985
> Cover art by Robert J. Szmidt; translated by Zbigniew A. Królocki and Robert J. Szmidt

## Conan Ryzykant

Contains *Ludzie Czarnego Kręgu (The People of the Black Circle); Pelzajacy Cién (The Slithering Shadow); Bębny Tombalku (Drums of Tombalku); Szmaragdowa Tón (The Pool of the Black One)*
1st Edition, Wydawnictwo PiK, HB, 1992
> Cover art by Frank Frazetta; illustrations by Zbigniew Mielnik; translated by Zbigniew A. Królocki

## Conan: Skarby Gwalhura

Contents *Skarby Gwalhura (Jewels of Gwahlur?)*
1st Edition, SFERA, PB, 1984
> Cover art and 2 interiors by Robert Szmidt; back cover: Piotr Surmiak; translated by Zbigniew A. Krolicki

## Conan: Strażnicy Larsha / Okrwawiony Bôg

Contains *Strażnicy Larsha (The Hall of the Dead); Okrwawlony Bôg (The Bloodstained God)*
1st Edition, SFERA, PB, 1986
> Cover art by Robert P. Sznitte; translated by Zbigniew A. Królicki

## Conan Uzurpator

Contains *Skarb Tranikosa (The Treasure of Tranicos); Wilhi na Granicy (Wolves Beyond the Border); Feniks na Mieczu (The Phoenix on the Sword); Szkarlotina Cytadela (The Scarlet Citadel)*
1st Edition, Wydawnictwo PiK, HB, 1992
> Cover art by Frank Frazetta; interior illustrations: 4 full page and 3 spot by Piotr Stanek; translated by Zbigniew A. Królicki

## Conan Wojownik

Contains *Czerwone Ćwieki (Red Nails); Skarby Gwalhura (Jewels of Gwahlur); Za Czarną Rzeką (Beyond the Black River)*
1st Edition, Dom Ksiegarsko-Wydawniczy ART, HB, 1991
> Cover art by Frank Frazetta; translated by Zbigniew A. Królicki

## Conan Z Cynerii

Contains *Okrwawiony Bóg (The Bloodstained God); Córka Lodowego Olbrzyma (The Frost Giant's Daughter); Królowa Czarnego Wybrzeża (Queen of the Black Coast); Dolina Zaginionych Kobiet (The Vale of Lost Women); Pysk w Ciemności (The Snout in the Dark)*
1st Edition, Dom Księgarsko-Wydawniczy ART, HB, 1991
> Cover art by Frank Frazetta; interiors by Zbigniew Mielnik; translated by Zbigniew Królicki; black boards with white lettering

## Conan Z Cimmerii

Contains *Era Hyboryjska, Pt. 1 (The Hyborian Age); Dom Pelen Latrów (Rouges in the House); Cora Lodowego Olbrzyma (The Frost Giant's Daughter); Królowa Czarnego Wybrzeża (Queen of the Black Coast); Narodzi się Wiedźma (A Witch Shall Be Born); Pelzający Cień (The Slithering Shadow)*
1st Edition, Wydawnictwa ALFA, PB, 1988
Cover art by Robert Bury; translated by Stanislaw Plebański: A Witch Shall Be Born, Rogues in the House, The Hyborian Age; Stanislaw Czaja: The Frost Giant's Daughter, Queen of the Black Coast; Lukasz Piother: The Slithering Shadow

## Conan: Za Czarną Rzeka

Contains *Beyond the Black River*
1st Edition, Sokibus f, PB, 1986
Translated by Zbigniew A. Królicki

## Conan Zdobywca

Contains *Conan the Conqueror*
1st Edition, Wydawnictaw PiK, HB, 1993
Cover art by Frank Frazetta; illustrations by Marian Knobloch; translated by Zbigniew A. Królicki; black binding, white lettering w / dj art imprinted on binding

## Conan Zdobywca

Contains *Tajemnica Świąttni Kalliana (The God in the Bowl); Dolina Zaginionych Kobiet (The Vale of Lost Women); Czarny Kolos (Black Colossus); Cienie w Blasku Księzyca (Shadows in the Moonlight); Cienie w Zamboula (Shadows in Zamboula); Szmaragdowa Tón (The Pool of the Black One); Feniks na Mieczu (The Phoenix on the Sword)*
1st Edition, Swiat Fantasy, PB, 1987
Translated by Zbigniew A. Królicki

## Czerwone Cienie

Contains *Nocne Skrzyoła (Wings in the Night); Dzieci Asszuru (The Children of Asshur); Prawa Dloń Przeznaczenia (The Right Hand of Doom); Czerwone Cienie (Red Shadows); Grzechot Kości (Rattle of Bones); Zamczysko Diabła (The Castle of the Devil); Ostrze Braterstwa (Blades of the Brotherhood); Solomon Kane Wraca w Rodzinne Strony (Solomom Kane's Homecoming) (v)*
1st Edition, Wydawnictwo PiK, HB, 1992
Cover art by Tadeusz Luczejko; translated by Andrzej Leszczyński

## Dolina Grozy

Contains *Dolina Grozy (The Valley of the Worm); Zemsta Spod Ziemi (Worms of the Earth)*
1st Edition, Wydawnictwo Iskry, PB, 1986
Cover art by Tadeusz Luczejko; translated by Piotr Cholowa

## Jastrzebie Outremeru

Contains *Jastrzebie Outremeru (Hawks of Outremer); Krew Belshazzara (The Blood of Belshazzar); Niewolnica (The Slave-Princess)*
1st Edition, Wydawnictwo Andor, PB, 1991
Cover art by Ryszard Janiczewski; translated by Jacek Ring

## Krwawy Monolit

Contains *Golebie z Piekiel (Pigeons from Hell)*
1st Edition, Wydawnictwo Andor, PB, 1993
Cover art by Luis Royo; translated by Katarzyna Pawlak

**Krolowie Nocy**
> Contains *Kings of the Night*
> 1st Edition, PB
>> Translated by Janusz Kopka

**Księżyc Czaszek**
> Contains *Powrót su Richarda Grenville'a (The Return of Sir Richard Grenville) (v); Księżyc Czaszek (The Moon of Skulls); Czaszki Między Gwiazdami (Skulls in the Stars); Stąpania Wewnątrz (The Footfalls Within); Wzgórza Umarłych (The Hills of the Dead); Hawk z Basti (Hawk of Basti)*
> 1st Edition, Wydawnictwo PiK, HB, 1992
>> Cover art and illustrations by Tadeuz Luczejko; translated by Andrzej Leszczynski

**Ludzie Czarnego Kregu**
> Contains *The People of the Black Circle*
> 1st Edition, Wydawnictwo Iskry, PB, 1988
>> Cover art by Tadeusz Luczejko; translated by Zbigniew A. Krolicki

**Nie Kopcie Mi Grobu**
> Contains *Hiena (The Hyena); Serce Starego Garfielda (Old Garfield's Heart); Człowiek Lezący na Ziemi (The Man on the Ground); Umarli Pamiętają (The Dead Remember); Nie Kopcie mi Grobu (Dig Me No Grave); Dzika Woda (The Valley of the Lost); Hiszpańskie Złoto na Diabelskim Koniu (Spanish Gold on Devil Horse); Bębny w Górach Zachodzącego Słońca (Drums of the Sunset); Dzieci Nocy (The Children of the Night); W Lesie Villefere (In the Forest of Villefere); Wąż ze Snu (The Dream Snake)*
> 1st Edition, Wydawnictwo Andor, PB, 1994
>> Cover art by Piotr Szalkowski; translated by Katarzyna Pawlak, Grzagorz Prusinowski & Pawel Stasiak

**Płomień Assurbanipala**
> Contains *Skrzydla Wśród Nocy (Wings in the Night); Płomien Assurbanipala (The Fire of Asshurbanipal); Potwór na Dachu (The Thing on the Roof)*
> 1st Edition, Wydawnictwo Iskry, PB, 1986
>> Cover art by Tadeusz Luczejko; translated by Piotr R. Cholowa

**Przeklénstwo Zlotej Czaszki**
> Contains *Dom Arabu (The House of Arabu); Jasnowlosa Bogini Bal-Sagoth (The Gods of Bal-Sagoth); Dolina Zaginionych (The Valley of the Lost); Glos El-lila (The Voice of El-lil); Prezeklénstwo Zlotej Czaszki (The Curse of the Golden Skull); Wyspa Eonów (The Isle of the Eons)*
> 1st Edition, Wydawnictwo PiK, HB, 1993
>> Cover art by Olivieri Berni; interiors by Piotr Stanek; translated by Zbigniew A. Królicki; black binding, white lettering

**Robaki Ziemi**
> Contains *Bębny Piktów (The Drums of Pictdom) (v); Zaginiona Rasa (The Lost Race); Ludzie Cieni (Men of the Shadows); Królowie Nocy (Kings of the Night); Pieśń Rasy (A Song of the Race) (v); Robaki Ziemi (Worms of the Earth); Fragment / Ciemny Posąg (The Dark Man)*
> 1st Edition, Wydawnictwo PiK, HB, 1994
>> Illustrations by Artur Przebindowski; translated by Piotr W. Cholewa ("The Dark Man") & Jaroslaw Kotarski (remainder)

**Szable Szahrazaru**
> Contains *Przekleństwo Szkarłatnego Boga (The Curse of the Crimson God); Skarby Tartaru (The Treasures of Tartary); Szable Szahrazaru (Swords of Shahrazar)*
> 1st Edition, Wydawnictwo PiK, HB, 1992
>> Cover art by Tadeuz Luczejko; translated by Piotr Leszczyński

## Trupioglowy

Contains *Skull-Face*
1st Edition, Wydawnictwo Arka & Wydawnictwo Dilmun, PB, 1991
> Cover art by Janusz Oblucki; translated by Anna Reszka

## Wedrowcy Z Valhalli

Contains *Wedrowcy z Valhalli (Marchers of Valhalla); Jezdziec Gromu (The Thunder-Rider); Zmierzch Ponurego Boga (The Grey God Passes)*
1st Edition, Wydawnictwo ANDOR, PB, 1991
> Cover art by Ryszard Janiczewski; translated by Jacek Ring

## Wilcza Glowa

Contains *Czarny Pies Śmierci (Black Hound of Death); Ponury Wiatr Dmie (Black Wind Blowing); Czarny Canaan (Black Canaan); Gołębie z Piekla (Pigeons from Hell); Wilcza Glowa (Wolfshead); "Z Miłości do Barbary Allen" ("For the Love of Barbara Allen")*
1st Edition, Wydawnictwo PiK, HB, 1994
> Cover art and interiors by Dariusz Rzontkowski; translated by Jan S. Zaus & Irena Ciechanowska-Sudymont

## Wysłańcy Walhalli

Contains *Akwaforty na Sloniowej Kości (Etchings in Ivory); Plonacy Marmur (Flaming Marble); Czaszki i Orchidee (Skulls and Orchids); Medaliony z Ksiezyca (Medallions in the Moon); Bogowie Zapomniani (The Gods That Men Forget); Krwawniki i Heban (Bloodstones and Ebony); Ogród Strachu (The Garden of Fear); Brachan Celt (BrachEn the Celt); Jeździec Gromu (The Thunder-Rider); Lud Mroków (People of the Dark); Wysłańcy Walhalli (Marchers of Valhalla); Kurhan na Przylądku (The Cairn on the Headland)*
1st Edition, Wydawnictwo ARKA, HB, 1992
> Cover art by Janusz Oblucki; translated by Zbigniew A. Królicki

## Zakazane Miasto Gothan

Contains *Polityka i Rewolwery (Pistol Politics)*
1st Edition, Wydawnictwo Andor, PB, 1993
> Cover art by Luis Royo; translated by Pawel Stasiak, Jacek Medrzycki & Grzegors Prusinowski

## Zaginiona Dolina Iskandera

Contains *Córka Erlik-chana (The Daughter of Erlik Khan); Zaginiona Dolina Iskandera (The Lost Valley of Iskander); Jastrzab z Gór (Hawk of the Hills)*
1st Edition, Wydawnictwo PiK, HB, 1993
> Cover art by Tadeusz Luezejko; interiors by Marian Knobloch; translated by Piotr Leszczyński; black binding w/ white lettering

## Zmierzch Nad Stonehenge

Contains *Zmierzch nad Stonehenge (Twilight on Stonehenge) (v); Czarny Monolit (The Black Stone); Płomień Asurbanipala (The Fire of Asshurbanipal); Skarb Jukatanu (The Thing on the Roof); Arkham / Nie Kop mi Grobu (Dig Me No Grave); Mury Mekki (Silence Falls on Mecca's Walls) (v); Dolina Czerwia (The Valley of the Worm); Czarne Morza (Black Seas) (v); Cień Bestii (The Shadow of the Beast); Szepty Nocnych Wiatrów (Whispers on the Nightwinds) (v); Serce Starego Garfielda (Old Garfield's Heart); Wygnaniec z Atlantydy (Exile of Atlantis); Ostatnie Słowa (The Last Words He Heard) (v); Cień Szarego Boga (The Grey God Passes); Otwarte Okno (An Open Window) (v)*
1st Edition, Wydawnictwo GEA Sp. z.o.o., HB, 1994
> Cover art by Melvyn Grant; illustrations by Piotr Gancewski; translated by Aldona Szpakowska (Dig Me No Grave), Ewa Witecka (Exile of Atlantis), Andrzej Sawicki (Foreword, The Black Stone, The Fire of Asshurbanipal, The Thing on the Roof, Arkham), Piotr Ogorzalek (remainder)

# PORTUGESE (All these published in Brazil)

## Conan - Espada & Magia #1 (Conan - Sword and Sorcery #1)

Contains *A Torre do Elefante (Tower of the Elephant); A Filha do Gigante de Gelo (Frost Giant's Daughter); O Deus na Tigela (God in the Bowl); Vingança (Revenge/Vengeance?); A Fênix na Espada (The Phoenix on the Sword)*

1$^{st}$ Edition, Unicórnio Azul, PB, date unknown
    Based on Lancer/Ace versions of the stories; don't know what that "Revenge" story is

## Conan - Espada & Magia #2 (Conan - Sword and Sorcery #2)

Contains *A Mão de Nergal (Hand of Nergal); A Libertação de Thugra Khotan (The Release of Thugra Khotan - likely Black Colossus)*
1$^{st}$ Edition, Unicórnio Azul, PB, date unknown
    Based on Lancer/Ace versions of the stories

## Conan - Espada & Magia #3 (Conan - Sword and Sorcery #3)

Contains *O Focinho na Escuridão (The Snout in the Dark); O Salão dos Mortos (Hall of the Dead); A Maldição da Lua Crescente (Curse of the Crescent Moon - likely A Witch Shall Be Born)*
1$^{st}$ Edition, Unicórnio Azul, PB, date unknown
    Based on Lancer/Ace versions of the stories

## Conan - Espada & Magia #4 (Conan - Sword and Sorcery #4)

Contains *A Rainha da Costa Negra (Queen of the Black Coas); O Vale das Mulheres Perdidas (Vale of Lost Women)*
1st Edition, Editora Mercuryo Ltda, PB, 1995
    Cover art by Maria Amelia de Azevedo & Ed Imparato; translated by Júlia Bárány & José Antonio Ceschin

## Conan - Espada & Magia #5 (Conan - Sword and Sorcery #5)

Contains *O Poço Macabro (Pit/Pool Macabre? Maybe Pool of the Black One?); A Lâmina de Fogo (The Flame Knife)*
1$^{st}$ Edition, Unicórnio Azul, PB, date unknown
    Based on Lancer/Ace versions of the stories

## Conan Espada & Magia: A Lamina De Fogo

Contents unknown
1$^{st}$ Edition, Editora Mercuryo Ltda (Unicornio Azul), 1995,Brazil, PB

## Conan Espada & Magia: A Maldicao Da Lua Crescente

Contents unknown
1$^{st}$ Edition, Editora Mercuryo Ltda (Unicornio Azul), 1995, Brazil, PB

# Magos (Wizards)

Contains *Povo do Círculo Negro (People of the Black Circle)*
1$^{st}$ Edition, Editora Melhoramentos, PB, 1990
    Edited by Isaac Asimov; based off of ISAAC ASIMOV'S MAGICAL WORLDS OF FANTASY #1: WIZARDS

**Pregos Vermelhos (Red Nails)**
> Contains *Red Nails*
> 1st Edition, Newton-Compton, PB, 1996
>> As part of their collection called "Fantásticos Econômicos", something like "Cheap Fantasy" - "cheap" as opposed to dear, or expensive

# ROMANIAN

**Conan**
> Contains *Era Hiboriană (The Hyborian Age), Pt. 1; Turnul Elefantului (The Tower of the Elephant); În Lăcasul Mortii (The Hall of the Dead); Zeul din Sarcófag (The God in the Bowl); Noaptea Hoţilor (Rogues in the House); Mâna Lui Nergal (The Hand of Nergal)*
> 1st Edition, Editura Fantasia, PB, 1994
>> Cover art and illustrations by Tudor Popa; translated by Junona Tutunea

# RUSSIAN

**Chas Drakona**
> Contains *Lyudi Chernogo Kruga (The People of the Black Circle); Chas Drakona (The Hour of the Dragon); Plamen Ashurbanipala (The Fire of Asshurbanipal); Tvar na Krishe (The Thing on the Roof); Kryliya v Nochi (Wings in the Night); Golubi iz Ada (Pigeons from Hell)*
> 1st Edition, Eridan, HB, 1990
>> Printed in Belarus

**Chernye Kanaan**
> Contains *Zhivuschie Pod Usypainitsami (The Dwellers Under the Tomb); Povelitel Koltsa (The Haunter of the Ring); Dom Okruzhennyi Dubami (The House in the Oaks); V Lesu Willefer (In the Forest of Villefere); Kogda Voskhodit Poinaia Luna (Wolfshead); Chernye Kanaan (Black Canaan); Luna Zimbabwi (Moon of Zembebwei); Golubi Ada (Pigeons from Hell); Dolina Sginuvshykh (The Valley of the Lost); Serdtse Starogo Garfilda (Old Garfield's Heart) Prishelets iz Tmy (The Noseless Horror); Chernye Kamen (The Black Stone); Grokhut Trub (A Thunder of Trumpets); Dom Ereljbu (The House of Arabu)*
> 1st Edition, Olma Press, HB, date unknown

**Chernuy Kamen**
> Contains *Plamya Ashybanipala (The Fire of Asshurbanipal); Chernuy Kamen (The Black Stone); Grohot Trub (A Thunder of Trumpets); Delenda Est; Obitateli Chernava Poberezhya (The People of the Black Coast); Dom Ereybu (The House of Arabu)*
> 1st Edition, Severo-Zapad, HB, 1997
>> Cover art by Ken Kelly

**Conan – Corsar**
> Contains *Ogneyl Nozh (The Flame Knife)*
> 1st Edition, Eridan, HB, 1993
>> Translated by V. Velesko & V. Karachevski; blue binding, gilt lettering

**Conan Eternal**
> Contains *The Hall of the Dead; The God in the Bowl; The Hand of Nergal; The Vale of Lost Women; The Snout in the Dark; The Flame Knife; The Drums of Tombalku; Black Stranger; Wolves Beyond the Border*
> 1st Edition, Eksmo, HB, 2003
>> Collection of REH derivatives and pastiches, mostly from the Lancer/Ace series

**Conan I Iztochnik Sudeb**

Contains *Barabani Tombalku (Drums of Tombalku)*
1st Edition, Severo–Zapad (Troll), HB, 1996
> Cover art by A. Ariskin; illustrations by A. Shirkin; translated by N. Baulina

## Conan Iz Cimerii (Conan the Cimmerian)
Contains *Letter to P. Schuyler Miller; Hyboriyskaya Era (The Hyborian Age, Pt. 1); Bashnya Slona (The Tower of the Elephant); Splosh Negodyai v Dome (Rogues in the House); Doch Ledyanova Giganta (The Frost-Giant's Daughter); Koroleva Chernava Poberezhya (Queen of the Black Coast); Sokrovishta Gwalura (Jewels of Gwahlur); Chernuy Collos (Black Colossus); Zheleznoi Demon (The Devil in Iron); Teni v Lammon Yvete (Shadows in the Moonlight); Roditsya Vedma (A Witch Shall Be Born); Prizraki Zambulii (Shadows in Zamboula); Ludi Chernova Kruga (The People of the Black Circle); Polzuchaya Ten (The Slithering Shadow); Gwozdi a Krasnimi Shiyapkamy (Red Nails); Po tu Staronu Chernoy Reki (Beyond the Black River); Feniks na Meche (The Phoenix on the Sword); Alaya Citadela (The Scarlet Citadel); Chas Drakona (The Hour of the Dragon); Hyboriskaya Era (The Hyborian Age, Pt, 2)*
1st Edition, Eksmo, HB, 2003
> Translators include M. Semenova; E. Haeckaya; M. Uspenski; A. Prutskola; A. Zimerman; A. Kononova; V. Karchevsky

## Conan, Varvar Iz Cimmeria
Contains *Voznaprazhdenie (Recompense) (v); Siyn Thora (Thor's Son) (v); Cimmeria (v)*
1st Edition, Troll, HB, 1996
> Troll and AST are imprints of Severo Zapad

## Gentelmen S Medvezhey Rechki
Contains *Gentelmen S Medvezhey Rechki (A Gent from Bear Creek (novel))*
1st Edition, Yanus, PB, 1992
> Cover art and illustrations by A. Gorbunov; translated by A. Zimerman

## Koghot Drakona
Contains *Dabruy Titzar (The Good Knight); Osobnyak Podozrenuy (The House of Suspicion); Povesa iz Naif-River (Knife River Prodigal); Moushki Hartuma (The Guns of Khartum); Istorii o Stivene Allisone (The West Tower); Bronzovoi Pavlin (The Brazen Peacock); Doul Chernuy Veter (Black Wind Blowing); Yarost Medvedya (The Black Bear Bites); Kak Izbavitsya ot Trusa (The Extermination of Yellow Donory); Skachuschuy s Gromon (The Thunder Rider); Kopie i Kluik (Spear and Fang)*
1st Edition, Severo-Zapad, HB, 1999
> Cover art by Ken Kelly

## Konan I Gorod Pleneniych Doush
Contains *Doch Ispolina Ida (The Frost Giant's Daughter); Coroleva Chernova Poberezhya (Queen of the Black Coast); Chernaya Ten (Shadows in the Moonlight); Volchyi Rubezh (Wolves Beyond the Border); Sokrovishta Tranikosa (The Treasure of Tranicos)*
1st Edition, Severo-Zapad (Troll), HB, 1996
> Cover art by Andrey Aryskin

## Konan I Povelitely Peshter
Contains *Zheleznyi Demon (The Devil in Iron); Alyie Koghty (Red Nails); Socrovishta Gvalura (Jewels of Gwahlur); Za Chernoy Rekoy (Beyond the Black River)*
1st Edition, Severo-Zapad, HB, 1993
> Cover art by Vladislav Asadulin; translators: "The Devil in Iron" by E. Kravitzkayr; "Red Nails," "Jewels of Gwahlur," "Beyond the Black River" by A. Zimmerman

## Krov Bogov

Contains *Krov Bogov (Blood of the Gods); Strana Kinzhalov (The Country of the Knife); Sin Balovo Volka (Son of the White Wolf); Poyavienie El Boraka (The Coming og El Borak); Raskar Hoda Hana (Khoda Khan's Tale); Zheleznuy Voinn (The Iron Terror); Raskaz o Koitze Raji (The Tale of the Rajah's Ring); Lal Singh - Ricar Vostoka (Lal Singh, Oriental Gentleman); Ispanskoe Zoloto (Spanish Gold on Devil Horse); Nozh, Pulya i Petiya (Knife, Bullet and Noose)*
1st Edition, Severo Zapad, HB, 1988
> Cover art by Ken Kelly

## Lik Smercha

Contains *Kulachyi Boetz (Circus Fists); Vikingi v Boxerskih Perchatkah (Vikings of the Gloves); Noch Bitvyi (Night of Battle); Kitaiskie Zabavuy (The Slugger's Game); General Stalnyi (General Ironfist); Boy Bez Pravil (Sluggers on the Beach)*
1st Edition, Severo-Zapad, HB, 1998
> Translated by S. Sokolin

## Moichanie Idola

Contains *Hozyain Sudbui (Skull-Face); Povelitel Mertvuih (Lord of the Dead); Chemaya Kniga (Names in the Black Book); Socrovishte Tartara (Treasure of Tartary); Moichanie Idola (The Trail of the Blood-Stained God); Yastreb Hoimov (Hawk of the Hills); Letters: to Farnsworth Wright, ca. June 1930 ("I have long looked . . ."); to HPL, ca. August 1930 ("Let me first thank you . . .); to TCS, ca. August 1930 (not sure which letter ); To H.P. Lovecraft (not sure which letter); to TCS, ca. September 1930 (not sure which letter)*
1st Edition, Severo-Zapad, HB, 1999
> Cover art by Ken Kelly; Translators: "Skull-Face" by G. Usova; "Lord of the Dead" by I. Burova; "Names in the Black Book" by A. Curych; "The Treasures of Tartary" by N. Druzhinia; "The Trail of the Bloodstained God" by N. Druzhinina; "Hawk of the Hills" by M. Riner

## Prizraki Zambuli

Contains *Shadows in Zamboula*
1st Edition, Journalist Fund of Byelorussia, PB, 1990
> Art by M. Kopilova & Z. Pehovskoya

## Solomon Kein

Contains *Luna Cherepov (Skulls in the Stars); Desnitza Sudbuy (The Right Hand of Doom); Bagrovie Teniy (Red Shadows); Perestuk Costey (Rattle of Bones); Luna Cherepov (The Moon of Skulls); Klinky Bratsva (Blades of the Brotherhood); Holmuy Mertvih (The Hills of the Dead); Bastiyskiy Yastreb (Hawk of Basti); Deti Ashura (The Children of Assur); Pogibshiy Drug (The Return of Sir Richard Grenville) (v); Vozvrashtenie Solomona Keina (Solomon Kane's Homecoming) (v)*
1st Edition, Azbuka, PB, 1997

## Tzar Kull

Contains *Begstvo iz Atlantidyi (Exile of Atlantis); Tzarstvo Tenei (The Shadow Kingdom); Altar i Scorpion (The Altar and the Scorpion); Koshka Delcardii (Delcardes' Cat); Cherep Melchaniya (The Skull of Silence); Sim Toporom ya Boudou Pravit (By This Axe I Rule); Uodar Gonga (The Striking of the Gong); Zerkalo Tuzun-Tuna (The Mirrors of Tuzun Thune); Mechi Purpurnova Ritzarstva (Swords of the Purple Kingdom); Oscorblenie ("Thus," said Tu . . ."); Chernii Gorod (The Black City); Rasskaz Picta ("Three men sat . . ."); Tzar i Dub (The King and the Oak) (v)*
1st Edition, Azbuka, PB, 1997
> Translators: C. Trotsky: Exile of Atlantis, The Shadow Kingdom, The Altar and the Scorpion, Delcardes' Cat, The Skull of Silence, By This Axe I Rule!, The Striking of the Gong, The Mirrors of Tuzun Thune, all poetry; M. Pirus: Swords of the Purple Kingdom, The Black City, fragment ("Three men sat . . ."), fragment ("Thus" said Tu . . .")

## Vozvrashtenye Conana

Contains *Dragocenasty Tranicosa (The Treasure of Tranicos); Volki po to Storonu Granicyi (Wolves Beyond the Border); Tigri Morya (Tigers of the Sea); Mechy Severnova Morya (Swords of the Northern Sea); Noch Volka (The Night of the Wolf); Mrezkoe Svyatilistye (The Temple of Abomination); Bogi Bel-Sagota (The Gods of Bal-Sagoth); Krasniye Teni (Red Shadows)*
1st Edition, Eridan, HB, 1993
> Translated by A. Ivanova and N. Karcheski; printed in Belarus

## Zhivushtiye Pod Usiypainitzami

Contents unknown
1st Edition, Lenizdat, Russia, PB

## Znak Ognya (Three-Bladed Doom)

Contains *Znak Ognya (Three-Bladed Doom); Doch Eriik Hana (The Daughter of Erlik Khan); Zateryanaya Dolina Iskandera (The Lost Valley of Iskander); Lev Tiveriaduy (The Lion of Tiberias)*
1st Edition, Severe Zapad, HB, date unknown

# SPANISH

## Almuric

Contains *Almuric*
1st Edition, Miraguano Ediciones, PB, 1987
> Cover art by Frank Frazetta; translated by Francisco Arellano

## Clavos Rojos

Contains *Red Nails*
1st Edition, Quepuntoes Crom, PB, 2001
> Cover art and illustrations by Juan Jose Ryp; additional illustrations by Antonio Vazquez; translated by Leon Arsenal

## Conan

Contains *Letter to P. Schuyler Miller, March 10, 1936 ("I am indeed . . ."); La Era Hyborea, Part 1 (The Hyborian Age); La Torre del Elefante (The Tower of the Elephant); El Aposento de los Muertos (The Hall of the Dead); El Dios del Cuenco (The God in the Bowl); Villanos en la Casa (Rogues in the House); La Mano de Nergal (The Hand of Nergal)*
1st Edition, Ediciones Forum S.A., PB, 1983
> Cover art by Franc Reyes; translated by Beartriz Oberländer
Ediciones Martinez Roca, S.A., PB, 1995
> Cover art by Ken Kelly; translated by Beartriz Oberländer

## Conan de Cimmeria

Contains *Una Deidad Manchado de Sangre (The Bloodstained God); La Hija del Gigante Helado (The Frost-Giant's Daughter); La Reina de la Costa Negra (Queen of the Black Coast); El Valle de las Mujeras Perdidos (The Vale of Lost Women); Un Hocico en la Oscuridad (The Snout in the Dark)*
1st Edition, Editorial Bruguera, S.A., PB, 1973
> Cover art by Frank Frazetta; translated by Fernando Corripio

## Conan de Cimmeria III

Contains *The Servants of Bit-Yakin (Jewels of Gwahlur); Beyond the Black River; The Black Stranger; The Man-Eaters of Zamboula (Shadows in Zamboula); Red Nails; Untitled Notes; Wolves Beyond the Border (early draft); Wolves Beyond the Border (later draft); The Black Stranger (early synopsis); The Black Stranger (later synopsis); The Man-Eaters of Zamboula (synopis); Red Nails (draft); letter to P. Schuyler Miller, March 10, 1936; plus a map of the Hyborian Age*

1ˢᵗ Edition, Timon Mas, HB, October 2006
> Edited by Patrice Louinet and Rusty Burke; based on the Wandering Star ROBERT E. HOWARD'S COMPLETE CONAN OF CIMMERIA, VOLUME 3, which may or may not see publication; cover and extensive interior artwork by Greg Manchess; this particular volume has dust jacket AND slipcase, all plates in color, with sewn-in cloth bookmark

## Conan El Aventurero

Contains *El Pueblo del Ciculo Negro (The People of the Black Circle); La Sombra Deslizante (The Slithering Shadow); Los Tambores de Tombalku (Drums of Tombalku); El Estanque de los Negros (The Pool of the Black One)*
Editorial Bruguera, S.A., PB, 1973
> Cover art by Frank Frazetta; translated by Jaime Pineiro

Ediciones Forum, S.A., PB, 1983
> Cover art by Pablo Marcos; translated by Beartriz Oberländer

Ediciones Martinez Roca, S.A., PB, 1995
> Cover art by Ken Kelly; translated by Beartriz Oberländer

## Conan El Conquistador

Contains *Conan The Conqueror*
Editorial Bruguera, PB, 1973
> Cover art by Frank Frazetta; translated by Fernando Corripio

Ediciones Forum S.A., PB, 1983
> Cover art by Tony de Zuniga; translated by Beatriz Oberländer

Ediciones Martinez Roca, S.A., PB, 1996
> Cover art by Ken Kelly; translated by Beartriz Oberländer

## Conan El Guerrero

Contains *Unas Purpureas (Red Nails); Las Joyas de Gawlar (Jewels of Gwahlur); Más Allá del Rio Negro (Beyond the Black River)*
1st Edition, Editorial Bruguera, S.A., PB, 1973
> Cover art by Frank Frazetta; translated by Fernando Corripio

Ediciones Forum S.A., PB, 1983
> Cover art by Pablo Marcos; translated by Beatriz Oberländer

## Conan El Pirata

Contains *Halcones sobre Shem (Hawks Over Shem); El Coloso Negro (Black Colossus); Sombras a la Luz de la Luna (Shadows in the Moonlight); El Camino de las Águilas (The Road of the Eagles); Nacerá una Bruja (A Witch Shall Be Born)*
1st Edition, Editorial Bruguera, S.A., PB, 1973
> Cover art by John Duillo; translated by Fernando Corripio

Ediciones Forum, S.A., PB, 1983
> Cover art by Nestor Redondo; translated by Beartriz Oberländer

Ediciones Martinez Roca, S.A., PB, 1995
> Cover art by Ken Kelly; translated by Beartriz Oberländer

## Conan El Usurpador

Contains *El Tesoro de Tránicos (The Treasure of Tranicos); Lobos Más Allá de la Frontera (Wolves Beyond the Border); El Fénix y la Espada (The Phoenix on the Sword); La Ciudadela Escarlata (The Scarlet Citadel)*
1st Edition, Editorial Bruguera, S.A., PB, 1973
> Cover art by Frank Frazetta; translated by Fernando Corripio

Ediciones Forum, S.A., PB, 1983
> Cover art by John Buscema; translated by Beartriz Oberländer

Ediciones Martinez Roca, S.A., PB, 1996
> Cover art by Ken Kelly; translated by Beartriz Oberländer

## Conan El Vagabundo
Contains *Sombras en Zamboula (Shadows in Zamboula); El Diablo de Hierro (The Devil In Iron); La Daga-Llama (The Flame Knife)*
1st Edition, Editorial Bruguera, S.A., PB, 1973
  Cover art by John Duillo; translated by Jaime Pineiro
Ediciones Forum, S.A., PB, 1983
  Cover art by John Buscema; translated by Beartriz Oberländer
Ediciones Martinez Roca, S.A., PB, 1995
  Cover art by Ken Kelly; translated by Beartriz Oberländer

## El Reino De Las Sombras
Contains *El Reino de las Sombras (The Shadow Kingdom); Los Espejos de Tuzun Thune (The Mirrors of Tuzun Thune); El Jardin del Miedo (The Garden of Fear); Sonja la Rojo (The Shadow of the Vulture); En el Bosque de Villefère (In the Forest of Villèfère)*
1st Edition, Ediciones Obelisco, PB, 1987
  Cover art by Jordi Farré; translated by Francisco Arellano

## El Templo De Yun-Shatu
Contains *El Templo de Yun-Shatu (Skull-Face); El Canaan Negro (Black Canaan)*
1st Edition, Mateu, Editor, state unknown, 1948
  Cover art by. A. Lopezolonso; translated by Casa de Vall; published in Barcelona, it is unknown whether this book is actually in Spanish or Catalan

## El Tesoro De Tranicos
Contains *El Tesoro de Tranicos (The Treasure of Tranicos)*
1st Edition, La Factoria de Ideas, PB, 2000
  Cover art by Luis Royo; translated by Carlos Lacasa Martin

## Gusanos De La Tierra
Contains *Prefacio; La Raza Perdida (The Lost Race); Hombres de las Sombras (Men of the Shadows); Reyes de la Noche (Kings of the Night); Una Canción de la Raza (A Song of the Race) (v); Gusanos de la Tierra (Worms of the Earth); Fragmento (Untitled: "A grey sky . . ."); El Hombre Oscura (The Dark Man)*
1st Edition, Ediciones Martinez Roca, S.A., PB, 1987
  Cover art by Frank Frazetta; translated by Albert Solé

## La Cuidad Muerta
Contains *La Cuidad Muerta (The Fire Asshurbanipal); La Tumba India (The Horror from the Mound); El Valle del Gusano (The Valley of the Worm); La Cuidadela Escarlata (The Scarlet Citadel); Rufianes en la Casa (Rogues in the House)*
1st Edition, Mateu, Editor, HB, 1947
  Cover art by A. Lopezolonso; translated by Juan G. de Lauces; brown-red binding, gilt lettering

## Las Aventuras De Solomon Kane
Contains *Calaveras en las Estrella (Skulls in the Stars); La Mano Derecha de la Condenacion (The Right Hand of Doom); Sombras Rojas (Red Shadows); Los Negros Jinetes de la Muerte (Death's Black Riders; completed by Fred Blosser); Un Bailoteo de Huesos (Rattle of Bones); El Castillo del Diablo (The Castle of the Devil); Luna de Calaveras (Moon of Skulls); El Negro Boldon (The One Black Stain) (v); Las Espadas de la Hermandad (Blades of the Brotherhood); Las Colinas de los Muertos (The Hills of the Dead); Los Hijos de Asshur (The Children of Asshur); La Aparicion de Sir Richard Grenville (The Return of Sir Richard Grenville) (v); Alas en la Noche (Wings in the Night); Pasos en el Interior (The Footfalls Within); Hawk di Basti (Hawk of Basti); El Regreso al Hogar de Solomon Kane (Solomon Kane's Homecoming) (v); El Regreso al Hogar de Solomon Kane (Solomon Kane's Homecoming [variant version]) (v); The Return of Sir Richard Grenville(v)*
1st Edition, Anaya, HB, 1994
  Cover art by Pablo Torrecilla; translated by Javier Martin Lalanda; green binding, silver lettering

## Las Extranas Aventuras De Solomon Kane

Contains *Prologo; Craneos en las Estrellas (Skulls in the Stars); La Mano Derecha de la Maldicion (The Right Hand Of Doom); Sombras Rojas (Red Shadows); Resonar de Huesos (Rattle of Bones); Luna de Calavera (The Moon of Skulls); Las Colinas de los Muertos (The Hills of the Dead); Alas en la Noche (Wings in the Night); Los Pasos en el Interior (The Footfalls Within); La Sombra del Buttre (The Shadow of the Vulture)*
1st Edition, Valdemar, HB, 2003
    Translated by Leon Arsenal

## Las Mejores Historias De Horror

Contains *El Desafio del Mas Alla (The Challenge from Beyond)*
1st Edition, Editorial Bruguera, PB, 1969
    Edited by Forrest J Ackerman; an anthology

## Los Gusanos De La Tierra Y Otros Relates De Horror Sobrenatural (Worms of the Earth and Other Stories of Supernatural Horror)

Contains *Arkham (v); En El Bosque de Villefere (In the Forest of Villefere); La Serpiente del Sueno (The Dream Snake); La Voz de El-Lil (The Voice of El-Lil); Los Hijos de la Noche (The Children of the Night); Los Dioses de Bal-Sagoth (The Gods of Bal-Sagoth); LaPiedra Negra (The Black Stone); El Hombre Oscuro (The Dark Man); La Casa del Tejado (The Thing on the Roof); El Pueblo de la Oscuridad (People of the Dark); Los Gusanos de la Tierra (Worms of the Earth); El Hombre del Suelo (The Man on the Ground); El Corazon del Viejo Garfield (Old Garfield's Heart); El Valle del Gusano (The Valley of the Worm); El Jardin del Miedo (The Garden of Fear); Los Muertos Recuerdan (The Dead Remember); El Fuego de Asurbanipal (The Fire of Asshurbanipal); No Me Caveis una Tumba (Dig Me No Grave); Las Palomas del Infierno (Pigeons from Hell); La Sombra de la Bestia (The Shadow of the Beast); Una Ventana Abierta (An Open Window) (v)*
1st Edition, Valdemar, HB, 2001
    Translated by Santiago Garcia

## Noches En Zamboula

Contents unknown
1st Edition, Mateu, HB, 1949

## Rey Kull

Contains *Pológo (The Hyborian Age); Exilio de Atlantis (Exile of Atlantis); El Reino de las Sombras (The Shadow Kingdom); El Altar y el Escorpión (The Altar and the Scorpion); Abismo Negro (Black Abyss); La Gata de Delcardes (Delcardes' Cat); El Espectro del Silencio (The Skull of Silence); Jinetes del Sol Naciente (Riders Beyond the Sunrise); Con Esta Hacha Gobierno! (By This Axe I Rule); El Estruendo de Gong (The Striking of the Gong); Espadas del Reino Púrpura (Swords of the Purple Kingdom); Hechicero y Guerrero (Wizard and Warrior); Los Espejos de Tuzun Thune (The Mirrors of Tuzun Thune); El Rey y el Roble (The King and the Oak) (v); Epilogo*
1st Edition, Ediciones Martinez Roca, S.A., PB, 1993
    Translated by Jose M. Pomares

## Rostro De Calavera

Contains *Which Will Scarcely Be Understood (v); Wolfshead; The Black Stone; The Horror from the Mound; The Cairn on the Headland; Black Canaan; The Fire of Asshurbanipal; A Man-Eating Jeopard; Skull- Face; The Hyborian Age; Worms of the Earth; The Valley of the Worm; Skulls in the Stars; Rattle of Bones; The Hills of the Dead; Wings in the Night; The Phoenix on the Sword; The Scarlet Citadel; The Tower of the Elephant; Rogues in the House; Shadows in Zamboula; Lines Written in the Realization That I Must Die (v)*
1st Edition, ST, PB, 1987
    Introduction by HPL; from SKULL-FACE OMNIBUS, VOLUMES 1-3, Panther edition, translated by Albert Sole; published in Barcelona, Spain

**Rostro De Calavera**

Contains *Rostro de Calavera (Skull-Face); Cabeza de Lobo (Wolfshead); La Piedra Negra (The Black Stone); El Horror del Monticulo (The Horror from the Mound); Canaan Negro (Black Canaan)*
1st Edition, Ediciones Martinez Roca, S.A., PB, 1987
     Cover art by Salinas Blanch; translated by Albert Solé

# SWEDISH

**Conan**

Contains *A letter to P.S. Miller, March 10, 1936 ("I am indeed . . ."); Den Hyboriska Tidsaldern (The Hyborian Age), Pt. 1; Elefantens Torn (The Tower of the Elephant); De Dödas Sal (The Hall of the Dead); Guden I Skålen (The God in the Bowl); Skurkar I Huset (Rogues in the House); Nergals Hand (The Hand of Nergal)*
1st Edition, Aventyrsspel, PB, 1987
     Cover art by Boris Vallejo; translated by Bo Petersson

**Conan Äventyraren**

Contains *Den Svarta Cirkelns Män (The People of the Black Circle); Den Gäckende Skuggan (The Slithering Shadow); Tombalkus Trummor (Drums of Tomblaku); Den Svartes Bassäng (The Pool of the Black One)*
1st Edition, Target Games, PB, 1990
     Cover art by Frank Frazetta; translated by Kerstin Kvisler

**Conan Cimmeriern**

Contains *A letter to P.S. Miller, March 10, 1936 ("I am indeed . . ."); Den Hyboriska Tidsåldern (The Hyborian Age); Den Blodfläckade Guden (The Bloodstained God); Frostjättens Dotter (The Frost Giant's Daughter); Svarta Kustens Drottning (Queen of the Black Coast); De Förlorade Kvinnornas Dal (The Vale of Lost Women); Trynet i Mörkret (The Snout in the Dark)*
1st Edition, Aventyrsspel, PB, 1987
     Cover art by Boris Vallejo; translated by Gunilla Jonsson and Hathor Frapp

**Conan Förgöraren**

Contains *Skuggor i Zamboula (Shadows in Zamboula); Järndjävulen (The Devil in Iron); Flamkniven (The Flame Knife)*
1st Edition, Target Games AB, PB, 1989
     Cover art by Frank Frazetta; translated by Joakim Svahn

**Conan Harskaren**

Contains *Conan the Conqueror*
1st Edition, Target Games, PB, 1991
     Cover art by Maren; translated by Magnus Eriksson

**Conan Krigaren**

Contains *Röda Spikar (Red Nails); Gwahlurs Juveler (Jewels of Gwahlur); Bortom Svarta Floden (Beyond the Black River)*
1st Edition, Target Games AB, PB, 1991
     Cover art by Ken Kelly; translated by Magnus Eriksson

**Conan Piraten**

Contains *Hökar över Shem (Hawks over Sham); Den Svarta Kolossen (Black Colossus); Skuggor i Månskenet (Shadows in the Moonlight); Ömamas Stig (The Road of Eagles); En Häxa Skall Födas (A Witch Shall Be Born)*
1st Edition, Target Games, PB, 1989
     Cover art by Doug Beekman, translated by Kerstin Kvisler

### Conan Segraren

Contains *Tranicos Skatt (The Treasure of Tranicos); Vargar Bortom Gränsen (Wolves Beyond the Border); Symbolen pa Svärdet (The Phoenix on the Sword); Det Röda Citadellet (The Scarlet Citadel)*
1st Edition, Target Games, PB, 1991
> Cover art by Ken Kelly; translated by Henrik Nilsson

# TURKISH

### Fatih Conan

Contains *The Hour of the Dragon*
1st Edition, Ithaki Yaymlan, PB, 2001
> Translated by Dost Korpe; cover art by Frank Frazetta

### Fil Kulesi

Contains *Hyboria Cagi (The Hyborian Age); Fit Kulesi (The Tower of the Elephant); Oluler Salonu (Synopsis for The Hall of the Dead); Kutudaki Tanri (The God in the Bowl); Evdeki Haydutlar (Rogues in the House); Nergal'in Eli (The Hand of Nergal, fragment); Buz Devinin Kizi (The Frost-Giant's Daughter); Kara KryNann Kralicesi (Queen of the Black Coast); Kayip Kadinlar Vadisi (The Vale of Lost Women); Karanliktaki Burun (The Snout in the Dark, fragment)*
1st Edition, Ithaki Yaymlan, PB, 2003
> A reprint of part of CONAN CHRONICLES I (Millennium); same cover art by Howe; translated by Dost Korpe

### Karanlikta 33 Yazar

Contains *Cehennen Guvercinieri (Pigeons from Hell)*
1st Edition, Ithaki Yaymlan, PB, 2001
> Translated and edited by Somnez Guven; an anthology

# YUGOSLAVIAN

### Konan

Contains *Slonova Kula (The Tower of the Elephant); Dvorana Mrtvih (The Hall of the Dead); Bozanstvo u Zdeli (The God in the Bowl); Bitange u Kući (Rogues in the House)*
1st Edition, Niro Dečje Novine, PB, 1984
> Cover from movie *Conan the Barbarian*; based on the Lancer CONAN book

### Konan: Crni Kolos

Contains *Crni Kolos (Black Colossus), pt. 2; Senke na Mesečin (Shadows in the Moonlight); Staza Orlova (The Road of the Eagles); I Rodice se Vestica (A Witch Shall Be Born), part 1*
1st Edition, Niro Dečje Novine, Gornji Milanovac, 1985
> Cover by Frank Frazetta; translated by Branka Kostić-Jurišić

### Konan: Crni Lavirint

Contains *Senka Koja Gmiže (The Slithering Shadow); Bubmjeir Tombalkua (Drums of Tombalku; part 1)*
1st Edition, Niro Dečje Novine, PB, 1985
> Cover art by Frank Frazetta; translated by Branka Kostić-Jurišić

### Konan: Demonsko Ostrovo

Contains *Demonsko Ostrovo (The Devil in Iron), pt. 2; Plameni Nož (The Flame Knife); pt. 1*
1st Edition, Nire Dečje Novine, PB, 1985
> Cover art by Frank Frazetta; traslated by Branka Kostić-Jurišić

## Konan: Dragulji Gvahlura

Contains *Gradani u Svadi (Red Nails; part 2); Dragulji Gvahlura (Jewels of Gwahlur)*
1st Edition, Niro Dečje Novine, PB, 1985
Cover art by Frank Frazetta; translated by Branka Kostić-Jurišić

## Konan: Drvo Smrti

Contains *Drvo Smiti (A Witch Shall Be Born), pt.2 Senka u Zambuli (Shadows in Zamboula); Davo od Gvožda (The Devil in Iron), pt. 1*
1st Edition, Niro Dečje Novine, PB, 1985
Cover art by Frank Frazetta; translated by Branka Kostić-Jurišić

## Konan: Grad Lobanja

Contains *Nergalova Ruka (The Hand of Nergal); Okrvavijeni Bog (The Bloodstained God); Kći Diva Mraza (The Frost Giant's Daughter); Kraljica Crne Obale (Queen of the Black Coast); pt. 1*
1st Edition, Niro Dečje Novine, 1984
Cover art by Frank Franzetta

## Konan: Opkoljeni Vukovi

Contains *Opkoljeni Vukovi (The Flame Knife), pt. 2 / Ljudi iz Crnog Kruga (The People of the Black Circle), pt.1*
1st Edition, Niro Dečje Novine, PB, 1985
Cover art by Frank Frazetta

## Konan: Princ Čarobnjaka

Contains *Reptil Napada (The People of the Black Circle), pt.2*
1st Edition, Niro Dečje Novine, PB, 1985
Cover art by Frank Frazetta; translated by Branká Kostić-Jurišić

## Konan: Prokletstvo Monolita

Contains *Kraljica Crne Obale (Queen of the Black Coast), pt. 2; Dolina Izgubljrnih Žena (The Vale of Lost Women); Rilica iz Mraka (The Snout in the Dark); Jastrebovi nad Šemom (Hawks over Shem); Kupola od Šlonovače (Black Colossus), pt. 1*
1st Edition, Niro Dečje Novine, PB, 1985
Cover art by Frank Frazetta

## Konan: Tajanstveni Gazal

Contains *Tajanstveni Gazal (Drums of Tombalku; part 2); Bazen Crnog Stvorenja (The Pool of the Black One); Crveni Nokti (Red Nails; part 1)*
1st Edition, Niro Dečje Novine, PB, 1985
Cover art by Frank Frazetta

# A SAMPLING OF COMICS
# ADAPTING REH MATERIAL

Most people are aware of the adaptation of REH's most famous character, Conan, in such comics as SAVAGE SWORD OF CONAN, CONAN THE BARBARIAN, KING CONAN, and CONAN SAGA. There is even now a new Conan comic being produced by Dark Horse. Marvel and Dark Horse also sold titles relating to King Kull and Solomon Kane. All of these used a mixture of REH original works along with partial or full pastiche, written by various authors. I have not tried to identify the issues that most closely correspond to various REH stories in those titles, as the closeness of the interpretation is an open question. In some case, only the title is retained from the original story. In any case, there are several good sources online to find information on those comics.

Listed here are some not so well known or obvious titles where one can find graphical adaptations of REH original material.

These are SORTED BY PUBLISHER, THEN BY TITLE. IF PUBLISHER IS UNKNOWN, THEN BY TITLE. The list includes both English and some non-English appearances. I have included what information I have, but in many cases my information is limited. Poetry is indicated by (v).


**Blackthorne**
KULL 3-D
RED SONYA 3-D
SOLOMON KANE 3-D

**Bladkompaniet (Norway)**
They publish the currently produced SAVAGE SWORD OF CONAN magazines in Norway

**Conquest**
THE VULTURES OF WHAPETON
> Contains *The Vultures of Whapeton*
> May 1991

ROBERT E. HOWARD'S BLOOD AND THUNDER
> Contains *Law Shooters of Cowtown*
>> Written by Rick McCollum

ROBERT E. HOWARD'S SONGS OF BASTARDS
> Contains *Songs of Bastards*
> 1992
>> Cover by Marcus Boas, interior work by Maelo Cintron

LORD OF THE DEAD
> Contains *Lord of the Dead*
> 1992
>> Cover by Marcus Boas, interior work by Felix Ortega

## Corporacion Editorial Mexicana, SA (Mexico)
CUENTOS DE ABUELITO – LA REINA DE LA COSTA NEGRA (STORIES OF MY GRANDFATHER – QUEEN OF THE BLACK COAST) #17

> **The very first Conan comic series**; approximately 18 issues, first published in the early 1950's; approximately 4 inches square; cover is same paper as interior; e.g., Volume 1, #17, November 17, 1952

## Crom the Barbarian
Issued in the 1950s, unknown publisher; an attempt to pastiche?

## Cross Plains Comics (all edited by Richard Ashford)
MYTH MAKER

> Contains *Spear and Fang; The Dream Snake; Dermod's Bane; Men of the Shadows (v); An Open Window (v); The Song of a Mad Minstrel (v, partial); Moon Shame (AKA Moon Woman, v, partial); Chant of the White Beard (v); Rune (v); The Tempter (v, partial)*
> July 1999
>> Several poems were intentionally diced and spliced, hence the "partials" above; first printing was limited to around 9000 copies

REH: A SHORT BIOGRAPHY OF ROBERT E. HOWARD

> August 1999
>> Written by Rusty Burke; contains possibly the currently most accurate short biography of REH, along with old Marvel artwork from Neal Adams, John Bolton, John Buscema, Howard Chaykin, Tim Conrad, Richard Corben, Gene Day, Phillippe Diederich, Michael Golden, Kelley Jones, Michael Kaluta, Gil Kane, Rafael Kayanan, Roy Krenkel, Mike Mignola, Rudy Nebres, Alex Nino, Mike Ploog, Sandy Plunkett, Tim Sale, John Severin, Bill Sienkiewicz, Barry Windsor Smith, Boris Vallejo, Michael Whelan, Berni Wrightson, plus some REH related photos, and a Roy Thomas intro

ROBERT E. HOWARD'S WOLFSHEAD

> Contains *In the Forest of Villefere; Wolfshead*
> August 1999

ROBERT E. HOWARD: THE HORROR COLLECTION

> Contains *The Black Stone; Horror from the Mound; Dig Me No Grave; The Thing on the Roof; Hope Empty of Meaning (v)*
> August 2000
>> Reprints from various Marvel titles

WORMS OF THE EARTH

> Contains *Worms of the Earth*
> October 2000
>> Also a set of 4X6 promotional cards available

## Dark Horse
CORMAC MAC ART
Four part miniseries in 1990, VERY loosely based on some original REH stories

ALMURIC
Contains *Almuric*
1991

> Adapted by Roy Thomas and Tim Conrad, reprint of Epics Illustrated version

IRONHAND OF ALMURIC
Sequel to Almuric

KINGS OF THE NIGHT
2-parter

## DC
Captain Marvel had a villain of old named King Kull, maybe created by Otto Binder, not the same as REH's, still turns up from time to time

## Eclipse
PIGEONS FROM HELL
    Contains *Pigeons from Hell*
    1<sup>st</sup> Edition, HB and TPB, 1988
        By REH and Scott Hampton; illustrated by Scott Hampton; introduction by Ramsey Campbell; a graphic novel pretty accurately based on the REH story; HB limited to 1000 numbered copies, signed by Scott Hampton

## Epic Illustrated (a Marvel publication)
Volume 1, #2
    Contains *Almuric*
    Summer 1980
        Part 1 of 4; adapted by Roy Thomas and Tim Conrad; later reprinted by Dark Horse

Volume 1, #3
    Contains *Almuric*
    Fall 1980
        Part 2 of 4

Volume 1, #4
    Contains *Almuric*
    Winter 1980
        Part 3 of 4

Volume 1, #5
    Contains *Almuric*
    April 1981
        Part 4 of 4

## Espee (Netherlands)
Gummi #1, 1977, Conan story
    Later issues also contained Conan stories, including "The Frost Giant's Daughter"

## Forum (Spain)
European publisher of Marvel Conan material, 1982-1990; sales especially good in Spain, Scandinavia, Turkey and Brazil; lots of reprints, in color and black and white; published some original Conan material in the 1990s, supposedly 8 short pieces and 55 long stories

## Harrier Comics (UK)
DEATHWATCH #1
    July 1987
        Story about folks who hunt down and kill evil things, goes after Zuvembies in Blassenville Manor, of "Pigeons from Hell" fame

**IDW Publishing**
SPOOKHOUSE 2, 2004
 Contains *Pigeons from Hell*
 Reprinted Scott Hampton's PIGEONS FROM HELL graphic novel, previously published by Eclipse

**Junior Press (Netherlands)**
CONAN DE BARBAAR SPECIAL
Dutch reprints of Marvel's CONAN THE BARBARIAN, beginning with CDBS #1, which reprinted CtB #58-61; subsequent issues also reprint multiple issues of CtB her issue of CDBS

**La Reina de la Costa Negra (Mexico)**
A Conan comic series, likely based on the earlier Cuentos de Abuelito Mexican comic; this is also a Mexican comic book ca. 1958-1966, went at least 45 issues; very rare

**L'Echo des Savane (France)**
#8
Reprints of B&W Conan comics, in French

#9
Reprints of B&W Conan comics, in French; possibly additional issues as well

**Lone Star Press**
PANTHEON #6
Features an appearance by the Howard House in Cross Plains

**Marvel**
CHAMBER OF CHILLS #2
 Contains *The Horror from the Mound*
 January 1973

CHAMBER OF CHILLS #3
 Contains *The Thing on the Roof*
 March 1973

CREATURES ON THE LOOSE #10
 Contains *The Skull of Silence*
 March 1971

THE HAUNT OF HORROR #1
 Contains *Usurp the Night*
 June 1973
  A sci-fi pulp digest, only two issues

JOURNEY INTO MYSTERY #1
 Contains *Dig Me No Grave*
 October 1972

MARVEL PREMIERE #33-34
 Contains *Red Shadows*
 December 1976 & February 1977
  Adaptation by Roy Thomas, artwork by Howard Chaykin

MARVEL PREVIEW #19
  Contains *The Footfalls Within*
  October 1979

MARVEL SUPER SPECIAL #2
  Contains *Revenge of the Barbarian! (Black Vulmea's Vengeance)*
  1978

MASTERS OF TERROR #1
  Contains *The Horror from the Mound*
  July 1975
    Published under the "Curtis" imprint

MASTERS OF TERROR #2
  Contains *Dig Me No Grave*
  September 1975
    Published under the "Curtis" imprint

MONSTERS UNLEASHED #1
  Contains *Skulls in the Stars*
  1973
    Adapted by Roy Thomas and Ralph Reese; published under the "Curtis" imprint

SUPERNATURAL THRILLERS #3
  Contains *The Valley of the Worm*
  April 1973

THE SWORD OF SOLOMON KANE #1
  Contains *Red Shadows*
  September 1985
    Limited Series of 6 issues, adaptation by Ralph Macchio and Bret Blevins

THE SWORD OF SOLOMON KANE #3
  Contains *Blades of the Brotherhood*
  January 1986

THE SWORD OF SOLOMON KANE #5
  Contains *The Hills of the Dead*
  May 1986

THE SWORD OF SOLOMON KANE #6
  Contains *Wings in the Night*
  July 1986

## Millennium
ROBERT E.HOWARD'S THE BLACK REAPER
  Contains *Destiny ("I think I was born . . ."); Black Seas; Empire; The Call of Pan; A Far Country; Flaming Marble; Symbols; Musings ("The little poets . . "); Musings ("To every man . . "); Love (all v)*
  1995 (no date on book)
    Artwork by Terry Pavlet, Carlos Phoenix Jimenez, Charles Lang, and Mark AW Jackson; At least two cover variations, plus a "deluxe" book signed by a few of the artists

**Oberon (Netherlands)**
CONAN DE BARBAAR ("Conan the Barbarian")
Reprinting Marvel's CONAN THE BARBARIAN, two reprints per issue, starting with #1, January 1981, which contained CtB #1 and #2

CONAN DE BARBAAR Graphic Novels (also known as "Comic-Albums"), Reprinting mostly SAVAGE SWORD OF CONAN, in color, starting with #1, 1979, Reprint of SSOC #38

PEPTOES
Reprints CONAN THE BARBARIAN, in B&W, starting with #1, 1974, which reprints CtB #1

**Panini, S.A. (Marvel Italy)**
Published a series of original Conan stories in Italian comics ("Fumettos"), 15 long stories, very adult-oriented, very violent and sexually graphic; Marvel refused to let these get to US, too adult; did not get received well, and died shortly thereafter

**Real Free Press (Netherlands, in English)**
RED BLADES OF BLACK CATHAY
1975

**Star-Studded Comics**
#14
> Contains *Gods of the North*
> December 1968
>> First Conan comic in English; artwork on this story by Larry Herndon, Steve Kelez and Alan Hutchison

# TEN BEST STORIES FOR THOSE WHO HAVE NEVER READ REH BEFORE

by Rusty Burke, series editor for the Wandering Star Library of Classics

As with any top ten list I have ever done, this comes with the caveat that it could change within the next ten minutes. But I think that if you've never experienced REH, or want to introduce his work to someone who has never read it, these would be good starters. I'm not going to attempt to rank these, so I'll list them in alphabetical order.

### "The Dark Man"
The 11th-century Irish adventurer Turlogh Dubh O'Brien pursues the Vikings who kidnapped a young woman of his clan – a clan that outlawed him. Along the way, he comes upon a mysterious statue which had apparently been the object of a fight to the death between a band of Danes and another group of small, dark men. The statue accompanies Turlogh to the steading of the Viking raiders, where it is mute witness to a ferocious battle. When the story was originally published in *Weird Tales*, some readers complained it was not "weird" enough, so subtly does Howard handle the fantastic elements. By the time he wrote this story, Howard had absorbed a considerable amount of Irish literature, and it shows in the lilting dialogue and poetic diction, as well as in the elegiac final paragraphs.

### "The Fightin'est Pair"
Though chiefly known for his heroic fantasy, Howard found considerable success in other genres. An ardent student of boxing, he wrote 31 stories about a brawling merchant seaman named Steve Costigan, whose riotous misadventures entertained readers of *Fight Stories*, *Action Stories*, *Jack Dempsey's Fight Magazine*, and others. Steve is an iron man, with a heart of gold and a head of wood. In this story, Steve's white bulldog, Mike, is kidnapped in Singapore, and the madcap mayhem that ensues has a little bit of everything that makes the Costigan series so enjoyable, including vivid fight action, colorful dialect, and not least the heart-warming bond between a man and his dog.

### "'For the Love of Barbara Allen'"
The poet laureate of violence had a tender side, too, and it, as well as his love of folk music, is on display in this tale of a love that transcends war and death.

### "Swords of the Hills" (published as "The Lost Valley of Iskander")
Pursued by the murderous followers of a man whose plotting he has unmasked, Francis X. Gordon, a former Texas gunslinger whose exploits in the Middle East and Central Asia have earned him the name "El Borak" ("the Swift"), discovers in the mountains of Afghanistan a city built by Alexander the Great and inhabited by descendants of the soldiers he left to man it. With them he must thwart the evil ambitions of Gustav Hunyadi, who hopes to stir up religious war in Central Asia and send hordes of fanatics against the Indian border.

### "Queen of the Black Coast"
Conan of Cimmeria meets Bêlit, "the wildest she-devil unhanged," leader of a crew of savage corsairs. In search of a fabled treasure, they sail up a haunted river to an encounter with the last, bestial survivor of an ancient race. "Mystery and terror are about us, Conan, and we glide into the realm of horror and death." Part heroic fantasy classic, part love story, all REH.

**"The Shadow Kingdom"**
Frequently cited as the first "sword and sorcery" story, this tale of Kull, the Atlantean barbarian who usurped the throne of the most powerful kingdom in the world, is a masterpiece of purest paranoia. Snake-men, remnants of an age when men and beasts vied for control of the world, able to take on the semblance of any man they wish, have infiltrated Kull's palace and plan to kill him and put on the throne in his stead one of their own with his likeness. With the Pictish warrior Brule as his guide, Kull must thread the dim halls and secret passages of the palace to defeat an enemy who may lurk behind the guise of his friends.

**"The Shadow of the Vulture"**
Inspired by the exploits of historical swordwomen, Howard created the fiery-tressed warrior Red Sonya of Rogatino. Unlike later imitations, Sonya has sworn no vows against men – she just demands to be treated with respect, as an equal and comrade-at-arms. On the walls of Vienna during Suleyman the Magnificent's 1529 siege, she meets Gottfried von Kalmbach, late of Suleyman's prison, a doughty fighting man but a noble toper. Together they must fight against the sultan's Janizaries, and keep his captain Mikhal Oglu from presenting Gottfried's head to the sultan as a gift.

**"Sharp's Gun Serenade"**
Breckinridge Elkins, mighty of stature and small of brain, was the hero of one of Howard's most popular series, his slapstick misadventures appearing in every issue of *Action Stories* for a period of over two years and spawning similar characters for other magazines. The manic, exaggerated mayhem is rather like turning Pecos Bill loose in a Keystone Kops feature. In this tale, Breck assists a friend in trying to prevent a suicide, and ends up fighting the entire town of Chawed Ear in an attempt to bring culture and education, in the form of a pretty young school marm, to his home in Bear Creek. "Bear Creek is goin' to have culture if I have to wade fetlock deep in gore to pervide it," he swears. Though better known for dark fantasy, Howard had a broad, rollicking sense of humor and a knack for regional dialect that make his humorous westerns among the best of their kind.

**"The Tower of the Elephant"**
The young Conan, still new to the ways of "civilization," joins an older thief in a daring attempt to steal a fabulous jewel called The Elephant's Heart from a powerful sorcerer. Only Conan survives to enter the tower, and there meets the weird, alien being that gives the tower its name. At the creature's behest, Conan brings to the sorcerer Yara "a list gift and a last enchantment." One of Howard's most popular stories (and, I admit, the one that – in its first comic-book incarnation – introduced *me* to Howard and Conan).

**"Worms of the Earth"**
One of REH's darkest, most powerful tales, about which H.P. Lovecraft said, "Few readers will ever forget the hideous and compelling power of that macabre masterpiece, 'Worms of the Earth.'" The Pictish king, Bran Mak Morn, seeking to revenge himself upon the Roman occupiers of Britain after watching, helpless, as one of his subjects was unjustly executed, drives a hellish bargain with an unimaginably ancient and loathsome race, at the peril of his soul. "I fight Rome... By steel and fire I will fight her – and by subtlety and treachery – by the thorn in the foot, the adder in the path, the venom in the cup, the dagger in the dark; aye... and by the worms of the earth!"

# THE TOP TEN ARTISTS OF ROBERT E. HOWARD WORKS

## by Bill Cavalier

(in descending order):

### 10. Margaret Brundage
Ah, the Princess of Pastels, Cover Artist for the legendary WEIRD TALES magazine. Mrs. Brundage did nine covers for Conan yarns, and singled out Howard's Conan stories as being her favorite to illustrate. She only depicted Conan three times (and very poorly), but she could paint Conan's naked female companions like there was no tomorrow!

### 9. Rick McCollum
McCollum is certainly one of the most prolific Howard illustrators of all time, primarily through his long-time membership in the Howard APA, REHupa. His detailed black and white Howard work has also been featured in comic books (Blood and Thunder, Ashley Dust) and several of James Van Hise's publications. Rick may well have done more depictions of Howard and his characters than any artist!

### 8. Hugh Rankin
Rankin was an interior illustrator for Weird Tales, and did a fair amount of Howard illustrating. He's on this list because Howard himself said, "I am sort of a fiend about Rankin's illustrations myself…" Howard meant to collect Rankin's drawings of his work and display them on a panel. What a display THAT would make at the Howard House!

### 7. Steve Fabian
Longtime fan favorite Steve Fabian's Howard work has appeared for four decades now. His distinctive ink and crayon-shaded coquille board drawings have been featured in portfolios, fan & pro magazines, and his color work is most recently featured on the ten book WEIRD WORKS OF ROBERT E. HOWARD series from Wildside Press.

### 6. Roy Krenkel
The most notable Howard work done by Roy Krenkel was his magnificent work in the Don Grant editions of THE SOWERS OF THE THUNDER and THE ROAD TO AZRAEL. He also painted the fine cover to the Lancer edition of KING KULL, as well as contributing hundreds of drawings and sketches to Howard zines of the 70's (most notably AMRA). Krenkel is also well known as inspiration and mentor to Frank Frazetta.

### 5. Barry Windsor-Smith
BWS was known as just plain ol' Barry Smith in his hey-day as an illustrator of Robert E. Howard. He is most remembered for his magnificent if tumultuous run as the artist for the Marvel Comics CONAN title in the early 1970's. BWS began as a Jack Kirby clone with Conan #1, and rapidly evolved into one of the most memorable of all Conan artists. His work was featured in the bulk of the first 24 Marvel Conans and culminated with his 64 page masterpiece adaptation of REH's RED NAILS. After leaving the Conan comic, BWS produced two much sought-after REH collections: THE ROBERT E. HOWARD PORTFOLIO and the TUPENNY CONAN PORTFOLIO. Smith later returned to do some Conan work with covers for Marvel's Conan Saga, as well as the great CONAN VS. RUNE one-shot comic, also for Marvel.

## 4. Ken Kelly

Kelly found prominence in two separate decades as a Robert E. Howard illustrator. In the 70's, his Frazetta-influenced work found its way onto the 16 volume Howard set done by Berkley Publishing, and in the 90's he was the cover artist for the seven volume Baen editions. Kelly's wonderfully vibrant Berkley paintings are the better of the two series, in this reviewer's opinion. By the time the Baen covers came around, his work had become rather run-of-the-mill. The Berkley work was also collected as a 1977 calendar, and puts him high on the list.

## 3. Jeff Jones

The highly distinctive work of Jeff Jones graced the covers of the 12 1970's Zebra editions of Howard's stories, and along with his (then) benchmark SOLOMON KANE work for Don Grant, earns him the #3 spot. Working in the shadow of Frazetta, Jones was one of the most prolific fantasy cover artists of the 70's and 80's. His bold, colorful painting style no doubt increased the popularity of Robert E. Howard's words during the 70's Howard Boom.

## 2. Gary Gianni

There's little doubt that Gary Gianni is THE Howard artist of the last decade. He has illustrated three of the five Howard books published by Wandering Star since 1998 with a classical style reminiscent of both N.C. Wyeth (painting) and Joseph Clement Coll (ink drawings). Gianni's work for the complete SOLOMON KANE volume has eclipsed the Jeff Jones RED SHADOWS book and established a new benchmark for all Howard illustrating. The Solomon Kane Gianni illustrated book may quite possibly be the crown jewel of Howard illustrative efforts. On the strength of Gary's SOLOMON KANE, BRAN MAK MORN and CONAN Volume Two efforts, I rank him as the #2 Howard artist.

## 1. Frank Frazetta

Was there any doubt? Frank Frazetta's iconic masterpiece is the cover to the Lancer edition CONAN THE ADVENTURER, and in this reviewer's mind is the only image needed to rate Frazetta as the #1 Howard artist of all time. His depiction of Conan standing brace-legged atop battlefield carnage is THE benchmark image of the Conan of Robert E. Howard. Frazetta painted other Conan covers for Lancer, and while they are all iconic in a lesser way, his (now entitled) THE BARBARIAN is the quintessential Robert E. Howard illustration. Additionally, Wandering Star used scores of Frazetta's works cobbled from various sources to illustrate their 1999 volume THE ULTIMATE TRIUMPH. Simply put, Frazetta is THE Howard artist.

# THE TOP TEN POEMS BY ROBERT E. HOWARD

selected and with some defense of choices
by Frank Coffman, Professor of English and Journalism
Rock Valley College

I have stated on many occasions — both in print and in person — that Robert E. Howard was a far greater poet than is generally recognized. I believe the scope and quality of his poetic achievement is being more and more noted as the centenary of his birth approaches. This is a good thing, since Howard's breadth of talent as both poet and author has been somewhat eclipsed by the immense popularity of the stories of Conan the Cimmerian. While the Conan stories assured Howard of fame as the creator of the "Sword and Sorcery" genre, they served to some degree to hold back the general awareness of his other worthy works. But Robert E. Howard was far from being a "one trick pony." The renewed interest in his work and in the imaginative genres of popular fiction in general over the latter 20th century and since will, I believe, eventually bring the general acceptance and final appreciation of his talents as a writer — as his tombstone reads: "Author and Poet."

Selecting the "Top Ten" poems by any poet of merit is, at best, hazardous to some degree. The old adage about not being able to please everyone certainly applies. Since Howard wrote considerably more than ten excellent poems, such a choice must always be a matter, to some degree, of personal taste on the part of any selector. I've decided to attack this thorny problem by making selections based upon a triad of criteria: first, I wanted to show the spectrum of Howard's poetic genius across several forms and themes, even though more than a single poem in any given form or on any particular topic might be worthy of inclusion; second, I attempted to choose the most representative poem of true quality and display of creative genius in each of the several types or topics; third and finally, the task was then to rank the selections in an order that would make sense — or at least be defensible.

While perhaps no one will agree with my exact selections or order of merit and importance, I hope that many will agree with the inclusion of some and that most readers will acknowledge the overall quality of this representative sample of the poetic achievement of "The Bard of the Post Oaks."

Are they my exact ten personal favorites? That would be telling. I'll leave it to the reader to explore and either applaud or debate the selections

Frank Coffman — Elgin, Illinois, 7 November 2005

## 10. "Private McGrath of the A.E.F."

More than a simple blend of the Howardian interests in boxing and warfare, "Private McGrath" is a poem in the traditions of Rudyard Kipling's *Barrack Room Ballads* — narratives of the common British soldier (as with "Gunga Din" and "Danny Deever") — and Robert W. Service's poetry of the Klondike gold rush and the fine modern ballads of the frozen North (as with "Sam McGee" and "Dan McGrew").

It is also a good representative example of Howard's small contribution of poems with a direct connection to the real times and important events through which he matured. Future criticism needs to pay greater attention to the world and national events of Howard's childhood and youth: The Great War, the great influenza epidemic, the Great Depression.

Had he chosen to live, I believe both his poetry and his fiction might have turned to matters historical and "real life" contemporary issues.

## 9. "The Singer in the Mist"

The best and rightly most well-known of the "Sonnets out of Bedlam." The possibly autobiographical nature of these sonnets needs to be further explored, but the notion of "monstrous spells" laid upon the speaker in the poem and the resultant need to travel "strange highroads" certainly could be applied to Howard.

## 8. "The Poets"

The best of the several poems of literary comment and criticism, which includes the more-often-cited "Which Will Scarcely Be Understood" and "Song of the Mad Minstrel." It is a poetic essay bemoaning Howard's perception of both the fleeting nature of fame and the general lack of appreciation of poetry — perhaps art itself.

## 7. "Autumn"

Brief, but to his point of the advance of an age of decadence and a gradual loss of touch with tradition and the heroic ages of poetry and song – and of reverence for poetry and song themselves: "Now is the harp of Homer flecked with rust…."

A grimmer poem, but an extension of the same theme with even greater notes of disillusionment mixed in is the often quoted and noted "Always Comes Evening."

## 6. "Miser's Gold"

As fine an example of the sonnet used as narrative as exists in English language literature. The poem is a masterpiece of compactness and an amazing utilization of the scant space of the 14-liner. Different voices speak, the back-story is filled in with just enough detail, and the ending surprises us almost as much as it does the unlucky thieves. The poem allows the reader to fill in the plot and become engaged in the story — brief and poignant as it is.

## 5. "The Tempter"

One must include this classic on the theme of suicide, not only because of the often-discussed and often-emphasized (perhaps too often) ending of Howard's life, but because of the qualities of the poem. Its driving rhythms and insistent rhymes pull the reader forward through this powerful poem — much as "the Tempter" is pulling the other voice in the poem to a different conclusion.

## 4. "The Adventurer"

One of the more interesting of Howard's poems because he takes time to marvel in the power of the imagination and his own developed ability to travel "world's away" as Dickinson says or into the "realms of gold" as Keats has it. A well-wrought poem on the wondrous power of the mind's eye.

## 3. "The Ballad of King Geraint"

"King Geraint" is an extended narrative poem, inspired without doubt by Chesterton's *Ballad of the White Horse* and, likely, the French national epic, *The Song of Roland* (probably the Moncrieff translation).

As an extended narrative, it marks Howard's only foray into that genre, important in the annals of American poetry, but already dying out in Howard's day. The long heroic poem or epic is, sadly, a thing of the past it seems. Had Robert E. Howard lived, he might have sustained the form for at least another generation and possibly influenced poetic narratives that went unwritten without his mature influence.

## 2. "Recompense"

Howard's recompense as poet and author was the knowledge that he had gone where few have power to go. Through the mingled fires of imagination, untamed spirit, and heroic zest for fame, Howard traveled vicariously, intellectually, and imaginatively to *elsewheres* and *elsewhens* in both his fiction and his poetry. "Recompense" catalogues some of these excursions.

The poem makes fine use of rhetorical and poetical parallelisms and the striking images typical of all of Howard's work — both poetry and prose.

Like "The Adventurer" the poem is a tribute to the power of the creative imagination and the power of language itself.

**1. "Cimmeria"**

One of the very few examples of Howard's use of blank verse and without doubt not only the best blank verse in terms of flow of language and poetic form, but it is, most likely, the most important poem (at least for Howard himself, his career and subsequent fame) that he ever wrote.

All indications are that this poem, composed during that seminal time when the character of Conan was emerging to take his place in literature and establish firmly both the genre of Sword & Sorcery and Howard's basis of fame, had an almost mystical origin, welling from the depths of Howard's creative genius.

It is also a truly fine example of blank verse, a form important in the literature of the English language as the most common of our heroic measures. It is, perhaps, the epic seed from which all of Cimmeria and the great Cimmerian grow.

# THE TOP 10 SAILOR STEVE COSTIGAN STORIES AND WHY ON EARTH YOU SHOULD SEEK THEM OUT

by Mark Finn

Asking me to pick my favorite funny boxing stories of REH is just plain mean-spirited; I'll rank 'em differently every time I do it. However, while the rankings may change from day-to-day, the stories won't. Howard's prodigious boxing canon has only recently begun to enjoy the same critical scrutiny and respect as his fantasy works. The stories below should be read by anyone interested in a complete and balanced picture of Howard as a writer; he was funny, self-deprecating, clever, and an ardent student of "the squared circle." Above all else, Howard was a veteran tall-tale teller, and the boxing stories showcase the author at his most hyperbolic and entertaining.

**"Pit of the Serpent"**
You have to start the series here, as you get the first glimpse of that lovable dullard, Steve Costigan. Thankfully reprinted often enough to be readily available. This was the start of Howard's first great commercial success; a character close to his heart because, at heart, Steve Costigan *was* Robert E. Howard.

**"The Bull Dog Breed"**
This story completes what "Pit of the Serpent" started. Costigan and Mike, his white bulldog, are a matched set, as this story demonstrates. Of the two, Costigan is the (ahem) brains, and Mike is the heart. Not as funny as the rest of the Costigan stories, but "The Bull Dog Breed" is still a great story, and an amazing example of Howard's "Iron Man" thesis.

**"Viking of the Gloves"**
Costigan passes himself off (not very well) as a Swede in order to pick up a fight card. While all of his shipmates bet on him to win, the captain of the Sea Girl (Costigan's ship), unaware of Costigan's ruse, bets the ship that he'll lose. A classic "rock and a hard place" Howard plot, turned on its ear by the antics of the dopey sailors.

**"Texas Fists"**
This story brings Steve Costigan back home to Texas, and presupposes the later funny cowboy character, Breckinridge Elkins. Costigan is shanghaied by ranchers to fight for them against a rival mining camp. This was the first "tall tale" Costigan story that Howard wrote, and his later boxing yarns incorporated this exaggeration. Terrific use of language and dialect as all of the Texans congregate for the first time in Howard's fiction.

**"Sluggers of the Beach"**
Based on one of the many prizefights that Howard watched, this story starts out funny and becomes even funnier as Costigan piles complications onto his simple plan of vengeance. Throw a little buried treasure and some revolutionaries into the mix and "Sluggers of the Beach" stands out as a particularly fine story.

**"Sailor Costigan and the Destiny Gorilla"**
Perhaps the best "sucker for a dame" tales in this series, and the best punch line of the series, too. Costigan, ever defiant, makes enemies of the local gang, on top of having to vanquish the man who stands between him and true love.

**"Sailor Costigan and the Swami"**
Costigan quits the ship and while pondering his fate, consults a swami who tells him to become a fight promoter. Costigan learns the hardships of fight promotion—he gets stiffed, loses a fighter, refunds money, has to ref the fight (the combatants keep clinching), riots, madness, and a typhoon which destroys the place! A great set-up, and a terrific pay-off, like a well-told joke.

**"Cultured Cauliflowers"**
Costigan rubs elbow with the upper crust of San Francisco, in an exhibition match that ends up very real, and in the process manages to take apart a high society mansion. Mike gets in on the acts of mayhem, too. All the action of a keystone cops movie, plus a great set-up for Costigan to be wearing "fancy duds."

**"Waterfront Fists"**
Costigan at his unreliable-narrator best! The big, dumb sailor doesn't know when he's in trouble, when he's out of trouble, and when he's being taken on a ride. The port is full of sailors who want a fight, crooked promoters, and triple-crossing gangster molls on the take. This is one of the better examples of the Costigan series. A great mix of action and humor.

**"The Fighten'est Pair"**
When Mike is dognapped, Costigan cuts a bloody swath through Singapore trying to find him. Costigan's efforts to fight without Mike at his side are heart-breaking, and the results of the sign posted offering a reward for the return of Mike result in one of the most memorable Costigan stories of all.

# THE EDITOR'S FIVE FAVORITE REH CHARACTERS

by Paul Herman

I am one of the few folks I know who has actually read ALL of REH's published stories, giving me a pretty broad scope of view. Different people have different favorite characters, that no doubt strike a chord of some kind with each. These are just mine.

### 5. Cormac Fitzgeoffrey
THIS is the predecessor for Conan, not Kull. The Kull stories had a barbaric king in the ancient past, and that's about as far as the similarities go. To see where Conan came from, take a look at the Cormac Fitzgeoffrey stories, written just before the Conan stories, and sold to a different market. A ferocious barbarian, unquestionably big and strong and fierce, there are no apologies for this character, he is dark and grim and lethal. Being in a historical setting, REH was limited to what his hero could achieve, as he couldn't rewrite history, and you can almost feel the frustration in REH in these stories, his heroes hands tied, can't alter it. In my opinion these stories led to REH taking this character and dropping him into a Kull-like setting, so that he COULD be the Great Changer of Things. See for yourself.

### 4. Turlogh Dubh O'Brien
It's a shame there are not more stories featuring this character. An unapologetic Celt, incredibly loyal, full of unquenchable hate for some, a soft heart too, a good fighter, he embodies so many of the perceived characteristics of Celts that REH loved so much. And REH was using him at a time when he was writing some of his best material, including "The Dark Man" and "The Gods of Bal-Sagoth".

### 3. Breckinridge Elkins
The super-hillbilly, REH's ultimate fighter, would have whooped Conan in a fight, fair or not. Dumb as a brick, loyal and trusting, but could clean out a bar of rowdies in wonderfully short order. And gets to tell his own stories in his own way, which just make you smile again and again. Developed out of Sailor Steve Costigan, if you asked me, and definitely one of REH's peak characters.

### 2. Solomon Kane
Not big and heavy like Conan or Breck, SK was a sword fighter first, though he could do everything else as well, of course. And SK fought for a cause, a fascinating character who you constantly believe is just a little bit crazy, but in a good way, unless you make him angry. A fighter for God who doesn't compromise, and the stories are the same, no compromises.

### 1. Conan
Duh. Almost always the character that drags folks into reading more and more REH. One of REH's peak characters, along with Breck Elkins, and one that represents so many different things to so many different people. It is always amazing to see how the original Conan stories evoke different responses in different folks, from those that see only babes and swords and violence, to those that see populism, to the importance of individualism, to hatred, to anti-social teachings, to heroism. A brilliantly conceived character, generally in some of his very best stories.

# AFTERWORD

And so the Neverending Hunt will continue. As you can see from these listings, there are still lots of holes to fill in, lots of details to discover and add into the margins. And with the current REH publishing boom, there will be more and more publications to keep adding to the lists.

And who knows, the Next Great Biblio may be strictly an online version, allowing hyperlinks and constantly updated information. Maybe at HowardWorks, maybe at Wikipedia, maybe at some plot of cyberspace that hasn't been created yet. Maybe it'll be a little space stored in your hyperbook.

Here's hoping the next one will be twice as big again.

Paul Herman

www.ingramcontent.com/pod-product-compliance
Lightning Source LLC
Chambersburg PA
CBHW080408270326
41929CB00018B/2948